Special Edition

USING
OS/2® Lotus®
SmartSuite®

Written by

Robert L. Weberg

with

Derek S. Anderson
Lenny Bailes
Elaine Marmel
Sue Plumley

que

Special Edition, Using OS/2 Lotus SmartSuite

Copyright© 1995 by Que® Corporation

You may reach Que's direct sales line by calling 1-800-428-5331.

Library of Congress Catalog No.: 95-68259

ISBN: 1-7897-0272-X

97 96 95   4 3 2 1

Interpretation of the printing code: the rightmost double-digit number is the year of the book's printing; the rightmost single-digit number, the number of the book's printing. For example, a printing code of 95-1 shows that the first printing of the book occurred in 1995.

Special Edition, Using OS/2 Lotus SmartSuite is based on Versions 1.1 and 2.0 of Lotus SmartSuite for OS/2.

Screen reproductions in this book were created with Collage Complete from Inner Media, Inc., Hollis, NH and with Print Screen from Mitnor Software, Broken Arrow, OK.

Publisher: Roland Elgey
Vice President and Publisher: Marie Butler-Knight
Associate Publisher: Don Roche, Jr.
Editorial Services Director: Elizabeth Keaffaber
Director of Marketing: Lynn E. Zingraf

Credits

Managing Editor
Michael Cunningham

Acquisitions Editor
Deborah Abshier

Product Director
Kathie-Jo Arnoff

Product Development Specialists
Lorna Gentry
Lisa D. Wagner

Technical Editors
Kim Libeth Fanta
Elaine Marmel
Sue Plumley

Production Editor
Julie A. McNamee

Editors
Lori A. Lyons
Theresa Mathias
Lisa M. Gebken
Thomas F. Hayes
Kezia Endsley
Geneil Breeze

Assistant Product Marketing Manager
Kim Margolius

Technical Specialist
Cari Skaggs

Acquisitions Assistant
Tracy M. Williams

Operations Coordinator
Patricia J. Brooks

Editorial Assistant
Jill L. Pursell

Book Designer
Sandra Stevenson Schroeder

Cover Designer
Dan Armstrong

Production Team
Steve Adams, Claudia Bell,
Kim Cofer, Chad Dressler,
DiMonique Ford, Karen Gregor,
Aren Howell, John Hulse,
Barry Jorden, Bob LaRoche,
Beth Lewis, Alan Palmore,
Linda Quigley, Clair Schweinler,
Kris Simmons, Michael Thomas,
Scott Tullis, Elaine Voci-Reed,
Jody York

Indexer
Kathy Venable

Composed in *Stone Serif* and *MCPdigital* by Que Corporation

About the Authors

Robert L. Weberg is a Lotus Notes Application Developer for a major banking corporation in Chicago, IL. He has developed applications and business systems in Lotus Notes, Ami Pro, Lotus 1-2-3, Approach, Paradox, and Word for Windows. Robert recently coauthored *Using Lotus SmartSuite 3, Special Edition* and *Using 1-2-3 Release 5 for Windows, Special Edition* and was the technical editor for *Easy Freelance Graphics 2.0.* He has a B.S. in Finance from the University of Iowa and an M.S. in Finance and Decision Sciences from Georgia State University. Robert resides with his wife Anna in Bartlett, IL. He can be reached directly on CompuServe at 71714, 2276.

Derek S. Anderson is the Systems Development Manager for Haas Publishing Companies in Atlanta, GA. He has been active in the PC development community for the past six years, spending the first three as an instructor of end-user PC applications, before joining Haas. Currently, he manages a programming staff that is developing Wide Area Network applications. Derek is a frequent speaker at PC conferences, and most recently served as a contributing author on Que's *Using Paradox 5 for Windows, Special Edition* book.

Lenny Bailes is a writer, teacher, and consultant who lives in the San Francisco Bay area. He is a frequent contributor to *OS/2 Magazine,* and the co-author of *Multitasking and Memory Management Beyond 640K* (Windcrest/McGraw-Hill, 1992), *The Byte DOS Programmer's Cookbook* (Osborne McGraw-Hill, 1994), and *Using OS/2 Warp, Special Edition* (Que, 1994). His columns and reviews also appear in *Microtimes, Computer Shopper,* and *Boardwatch Magazine.*

Elaine Marmel is President of Marmel Enterprises, Inc., an organization specializing in assisting small- to medium-sized businesses computerize their accounting systems. Elaine spends most of her time writing and is the author of *Word for Windows 2 QuickStart* (also translated into Portuguese and Thai), *Quicken 1.0 for Windows Quick Reference, Quicken 6 for DOS Quick Reference, Using Quicken 2.0 for Windows, The PC User's Mac/The Mac User's PC, Word for Windows 6 Solutions, Word for the Mac Solutions, 1-2-3 Release 4 for Windows Solutions,* and *Que's Guide to Using Lotus Organizer 2 for Windows.*

In addition, Elaine is a contributing editor to *Inside Timeslips* and *Inside Peachtree for Windows*, monthly magazines published about Timeslips 5 and Peachtree for Windows.

Sue Plumley owns and operates Humble Opinions, a consulting firm that offers training in popular software programs as well as network installation and maintenance. Sue is the author of 12 Que books, including *Crystal Clear DOS, Crystal Clear Word 6,* and *Microsoft Office Quick Reference.* She is the coauthor of 16 additional books, including *Using WordPerfect 6 for DOS, Using OS/2 2.1,* and *Using Microsoft Office.*

Trademarks

Contents at a Glance

A New Way to Work

Using 1-2-3

Using Ami Pro

Using Freelance Graphics

Working Together

Communicating

Appendixes

Contents

8 Using Formulas and Functions   169

III Using Ami Pro   245

12 Creating and Editing Documents   247

13 Formatting Text and Documents   265

14 Proofing and Printing Documents   287

15 Managing, Organizing and Importing Files   303

16 Changing Views and Creating Outlines, Styles, and Revisions 325

17 Working with Frames, Tables, and Charts 345

21 Entering Slide Content   409

22 Working with Objects   425

23 Drawing Shapes, Curves, and Lines   443

V Working Together with Lotus SmartSuite Applications 507

Introduction

Lotus SmartSuite Release 2.0 for OS/2 is the only complete desktop suite developed specifically for IBM's OS/2 operating system. The SmartSuite is a composite of four useful business applications: Ami Pro 3.0b for OS/2, 1-2-3 Release 2.1 for OS/2, Freelance Graphics 2.1 for OS/2, and cc:Mail 1.03 for OS/2. The SmartSuite applications provide a unique level of integration and reflect the Lotus strategy of "working together" which focuses on usability, cross-platform integration, networked applications, and working with other users.

By using the SmartSuite applications you'll be able to work more efficiently and effectively by entering text or data in only one program, and then copying or linking that data to other programs for a different presentation or analysis.

Besides sharing information between programs, you save time and energy when working with the SmartSuite applications. The programs are designed to look and act alike; the tools, menus, procedures, and functionality are very similar—if not exactly alike—across applications. Plus, two of the applications, 1-2-3 and Freelance, have the ability to share common directories and various tools. These similarities reduce the learning curve as you work from program to program.

Most industry experts agree that application suites are becoming necessities in the business computing environment. Corporations find that suites encourage increased productivity and support among their employees, reduce computing anxieties, lighten support load on help desks, and save licensing costs. *Special Edition Using OS/2 Lotus SmartSuite* presents the instruction, features, and ideas you need to learn this new way of working with the integrated software suite.

Que's experience with Lotus SmartSuite and OS/2 users has helped produce this high-quality, highly informative book. But this type of book doesn't evolve overnight. *Special Edition Using OS/2 Lotus SmartSuite* combines the talents of a diverse collection of experts chosen for their understanding of the SmartSuite products, as well as their ability to write clear instructional text. The experts who worked on this book include managers, consultants, training specialists, systems analysts, and technical magazine authors. They have taught others how to use the SmartSuite to build many types of business applications, plus answer users questions quickly, clearly, and completely. This experience, combined with Que's professional publishing and editorial team, brings you outstanding tutorial and reference information. Each author covers, in detail, an application in the SmartSuite that he or she specializes in: Ami Pro, Lotus 1-2-3, Freelance Graphics, Lotus Notes, cc:Mail, and integration—sharing data between the applications.

This collaborative approach gives the most concise information about individual applications and expert advice on common features, problem-solving, and program integration. Along with the four applications included in Lotus SmartSuite, this book includes special coverage of Lotus Notes because of its growing importance in allowing users to share information. *Special Edition Using OS/2 Lotus SmartSuite* provides detailed, comprehensive information to let you take advantage of Lotus SmartSuite within the OS/2 operating environment.

Who Should Use This Book?

Special Edition Using OS/2 Lotus SmartSuite is the logical choice for any user utilizing two or more of the SmartSuite applications: corporate personnel, consultants, home-office workers, students, faculty, and computer-support staff. It's also useful for anyone new to these applications who wants to quickly get up and running with the SmartSuite.

This book assumes that you know either the new OS/2 Warp or any version of OS/2 from 2.1 and up, but are not familiar with all the applications in the SmartSuite. However, recognizing the importance of how the SmartSuite applications interact with OS/2, several chapters detail these system integration features.

Special Edition Using OS/2 Lotus SmartSuite can help you integrate two or more of the SmartSuite applications, exchange data and other information between applications, and collaborate effectively with coworkers on a project.

How This Book Is Organized

Special Edition Using OS/2 Lotus SmartSuite is designed to complement the documentation that comes with the SmartSuite applications. It includes step-by-step information for users searching for instructions on any of the SmartSuite applications, as well as comprehensive coverage and expert advice for intermediate and experienced users. After you become proficient with the SmartSuite applications, you can use this book as an accessible desktop reference.

Special Edition Using OS/2 Lotus SmartSuite is divided into the following six parts and two appendixes:

Part I, "Learning a New Way To Work with OS/2 and the SmartSuites," introduces you to the SmartSuite and to the new ways of working that the suite presents. In Chapters 1 and 2, you learn about the common features shared by the applications that let you launch applications and switch from program to program. The third chapter deals with managing file and work areas in the applications using the powerful features of the OS/2 Workplace Shell. Part I helps you understand the basic similarities of the programs and the OS/2 environment and prepares you for the more detailed information in the rest of the book.

Parts II through IV cover the essentials of 1-2-3, Ami Pro, and Freelance Graphics. Chapters 4 through 11 introduce you to 1-2-3 worksheets. Chapters 12 through 19 show you how to use Ami Pro to create professional documents. Chapters 20 through 26 introduce you to creating impressive presentations in Freelance Graphics. By reading the chapters about a specific application, you can learn and discover how to use that program's functionality to its full potential.

Part V, "Working Together with Lotus SmartSuite Applications," covers the concept of integrating the SmartSuite products with each other. Chapters 27 through 29 show you how to share data between programs by cutting and pasting, linking data, and creating integrated project files and folders on the OS/2 Desktop.

Part VI, "Communicating with Others Using the Lotus Suite of Products," includes information about using the SmartSuite applications with cc:Mail and Lotus Notes. Chapter 30 covers how to use cc:Mail with the SmartSuite applications by sending files, attachments, and creating reusable message templates. Although Lotus Notes isn't included with SmartSuite, Lotus designed the SmartSuite applications to work with Notes. Chapters 31 through 34 show you how to use Lotus Notes to share files for collaboration with your colleagues.

Appendix A guides you through installing the SmartSuite applications. Appendix B teaches you how to customize your SmartIcon palettes. Appendix C describes the Value Pack containing the added SmartCenter application and other features new with version 2.0 of OS/2.

Finally, you'll find a comprehensive general index.

Conventions Used in This Book

The writing and instructions in this book focus on consistency. The goal is to use recognizable text and formatting to maintain consistent instructions in all the chapters. The following examples represent the conventions used in this book to help you distinguish between the different elements.

Keyboard and Mouse Representations

SmartSuite for OS/2 allows you to use both the keyboard and mouse to choose and activate menu commands and dialog box option items: you can press a letter or you can select an item by clicking it with the mouse.

In most cases, keys are represented as they appear on the keyboard. On your keyboard, key names like Page Up may be spelled out or abbreviated differently (PgUp). When two keys appear together with a plus sign, such as Ctrl+Esc, press and hold the first key as you press the second key. When two keys appear together without a plus sign, such as End Home, press and release the first key before you press the second key.

The hot keys for option and menu commands are printed in boldface type: **F**ile, **O**pen, for example.

Names of the dialog boxes and dialog box options are initial capped letters.

Messages that appear on-screen are printed in a special font: Document 1.

Text you type appears in **boldface.**

New terms are introduced in *italic* type.

Uppercase letters are used to distinguish file and directory names.

The following example shows a typical command sequence:

1. Choose **F**ile, **O**pen; or press Ctrl+O.

Margin Icons

The programs included with the SmartSuite provide SmartIcons for your con-
venience. By clicking a button in the SmartIcons set, you can quickly execute
a command or access a dialog box. Chapters in this book often contain
SmartIcons in the margins, indicating which button you can choose to
quickly perform a task.

Notes, Tips, Cautions, Troubleshooting, and Cross-References

> **Note**
>
> This paragraph format indicates additional information or notations that may help
> you avoid problems or that should be considered when using the described features.

Tip
This format
suggests easier or
alternative meth-
ods of executing a
procedure. Tips
can be invaluable
to your SmartSuite
experience.

> **Caution**
>
> The Caution paragraph format warns you about hazardous procedures (for example,
> activities that clear desktops or delete files).

> **Troubleshooting**
>
> The Troubleshooting information provides guidance on how to find solutions to
> common problems or situations in a problem/solution format.

Special Edition Using OS/2 Lotus SmartSuite has cross-references in the margin
to help you access related information in other parts of the book, as follows:

Right-facing triangles point you to related information in later chapters.
Left-facing triangles point you to information in previous chapters.

◀ See "Section
   title," p. xx

Part I

Learning a New Way to Work with OS/2 and the SmartSuites

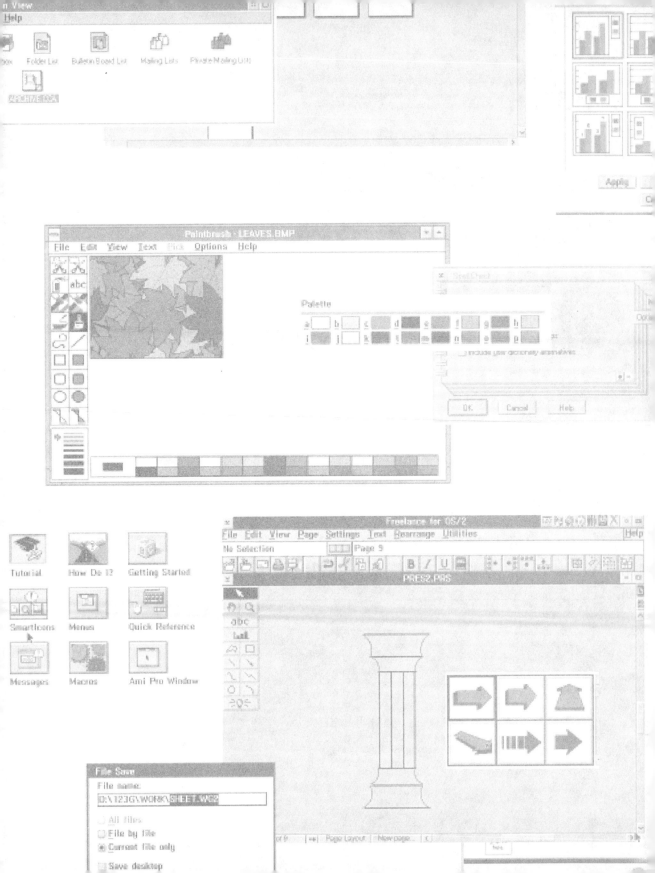

Chapter 1

New Ways of Working with OS/2

by Robert L. Weberg

With bundled suite packages available in the market today, you can purchase a family of applications that are integrated and cosmetically similar. The basic concept behind a family of office applications is to make teamwork and sharing information and files easier and more effective. Using a bundled office suite—an integrated group of business applications—you can produce a professional looking, complete document in half the time.

The Lotus SmartSuite for OS/2 bundle is a perfect example of tight and efficient integration. The SmartSuite applications provide many features that help you produce professional looking documents, analyze data and information, share files between the product family, and follow and revise the work of others. You can even share and send files through cc:Mail and integrate the SmartSuite with the groupware product Lotus Notes.

In this chapter, you learn to:

- Use the advantages of Lotus SmartSuite

- Recognize the important features of each SmartSuite application

- Determine which SmartSuite application to use

Taking Advantage of SmartSuite

Lotus SmartSuite for OS/2 offers four applications to help you produce business documents quickly and practically. The applications included in SmartSuite incorporate a word processor, spreadsheet program, presentation software, and an electronic mailing package. You can use each application by itself or in conjunction with any of the other applications in the SmartSuite.

The applications are:

- 1-2-3 Release 2.1

- Freelance Graphics Release 2.1

- Ami Pro Release 3.0b

- cc:Mail for OS/2 Workplace Shell 1.03

When you choose to use the applications together to integrate your work, you reap the countless benefits of SmartSuite; sharing data may be the most important advantage of this group of applications. You can enter data into one application, for example, and then copy or link the data into another application. You can create a report in one program and use the text to build a presentation in another, import data from a spreadsheet into a presentation, import data to create a chart, and then spell check your files.

By using SmartSuite, you save time and money, improve work flow by copying and linking data, and reduce errors, ensuring the accuracy and integrity of your data. As you work with SmartSuite for OS/2, you will find many advantages, including the following:

- Cost savings because buying the SmartSuite costs less than purchasing each individual application.

- The only full-featured desktop business suite built specifically for IBM's OS/2 operating system.

- A lower training curve made possible by the design and use of common interfaces.

- Flexibility to switch quickly and easily between documents or applications using SmartIcons and the OS/2 Workplace shell.

- Ability to share information between documents and applications.

- Ability to share resources and common tools between applications.

Using the OS/2 Workplace Shell

Lotus SmartSuite for OS/2 2.0 is the only complete desktop suite of native business applications written for OS/2 2.1 and the newly released OS/2 Warp.

Featuring all 32-bit native OS/2 applications, the suite takes advantage of 32-bit memory management, the drag-and-drop feature of the OS/2 Workplace Shell interface, the usage of Work-Area folders to store related documents, time-saving benefits of multithreading, and the added security of working in a true multitasking environment.

The OS/2 Workplace Shell is an exciting world of icons, objects, and folders. You can simply drag-and-drop Lotus data file objects, such as an Ami Pro document or a Freelance presentation, to a printer or shredder device icon. Or you can even arrange your Lotus data file objects in a project-related Work-Area folder and then double-click any SmartSuite for OS/2 application file icon to load the associated program and file.

With *multithreading* you can easily perform separate operations in the same application, such as printing a daily expense report in 1-2-3 while another process, such as the Solver in 1-2-3, runs in the background to find solutions to a multi-variable problem. You save time by having the applications work on multiple tasks at the same time.

True *multitasking* lets you perform tasks in one application while other tasks are carried out simultaneously in other applications. For example, a user can work on a budget in 1-2-3 while Ami Pro prints a lengthy proposal document.

The SmartSuite bundle also provides compatibility with the Windows versions of those applications, as well as a high degree of cross-platform integration. This "working together" strategy allows applications to function across platforms and systems, and allows users to work and communicate with other people in a networked environment.

SmartSuite applications optimize their definitive integration features with the personal computing power of OS/2. In fact, these bundled products represent the simplest means of purchasing, installing, and supporting a suite of full-featured, integrated desktop business applications.

Sharing a Common Interface

Most OS/2 programs are cosmetically similar in look and feel; for example, many of the window elements—such as scroll bars, title bars, rulers, and menus, are nearly the same. SmartSuite applications share common interfaces, including SmartIcons and common behavior, and a standardized appearance and usage that takes advantage of the OS/2 Workplace Shell.

Figure 1.1 shows the top parts of 1-2-3, Freelance Graphics, and Ami Pro screens for you to compare.

Fig. 1.1
Although each
application has
elements unique to
it, all SmartSuite
applications have
many elements in
common.

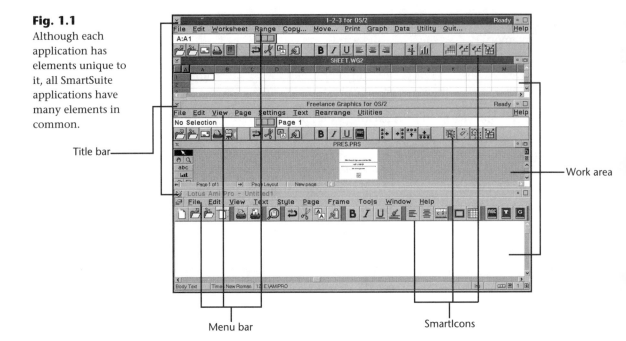

Title bar

Work area

Menu bar

SmartIcons

Each application uses similar window elements, menus, dialog boxes, and
commands. In fact, many of the same commands can be found listed in the
same menus of each application. For example, the File menu of all SmartSuite
applications contains Open, Save, and Print commands. The Edit menus all
contain Undo, Cut, Copy, and Paste, as well as other similar editing commands—such as Paste Special or Paste Link. Resulting dialog boxes and outcomes from these commands are similar, if not exactly the same.

▶ See "Using
Dialog Boxes,"
p. 42

Figure 1.2 shows the File Open dialog box in 1-2-3 and figure 1.3 shows Ami
Pro's Open dialog box. The 1-2-3 File Open dialog box is identical to the one
that appears when using Freelance Graphics. Notice that the dialog boxes
include areas for the file name, drive, directory, a list of files, and the file type.

▶ See "Using
Online Help,"
p. 53

Additionally, the SmartSuite applications share many shortcut keys, mouse
functions, macros, and SmartIcons, as well as the Help feature. Learning one
of the SmartSuite applications makes learning any of the other applications
easier because you have already learned the basics.

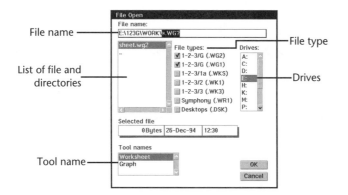

File name

List of file and
directories

Tool name

File type

Drives

Fig. 1.2
In the 1-2-3 File
Open dialog box,
change directories
by double-clicking
the name of the
directory in the
list. This dialog
box looks identical
to the Freelance
Open File dialog
box.

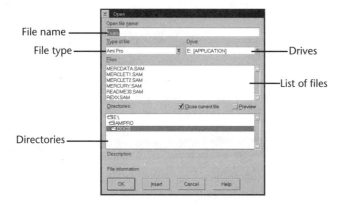

File name

File type

Directories

Drives

List of files

Fig. 1.3
Double-click the
directory folder
whose contents
you want to view
in the Ami Pro
Open dialog box.

I

A New Way to Work

Note

Even though there are many common elements between the SmartSuite applications, there are also many unique features to each application. 1-2-3, for example,
includes the Range menu that presents commands unique only to the spreadsheet
program. Also, the View menu in Freelance and the View menu in Ami Pro contain
some similar and completely different commands that suit each individual program.

Switching Tasks

When you work with several documents or applications at one time, you
can switch between the documents or to another program as you work.
SmartSuite enables you to quickly move around open documents so you
can complete your work as effectively as possible.

▶ See "Switching between Applications," p. 68

▶ See "Cutting, Copying, and Pasting," p. 49

Using the SmartIcons within each application or the Lotus Application Manager tool, you can switch from one open application to another while leaving the original program up and running in the background. The Lotus Application Manager is a stand-alone program that lets users work easily among different SmartSuite applications and Lotus Notes. After starting this program, a palette of SmartIcons resides on the OS/2 Workplace Shell desktop when OS/2 applications are minimized or fits into the upper-right hand corner of an application's title bar when maximized. A simple click on the desired icon allows you to start SmartSuite applications and switch between SmartSuite applications, Lotus Notes, and an OS/2 window.

Additionally, by using the Desktop Control menu in 1-2-3 and Freelance you can display the Window menu so you can move easily between documents or even tile and stack the document windows. In Ami Pro, you can use the Window menu to tile and cascade windows to display more than one document on-screen at a time.

Figure 1.4 illustrates a switch to 1-2-3 to pick up some figures for a report in Ami Pro using the Lotus Application Manager. Figure 1.5 shows how to use the Window menu within the Desktop Control menu in 1-2-3 and Freelance.

Note

▶ See "Switching between Documents," p. 67

To switch between open documents in Ami Pro you need to open the Window menu and choose the desired document window in the numbered list.

Fig. 1.4

The active window is the Ami Pro window; to change back to 1-2-3, just click the document window or the 1-2-3 SmartIcon in the Lotus Application Manager.

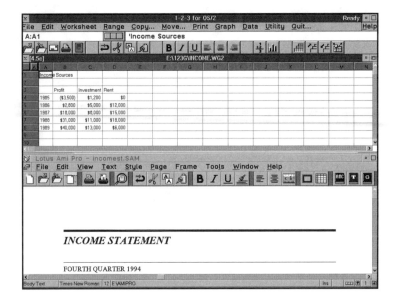

Desktop Control menu

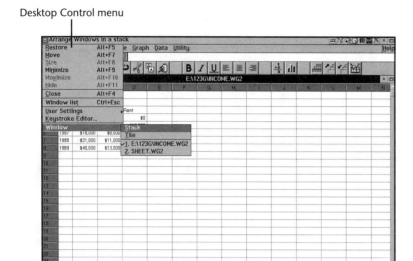

Fig. 1.5
The Desktop
Control menu also
allows you to
switch between
and tile or stack
the open windows
in your current
application.

A New Way to Work

Sharing Data

Sharing data between SmartSuite applications is one of its major advantages. OS/2, of course, enables you to cut, copy, and paste text and graphics from one program to another through the OS/2 Clipboard. SmartSuite applications also support these editing techniques.

► See "Cutting, Copying, and Pasting," p. 49

Additionally, SmartSuite supports DDE (Dynamic Data Exchange). Using this feature, you can link data from the source file to another file, and you can be sure that the data is automatically updated whenever you revise it.

► See "Understanding Links," p. 526

Figure 1.6 illustrates a linked spreadsheet in an Ami Pro document.

Sharing Resources and Tools

In addition to sharing data and other information between the SmartSuite applications, Lotus also provides several resources you can use with the applications: the Shared Graph Tool, common directories, Lotus Application Manager, Workplace Shell Integration (Drag and Drop), VIM-Mail Enabling with attached files, common Spell Check dictionaries, shared clip art and symbols, and the ability to create time-saving Desktop files.

► See "The Shared Graph Tool," p. 129

Fig. 1.6

Linking the data in the table means you can change the numbers or formulas in 1-2-3; they automatically change in the Ami Pro document.

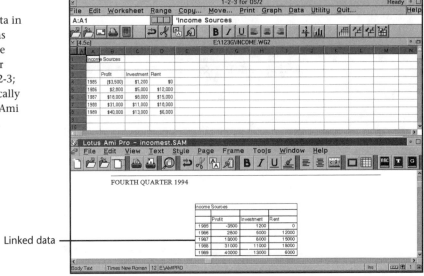

Linked data

Since 1-2-3 and Freelance Graphics share the same Graph Tool and most File menu commands, you can often use the two applications as if they were one. You can open worksheet (.WG2), desktop (.DSK), presentation (.PRS), and graph (.GPH) files from either 1-2-3 or Freelance Graphics. Also, 1-2-3 and Freelance Graphics can install in one directory and share many of the same files and configuration information. This directory structure saves launch time, memory, and disk space.

Another great feature of integrating 1-2-3 and Freelance is the ability to save your desktop setup as a (.DSK) file. A desktop file integrates the graph, worksheet, and presentation files you have on your desktop and remembers their names, placement, links, and status. Desktop files are great file containers and save the time it would take to open individual files, link them together, and position them.

You can import 1-2-3 worksheets into Ami Pro and display the data in a table, which allows you to present spreadsheet data in proposals and reports. You can paste graphs, clip art, and symbols from Freelance into Ami Pro to keep your documents and presentations consistent with company standards.

SmartIcons

The SmartSuite applications share many SmartIcons (buttons representing functions) that you can use across applications. A SmartIcon icon set is a palette that contains icon buttons representing certain automated actions, such as opening a file, cutting a selected object, and so on. Figure 1.7 illustrates Freelance Graphics, 1-2-3, and Ami Pro tiled on-screen so you can compare the default SmartIcon sets.

Default SmartIcons

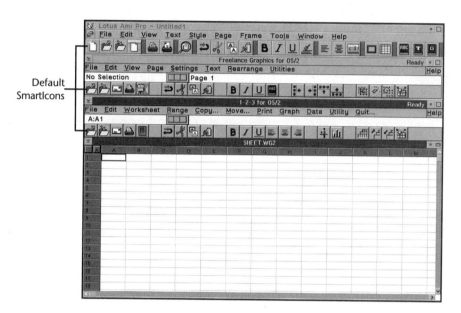

These SmartIcons enable you to perform such tasks as copying and pasting data between applications, running built-in macros, activating spell checking, and so on. Using the SmartIcons within each application saves you time and frustration.

Custom Dictionary

Ami Pro, Freelance, and cc:Mail have common spell dictionaries which allow you to share a custom dictionary and save resources (1-2-3 for OS/2 doesn't contain a spell checker). You can create a custom dictionary that includes proper names and other words unique to your company or business, plus

Tip

To view a description of a SmartIcon button in the title bar, click the right mouse button on the desired icon.

Fig. 1.7

The SmartIcon palettes or sets for each application contain similar SmartIcons and actions.

▶ See "Using the SmartIcons," p. 39

▶ See "Using Custom Dictionary and Language Options," p. 291

I

A New Way to Work

Tip

Your custom dictionary, LTSUSER1.DIC, is a text file located in your program directory.

▶ See "Inserting Symbols and Other Graphics," p. 416

switch to a different spell checking language. The custom user dictionary can be shared with other Lotus products not in the SmartSuite for OS/2, such as Ami Pro and 1-2-3 for Windows.

Clip Art and Symbols

Ami Pro includes many clip art files in the C:\AMIPRO\DRAWSYM directory as well as a few TIF (Tagged Image Format) art files. You can cut and paste any clip art from Ami Pro to one of the other applications. Figure 1.8 shows an Ami Pro clip art file in a Freelance Graphics presentation.

Additionally, Freelance Graphics contains many symbols and other pictures, including arrows, people, computers, animals, and so on. You can use these symbols in several of the applications by cutting or copying the symbol from your Freelance Graphics presentation slide, switching programs, and pasting in a different application. Figure 1.9 shows a Freelance Graphics symbol being pasted into Ami Pro.

Fig. 1.8

Select the art and press Shift+Insert to copy it; then switch programs and position the insertion point. Press Ctrl+Insert to paste the copied picture.

▶ See "Copying from Ami Pro to 1-2-3 and Freelance," p. 516

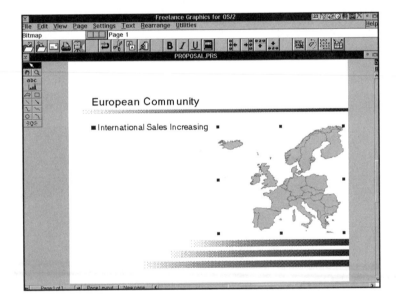

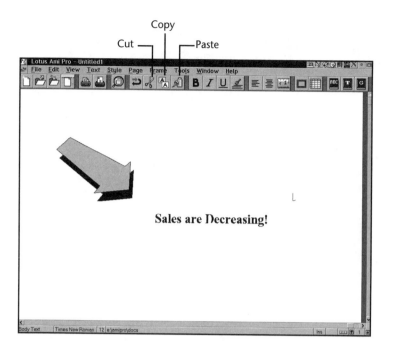

Fig. 1.9
Select a symbol
and cut or copy it,
switch programs,
and then paste the
symbol.

I

A New Way to Work

Graph Tool

Both 1-2-3 and Freelance Graphics use a common, graphical charting tool
called the Graph Tool that provides a consistent user interface for charting
graphs from within either product. The Graph Tool is a separate tool that
runs on the desktop and can be run seamlessly from either 1-2-3 or Freelance.

With the Graph Tool you can create and edit graphs and quickly choose a
format for your graph from an on-screen gallery of over 60 predefined graph
styles. After creating or editing graphs in the Graph Tool window, the resulting graphs are part of your presentation or worksheet file. You can create a
graph from 1-2-3 worksheet data and then use the very same graph in a
Freelance presentation. Because 1-2-3 and Freelance share the same Graph
Tool, you can edit the presentation graph in Freelance without affecting the
data in 1-2-3, and if you change the source data in 1-2-3, the Freelance graph
updates (see fig. 1.10).

▶ See "The Shared
Graph Tool,"
p. 129

▶ See "Using the
Graph Tool,"
p. 471

Fig. 1.10

A graph being shared between 1-2-3 and Freelance.

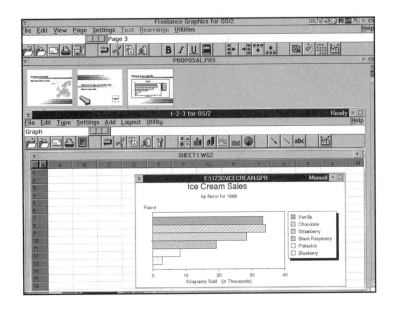

Identifying the Applications

The SmartSuite applications give you the resources to create various business documents. Using Ami Pro, you can create letters, brochures, reports, envelopes, newsletters, and so on. 1-2-3 enables you to organize, manipulate and analyze data. Freelance Graphics provides a tool for creating professional looking presentations and slides to show your customers or to include with company reports. cc:Mail allows you to communicate electronically with your coworkers and send file attachments.

Each application in the SmartSuite has its own specific purpose. You can create a worksheet in the word processor (using tables), but it's easier and more efficient to create and analyze the data in the spreadsheet program. Additionally, with easy task-switching and methods of sharing data, your work will be easier if you use each application as it is intended, as described in this section.

What Is 1-2-3 Release 2.1?

Lotus 1-2-3 Release 2.1 for OS/2 is a spreadsheet application intended for managing, calculating, analyzing, and presenting data. With 1-2-3, you can create worksheets and charts, and solve what-if problems. 1-2-3 offers the tools for producing advanced worksheets, customizing 1-2-3, automating procedures by writing macros, and creating database tables within the application. 1-2-3 takes advantage of the Presentation Manager graphical user interface while maintaining compatibility with other releases of 1-2-3, including 1-2-3 Release 3 for DOS and 1-2-3/G.

In addition to creating analytical worksheets and ranges, entering and editing data in cells, inserting and deleting columns and rows, calculating with formulas and functions, and other basic operations, 1-2-3 enables you to perform the following:

- Enhanced integration of 1-2-3 into the OS/2 Workplace Shell; the ability to drag and drop files to program objects, folders, and device objects, like printers.

- Open, copy, move, and delete files by dragging and dropping icons in the OS/2 Workplace Shell; even attach a file to a cc:Mail message by dropping it on an open cc:Mail message.

- Format and change fonts, numbers, borders, styles, row and column size, and so on.

  ▶ See "Formatting Numbers for Clarity," p. 108

- Print and preview the entire worksheet or only a range, and specify print options according to your printing needs.

- Create charts using the Graph Tool to illustrate the data. Charts can include axis titles, tick marks, labels, and legends.

- Data Protect and Password Protect access to worksheets and ranges within worksheets; plus annotate worksheets using descriptive Notes.

- Use the Backsolver and Solver to analyze what-if problems such as "What happens to our market share if sales increase by 5%?"

  ▶ See "Entering Worksheet Calculations," p. 89

- Create and use database tables and query tables.

- Customize SmartIcons and palettes; plus assign macros to them to help speed and automate your work.

- Create powerful macros that automate tasks and speed up repetitive or complex tasks within worksheets.

- Perform statistical analysis to track and organize your business activities over time.

Figure 1.11 shows the default 1-2-3 worksheet window.

Fig. 1.11

1-2-3 offers an easy-to-use graphical interface that is very similar to Freelance and other OS/2 applications.

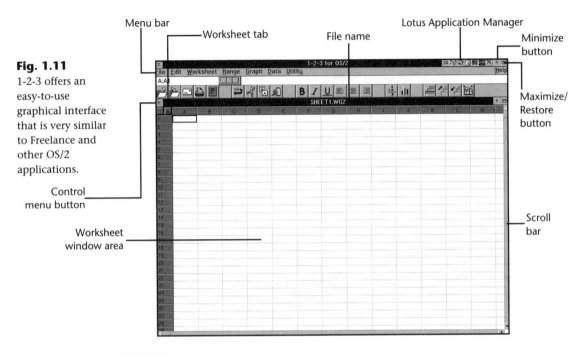

What Is Ami Pro Release 3.0b?

▶ See "Placing Text in Your Document," p. 250

Ami Pro is a powerful, flexible and beneficial word processing program you can use to produce most of your business documents. In addition to entering and editing text, you can use Ami Pro to check spelling and grammar, format text, and modify page layout.

Not only can you perform basic word processing functions in Ami Pro, you can also perform the following tasks that make Ami Pro closely resemble a desktop publishing application:

- Create and modify paragraph styles that enable you to easily format and make global changes to your documents.

- Organize long documents using outlines and designating outline styles, outline levels, and numbering.

- Review and proofread documents by checking spelling, grammar, and making use of the thesaurus.

- Print documents, envelopes, labels, and more.

- Create footnotes, headers and footers, tables of contents, indexes, and other available reference tools.

- Create and modify frames to hold text or pictures.

- Create and modify tables for columnar text and other data; use formulas, tabs, footnotes, and other features within the tables you create.

- Create and edit drawings, shapes, and objects; and save for use in Ami Pro or other applications.

- Create charts and modify them using the Ami Pro Charting functions.

- Track revisions to documents using revision marking and notes, and compare documents, which is especially helpful for projects utilizing more than one author.

- Merge data files and documents to create mail merge letters, labels, envelopes, and so on.

- Create time-saving documents called Automated Style Sheets to encourage document standardization, which in turn enhances your company's image.

- Build powerful macros that can be saved to automate your repetitive word processing tasks.

- Integrate Ami Pro with the other SmartSuite Programs.

Figure 1.12 illustrates the Ami Pro screen for comparison with the other SmartSuite applications.

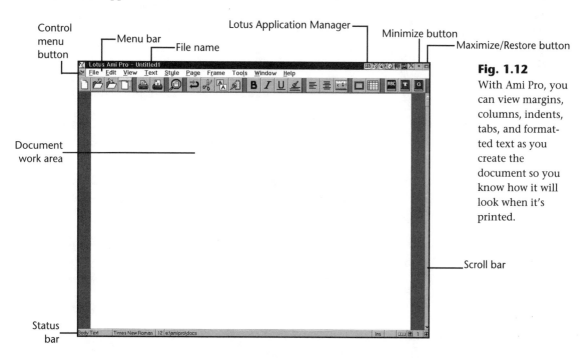

Fig. 1.12
With Ami Pro, you can view margins, columns, indents, tabs, and formatted text as you create the document so you know how it will look when it's printed.

What Is Freelance Graphics Release 2.1?

Freelance Graphics is a presentation program that enables you to create printed presentations to show customers or coworkers, eye-catching slide shows, and overhead transparencies. A presentation is generally used to help sell a product or idea, or to illustrate specific data, such as sales numbers, new services, product lines, and so on. Freelance automates the process of creating a presentation.

In addition to entering and editing text, formatting text, and enhancing a presentation using symbols, bullets, and other images, you can also do the following with Freelance Graphics:

▶ See "Entering and Editing Text," p. 411

- Create text slides that include data-driven charts and edit them by adding titles, notes, axis labels, and other charting features.

- Print a presentation with headers and footers, and even print up to six presentation pages on a handout for distributing to audiences.

- Create a screen show production of your presentation to use as the delivery medium for informal meetings, demos at trade shows, or mobile sales and marketing presentations.

- Use drawing tools to create, edit and annotate illustrations to make your presentation more attractive.

▶ See "Working in a New Presentation," p. 394

- Create a presentation using Freelance Graphics' pre-formatted SmartMasters for titles, bulleted lists, charts, and so on.

- Make global changes to a presentation for a quick and easy update process.

- Change and modify the colors of text, shapes, backgrounds, and other objects.

- Use SmartMaster backgrounds for industry-specific and international subjects, such as worldwide landmarks, agriculture, and maps.

- Add ready-made artwork, scanned images, and even choose from an installed library containing hundreds of symbols spanning broad subject matters.

- Integrate Freelance Graphics with 1-2-3 for OS/2 by graphing worksheet data and sharing the graph results.

Figure 1.13 illustrates the Freelance Graphics screen with a default presentation slide.

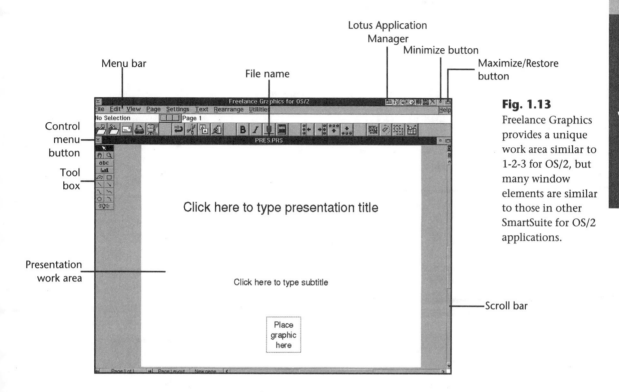

Fig. 1.13
Freelance Graphics provides a unique work area similar to 1-2-3 for OS/2, but many window elements are similar to those in other SmartSuite for OS/2 applications.

What Is cc:Mail 1.03?

cc:Mail Desktop for OS/2 WPS is a powerful and flexible electronic mailing package that takes full advantage of OS/2 Workplace Shell's object-oriented interface. It allows you to exchange messages and attachments with not only other cc:Mail users but other users utilizing Vendor Independent Messaging Interface (VIM) mailing applications.

This powerful communication package allows you to send and receive virtually anything that can be created on your workstation as mail. Organizing messages is more intuitive and faster. Mail functions such as Inboxes, Message folders, Message templates, and Directories are represented by objects within the cc:Mail folder. The cc:Mail work area and folder appear in figure 1.14. You can move these objects to desired locations, quickly move between objects, attach documents, and delete and organize message objects by dragging and dropping them within the OS/2 Workplace Shell.

Fig. 1.14

cc:Mail allows you to exchange messages and attachments with users using other mail and messaging systems.

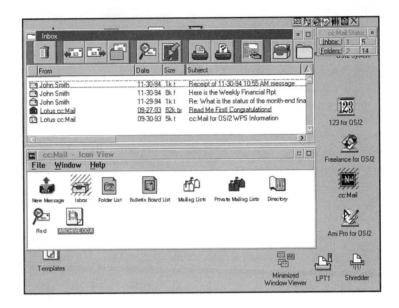

▶ See "Sending a cc:Mail Message from within the SmartSuites," p. 575

▶ See "Using the Mail Database," p. 591

In addition to sending and receiving messages, cc:Mail also allows you to perform the following functions for more effective electronic communication.

■ Create, edit, and maintain public and private electronic mailing lists.

■ Create Message Templates Objects which allow you to create new mail messages directly from the desktop, and even drag-and-drop file attachments onto the object for automatic routing to predefined recipients.

■ Search for messages contained in your inbox, folders, or bulletin boards.

■ Establish message priorities to indicate the urgency of the message and even request a return receipt for mail certification at the time the recipient opens the mail message.

■ Spell check your messages before sending and routing to individuals.

■ Attach files to messages without leaving your SmartSuite application or even drag and drop file attachments from cc:Mail to open or launch the attached file.

■ Receive notification of incoming mail via your inbox in the cc:Mail status window.

■ Store, retrieve, move, trash, and archive messages.

From Here...

Now that you are familiar with a new way of working by using the Lotus SmartSuite applications, refer to the following chapters to learn more about the common features shared by the applications:

■ Chapter 2, "Using Common Features," shows you the intricacies of utilizing the OS/2 Workplace Shell including how to launch the applications, open and close files, move between programs and documents, use menus and dialog boxes, enter and edit text, and use the Help feature.

■ Chapter 3, "Managing Files and Work Areas," shows you how to name, save, and print files; and describes the work areas of the SmartSuite applications and the OS/2 Workplace Shell.

I

A New Way to Work

Chapter 2

Using Common Features

by Lenny Bailes

One advantage of using OS/2 applications is that all OS/2 applications have common elements: menus, title bars, scroll bars, dialog boxes, and so on. Additionally, many features, such as Cut and Paste, macros, and many short-cut keys, work the same way in all OS/2 applications. SmartSuite takes these similarities a step further by using many common elements, features, and commands in all the SmartSuite applications.

Once you learn, for example, to use the SmartIcons in Ami Pro, you can easily apply that knowledge to Freelance Graphics or 1-2-3. Similarly, after you learn which menus contain specific commands, you can find many of those commands in the same menus in the other applications. Applying common features to the SmartSuite applications makes it easier for you to get to the task at hand, learning only the new features particular to the program.

In this chapter, you learn how to:

- Open and exit applications

- Use menus, commands, and dialog boxes

- Enter, select, and edit text

- Copy and move text

- Format text

- Manage objects

- Use online Help

Opening Applications

As with any OS/2 application, you can open—or *launch*—a SmartSuite program by using any of several methods. You can use the mouse or the keyboard, or a combination of both. You can open an application from an object on the OS/2 desktop, from the OS/2 Drives Object, or by typing its name at an OS/2 command prompt. You can also have a program open automatically when OS/2 starts or use the Lotus Application Manager to launch or switch between SmartSuite applications.

Launching from the Desktop

OS/2's Workplace Shell provides groups of related programs or data files together in a desktop object called a *folder*. When the folder is opened, individual icons within it represent programs or data files. To open a program using the mouse, double-click a folder to open it, then double-click the program's icon. To open a program using its menu, right-click the program icon. Then, choose **O**pen from the object's pop-up menu. As a shortcut, you can select the program icon with the mouse or keyboard and press Enter to open the application.

Figure 2.1 Illustrates the OS/2 Desktop with the Lotus Applications folder displayed. The 1-2-3 for OS/2 program icon is selected, and its pop-up control menu is displayed.

Launching from the Drives Object

You can open applications from the OS/2 Drives Object. Double-click the Drives Object, which may be located on the Desktop or the Launch Pad, but can always be found in the OS/2 System Folder. Double-click the correct drive and directory. Then locate the EXE (executable file) in the open folder that represents the directory. For example, to open Lotus 1-2-3, locate the 123G folder/directory and the 123G.EXE file. To open the application file with the mouse, double-click the EXE file name. You can also select the file name and press Enter to open the application.

Fig. 2.1

Select the program icon, open the control menu and choose Open to launch an application.

Figure 2.2 illustrates the 123.EXE file selected and ready to open from the 123G folder in the "Drive E" Drives Object.

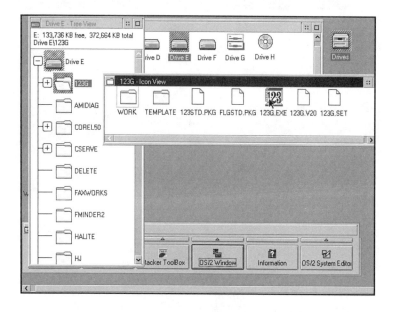

Fig. 2.2

Select the program file's icon/object.

Launching Automatically with the Startup Folder

If you use a specific program every time you boot OS/2, you can place that program's icon in the OS/2 Startup folder and the program automatically opens each time you boot OS/2. Naturally, you can close the program at any time, and you can remove it from the Startup folder if your needs change.

To place a program icon in the Startup folder, open the program's folder and the Startup folder. The Startup folder is located within the OS/2 System folder. Holding down the Ctrl+Shift keys and the right-mouse button, drag the program icon from its folder to the Startup folder (You can also right-click the icon, select Create Shadow from its pop-up menu, select the Startup folder from the resulting dialog box, and click **C**reate). The next time you boot OS/2, any program whose icon is in the Startup folder opens as well.

Figure 2.3 shows the 123G folder from Drive E, and the Startup folder nested within the OS/2 System Folder. The 123.EXE file object is dragged to the Startup folder while the Ctrl and Shift keys are held down. This makes a "Shadow Object" in the Startup folder so each time OS/2 boots, 1-2-3 opens too.

Fig. 2.3
Drag the program icon to or from the Startup folder to add or remove programs from startup at boot time.

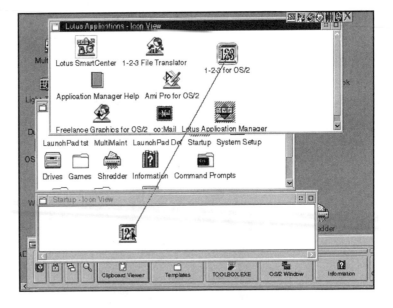

Launching with Application Manager

To help you integrate your SmartSuite applications, Lotus has added an extra tool, called the Lotus Application Manager. You can use Lotus Application Manager to quickly open new programs or switch between programs that are already open. The Application Manager, which displays six Lotus icons, appears in the upper-right corner of the desktop after it has been started. (To start Application Manager, double-click its icon in the Lotus Application folder.) If you're running a SmartSuite application in a maximized window, the Application Manager icon bar appears in the upper-right corner of the application's title bar.

Figure 2.4 shows the Lotus Application Manager in the upper-right corner of the Ami Pro window.

Tip
You can make the Application Manager start automatically when you boot OS/2 by creating a shadow of it in the OS/2 Startup folder.

Lotus Application Manager

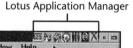

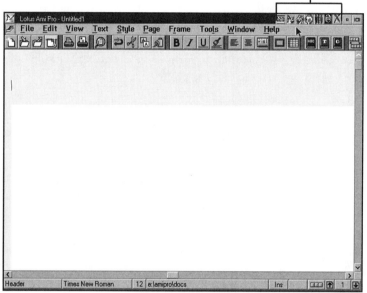

Fig. 2.4
Lotus Application Manager icons enable you to quickly open or switch to applications in the Suite.

A New Way to Work

To launch or switch to a program in the Application Manager, click the representative program icon. If the program isn't already open, Application Manager launches it; if the application is open, Application Manager switches to that program without closing the original application. Selecting the red X at the extreme right closes the Application Manager.

Caution

If your system has limited memory, it may not be able to handle three, four, or five open applications at one time. Close any programs not in use and check into purchasing more RAM for your computer.

Launching from Lotus SmartCenter

In addition to the Application Manager, SmartSuite now includes a more full-featured, user-configurable toolbar called the Lotus SmartCenter. SmartCenter was formerly available as part of a separate package called the SmartSuite Value Pack. If your copy of SmartSuite doesn't include the Lotus Value Pack diskettes, you can request them free of charge from Lotus Customer Support.

As with the Application Manager, when you double-click the SmartCenter object, a new toolbar is displayed on the desktop. The SmartCenter toolbar contains icon options to launch SmartSuite applications, among its many other useful features. A built-in balloon help feature shows you the function of each icon on the toolbar when you point to it with the mouse. (Let the mouse hover over a selected icon for several seconds, as shown in figure 2.5 to pop up a balloon description of its function.) To start 1-2-3, Freelance Graphics, Ami Pro, the cc:Mail Inbox, or a windowed OS/2 session, click the appropriate icon in the center of the toolbar.

Fig. 2.5

Lotus SmartCenter contains a superset of the options in Application Manager. A balloon caption describes each icon's function.

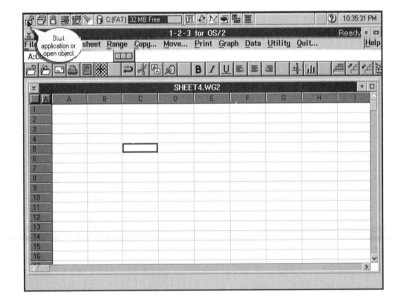

▶ See "Lotus SmartCenter," p. 691

The SmartCenter toolbar can also be configured to launch non-SmartSuite applications. To learn more about SmartCenter's additional features and display options, click the question mark icon toward the right end of the toolbar.

Launching from an OS/2 Command Prompt

You can launch SmartSuite applications, or any other OS/2 program from a text-based OS/2 command prompt. For instance, to start Ami Pro, open an OS/2 command prompt from the Application Manager (second icon from the right edge), or the OS/2 System Command Prompts folder. Change to the \AMIPRO directory on the appropriate drive, type **amipro.**, and press Enter.

Launching from the Warp Launch Pad

If you are using OS/2 Warp, v. 3.0, you have the option of starting applications from the Launch Pad. Consult your Warp manual for details on how to do this.

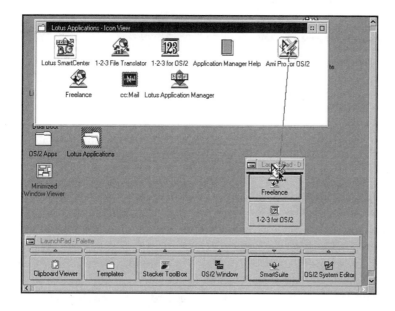

Fig. 2.6
Add an application to the Warp, v. 3 Launch Pad by dragging it to the main icon window, or to one of the nested drawers.

Closing Applications

OS/2 provides several ways for you to close applications. You can use the **F**ile menu, a mouse shortcut, keyboard shortcut, or the OS/2 Window List. Close an application when you're finished using it so system memory can apply to other open applications and documents. Most OS/2 programs close the same way. To close an application, do one of the following:

■ Choose **F**ile, **E**xit. (For Lotus 1-2-3, select the **Q**uit option at the right end of the menu bar unless you have enabled the CUA menus. Freelance has no Exit or Quit command on its menus, and must be closed by one of the other methods listed on the following page.)

■ Press Alt+F4 or click the Control menu and choose Close.

■ Double-click the Control menu (located in the left corner of the title bar of the application).

■ Press Ctrl+Esc (or click the Desktop with both mouse buttons held down) to display the Window List. Point to the application, click the right-mouse button and choose **C**lose.

When you close an application, if you haven't saved recent changes to your documents a dialog box appears reminding you to save changes before closing. You can choose to save, ignore the exit command, or close the application without saving the document.

Note

If you're running a DOS application in OS/2, close the application as you normally would in the DOS environment. To exit the MS-DOS Prompt, type **exit** and press Enter. Windows programs can be closed in the same way as native OS/2 applications.

Viewing Parts of the Window

All OS/2 applications have common elements so they are easier to learn and use, including scroll bars, Control menus, title bars, and so on. In addition to the common OS/2 elements, SmartSuite incorporates similar window elements in its programs. For example, SmartIcons provide shortcuts for commands and other tasks you perform while working in the SmartSuite applications. Many of the SmartIcon sets are similar, as are many buttons within the sets. Finally, many of the menus and commands in each of the SmartSuite applications are similar and easy to learn and use.

Note

Although most windows include the same elements, there are some differences between the window elements in an application window and a document window. All windows, for example, contain a Control menu, but only document windows use scroll bars.

Viewing Common Window Elements

The SmartSuite applications are fashioned after other OS/2 applications and contain window elements common to all OS/2 programs. Figure 2.7 shows the Lotus 1-2-3 screen with common elements of the OS/2 applications labeled.

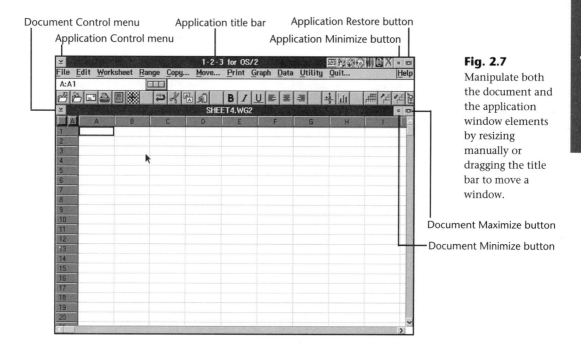

Fig. 2.7
Manipulate both the document and the application window elements by resizing manually or dragging the title bar to move a window.

Many window elements are common to both application and document windows; other features pertain only to one or the other window type. Table 2.1 describes the common window elements and their uses.

▶ See "Controls To Manage Your Work," p. 78

Table 2.1	Common Window Elements	
Element	**Location**	**Description**
Control menu	Upper-left corner of a window's title bar	Opens to view commands directly related to manipulating the application or window, such as minimizing or maximizing, closing, or switching to another application or document.

(continues)

Table 2.1 Continued

Element	Location	Description
Title bar	Top of window	Names the application and document; drag title bar to reposition window.
Minimize button	Small square button in the upper-right corner of a window	Shrinks the window to an icon.
Maximize button	Large square button in upper-right corner of window	Enlarges the window to fill the work area. When a window is maximized, you can click this button to return the window to its previous size.
Menu bar	Directly below the title bar of an application window	Displays a list of related commands, or opens the menu. Click a menu name or press the Alt key to activate the menu bar and then press the underlined letter to open a specific menu (**F**, for example, in **F**ile).
SmartIcons	Below the menu bar or positioned anywhere when customized	Click a button on the SmartIcon toolbar to perform an action or command.
SmartIcon button	Directly underneath the Help menu to the right	Displays the SmartIcon sets available.
Scroll bars	On right side and bottom of a document window	Click in the scroll bar to move around in the document window.
Scroll arrows	At the ends of the scroll bars	Click once to move the cursor one line at a time, in that direction; hold down the mouse button to move continuously.
Scroll box	Inside the scroll bars	Drag the scroll box to another position in the scroll bar to move within the document window.
Window border	Narrow line surrounding document and application windows that are not maximized	Move mouse pointer over border until a double-headed arrow appears; then drag the border to resize the window.

Using the SmartIcons

SmartIcons are part of the common interface Lotus applies to the SmartSuite applications. All SmartIcons work the same way, with each icon representing a commonly used command, feature, or function that activates when you click the button. SmartIcons save you time because you can apply the functions of these buttons to other Lotus applications once you learn the icon sets. Although all SmartSuite applications share common buttons that perform the same tasks in any program, each SmartSuite application also has SmartIcon buttons unique to the program. For a complete discussion of each program's SmartIcons, see the chapter on the individual application.

Using Menus and Commands

The menu bar is located below the title bar of an application. Each menu contains related commands that display when you open the menu. Commands let you perform tasks such as searching for specific text, formatting text, inserting a picture, and so on. Some commands require that you select text or graphics before performing the task; for example, you must select text before you can cut or copy it.

To make using the SmartSuite applications even handier, Lotus has used many of the same menus and commands, in similar placement, within each of the applications. Learning the uses of these commands in one program gives you a head start when learning another SmartSuite application.

Using a Menu

Listed on any menu in any OS/2 application are related commands that let you manage files, get help, edit text, and so on. When you open a menu, a list of related commands drops down from the menu bar. To open a menu, do one of the following:

- Click the menu name with the mouse.

- In Ami Pro, press Alt plus the underlined letter in the menu name. For example, press Alt+**F** to open the **F**ile menu. In 1-2-3 and Freelance, pressing and releasing Alt will activate the menu bar. You can then type the letter of the menu.

- Press the Alt key, and use the left- or right- arrow key to highlight a menu's name; press Enter to open the menu.

Tip

To find out what any SmartIcon can do, point the mouse at the icon and press and hold the right mouse button. A description appears in the application title bar, temporarily replacing the application name.

▶ See "Using SmartIcons," p. 674

I

A New Way to Work

If you accidentally open the wrong menu, you can do one of the following:

- Press the Esc key once to close the menu, but leave the menu bar highlighted; then highlight another menu

- Press the Esc key twice to close the menu and deactivate the menu bar.

- Click another menu.

- Click outside the menu to close it.

- Press the Alt key again.

Using Commands

When you open a menu, a list of commands drops down from the menu bar, and you can choose the command you want the application to perform. Commands are directly related to the menu name; for instance, the **F**ile menu contains commands related to files—**S**ave, **P**rint, **O**pen, and so on. To choose a command, click the command name or press the underlined letter in the command.

> **Note**
>
> Many commands are followed in the menu list by a combination keystroke you can use as a shortcut. For example, Alt+Bksp (backspace) is a shortcut for **U**ndo. You can only use the shortcut if the menu is closed, so remember the shortcut for the next time you need the command.

Some commands automatically perform an action; others display a dialog box. Still other commands display a secondary, or *cascading*, menu. All menus in OS/2 applications use similar symbols—the ellipsis, arrow, or checkmark—to indicate the result of choosing a command.

The indicators for commands in most OS/2 applications are:

- *Ellipsis.* Three dots after a command indicates that a dialog box containing additional options and choices will appear when you choose that command.

- *Arrow.* An arrow to the right of the command indicates a secondary or cascading menu containing more related commands will appear.

- *Checkmark.* A checkmark in front of a command indicates that the command is active. Commands using checkmarks appear in groups; only one command within the group can be active at any time.

Figure 2.8 illustrates the **V**iew menu in Ami Pro. Only one checkmark appears in each group of viewing commands.

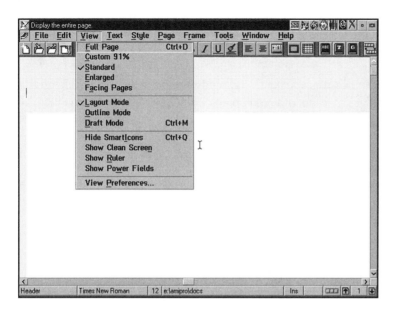

Fig. 2.8
When you choose a command, a brief description of the command appears in the title bar.

Using SmartSuite Menus and Commands

The SmartSuite applications share several menus and commands which produce similar results.

Common Menus

All the SmartSuite applications use the menus listed in table 2.2.

Table 2.2	Common Menus in SmartSuite
Menu	**Common Commands**
File	New, Open, Save, Save As, Print, Exit
Edit	Undo, Cut, Copy, Paste, Paste Special, Link or Link Options
Help	Contents, Keyboards, How Do I?, Index (123 and Freelance), About

Note

Some of the File and Edit options are not present in Freelance Graphics or within the cc:Mail utilities. In order to see these menu options in 1-2-3, you must select CUA Menus from the User Settings, Preference dialog box under the Utility menu.

Each menu contains related commands; for example, the Edit menu in Ami Pro contains, among other commands, Undo, Cut, Copy, Paste, Paste Link, Paste Special, Find and Replace, Go To, and Insert. Again, Lotus makes learning and using the SmartSuite applications easier by placing many of those commands in other applications in the suite. The commands also perform the same task, in a similar way, no matter which application you use.

Shortcut-Key Combinations

The SmartSuite menus provide several shortcut-key combinations you can use to activate a command. Key combinations display to the right of many commands in the application menus. Some commands perform tasks without further input; others display a dialog box for more information. Pressing a shortcut-key combination evokes the same response as if you had opened the menu and selected the command.

Using Dialog Boxes

When you choose a command with an ellipsis, a dialog box appears, asking for more or related information. Dialog boxes may be as simple as a message—such as: Spell checking is complete.— or as complicated as Ami Pro's Font dialog box, in which you choose typeface, size, attribute, and color.

Tip

To close a dialog box without making any changes, press the Esc key; pressing Esc is the same as choosing the Cancel command button.

No matter what type of dialog box appears, you must communicate, (or have a dialog) with it. In many cases, you can't continue your work until you at least acknowledge the dialog box, choosing OK, for example. OK is a command button that signifies you accept the changes you just made to the dialog box and closes the box. On the other hand, you can choose the Cancel command button to close the dialog box without making any changes. A shortcut for choosing OK is to press Enter; a shortcut for Cancel is to press the Esc key.

All dialog boxes have some common features and symbols. For example, dialog boxes look and act like windows. Dialog boxes also have other elements that allow you to communicate with them. Figure 2.9 illustrates some common elements. In Ami Pro, additional options are accessible by clicking the tabs on the right side of the dialog box. Lotus 1-2-3 and Freelance dialog boxes have a slightly different format. Instead of tabs, additional options may be accessible from radio buttons.

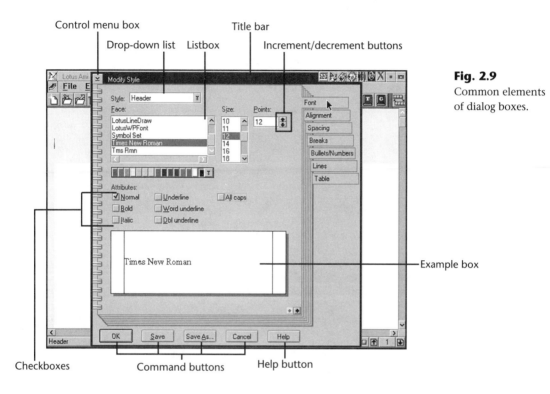

Fig. 2.9
Common elements of dialog boxes.

Table 2.3 lists and describes the common elements in the SmartSuite application's dialog boxes.

Table 2.3 Common Dialog Box Elements	
Element	**Description**
Title bar	Displays the name of the dialog box; drag the title bar to move the dialog box on-screen
Group	A boxed-in grouping of related options or choices
Option buttons	Round radio buttons representing options; within one group, you can choose only one option
Checkboxes	Square boxes representing choices within one group; you can choose as many or as few checkboxes as you want

(continues)

Table 2.3 Continued

Element	Description
Listbox	A box containing choices; sometimes you can choose only one option and sometimes you can choose several
Example box	A display or preview of the formatting selections so you can view changes before accepting them
Increment/Decrement buttons	A text box with an up and down arrow attached; click an arrow to change the value in the box
Text box	A box in which you can type an option or choice; generally connected to a listbox from which you can choose instead of entering text
Drop-down list	A text box with an underlined down arrow attached; click the down arrow to display a list of more choices
Command buttons	Buttons that let you close the dialog box (OK or Cancel), or take some other action as indicated on the face of the button; command buttons with an ellipsis following the label (tunnel-through command buttons) open additional dialog boxes

Note

Using the mouse to move around and make choices in a dialog box is much easier than using the keyboard. If you must use the keyboard however, use the Tab and arrow keys to move around, highlight your choice, then press Enter to select the choice.

Entering, Selecting, and Editing Text

To create a letter, worksheet, database, calendar, or other document, you must first enter text. After you enter the text, you can format, proof, delete, modify, or otherwise edit it; but you must first select it. No matter what application you're using, you must first identify the text before you can perform any editing tasks on it.

The SmartSuite applications use similar methods of entering, selecting, and editing text, as well as a few specialized techniques. This section covers only the common ways of entering, selecting, and editing text; see the chapter concerning the specific application for any specialized methods.

Entering Text

In the SmartSuite applications, you can enter text into a document, cell, text block, or text box. When you want to enter text, move the mouse over the area—a box, blank page, or text box—and the mouse pointer changes to an I-beam cursor. Click the mouse; a blinking vertical line, or cursor, appears. The cursor moves for every character you type. The position where the cursor is blinking is also called the *insertion point*. Figure 2.10 illustrates entering text in Ami Pro.

A New Way to Work

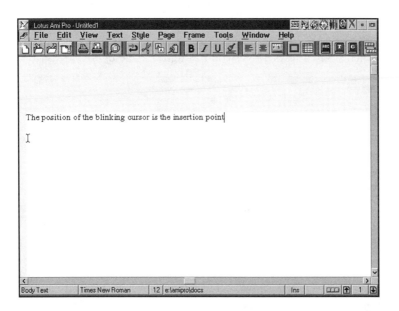

Fig. 2.10
Click the I-beam to position the insertion point; as you type, the blinking cursor moves.

> **Note**
>
> In Freelance Graphics, you can create text boxes by clicking the text tool and dragging it to make the size box you want. When you release the mouse button, the blinking cursor appears in the text box. In Ami Pro, you can do this by selecting **C**reate Frame from the **F**rame menu. When you double-click the Ami Pro frame, the blinking cursor appears within the box.

To type in a cell (in a 1-2-3 or an Ami Pro table, for example), click the I-beam and begin typing. You can enlarge the cell one more line by pressing Enter or by allowing the text to wrap to the next line when it reaches the right side of the cell.

Moving Around the Screen

After entering information in any of the SmartSuite applications, you need to move around the screen so you can edit or add information. Moving around is a similar process in all the programs. You can use either the mouse or the keyboard to move around on-screen, or you can use a combination of both.

Using the Mouse To Move Around the Screen

Use the scroll bars, scroll arrows, and scroll boxes to move around a document, presentation, slide, or worksheet that doesn't all fit into view on-screen. Dragging the scroll box moves you up and down (vertical scroll bar) or from left to right (horizontal scroll bar) quickly. Clicking the up, down, right, or left scroll arrows moves you through the document slowly.

> **Caution**
>
> Be careful when using the scroll bars because even though the screen moves, the insertion point remains in the same position. Do not forget to click in the new on-screen location.

Using the Keyboard To Move Around the Screen

The movement keys on your keyboard work well to move the insertion point on-screen in the SmartSuite applications. Use the following movement keys to move the insertion point on-screen:

- Use the directional arrow keys to move one character to the left or right, or one line up or down.

- Use the PgUp and PgDn keys to move one screen up or down (in Freelance, this changes slides).

- Pressing Ctrl+Home moves the insertion point to the beginning of the document or worksheet; pressing Ctrl+End moves to the end of the document. (In Freelance these keys move the insertion point to the beginning or end of a text box.) In 1-2-3 End+Home moves to the end of the document.

▶ See "Navigating the Worksheet," p. 86

- Home moves the insertion point to the beginning of a line; End moves it to the end of a line.

Selecting Information

When you reach the point where you want to add, delete, or edit, you may need to select the information to make a change. Before you can cut or copy information, or change spacing, typefaces, or attributes, you must select it. You can delete information after you select it or replace selected information with new information. Selecting it, or designating it as the information that the next action will affect, is similar in all of the SmartSuite applications.

To deselect something, click the mouse anywhere on-screen, or press one of the arrow keys.

Selecting Information with the Mouse

The easiest way to select information is by using the mouse. Click the mouse at the beginning of the item to be selected and drag it to the end of the item. You can also select information with a mouse by doing the following:

- Double-click a word or object to select it.

- Click at the beginning of the selection while pressing and holding the Shift key. Click at the end of the selection.

Figure 2.11 shows selected, or highlighted, text in Ami Pro.

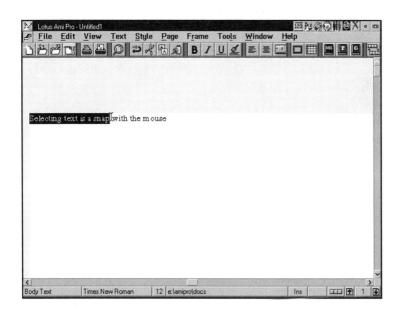

Tip

You can apply formatting—such as alignment, indents, and tabs—to text by positioning the insertion point within the text to be modified.

Tip

Text selection can be dependent on the view; you can only select text in Freelance Graphics when in current page view.

Fig. 2.11

Text or objects that are selected can be edited or easily deleted and replaced.

I

A New Way to Work

Selecting Text with the Keyboard

You can use many keys to select information on-screen in any of the SmartSuite applications. To use the keyboard for information selection, do the following:

- Press Shift+left or right arrow to select one character to the left or right of the cursor. Make sure 1-2-3 is in edit mode and you've opened a text block in Freelance.

- Press Shift+up or down arrow to select from the insertion point to the same point above or below the insertion point. (In 1-2-3, this will shift to the cell above or below the one you were editing.)

▶ See "Entering Data," p. 81

- Press Shift+Home or End to select from the insertion point to the beginning or end of a line. Shift+End doesn't work in 1-2-3.

▶ See "Placing Text in Your Document," p. 250

- In 1-2-3, press Ctrl+Shift+left or right arrow to select five characters to the left or right; continue to press the arrow to continue selecting five characters at a time. (In Freelance and Ami Pro, Ctrl+Shift+left or right arrow will select a complete word.)

Editing Text

OS/2 applications provide many methods of editing text. You can add, delete, or type over it. Following are the common methods of editing text in the SmartSuite applications:

- Press Backspace to delete the character to the left of the insertion point. Make sure 1-2-3 is in edit mode.

- Press Del to erase the character to the right of the insertion point; hold the key down to erase more characters. In 1-2-3 and Freelance, pressing delete erases all data in the highlighted cell; change to edit mode first.

- Choose **E**dit, **U**ndo to erase the typing you just performed; alternatively, press Alt+Backspace to undo typing.

- Position the insertion point at the beginning of the text you want to delete. Press the Ins key and begin typing; each character you enter replaces one existing character.

- Select the text you want to replace and begin typing. The new text replaces the selected text.

Copying and Moving Data

When you move or copy data, you transfer the data to the OS/2 Clipboard. Using the Clipboard, you can transfer or copy data from one document to another, one worksheet or presentation to another, or from one application to another. You could create a worksheet in 1-2-3 and copy it to a business report in Ami Pro; imagine the time and work it would save. Moving and copying data is similar in all OS/2 applications and in the SmartSuite programs.

▶ See "Editing Text," p. 254

Cutting, Copying, and Pasting

To move data, cut it; to copy data, use the **C**opy command. The data remains on the Clipboard until you paste it or cut or copy another selection of data to the Clipboard. Follow these steps to cut, copy, and paste:

1. Select the information to be cut or copied.

2. Do one of the following:

Choose **E**dit, Cu**t** to move the text, or **E**dit, **C**opy to make a duplicate of the text.

Press Shift+Del to move or cut the text, or Ctrl+Ins to copy it.

Click the Cut or Copy SmartIcon on the Default SmartIcon bar.

3. Do one of the following:

Move to a new place in the file by using the scroll bars or keyboard.

Choose **F**ile, **O**pen to open another document.

Press Ctrl+Esc to display the Window List and choose another application or use the Lotus Application Manager to switch to another application.

4. Position the insertion point.

5. Do one of the following to paste the text at the insertion point:

Choose **E**dit, **P**aste.

Press Shift+Ins.

Click the Paste SmartIcon in the Default SmartIcon bar.

Tip

You can also cut or copy objects, such as pictures, charts, and tables.

So, to copy and paste data, simply select the data, press Ctrl+Ins, reposition the insertion point, and press Shift+Ins. The data appears at the insertion point.

Formatting Text

Whether you're creating a business report, sales presentation, or budget worksheet, you can format the text in your document by using similar methods in the SmartSuite applications. *Formatting* text includes modifying the typeface, changing the size of the text, applying text attributes (bold, italic, and so on), and changing alignment. These are the shared formatting methods in the applications, even though each individual application may let you change indents, apply tabs, adjust spacing, and so on.

> **Note**
>
> Ami Pro and Freelance Graphics both offer additional formatting with Styles and SmartMasters. See the sections about the individual application for more information.

Changing the Font

Changing the font includes choosing typeface, type size, and text attributes. You can use the Font dialog box to change all of these formats at one time and work more efficiently. The Font dialog boxes in Ami Pro, 1-2-3, and Freelance Graphics are similar. Figure 2.12 illustrates the Font dialog box in Ami Pro.

Fig. 2.12
Use the Font dialog box to choose the face, size, attributes, and color for the selected font and preview what you have chosen before accepting changes.

To use the Font dialog box, follow these steps:

1. Select the text, or cell, containing the text to be formatted.

2. In Ami Pro, choose **T**ext, **F**ont; in Freelance Graphics, choose **T**ext, **F**ace. In 1-2-3, choose **R**ange, **A**ttributes Font. The appropriate Font dialog box appears.

3. Choose the Face, Size, Attribute, and Color you want to apply to the selected text.

4. Choose OK to accept the changes and return to the document.

> **Tip**
> You can use the SmartIcons to apply bold, italic, or underline attributes to selected text.

Troubleshooting

When I print, the fonts look different on paper than on my screen.

If this occurs in Freelance, choose **U**tilities, **P**references, **A**lways Use Outline Fonts. If it occurs in 1-2-3, choose **R**ange, **A**ttributes, **F**ont, **S**etup and switch the display from **S**creen to **P**rinter.

Changing Alignment

In addition to formatting fonts in the SmartSuite applications, you can change text alignment by using the keyboard shortcuts or the SmartIcons in the various programs.

To use the SmartIcons for aligning (left, right, or center), and justifying, select the text or position the insertion point in the text, and click the SmartIcon. (In 1-2-3, select the cell or cells. In Freelance, open the text block.)

To use the keyboard shortcut in Ami Pro, position the insertion point in the text, and press one of the following:

Ctrl+L	Left-aligned
Ctrl+R	Right-aligned
Ctrl+C	Center-aligned
Ctrl+J	Justified

▶ See "Changing Paragraph Attributes," p. 272

▶ See "Styling Entries for Emphasis," p. 112

A New Way to Work

Managing Objects

Objects can include clip art or other pictures, charts, tables, or graphs. Objects can be created within some programs; or they can be imported, linked, embedded, or copied from one application to another. Managing objects—copying, deleting, moving, and selecting—is similar in the SmartSuite applications.

Selecting, Resizing, and Moving an Object

▶ See "Using Graphics with Ami Pro," p. 353

▶ See "Inserting Symbols and Other Graphics," p. 416

Whether the object is a picture, chart, table, or other graphic, you can select it just like you select text. After you select the object, you can manipulate it and format it as well. To manipulate an object, do the following:

■ To select an object in one of the SmartSuite applications, click the object. Small black boxes, or *handles*, appear on the corners and sides of the object to indicate that it's selected (see fig. 2.13).

■ To move a selected object, position the mouse pointer anywhere within the borders of the object and drag it to a new position. The object moves with the mouse.

■ To resize a selected object, position the mouse pointer on one of the handles; the pointer changes to a double-headed arrow (in 1-2-3 the pointer changes to a + sign and in Freelance it remains a single arrow). Drag the handle toward the center of the object to reduce its size; drag the handle away from the center to enlarge the object.

■ To delete a selected object, press Del.

Formatting the Object

In every SmartSuite application, you can format an object by selecting it and then using a formatting menu—such as the Chart, Table, or Frame menu—or by double-clicking the object. When you double-click an object, a dialog box appears, from which you can modify the entire object or a portion of it.

▶ See "Frame Options," p. 348

When you work with a graph in either 1-2-3 or Freelance, for example, and then double-click it, the graph is opened in a window of its own. You can then modify it with options in the **S**ettings and **A**dd menus. If you double-click a specific part of the chart, the Line and Color, Titles, Heading, or Legend dialog box may appear for further editing and formatting. Once a 1-2-3 or Freelance chart appears in its own window, you can bring up the Type Gallery dialog box from the Type menu (see fig. 2.14).

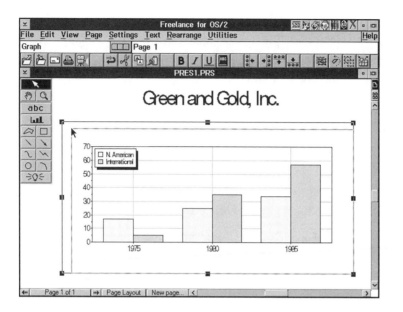

Fig. 2.13
Double-click a chart to open it in a separate window.

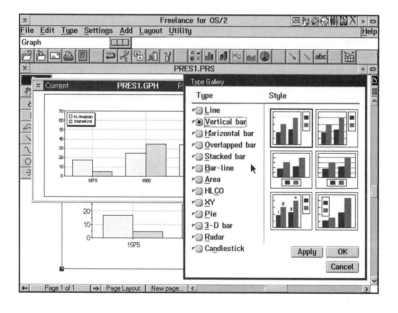

Fig. 2.14
To display the Type Gallery dialog box, choose **T**ype, **G**allery; make changes and choose OK to return to the chart.

Using Online Help

The Help feature of the SmartSuite applications provides extensive, online assistance when you're working. (Online means that Help is available, on-screen, at the click of a mouse.) You can use the Help menu to gain information about specific topics, keyboard shortcuts, procedures, and more.

Using the Help Commands

The Help menu is similar in all the SmartSuite programs. You can choose from various categories, or Help commands, to get the assistance you need. The Help commands are as follows:

- *Contents.* (Ami Pro) Displays help topics in icon form to choose for more information, such as "What's New," "Menus," and "Error" messages.

- *Using Help.* (Ami Pro) Provides assistance in using the Help features.

- *Help Index.* (1-2-3, Freelance, and cc:Mail) Displays a series of help topics in text form to choose for more information.

- *How Do I?* (1-2-3, Freelance, and Ami Pro) Lists common procedures to choose from, and displays detailed steps to follow.

- *About.* Lists the release number, copyright information, free memory in your system, and so on.

To use the **H**elp menu, activate the menu and select a command. Figure 2.15 illustrates the Contents window in Ami Pro. Note that the icons represent general subjects. Select an icon to view more information about it.

Tip

In Ami Pro, if you're in a dialog box and need help about what to do next, click the help button—the question mark in the upper-right corner—for context-sensitive help.

Fig. 2.15

Click an icon to reveal underlined topics; click an underlined topic to reveal more information.

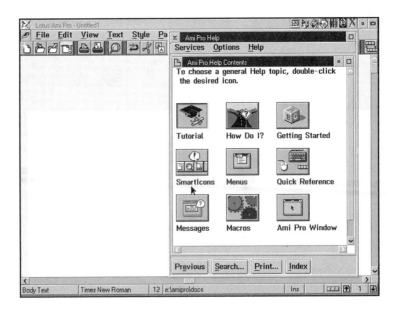

Note

Help windows are like any other window—they have a Control menu, a title bar, window borders, and so on. You can manipulate the window by moving it and resizing it.

From Here...

Now that you know the common commands, features, and workings of the SmartSuite applications, you are ready to move on to working with the applications. To continue your introduction to SmartSuite, you may want to review the following chapter:

■ Chapter 3, "Managing Files and Work Areas," shows you how to save, open, print, and close files and how to work with drives and directories.

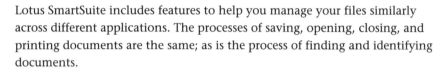
Chapter 3

Managing Files and Work Areas

by Lenny Bailes

Lotus SmartSuite includes features to help you manage your files similarly across different applications. The processes of saving, opening, closing, and printing documents are the same; as is the process of finding and identifying documents.

In this chapter, you learn how to:

- Save, open, and close documents

- Use drives and directories

- Print documents, spreadsheets, and other files

- Move between documents and applications

Working with Files

When you first open a SmartSuite application, a blank page or worksheet appears. (In Freelance, you're directed to load a new or existing presentation, first.) After entering text or other data, you save the document so you can come back to it later. Until you save the document, it exists only in your computer's memory; if you lose power or neglect to save the file, you lose the document.

When saving a file, you assign it a location on a specific drive and directory, and give it a name. When you finish working with the saved file, close it so

▶ See "Customizing Your Working Environment," p. 95

you can either work on another document or close the application. You can open a saved document later to review, revise, or print.

Saving, Opening, and Closing Files

Tip
When you first save a file, you must assign a location (drive name/directory) and a name to the file. Future changes will be saved under this assigned file name.

The dialog boxes you use to save and open files are similar in all the SmartSuite programs. Each dialog box has sections for a file name, drive, directory, file type, and so on. The procedure for closing files varies in each of the applications.

For example, you use the Save command or icon when you first save a file. The first time you save the file, a dialog box appears asking you to name the file and assign it a location on a drive and directory. Use the **S**ave command again to save changes to a file you have already named.

To save, open, or close a file, you can use a menu command, SmartIcon, or, in some of the applications, a shortcut key. Table 3.1 shows the different methods for saving, opening, and closing files in the SmartSuite applications.

▶ See "Working with Old and New Files," p. 102

▶ See "Saving Your Work," p. 102

▶ See "Saving a Presentation," p. 405

Table 3.1   Saving, Opening, and Closing Files

Task	SmartIcon	Menu Command	Shortcut Key
Save		File, Save	Ctrl+S
Save As		File, Save As	None
Open		File, Open	Ctrl+O
Close	(Ami Pro Only)	File, Close	Ctrl+F4

Note

For 1-2-3 and Freelance, files are closed by double-clicking the control menu in the document window.

Note

After entering changes, if you try to close a file without saving it first, a dialog box appears asking whether you want to save. Choose OK or Yes to save the file, No to close without saving changes or naming the file, or Cancel to return to the file without closing.

> **Note**
>
> In Ami Pro, at the bottom of the **F**ile menu is a list of the three most recently opened files, including drive, directory, and file name. Files opened from the floppy drive don't display in the recently opened list.

Troubleshooting

Sometimes I can't open a file, or I can open it but not save my changes.

The file may be password-protected. If this is the case, you must know the password to save changes to the file.

I can't tell the difference between file types.

Refer to the three-letter extension: for example, SAM is an Ami Pro document, WG2 is a 1-2-3 file, and so on.

Tip
Starting a new file is also the same in all the SmartSuite applications. Choose **F**ile, **N**ew or choose the New SmartIcon to open the New dialog box.

Using File Dialog Boxes

When you open the Save As or Open dialog boxes, the application displays the default drive, directory, and, in some of the applications, a list of file names. The default drive and directory usually hold the program's files. For example, Ami Pro documents are stored in the C:\AMIPRO\DOCS directory; 1-2-3 worksheets are stored in the C:\123G and 123G\WORK directories. A file name consists of up to eight characters, a period, and a three-character extension. The extension identifies the program: SAM is the extension, for example, for Ami Pro. Figure 3.1 shows the Ami Pro Save As dialog box.

Tip
To access the list of files in the Freelance File Save dialog box, click the List Files button.

> **Note**
>
> You can customize the default document directories in some of the SmartSuite programs. See Chapter 15, "Managing, Organizing, and Importing Files," for more information about customizing Ami Pro and Chapter 4, "Introducing the 1-2-3 Worksheet," for modifying 1-2-3.

The following elements appear in a Save As dialog box in all the SmartSuite applications:

- *File **N**ame text box.* Type the name of the file, with up to eight characters. You can let the program fill in the period and extension for you, or you can add your own.

■ *Command buttons.* Choose OK to accept your choices (in cc:Mail, choose Save); choose Cancel to close the dialog box without saving.

Fig. 3.1
The Save As File **N**ame text box is highlighted. Type the eight-character file name—the program adds the extension.

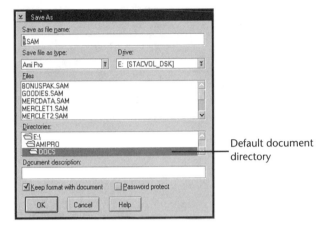

Default document directory

Working with Drives and Directories

In Freelance and Ami Pro, The Save As and Open dialog boxes include a Drive pop-up listbox and a Directories listbox from which you can choose. (In 1-2-3, only the Open dialog box has these features.) The different applications use a specific directory to store text or data files: for example, Freelance Graphics presentation files are stored in C:\123G\WORK, if you installed Freelance Graphics in a shared directory with 1-2-3. If you installed Freelance Graphics in its own directory, the presentation files are stored in [D:]\FLG\WORK. WORK is the specific directory for presentation files. You can, of course, change the directories and drives you save your files to. In the Save or Save As options for 1-2-3, if you want to change the location where a file is stored you must manually enter a drive and directory name into the File Name dialog box. 1-2-3 has a separate option for bringing up a drive/directory listbox to change the default working directory. This is accomplished by selecting the Directory option from the File menu.

Drives

To change to a different drive, such as a floppy or network drive when opening a new file, use the Drive pop-up listbox (see fig. 3.2). (In Freelance, you must first click the List Files button.) Choose the drive you want. New directories display in the Directories listbox.

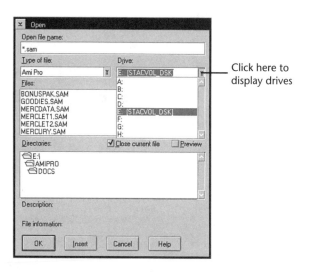

Click here to display drives

Fig. 3.2
You must insert
a disk before the
application can
access the high-
lighted drive.

I

A New Way to Work

Note

Drives A and B are usually reserved for floppy disk drives and C is reserved for the first hard drive partition. Drives D, E, and so on can be used for hard drive partitions, removable tape drives, or network drives.

Directories

The hard drive on your computer is organized with directories and sub-directories, similar to how you organize a filing cabinet. The entire drive is like the cabinet and is called the *root directory*. The root directory contains all of the other directories—such as DOS, OS2, DESKTOP, Windows, Ami Pro, and so on—and some program files such as AUTOEXEC.BAT and CONFIG.SYS.

Each *directory* extending from the root directory is like a drawer in the filing cabinet. Each drawer holds file folders, or *subdirectories;* and each subdirectory holds *files* (refer to fig. 3.2).

To change directories in a file dialog box, double-click the *parent directory,* which holds the other directories. In figure 3.2, E:\ is the parent directory of AMIPRO. AMIPRO is the parent of DOCS. So, double-clicking AMIPRO displays the directories on the same level as the DOCS directory (see fig. 3.3).

You can double-click the parent of a directory to see all directories on that same level. To see all directories on the drive, double-click the E:\ or root

Tip
The file folder icon to the left of the directory is open when you are viewing its contents. You can double-click file folders that appear closed to view their contents.

directory. (In figure 3.3, E is the root directory.) Opening directories works in the same way; to see the subdirectories in any directory, double-click that directory.

Fig. 3.3
AMIPRO is the parent directory not only to DOCS, but to DRAWSYM, ICONS, and MACROS as well.

> **Note**
>
> In 1-2-3, you can only access drives and directories in the File Open file dialog box. In the File Save dialog box you must manually enter information if you want to change the drive and directory path. For example, to save a worksheet called JAN.WG2 in a directory called C:\WORK\JANUARY, type the path and file name in the file name area in the File Save dialog box. 1-2-3 also allows you to change the default working directory by selecting the Directory option from the File menu. The 1-2-3 File, Directory feature is equivalent to the drive and directory listboxes that appear in the Save and Save As menus of the other SmartSuite applications.

Working with File Types

Each application uses its own file type when it saves a file. In the file dialog boxes, notice the extension added to the file names. By default, the files save as the application's file type. The following is a list of the SmartSuite application file types:

■ SAM for Ami Pro

■ PRS for Freelance Graphics

■ WG2 for 1-2-3 Worksheets

■ GRH for 1-2-3 Graphs

When you save a file in any of these applications, the application automatically adds the three-character extension so you can easily find the file again for later use. When you access the Open dialog box, the application automatically lists the files with that same three-character extension.

> **Note**
>
> Notice the use of the wild card and extension in the Open File Name text boxes when you first access an **O**pen dialog box. The wild card, asterisk (*), used in conjunction with the extension, tells the program to list all files in the directory that end with that specific extension; for example, *.SAM means list all files ending in SAM.

You can save files with a three-letter extension other than the designated default extension. You can also open files created in other programs by changing the file type. Figure 3.4 shows the Ami Pro Open dialog box with a 1-2-3 file about to be opened. To get to the point where the figure is, you must first change directories, choose the file type, and type or choose the file name from the list. You can then choose OK to open the file. In this case, Ami Pro asks questions about how much of the worksheet you want to open.

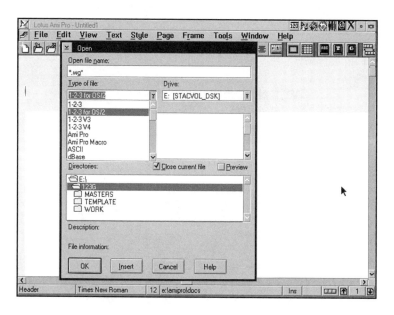

Fig. 3.4
Change the file type to open a file from a different application.

> **Note**
>
> Although 1-2-3 can't directly open or import Microsoft Excel spreadsheets, you can place them in a 1-2-3 window via Ami Pro and the Clipboard. In Ami Pro, choose **File, O**pen. In the **T**ype of File listbox, choose Excel. After the spreadsheet appears in Ami Pro, select the desired cell range with the mouse and copy it to the Clipboard. Now start up 1-2-3 and open a new spreadsheet file. Import the Excel range by choosing **E**dit, **P**aste.

Printing Files

The SmartSuite applications let you print your files in similar ways. Using similar Print and Printer Setup dialog boxes between programs, Lotus makes it easier for you to efficiently print your documents, worksheets, and presentations. In addition to using the menu command to print, you can print a file by using a shortcut key (if available) or a SmartIcon.

Printing and Print Options

You can print one or more pages, worksheets, slides, or other document types; or you can print a specific range or selection. To open the Print dialog box, press the Ctrl+P shortcut-key combination (available only in Ami Pro), click the Print SmartIcon, or use the menu command. To print a file, choose **File, P**rint. In 1-2-3 or Freelance Graphics, choose **P**rint, Print Worksheet or Print Presentation from the set of submenu options. The Print dialog box for Ami Pro appears in figure 3.5.

Fig. 3.5
The Ami Pro Print dialog box presents choices for specific page range and number of copies, as well as buttons to access page setup options.

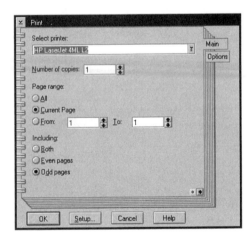

The following is a description of the common options in the SmartSuite Print dialog boxes. (In 1-2-3 and Freelance, some of these options appear in the dialog box that appears when you select Print, Options.)

- Choose to print **C**urrent Page, **A**ll pages in the file, or specify the page numbers you want to print.

- Choose the **N**umber of Copies you want to print.

- Choose the Page Setup command button to change page orientation, page size, margins, and so on.

▶ See "Printing the Worksheet," p. 215

> **Note**
>
> Each application offers other printing options; for more information, see the chapters on the individual SmartSuite applications.

Changing Printer Setup

Changing the printer setup is also similar in the SmartSuite applications. You can choose the fonts, page size, orientation, paper source, and so on, all in the Printer Setup dialog box. To display the Printer Setup dialog box, choose **F**ile, Prin**t**er Setup. Depending on the application, you may need to choose which printer you want to modify or choose a Setup command button. The Options dialog box appears (see fig. 3.6).

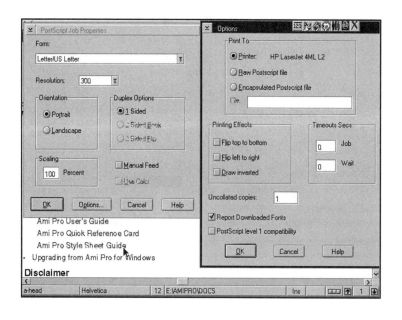

Fig. 3.6
You can display the Options dialog box to choose a printer and select other options.

The following is a list of common features in the Setup dialog box in Ami Pro with an HP LaserJet 4 PostScript printer. Depending on your printer, you may see other options in the Setup dialog box.

- *Form/Paper Size.* Specify which paper bin or tray you want to use. Choose the size you want to print, such as letter, legal, commercial envelope, and so on.

- *Orientation.* Choose Po**r**trait or **L**andscape.

- *Resolution.* Set the resolution of the printer output in dots per inch. (300 dots per inch is standard on most laser printers.)

- *Scaling.* Choose a percentage by which to enlarge or reduce the printed document, if applicable.

- *Duplex (Features).* Choose options specific to your printer, such as double-sided printing, envelope printing, and so on.

- *Output Format.* (Accessible after choosing O**p**tions.) Choose a format specific to your printer, such as PostScript, Encapsulated PostScript, HP PCL 4 or 5, and so on. This menu also lets you determine whether the Postscript driver will report system or downloaded fonts as printer fonts, and enable support for Postscript Type I font on older, Postscript Level 2 printers.

Troubleshooting

I received a message stating Cannot find a printer driver. *What should I do?*

Choose File, Print, Destination in 1-2-3 or Freelance or File, Printer Setup in Ami Pro and select a printer. Make sure you specified the appropriate printer in the dialog box. If you didn't, you may need to install your printer with the OS/2 Selective Install object, located in the OS/2 System Setup folder.

I can't print in Landscape Orientation.

To print in landscape mode, your printer, the font, and the printer driver must support Landscape printing. In Print Setup, change orientation to Landscape. If you changed the orientation to landscape and still can't print landscape, check your printer manual to make sure your printer supports this mode.

Switching between Documents

In all SmartSuite applications except cc:Mail, you can open several files at one time and switch between them. This way you can refer to other documents, share data, edit, and so on. You can also display two or more files on-screen at the same time. To switch between files in 1-2-3 and Freelance Graphics:

1. Make sure both documents are in resizable windows, rather than maximized windows. The rectangle in the upper-right corner of the document window controls this setting.

2. Resize the current document window with the mouse so that part of the other document window is visible on the screen.

3. Click the document window you want to make current while holding down the left mouse button. You may also switch between document windows by pressing Ctrl+F6.

When you click the title bar of any window, that window becomes active. An active window has a dark title bar. All menu commands, SmartIcon buttons, and shortcut-key combinations apply to the active window.

You can also open several files and then minimize them until you need them. To minimize a file window, click the Minimize button. The document changes to a small icon that appears in the application window. Figure 3.7 shows two worksheets in 1-2-3 minimized and a new file window adjusted so you can see the two icons.

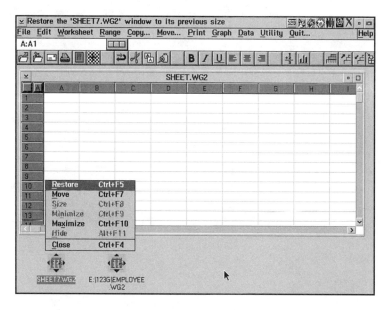

Tip
By default, Ami Pro closes the current document before opening a new one. You can disable this feature by removing the check from the **C**lose Current File checkbox in the Open dialog box.

Fig. 3.7
You can click a document icon to reveal the Control menu, then choose the **R**estore command to open the window.

Switching between Applications

Tip
Double-click a
document icon
to open the
document.

One of the most useful advantages of using Lotus SmartSuite is the capability to switch between similarly constructed applications. You can work in two, three, or four applications without closing them—for example, all you have to do is switch from Ami Pro to 1-2-3, or from cc:Mail to Freelance Graphics. Switching between applications which recognize one another makes it easier and more efficient for you to share data.

◀ See "Taking
Advantage of
SmartSuite,"
p. 9

You can switch between applications by doing any of the following:

- Click the application's icon in the Lotus SmartCenter or Lotus Application Manager.

- Press Alt+Tab to move from one open application to another.

- If part of an application window shows, click it to bring the window forward.

- Press Ctrl+Esc, or open the application's Control menu and choose Window List, to display the OS/2 Window List. Select the application and double click with the left mouse button.

Figure 3.8 illustrates the Window List with several applications listed.

Fig. 3.8
Use the Window
List, the keyboard,
the Lotus Applica-
tion Manager,
or the Lotus
SmartCenter to
switch between
applications.

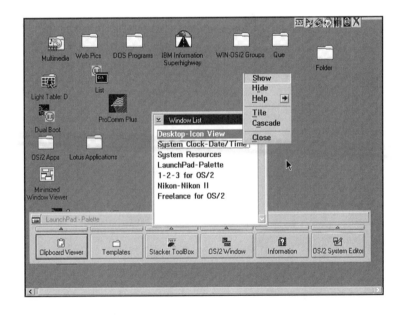

Troubleshooting
My system slows down when I switch between applications.
You need more RAM. Try closing unused applications and leaving only two or three applications open at one time.

From Here...

Now that you understand what the SmartSuite applications have in common, you're ready to learn each program's specific benefits, features, and application. Refer to the following chapters:

- Chapter 4, "Introducing the 1-2-3 Worksheet," introduces 1-2-3 by discussing advantages of the program, defining terms specific to 1-2-3, describing basic data entry and navigation throughout the worksheet, and how to use ranges and calculations in the worksheet.

- Chapter 12, "Creating and Editing Documents," is an introductory chapter for using Ami Pro that shows you how to place and edit text, define files, save documents, and create new documents.

- Chapter 20, "Getting Started with Freelance Graphics," teaches you how to display rulers and use SmartMasters, objects, and layouts in the presentation program.

Part II

Using 1-2-3

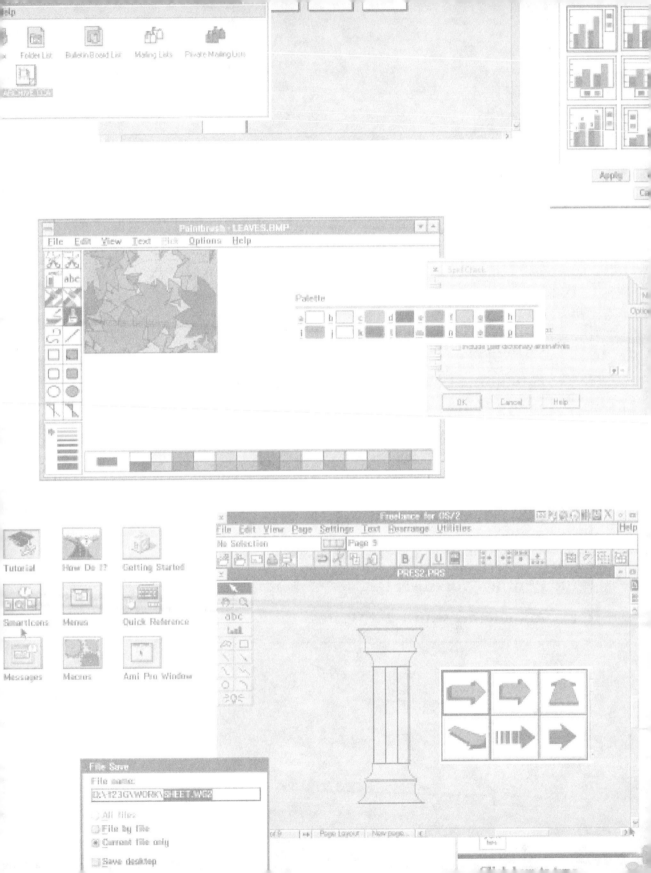

Chapter 4

Introducing the 1-2-3 Worksheet

by Elaine Marmel

Even people who have used computers extensively might never have seen an electronic spreadsheet because the nature of their work doesn't require this tool. For those who work extensively with numbers, however, the spreadsheet is the heart of Lotus SmartSuite for OS/2. The spreadsheet, they might suggest, is the starting point for most SmartSuite chores; it's the glue that holds the other applications together.

This chapter introduces 1-2-3. It explains what an electronic spreadsheet is and what it can do. It explores the controls available in 1-2-3, shows how to use those controls to store numbers and other data, and how to use them in calculations. The chapter ends by explaining how to save the work you've done in 1-2-3 so you can retrieve it later, to re-examine, edit, or add to it.

In this chapter, you learn:

- Exactly what an electronic spreadsheet is

- What types of tasks an electronic spreadsheet can accomplish

- How to store numbers and text in a 1-2-3 worksheet

- Methods for navigating in the worksheet

- How to perform calculations with your worksheet data

- Commands that customize 1-2-3's appearance and behavior

What Can an Electronic Spreadsheet Do for You?

The worksheet is the "1" in 1-2-3. At its simplest, an electronic spreadsheet is an expensive desktop calculator. Beyond simple calculations, though, 1-2-3 can save lists and tables of numbers for you to use again and again in calculations. It also stores formulas that you can reuse from one set of numbers to another, decreasing the amount of time you spend punching keys.

Reusability is a hallmark of the electronic spreadsheet. You lay out the formulas and text in a spreadsheet that describe your business calculations, and you can save the sheet's structure and reuse it with new data time after time.

Imagine having a fill-in-the-blanks mortgage calculator, or a single spreadsheet that you can use each week to report your travel expenses. Imagine being able to prepare budgets by drawing information from many worksheets (often provided by other users) into one worksheet. Along with numbers and calculations, 1-2-3 lets you store text entries. These entries label your calculations and describe the relationships among your data. Because you lay out the numbers, calculations, and labels as if on a large piece of paper, the end product can be a detailed report about any aspect of your business (see fig. 4.1).

Database management is the "2." 1-2-3 offers basic database management tools—the capability to store records in worksheet files, to arrange records alphabetically and numerically, to locate records that fit a profile (such as "all people from Florida," or "all employees making more than $42,000"), and to calculate subtotals by category such as department, gender, region, or years of employment. 1-2-3's database functions work well on smaller databases; a small database might contain 1500 records, each of which has 15 fields. For larger databases, you should use a tool specifically designed to handle database tasks to gain efficiency and speed.

Plotting graphs of numbers is the "3" in 1-2-3. Your worksheet software has an impressive graph-drawing facility. You enter numbers in the worksheet, click a few times with the mouse, and a graph appears almost instantly. Graphs can eliminate the gray from your reports and increase understanding for coworkers and managers who prefer visual over verbal input.

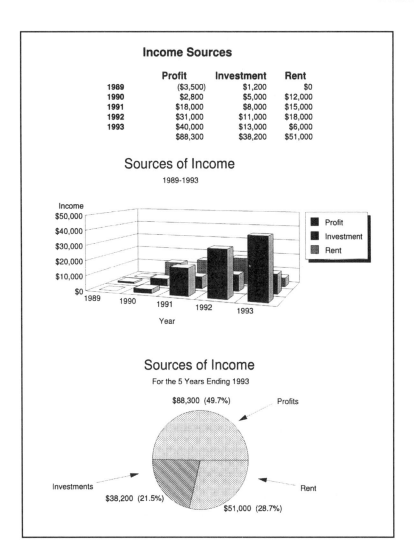

Fig. 4.1
In a 1-2-3 worksheet, you can create reports like this that include graphs.

What Is a Worksheet?

Lotus Development Corporation chose to use the term *worksheet* to mean spreadsheet. The meanings of both words are interchangeable. Arguably, any piece of paper, divided into rows and columns, can be a *spreadsheet*—a surface on which to write numbers, work out calculations, and, perhaps, make notes about what the numbers and calculations mean.

At its very simplest, an electronic spreadsheet satisfies this definition with the great distinguishing characteristic being the departure from paper. An electronic spreadsheet such as 1-2-3 is a computer program that acts as a surface on which to write down numbers, perform calculations, and label your work.

1-2-3's worksheet is a little more rigid than a piece of paper while you work. For numbers to be useful, they must reside at specific locations. These locations, called *cells*, are at the intersections of columns and rows—just like the spaces in which you write on a piece of ledger paper.

There are 256 columns in each 1-2-3 worksheet. Each column has a letter, or a pair of letters to identify it. Reading from left-to-right, the first column is A, the second B, and so on through column Z. The column after Z is AA, the next is AB, and so on. This progression continues through column IV.

A 1-2-3 worksheet has 8,192 numbered rows. In effect, then, there are 2,097,152 cells on the worksheet—a piece of ledger paper with that many spaces would be rather large. You identify a cell by naming both its column letter and its row number. So the cell in the top-left corner of the sheet—that is, the first row of the first column—is cell A1. The cell at the bottom-right corner is IV8192. These column-letter and row-number combinations are called *cell addresses*. Figure 4.2 shows the top-left corner of 1-2-3's worksheet as it appears on screen.

Fig. 4.2

In a 1-2-3 worksheet, letters identify columns; numbers identify rows. Use the combination of a column letter and a row number to identify a cell. Cell A1 is outlined in the figure.

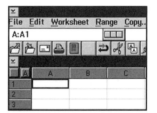

To store a number in 1-2-3, you type it in a cell. To perform a calculation, you enter a formula in a cell. To label the numbers and formulas, you type words into cells. As you can see, most of your work in the worksheet involves entering information into cells and, consequently, navigating from cell to cell using the scroll bars and direction keys. Later in this chapter, you'll learn how to move around a worksheet.

A Ledger Paper Notebook

Actually, a 1-2-3 file contains 256 worksheet pages, each having the described 256 columns and 8,192 rows. Lotus calls each of these pages *sheets*. Typically, you distribute information among several pages. For example, one page might hold budget data for Department 1, another might hold budget data for Department 2, and a third might hold formulas that calculate the total budget. When you use the sheets in this way, your worksheet file takes on a three-dimensional character.

Each sheet has a letter that identifies the sheet. These letters are A through IV, just like the columns of a single sheet. Figure 4.3 shows three sheets in a 1-2-3 worksheet file.

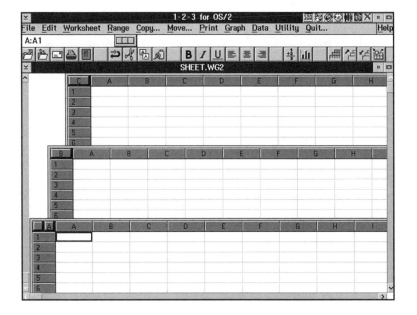

Fig. 4.3
In perspective view, you can see sheets contained in a worksheet file. The letter identifying each sheet appears in the upper-left corner of that page.

II

Using 1-2-3

You might guess that a column letter and row number alone can't describe a cell's location in a 3D worksheet file. A complete address consists of the page letter followed by a colon and then the location within the sheet. The address of cell A1 in sheet B is B:A1.

The Current, or Active, Cell

Even though you have many pages in a worksheet file and therefore many cells available, you can enter data into only one cell at a time—the *active cell* (also called the current cell). That's the cell that has a black box (called the *cell pointer*) around it.

Coincidentally, its address appears at the top-left of the screen between the menu and SmartIcon bar. In figure 4.4, the cell pointer is in cell A:A1. There are many ways to make a different cell current—for example, clicking a cell moves the cell pointer to it—you read about these alternative ways in later sections of this chapter.

Fig. 4.4
The current cell contains the cell pointer. Also, its address appears near the top-left corner of 1-2-3's display.

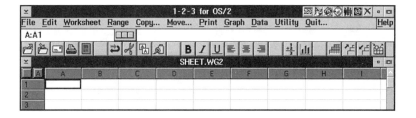

Controls To Manage Your Work

There's more to working in 1-2-3 than merely entering information in cells and moving from place to place. To that end, the software surrounds the worksheet area of the display with many controls, most of which are familiar even to a casual OS/2 user. Other controls are omnipresent throughout SmartSuite, so they may be familiar if you already work with another SmartSuite application.

Tip
Any action—formatting, deleting, copying, and so on—affects the active cell or cells.

As in all OS/2 applications, 1-2-3's main window contains sizing controls (Minimize, Maximize, and Restore buttons) in its top-right corner and a Control menu box in its top-left corner. The worksheet resides in a window with its own sizing controls and Control menu box.

The right and bottom borders of the worksheet window contain scroll bars that let you move the worksheet around behind the window—necessary because of the enormous size of the sheet and the limited size of the computer display. You can see all these controls in figure 4.5.

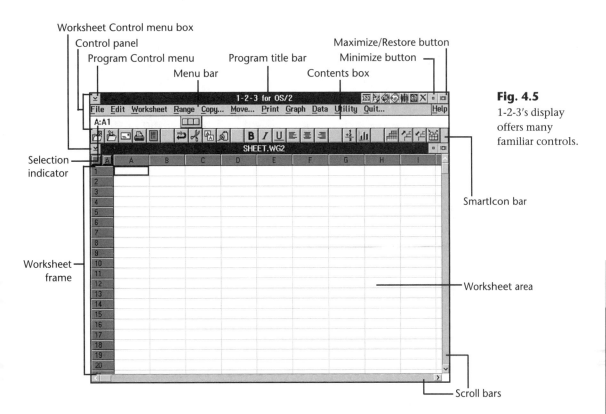

Worksheet Control menu box

Control panel

Program Control menu

Menu bar

Program title bar

Maximize/Restore button

Minimize button

Contents box

Selection indicator

Worksheet frame

Fig. 4.5

1-2-3's display offers many familiar controls.

SmartIcon bar

Worksheet area

Scroll bars

The Control Panel

The area above the worksheet in 1-2-3's display is the control panel. Normally, the control panel holds 1-2-3's main menu and a collection of boxes that provides information about your activity in the worksheet. The box at the far left is the selection indicator. The icon to the right of the selection indicator controls the display of the SmartIcon bar, which you will learn about in later sections. The large white space that stretches to the right of the SmartIcon display control is actually a box—the Contents box. Its purpose becomes apparent when you learn how to enter information into a worksheet.

The Main Menu

1-2-3's main menu resides in the Control panel. As with menus in most software programs, 1-2-3's menus contain commands you use to perform various functions, such as opening or saving a worksheet. The menus you see by

Tip
To use CUA menus, choose **U**tility, **U**ser Settings, **P**references. In the resulting dialog box, choose CU**A** menu and then OK to save.

default mimic the original 1-2-3 product for DOS. You can set your preferences so that you use a CUA (Common User Access) Interface; with CUA menus, the Print, Copy, Move, and Quit commands disappear from the main menu but appear on either the **F**ile menu or the **E**dit menu.

You can access these pull-down menus either by clicking the mouse, or by pressing the Alt key. Or, if you have worked with 1-2-3 on another software platform, you may be familiar with the slash key (/) method of accessing menus; this method is also available in 1-2-3 for OS/2.

SmartIcons

A prominent feature of 1-2-3's display is common to all the SmartSuite products: SmartIcons. Each icon on the palette near the top of the worksheet represents some task that you might otherwise perform by making selections from menus. Although the images on the icons are supposed to alert you to their uses, sometimes their meanings aren't always obvious.

If you need help remembering what a SmartIcon does, move the mouse pointer to it and click and hold the right mouse button. A short description of the SmartIcon's purpose appears in the program title bar, temporarily replacing "1-2-3 for OS/2" (see fig. 4.6).

Description of SmartIcon's purpose

Fig. 4.6
The purpose of a SmartIcon appears in the program title bar when you point at the SmartIcon and press and hold the right mouse button.

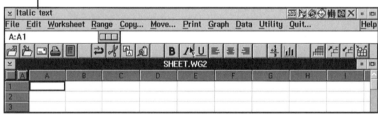

Status Bar

For those of you who have used 1-2-3 for DOS or 1-2-3 for Windows, you may be looking for the status bar. 1-2-3 for OS/2 does not use the status bar like other versions of 1-2-3. You will find the mode in which you are operating at the right edge of the program title bar. You will find information about the options you've established for selected cells in the worksheet at the left edge of the worksheet title bar (see fig. 4.7).

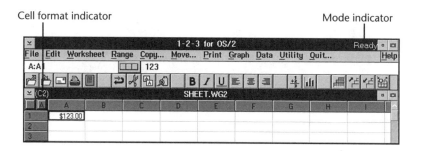

Cell format indicator   Mode indicator

Fig. 4.7
Instead of a status bar, 1-2-3 for OS/2 uses the program title bar and the worksheet title bar to display operating information.

Entering Data

Being familiar with 1-2-3's display doesn't get any work done. However, after the brief orientation, you're ready to exploit the power of this gigantic piece of electronic ledger paper. For most of us, the first step is to enter information into cells.

Entering Numbers

Almost all spreadsheet computing involves numbers, so entering a few in the worksheet is a good way to get started. To enter a number in a specific cell, simply activate the cell by clicking it and then type the number. As you type, the number appears in the contents box at the top of the display. Also, the Cancel and Confirm buttons appear to the left of the contents box, as shown in figure 4.8.

Tip
If you're using the Lotus Application Manager, you won't be able to see the mode indicator because the Application Manager covers it up unless you use the Restore button to make the 1-2-3 screen a little smaller.

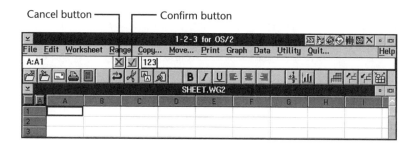

Cancel button ——   —— Confirm button

Fig. 4.8
The control panel changes as you type an entry in a worksheet cell.

When you've typed all the number's digits, press Enter or click the Confirm button. The number appears aligned to the right side of the cell, as shown in figure 4.9.

Fig. 4.9
By default, 1-2-3 aligns numbers at the right boundaries of their cells, as you see in cells B2, B3, and B4.

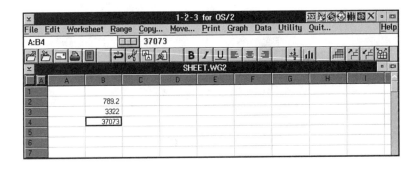

Tip
You can realign cell contents by activating the cell and clicking one of the align SmartIcons.

▶ See "Formatting Numbers for Clarity," p. 108

If you type a number, but decide you don't want to store it in the cell, before you press Enter, press Esc or click the Cancel button.

> **Note**
>
> If a number you enter has more digits than can fit in the cell, 1-2-3 displays the number in scientific notation. For example, if you enter 1234567890 in a cell, 1-2-3 displays the number as 1.235E+09. You can alleviate this problem by adjusting the column width.

▶ See "Changing Column Width and Row Height," p. 116

Troubleshooting

After I make an entry, the cell pointer is stuck. When I click another cell, or press a direction key, the computer beeps and nothing happens.

Look for the word Edit at the right edge of the program title bar at the top of the screen. If it appears there, something is wrong with the entry you just typed. Chances are you were typing a formula and made a mistake. It's also possible that you unintentionally started an entry with a reserved character such as @ or . (a decimal point). Either press Esc once or twice to clear the entry, or figure out what's wrong and edit the entry as explained in the next few pages.

Entering Text

When you want to label the numbers in a worksheet to show what the numbers represent, simply find a nearby cell to hold a new entry and type the appropriate word or words. For example, suppose the numbers in figure 4.9 represent ice cream sales for various flavors. To label the column, click cell B1, type **Volume Sales (Gallons)**, and press Enter or click the checkmark (Confirm) button. To identify sales volume for vanilla, click cell A2 and enter **Vanilla**.

As with numbers, when you type a label, the characters show up in 1-2-3's contents box. But here's a twist: when you press Enter to store a label, 1-2-3 inserts a label prefix character in front of it. By default, the *label prefix* is an apostrophe. It appears only in the contents box, and not in the worksheet. A label prefix is not part of the label, but as you'll see in Chapter 5, "Formatting Data and Working within the Worksheet," the prefix serves the important purpose of determining how the label will align within the cell. Figure 4.10 shows a worksheet with labels that clearly identify the numeric entries.

▶ See "Aligning Data," p. 118

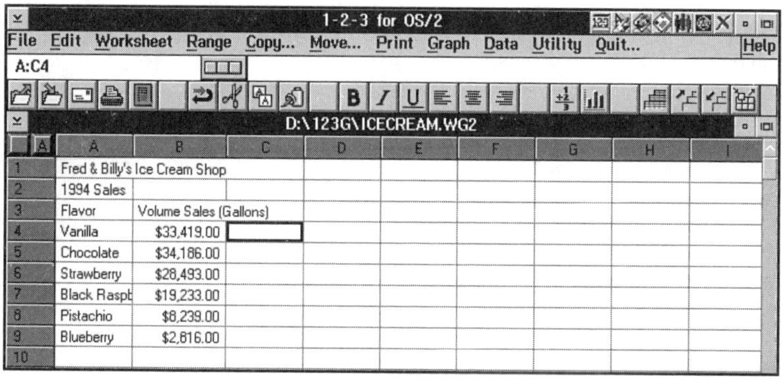

Fig. 4.10
A typical worksheet contains numbers and labels that describe some aspect of a business.

Note

When a label is too wide to fit in a cell, 1-2-3 lets it extend over adjacent cells (check out cells A1 and B3 of fig. 4.10). However, if there is data in an adjacent cell, 1-2-3 visually cuts the label short (as in cell A7); all the label's characters remain in the cell—you just can't see all of them. You can adjust a column's width to accommodate a long label. To do this, click any cell in the column. Then, open the **W**orksheet menu and choose the **C**olumn command. From the Worksheet Column dialog box, choose **F**it Largest. When you choose OK, the column's width changes to fit the column's widest entry.

Entering Dates and Telephone Numbers

Sometimes, you want to include dates or phone numbers in worksheets as information only. In these cases, dates and phone numbers are not really numbers; they are labels. The problem arises when you try to type a date or phone number and 1-2-3 assumes all entries that begin with numbers are, in fact, numbers. So, 1-2-3 treats the entry as a number instead of a label.

Tip

1-2-3 can store the time of day. To enter a time, select a cell and type an entry in a standard time format such as HH:MM:SS. Don't forget to precede the entry by an apostrophe or format the cell as a time entry.

To enter a date or a phone number, you can tell 1-2-3 that the information you are entering should be treated as a label by preceding the date or phone number with an apostrophe.

Troubleshooting

I typed a date into cell C3 by typing 1/1/95 and instead of the date, I got 34700. What's wrong?

For 1-2-3 to display a date in a cell, you must either define the date as a label by preceding it with an apostrophe, or you must define the formatting for that cell as date formatting.

Later in this chapter, you'll see that you can use dates in mathematical calculations just like you use other numbers. Chapter 5 teaches more about formatting dates to control how they appear in the sheet, and Chapter 7 explains how to manipulate dates mathematically in terms of days, months, weeks, and years.

Fixing Mistakes

Rare, indeed, is the perfect typist. But don't worry about any errors you might make as you're typing worksheet entries. If you recognize an error within a few characters of making it, simply press Backspace until you wipe it out. Then resume typing to make the correction.

If you realize that you made an error 10 or 15 characters earlier in a very long entry, press F2 to enter edit mode, and make the correction. For example, suppose you've typed **All Octuber sales were adjusted**, you haven't yet pressed Enter, and you notice that you misspelled October. Or suppose you notice the mistake after you press Enter, but before you move the cell pointer to a different cell. Proceed as follows:

1. Press F2. Note that the far right edge of the program title bar shows the word Edit.

2. Use the direction keys to move the insertion point between the *u* and the *b* in Octuber—or click between them with the mouse pointer. (Table 4.1 lists the effects of the direction keys when 1-2-3 is in edit mode.)

3. Press Backspace to remove the *u* from the label, and then type **o**.

4. Press End to return the insertion point to the end of the entry.

5. Continue typing the entry. Editing keys appear in table 4.1.

Table 4.1 1-2-3's Editing Keys	
Key	**Action**
⬅	Moves insertion point left one character.
➡	Moves the insertion point right one character.
⬆	Stores entry and moves cell pointer up one cell.
⬇	Stores entry and moves cell pointer down one cell.
Home	Moves insertion point to beginning of the entry.
End	Moves insertion point to end of the entry.
Backspace	Deletes character to the left of the insertion point.
Del	Deletes character to the right of the insertion point.
Enter	Stores the entry in the cell and leaves the cell pointer in place.

When you complete a cell entry and then discover an error in it, you can replace the entry or edit it. To replace an entry, click the cell and simply type a new one on top of it. To edit an entry, make its cell active, and then press the Edit key (F2). Alternatively, double-click the cell that contains the entry. In any case, with 1-2-3 in edit mode, use the appropriate keystrokes from table 4.1 to make modifications.

Tip

To clear the contents of a cell after completing an entry in it, select the cell and press Del.

Caution

Don't erase the contents of a cell by selecting it and pressing the spacebar. 1-2-3 then stores a blank character in the cell (you'll see an apostrophe in the cell if you select it). Every cell that 1-2-3 must store increases the size of your worksheet—the larger your worksheet, the longer it takes to open it and save it.

II

Using 1-2-3

Navigating the Worksheet

Moving the cell pointer from cell to cell is crucial to completing any serious spreadsheet project. Earlier sections in this chapter briefly explained some ways to move the cell pointer. However, when you're familiar with all the navigation tools, you can complete your work much more efficiently.

Using the Mouse

As you know, you can make any cell current simply by clicking it. If the desired cell isn't visible on the display, use the scroll bars to move the worksheet behind the worksheet window until the cell is visible. Then click the cell.

 Sometimes the desired cell is on a sheet other than the current one. In that case, click the Perspective View SmartIcon to display three sheets simultaneously (1-2-3 can display up to five sheets simultaneously). Use the Next Sheet SmartIcon or the Previous Sheet SmartIcon to display the appropriate page. Then navigate within the correct sheet, as before.

You may open more than one worksheet at a time. To move between worksheet files, click the title bar of the worksheet you want to use. If you can't see the title bar, you can drag the title bar of the current worksheet until you see the title bar of the worksheet you want. Or, open the program Control menu and choose the **W**indow command. Then, choose the worksheet you want to view from the list (see fig. 4.11).

Fig. 4.11
From the program control menu, you can select a worksheet file to view.

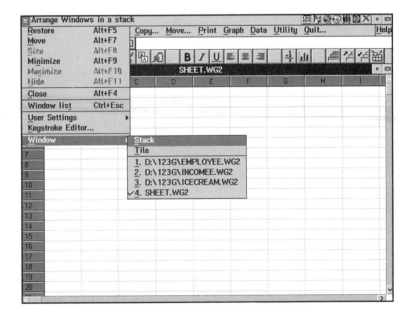

Using the Keyboard

Originally, the only way to navigate a worksheet was to press keys on the keyboard. Although the mouse has become a popular alternative, keystrokes often remain the most efficient route for cell-to-cell movement.

Direction Keys

The direction keypad offers tools for run-of-the-mill movements in the sheet. Table 4.2 lists the direction keys and the actions they initiate with the cell pointer.

Table 4.2 Direction Keys	
Key	**Action**
↑	Moves cell pointer up one cell
↓	Moves cell pointer down one cell
←	Moves cell pointer left one cell
→	Moves cell pointer right one cell
PgUp	Moves cell pointer up one screen
PgDn	Moves cell pointer down one screen
Home	Moves cell pointer to cell A1 of the current sheet in the file
Tab or Ctrl+→	Moves cell pointer right one screen
Shift+Tab or Ctrl+←	Moves cell pointer left one screen
Ctrl+PgUp	Moves cell pointer to the next sheet in the file
Ctrl+PgDn	Moves cell pointer to the previous sheet in the file
Ctrl+Home	Moves cell pointer to top-left corner of first sheet in the file
Ctrl+F6	Moves the cell pointer to the next open worksheet file

Tip
To display a list of open worksheets and select one to view, press Alt+Spacebar and then choose the **W**indow command.

End-Arrow Sequences

Pressing the End key on the direction keypad activates the End indicator near the right end of the worksheet title bar. With the indicator on, most of the cursor keys initiate different cell pointer movements than they do with the indicator off. The effects of pressing End+→ illustrate the use of the End key with other arrow keys as well. There are three possible scenarios:

- If the current cell is blank, pressing End+→ moves the pointer right to the first nonblank cell, or to the edge of the worksheet if there is no data to the right.

- If both the current and the adjacent cell to the right contain entries, pressing End+→ moves the pointer to the last contiguous data cell in the row.

- If the adjacent cell to the right of the current cell is blank, pressing End+→ moves the pointer to the next data cell in the row, or to the edge of the worksheet if there is no data to the right.

Figure 4.12 illustrates outcomes of pressing End and then an arrow key, depending on what information resides along the path of the cell pointer.

Fig. 4.12

Press End and then Down in this worksheet, and the pointer moves as shown by the arrow labeled 1. Press End Down again and the pointer makes jump 2. The fourth End Down sequence sends the pointer to the bottom of the worksheet—cell E8192.

	A	B	C	D	E	F	G	H
1	Eagle Products Incorporated							
2		Total Widgets Produced (in thousands)						
3			Product A	Product B	Product C			
4	1985	2,431	1,564	5,487				
5	1986	2,564	1,634	5,879				
6	1987	2,532	1,576	6,845	1			
7	1988	2,687	1,768	7,456				
8	1989	2,785	1,954	8,456				
9	1990	2,987	2,145	9,345				
10								
11								
12		Summary by Product			2			
13								
14			Product A	15986				
15			Product B	13555	3			
16			Product C	10991				
17					4			

Here are some other useful End key sequences:

- End followed by Home moves the cell pointer to the bottom-right corner cell of the current sheet's active area. That's the area defined by the far-right and bottom-most cell containing information.

- End followed by Ctrl+PgUp moves the cell pointer straight down through sheet pages in the file to the same cell in the last worksheet.

■ End followed by Ctrl+PgDn moves the cell pointer straight up through sheet pages in the file to the same cell in the first worksheet.

■ End followed by Ctrl+Home sends the pointer to the bottom-right corner of the file's active area. That's the area defined by the far-right column, the bottom row, and the last sheet containing an entry.

The Go To Feature

If you know the address of the cell you want to view, but it happens to be in a different worksheet file or several sheets or dozens of rows and columns away, choose **R**ange, **G**oto. Alternatively, press F5. This activates the dialog box shown in figure 4.13, which displays open worksheets. Type, in the unlabeled text box, the address of the cell that you want to make active. Then choose OK or press Enter.

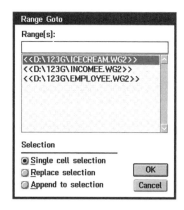

Tip
To move to a different sheet in the file, be sure to include the sheet letter. For example, type AB:A2 to move to page AB cell A2 in the current worksheet.

Fig. 4.13
Press F5 or choose Range, Goto to display the Range Goto dialog box.

Entering Worksheet Calculations

If you never learn more about 1-2-3 than entering numbers, labels, and dates, you'll miss out on the true power of worksheet software: its capability to perform calculations. Sure, any pocket calculator can do math, but the worksheet goes a step further. With it you can write a formula once, and use that formula to return answer after answer without retyping it.

> **Note**
>
> For quick-and-dirty calculations, equivalent to those you get from a pocket calculator, simply type an expression as if to enter it into a cell. For example, to add 8, 10, and 23, type **+8+10+23**. Then, rather than pressing Enter, press function key F9. The result of the formula appears in the contents box. Press Esc twice to clear the result, or press Enter if you want to enter the sum in the worksheet.

Simple, Reusable Formulas

After you enter some values in a sheet, you can write simple formulas to use the values in calculations. Consider the numbers in figure 4.14. To add the first two numbers, you can type the formula **+B2+B3** into cell B4. It's simple algebra, meaning, "Add the value found in cell B2 to the value in cell B3, and show the result here."

Fig. 4.14
Only a formula's result appears in the worksheet cell; the actual formula appears in the edit box in the control panel.

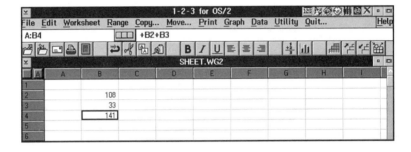

Tip
If you omit the sheet letter of a cell address when you write a formula, 1-2-3 assumes the formula refers to cells in the current sheet.

Troubleshooting

Instead of typing cell addresses to add two numbers, can't I just type the two numbers, like you said earlier?

Yes, but you lose the power of the electronic spreadsheet. By typing the cell addresses in your formula, you can change the numbers in the other two cells and calculate a new result without changing the formula.

As you'll see in Chapter 8, "Using Formulas and Functions," 1-2-3 performs subtraction, multiplication, division, exponentiation, and other important operations. You'll also discover several ways to go about building formulas.

► See "Revisiting Basic Calculations," p. 169

The point to get here is that formulas are not one-shot calculations. Rather, each time you change a number to which the formula refers, the formula recalculates its result to reflect the change! So if you were to replace 33 in cell B3 of figure 4.14 with 44, the formula in cell B4 would immediately display the result 152.

Basic @Functions Abbreviate the Complex

Sometimes a formula that uses simple math becomes very long. For example, one formula to add up all the entries in figure 4.15 is +B2+B3+B4+B5+B6+ B7+B8+B9+B10+B11, as you can see in the figure. Fortunately, 1-2-3's designers believed that you shouldn't have to enter such a mess. To simplify matters, they created a collection of tools called @functions.

> **Note**
>
> Pronounce the expression @function as *at-function*. Pronounce @SUM as *at-sum*. Use this standard to pronounce all @function names.

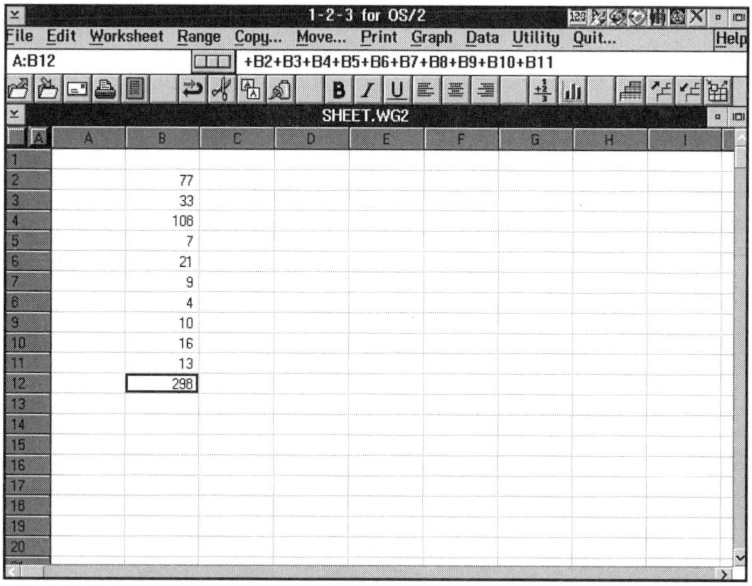

Fig. 4.15
The formula in cell B12 of this worksheet is rather cumbersome. Imagine how messy it would be if it added values from 100 or more cells.

Perhaps the most-used @function is @SUM. It adds up all the values in a list. To sum the entries in cells B2 through B11, you use the formula @SUM(B2..B11). The function uses a range reference to identify which cells to sum (read on for more about ranges).

▶ See "Working with @Functions," p. 179

1-2-3 provides hundreds of @functions to simplify many types of calculations. Some functions perform financial calculations; others perform statistical calculations; and still others handle trigonometry. There are even @functions that manipulate label entries.

Selecting Ranges

One very important worksheet concept is that of the range. A *range* is any rectangular or cubical collection of contiguous cells. The address of a range is the address of its top-left corner cell separated by at least one period from the address of its bottom-right corner cell. So, B3..D12 identifies a range that begins with cell B3 and is 10 rows deep by three columns across. The expression B:D1..E:F4 is a range that spans four rows, three columns, and four sheets.

Many tasks in 1-2-3 involve more than a single cell. As you've seen, you use range references to simplify potentially complicated formulas. Eventually, you might want to change the font of all the entries in a table, or draw a box around a range of cells. Range references also come in handy for these tasks.

Uses for ranges arise so often that 1-2-3 includes powerful facilities for working with them. You can select (or specify) a range in several ways:

- ■ Dragging with the mouse

- ■ Typing

- ■ Using the directional keys

Tip
To highlight a range quickly, click the first cell in the range, hold down the Shift key, and click the last cell. This also works when selecting text in Ami Pro and Freelance Graphics.

Dragging the Mouse To Highlight a Range

One way to specify a range, for whatever use, is simply to click-and-drag from its top-left corner cell to its bottom-right corner. A highlight stretches over the underlying cells as you drag, and remains in place when you release the mouse button (see fig. 4.16). You can begin many procedures by selecting a range this way, and then issue commands by accessing menus or clicking SmartIcons.

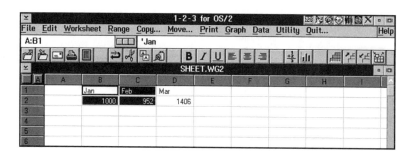

Fig. 4.16
You begin many
procedures by
selecting a range.
1-2-3 identifies a
selected range by
highlighting it.

Typing a Range Address

A second way to specify a range is to type its address. As you learn in later
sections, many of the dialog boxes you face as you issue commands in 1-2-3
require that you specify a range. When you face such a dialog, simply activate
the appropriate text box, and type the desired range address, preceded by a
plus sign (+).

Using the Direction Keys To Highlight a Range

A third way to specify a range is to highlight it using the direction keys. For
example, suppose you want to erase the contents of range B1..C2—that's the
highlighted range in figure 4.16. First, select cell B1. Then, while holding
down the Shift key, press ⊡+⊡. A highlight expands in the direction of each
arrow key you press. When you release the Shift key, the range remains highlighted; press Del to erase its contents.

Data-Entry Shortcuts

As suggested earlier in this chapter, most worksheet users spend a lot of time
entering data. Fortunately, more than 10 years of worksheet technology has
given rise to a variety of mechanisms that speed the entry of data. Learning
some of the shortcuts can save you a lot of time and effort.

Copying Entries

Have you entered a label you can reuse throughout your worksheet? Is there a
number or a date that must appear repeatedly? If so, then copy it! Here's how
to copy a cell or a range:

1. Select the cell or range to copy.

2. Choose **C**opy from the menu bar. The Copy dialog box appears.

3. Click the To text box.

4. In the worksheet, click the top-left cell of the range that receives the copied data.

5. Click the OK command button or press Enter.

Troubleshooting

The cell I need to click (that will receive the copied data) is behind the Copy dialog box. How can I get to it?

You can click the To text box and then minimize the Copy dialog box by clicking the button in the upper-right corner of the dialog box. Once the dialog box is minimized, click the cell that represents the upper-left corner of the range that will receive the data. Restore the Copy dialog box (click the button in the upper-right corner of the dialog box) so you can click OK.

▶ See "Copying Worksheet Data," p. 142

Copying cells can have various ramifications depending on the cell contents and on the dimensions of the source and target ranges of the copy operation.

Generating Number Sequences

1-2-3 has a special feature to enter sequences of increasing numbers. Here's how to enter the values 1 through 15 down a column almost instantly:

Tip
For dates and times to appear properly in ranges you fill, the ranges must be properly formatted.

▶ See "Formatting Numbers for Clarity," p. 108

1. Select the range of cells into which you want to place sequential information.

2. Choose **D**ata, **F**ill. 1-2-3 displays the Data Fill dialog box (see fig. 4.17).

3. Type the beginning number in the Start text box.

4. Type the number by which you want to increment in the Step text box.

5. From the Series option buttons, choose the method you want 1-2-3 to use to calculate the fill numbers.

6. If you highlighted a range that spans multiple rows or columns, choose the **C**olumn option button to fill the range vertically or choose the **R**ow option button to fill the range horizontally.

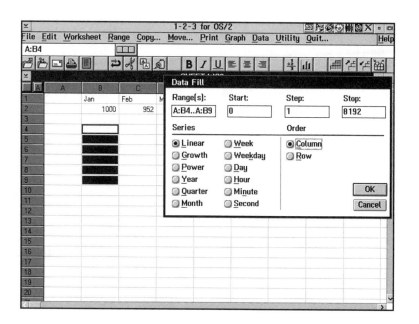

Fig. 4.17
The Range Fill dialog box quickly enters sequences of numbers, dates, and times into worksheet ranges.

Customizing Your Working Environment

As you enter data, labels, and formulas in 1-2-3, some aspects of the display may not appeal to you. So far, you're working with the default display settings. But 1-2-3 also provides a great deal of control over how its interface looks and acts. Studying these features helps you customize 1-2-3 so it better suits your preferences.

Locking Titles On

When you're working with dozens of rows of information, a worksheet can become a bit disorienting. Consider figure 4.18. The rows there contain both textual and numeric entries. However, no column headers are visible to tell you what the numbers represent.

There are, in fact, column headers in row 1 of the worksheet. They identify the columns as long as row 1 is on the display. The trick, then, is to lock row 1 on the display permanently so you can see the labels it contains even when you scroll deep down in the sheet. Here's how:

1. Position the row of headers—and any rows above them that you also want to lock on-screen—at the very top of the worksheet display window. In this case, pressing Home gets the job done.

2. Move the cell pointer to the row directly beneath the headers (see fig. 4.19).

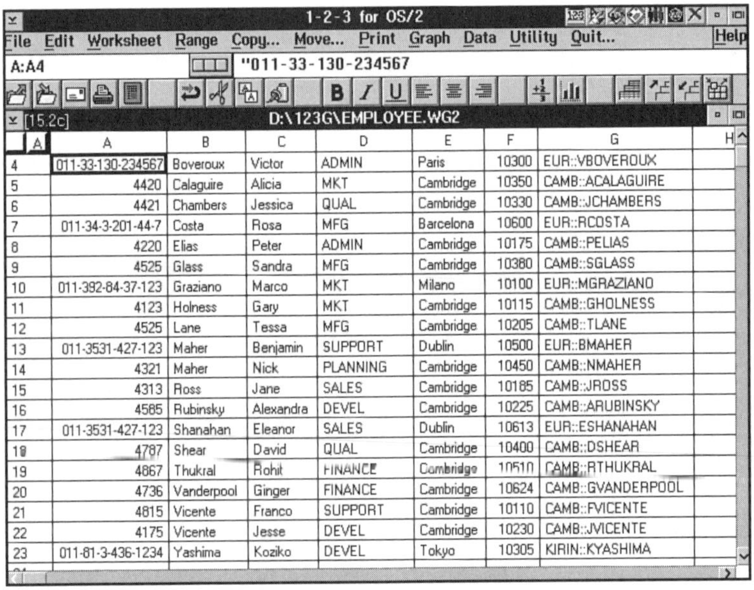

Fig. 4.18

It might be a challenge to remember what the data in each column represents in a very large worksheet.

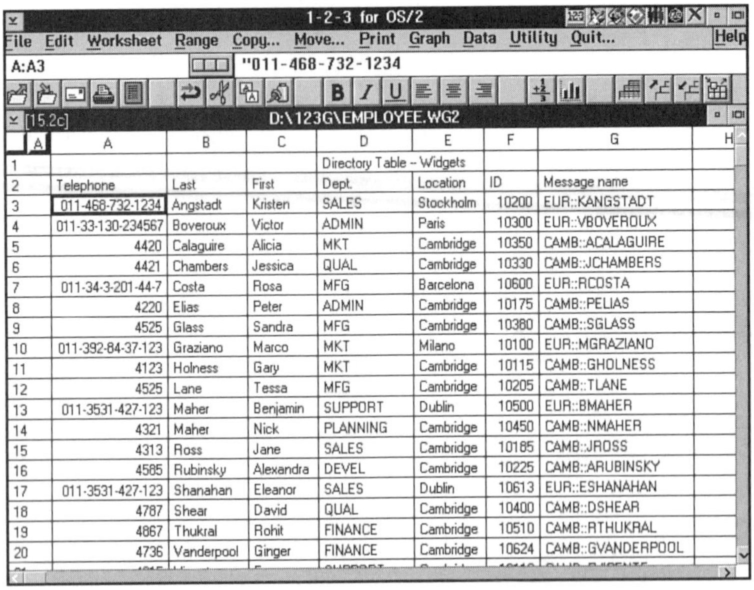

Fig. 4.19

1-2-3 locks on-screen any rows visible above the cell pointer when you establish horizontal titles.

3. Choose **W**orksheet, **T**itles.

4. Choose the **H**orizontal option button in the resulting dialog box (see fig. 4.20).

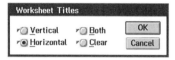

Fig. 4.20
The Worksheet
Titles dialog box
offers options for
locking rows,
columns, or both
on the display.

5. Choose OK or press Enter.

Neither selecting with the mouse nor navigating with direction keys moves the cell pointer into the titles area. However, with titles locked, it's much easier to interpret the contents of a sheet. Figure 4.21 shows the worksheet after scrolling down with its first two rows locked in as titles.

A:A14			4321				
	A	B	C	D	E	F	G
1				Directory Table -- Widgets			
2	Telephone	Last	First	Dept.	Location	ID	Message name
14	4321	Maher	Nick	PLANNING	Cambridge	10450	CAMB::NMAHER
15	4313	Ross	Jane	SALES	Cambridge	10185	CAMB::JROSS
16	4585	Rubinsky	Alexandra	DEVEL	Cambridge	10225	CAMB::ARUBINSKY
17	011-3531-427-123	Shanahan	Eleanor	SALES	Dublin	10613	EUR::ESHANAHAN
18	4787	Shear	David	QUAL	Cambridge	10400	CAMB::DSHEAR
19	4667	Thukral	Rohit	FINANCE	Cambridge	10510	CAMB::RTHUKRAL
20	4736	Vanderpool	Ginger	FINANCE	Cambridge	10624	CAMB::GVANDERPOOL
21	4815	Vicente	Franco	SUPPORT	Cambridge	10110	CAMB::FVICENTE
22	4175	Vicente	Jesse	DEVEL	Cambridge	10230	CAMB::JVICENTE
23	011-81-3-436-1234	Yashima	Koziko	DEVEL	Tokyo	10305	KIRIN::KYASHIMA
24							
25							
26							
27							
28							
29							
30							
31							

Fig. 4.21
The top two rows,
locked as titles,
remain visible even
when you scroll
down tens,
hundreds, or
thousands of rows
into the sheet.

You can clear established titles by choosing **C**lear from the Worksheet Titles dialog box.

Splitting the Worksheet Windows

As a worksheet file grows, you may feel frustrated that you can examine only one portion of it at a time. For example, you might want to review

Tip
To edit the titles,
first clear the
locked titles
by choosing
Worksheet, **T**itles,
Clear. When you
finish editing, use
the Worksheet
Titles dialog to
reestablish the
titles lock.

II

Using 1-2-3

information in an established table while you're building a new table in another sheet. No problem. Just split the worksheet into two horizontal or vertical windows.

With a split view, you can work in either window, adding data, writing formulas, and so on. You can even copy data from one window to the other—saving effort when you need to copy information from one sheet layer to another, or to some distant range in a single sheet.

Here's the hard way to split a window:

1. Move the cell pointer to a position that marks where you want the split to occur. For a horizontal split, there must be at least one row above and below the pointer; for a vertical split there must be at least one column on each side of the pointer.

2. Choose **W**orksheet, **W**indow. The Worksheet Window dialog box appears (see fig. 4.22).

Fig. 4.22

Use the Worksheet Window dialog box to split a window.

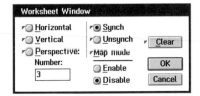

3. Choose **H**orizontal or **V**ertical.

4. Choose either the **S**ynch option button or the **U**nsynch option button. If you plan to view corresponding cells in different sheets, you might prefer synchronized scrolling, where cell pointer movement in one window results in identical movement in the other. Do not use synchronized scrolling if you want to be able to move in one window without affecting the state of the other window.

5. Choose OK or press Enter.

Figure 4.23 shows 1-2-3 with the worksheet window split horizontally.

	1-2-3 for OS/2				

Fig. 4.23
With an unsynchronized window split, you can wander in one window, while keeping a specific range in view in the other.

File Edit Worksheet Range Copy... Move... Print Graph Data Utility Quit...   Help

C:D8   8456

D:\123G\EMPLOYEE.WG2

C	A	B	C	D	E	F	G	H
4	1985	2,431	1,564	5,487				
5	1986	2,564	1,634	5,879				
6	1987	2,532	1,576	6,845				
7	1988	2,687	1,768	7,456				
8	1989	2,785	1,954	8,456				
9	1990	2,987	2,145	9,345				
10								
11								
12		Summary by Product						

C	A	B	C	D	E	F	G	H
10								
11								
12		Summary by Product						
13								
14			Product A	15986				
15			Product B	13555				

Note

You might notice the **P**erspective option in the Worksheet Window dialog box (refer to fig. 4.23). Choosing this option is the same as clicking the Perspective View SmartIcon, but from the Worksheet Window dialog, you can choose to display up to five consecutive sheets at once.

To clear any window splits, select **C**lear from the Worksheet Window dialog box.

Fiddling with Minutia

There are dozens more ways to customize the way 1-2-3 looks and works. Some affect the overall 1-2-3 working environment, whereas others are specific to the current worksheet. Because the ways you can customize 1-2-3 are so numerous, I'm going to touch only briefly on each and try to point out ones you might find more important than others.

II

Using 1-2-3

Basic 1-2-3 Functioning

From the **U**tility menu, you can access the **U**ser Settings menu. From that menu, you can display four different dialog boxes, each of which lets you control some portion of 1-2-3's overall functioning (see figs. 4.24, 4.25, 4.26, and 4.27).

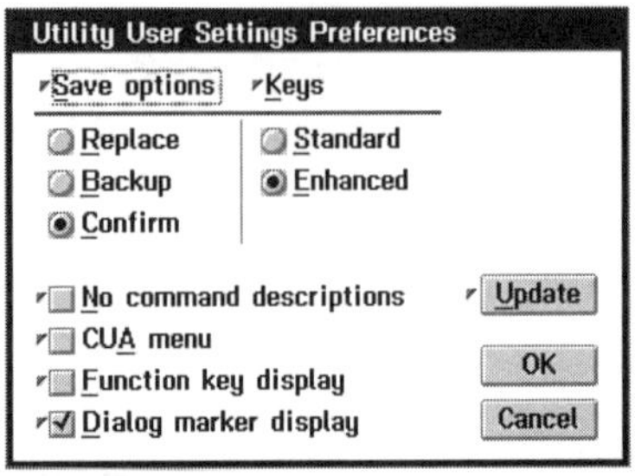

Fig. 4.24

In the Utility User Settings Preferences dialog box, you can tell 1-2-3 how to handle saving your files.

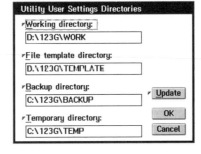

Fig. 4.25

In the Utility User Settings Directories dialog box, you can tell 1-2-3 where to store files. The working directory you specify determines the directory 1-2-3 displays when you choose to open a file.

Fig. 4.26

The Utility User Settings Startup dialog box lets you specify 1-2-3's behavior when you first start the program.

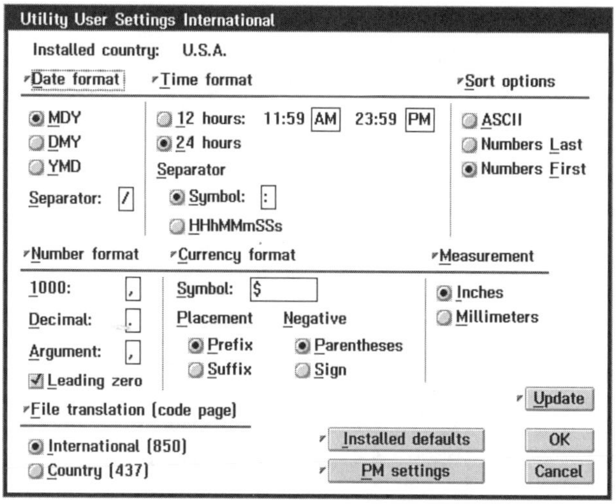

Fig. 4.27

In the Utility User Settings International dialog box, you can set default date, time, number, currency, and measurement formats as well as sort and file translation options.

Worksheet Settings

Using the choices on the **G**lobal menu, you affect the way the current worksheet looks and operates. Many of these options will mean more to you after you have read other sections in the book. For example, the dialog boxes you see when you choose **W**orksheet, **G**lobal, **F**ormat; and **W**orksheet, **G**lobal, **L**abel will mean more after you work through Chapter 5 and read about these dialog boxes.

You can see any of the following dialog boxes by choosing **W**orksheet **G**lobal and then the appropriate command (see figs. 4.28, 4.29, 4.30, and 4.31).

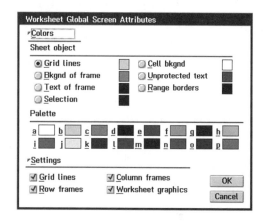

Fig. 4.28

In the Worksheet Global Screen Attributes dialog box, you can set colors for various screen objects as well as display or hide grid lines, column or row frames, and worksheet graphics.

II

Using 1-2-3

Fig. 4.29

You can tell 1-2-3 to display blanks for any cells whose value equals 0.

Fig. 4.30

You can prevent anyone from changing protected cells.

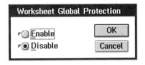

Fig. 4.31

You can manually recalculate large spreadsheets to save time during data entry by changing the default (automatic).

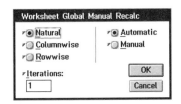

Working with Old and New Files

Given the knowledge to navigate and enter values, labels, and formulas, you know enough to build very useful worksheet models. There's not much point in building a worksheet, however, if you don't also know how to store it on disk so you can return to it later. And once you've saved a worksheet file, knowing how to retrieve it becomes a useful skill.

▶ See "Printing the Worksheet," p. 215

Even if you haven't built any new worksheets, you may have some 1-2-3 Release 2.x or 3.x (for DOS or Windows) files you want to use in 1-2-3 for OS/2. In that case, you can use 1-2-3's file-handling commands to open those files.

You can even save your newly created 1-2-3 for OS/2 worksheets in .WK1 and .WK3 file formats in case you need to share them with users who haven't switched to OS/2, but any features specific to 1-2-3 for OS/2 are lost when you save a .WK3 or .WK1 file.

Saving Your Work

Chapter 3, "Managing Files and Work Areas," tells you everything you need to know to save and open files in 1-2-3. But there are a few points worth adding:

- Using the default menus (non-CUA), each time you save a file, 1-2-3 produces the File Save dialog box shown in figure 4.32 when you choose the **F**ile, **S**ave command.

Fig. 4.32
If this is the first time you've saved, 1-2-3 offers a generic filename that you can replace easily.

- Using CUA menus, the first time you use the **F**ile, **S**ave command to save a file, 1-2-3 produces the File Save As dialog box, which looks very much like the File Save dialog box shown in figure 4.32. After you've saved the file once, the **F**ile, **S**ave command saves without even alerting you that the new version is replacing an existing version on the disk.

Tip
To use CUA menus, choose **U**tility, **U**ser Settings, **P**references. In the resulting dialog box, choose CU**A** menu and then OK to save.

- You can save a file you've already saved using a new name. If you're using the default menus, choose **F**ile, **S**ave. If you're using CUA menus, choose File Save **A**s. Then assign the new name and choose OK or press Enter in the resulting dialog box.

- You don't need to specify an extension when you type a new filename; 1-2-3 automatically appends .WG2. If you want to save the worksheet to a .WK3 or .WK1 format, simply specify the extension.

- Some formulas and graphic elements don't save in .WK1 or .WK3 file formats. 1-2-3 alerts you when it can't convert all the information from .WG2 format into another format.

- You cannot save a 3D file in the .WK1 format. To create a .WK1 worksheet file from 1-2-3 for OS/2, eliminate all but one sheet before saving.

- 1-2-3 does not create a separate format file (.FMT) for every worksheet file. Unlike Releases 2.x and 3.x for DOS, WYSIWYG formatting information resides in the worksheet file along with the data, labels, and formulas.

II

Using 1-2-3

Retrieving Your Work

Chapter 3 discusses how to open files in SmartSuite applications. Here are a few important points to consider:

- You can have several files open at once in 1-2-3. Chapter 7 includes information to help you work with several open files at once.

- There are a series of File Type checkboxes in the File Open dialog box. Use them to specify the file types you want to see in the list when you want to open files from earlier releases of 1-2-3, or from other spreadsheet and database management products such as Excel, Paradox, and dBASE.

- When you open a non-WG2 file in 1-2-3, the software keeps track of the extension of the original file. So, for example, a file named PROFITS.WK1 retains the name even as you add to or modify the worksheet. 1-2-3 tries to save using the original name and file format when you later choose **S**ave from the **F**ile menu.

Chapter 7 discusses further issues associated with opening worksheet files.

A Note about Help

As much as you learn about 1-2-3, there may be times when it's just not enough. In those instances, turn to the online help system. Chapter 2, "Using Common Features," explains specifics of working with online help in all SmartSuite applications. There are several additional tidbits to be aware of while using 1-2-3:

◀ See "Using Online Help," p. 53

- Help in 1-2-3 is context-sensitive. If you begin a command sequence, activate a dialog box, or get partway through a cell entry and then decide you need help, press F1. This activates 1-2-3's help system, offering a topic that very likely relates to whatever task you were performing. When you close the help session, you return to 1-2-3 exactly where you were when you pressed F1.

- There's no need to close Help when you want to return to the worksheet. Sometimes you get more out of a Help topic if you read a bit, go back to the worksheet to apply what you've read, read a little more in Help, and so on. After you've found a topic, leave Help open and click a worksheet. When you want to refer to Help, click **H**elp. You also can use the Window menu to switch to Help. Press Alt+Spacebar and then choose the **W**indow command.

From Here...

If you read all of this chapter, you have a solid understanding of basic spread-sheet concepts. You should be able to create useful models that represent your business data. Further chapters build on the foundation as follows:

■ Chapter 5, "Formatting Data and Working within the Worksheet," explores formatting cells and the worksheet, including number display, label alignment, and column and row sizing.

■ Chapter 6, "Working with Charts and Graphics To Present Your Data," explains how to use 1-2-3's worksheet publishing features to add drama to your worksheets.

■ Chapter 7, "Editing Worksheets," delves into issues you face as you build increasingly complex worksheet models.

II

Using 1-2-3

Chapter 5

Formatting Data and Working within the Worksheet

by Elaine Marmel

People don't typically use terms like "flair," "excitement," or "drama" to describe the contents of a spreadsheet model. In fact, a collection of numbers, formulas, and labels usually is downright boring—even when it shows an exceptional trend.

In 1988, spreadsheets gained the capability to display cell entries in more than one font. Programs suddenly offered tools to draw lines around cells, add shading effects, change the worksheet's colors, and even display charts alongside text and data. More importantly, users could print the worksheet almost exactly as it appeared on the display.

Today, these features are commonplace. So, you can use 1-2-3 for OS/2 to exploit all the spreadsheet publishing features and make your worksheets stand out in a sea of otherwise dreary computer printouts.

In this chapter, you learn how to:

- Make numbers appear as dollars, percentages, and more

- Change the appearance of a date or time entry

- Emphasize labels and numbers by using different fonts, colors, and lines

- Change column widths and row heights

- Realign cell entries

Tip

Here's a bit of trivia. 1-2-3's original design was to run on computers with two monitors: one to show the spreadsheet and one to display charts.

Formatting Numbers for Clarity

Numbers are numbers, but some numbers are more descriptive than others. A number that begins with a dollar sign, for example, indicates money. One followed by a percent sign has a different meaning than one followed by a British pound sign. So far you've learned only how to type numbers and perform calculations with them. Learning to format them helps you charge numbers with meaning.

◀ See "Entering Numbers," p. 81

When you want a number to appear with special punctuation, apply a numeric format. Consider the worksheet in figure 5.1. The numbers in columns C, D, E, and F appear as dollars, and the numbers in column G appear as percentages. To type numbers with this format, you apply a numeric format.

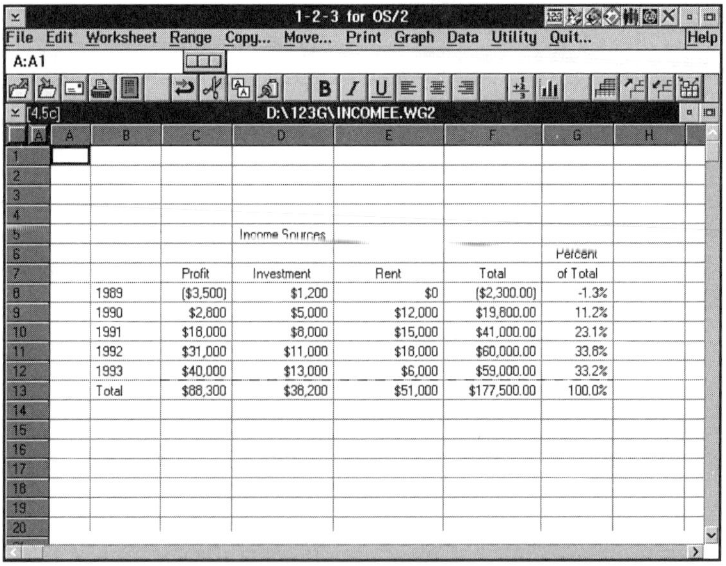

Fig. 5.1
The dollar amounts in columns C, D, E, and F and the percentages in column G are numbers and formulas, respectively. Numeric formats make them appear with dollar and percent punctuation.

The following sections describe several ways to apply numeric formats with 1-2-3.

Assigning Number Formats

Use the Range Format dialog box to specify the numeric format for a particular range of cells. To use the Range Format dialog box to change the formats of worksheet cells, follow these steps:

1. Select the cells to format.

2. Choose **R**ange, **F**ormat.

3. Make appropriate settings in the resulting Range Format dialog box and choose OK or press Enter (see fig. 5.2).

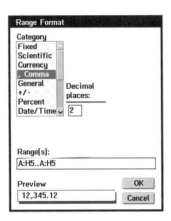

Fig. 5.2

As you change categories in the listbox, a sample of your selection appears in the Preview box at the bottom of the Range Format dialog box.

Use the sample entry in the box labeled *Preview* to guide you as you choose a display format. Some of the formats let you specify how many digits should appear after the decimal point; a text box for this information appears when you choose one of those formats. The currency symbol that appears if you choose the currency format is based on the country you chose when you installed 1-2-3 for OS/2.

To clear all number formats from the selected entries, choose Reset in the Category list in the Range Format dialog box.

You can create a number, date/time, or general format of your own design. Select User from the Category list in the Range Format dialog and then select one of the formats from the Format listbox. Use Appendix B, "Format Description Language," in the Graph Tool Handbook (which came with your SmartSuite as part of the Freelance books) to specify a form in the User format text box.

> **Note**
>
> You can set the format for your entire worksheet instead of just specific cells. Choose **W**orksheet, **G**lobal, **F**ormat to display a dialog box that looks almost exactly like the Range Format dialog box. By using the Worksheet Global Format dialog box, you can set the format for *all* cells in a worksheet, not just those in a selected range.

Using 1-2-3

The following is a list of formats and their descriptions:

General Format. Default format that 1-2-3 uses when you type a number in a new worksheet. It shows numbers without punctuation and fits as much of a number as possible within the space allowed by a cell's width. Type the entry **12345.6789** into a cell with general format, and 1-2-3 shows it as you've typed it—or in scientific notation if the cell is too narrow to fit all the digits.

Scientific Format. 1-2-3 uses the letter E and a plus or minus sign (+ or -) in place of the expression "x10" in its scientific notation. So, the familiar $6.73x10^6$ becomes 6.73E+06 in a worksheet cell with Scientific format. Large numbers entered into a cell formatted with the General format appear in scientific notation if the cell is too narrow to fit all the digits.

Fixed Format. Looks just like General formatting, but you can specify (and therefore limit) the number of decimal places you want displayed.

Comma Format. 1-2-3 displays commas to separate thousands. Like with Fixed formatting, you can specify the number of decimal places you want displayed for Comma formatting.

0.0 Applies the Comma format with no decimal places.

Currency Format. A variation of Comma formatting that includes a currency symbol with the number as well as commas and a specified number of decimal places. The currency symbol displayed depends on the country you selected when you installed 1-2-3 for OS/2.

$ Applies the worksheet's default Currency format.

Percent format. Multiplies the contents of a cell by 100 and displays the result as a percentage. When you choose Percent formatting, you can specify the number of decimal places you want displayed.

% Applies the Percent format with two decimal places.

Dates and Times Format. Date and time entries are numbers with a special format. To the computer, a date is an integer serial number that represents how many days have passed since December 31, 1899. A time is a decimal value that represents the percentage of a day passed since midnight, so the value .25 represents 6:00AM.

When you format a cell for date format and type a date in the mm/dd/yy format, 1-2-3 automatically converts the date into a serial number, but continues to show that number as a date. When you choose the Date/Time option in the Category selection box, the Number Format dialog box changes to offer a list of date and time formats such as MMo/DD/YY, DD-Mon-YY, HH:MMi:SS AMPM and HH:MMi using a 24-hour clock.

Automatic Format. Lets you type the number the way you want it to appear and 1-2-3 automatically formats the cell that way. When you include punctuation as you type an entry—such as a number that begins with a dollar sign and includes two decimal places—in a cell with automatic format, 1-2-3 changes the cell's format to match the entry. The cell no longer has automatic format. Choosing Automatic in the Range Format dialog box resets the cell in anticipation of a new entry.

+/- Format. A vestige of the original 1-2-3. With this format, a number appears as a sequence of plusses or minuses. If the number is 5, for example, five plus signs appear in the cell. If the number is -7, seven minus signs appear.

Text Format. Displays formulas literally as formulas rather than as the results of formulas. So, entered in a cell with text format, the expression @SUM(B2..B12) appears in the cell as @SUM(B2..B12) instead of a number. You can print your worksheet in this fashion to see the formulas that appear in various cells.

Label Format. Adds a label character to the cell, displaying any value entered into the cell as a label. You can use label formatting to format cells containing phone numbers, nine-digit ZIP codes, or dates you don't intend to use in mathematical formulas.

Hidden Format. Causes a cell to appear blank, although it contains an entry. You can still review the entry by selecting the cell; its contents appear in the edit box of the control panel.

▶ See "Working with @Functions," p. 179

Enclosing Values in Parentheses. Using the (Parens) option in the Category list, you can tell 1-2-3 to enclose all numbers in parentheses. Be aware that this format only makes numbers appear in parentheses; it does not make 1-2-3 treat them as negative numbers in calculations.

II

Using 1-2-3

Troubleshooting

To enter a dollar amount, I formatted a cell for currency and then entered the amount without a dollar sign ($) or commas. Only asterisks appeared in the cell.

You entered a very large dollar amount, and 1-2-3 tried to apply a special display format to it. Now the entry is too wide to fit in the cell. Later in this chapter, you'll learn how to increase the column's width; once the column is wider, the asterisks vanish, leaving the formatted number in place.

A cell can appear filled with asterisks whenever you format a cell and then enter a number too large to appear in the cell with the special formatting. You can always solve this problem by either widening the column or using a different format.

My formatted numbers appear as 3 and 6, but the formula that sums them returns 10.

The underlying values probably have a decimal component. For example, 3.49+6.48 equals 9.97. When you use a fixed format with no decimal places, however, the numbers appear as 3, 6, and 10. These are the same values rounded off. Don't confuse this with true rounding—the underlying values remain 3.49, 6.48, and 9.97; only their appearances change.

I typed a number starting with a dollar sign and including two decimal places in a cell formatted with automatic formatting, but 1-2-3 displays it as a very large percentage.

You must have entered a percentage in the cell sometime earlier. With automatic formatting, once 1-2-3 assigns a format to a cell, that format stays in effect until you override it via the Range Format dialog, or via a formatting SmartIcon. You can reapply automatic formatting to the cell so that 1-2-3 again assigns to the cell the formatting you type when entering data.

Styling Entries for Emphasis

Although it's important to make numbers descriptive, little about a formatted entry draws a reader's eye. If you want people to notice your worksheet reports, try changing fonts and font styles and adding lines and colors. Don't use these special effects to excess. A large title, a little shading, and a few lines on a page usually are enough to give your worksheet professional polish. If you use these special effects to excess, you produce garish reports whose appearance distracts the reader from the content, which is still the most important issue.

Setting Fonts and Attributes

To change an entry's font, select the cell containing the entry and choose **R**ange, **A**ttributes, **F**ont. 1-2-3 displays the dialog box shown in figure 5.3.

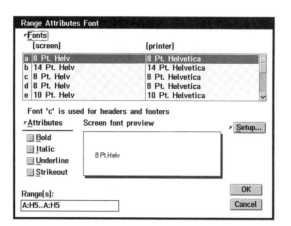

Fig. 5.3
The Range
Attributes Font
dialog box offers
one-stop shopping
for all your type-
face and type style
needs.

Select a font and font size from the Screen listbox and the Printer listbox.
1-2-3 measures font sizes in points. 1-2-3 uses Adobe Type Manager to pre-
install 20 combinations of fonts and point sizes.

If you want the selected entry to appear in boldface, italics, or both, choose
the appropriate checkbox under **A**ttributes. You also can specify an underline
attribute.

If you don't find a font or point size you want in the list, choose the **S**etup
command button on the right side of the dialog box. 1-2-3 displays the
Range Attributes Font Setup dialog box shown in figure 5.4.

Tip
The entry in the
box labeled *Screen
font preview* reflects
the selections you
make in the Font
and Attribute
dialog box.

II

Using 1-2-3

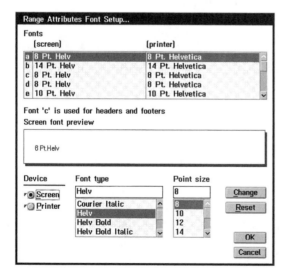

Fig. 5.4
In the Range
Attributes Font
Setup dialog box,
you can replace
one of the pre-
installed fonts
with a font of
your choice.

Figure 5.5 shows a worksheet with some titles set in a distinctive font and font size.

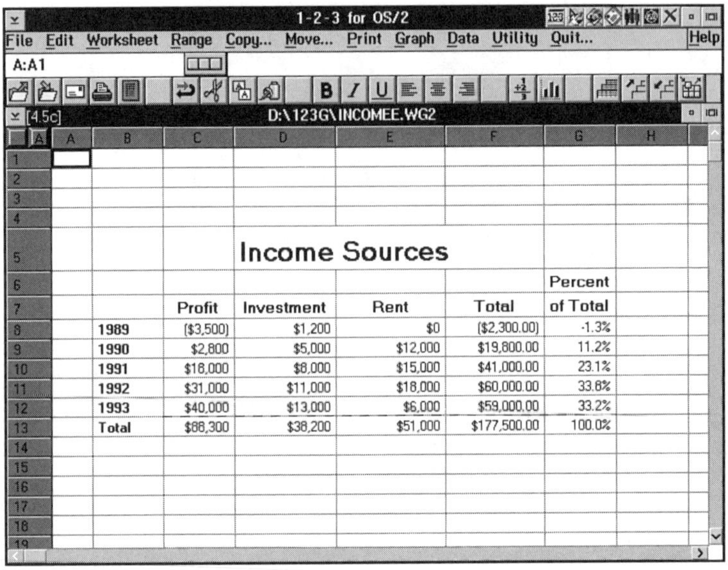

Fig. 5.5
Changing fonts and font sizes of just a few entries significantly changes the character of a worksheet.

Sometimes you want to add bold, italic, or underline to selected entries without changing the typeface or text color. Use the SmartIcons listed here:

B Sets the selected entries in boldface.

I Sets the selected entries in italic.

U Underlines the entries in the selected cells.

Adding Lines to Cells

Adding lines to your worksheet can enhance its appearance and clarify information. To add lines, you use the Range Attributes Border dialog box. Choose **R**ange, **A**ttributes, **B**order to display the dialog box shown in figure 5.6.

You use this dialog box in the same way you use the Range Attributes Color dialog box: choose an option button that describes the place where you want to draw lines and then from the available line styles, choose a solid line or any of several broken line styles. As you make selections in the dialog box, the Sample box instantly changes to give you an idea of how the settings affect the selected worksheet range.

```
┌─────────────────────────────────────────┐
│ Range Attributes Border                  │
│   Frame          Inside       Sample     │
│   ⊙ All          ⊙ All      ┌─────────┐  │
│   ⊙ Right        ⊙ Horiz    │         │  │
│   ⊙ Left         ⊙ Vert     │         │  │
│   ⊙ Top                     │         │  │
│   ⊙ Bottom                  └─────────┘  │
│   Line style                             │
│   a ▭    c ┄┄┄   e ▭    g ┄┄┄           │
│   b ┄┄   d ▭     f ┄┄                    │
│   Range(s):              ┌────────┐      │
│   A:A1..A:A1             │   OK   │      │
│                          ├────────┤      │
│                          │ Cancel │      │
│                          └────────┘      │
└─────────────────────────────────────────┘
```

Fig. 5.6
The Range Attributes Border dialog box applies lines to a selected range in a way very similar to the Range Attributes Color dialog box.

The option buttons under **F**rame place lines around the outside edges of the selected range (*not* around each side of a cell in the selected range). **L**eft, **R**ight, **T**op, and **B**ottom draw lines along the left, right, top, or bottom sides of the selected range. If you select two columns and then choose **F**rame **A**ll, you will draw a box around the outside of the pair of columns, perhaps implying that you want to group those two columns together.

As a shortcut, you can use the Worksheet formatting version of the SmartIcon bar and then click the Outline border SmartIcon shown in the margin to place an outline around the selected range.

The option buttons under **I**nside place lines around the inside edges of the selected range (*not* inside each cell in the selected range). To draw lines between columns, for example, you can select a range that spans the columns, and then choose **H**oriz or **V**ert. If you select multiple rows and columns and then choose **I**nside **A**ll, the resulting lines resemble a Tick Tack Toe board.

Tip
To draw lines around all edges of all cells in a selected range, choose **F**rame, **A**ll and then **I**nside, **A**ll in the Range Attributes Border dialog box.

Troubleshooting

I drew lines but now I want to remove them. There's no Reset command button in the Range Attributes Border dialog box. How do I get rid of the lines?

Select the range and then open the Range Attributes Border dialog box. Select the appropriate option button under **F**rame or **I**nside and then select Line style *d* and choose OK.

Changing Column Width and Row Height

Fitting a column's width to the entries it contains came up in Chapter 4, "Introducing the 1-2-3 Worksheet." In many situations, you may need to manipulate column widths and row heights. Sometimes a one- or two-character adjustment can make the difference between fitting all your data on one display or having a column spill over onto a second screen.

Drag To Change Width or Height

The quickest way to change a column's width or a row's height with the mouse is to drag in the worksheet frame. Move the mouse pointer into the frame to the right edge of a column whose width you want to change. The pointer changes into a doubled arrow, as shown in figure 5.7. Now drag left or right to widen or narrow the column.

Fig. 5.7

The mouse pointer changes to a pair of opposed arrows when it's in the zone to change a column's width.

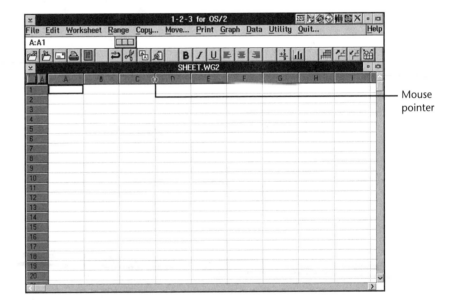

— Mouse pointer

To change the widths of several adjacent columns uniformly at once, follow these steps:

1. Select the first of the columns by clicking its letter in the frame.

2. Hold down the Shift key and click the letter of the last column. (Alternatively, simply drag from the first column letter to the last of the columns you want to resize.)

3. Move the mouse pointer within the frame to the left border of one of the selected columns until the pointer changes.

4. Drag to change the column's width.

5. Release the mouse button. The widths of all selected columns change.

Changing row heights is as easy as changing column widths. Simply drag the bottom border of the row in the worksheet's frame. By default, a row's height automatically fits its tallest entry. After you change the height, it remains fixed even if the sizes of its entries change.

Use Dialog Boxes To Make Adjustments

Several dialog boxes help you deal with column widths and row heights. To adjust column widths, as always, start by selecting the columns whose widths you want to change. Then activate the Column Width dialog box by choosing **W**orksheet, **C**olumn. The dialog box you see in figure 5.8 appears.

You can use the dialog box's controls to specify a width—in characters—for the selected columns, to set column widths so they fit their widest entries, or to reset columns to the worksheet's default column width—normally nine characters.

The dialog box you use to change row height appears in figure 5.9. Activate it by selecting **W**orksheet, **R**ow. 1-2-3 measures row heights in points and by default automatically changes a row's height to fit the largest font used in the row. When you change a row's height by dragging in the frame or by using the Set height control, 1-2-3 overrides the default. Restore the default setting and return the row's height to fit the largest font by choosing **R**eset Height.

II

Using 1-2-3

Fig. 5.9
Activate the
Worksheet Row
dialog box when
you want to
restore a row's
capability to
determine its own
height according
to the largest font
it contains.

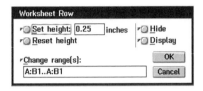

Aligning Data

Changing the alignment of entries within columns and rows isn't likely to add pizzazz to your worksheets, but it can add clarity. Simply centering entries in their cells or shifting them to the right sides of their cells, however, can make a worksheet much easier to interpret.

Aligning Data within Columns and Rows

Initially, when you type text into a cell, 1-2-3 uses the options set in the Worksheet Global Label dialog box. These options align the text at the left edge of the cell and numbers at the right edge of the cell. You can change these global alignments, and you can selectively change the alignment of cells in a worksheet to add clarity to your worksheet.

> **Note**
>
> The Worksheet Global Label dialog box looks and acts basically the same as the Range Label dialog box you see in figure 5.10.

To change the alignment of existing entries within their columns, follow these steps:

1. Select the range of entries you want to change the alignment for.

2. Choose **R**ange, **L**abel. The dialog box in figure 5.10 appears.

Fig. 5.10
The Range Label
dialog box lets
you control the
positioning of
entries within
columns and rows.

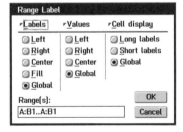

3. To set alignment for text that appears in the selected cells, choose one of the **L**abels option buttons. To set alignment for numbers that appear in the selected cells, choose one of the **V**alues option buttons. The **L**eft, **R**ight, and **C**enter buttons are self-explanatory. The **G**lobal button uses the alignment established in the Worksheet Global Label dialog box. If you select the **L**abel **F**ill option button, 1-2-3 fills the cell with whatever you type into the cell. If you type a word, the word repeats within the cell until the cell is filled. This option is particularly useful when you use a cell to hold a set of underscores, implying that the numbers below the underscore are the sum of the numbers above the underscore.

4. Use the **C**ell Display option buttons to tell 1-2-3 how to handle entries that extend beyond the edge of the cell. If you choose the **L**ong Labels option button (the default), 1-2-3 displays the entire entry when the cell immediately to the right is blank. If you choose **S**hort Labels, 1-2-3 truncates the entry to fit within the cell even if the cell immediately to the right is blank.

5. Choose OK to exit the dialog box.

Figure 5.11 shows the effects of the various alignment options.

Tip

1-2-3 Release 2.1 for OS/2 lets you change the alignment of numeric and formula entries as well as label entries.

II

Using 1-2-3

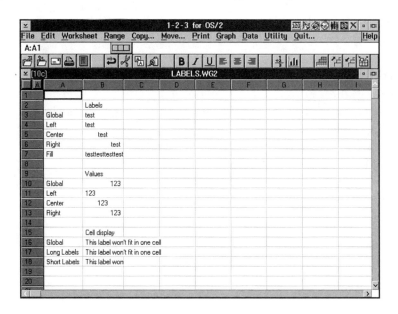

Fig. 5.11

Each cell in ranges B3..B7, B10..B13, and B16..B18 contains the labels and values. Column A lists the selected alignment options.

> **Note**
>
> You can establish a label's horizontal alignment within a column as you begin typing a label. To do this, type a label prefix character before typing the text of the label. To type the word **Salary** so that it appears centered in the cell, for example, type a caret (^) and then type the word. To left-align a label, just start typing. To right-align a label, start with quotation marks ("). 1-2-3 doesn't display the label prefix in the cell, but the prefix does appear in the control panel's edit box when you highlight the cell.
>
> A label prefix overrides any established alignment setting for the cell. So, if you have used the Range Label dialog box to center some text, typing **test** preceded by a quotation mark (**"test**) into the cell results in a right-aligned label.

Using Alignment SmartIcons

Three SmartIcons that change the alignment of worksheet entries reside on the Default Sheet palette.

 Aligns each entry to the left end of its cell.

 Centers each entry in its cell.

 Aligns each entry to the right end of its cell.

Making Entries Wrap

To change the way 1-2-3 handles long labels in selected cells, choose **R**ange, **J**ustify to display the Range Justify dialog box. By default, a very long label resides in one cell but appears to extend over adjacent cells unless those cells contain entries. When you justify an entry, 1-2-3 moves some of the text down to the next cell to keep all the text of a label within the column's width. Figure 5.12 shows two long labels—one with the default left-alignment, and the other after justifying the entry using a range of A3..B3.

Tip
Make sure the cell immediately below the text you want to justify is empty. Otherwise, 1-2-3 justifies that text, too.

Cells A3, A4, and A5 actually contain text (their counterparts in column B are empty). Justifying does not expand the height of the cell containing the original text. Instead, it adds rows and moves some of the text down to the next cell.

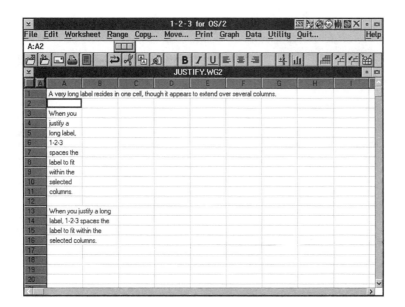

Fig. 5.12
The label in cell A1 has the default alignment, but cells A3..A11 show a long label justified into just column A, and cells A13..A16 contain a long label that was justified over cells A3..B3.

Understanding Worksheet Defaults

1-2-3's worksheet defaults initially show cells with black text on white backgrounds, fonts begin as 8-point Helvetica, labels align to the left of columns, and so on. All settings you make on a cell-by-cell or range basis override those default settings.

To change the defaults for the current worksheet, choose **W**orksheet, **G**lobal to produce the menu shown in figure 5.13. From this menu, choose the option that describes the type of default you want to change globally.

Periodically in this chapter, you've read about some of these options. For example, you read about the Worksheet Global Format dialog box and the Worksheet Global Label dialog box earlier in this chapter. In Chapter 4, for example, you learned about the Worksheet Global Screen Attributes dialog box and the Worksheet Global Zero Suppress dialog box.

◀ See "Customizing Your Working Environment," p. 95

Whatever settings you make in these dialog boxes take effect only in the current worksheet—even in a multisheet file. Equally important: settings you make here do not override settings you have made on a cell-by-cell or range basis. So, if you have already used the **R**ange menu options to change fonts, alignments, column widths, and formats of specific cells, those settings remain unaffected by changes to the defaults.

Fig. 5.13

Settings you make in the dialog boxes you see after choosing a command from the Worksheet Global menu replace the factory settings for the current worksheet.

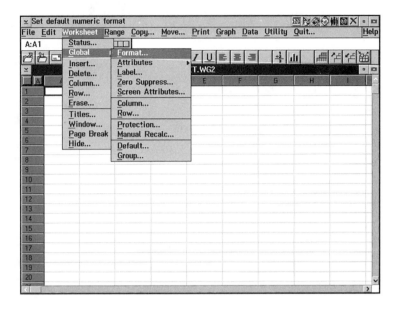

Caution

To apply worksheet default settings to all worksheets in a file, choose **W**orksheet, **G**lobal, **G**roup and enable group mode in the resulting dialog box. Unfortunately, activating group mode applies all range style settings from the current worksheet to all other sheets in the file. Use group mode only when the formatting of every worksheet in the file should match every other worksheet. Or activate group mode before you apply any range formatting so that all worksheets begin with the same defaults. Then deactivate group mode before you apply styles and formats unique to individual sheets.

From Here...

Chapters 4 and 5 presented the information you need to create relatively ornate worksheets that represent rather simple data and calculations. Further chapters in this section help you deal with larger and more complex spreadsheet models.

■ Chapter 6, "Working with Charts and Graphics To Present Your Data," helps you display numeric data as charts and graphs in your worksheet and incorporate illustrations into your worksheet.

- Chapter 7, "Editing Worksheets," delves into issues you face as you build increasingly complex spreadsheet models.

- Chapter 8, "Using Formulas and Functions," presents in-depth information on building formulas with and without @functions.

- Chapter 9, "Managing and Analyzing Data," deals with managing information stored in database format—both in the sheet and in files on-disk.

- Chapter 10, "Printing Worksheet Data," shows how to produce a print-out of your finished worksheet.

- Chapter 11, "Automating with 1-2-3 Macros," introduces the topic of spreadsheet automation with macros.

II

Using 1-2-3

Chapter 6

Working with Charts and Graphics to Present Your Data

by Elaine Marmel

In the last chapter, you learned how to add some pizzazz to the numeric portion of the data contained in a worksheet. But numbers aren't the whole story. In fact, most people agree with that old Chinese proverb, "A picture is worth a thousand words." Displaying numeric data in chart format often gets the point across when the numbers alone just aren't telling the story.

You can add pictures to a worksheet—pictures that are not charts but may help you tell your story. Suppose, for example, incorporating your company's logo would help drive home the fact that *your* company came up with the information in the attached report. You can include your company's logo in a 1-2-3 for OS/2 worksheet. But that's not all. 1-2-3 for OS/2 also contains a built-in charting facility that lets you easily display numbers in bar charts, pie charts, area charts, and line charts. The charting facility uses the Graph Tool, also used by Freelance Graphics.

In this chapter, you learn how to:

- Place professional-quality graphics in your worksheets
- Plot your numeric data on bar, line, and other types of charts

Using Illustrations in the Worksheet

Nothing adds more flair to a worksheet than a graphic image. Traditionally, you couldn't even display charts alongside the worksheet data on which they were based. Now you can do that and add graphics prepared in other programs such as Freelance Graphics.

Importing Pictures from Disk

You should be able to find slick graphics available electronically from many sources. Lotus Development Corporation, for example, markets a product called SmartPics that contains thousands of professionally drawn images of people, machines, buildings, symbols, and so on. You can download image libraries from online information services such as CompuServe, and you can buy disks and CD-ROMs of images through mail houses and retail stores.

1-2-3 can import images from disk into a worksheet as long as the images are computer graphics metafiles (.CGM). Follow these steps to import a graphic from disk:

1. Choose **Utility**, **D**raw, **F**ile Picture. You see the dialog box shown in figure 6.1.

Note

You may need to change directories to the \123G\ directory.

Fig. 6.1
From the Utility
Draw File Picture
dialog box, you
can select .CGM
files to import into
a 1-2-3 worksheet.

2. Navigate to the folder containing the desired image file on-disk.

3. Make sure a check appears in the ANSI (.CGM) checkbox to view .CGM files.

4. Highlight the file and choose the OK button to exit the dialog box.

1-2-3 imports the image into a graphics object superimposed on the worksheet. Click anywhere on the object to select it, and then use its sizing handles to make it fit where you want on the display. Figure 6.2 shows a worksheet that contains an imported CGM image.

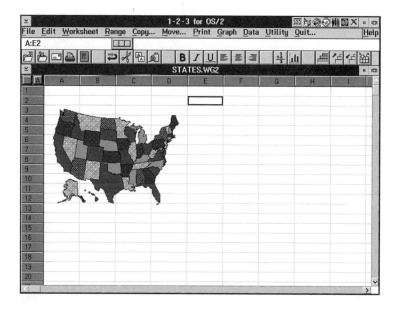

Fig. 6.2
The .CGM file containing an image of the United States came packaged with 1-2-3 Release 2.1 for OS/2.

Copying Images from Other Applications

Few image libraries come in the .CGM file format. You can, however, easily find libraries of images in .PCX or .TIF format. You probably can find libraries of .BMP graphics files also.

1-2-3 may not be able to import a .PCX, .TIF, or .BMP image from disk, but if you can view an image on your display in another program, you can get the image into a worksheet. The steps you use to copy an image into a worksheet closely resemble the procedures you use to copy information from another application into 1-2-3:

1. Open the image file in the other program, making sure you are opening a .PCX, .TIF, or .BMP file. Figure 6.3 shows the LEAVES.BMP wallpaper file, an image that comes with Microsoft Windows, open in Paintbrush (a Windows accessory program) and ready to copy.

II

Using 1-2-3

Fig. 6.3
Copying
LEAVES.BMP
from PaintBrush
into 1-2-3.

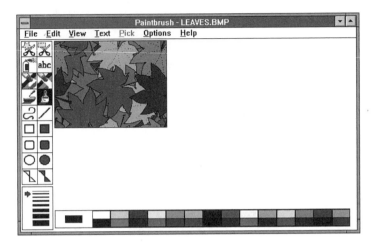

2. Select the image you want to copy.

3. Choose **E**dit, **C**opy.

4. (Optional) close the application.

5. Switch back to 1-2-3, place the insertion point where you want the graphic to appear; then choose **E**dit, **P**aste, or click the Paste SmartIcon.

6. When the graphic appears (see fig. 6.4), use its sizing handles to make it fit where you want it in the worksheet. You can move the graphic the same way you move information in any cell.

Fig. 6.4
After copying an
image into 1-2-3
from another
application, you
can move the
image or resize it.

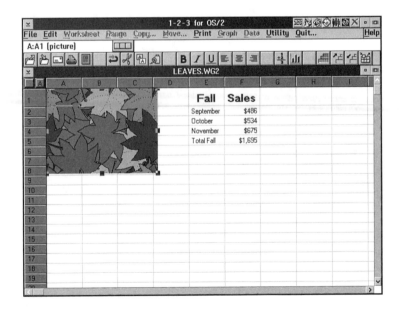

Creating Charts

The most meaningful graphics you're likely to add to a worksheet are charts that represent the worksheet's numeric entries. Sure, anyone can study lists of numbers to figure out what your worksheet's about, but many get the point more quickly when reviewing a chart of the data.

The process of charting worksheet data is so easy that it may seem trivial. The results, however, can be impressive and vital to reaching the people who review your work.

The Shared Graph Tool (between 1-2-3 and Freelance Graphics)

When you use 1-2-3 for OS/2's built-in charting facility, you use the Graph Tool to display numbers in bar charts, pie charts, area charts, and line charts. The Graph Tool is also used by Freelance Graphics, so if you already know Freelance, you don't need to learn anything new to use the charting facility in 1-2-3. In addition, because both programs use the Graph Tool, the link is seamless between files created in either program.

You can use graphs you create in 1-2-3 in presentations you create in Freelance Graphics. If you update the graph's data in 1-2-3, the updates are automatically reflected in the graph you create, even if you're using that graph in a Freelance presentation as opposed to a 1-2-3 worksheet.

When you view a graph, 1-2-3 automatically displays the Graph Tool. 1-2-3 may attempt to graph data in your worksheet, depending on the number of sets of data in the worksheet and whether you select any data (see fig. 6.5).

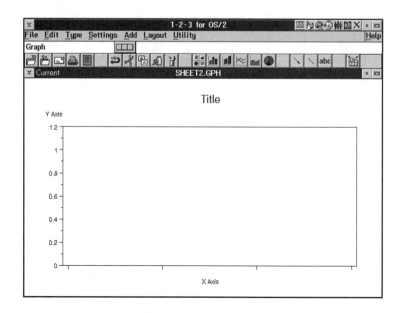

Fig. 6.5

When you have more than one set of data and you don't select any data, 1-2-3 displays an empty chart in the Graph Tool.

Creating a Chart Based on Worksheet Data

Before you create a chart, make sure you're dealing with data that makes sense in a graphical format. Actually, most spreadsheet information works fine in charts. Even if your first choice of chart types—say, a bar chart—doesn't look so hot, you usually can find one you like if you fiddle around enough. 1-2-3 can create several types of line charts, bar charts, pie charts, area charts, radar charts, XY charts, and high-low-close-open charts.

Consider the worksheet in figure 6.6. A chart based on the First Quarter Sales table (range A1..E10) can be useful, although a bit confusing because of the repeating elements—two rows for each name, and three rows for each product. The summary table, which suggests several useful charts, is a little easier to understand. A simple bar or line chart, for example, can compare the monthly sales of the sales representatives. Pie charts can illuminate the percentage of sales by month or by quarter.

Fig. 6.6

Charts based on the First Quarter Summary table are easier to interpret than ones based on the Sales Result table.

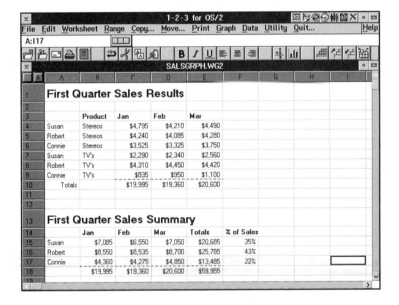

In any case, your first step in creating any chart is to create a default chart. Later, you can change the chart's settings to produce the type of chart you really want. To create a chart that compares the monthly sales by salesperson as reported in range A13..F18 of figure 6.6, follow these steps:

1. Select the range of data to plot—in this case, range A13..E18. Note that the range includes the title, row labels, and column headers that identify the table's contents; it does not include the calculated totals or percentages.

2. Choose **G**raph, **S**etup. You see the Graph Setup dialog box shown in figure 6.7.

3. Choose options and then choose OK. The graph appears in a separate window.

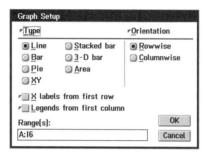

Fig. 6.7

You can tell 1-2-3 the type of graph to produce, how to orient the graph, and whether to use the first row or column for label and legend information.

Unless you have changed the defaults in the dialog box, 1-2-3 draws, in the Graph Tool, a line chart of rowwise orientation. If you placed checks in the checkboxes, the line chart includes labels from the first row of data and a legend from the first column of data. Figure 6.8 shows one possible outcome, a bar chart in its own window (the title of the window is the title of the worksheet with a .GPH extension). This window has the Graph Tool menus and a different SmartIcon bar.

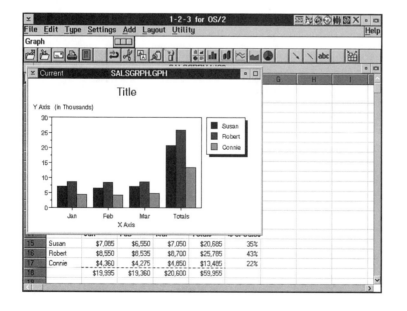

Fig. 6.8

Virtually all the elements of a chart are objects in and of themselves, although you can modify them only in the Graph Tool.

If you click outside the chart window, you return to the worksheet and the graph window moves to the background. You can use the Window command on the program control menu to switch back to the graph. Later, you'll learn how to place the chart directly into the worksheet.

Working with the Charting Tools

In the Graph Tool, you have access to all of 1-2-3's charting tools. This is handy because 1-2-3 only guesses how you want the chart to appear when you first draw it. You often need to make changes before a chart meets all your expectations. At a minimum, you will probably want to add a title to the chart.

Changing the Chart Type

The earlier example produced a bar chart, but suppose your personal prefer-ence is to have a line chart. To change the chart's type, open the **T**ype menu and choose the type of chart you want. If you're not sure or if you want to set a particular style for your type of chart, choose the **T**ype, **G**allery command. You see the Type Gallery dialog box shown in figure 6.9.

Note

A bar chart usually represents data by comparing one item to another, or by compar-ing different items over a period of time.

Fig. 6.9
With the Line option button selected, the Type Gallery dialog box shows six variations of line charts from which to choose.

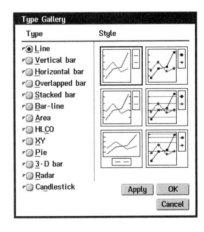

Click an option button in the Type list to see a sample of that type of chart. Click a box on the right side of the dialog box to select a particular style available for your type of chart. You can use the Apply button to apply the type and style to your data and preview your chart. Keep selecting types and styles until you find one you like or one that best represents your data. Your line chart might resemble the one shown in figure 6.10.

Tip
Line (and area) charts reveal a trend over a period of time.

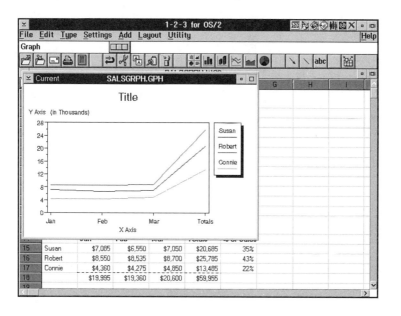

Fig. 6.10
You might prefer a line chart over a bar chart to represent your data.

Understanding Rowwise Versus Columnwise

In our charting example, 1-2-3 automatically uses each row of entries as a chart range. The first row becomes the chart's X-axis range. Successive rows become the A range, the B range, and so on. A chart can have as many as 23 ranges, although things can get confusing pretty quickly when you add more than three or four chart ranges.

Sometimes you want to plot data columnwise instead of rowwise. To do so *after* creating the chart, you must re-create the chart. Click outside the graph to redisplay the worksheet. Reselect the data and choose **G**raph, **S**etup. You see the Graph Setup dialog box again, where you can choose **C**olumnwise.

1-2-3 redraws the chart using columns as the chart ranges rather than rows, as you see in figure 6.11. 1-2-3 does maintain other elements you added to your chart, such as a title.

II

Using 1-2-3

Fig. 6.11

The bar chart created from the worksheet in figure 6.6 clusters each salesperson's bars when you set the columns as the data ranges.

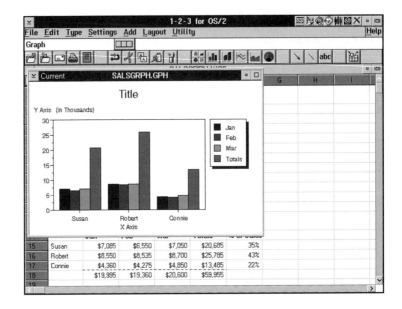

Editing a Chart Title or Axis Title

A chart wouldn't be very meaningful to readers if you showed them the default chart produced by 1-2-3—the one titled *Title*. You can change the title by double-clicking it. The text *Title* appears in the contents box, where you can edit it as you edit any label in 1-2-3. When you press Enter after making changes, the new title appears at the same location as the old title.

Troubleshooting

I need a second title for my chart. The first title doesn't tell the whole story. How can I do that?

Choose **A**dd, **T**itle. From the submenu, choose **S**econd. 1-2-3 adds a line below *Title* called *Second Title*. Edit it the same way you changed the title.

Follow the same procedure to provide meaningful labels for the x axis and the y axis. Double-click one of them and modify it in the contents box.

Controlling the Appearance of a Chart Axis

You can control the way 1-2-3 scales the chart's x axis and y axis. By default, 1-2-3 automatically chooses a scale that suits whatever data you chart. In some line and XY charts, however, you may want to limit the range of values that 1-2-3 plots.

Choose **S**ettings, **S**cale, **X** to use the Settings Scale X dialog box (see fig. 6.12) to specify whether 1-2-3 should show every label along the x axis, or show only every *n*th label. Choose **S**ettings **S**cale **Y** to use the Settings Scale Y dialog box (see fig. 6.13) to set limits for the y axis.

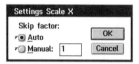

Fig. 6.12
You can control the values that appear on the x axis of a chart.

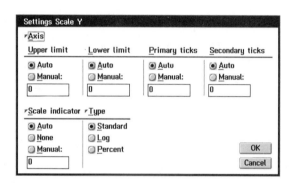

Fig. 6.13
You also can control the values that appear on the y axis of a chart.

You also can control the format of the numbers on the y axis of a chart. Choose **S**ettings, **N**umber Format. From the submenu, choose **Y** Labels. In the resulting dialog box (see fig. 6.14), you can set a number format using the formats you learned about in Chapter 5.

◀ See "Formatting Numbers for Clarity," p. 108

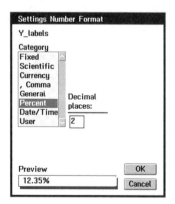

Fig. 6.14
Use the options in the dialog box to control the appearance of the numbers on the y axis.

Using 1-2-3

Changing Legend Elements

Every part of a chart is an element that you can manipulate independently. You can, for example, move the box that encloses the chart's legend in figure 6.11. To change the position of the legend, choose **S**ettings, **P**osition, **L**egend and use the Settings Position Legend dialog box to place the legend at the **B**ottom of the chart or on either the **L**eft or **R**ight sides of the chart. You also can adjust the location of the legend by dragging. Click the outline frame of the legend box so that its handles appear. Then drag to change the box's position.

Tip

Change the actual text that appears in the legend box. Double-click it and edit it in the contents box.

You also can change the font of the text within the legend box—and the colors that apply to the text. Click one of the text elements in the legend box; and then choose **S**ettings, **F**ont to change the font or **T**ext Style to change the color of the text.

Adding Text or Arrows to a Chart

Often, you wish you could be there to point out an important element to the reader on a particular chart. Using lines, arrows, and text, you can draw the reader's attention to the particular portions of the chart that you want to emphasize.

Suppose you want to use arrows to point out a trend in a bar chart. Follow these steps:

1. Click the Arrow SmartIcon. An arrow appears on your chart. Selection handles indicate it is already selected.

2. To change the position of the arrow, drag the center of the line of the arrow.

3. To change the direction of the arrow, drag either end of the arrow. Note that you may also change the size of the arrow when you change its direction.

Add text or a line to your chart in the same way, using the Text SmartIcon or the Line SmartIcon, both shown in the margin.

Changing the Style of Chart Elements

Once you have an element in place, you can change its appearance. You may want to change the colors of lines or bars, or you may want to use a different line style. You also can add background color to a particular element. Remember as you make these changes, that you don't want to distract the reader of the chart. You want your changes to emphasize the readability of the chart.

To modify the style of any element, select that element and then open the **S**ettings menu and choose any of the last commands on the menu (see fig. 6.15). Depending on the selected element, only certain commands are available.

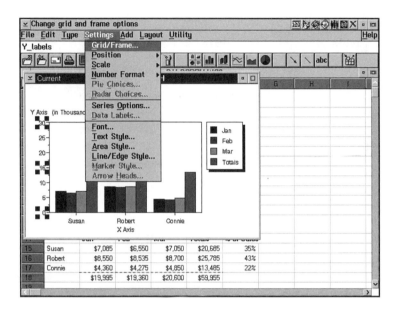

Fig. 6.15
Using the commands at the bottom of the Settings menu, you can change the style and color of any chart element.

When you choose one of these commands, you see a dialog box in which you can select a new color and, if appropriate, style for the element.

Using Graph Tool SmartIcons

The chart-editing SmartIcons speed your selection of a type for a selected chart. In addition, you find SmartIcons that let you quickly add lines, arrows, and text to your chart. As you found in 1-2-3, you can point at a SmartIcon and press the right mouse button to see its purpose displayed in the program title bar.

► See "Using SmartIcons," p. 674

Using the Same Data To Create Many Charts

Suppose you realize, after working intensively with the data in your worksheet, that you need to present different charts of the same data. You might, for example, want to show a line chart to emphasize a trend and then a bar chart to emphasize individual points of data. Or, you might want to present a rowwise chart and a columnwise chart of the same data.

II

Using 1-2-3

Tip

Try displaying the data in a line and area chart, or a 2D and 3D bar chart. Various chart types can emphasize or distort the effect of the data.

You don't need to retype anything in the worksheet. In fact, you don't even need to save separate graph files. You can store different chart views of the same data in your worksheet. The basic steps in the process include:

1. Set up the first chart and make it look the way you want, including titles, legend, arrows, axis modifications, and so on.

2. Switch to the worksheet and save this view of the chart.

3. Set up the second chart and make it look the way you want.

4. Switch to the worksheet and save the new view of the chart.

You know how to accomplish steps 1 and 3. Now you'll learn how to complete steps 2 and 4.

After you set up a chart and it looks the way you want, click the worksheet to switch back to it. Then, choose **G**raph, **N**ame. The Graph Name dialog box appears (see fig. 6.16).

Fig. 6.16

Using the Graph Name dialog box, you can save and then return to different charts you create of the same data.

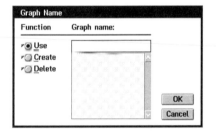

In the dialog box, type a name for the chart in the Graph Name text box and then choose the **C**reate option button and the OK button. 1-2-3 stores the settings for the first chart.

Create the second chart (**G**raph, **S**etup) and make it look the way you want. Then, repeat the process described, supplying a new name for the second chart.

> **Note**
>
> You can't use the Graph SmartIcon to create the second chart because the tool displays the original chart when you click it.

Switch between the two graph views by choosing **G**raph, **N**ame in the worksheet, selecting the appropriate view, and choosing the **U**se option button.

1-2-3 saves the different views you create when you store them in the worksheet using the Graph Name dialog box, so you don't need to save the graph file.

Placing a Chart into a Worksheet

Of course, we all want our charts to appear right beside the numbers that created them. And, so far, the charts in 1-2-3 all appear in the Graph Tool window. So, can you get them into the worksheet? Yep. Follow these steps:

1. In the Graph Tool, set up the chart the way you want it to appear in the worksheet.

2. Click anywhere in the Graph Tool window containing your chart, but make sure you *don't* select a chart element.

3. Choose the Copy SmartIcon; or choose **E**dit, **C**opy.

4. Switch back to the worksheet by clicking outside the Graph Tool window.

5. Position the cell pointer where you want the upper-left corner of the chart to appear. In this case, place the cell pointer beneath the table.

6. Choose the Paste SmartIcon; or choose **E**dit, **P**aste. The chart appears in your worksheet (refer to fig. 6.17).

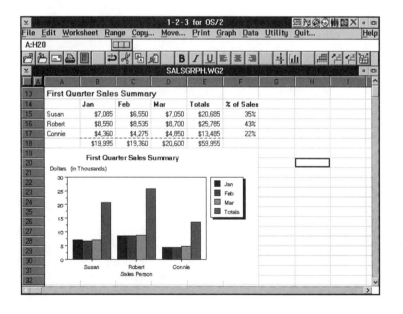

Fig. 6.17
After creating a chart in Graph Tool, you can easily incorporate it into your worksheet and then print both the numbers and the chart on the same page.

From Here...

Chapters 4 and 5 presented the information you need to create relatively ornate worksheets that represent rather simple data and calculations. Chapter 6 helped you display numeric data as charts and graphs in your worksheet and incorporate illustrations in your worksheet. Further chapters in this section help you deal with larger and more complex spreadsheet models:

■ Chapter 7, "Editing Worksheets," delves into issues you face as you build increasingly complex spreadsheet models.

■ Chapter 8, "Using Formulas and Functions," presents in-depth information on building formulas with and without @functions.

■ Chapter 9, "Managing and Analyzing Data," deals with managing information stored in database format—both in the sheet and in files on-disk.

■ Chapter 10, "Printing Worksheet Data," shows how to produce a printout of your finished worksheet.

Chapter 7

Editing Worksheets

by Elaine Marmel

A model is a representation of some aspect of your business, finances, or research. You use models to show—or to help you guess—how changes in your assumptions might change your bottom line. Virtually every spreadsheet you build is a model of sorts.

Spreadsheet users typically talk about building spreadsheet models. The term fits because creating a model involves combining dozens, hundreds, or thousands of small pieces that eventually make up a complete project. You work with the fabric of the spreadsheet, stretching, cutting, pasting, weaving, and otherwise manipulating it. When a part of the spreadsheet meets certain specifications, you can instantly reproduce it again and again for every part of your model that needs it. 1-2-3 is particularly well suited to building large models in a hurry. Understanding the tools saves you hours of painstaking typing and retyping.

In this chapter, you learn to:

- Reuse data and formulas by copying cells

- Move spreadsheet cells and ranges

- Make room for new entries among existing ones

- Remove unwanted entries from the spreadsheet

- Move data from one file to another

- Name ranges and exploit the names as your worksheet grows

Copying Worksheet Data

The single most important time-saving facility of 1-2-3 is its capability to copy cells, formulas, and ranges. This may not seem so important at first. After all, you rarely need to enter a particular label dozens of times, and it's even less common to need a single value in several dozen cells.

You realize the true power of copying cells when you begin to rely heavily on formulas. A quick overview helps you recognize opportunities to employ 1-2-3's copying capabilities.

General Effects of Copying Information

▶ See "Revisiting Basic Calculations" p. 169

The outcome of copying varies depending on whether you copy one cell to another, one cell to a range, or a range of cells to another range. Understanding the possible outcomes speeds you through many mundane spreadsheet chores.

Copying One-to-One Ranges

One consequence arises when you copy a source range of cells to a same-sized target range. If the target range exactly matches the dimensions of the source range—or is wider, taller, and deeper—1-2-3 will make an exact copy of the source range and place it starting in the upper-left corner of the target range. In figure 7.1, the empty gray area represents the selected target range before the copy operation is completed. Exceptions to this rule arise when you copy formulas (see "Effects of Copying Formulas," later in this chapter).

> **Note**
>
> Regardless of the dimensions of the source range, when you specify a single cell as the target range for a copying operation, 1-2-3 places the copy with its top-left corner cell starting in the target cell. Copying range A13..D19 to the target range A22 is equivalent to copying to range A22..D28.

Copying Ranges of Different Sizes

◀ See "Selecting Ranges," p. 92

A second consequence arises when you copy a single cell to a multicell range. Whatever the dimensions of the target, 1-2-3 places a copy of the source cell in every cell of the target range, as suggested by figure 7.2, which shows the target range after completing the copy operation.

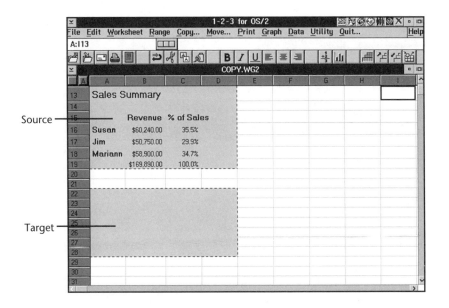

Fig. 7.1
Suppose you specify range A13..D19 as the range to copy and range A22..D28 as the range to copy to. The copy you see in the worksheet matches the original because the target range (empty but gray in this figure) is the same size as the source.

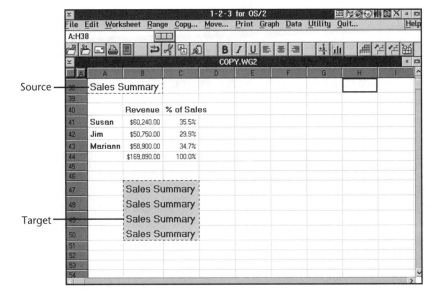

Fig. 7.2
Copying a single cell to a multicell range fills the range with copies in a snap.

Using 1-2-3

Copying Rows, Columns, or Sheets

A third consequence arises when you need to make several copies of a row range, column range, or spreadsheet range. If you specify some portion of a row as the source range, you can create several copies of it by specifying a target range within a single column. Use a portion of a column as the source, and a target range within a row results in multiple copies. The worksheet in figure 7.3 clarifies these statements.

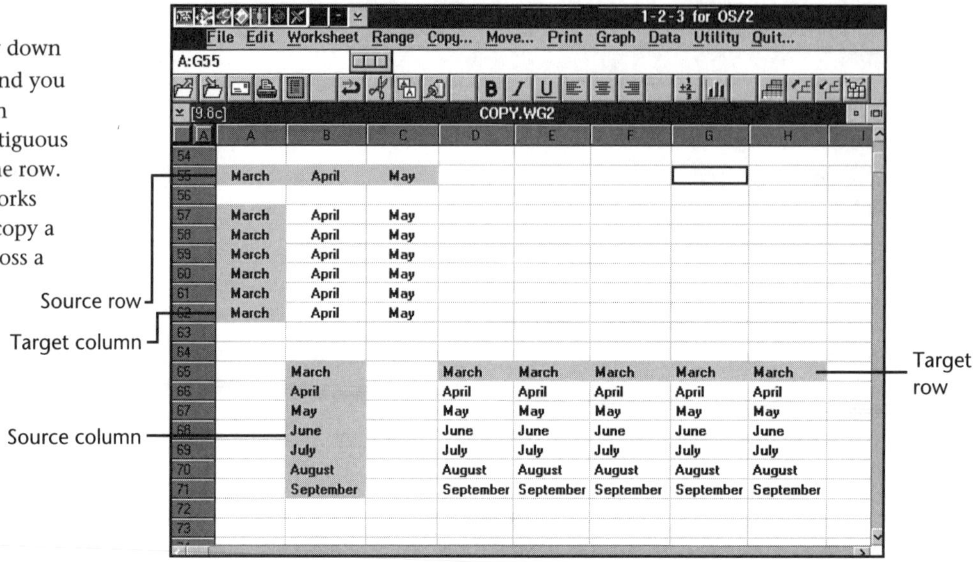

Fig. 7.3

Copy a row down a column and you end up with several contiguous copies of the row. This also works when you copy a column across a row.

When you copy a two-dimensional range down through a third dimension, 1-2-3 replicates the range in each layer along that third dimension. Typically, you copy through the third dimension when you need to create the same general structure of labels and formulas on several sheets—to report a different month's production results on each page, for example. Create one of the sheets; then copy it down through the stack.

Effects of Copying Formulas

◀ See "A Ledger Paper Note-book," p. 77

Simply copying cells and ranges speeds your work dramatically, even if you performed only the copying routines covered in the last few pages. But copying cells can save you even more time when it involves formulas. This procedure has to do with the way 1-2-3 "thinks" of the references in formulas.

Consider the expression +B3+C3 stored in cell D3. To 1-2-3, this means, "Add the value that is two cells to the left of the current cell to the value that is one cell to the left and place the answer in the current cell."

Similarly, the expression @SUM(B4..B7) entered in cell B8 means, "Sum the values that run from the fourth cell above this one through the first cell above it and place the answer in the current cell." The cell addresses appear for your benefit; they make it easy for you to identify which values 1-2-3 is adding.

1-2-3's interpretation of the references may seem trivial, but it's vital to most spreadsheet model building. Figure 7.4 shows a typical worksheet listing the monthly product sales of several sales people. Entering the data is painful enough, but who wants the added aggravation of typing a formula at the bottom of each column to calculate monthly sales totals for each month?

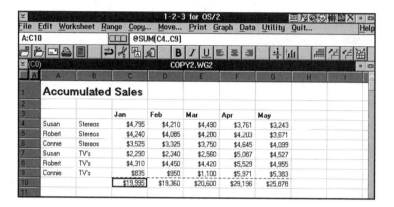

Fig. 7.4
1-2-3's use of relative references lets you write one formula and then copy it to add up the monthly sales totals.

Instead, you enter a single formula at the bottom of the first column—that's cell C10—and copy it across. One formula you might use is @SUM(C4..C9). Because it means "Sum the values in the current column that run from the fourth cell through the ninth cell," you can copy it to columns D through G to calculate their totals. Copied to cell D10, the formula becomes @SUM(D4..D9). In cell E10 it becomes @SUM(E4..E9). In all cases, the formula continues to refer to a certain number of cells in the same column in which the formula resides.

A cell or range reference that adapts to its position in the spreadsheet no matter where you copy the formula containing it is a *relative reference*. You'll discover dozens of ways to use relative references as you build more and more complex models.

> **Note**
>
> It's important to recognize that 1-2-3 copies everything about a cell. The cell contents, numeric formatting, label alignment, colors, and borders from the source all appear in the target cells. Nothing existing in the range the copied cells overwrite survives the event—1-2-3 wipes those cells clean and replaces their contents and formatting.

II

Using 1-2-3

▶ See "Using Cell and Range References in Formulas," p. 176

That was a big build-up of the various consequences of copying cells. So the big question becomes, "How do I copy cells?" Read on.

Using the Copy Command

For those of you who like working in dialog boxes, you can use the **C**opy command on the menu bar and let 1-2-3 prompt you for source and target ranges. You will find using this dialog box easier if you start by selecting the source range:

1. Select the range you want to copy.

2. Choose the **C**opy command. 1-2-3 displays the dialog box you see in figure 7.5.

3. Click the To box.

4. Click the worksheet and select the target range. Remember, you can click the upper-left corner of the target range without specifying the entire target range.

5. Click the OK button.

Fig. 7.5

When you click the worksheet, 1-2-3 changes the contents of the Copy dialog box to match the cell(s) you select in the worksheet.

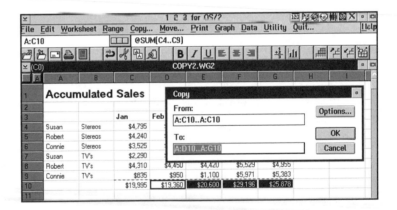

Note

Pasting a copied range doesn't necessarily end the excitement of copying and pasting. When you copy a range, 1-2-3 copies the selected range to the OS/2 Clipboard. The copy remains on the Clipboard until you perform another task that places information there. This means that after you copy a range to the Clipboard, you can paste it in the worksheet repeatedly. Simply select a target location and Paste, select another target and Paste, and so on.

Using Edit Copy and Edit Paste

The classic model for copying information is the Edit Copy and Edit Paste combo. Here's how to apply it in 1-2-3:

1. Select the source range to copy.

2. Choose **E**dit, **C**opy, click the Copy SmartIcon, or press Ctrl+Ins.

3. Select the target range.

4. Choose **E**dit, **P**aste, click the Paste SmartIcon, or press Shift+Ins.

Troubleshooting

I got a lot of work done, only to discover that I really needed the rows to be columns and vice versa. I thought I could copy the information—until I actually tried it and found out that I would need to copy one cell at a time. Do I need to start all over or is there an easy way to fix my mistake?

You can transpose the rows and columns using a variation of the **C**opy command. Select the range you want to switch and choose **R**ange, **T**ranspose. In the resulting dialog, choose **R**ows/Columns from the Transposition options. Then, click the To text box and click the worksheet to identify the location where you want the upper-left corner of the transposed information to appear. (You can place the transposed information on top of the existing information, but 1-2-3 overwrites what's already there, so be sure of your action.) When you choose OK, 1-2-3 reorganizes your information.

Using Edit Paste Special

A near hit at anything can be incredibly frustrating. You get tantalizingly close to your target, but the desired result eludes you. That can be the case with copying cells. You may already have entered data at the target, and now you want to copy only the numeric formats, and text and line styles from other cells. Or perhaps you want to copy the cell entries, but without disturbing the formatting and styling at the target range. Or, perhaps you don't really want to copy the formulas; instead, you want to copy the results of the formulas. The Paste Special command serves these purposes.

To use the Paste Special command, begin as if copying cells. That is, select a source range and copy it to the Clipboard. Then select the target range and choose **E**dit, Paste **S**pecial. 1-2-3 displays the dialog box shown in figure 7.6.

Fig. 7.6
The Paste Special
dialog box lets you
choose which
aspects of a copied
range to paste into
the target range.

Tip
If you like using
the Copy dialog
box, use the Op-
tions button in
that dialog box.
You see the Copy
Options dialog
box, which looks
suspiciously like
the Edit Paste
Special dialog box.

Tip
Removing the
check from the
Formulas
checkbox (under
Contents) tells
1-2-3 to copy
formulas to the
target range but
convert them to
values in the
target range.

Using the checkboxes under **T**ype of Entry, remove checks to avoid copying
labels, numbers, or formulas from the selected range. Using the checkboxes
under **C**ontents, remove checks to avoid copying formulas, values, notes, or
settings from the selected range.

Moving Worksheet Data

In most building projects, careful planning is paramount to getting acceptable results. Not so with building spreadsheet models. Sure, if you plan a
spreadsheet model, the time you take to build it will probably decrease. However, most spreadsheet developers discover that you can build a spreadsheet
and design it all at once—the tools for changing a spreadsheet's layout are so
powerful that there's little risk in getting trapped by your original design.

When you know how to insert and delete rows and columns and move cells
and ranges, you might come to use the spreadsheet to doodle your way to a
finished application.

On the surface, moving cells looks a lot like copying them. You specify a
range to move, and then a range to move it to. Everything from the source
ends up at the target, leaving a blank area in place of the range's original
entries. Depending on what you move, the effects of the procedure can be
profound. Moving cells involved in a formula can dramatically change the
formula's references, and even damage them so the formula returns an error
message.

Caution

The effects of moving cells can seriously damage a spreadsheet! It's important to
understand the possible outcomes before you begin. If you recognize that something
has gone wrong as a result of moving cells, you can recover instantly by choosing
Edit, Undo; or by clicking the Undo SmartIcon.

General Effects of Moving Information

If you have nothing more than numbers and labels in your worksheet, you can move ranges with impunity. Remember that when you paste a range, you cut from another location and obliterate the existing cells at the destination. This makes more sense when you see how moving cells can affect formulas.

Moving Formulas with Their Supporting Data

Consider the worksheet in figure 7.7. The entries in row 8 are @SUM formulas that add up values for the columns. So, B8 contains @SUM(B4..B7), C8 contains @SUM(C4..C7), and so on. Moving the entire range of values and formulas—range A3..F8—doesn't change much at all. The formulas retain their relationships relative to the data. The cell references change, but the formulas return the same subtotals.

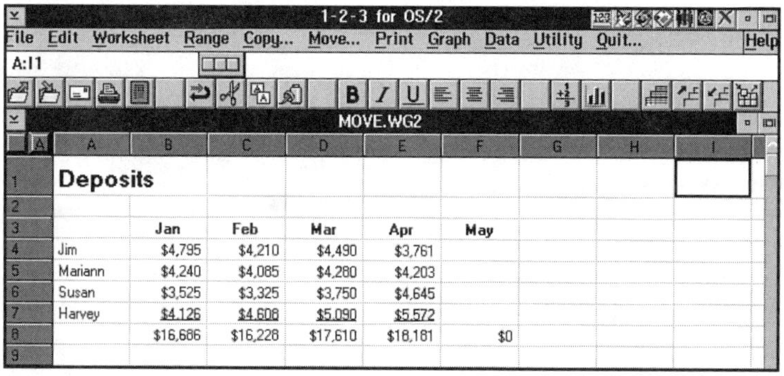

Tip

Always save a worksheet before making major changes. If you make a major mistake, you can revert to the saved copy.

Fig. 7.7

A typical model with a few summary formulas can illustrate the effects of moving worksheet ranges.

Moving Only Formulas

What happens if you move the formulas, but leave the data in place? As long as you use the Move command and don't drop the formulas on top of the data, the formulas retain their range references; they still calculate totals for January through April.

1-2-3 assumes you want to maintain the relationships between the formulas you create and the data they refer to no matter where you move the formulas.

Moving Only Data

If, in a single operation, you move all the data to which a formula refers using the Move command, the formula continues to refer to the data. This means that the formula's references must change to reflect the new location of the data in the worksheet. If you move range B4..B7 of figure 7.7 to cell B10, for example, the formula in cell B8 transforms to read @SUM(B10..B13); it continues the sum of the January data.

Moving Some Data, But Not All

Real weirdness arises when you move some, but not all, of the cells to which a formula refers. To 1-2-3, the two opposite corner cells of every range are very important, but the other cells are little more than debris. In most cases, the top-left and bottom-right corners are the important ones, but in formulas, that can change depending on how you specify the range references when you create them.

Once again, consider figure 7.7. If you move range E5..E6 over to column H, the formula in cell E8 doesn't know the difference; it continues to sum entries in range E4..E7. However, move cell E4 to cell G2, and you move the top-left corner of the formula's range reference. Now the formula in E8 becomes @SUM(G2..E7)—note that cells G2 and E7, the top-right and bottom-left corners, become critical in identifying the formula's range reference.

> **Caution**
>
> The most devastating result of moving cells arises when you dump a cell or range on top of another cell to which some formula refers. Refer once more to figure 7.7. Column F is ready and waiting to receive data, complete with the formula @SUM(F4..F7) in cell F8. Suppose you enter a column of values in range A10..A13, and later want to move those values into the May data area. Moving a range blows away all the original cells at the target—along with any references to them. So when the range of data hits cells F4 and F7, the formula in F8 becomes invalid and returns ERR.

Using the Move Command

The **M**ove command lets you work from a dialog box and move information. If you are moving a formula without moving the cells to which it refers, or you are moving cells to which a formula refers but you are not moving the formula, you get unexpected results using any method other than the Move command.

Like the **C**opy command, the **M**ove command lets you work in a dialog box, with 1-2-3 prompting you for source and target ranges. You will find using this dialog box easier if you start by selecting the source range:

1. Select the range you want to move.

2. Choose the **M**ove command. 1-2-3 displays the Move dialog box.

3. Click the To box.

4. Click the worksheet to select the target range (see fig. 7.8). Remember, you can click the upper-left corner of the target range without specifying the entire target range.

5. Click the OK button.

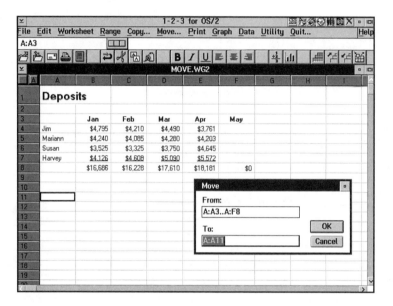

Fig. 7.8
When you click the worksheet, 1-2-3 changes the contents of the Move dialog box to match the cell(s) you select in the worksheet.

Using Edit Cut and Edit Paste

The classic mechanism for moving things is to start by cutting them from the application to the OS/2 Clipboard, and then pasting them from the Clipboard into a new location. Here's how this works in 1-2-3:

Caution

Unless you are moving both a formula and the data to which it refers, this method does not preserve the integrity of formulas. Use this method to move labels or numbers to which no formula refers.

---

1. Select the range you plan to move.

2. Choose **E**dit, Cu**t**, click the Cut SmartIcon, or press Shift+Del. The selected range becomes blank as 1-2-3 moves its contents to the Clipboard.

3. Select a cell that marks the location where you want to deliver the range you're moving. This cell should fall at the top-left corner of the destination range—the top-left corner cell of the range you're moving ends up here.

 4. Choose **E**dit, **P**aste, click the Paste SmartIcon, or press Shift+Ins.

> **Note**
>
> As with copying, when you Cut and Paste, a copy of the moved range remains on the Clipboard even after you first paste it until you cut or copy another item. You can paste the copy repeatedly as you do when you copy a range to the Clipboard.

Working with More Than One Range

There are times when you need to perform the same function on cells that are not contiguous so you can't select them as a range of cells. Or, at least you think you can't select them as a range of cells. In fact, 1-2-3 lets you work with *collections,* which are two or more sets of cells that are not adjacent

Tip
A collection can consist of single, non-contiguous cells, non-contiguous ranges, or a combination of the two.

For example, suppose you wanted to format cells B23..B27 and cells D23..D27 as currency, and cells C23..C27 and E23..E27 as percentages. You can treat cells B23..B27 and D23..D27 as a collection and format them at the same time. Then, you can treat C23..C27 and E23..E27 as another collection and format them simultaneously. The secret, as you have probably guessed, is in the way you select the cells. To select cells as a collection, follow these steps:

1. Select the first cell or set of cells as you normally do.

2. Select the second range by pressing and holding the right mouse button while you drag.

3. Repeat step 2 to add additional ranges to the collection (see fig. 7.9).

   To select a collection that spans worksheets, work in perspective view by clicking the Perspective View SmartIcon. Select the first range. Then, using the right mouse button, click the second worksheet and select that range. When you need to select a range in a sheet that you can't see, use the Next Sheet and Previous Sheet SmartIcons to navigate to the correct sheet and continue selecting.

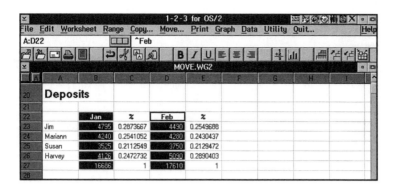

Fig. 7.9
Using collections,
you can select cells
or ranges that are
not adjacent.

Tip
You can't move a
collection. You
can, however,
copy a collection
using the Copy
command.

Inserting Rows, Columns, and Sheets

Sometimes you simply need more space (not personal space, but space in a
worksheet). Use 1-2-3's tools for inserting blank columns, rows, or sheets into
a file.

You can make insertions anywhere, but use caution. When a row or column
you insert falls within a range referenced in a formula, no problem—the
formula's reference expands accordingly. But, when you insert a row or column at the edge of a range referenced in a formula, the formula's reference
does not expand.

The worksheet in figure 7.10 is an updated version of the one in figure 7.7. It
happens to be missing deposits that were collected by Constance. To add
those deposits, you might insert a row above or below the existing records.
Then you'd have to rewrite the formulas in row 8 to incorporate the new
data. However, if you insert a row in the records as shown in figure 7.11, the
summary formulas adjust automatically to include the row. The formulas
automatically incorporate Constance's entries in their calculations.

Inserting Rows or Columns

Suppose that you decide to insert a new row. Do the following:

1. In the worksheet frame, click the number of the row above which you
want to make the insertion. 1-2-3 highlights the entire row. To insert
several rows at once, drag in the frame from the selected row down over
as many rows as you want to insert.

2. Choose **W**orksheet, **I**nsert. You see the dialog box that appears in figure
7.12.

3. Choose the **R**ow option and choose OK.

II

Using 1-2-3

Fig. 7.10

Inserting a row at either arrow makes room for data, but with a shortcoming: the formulas in row 8 don't incorporate the new row.

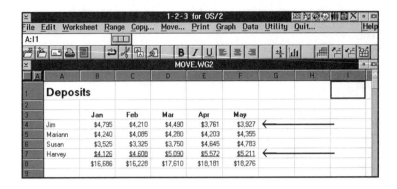

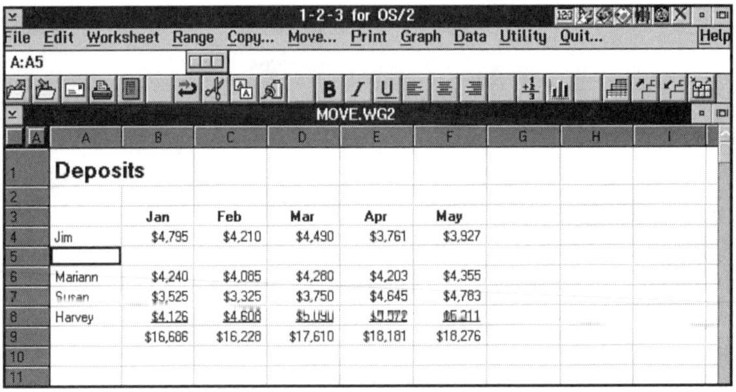

Fig. 7.11

The formulas in row 8 incorporate cells in a new row if you insert it between rows 4 and 7 as a new row appears here.

Fig. 7.12

Using the Worksheet Insert dialog box, you can insert all or part of a row, column, or sheet.

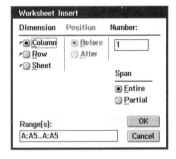

Inserting an entire row might split important ranges not visible on the display. Make sure before you proceed that there are no tables or referenced ranges outside the visible area that an insertion will affect. Alternatively, limit the rows affected by an insertion as follows:

1. Select a range within which 1-2-3 should insert rows. For example, to insert three rows within columns B, C, D, E, and F starting at row 5, select range B5..F7.

2. Choose **W**orksheet, **I**nsert.

3. In the dialog box, select the **R**ow option and, under the Span options, choose the **P**artial option. Then click OK.

Inserting a column is just like inserting a row:

1. Click in the worksheet frame the letter of the column to the right of where you want to insert. Drag from there to the right over as many columns as you want to insert.

2. Choose **W**orksheet, **I**nsert and complete the dialog box.

Inserting Sheets

Each 1-2-3 worksheet initially contains 256 sheets. But suppose you decide that the first sheet (in which you have been working) should really be the second sheet in the file. To insert a worksheet in front of a file's first worksheet, follow these steps:

1. Go to the file's top worksheet.

2. Choose **W**orksheet, **I**nsert. The Worksheet Insert dialog box, shown earlier in figure 7.12, appears.

3. Activate the **S**heet option and click OK.

Tip
Pressing Ctrl+Home will quickly take you to the top worksheet.

Troubleshooting

Several formulas in one of my worksheets were calculating sums that were at least twice what they should have been. I discovered that the formulas referred to several extra columns of data.

You must have moved some cells to which the formulas referred. If you move the bottom-right or top-left cell of the range to which a formula refers, the formula's reference changes. It can possibly end up summing too many columns or rows.

A row of ERRs appeared in one of my spreadsheets and I discovered the row contained summary formulas that read @SUM(ERR). Originally they read @SUM(B3..B9), @SUM(C3..C9), and so on.

Did you move data into range B3..E9? Or, did you delete row 3 or row 9? Either action damages the original formula's range references and results in the ERR expressions.

(continues)

II

Using 1-2-3

> (continued)
>
> *I've tried to insert rows in the spreadsheet, but I keep getting the error message,* Cannot move or copy data beyond worksheet boundaries.
>
> You've been busy. There must be an entry in the very last row of your worksheet (row 8192). If you don't think there should be an entry there, go to the bottom row and scan across it—remember how to navigate using the End and Direction key sequences—to find the problem. If you're certain that extraneous entries near the bottom of the sheet aren't important, simply delete the rows that run from your last worksheet entry to the bottom of the sheet.

Deleting Data and Styles

What if you build it and they don't come? Well, you don't have to live with it—you can simply remove it from the worksheet. If you're like most people, time and again you'll decide that something you've built simply doesn't belong in your spreadsheet model.

Erasing Cell Entries

Suppose you just need to remove the data from a range. The range contains styles and formats as well as data, and you want to leave those in place so future entries assume the characteristics of the current ones. Figure 7.13 shows one such scenario. You closed out the 1994 fiscal year, and want to reuse the spreadsheet for 1995. Follow these steps to clear the data from range B4..E8, but leave the dollar formats and vertical cell borders in place:

1. Select the range.

2. Choose **E**dit, Cl**e**ar; or press Del.

> **Caution**
>
> Using Edit, **C**lear or pressing Del to erase data does not preserve the deleted entries on OS/2's Clipboard.

Clearing Styles and Attributes

If you don't care for the look you established in a range, correcting it can be laborious. To clear a range format, you select the range, choose **R**ange,

Format, and click the Reset button at the end of the category list in the resulting dialog box. To clear font and font attribute settings, you need to remember the spreadsheet defaults, and then change the settings back via the Range Attributes Font dialog box. The same applies for resetting the lines and colors applied to a range.

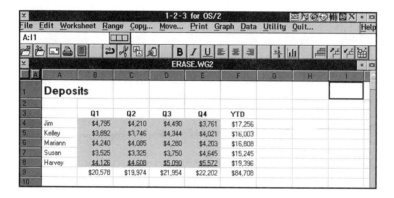

Fig. 7.13
Erasing the data in range B4..E8 leaves formatting and formulas in place, while clearing the spreadsheet to receive data for the next fiscal year.

You can do all those things, or you can use a shortcut to clear a range's style settings:

1. Select the range to clear.

2. Choose **E**dit, **C**ut; or click the Cut SmartIcon.

3. Choose **E**dit, Paste **S**pecial.

4. Remove the check from the **S**ettings checkbox and click OK.

Deleting Rows, Columns, and Sheets

Another way to remove unwanted information from a spreadsheet file is to delete the entire row(s), column(s), or sheet(s) containing the information. To delete rows and columns, follow these steps:

1. Drag in the worksheet border to select the rows or columns to delete.

2. Choose **W**orksheet, **D**elete.

3. In the resulting dialog box, select the option that describes what you want to delete (see fig. 7.14). Then click OK.

II

Using 1-2-3

Fig. 7.14

You can delete all or part of a row, column, or sheet in the Worksheet Delete dialog box.

> **Caution**
>
> Be careful about deleting rows, columns, and sheets! Don't delete rows, columns, or sheets to which formulas specifically refer. Deleting the critical corner cells of ranges invalidates the formulas that refer to them. Deleting any cell whose address appears explicitly in a formula invalidates the formula.

Deleting an entire row might damage spreadsheet entries not visible on the display. Make sure there are no entries or ranges outside the visible area that are affected by a deletion before you proceed. You can, alternatively, delete only part of a row, column or sheet.

Deleting entries in part of a row, column, or sheet differs from deleting part of a row, column, or sheet. When you delete entries, the original cells remain, but their contents disappear. When you delete cells, both the cell and its contents disappear, potentially changing the shape of a range containing a formula.

To avoid damaging spreadsheet entries not visible on the display or potentially changing the shape of a range containing a formula, limit the rows affected by a deletion as follows:

1. Select a range that you want 1-2-3 to delete. For example, to delete three rows in columns B, C, D, E, and F starting at row 5, select range B5..F7.

2. Choose **W**orksheet, **D**elete.

3. Activate the **R**ow option and the **P**artial option. Then click OK.

Copying or Moving between Worksheets

As you become prolific at building spreadsheets, you might discover that information stored in one spreadsheet file would be very useful in other files.

In these instances, being able to copy or move data from one file to another can save time and effort. 1-2-3 and the OS/2 interface make the task easy.

Working with Multiple Files in RAM

1-2-3 can manage many files in RAM at one time. To have more than one file open, simply open one (choose **F**ile, **O**pen; or use the Open SmartIcon) and then open a second one without closing the first. Or add a new file by choosing **F**ile, **N**ew.

> **Caution**
>
> If you are moving data, remember that using the Edit, Cut command or the Cut SmartIcon may not preserve the integrity of formulas. Unless you are moving *both* a formula and the data to which it refers, use the Move command.

Here's how to copy or move information from one file to another:

1. Make the window holding the source range the active window by clicking a visible portion of the window, choosing the appropriate name from the **W**indows menu, or pressing Ctrl+F6.

2. Select the source range to copy or move.

3. Choose the **E**dit, **C**opy or Cu**t** command, using whichever method you prefer.

4. Switch to the window holding the worksheet that will receive the data. Again, click any visible portion of that worksheet, choose its name from the **W**indow menu, or press Ctrl+F6.

5. Click the top-left corner cell of the desired destination.

6. Choose the **P**aste command, again using whichever method you prefer.

Except under circumstances discussed in the next chapter, copied formulas assume addresses in the new file—relative to where you paste them. Moved formulas behave a bit differently, assuming you move them using the **M**ove command:

- If you move data to which a formula refers, 1-2-3 adjusts the formula.

- If you move a formula without moving the cells to which it refers, 1-2-3 does not adjust the formula.

- If you move both a formula and the cells to which it refers, 1-2-3 adjusts everything.

Extracting to Files

A second way to share information among files is to extract the data to a new disk file. The new disk file can become the basis for an entirely new spreadsheet model, or you can combine it into another spreadsheet, as you'll see in a moment. Extracting information to a new disk file is particularly useful when the spreadsheets you're working with are so big that you're running low on system resources.

To extract a range into a new disk file, follow these steps:

1. Select the range to extract. The range can be a collection as long as the collection resides in one worksheet.

2. Choose **F**ile, **X**tract. 1-2-3 displays the dialog box you see in figure 7.15.

Fig. 7.15

Use the File Xtract dialog box, you can place part of one worksheet into a new file, copying formulas or actual values.

3. Using the **F**ormulas option, tell 1-2-3 to place formulas from the current worksheet into the new file or convert the formulas to values and place values in the new worksheet.

4. Type a new name for the file in the text box labeled File name. If the filename you type exists, be aware that 1-2-3 overwrites the data in that file.

5. Click OK to close the dialog box.

1-2-3 creates copies of all labels, data, formatting, styling, and formulas and places them starting in cell A1 of the new file, leaving the source range itself unchanged. All formula references in the extract file switch to that file.

Suppose you extract range B2..C5, and a formula in C5 refers to cell E5. In the target file, the range shifts up and to the right to begin in cell A1. So the formula now resides in cell B4. The formula's reference to E5 also shifts and refers to cell D4 in the new file.

Combining from Files

Combining ranges from disk files into the current file has more uses than simply copying data. You might use the capability to create consolidations of information gathered from several sources—other departments or coworkers, for example. To combine an entire file, or selected ranges from files, follow these steps:

> **Caution**
>
> To avoid losing data because you accidentally combine information on top of existing information, be sure to save the file before you combine.

1. Move the cell pointer to the top-left corner cell of the range that will receive the incoming data. Be aware that the data that comes in affects any data currently at the location you choose.

2. Choose **F**ile, **C**ombine. 1-2-3 displays the dialog box you see in figure 7.16.

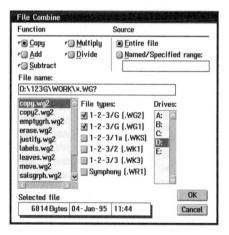

Fig. 7.16

You can combine all or part of files, and you can control the way 1-2-3 handles the data that comes into the worksheet.

3. Select the file you wish to combine in the File Name listbox.

4. Choose the **E**ntire File or **N**amed/Specified Range option to determine whether to incorporate the entire file, or just a range from the file. If you specify **N**amed/Specified range, type the address of the range you want to combine from the disk file.

5. Choose the action 1-2-3 should take with the incoming numeric entries by selecting from options under the heading, Function:

  ■ **C**opy causes 1-2-3 to replace any entries in the current worksheet that happen to correspond with entries incoming from the disk file; entries that correspond with blank incoming cells remain intact.

  ■ **A**dd, **S**ubtract, **M**ultiply, and **D**ivide each have the predicted effect. None of them affects any labels or formulas, but all change the values. For example, **A**dd causes 1-2-3 to add the incoming numbers to corresponding numbers in the current file. **S**ubtract subtracts incoming numbers from corresponding numbers in the current file. Use these options when you're consolidating identically laid out ranges from several sheets into a single summary worksheet.

6. Click OK to close the dialog box.

Annotating Cells

Occasionally, you'll wish to write yourself a note about the contents of a particular cell. You may want to print that note so the person who reviews your worksheet can also see it. Using the Note feature of 1-2-3, you can annotate cells. Then you can create a table of the notes (similar to a table of footnotes in a research paper) and print the table, which contains the cell reference and the note you created.

To annotate a cell, follow these steps:

1. Place the cell pointer in the cell about which you want to create a note.

2. Choose **U**tility, **N**ote. You see a dialog box similar to the one shown in figure 7.17.

Fig. 7.17

By annotating cells, you can clarify issues for the reader of your worksheet.

3. In the **N**ote text box, type the information you want included in the note.

4. Choose the OK button to save the note.

To create a two-column table that lists the notes you created and the cells you created them for, follow these steps:

1. Place the cell pointer in the upper-left corner of the range where you want the table to appear. Remember, the table overwrites any data that resides at the location you choose.

2. Choose **U**tility, **N**ote. You see the Notes dialog box (refer to fig. 7.17).

3. Click the **O**ptions checkbox. The dialog box expands to include additional options (see fig. 7.18).

Fig. 7.18
When you create a table of notes, 1-2-3 shows you a list of the notes in your worksheet.

4. Click the **T**able button. The current cell appears in the contents box, along with the insertion point.

5. Choose OK. 1-2-3 creates a Note Table, placing cell references in the first column of the table and note text in the second column of the table.

When you print the worksheet, you can include the Note Table as part of the print range to print the notes.

Naming Ranges

Range addresses can be tedious. There's not much meaning in the expression @SUM(B4..B8). Sure, it totals the entries in range B4..B8, but what the heck lives in that range? If you had to describe your formulas to non-spreadsheet users, you might be at a loss to get across your point. Life would be easier if you could refer to ranges by names that describe their contents. The expression @SUM(Q1DEPOSITS) is almost self-explanatory.

II

Using 1-2-3

Assigning Range Names

You can assign names to cells and ranges. Incredible as it may seem, 1-2-3 calls such names Range Names. Here's how to assign one:

1. Select the cell or range you want to name.

2. Choose **R**ange, **N**ame. From the submenu, choose **C**reate. 1-2-3 produces the dialog box shown in figure 7.19.

Fig. 7.19

If you open the listbox in the Range Name Create dialog box, you see the range names that exist in the worksheet.

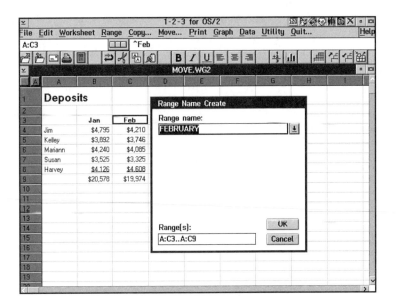

3. Type a name in the Range name text box.

4. Click OK.

Tip

Use descriptive range names. There's little point in a range name that doesn't identify the contents of its range.

After you assign a name, you can type it in place of a range address when you enter a formula, or when you must specify a range while issuing a command in 1-2-3. 1-2-3 shows the range name in place of the range reference in any formula that refers to it. However, the underlying formula references are still relative. If you copy the formula, the formula's new version in the target range adjusts to its location in the worksheet and loses the range name reference.

> **Caution**
>
> Named ranges act just like ranges referenced by formulas when you move cells and insert and delete rows, columns, and worksheets. If you move one corner of a named range without moving the critical opposing corner, you change the dimensions of the range. Likewise, if you move cells onto a critical corner of a named range, or delete a row or column that contains a critical corner, you blow out the range name completely.

Deleting Range Names

If you decide a range name is no longer useful, choose **R**ange, **N**ame, **D**elete. 1-2-3 displays the Range Name Delete dialog box. Open the Range Name listbox and click the range name you want to delete. Click the OK button.

> **Note**
>
> Deleting a range name does not delete any data. If a formula referred to the named range, the formula reverts to using cell names.

Assigning Labels as Range Names

When you name a single cell, it's a good idea to label the cell with an entry in the spreadsheet as well. For example, consider the worksheet in figure 7.20. It converts measurements in feet to measurements in meters. The labels in cells B5 and B7 make it clear which cell holds measurements in feet and which holds measurements in meters. After creating this portion of the worksheet, you might decide to name the cells that contain actual feet and meters values. The presence of labels can speed the task, because you can use the labels you placed in the worksheet as your range names.

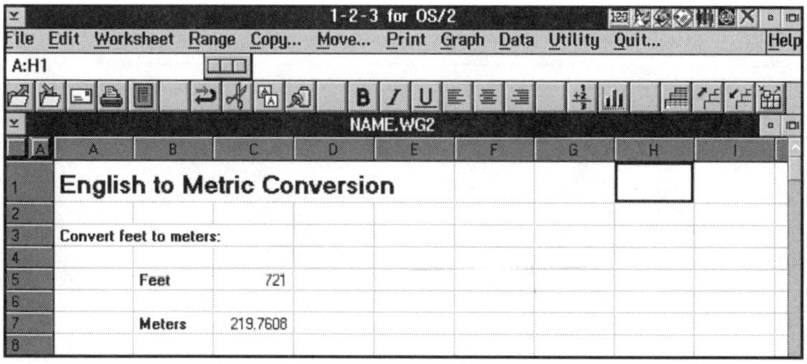

Fig. 7.20
This worksheet's meaning is clear because of the labels in cells B5 and B7. Those labels happen to match the names given to cells C5 and C7.

As you expect, the process of assigning labels as range names begins with selecting a range that contains the labels you want to use as names. 1-2-3 lets you use labels that appear either to the left, right, above, or below the cells you want to name. In addition, you can use 1-2-3's Intersect option, which allows you to name cells in an entire range except for the cells in the first row and column of the selected range.

The first row and column usually contain the labels 1-2-3 should use as the range names. If you intend to use the **I**ntersect option, the range you select should contain not only the labels, but also the cells you want to name.

1. Select the range that contains the labels—in the example, select B5..B7.

2. Choose **R**ange, **N**ame, **L**abels.

3. In the resulting dialog box (see fig. 7.21), click the option that identifies the relationship between the selected range and the range you want to name. By default, 1-2-3 uses the labels in the selected range as names for cells in the column to the right of the selected range. Choose **L**eft, **U**p, **D**own or **I**ntersect to change the direction of the cells to which 1-2-3 assigns names.

4. Click OK to close the dialog box.

Fig. 7.21

Use the Range Name Labels dialog box to assign range names to cells using labels that exist in the worksheet.

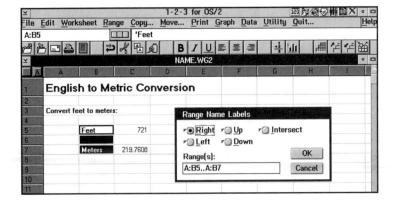

In any case, the Range Name Labels dialog box assigns several single-cell range names at once. In the example worksheet, selecting B5..B7, and using the Range Name Labels dialog box assigns the name *Feet* to cell C5 and *Meters* to cell C7.

Troubleshooting

I'm certain I assigned a range name that spans to the bottom of the worksheet. Now I can't find any sign that the name existed.

If the range name extended to the last row of the worksheet, and you then inserted rows, you destroyed the name. 1-2-3 loses a range name's reference without warning if inserting rows or columns expands the name beyond the edge of the worksheet.

I assigned range names to ranges B4..B8, C4..C8, and D4..D8. I didn't delete them, but now they're gone.

You might not have deleted the names per se, but perhaps you deleted a range of rows that included rows 4 through 8—or you deleted a range of columns that included B through D. Deleting the cells that a range name identifies also deletes the range.

From Here...

You're on the way to building worksheets in the most efficient way possible. Now it's time to learn about the most powerful spreadsheet feature: the spreadsheet calculation engine. When you understand all the tools available to drive your spreadsheet's calculations, you can build models to solve virtually any business problem. For more information to help you analyze the numbers you enter in your spreadsheet models, look into these chapters:

- Chapter 8, "Using Formulas and Functions," presents in-depth information on building formulas with and without functions.

- Chapter 9, "Managing and Analyzing Data," deals with managing information stored in database format—both in the worksheet, and in files on disk.

- Chapter 10, "Printing Worksheet Data," shows how to produce a printout of your finished spreadsheet.

- Chapter 11, "Automating with 1-2-3 Macros," introduces the topic of spreadsheet automation with macros.

II

Using 1-2-3

Chapter 8

Using Formulas and Functions

by Elaine Marmel

II

Using 1-2-3

1-2-3 is among the most powerful calculating tools available to common (we're defining "common" here as "low-budget") mortals—definitely more powerful than a desktop calculator. From basic addition, subtraction, multiplication, and division, to complex amortization, net present value, and interest accrual calculations, 1-2-3 handles all with equal ease. This chapter explores many aspects of performing calculations in a 1-2-3 file.

In this chapter you will learn:

- Basic formula-writing methods

- Standard mathematical operators

- Differences between relative and absolute formula references

- How to enter and track down needed functions

- How to link worksheet files with formulas

Revisiting Basic Calculations

You built a simple addition formula in Chapter 4, as well as a formula that used the @SUM function. Since then, you've seen the @SUM function in several examples that explore various operations of the spreadsheet software. In all those instances, you simply typed a formula to enter it into a cell. You can build formulas in several ways, however, and becoming familiar with all of them is useful. You can rely on different methods, depending on the situation.

Typing To Build Formulas

You can always type every character that makes up a formula. This method is often the most time-consuming and error prone, but it serves well when the formula must refer to cells scattered around a large worksheet file. It's also necessary when you employ certain functions or when you write certain types of string-handling formulas (explained later in this chapter).

Using the Direction Keys

A second way to build formulas involves pointing with the direction keys. The term seems to apply to working with a mouse, but it predates mouse-driven PCs by more than a year. Pointing with direction keys can be quick after you develop a knack. If you've been using any of the direction techniques discussed in Chapter 4, you will take to this method of formula-building easily.

Take a look at figure 8.1. Your mission in that worksheet is to build two formulas. One formula should subtract the In Stock animals from the Committed animals to calculate how many more animals the Home Pet Shopping Network must procure to fulfill orders received during their midnight madness sale. The second formula should total two columns to calculate how many critters the network sold and how many are in stock.

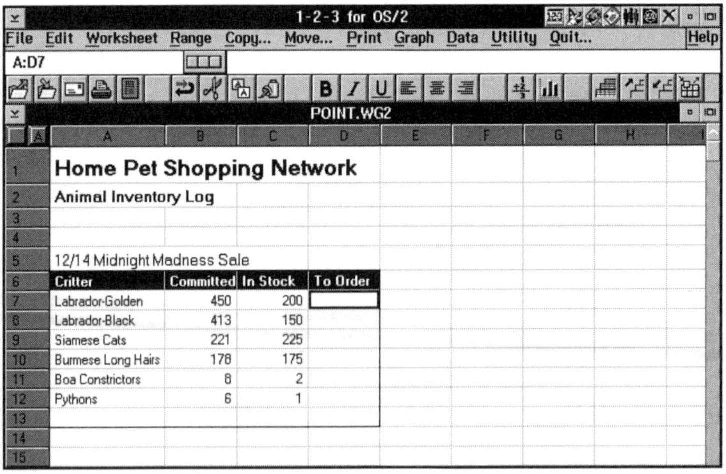

Fig. 8.1
You can type, point with the direction keys, or click and drag with the mouse to build formulas for column D and row 13 of this worksheet.

To write the first formula, follow these steps:

1. Move the cell pointer to cell D7.

2. Type a plus sign. When you start a cell entry with a plus sign, 1-2-3 "knows" you're creating a formula and frees the cell pointer to move in response to presses of the direction keys.

3. Press the ← key twice. Notice that the cell pointer moves left, even though you've started typing a cell entry. What's more, the address of the cell holding the pointer (B7) appears after the plus sign in cell D7.

4. With the cell pointer in cell B7, type a minus sign. This step effectively selects cell B7 as the first reference in the formula you're writing. The cell pointer jumps back to D7, ready for you to point to the next cell in the formula.

5. Press the ← key once to highlight cell C7. You can see in the control panel that the formula is complete.

6. Press Enter to store the finished formula in cell D7.

This formula uses single-cell references to perform a subtraction operation. The next formula, a summary formula, uses an @SUM function that requires a range reference. The procedure for building the formula is a bit different. To build the formula, follow these steps:

1. Move the cell pointer to cell B13.

2. Type the characters **@SUM(** or **@sum(**—case isn't important in typing an @function. When the first element of a formula is an @function, you don't need to start by typing a plus sign. Because the next element you need to enter is a cell or range reference, 1-2-3 frees the cell pointer to move in response to the direction keys.

3. Press ↑ six times. The cell pointer comes to rest in cell B7—the first cell in the range you want to sum. Note that 1-2-3 reflects this location in the contents of the control panel.

4. Anchor the pointer in cell B7 by pressing the period key (.). The reference to cell B7 in the control panel becomes a range reference that reads B7..B7.

5. Press ↓ five times, or press End ↓. In either case, the cell pointer stretches to highlight range B7..B12.

II

Using 1-2-3

6. Press Enter to store the formula in cell B13. 1-2-3 automatically adds a closing parenthesis because it recognizes that you haven't. If you prefer, you can type the closing parenthesis before you press Enter.

Pointing with the Mouse

Same scenario, different procedure. To create the subtraction formula by using the mouse instead of the direction keys, follow these steps:

1. Click cell D7 to select it.

2. Type a plus sign to begin the formula.

3. Click cell B7.

4. Type a minus sign.

5. Click cell C7.

6. Click the Confirm button (checkmark) that appears next to the edit line in the control panel.

To create the @SUM formula by using the mouse instead of the direction keys, follow these steps.

1. Click cell B13 to select it.

2. Type **@SUM(**.

3. Click and drag from cell B7 to cell B12.

4. Click the Confirm button in the control panel.

Whichever method of entering formulas you use, remember that you can copy the subtraction formula down column D to calculate the shortfall and surplus for each type of animal. You also can copy the summary formula to cell C13 to calculate the total number of critters in stock.

Understanding How 1-2-3 Does Math

OK, enough addition, subtraction, and summing. You don't have to be a mathematician to perform other types of calculations. You just need the right operators and an understanding of how 1-2-3 processes them. Remember, in math an *operator* is a symbol that tells the program what mathematical operation to perform with the numbers. The operators that 1-2-3 recognizes for common math aren't exactly what you learned in grade school, but they're close.

Common Operators for Common Math

The following table lists the operators that 1-2-3 recognizes along with descriptions of the operations they perform.

Operator	Function
+	Addition
−	Subtraction
*	Multiplication
/	Division
^	Exponentiation

Logical Operators

While working in a spreadsheet, you often use a particular branch of mathematics called Boolean algebra, or conditional math. In Boolean algebra, a formula's result can be 1 (representing true) or 0 (representing false). You use such expressions to ask questions about numbers, such as, "Did second-quarter sales exceed first-quarter sales?" or "Did output from the Sudbury plant match or exceed output from the Dorchester plant?" Express these questions mathematically, and when the answer is yes, the result is 1. Otherwise, the result is 0. The following table lists the logical operators and descriptions of the comparisons they perform.

Operator	Description
<	less than
>	greater than
=	equals
<>	does not equal
<=	less than or equal to
>=	greater than or equal to
#NOT#	is not
#AND#	logical and (to create complex conditional statements)
#OR#	logical or (to create complex conditional statements)

Order of Precedence

The order of precedence in mathematics describes the order in which you perform calculations in a complex formula. 1-2-3 follows the order of precedence you learned in high school math. That is, 1-2-3 solves a formula one expression at a time, reading from left to right, but it solves operations of high precedence before considering operations of lower precedence. First, 1-2-3 solves all exponentiation—raising a number to a power. Then it solves all multiplication and division. Finally, it solves all addition and subtraction operations. If logical expressions are also in the formula, 1-2-3 solves them last.

You can override the natural order of precedence by enclosing expressions in parentheses. Consider this formula:

+B3+7*B8^3/B12–17

1-2-3 resolves the formula in this order:

1. Raise the value in B8 to the third power (cube it).

2. Multiply that result by 7.

3. Divide that result by the value in B12.

4. Add the value in B3 to that result.

5. Subtract 17 for the final result.

Throw in a few parentheses, and you can change the order dramatically. One example is:

+(B3+7)*B8^(3/B12)–17

1-2-3 resolves all parenthetical expressions first, working left to right through the formula; then it follows the original precedents to resolve any remaining expressions:

1. Add the value in B3 to 7.

2. Divide 3 by the value in cell B12.

3. Raise the value in B8 to the power calculated in step 2 (3/B12).

4. Multiply the result of step 1 by the result of step 3.

5. Subtract 17 to determine a final result.

The Concatenation Operator

1-2-3 recognizes one other operator. It might seem a bit odd because it works with strings rather than numbers. A *string* is any sequence of characters that does not have a numeric value. In 1-2-3, all label entries are strings. All strings are not necessarily labels, however, because you can use a literal string in a formula much as you might include a number in a formula. The operator that enables you to use literal strings is the ampersand (&).

You add the two literal numbers 7 and 3 in 1-2-3 with the formula +7+3. You add the literal strings Jeremy and Anderson with the formula

> +"Jeremy"& "Anderson"

The result of this string addition, or *concatenation* in computer terms, is the string JeremyAnderson. To have the formula include a space between the concatenated names, simply build it into the formula. The expression becomes

> +"Jeremy"&" "&"Anderson"

Note that a single character space is within quotation marks between the ampersands.

Concatenate strings stored in cells by using references to the cells rather than literal strings in your formulas. The expression +A1&B1 concatenates strings stored in cells A1 and B1. If one of those cells is blank or contains a value rather than a string, the formula returns ERR. No mathematical precedent exists for adding—or concatenating—numbers and strings.

It is possible, however, for a string to look like a number—consider phone numbers, as discussed in Chapter 4. You can create such a string by typing a label prefix followed by several digits and storing the entry in a cell. Of course, to create a literal string that looks like a number, simply enclose the numbers in quotes, as you see in the following expression:

> +"Sandy and "&A1&" 149 "&B1

The expression concatenates a string in cell A1 to the literal string *Sandy and*. Then it concatenates the literal string 149, and finally it concatenates a string from cell B1. Cells A1 and B1 could contain any literal information; you could even change the contents of cells A1 and B1 to create a different concatenation.

Using Cell and Range References in Formulas

So far, you've explored some important aspects of cell and range references in formulas. You know several ways to create such references, and you know how inserting and deleting rows, columns, and sheets, and moving ranges can affect references built into formulas. You also know how relative references make the formulas you write versatile—you can copy those formulas across rows and down columns to reuse them ad infinitum. But there's one exciting tidbit about formula references you haven't yet examined.

All Things Relative...

Before getting into the exciting tidbit, you might benefit from a quick review. As you build formulas by pointing with the direction keys or clicking and dragging with the mouse, 1-2-3 automatically creates relative references. 1-2-3 thinks of relative references a bit differently than it displays them in the sheet.

◄ See "General Effects of Copying Information," p. 142

As you might remember, to 1-2-3, the expression +B5+C5 entered into cell D5 means "Add the value that resides two cells to the left to the value that resides one cell to the left." Copied down to cell D6, the references in the copy retain their meaning to 1-2-3. Because the copy of the formula is in D6, however, the cell two to the left is B6, and the cell one to the left is C6; the formula calculates a different result based on cells relative to its new position in the worksheet.

...But There Are Absolutes

The exciting tidbit is this: Formula references don't have to be relative. At times, you might want a formula to refer to a constant, such as a conversion factor or when you are trying to calculate a percentage for several cells all based on the same total amount. Consider the worksheet shown in figure 8.2. It reports revenues generated by sales of three representatives and the percentage of sales for which each sales representative is responsible. A sales commission percentage resides in cell C17, and the need is for a formula that calculates commissions for all three sales representatives.

The formula +B20*D17 entered in cell D20 returns the correct commission for Susan. If you copy the formula down the column, however, the formula's results are incorrect for Jim and Mariann. You can hard-code the commission percentage into the formula by entering it as +B20*.125, but if the commission amount changes (Oops! Your department went over budget), you have to edit the formula and copy it down the column again. The story changes if the formula uses an absolute reference to cell D17.

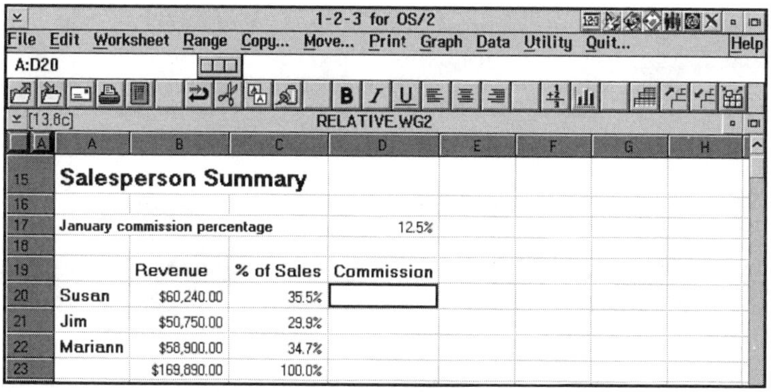

Fig. 8.2
With relative
references only,
a commission
formula you copy
down column D
would be of
limited usefulness.

An absolute reference remains fixed on a cell or range even in copies of a formula that contains it. To create such a reference, place a dollar sign ($) in front of the sheet number, column letter and row number of each cell address in the reference. An absolute reference to cell D17 is $D$17, and an absolute reference to range A:B20..B22 is A:$B$20..$B$22.

With this tidbit, you can write a versatile formula to calculate the sales commissions. In cell D20, enter +B20*$D$17. Copied down the column, the formula becomes +B21*$D$17 in cell D21, and +B22*$D$17 in cell D22.

Actually, the formulas in column C of figure 8.2 contain an absolute reference to compute each sales rep's percentage of sales. The formula in cell C20 is +B20/$B$23, and it was copied down the column when the worksheet was created.

Creating an Absolute Reference

1-2-3 offers a shortcut to creating absolute references as you build and edit formulas. Sure, you can type dollar signs if you build a formula by typing it character by character. But those of you who build formulas by pointing with the direction keys or clicking and dragging with the mouse can use function key F4 to create absolute references.

To build the percentage-calculating formula for cell C20 of figure 8.2, follow these steps:

1. Select the cell that is to receive the formula (C20).

2. Type a plus sign to start the formula.

3. Click cell B20, or press ↵ to highlight it.

4. Type a division symbol (/).

◀ See "A Ledger
Paper Note-
book," p. 77

5. Click cell B23, or use the direction keys to navigate there. The formula that appears in the control panel reads +B20/B23 at this point.

6. Press function key F4. 1-2-3 inserts dollar signs to make absolute the last reference you established. The formula now reads +B20/$B$23.

7. Press Enter or click the checkmark icon to store the entry.

Note

If you're working in a multisheet file, the absolute references you create with the F4 function key include sheet letters.

Mixing References

An absolute reference doesn't have to fix both the column and row addresses. If you prefer, you can make just the column reference absolute while the row reference remains relative. Likewise, you can fix the row reference while leaving the column reference free to change.

In 3D files, you might even make a formula's sheet references absolute, but leave the column and row references relative. Figure 8.3 shows one scenario in which you might use a mixed absolute and relative reference.

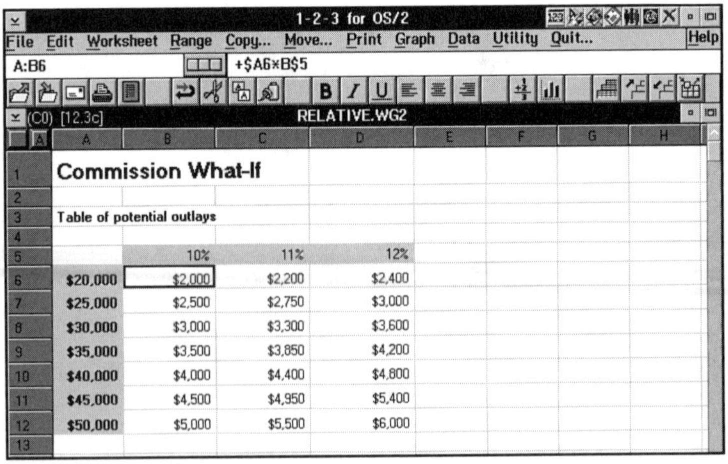

Fig. 8.3

A single formula that employs mixed relative and absolute references calculates every result in this table when copied throughout the table area.

The left column of the table contains sales revenue amounts that a representative is likely to generate in one month. The top row of the table contains commission amounts that your company might award in an upcoming month. The table values are the commission amounts you pay for each revenue amount at one of the commission percentages.

The formula that calculates the table values contains two mixed references. In cell B6, the formula is +$A6*B$5. The first reference's column component is absolute—it must always refer to column A. Its row reference is relative and so changes to refer to cell A7 in row 7, A8 in row 8, and so on.

The row component of the formula's second reference is absolute, and that reference's column component is relative. This reference must always refer to a cell in row 5, although when copied to column C it refers to C5, and in column D it refers to D5.

Working with @Functions

Yes, it is possible to express every mathematical calculation using basic math operators (+, −, *, /, ^) and logical operators. But, using @functions in 1-2-3 is usually more efficient.

Function Categories

Working with @SUM should have convinced you by now that functions are powerful and easy to use. Think of them as prewritten formulas, some so complex that only a mathematician, CPA, or statistician could write them. Fortunately, you rarely need even a rudimentary understanding of how a function performs its calculation. If you know what you want to calculate, a function might be able to do it for you even when you don't remember how.

1-2-3 divides functions into 10 categories. Each category includes functions that perform similar types of calculations. Their descriptions follow:

Calendar Functions. Manipulate date and time serial numbers and return such information as:

- The year, month, or day of a month that a date serial number represents

- The hour, minute in an hour, or second in a minute that a time serial number represents

- The name of a day or month that a serial number represents

- The number of days in the month and the number of days left in the month that a date serial number represents

- The quarter in which a date serial number falls

- The number of days, months, and years between two dates

- The current date or time

II

Using 1-2-3

One very useful calendar function is @NOW. Its syntax is, simply, @NOW, and it returns the full serial number (both date and time) of the moment according to your computer's built-in clock. When you format the cell for dates, what you see depends on the date format you select.

Another important function is @DATE. Its syntax is @DATE(YY,MM,DD), and it returns the serial number for the date its arguments identify.

► See "Calculating Database Statistics Using @Functions," p. 201

Database functions. Perform statistical calculations—sums, averages, standard deviations, and so on—with information stored in database tables. These functions enable you to identify categories of information to single out of a larger information set. The functions calculate their results by using only the selected data. Check out Chapter 9 for a more thorough explanation of database functions.

◄ See "Assigning Number Formats," p. 108

Financial Functions. Spreadsheets include financial functions for the original target users of the software. The electronic spreadsheet was supposed to be the software equivalent of ledger paper. Because number crunchers were going to be using these things anyway, it made sense to include some high-powered functions to reduce the tedium of the more common business calculations. The financial functions perform these types of calculations:

- Annuity calculations such as loan amortization, future value, various interest-related calculations, present value, term-related calculations, and so on

- Bond calculations such as accrued interest, annual duration, price as a percentage of par, and yield at maturity

- Capital budgeting tools to calculate IRR, NPV, and Modified IRR

- Depreciation, including linear, declining balance, double-declining balance, and sum-of-the-year's digits

- Compound interest calculations to determine the periods needed for an investment to reach a target value, or to determine the interest rate needed to grow in investment to a target value

One generic business calculation is calculating payments on a loan. 1-2-3's @PMT is perfect for the task. Its syntax is @PMT(principal,interest,term), and it returns the amount you pay each period at a specified interest rate. So, for a 30-year (360-month) fixed rate mortgage on $85,000 at 8.5% per year (.708333% per month), the function reads @PMT(85000,8.5%/12,360). Its result? The monthly payment is $653.58.

Information Functions. The information category includes functions that return information about the spreadsheet software, such as the name of the current file, the width of a specified column, and so on. You normally do not find uses for these functions in run-of-the-mill worksheets, but the need for such functions arises often when you're writing macro-driven applications. Macro programs (explained in Chapter 11) can call on functions from this category to learn what worksheet settings are in effect and to make decisions based on those settings. This category includes functions to:

- Count the number of columns, rows, or sheets that a range spans

- Build a cell address based on Cartesian coordinates measured from the upper-left corner cell of the worksheet file

- Convert a sheet letter into a number that represents the sheet's position in the file, or convert such a number back to the letter of the sheet it identifies

- Determine attributes such as label alignment, cell format, cell borders and colors, font size and typeface, column width and row height, and so on about a specified cell or the current cell

One example of an Information function is @ROWS. This function counts the number of rows in a specified range. So, @ROWS(B3..B9) returns 7—there are seven rows in range B3..B9. You might use such a function to count the number of items in a list. Should you add or delete items using techniques discussed in Chapter 7, 1-2-3 can update the result of an @ROWS function dynamically.

◄ See "Inserting Rows, Columns, and Sheets," p. 153

Logical Functions. All but one of the functions in this group return a Boolean result: 1 or 0. As explained earlier, in a Boolean calculation, the result 1 represents a true condition; the result 0 represents a false condition. Your formulas use functions of this type to determine certain information about cells, ranges, and the worksheet in general.

The one logical function that doesn't necessarily return a Boolean result uses Boolean algebra to decide which result it should return. That function, @IF, is surprisingly useful. The logical functions can:

- Determine whether a specific add-in, add-in function, or add-in macro exists in RAM

- Reveal the status of specified cells, such as: Is the cell empty? Does it contain a value?

- Evaluate whether a formula returns a string, a number, or an error result

Using 1-2-3

The syntax for @IF is

@IF(condition,result_if_true,result_if_false)

The condition argument is an expression whose result is either 1 (for true) or 0 (for false). When condition is true, the function returns the value of the result_if_true argument. When condition is false, the function returns result_if_false. So, the formula @IF(A1>7,"Buy","Sell") returns the string *Buy* when the value in cell A1 is greater than seven. Otherwise, it returns the string *Sell*.

Lookup Functions. This odd category of functions has the purpose of finding discrete items in lists and tables. Such functions belong in 1-2-3 because a worksheet leads its users to store information in these common data structures. These functions use various strategies to select the values they return:

- One chooses an item from a list of cell references, values, and strings that you build right into the formula.

- Several look up values in the top row or left column of a table and return associated values from within the table.

- Some return the cell address of the maximum or minimum values in a specified range.

- One returns the contents of a cell identified by an address stored in another cell.

Perhaps the easiest Lookup function to explain is @CHOOSE. Its syntax is

@CHOOSE(selector,item1,item2,item3,etc...)

The value of selector determines which item argument @CHOOSE returns. If selector is 0, the function returns item1. When selector is 1, the function returns item2, and so on. The item arguments can be values, strings, and even formulas that include other @functions.

Mathematical Functions. Most of these are the functions you expect to find on a calculator. They calculate values you used extensively in high school math classes such as sines, cosines, tangents, and logarithms. They also perform rounding operations, generate random numbers, calculate factorials, and perform a host of obscure numerical manipulations.

◀ See "Formatting Numbers for Clarity," p. 108

The @ROUND function stands out among the mathematical @functions. It rounds a value off to the number of decimal places you specify. Its syntax is

@ROUND(value,decimals). The expression @ROUND(3.1415,2) returns 3.14—note that this result is truly 3.14, and not merely the number 3.1415 rounded visually by a numeric format, as described in Chapter 5.

Statistical Function. Calculates statistics. That's a lame way of saying that these functions determine the average, standard deviation, sum, variance, maximum, minimum, count (as in total number of items), and other aspects of a list of information. To perform regression analysis, you use menu commands.

Text Functions. Manipulate strings vaguely the way other functions manipulate numbers. The functions in this category can cut characters from either end of a string or from its center. They can convert a string's characters from upper- to lowercase and back, and they can return strings in which every word's first character is capitalized with remaining characters in lowercase. Some of these functions can convert numbers into strings and convert strings that look like numbers into actual numbers.

For example, to convert a string into uppercase, use the function @UPPER(string), where string is a reference to the cell that contains the string.

To return a string in which each word begins with a capital letter, use the expression @PROPER(string).

Getting Help with Functions

So many functions are offered that you are unlikely to memorize the list. Most users learn a few that they use again and again and then never take full advantage of the vast power these tools provide. If you're at a loss, try using Help. Because 1-2-3's Help system is context-sensitive, you can score quickly with it if you guess a function's name before going into Help.

Suppose, for example, you vaguely remember that a function to calculate straight-line depreciation is available. If you guess that the function is @SL, simply type those characters and then press F1 (Help). Even if your guess is wrong (it is in this case), 1-2-3 activates Help at the @Function Index (see fig. 8.4).

As you move the pointer over an @Function, the pointer changes to a pair of question marks (??). Click the @Function you think you want to use, and 1-2-3 presents a description of the @Function as well as a syntax example showing the arguments for the @Function (see fig. 8.5).

Tip

If you correctly guess an @Function's name, 1-2-3 displays the help for that @Function instead of the index.

II

Fig. 8.4
Pressing F1 activates 1-2-3's Help system in the @Functions topic if you make a wrong guess at a needed function's name.

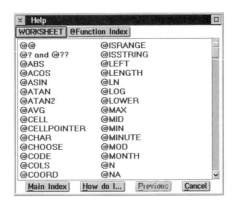

Fig. 8.5
If you guess a needed function's name properly, type your guess and press F1. 1-2-3 rewards you by opening Help to the page that describes the function.

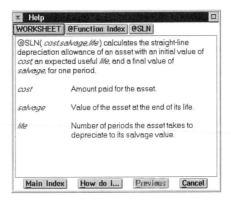

> **Note**
>
> In most cases, a function's arguments can be values or literal strings, cell and range references, and even other functions. The Help system and the @Function List dialog box can help you figure out which types of arguments are valid for the functions you're using.

Using the SmartSum SmartIcon

Don't miss the SmartSum SmartIcon shown here in the margin. Consider the worksheet in figure 8.6. All it needs is a row of @SUM formulas below the bottom row of data, and a column of @SUM formulas next to the right-most column. The quickest way to create them is to follow these steps:

1. Select the two ranges that will receive the subtotals. To select more than one range at a time (a collection), drag across one range, and then hold down the right mouse button while dragging across the next range. In this example, drag over range B8..E8, hold down the right mouse button, and drag over range F4..F7.

2. Click the SmartSum SmartIcon.

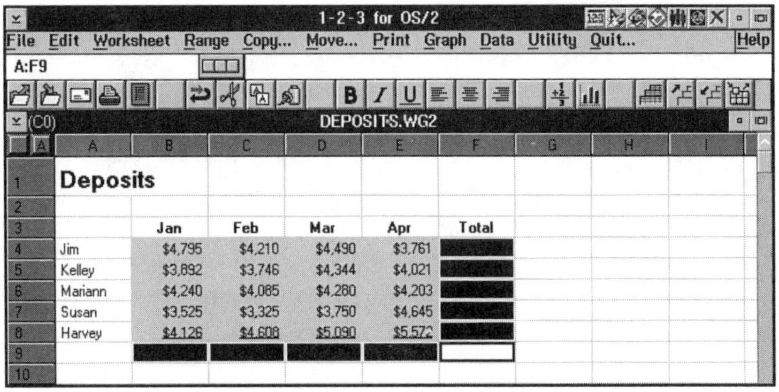

Fig. 8.6
After you've entered data, the Quick Sum function can enter @SUM formulas in a snap.

1-2-3 analyzes the relationships of the target cells to surrounding worksheet entries. It finds columns of numbers above the selected cells in row 8, so it builds @SUM functions to total those columns. At the same time, 1-2-3 finds rows of data next to the selected cells in column F; it writes appropriate @SUM functions there that total the rows.

Troubleshooting

I typed a complex formula, but when I pressed Enter, 1-2-3 stored it as a label.

You might have left off the @ sign or the plus sign. Take a closer look; this mistake is easy to overlook.

When I press Enter, the computer beeps and the formula doesn't go into the cell. I can't even move the cell pointer.

There's a mistake in the formula. Perhaps you misspelled a function's name, or you left out a needed parenthesis in the middle of the formula. The position of the insertion point can help you track down the error. It usually moves to the left of a word or character that doesn't seem to fit in the formula. When you fix the formula, you can finish the entry. Or, press Escape to clear the faulty entry and start over.

I finish typing a formula, and it goes into the cell without a problem, but the formula's result is ERR.

The cause of this problem can be elusive. Perhaps the formula includes a reference to a range name, but the range name doesn't exist in the worksheet file. Or, maybe you mistyped a cell or range address—for example, you typed SS8 rather than S8—so 1-2-3 is trying to interpret it as a (nonexistent) range name. If it's a linking formula, you might have mistyped the filename, or the intended file might not even reside on-disk. It's even possible the formula includes an expression that causes division by zero (dividing a number by zero isn't possible with the use of imaginary numbers).

II

Using 1-2-3

Creating Formulas That Link Files

One last area of exploration remains in the realm of building formulas: formulas that link files. One reason to link files is to save file load time and system RAM as you build larger and larger worksheets. Another reason is to offload little-used tables, or data structures whose contents rarely change, to simplify an otherwise complex file. Formulas in the main file can refer to tables and data structures in other spreadsheets still on-disk.

In a classic catch-22, building file-linking formulas is easiest when both the file to hold them and the file to which the formulas link are opened in RAM. Consider the display shown in figure 8.7. Suppose the worksheet on the left contains totals you want to report in the worksheet on the right. Values that support the totals might change as further sales records come in, but you need to build the summary spreadsheet now. By linking to the NWDIST worksheet, you ensure that formulas in the summary sheet take into account any new activity recorded in the Northwest District.

Fig. 8.7

Open two sheets at once when you need to build formulas that link them.

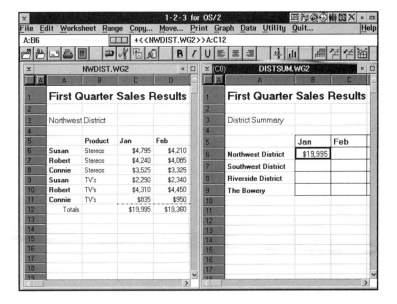

With both files opened, building a linking formula is as easy as following these steps:

1. Click the cell that is to contain the linking formula. In this case, the formula goes into cell B6 of the DISTSUM worksheet. That formula is a link to the January sales total in cell C12 of the NWDIST worksheet.

2. Type a plus sign.

3. Click the cell to which you want to link: cell C12 in the NWDIST worksheet.

4. Press Enter to complete the formula. The formula appears as some variation of

> +<<NWDIST.WG2>>A:C12

The first component of the formula is a linking statement that identifies the linked file. Following that is a reference to the target cell—including the sheet letter and cell address.

Knowing that information, you also know how to create linking formulas while the target file is closed rather than opened in RAM: Simply type the full reference to the cell or range that you want to link. Include the path to the target file enclosed in paired angle brackets if the target file does not reside in the default working directory.

> **Note**
>
> After you've established a linking formula, copying it across a row or down a column creates more linking formulas. The one suggested in the example links to January's total, but the worksheet also reports totals for March and April. No problem. Copy the formula from cell B6 in the DISTSUM file to range C6..D6, and the resulting formulas link to the NWDIST worksheet.

From Here...

This overview of working with formulas and formula references gives you a solid grounding in some of the most important spreadsheet concepts. As you continue to learn about 1-2-3, you'll put formulas to uses that would be difficult to explain at this juncture. The topic will come up again as you work with the spreadsheet's database-handling capabilities, and yet again as you learn to automate your worksheets with macros. See the following chapters to learn more about working with spreadsheet concepts:

- Chapter 9, "Managing and Analyzing Data," deals with managing information stored in database format—both in the sheet and in files on-disk.

- Chapter 10, "Printing Worksheet Data," shows you how to produce a printout of your finished worksheet.

II

Using 1-2-3

■ Chapter 11, "Automating with 1-2-3 Macros," introduces the topic of worksheet automation with macros.

Chapter 9

Managing and Analyzing Data

by Elaine Marmel

Lotus Development Corporation will tell you that for many years 1-2-3 was the most popular database manager on the market. Scary, but true, virtually every user ends up building a database in the spreadsheet eventually. But then, it's hard to avoid building a spreadsheet database because it's easy. Enter some column headers, list some data beneath them, and you're managing data. What's more, the data is in a standard database format!

That column and row format gives you great power over the data. With a database, you can quickly arrange information in alphabetical or numerical order; you can find, edit, and delete information easily; you can query the database to locate information that meets criteria you specify; and you can rapidly calculate subtotals and other statistics on specific categories of the data.

Even if you don't anticipate doing any of these things in 1-2-3, you may be surprised that some of the database-handling tools can dramatically reduce your effort at other tasks.

Although many of 1-2-3's most sophisticated data-analysis tools relate in some way to databases, there are a few that work as well with any spreadsheet-based data structure, such as what-if tables and automatic regression analyses. This chapter explores many of 1-2-3's most powerful data management and analysis tools.

In this chapter, you learn about:

- Database management—sorting, querying, and reporting

- What-if tables

- Regression analysis

- External database access

The "2" in 1-2-3

In 1-2-3, 1 stands for spreadsheet, 2 stands for database, and 3 stands for graphics. It's time to examine the 2 more closely. If you've worked with stand-alone database managers in the past, database management in the spreadsheet will be a snap.

Technically, a database is no more than a set of related information. For 1-2-3 to be able to manage a set of related information effectively, however, you must arrange the information in a specific format. So, for the sake of this discussion, a database is a set of related information stored in a specific layout. Figure 9.1 shows a list of information that 1-2-3 recognizes as a database.

Each row in a 1-2-3 database is a record. A record contains all pertinent information about an item. Each discrete element of a record is a field. In a 1-2-3 database, the columns define the fields, and you identify each field's contents by placing a header at the top of its column.

A record in an employee database may contain fields for such information as the employee's name, social security number, date-of-hire, home address, and so on.

Sorting a Database

One very easy way to prove the power of a database is to use one to arrange records in alphabetical or numerical order. Sorted this way, the records readily reveal groupings so you can track down information about a specific item. Suppose you want to review all of Charlotte's records in the database of figure 9.1.

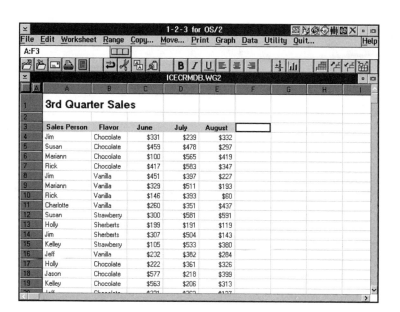

Fig. 9.1
A collection of employee records, a library card catalog, the stock quotes in the newspaper, and even these sales results are examples of databases. The database in this figure continues in rows below those you can see.

Alphabetizing the records based on Sales Person field entries groups Charlotte's records to make your job easy. Here's how to do it:

1. Select the entire range of records to sort. In this database, that's range A4..E40.

> **Note**
>
> The range to sort should not include database field headers. Also, don't include any blank rows—if you do, they appear at the top of the data after you sort. It should, however, include all columns for each record.

2. Choose **D**ata, **S**ort. The Data Sort dialog box appears, as shown in figure 9.2.

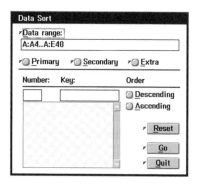

Tip
If you're not sure of what you're doing, save your worksheet before you sort. That way, you know you can recover your work if the sort doesn't work.

Fig. 9.2
The Data Sort dialog box gives you complete control over the ordering of records.

II

Using 1-2-3

3. Click the **P**rimary button. If A:A4 doesn't appear in the Key text box as the default entry, type **A4** into that box.

4. Choose a sort order. **A**scending arranges records alphabetically or in ascending numerical order. **D**escending puts records in reverse-alphabetical or descending numerical order. Ascending is appropriate for this sort. Once you choose the sort order, 1-2-3 lists the key in the listbox.

> **Note**
>
> The cell you specify in the Key text box is a sort key. A sort key need not fall on the first row of the range to sort. It can be any cell in the column—even one outside the database range.

Were you to choose **G**o at this point, 1-2-3 would sort the records by the entries in the Sales Person column. But wouldn't it be even more convenient if each rep's records were in order by product line? You control this by adding a second sort key, as in the following steps:

1. Click the **S**econdary button in the Data Sort dialog box.

2. Either type the address of a second sort key or click with the mouse first in the Key text box and then in the worksheet. In this case, you specify any cell in column B.

3. Choose a sort order and 1-2-3 adds the secondary key to the sort list (see fig. 9.3).

Fig. 9.3
1-2-3 adds sort keys to the list after you select a key and an order.

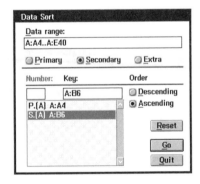

Tip
If the sort doesn't look right, choose the Undo SmartIcon. You may get a warning, but 1-2-3 will undo the sort.

4. Close the dialog box by clicking **G**o. The first 20 rows or so of the sorted database appear in figure 9.4.

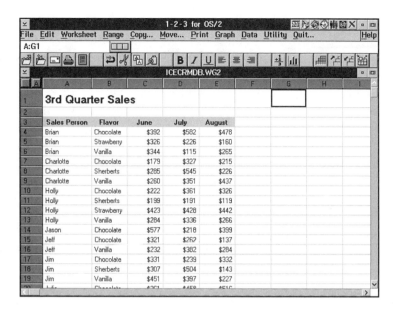

Fig. 9.4
When sorted, each salesperson's record appears in one group. Notice that the use of two sort keys placed everyone's records in order by flavor.

Troubleshooting

I use equal and minus signs as dividing lines in my worksheets. When I sort, however, the lines get mixed with the database I'm sorting.

Don't use cell entries to delineate worksheet areas. If you plan to sort, you can't rely on style options such as lines and shading either—they all sort with the cells containing them. If you need to sort a list, don't try to make it look beautiful. If you must include styles, wait until you've done the sort, save your worksheet, add your styles, and print. Then, either save the worksheet under a new name or don't save it (to avoid saving the styles in the list you need to sort). By the way, the effect you describe is the same one that occurs when you include blank rows in the sort range.

I sorted a database and now a whole column of entries is mixed up—the entries no longer fall within the correct records.

It sounds as if you sorted some, but not all of the columns in the database. Make sure you select all of the columns and rows in a database (except the field headers) before you launch into the sort operation. To recover, try using the Undo SmartIcon and then respecify your sort.

Managing Data

The point of storing information in a database is that it makes the information easy to manage. Manage in this context means to store information, edit it, track down specific pieces of it, and delete unwanted or outdated entries. 1-2-3 offers a few commands to speed you through these tasks with minimal involvement on your part.

Adding Records

Many databases grow or change indefinitely. You may start with certain information when you create the database, but after that, you add new information or modify the existing records to reflect changes in your business. Perhaps the simplest way to add new records to a database is to type each one in the spreadsheet directly beneath the last record—in the sample worksheet, you add new records in rows 41, 42, and so on.

Tip

To name a database, select all records and field names in the table and choose **R**ange, **N**ame, **C**reate.

The one drawback to this approach is that any range names associated with the database don't know about the new entries. So, if the database in figure 9.1 (range A3..E40) had the name *flavor_sales*, you need to reassign the database's name after adding records in rows 41 and beyond if you choose to append records this way.

Alternatively, you can enter new records in a separate range, spreadsheet, or file, and then use a menu command to have 1-2-3 add them to the existing database; using this approach, 1-2-3 automatically adjusts the database's range name. So, for example, if you use the command to move the records shown in figure 9.5 into the database in figure 9.1, 1-2-3 automatically adjusts the flavor_sales name to cover range A3 to E43.

◀ See "Naming Ranges," p. 163

Alone, the automatic name adjustment is nice, but there's a second advantage to 1-2-3's capability to append database records automatically: when you work with external databases such as dBASE and Paradox files, it's very convenient to enter records in the spreadsheet and then have 1-2-3 move them to the external file. There's one procedure to suit all circumstances:

1. Place the new records in a separate range either outside your database range or in another worksheet. Make sure the layout of the new records matches the basic layout of the database. The new records should reside in a set of rows and columns whose fields match those of the target database—including both the field headers and the types of data the fields contain. You use the field headers as a *criterion* range and the data you place below the field headers as an *output* range when you add records. Figure 9.5 shows a range of new records ready to add to the database in figure 9.1.

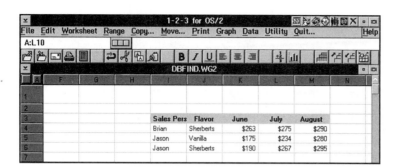

Fig. 9.5
Records you want
to append to a
database must be
in a layout that
matches that of
the database—
including match-
ing field headers to
identify the
columns.

2. If you named your original database range, skip to step 3. Otherwise,
select the original database records.

3. Choose **D**ata, **Q**uery. The Data Query dialog box appears, as shown in
figure 9.6.

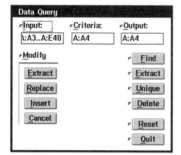

Fig. 9.6
The Data Query
dialog box is a
multipurpose
dialog box. When
adding records to a
database, make
sure that you
include the field
headers in both
the Input and the
Criteria ranges.

4. If you have given the database a range name, type the range name into
the **I**nput text box. Otherwise, the **I**nput text box should contain the
range of the database to which you want to add the records, including
the field headings of the original database. In this case, the database is
in range A3..E40, so enter that range in the text box. When working
with an external database, you enter the database's name rather than a
range address.

5. In the **C**riteria text box, click and then select any cell in the row containing the field headers of the new data you want to add. In the example, you can choose I3, J3, K3, L3, or M3.

6. In the **O**utput text box, type or specify the range that contains the new
data you want to add to the database and the field names for that data.
In the example, you select I3..M6.

7. Choose **Insert**.

1-2-3 copies the new records to the rows beneath the database. If you've assigned a range name to the database before appending records, 1-2-3 automatically extends the name downward to include the additions.

Note

It's good practice to assign a range name to the range holding a spreadsheet database. Doing so gives you a third way to specify the target database for database management operations. Suppose, for example, that the database in figure 9.1 has the name *flavor_sales*. When you need to specify the database as in step 4 of the previous procedure, select the contents of the appropriate text box and press F3. 1-2-3 displays a listbox of range names from which you can make a selection.

Finding Records

As a database grows, it starts to conceal information. How quickly can you locate a specific record in a list of several hundred or thousand? That depends on how you approach the task. Scanning the database visually row-by-row may be time-consuming. However, you could have 1-2-3 find and highlight the records so you can spot them more quickly.

Again, you use the Data Query dialog box, but you need only to specify an input range and a criteria range to find records. The criteria range consists of two rows, both completely outside the original database, which serve as the input range. The first row of the criteria range should contain the field headings exactly as they appear in the original database.

The second row of the criteria range contains the information 1-2-3 uses to find records. You can search for exact matches, or you can include a formula. For example, you can search for all of Jim's sales records (exact match) by typing **Jim** into the cell below the field name Sales Person. Or, you can search for all sales records where June's sales were greater than $550 by typing **>550** under the field heading June.

Search the database for all sales in June that were greater than $550; type **>550** in the cell immediately below the field header June. Figure 9.7 shows a criteria range set up to search for June sales greater than $550.

Fig. 9.7
When finding
records, the criteria
range shows what
you're looking for.

Criteria range

Now that you have set up what you want to find, follow these steps to find
the records:

1. If you named the database range, skip to step 2. Otherwise, select the
   database that contains records you want to find.

2. Choose **D**ata, **Q**uery. The Data Query dialog box appears (refer to
   fig. 9.6).

3. If you named the database range, type the range name in the **I**nput text
   box or press F3 to see a list of range names.

4. In the **C**riteria text box, specify the criteria range. In the example, the
   criteria range is K8..K9. Then choose **F**ind.

1-2-3 highlights the first record it finds that matches the criteria, as shown in
figure 9.8. Use the direction keys to view the records 1-2-3 found. You can go
both up and down in the list. When you finish reviewing records, press the
Esc key to redisplay the Data Query dialog box, which you can simply close
by choosing **Q**uit.

Tip
While finding
records, you might
find it useful to
turn on horizontal
titles so that field
headers always
appear.

II

Using 1-2-3

> **Note**
>
> Establishing criteria is the secret to making the Find command powerful. When estab-
> lishing criteria, use all the mathematical operators you read about in Chapter 8. You
> can also establish AND and OR conditions. To set up AND conditions, specify the
> criteria on the same row underneath different field headers. For example, to find
> records where sales in June and July were greater than $550, place >550 underneath
> both the June field header and the July field header. Remember, an AND condition
> reduces the number of records you see.
>
> (continues)

◀ See "Common
Operators for
Common
Math," p. 173

(continues)

OR conditions show you more records. To set up an OR condition, place the criteria on different rows under the field headings and then expand the criteria range to include both rows. Using the criteria field headers shown in figure 9.7, you can see records where sales in June were greater than $550 or sales in July were greater than $400 by placing >550 in cell K9 and >$400 in cell L10.

By the way, it is perfectly legitimate, if you want to see both Jim's and Susan's records, to type **Jim** in Cell I9 and **Susan** in Cell I10.

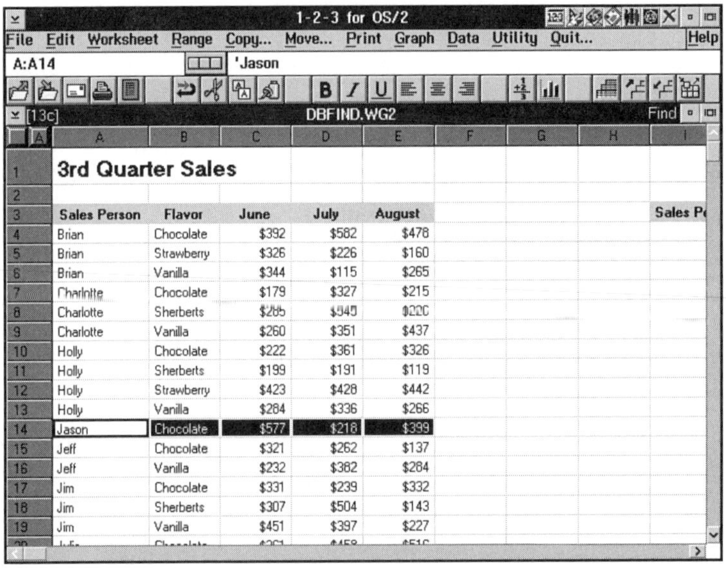

Fig. 9.8
When you use the
Find command,
1-2-3 highlights
the first record
that meets the
criteria. Horizontal
titles have frozen
the field headers
in this picture

Deleting Records

Relationships change. A supplier that handled your business in its younger days may not keep up as the business grows, or some of your customers may move out of the area. Whatever the database, it's likely you'll need to delete records from time to time—a process quite similar to that of finding records. Like finding records, deleting them also involves an input range, a criteria range, and an output range in which you specify criteria that describe the records to delete and the Data Query dialog box. Here's how you use it to remove the records for Jason, who no longer works for you:

1. Using the criteria range you created when finding records, define the criteria that describes the records you want to delete. In this example, you type **Jason** in cell I9, just below the Sales Person field header.

2. If you named the database range, skip to step 3; otherwise, select the database range.

3. Choose **D**ata, **Q**uery. 1-2-3 displays the Data Query dialog box (see fig. 9.9).

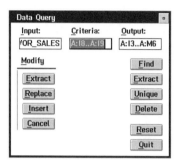

4. Make sure the **I**nput text box contains the original database range.

5. In the **C**riteria text box, specify the cells containing the criteria range. In the example, you specify I8..I9.

6. Choose **D**elete. 1-2-3 displays a confirmation box; choose **D**elete again. 1-2-3 then deletes all records that match the criteria. When you're using a spreadsheet-based database, any range names associated with the database adjust automatically to account for the missing data.

Extracting Records

Sometimes, you're just not sure you want to delete those records; you want to look at them first. Or, perhaps you've found a group of records that you want to be able to print—as a group. Use the **E**xtract button in the Data Query dialog box to copy records out of the database range and into a separate area of the worksheet.

The **E**xtract command works the same as the **D**elete and **F**ind commands, except that you must specify an output range along with the input range and the criteria range.

The output range, as you might expect, must meet some special criteria. The output range must appear outside the original database, and you need to copy the row headers from original database to the top row of the output range. When you specify the **O**utput range in the Data Query dialog box, you must specify a range large enough to hold all the records that 1-2-3 might extract. Therefore, it's a good idea to set up the output range so that its size can exactly match the original database's size—that way, the output range is never too small.

Keeping these facts in mind, set up the output range field headers in Row 3. That way, you can easily identify the last row you need in the output range, because it will be the same as the last row of the database. In this example, place the output range field headers in cells O3..S3.

Now try to extract Holly's records following these steps:

1. Using the criteria range you created when finding records, define the criteria that describes the records you want to extract. In the example, you type **Holly** in cell I9, just below the Sales Person field header.

2. If you named the database range, skip to step 3; otherwise, select the database range.

3. Choose **D**ata, **Q**uery. 1-2-3 displays the Data Query dialog box (refer to fig. 9.9).

4. Make sure the **I**nput text box contains the original database range.

5. In the **C**riteria text box, specify the cells containing the criteria range. In the example, you specify I8..I9.

6. In the **O**utput range, specify the range you set up before you started these steps. Remember, the output range must include the field headers and be large enough to accommodate all the data that 1-2-3 might extract. In the example, the output range is O3..S43.

7. Choose **E**xtract. 1-2-3 copies all records that match the criteria into the output range.

Eliminating Duplicate Records

Regardless of how careful you are while entering records in a database, the nature of the beast is such that you will end up entering duplicate records. If you're in a situation where more than one person enters data into the database, it's a sure bet that duplicate records appear.

You can sort your records and then try to "eyeball" them to find duplicates and then delete those. But 1-2-3 has a tool you can use to re-create your database and eliminate the duplicates as you do it. You again use an input range, a criteria range, an output range, and the Data Query dialog box. As you might expect, set up field headers for a criteria range and make sure the row immediately below the criteria range field headers is blank.

Then, as you did when you extracted records, set up the field headers for the output range alongside the original database. Make sure the area below the output range is empty, or you might write over it.

Open the Data Query dialog box and specify the input range as the original database. When you specify the criteria range, choose only one field header. When you select a field header with a blank cell below it, you tell 1-2-3 to select all records in the input range. For the output range, select the row of field headers only. Select the **U**nique button, and 1-2-3 rewrites your database—without duplicate records—into the output range.

> **Note**
>
> If the area below the field headers of the output range isn't blank, any data that appears there is destroyed. When you specify the output range, you can specify the entire range instead of just the field headers, but then you run the risk of 1-2-3 not having enough room in the output range.

Using Number-Crunching Tools

As you might have hoped, there are still more data-analysis tools built into 1-2-3. Some offer further shortcuts for accessing and summarizing data stored in databases. Others help you perform *what-if analyses*—operations where you substitute value after value into a set of calculations until you figure out which values offer the optimum solutions to your business problems.

Calculating Database Statistics Using @Functions

Database @functions let you calculate totals, averages, and other statistics from records in a database. The idea is quite simple: an @SUM function totals all the entries in a target column. The @DSUM function totals all the entries that meet specific criteria.

◄ See "Working with @Functions," p. 179

For example, consider the database in figure 9.10.

What if your interest with this database is no more than to calculate the total of all chocolate flavor sales in July? This is a perfect application of @DSUM. One appropriate formula is

>   @DSUM(A3..E19,"July",B3..B4)

A database @function's syntax is

>   @DFUNC(database,field name,criteria)

Tip
You can include several tables in a query by naming them and separating them with commas.

and, unlike the queries you have been doing, you don't set up ranges; you type the @function into a cell where you want the answer to appear.

◀ See "Using Cell and Range References in Formulas," p. 176

@DFUNC represents one of the database @functions listed next. The *database* argument identifies an in-sheet database or an external database that's connected to the file. The *field name* argument identifies the field that contains values to use in the function's calculations. The *criteria* argument is a range of at least two rows—the top row must contain a field name and the second row contains the actual criteria. Functions that use this syntax include:

- @DAVG—Averages the selected entries.
- @DCOUNT—Counts the selected entries.
- @DGET—Returns a unique entry from the database.
- @DMAX—Returns the largest of the selected values.
- @DMIN—Returns the smallest of the selected values.
- @DSTD—Calculates the population standard deviation for all selected entries.
- @DSTDS—Calculates the sample standard deviation for all selected entries.
- @DSUM—Sums the selected entries.
- @DVAR—Calculates the population variance of the selected entries.
- @DVARS—Returns the sample variance of the selected entries.

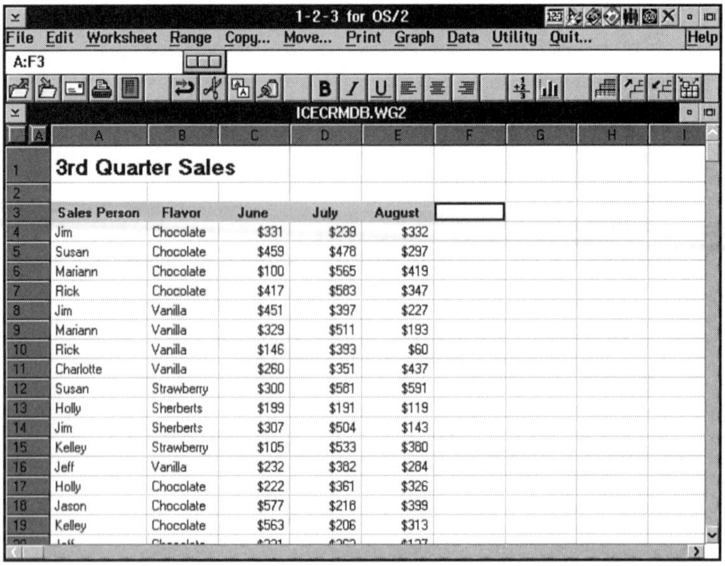
1-2-3 for OS/2
File Edit Worksheet Range Copy... Move... Print Graph Data Utility Quit... Help
A:F3
ICECRMDB.WG2
A B C D E F G H I
3rd Quarter Sales
Sales Person Flavor June July August
Jim Chocolate $331 $239 $332
Susan Chocolate $459 $478 $297
Mariann Chocolate $100 $565 $419
Rick Chocolate $417 $583 $347
Jim Vanilla $451 $397 $227
Mariann Vanilla $329 $511 $193
Rick Vanilla $146 $393 $60
Charlotte Vanilla $260 $351 $437
Susan Strawberry $300 $581 $591
Holly Sherberts $199 $191 $119
Jim Sherberts $307 $504 $143
Kelley Strawberry $105 $533 $380
Jeff Vanilla $232 $382 $284
Holly Chocolate $222 $361 $326
Jason Chocolate $577 $218 $399
Kelley Chocolate $563 $206 $313

Fig. 9.10
Database @functions come in handy when you want to calculate a few statistics for selected records in a database such as this.

The arguments of a database @function can include references to spreadsheet cells that contain criteria or field identifiers. So, if you want to calculate July totals for all the flavors listed in the database, you can resort to a scheme like the one shown in figure 9.11. There, @DSUM, @DMIN, and @DMAX functions have references to column H in their criteria arguments (the edit line in the control panel reveals the references of the formula in cell I4). As a result, each calculates a result for the corresponding product in column H.

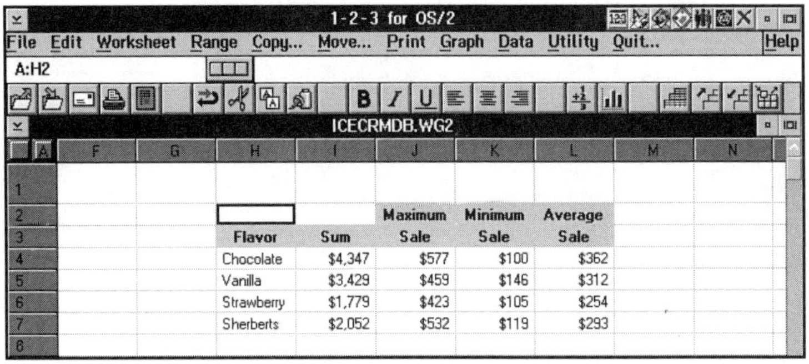

Fig. 9.11
This table uses @DSUM and @DMIN and @DMAX to return databases statistics for each flavor identified by the entries in column H.

Creating a Frequency Distribution

Another powerful feature is 1-2-3's capability to count the number of entries in a range of numbers. The word *range* here does not refer, as usual, to 1-2-3's range specification functions. Instead, range refers to a set of numbers with a lower and upper boundary. You probably remember this concept from school, although you may not have been aware of it. Your teachers who graded on a curve needed to know the number of scores within a given range. They used frequency distribution logic to help set the curve.

Suppose you wanted to know how many entries in the month of August represented sales falling in the ranges listed here:

Less than $100

$100—$200

$200—$300

$300—$400

$400—$500

Greater than $500

In 1-2-3, you set up a *bin range* that represents the range of values. In the bin range, you specify only the number representing the upper limit of the range.

Make sure you set up the bin range so that the column immediately to the right of the range is empty. Figure 9.12 shows how you might prepare to calculate a frequency distribution for August sales.

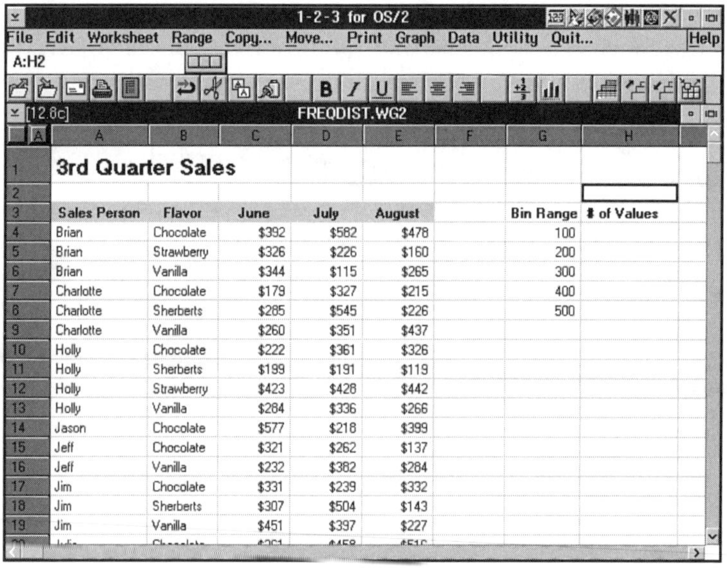

Fig. 9.12

1-2-3 places the frequencies into the column next to the bin values. Any values higher than the highest bin value appear immediately below the rest of the frequencies.

To calculate a frequency distribution on the example data, try this:

1. In an unused area of the worksheet, type in the bin values. Remember, the bin values represent the upper end of the range.

2. Choose **D**ata, **D**istribution. 1-2-3 displays the Data Distribution dialog box shown in figure 9.13.

Fig. 9.13

Specify the range containing the values whose frequencies you want to count and the range containing the bin values.

3. Specify the range containing the values you want to count in the Values text box. In the example, the Values range is E4..E40.

4. Specify the range containing the bin values in the **B**in range text box. In the example, the bin range is G4..G8.

5. Choose OK. In the column next to the bin range, 1-2-3 displays the number of values it counted that fell below the related bin value. If any values were larger than the largest bin value, the number of those values appears at the end of the column (see fig. 9.14).

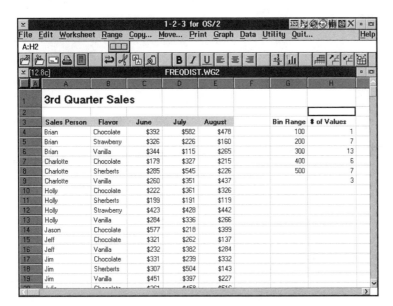

Fig. 9.14

In the column next to the bin values, 1-2-3 displays the resulting frequency distribution.

Note

As you can tell from the example, you don't need information in a database to calculate a frequency distribution. You can create a frequency distribution for any two column list in which the values in one column fall within a set of ranges.

Generating What-If Tables

The what-if table (also called a data table) may well be the quintessential spreadsheet analysis tool. Here's the basic concept: you develop some sequence of calculations that somehow ties into a single variable—identified as the *input cell*. The what-if table can substitute values from a list into the input cell one-by-one, and calculate the results of formulas that rely on it. For each substitution, 1-2-3 recalculates the spreadsheet and stores the formula results in the table. Figure 9.15 shows a very simple scenario that takes advantage of this facility.

Fig. 9.15

A one-way what-if table calculates the results of formulas that depend, in some way, on a single variable cell.

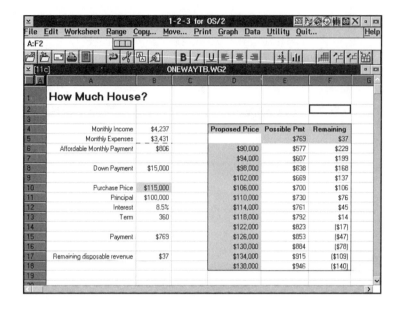

Column B of the spreadsheet contains several hard values and formulas. Cell B6 calculates how much money is left to pay the mortgage each month after paying all other expenses, so its formula is simply +B4-B5. Cell B8 contains a value—one possible down-payment for the purchase of a new house—and cell B10 contains another value—a possible purchase price for the house.

B12 and B13 contain values for the proposed interest rate and length of the mortgage loan. The remaining entries calculate how much money will be left after making the mortgage payment. Cell B11 contains the formula +B10-B8. Cell B15 contains the formula @PMT(B11,B12/12,B13) and cell B17's formula is +B6-B15.

However, you're not sure yet how much you're going to spend on a house. If you knew what your break-even point was, you might set an upper limit on a house price. Of course, you might also want to see what a small change in the purchase price does to the bottom line. The variable, then, is the purchase price, and the variable cell is B10. The table in columns D, E, and F provides the desired information. Here's how you might create such a table:

Tip

Here's a great place to use 1-2-3's **D**ata, **F**ill command.

1. Enter possible values for the purchase price down the left column of the table area (column D in the example worksheet)—these are the values that 1-2-3 substitutes into the variable cell when it generates the table.

2. In the top row of the table—row 5 in the example spreadsheet—enter formulas whose results change depending on the variable cell. In this case, there are two formulas. The one in cell E5 is +B15. It simply returns the monthly payment from cell B15—an amount that's bound to change if the purchase price changes. The formula in cell F5 is +B17. It returns the revenue remaining amount.

3. If you want, add column headings, shading, and a frame as in the illustration, although they aren't necessary in calculating the table.

◀ See "Styling Entries for Emphasis," p. 112

4. Select the table range. In this case, that's range D5..F18.

5. Choose **D**ata, **T**able **1**. The dialog box shown in figure 9.16 appears.

Fig. 9.16
The Data Table menu lets you make settings for one-way, two-way, and three-way tables, and the Data Table dialog box lets you describe the table range and the value you want to change.

6. Specify the variable cell—in this case, cell B10—as the Input cell. Then choose OK. 1-2-3 fills the table with values.

A calculated what-if table has no link to the data on which it's based. If you change assumptions that feed the table or modify any formulas, you must re-issue the What-if Table command to recalculate the table's values.

You create what-if tables with two or three variables much as you do tables with one variable. However, with either of these tables, 1-2-3 can calculate the result of only a single formula. A data table with two variables might be changing both the purchase price and the interest rate. To prepare a two-variable table, enter the second variable across the top row of the table leaving the upper-left corner of the data table range blank (in the example, the blank cell is D5). Then specify any formula cell whose result you want reported in the table.

A three-variable table might involve changing the purchase price, the interest rate, and the term of the loan. Because a three variable table is three-dimensional in nature, you use successive spreadsheet layers and create copies of a two-variable table.

The top-left corner of each table (the one you left blank in the two-variable table) holds a unique value for the third variable.

Pinpointing a Target with BackSolver

Although generating a what-if table gives you a good idea of how your bottom line changes depending on how some variables change, there's nothing quite like precision science. Wouldn't it be nice to know the exact break-even purchase price? Or how about setting a target amount for the revenue remaining so you know how much house you can buy and still have money left for other investments? You can get the answers in a flash with BackSolver:

Caution

BackSolver overwrites the current value for the By Changing Cell; therefore, save your file before using BackSolver or use Undo afterwards to replace the original value.

---

1. Choose **U**tility, **B**ackSolver. The dialog box shown in figure 9.17 appears.

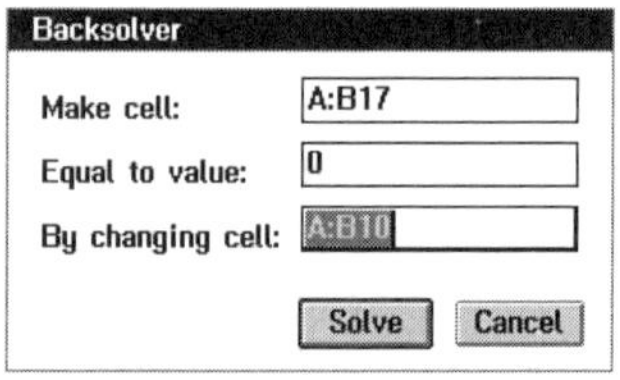

Fig. 9.17
Determine the maximum purchase price for a house you can afford given your monthly income and expenses.

2. In the Make Cell text box, specify which cell contains the formula whose result you want to control—that's cell B17 in the spreadsheet in figure 9.15.

3. In the Equal to Value text box, type the value that you want the formula to return. To find the break-even point in this model, type **0**. To leave $120 a month for investment purposes, type **120** in the box.

4. In the By Changing Cell text box, specify a cell whose contents 1-2-3 can change to arrive at the specified result. In this case, 1-2-3 should change the purchase price cell, cell B10.

5. Choose Solve. 1-2-3 enters a value in the purchase price cell that makes the revenue remaining formula equal the target value. In the example, if the target is 0, the purchase price is $119,823. If the target is $120, the purchase price is $104,217.

Performing Regression Analyses

When you work with processes, or with demographics, it's often important to know how much one event or outcome relies on others. For example, does a production line produce more on hot days than on cool days? Is a person from New York more likely to buy your product than a person from Alabama?

If you're asking such questions, you may already have notions as to their answers. Still, you may want some hard evidence to present to a boss or co-worker so they'll see that your hunch is correct. A regression analysis can provide the support you want.

Simple Linear Regression

A regression analysis tells you how much influence one or more variables (the independent variables) have on a single variable (the dependent variable). When the temperature (the independent variable) rises, does productivity (the dependent variable) also rise? Here's how you create a regression analysis to find out:

1. Collect some measurements and enter them into a spreadsheet. For each measurement, record the value of the dependent variable in one column, and the value of the independent variable in the column to its right. Figure 9.18 shows how this might look for the production scenario—a day's output in column A, and the day's average temperature in column B.

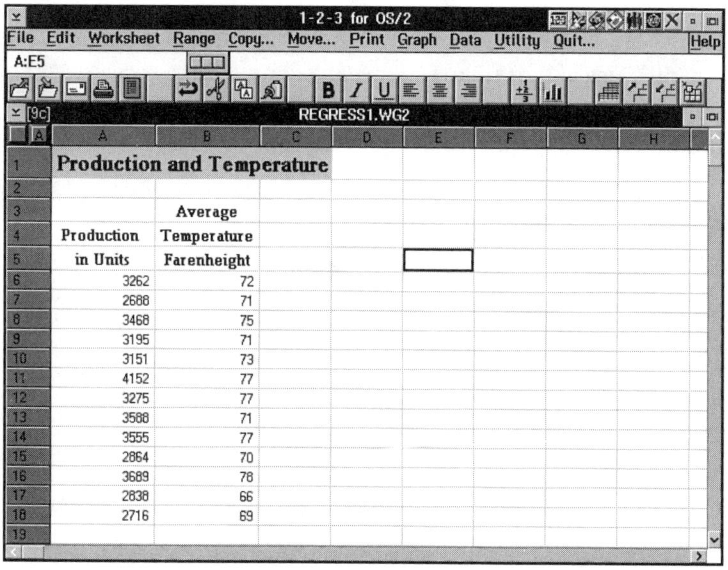

Fig. 9.18
Does a change in temperature (the independent variable) somehow affect a manufacturing facility's production output (the dependent variable)?

2. Select the column of independent variables—range B6..B18 in the example worksheet.

3. Choose **D**ata, **R**egression from the resulting menu. The dialog box shown in figure 9.19 appears.

Fig. 9.19
The X-range setting identifies the columns of independent variables. The Y-range setting identifies a single column of dependent variables.

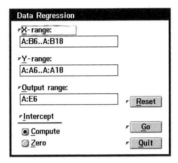

4. Specify range A6..A18 as the Y-range—1-2-3 has already established the selected range as the **X**-range setting. The **X**-range and **Y**-range must span an equal number of rows.

5. Specify a range to receive the results of the regression analysis. This can be a single-cell reference, but be aware that the results replace any data that already reside at the target. This example uses cell E6 as the **O**utput range.

6. Choose **G**o.

Tip
Use the **R**eset button in the Data Regression dialog box to clear all range text boxes and reset **I**ntercept to **C**ompute.

Your regression results should be similar to what appears in figure 9.20. In this case, they reveal that there is, indeed, a correlation between a change in temperature and a change in productivity. The R Squared value of .5709856 indicates that the temperature may account for 57 percent of the variation.

Note

What productivity can you expect if the temperature hits 80 degrees? The regression results give you a way to write a regression formula and make a reliable prediction. The standard regression formula is, Y=Constant+(X Coefficient * X). So, to predict output for an 80-degree day in the example, you write the formula +H7+(G13*80). The result is 3,890 and change.

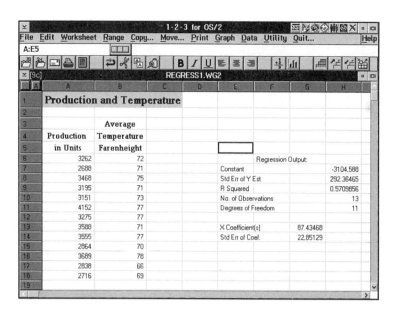

Fig. 9.20
The regression
results provide
enough detail that
you can write a
regression formula
to predict
productivity for
any temperature.

Multiple Regression

To improve your ability to predict an outcome, you might measure more
than one independent variable and perform a multiple regression analysis. In
the case of productivity, you might guess that more work gets done on a
Tuesday, Wednesday, and Thursday than on a Monday and Friday. So, for
every temperature/production pair you measure, you also record the weekday
of the measurement.

1-2-3 can't regress weekday names, so you need to convert the weekdays into
usable numbers. The best choice may be Boolean true/false values—say, false
(0) for Mondays and Fridays, and true (1) for Tuesdays, Wednesdays, and
Thursdays. Figure 9.21 shows the production data with added weekday information, showing 1 for values that occurred on either Tuesday, Wednesday, or
Thursday.

◀ See "Logical
Operators,"
p. 173

To perform the multiple regression, follow these steps:

1. Select all the columns holding independent variables—1-2-3 can handle
   as many as 75. In this case, you select range B6..C18.

2. Choose Data, Regression to display the Data Regression dialog box.

3. Make sure the Y-range setting is still range A6..A18, and that the Output
   range setting is still cell E6.

4. Choose **G**o.

II

Using 1-2-3

Fig. 9.21
Data gathered haphazardly over several weeks show Monday and Friday production as zeros and Tuesday, Wednesday, and Thursday production as ones.

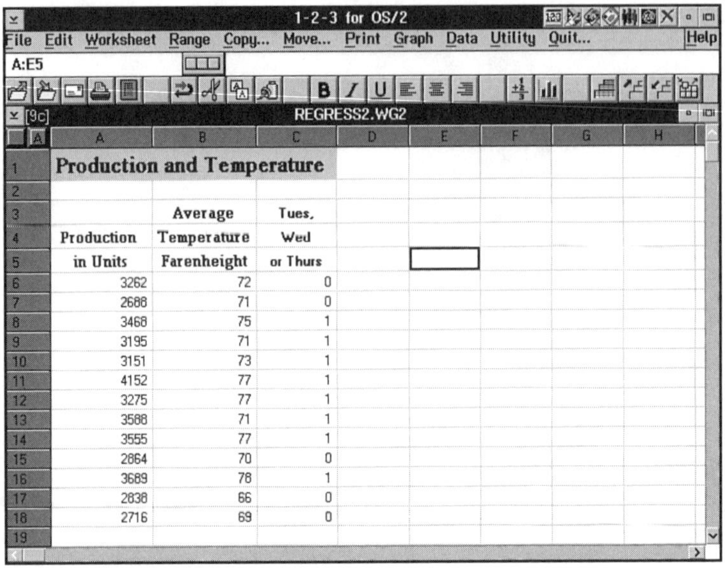

	A	B	C
1	Production and Temperature		
2			
3		Average	Tues,
4	Production	Temperature	Wed
5	in Units	Farenheight	or Thurs
6	3262	72	0
7	2688	71	0
8	3468	75	1
9	3195	71	1
10	3151	73	1
11	4152	77	1
12	3275	77	1
13	3588	71	1
14	3555	77	1
15	2864	70	0
16	3689	78	1
17	2838	66	0
18	2716	69	0

The resulting output, shown in figure 9.22, shows two X Coefficients, one for each independent variable. In this example, the new R Squared value is .6604175, meaning that the temperature and weekday together account for about 66 percent of the variation in productivity.

Fig. 9.22
Output from a multiple regression looks quite like the output from a simple regression. The only difference is the addition of X Coefficients that coincide with added variables.

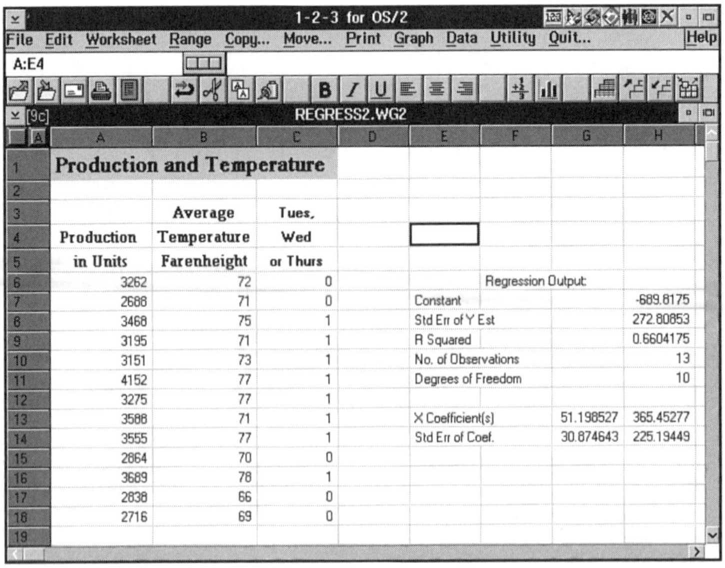

	A	B	C	D	E	F	G	H
1	Production and Temperature							
2								
3		Average	Tues,					
4	Production	Temperature	Wed					
5	in Units	Farenheight	or Thurs					
6	3262	72	0			Regression Output:		
7	2688	71	0		Constant			-689.8175
8	3468	75	1		Std Err of Y Est			272.80853
9	3195	71	1		R Squared			0.6604175
10	3151	73	1		No. of Observations			13
11	4152	77	1		Degrees of Freedom			10
12	3275	77	1					
13	3588	71	1		X Coefficient(s)		51.198527	365.45277
14	3555	77	1		Std Err of Coef.		30.874643	225.19449
15	2864	70	0					
16	3689	78	1					
17	2838	66	0					
18	2716	69	0					

> **Note**
>
> The regression formula for a multiple regression is
>
> $$Y = Constant + (X\ Coefficient * X_1) + (X\ Coefficient * X_2) + (X\ Coefficient * X_n)$$
>
> So, you can more accurately predict the production output for a given day when you specify a weekday as well as an average temperature. In the example worksheet, the regression formula to predict productivity on an 80-degree Monday or Friday becomes +H7+(G13*80)+(H13*0). To predict productivity for an 80-degree Tuesday, Wednesday, or Thursday, the formula is +H7+(G13*80)+(H13*1). The first returns 3,406 units; the second returns 3,772 units.

◀ See "Understanding How 1-2-3 Does Math," p. 172

From Here...

At this point there's little you can't do with 1-2-3. This section has delved into virtually every aspect of building spreadsheet models from basic data-entry through complex calculations.

You explored how to prepare an attractive spreadsheet presentation, how to manage large amounts of data, and how to perform in-depth analysis of all kinds. In the last two chapters of the section, you'll find the following kinds of information:

- Chapter 10, "Printing Worksheet Data," shows you how to produce a printout of your finished worksheet.

- Chapter 11, "Automating with 1-2-3 Macros," introduces the topic of worksheet automation using macros.

II

Using 1-2-3

Printing Worksheet Data

by Elaine Marmel

Between disk drives, keyboards, monitors, and online communications, it's amazing that a computer can do all that it does. It's even more amazing that you can transfer what you create on the computer to paper with virtually no effort! And, with laser and color printers, printouts can be of such high quality that they can go directly from your office to a binding service and become part of a professionally produced publication—indistinguishable from material produced by a graphics design service or a book publisher.

Before you see your creations in print, though, you need to know how to make them. There's little to challenge you here. You probably gained a general understanding of printing back in Chapter 3; however, there are several things to consider as you prepare to produce a spreadsheet printout.

◀ See "Printing Files," p. 64

In this chapter, you learn:

- The quickest path to printing

- How to view a printout without committing it to paper

- Ways to control printing details: headers, page orientation, and so on

- How to control the pagination of a printout

Printing the Worksheet

Printing is usually the last thing you do with a spreadsheet. And, sometimes, it's something you need to do in a hurry. At least once in your career, you're likely to cram a six-hour project and finish two minutes after the fateful meeting starts. At times like this, you simply can't afford to fiddle with menus and dialog box controls. You need the printout now.

 The quickest way to print anything in 1-2-3 is to select a range and click the Print SmartIcon. 1-2-3 immediately prints whatever range you selected.

> **Caution**
>
> If you only select a single-cell range, that's all 1-2-3 prints—even if the cell is blank.

That's it. 1-2-3 manages pagination automatically; anything that doesn't fit on the first page spills over onto subsequent pages. In fact, 1-2-3 paginates both horizontally and vertically. This means that if the spreadsheet is too wide for the paper, 1-2-3 cuts excess columns off to print on separate pages. And, when a spreadsheet has too many rows to fit on a page, 1-2-3 fills the first page from top-to-bottom, skips to the next page, and so on until it delivers your entire spreadsheet on paper.

If you have time, you might decide you don't like the way 1-2-3 paginated the printout. You also might lament the absence of page headers and footers, the sizes of the margins, or the orientation of the printout on the page (1-2-3 automatically prints in a portrait rather than a landscape orientation). *Portrait orientation* means the page is taller than it is wide—like this page. *Landscape orientation* rotates the page so it's wider than it is tall. Finish that project ten or twenty minutes before it's due, and you have plenty of time to control virtually every aspect of the printout.

Previewing a Printout

Before you start experimenting with your spreadsheet's print settings, how about a quick ecology discussion? 1-2-3 prints the spreadsheet pretty much as it looks on your display. But there are settings you can control that take effect between the spreadsheet and the printer. Page headers and footers, for example, don't appear in the spreadsheet, but they show up on paper. What a shame to discover you omitted headers and footers only after creating a ten-page printout. Worse, what if you accidentally specified more print range than needed, or the specified range is a few characters too wide for the paper? Again, it's a waste to print before learning of potential problems. Preview the document before printing, and you'll save reams of paper—and just think about the forests you'll save.

Activating Preview

There are several ways to launch into the Print Preview facility. You'll discover all of them as you become more proficient with 1-2-3. For now, try this:

1. Select the range you want to print. Select several adjacent sheets by holding down the Ctrl key as you click the sheet tabs or selected cells in the sheets. Alternatively, you can select a limited range that spans several adjacent rows, columns, sheets, or all three.

2. After selecting what you want to print, click the Print Preview SmartIcon. 1-2-3 displays the print job in a separate window on your worksheet (see fig. 10.1).

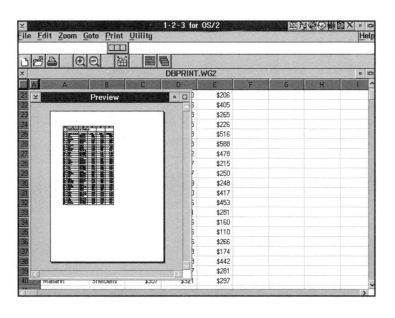

Fig. 10.1

1-2-3's Print Preview facility shows how your spreadsheet will look on paper.

Unfortunately, 1-2-3 doesn't help to orient you in the document unless you select several rows. Then, Print Preview shows a number of pages and screens the area on each page that displays.

Zooming a Preview

Because you're not sure "where you are" while looking at the small graphic in the Preview window, the first order of business is to orient yourself. Being able to read what's in the window would help. To accommodate you, the Preview facility has a zoom feature. There are additional levels of magnification. The smallest magnification shows how the data will lay out on the pages (see fig. 10.1); the second magnification shows the view somewhat

Tip

If you maximize the Preview window, you have only two levels of magnification: readable and unreadable. You're not *supposed* to be able to read the second magnification level—read on.

II

Using 1-2-3

larger. The third magnification gives you an indication of where text falls in the columns or rows. The text is *greeked*—too small to read but large enough to see how it fills a column or row. The fourth magnification enables you to zoom in and read data on any page. You can scroll between pages in this preview window (see fig. 10.2) and you can even maximize the Preview window to view more of the page—margin to margin.

Fig. 10.2
Good news—by zooming, you can magnify the information that appears in the Print Preview window so that you can actually read it.

The three ways to change magnification are:

- Click a mouse button. To zoom in (magnify to read) on the image, click the left mouse button. To zoom out (view the layout), click the right mouse button. Each click changes the magnification level by one.

- Click the zoom-in and zoom-out icons. They have the same effect on the Preview window as clicking the right and left mouse buttons.

- Use the commands on the **Z**oom menu at the top of the screen. (By the way, did you notice that the Preview window has its own menus?)

Navigating the Preview

Now that you can read what you're looking at, you may want to move around. The easiest way to navigate the Preview is to use the directional keys on the keyboard or the commands on the **G**oto menu. The directional keys and the commands on the **G**oto menu work just like the directional keys in a worksheet. For example, pressing the Home key (or choosing **G**oto, **H**ome) takes you to the upper-left corner of the Preview window. You also can use the scroll bars to move around the Preview window.

Printing from the Preview Window

If you like what you see in the Preview window, click the Print SmartIcon, or choose **P**rint, **P**rinter. The Preview window continues to display and the information you're currently previewing prints.

Exiting the Preview Facility

End a preview session by double-clicking the Preview window's control box.

If you simply click in the worksheet, the Preview facility remains open. Yes, you can then switch back to the Preview window. Can you modify the printer range by selecting another range in the worksheet and previewing it? Unfortunately, no. If you try to change the print range, 1-2-3 *adds* to the original print range instead of replacing it.

Enhancing the Printout

You don't have much control in the way 1-2-3 prints. The few things you can control, however, can have an enormous effect on your results. You'll produce much more attractive printouts after a quick look at the print settings you can control.

Specifying a Print Area

If 1-2-3 does an unacceptable job of paginating a printout, you might be able to control things by simply specifying a print area rather than printing the entire spreadsheet. For example, suppose your spreadsheet contains a database in columns A through F that exactly fits the display, but it also has a summary table off to the right in columns J through N. If you print the entire sheet, 1-2-3 might cut the summary table into several pages, and produce some blank pages. In figure 10.3, some data resides in column Z, with several blank columns to the left of column Z.

Instead, select individual ranges to print the various structures in a sheet. There are two ways to accomplish this:

◀ See "Naming Ranges," p. 163

- Choose a range, preview it, and print it. Then choose a new range, preview it, and print it. Continue until you've printed everything of importance.

- Choose **F**ile, **P**rint, **P**rint Worksheet to activate the dialog box shown in figure 10.4. Then specify multiple ranges to print in a single operation by establishing the first range to print in the **R**ange text box. Immediately after the range's address, type a comma. Then indicate the second

Tip

You can preview the print job before you print by selecting the **S**creen Preview checkbox.

II

Using 1-2-3

range to print, type another comma, and so on until you list all the needed ranges. Choose **G**o when you're ready to print and 1-2-3 places the job in the print queue. Choose **Q**uit to close the dialog box.

Fig. 10.3

Printing an entire sheet that contains various tables near columns Z and AA can result in poor pagination, and even blank pages.

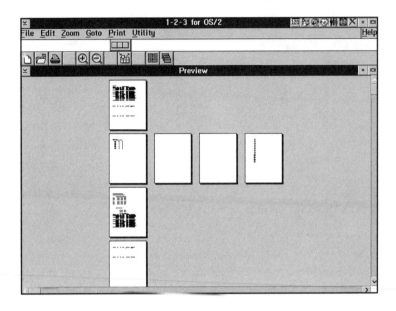

◀ See "Sorting a Database," p. 190

The downside of this second approach is that 1-2-3 doesn't paginate automatically between ranges in the list (depending on your needs, that can be a plus as well). If you use this approach, you may need to manually insert page breaks in the spreadsheet before committing the ranges to paper. For more information on inserting page breaks, see "What You See Is What You Get" later in this chapter.

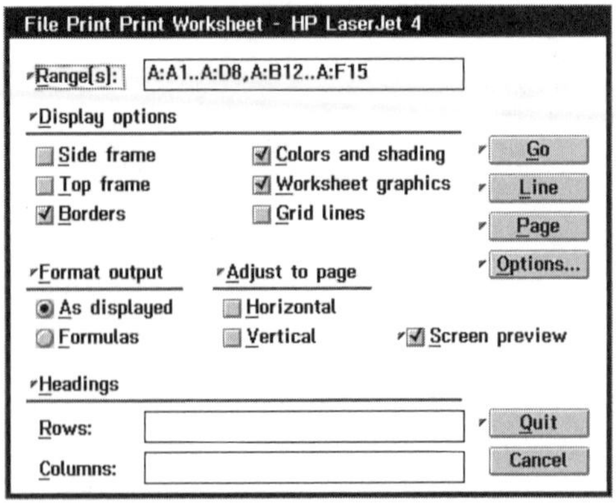

Fig. 10.4

You can print selected non-contiguous ranges using the File Print, Print Worksheet dialog box. You can also establish settings that control how 1-2-3 transfers a spreadsheet to paper.

Adjusting Page Settings

You can adjust the settings for most of the printing features you control through two dialog boxes: the File Print, Print Worksheet dialog box you saw in figure 10.4, and the File Print Options dialog box shown in figure 10.5.

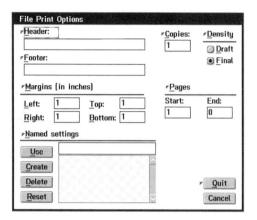

Fig. 10.5

The File Print Options dialog box lets you create headers and footers and control the number of copies you print.

Each dialog box controls several different aspects of printing. For example, you can determine the ranges you want to print in the File Print, Print Worksheet dialog box, and you can rotate the page from portrait to landscape orientation. In the File Print Options dialog box, you can control information that 1-2-3 should repeat on every page of the printout and set margins for each page.

There are a couple of ways to activate the File Print Options dialog box:

■ Choose **F**ile, **P**rint, **O**ptions.

■ In the File Print, Print Worksheet dialog box, choose the **O**ptions button—the title of the resulting dialog box is different, but the available options are the same.

Adding Headers and Footers

What about page numbering and document time-stamping? How about putting your name or your department name, or a label to uniquely identify the report—no matter what page the reader is studying? Adding headers and footers can give a printout extra polish and make it easier to read.

Use the **H**eader and **F**ooter text boxes of the File Print Options dialog box to add information that will appear at the top or bottom of every page of your printout. Here comes the tricky part: you can divide each box into three

Tip

You can change the font, size, and style of the header or footer in the Worksheet Global Attributes Font dialog box.

Tip
Use vertical bars without text for center and right alignment.

parts. Suppose you want to include the department name, the date, and the page number, in that order, in a footer. Type the information in the **F**ooter text box, separating each item with a vertical bar (|). 1-2-3 aligns the information to the left of the first vertical bar with the left margin. The information between the first and second vertical bars appears centered in the footer. And, as you expect, 1-2-3 aligns the information to the right of the second vertical bar with the right margin (see fig. 10.6).

Fig. 10.6
You can control the alignment of information that appears in a header or footer so that information appears on the left or right edge or in the center of the header or footer.

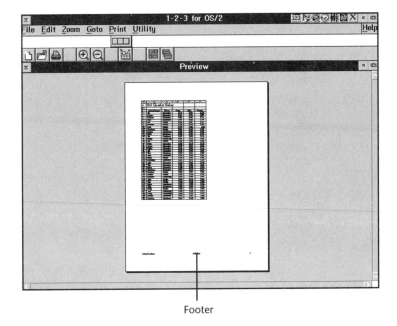

Footer

So, that's nice, but if you put in a page number, the same page number prints on every page. Further, you'd really like *today's* date to print, not the same date every time you print. 1-2-3 uses special characters that you include in a header or footer to accomplish tasks like these:

■ Place the @ sign in the **H**eader or **F**ooter text box. Wherever the @ sign appears, 1-2-3 substitutes the current date when printing.

■ Put a plus sign (+) in the text box. 1-2-3 substitutes the current time in place of the plus sign.

■ Place a pound sign (#) in the box. At the time of printing, 1-2-3 replaces it with the number of the current page.

■ Use a double pound sign and a page number to start numbering at that page number. ##20, for example, numbers the page as 20.

Changing the Page Orientation

Changing the page orientation in 1-2-3 is a snap. Choose **F**ile, **P**rint, **D**estination. From the resulting dialog box, choose the **S**etup button. You see a dialog box similar to the one in figure 10.7.

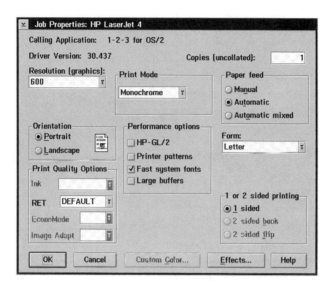

Fig. 10.7
Use this dialog box to specify portrait or landscape orientation. The setting remains in effect for the rest of the 1-2-3 session unless you change it again.

Select the appropriate button to print either **P**ortrait or **L**andscape. Figure 10.8 shows a spreadsheet range previewed in landscape orientation—an arrangement you might choose when the print range is too wide to fit the page in portrait orientation.

Controlling Margins

After you choose a page orientation, you might consider changing the margin settings. Use wide margins if your spreadsheet is packed with data and people might need to make notes on the printout. Use narrow margins when you're trying to squeeze just one more column or a few more rows on each page.

After you establish margins in the File Print Options dialog box, consider changing the alignment of the printout in the margins. In the File Print, Print Worksheet dialog box (refer to fig. 10.4), select the **V**ertical and **H**orizontal checkboxes to move the entire print range to the middle of the page. These options are particularly useful for designing title pages or for aligning custom-sized graphs on the printout.

II

Using 1-2-3

Fig. 10.8

Print with landscape orientation if your print range contains too many columns to fit in the portrait orientation.

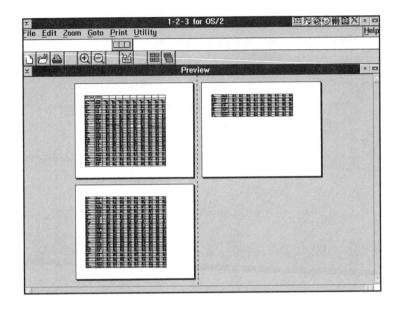

Including the Spreadsheet Frame

If you want, you can suppress the printing of drawn objects, such as charts and graphics, you've added with the drawing tools. You also can choose not to print the spreadsheet grid lines. If you're sharing your work with other spreadsheet developers (who are as moved as you are by cell and range addresses), you might want to print the spreadsheet frame along with the range it prints. The checkboxes to change these settings are in the File Print, Print Worksheet dialog box (refer to fig. 10.4).

> **Note**
>
> Gridlines, borders, and graphics don't print if you don't select the checkboxes in the Worksheet Global Screen Attribute dialog box, regardless of the settings in the Print dialog box.

When you want to share your work with other spreadsheet developers, you might also want to print a version on which you change your Format Output options to print formulas. In this case, 1-2-3 prints a list of each cell address and its contents. If a cell contains a formula, you see the formula, not the results of the formula (see fig. 10.9).

C:A1: 'Eagle Products Incorporated
C:A2: '   Total Widgets Produced (in thousands)
C:A4: '1985
C:A5: '1986
C:A6: '1987
C:A7: '1988
C:A8: '1989
C:A9: '1990
C:B3: 'Product A
C:B4: (,0) 2431
C:B5: (,0) 2564
C:B6: (,0) 2532
C:B7: (,0) 2687
C:B8: (,0) 2785
C:B9: (,0) 2987
C:B12: 'Summary by Product
C:C3: 'Product B
C:C4: (,0) 1564
C:C5: (,0) 1634
C:C6: (,0) 1576
C:C7: (,0) 1768
C:C8: (,0) 1954
C:C9: (,0) 2145
C:C14: 'Product A
C:C15: 'Product B
C:C16: 'Product C
C:D3: 'Product C
C:D4: (,0) 5487
C:D5: (,0) 5879
C:D6: (,0) 6845
C:D7: (,0) 7456
C:D8: (,0) 8456
C:D9: (,0) 9345
C:D14: @SUM(B4..B9)
C:D15: @SUM(B5..B10)
C:D16: @SUM(B6..B11)

Fig. 10.9
You can help others see how you got your answers by printing your worksheet formulas.

II

Using 1-2-3

Repeating Columns and Rows

Some spreadsheets contain data you'd like to see on every page of a printout. I'm not talking about headers and footers here. Instead, consider a database worksheet. It's nice to have field headers on every page—no matter where the pages break. 1-2-3 calls these repeating rows or columns *headings*. Headings act, in a sense, like worksheet titles that you set using the **W**orksheet menu.

To establish headings, use the File Print, Print Worksheet dialog box. In the **H**eadings section of this dialog box, specify range references to columns or rows.

◄ See "Locking Titles On," p. 95

There's a frustrating aspect to headings: usually you want them on every page *except* the first page of a printout. Refer to the printout in figure 10.10. As the first page of the printout, it has a main title and a row of field headers across the top of the database. If you set the field headers as print titles, they appear above the main title as well as at the top of the database. On each subsequent page, they're fine, but on the first page they're a mess.

Fig. 10.10
Adding headings can cause a confusing printout, but you can solve the problem by changing the range you select to print.

A:	A	B	C	D	E	F	G	H
1	3rd Quarter Sales							
2								
3	Sales Person	Flavor	March	April	May	June	July	August

A:	A	B	C	D	E	F	G	H
1	3rd Quarter Sales							
2								
3	Sales Person	Flavor	March	April	May	June	July	August
4	Jim	Chocolate	$417	$393	$331	$331	$239	$332
5	Susan	Chocolate	$451	$351	$459	$459	$478	$297
6	Mariann	Chocolate	$329	$581	$100	$100	$565	$419
7	Rick	Chocolate	$146	$191	$417	$417	$583	$347
8	Jim	Vanilla	$260	$504	$451	$451	$397	$227
9	Mariann	Vanilla	$300	$533	$329	$329	$511	$193
10	Rick	Vanilla	$199	$382	$146	$146	$393	$60
11	Charlotte	Vanilla	$307	$361	$260	$260	$351	$437
12	Susan	Strawberry	$105	$218	$300	$300	$581	$591
13	Holly	Sherberts	$393	$206	$332	$199	$191	$119
14		Sherberts	$351	$262	$297	$307	$504	$143

A:	A	B	C	D	E	F	G	H
1	3rd Quarter Sales							
2								
3	Sales Person	Flavor	March	April	May	June	July	August
60	Holly	Sherberts	$393	$206	$332	$199	$191	$119
61	Jim	Sherberts	$351	$262	$297	$307	$504	$143
62	Kelley	Strawberry	$581	$360	$419	$105	$533	$380
63	Jeff	Vanilla	$191	$406	$347	$232	$382	$284
64	Holly	Chocolate	$504	$115	$227	$222	$361	$326
65	Jason	Chocolate	$533	$545	$193	$577	$218	$399
66	Kelley	Chocolate	$382	$458	$60	$563	$206	$313
67	Jeff	Chocolate	$361	$498	$437	$321	$262	$137
68		Sherberts	$21	$58	$591	$532	$360	$206

Tip
Choose **F**ile, **P**rint **O**ptions to display the File Print Options dialog box.

The classic work-around to the problem is never to include the rows you intend to print as headings in your print range. In the case of printing a database, you'd specify only the records of the database as the print range, and omit the row of field headers. Then specify the row of field headers as the print headings row.

Saving for the Future

If you like the overall print options you establish for a spreadsheet, you might want to use the same settings in other sheets. For that matter, your company or department might have standard headers, footers, and margin settings that everyone is supposed to use when they create reports. In either case, click the **C**reate button in the File Print Options dialog box to activate the **N**amed Settings text box. Specify a name to save your print options settings under. To activate the settings, highlight them in the list and choose the **U**se button.

What You See Is What You Get

Occasionally, you might want 1-2-3 to place page breaks in locations other than the natural ones. Setting a page break is simple: click a cell in the row or column where you want the page break to fall. Choose **W**orksheet, **P**age Break. 1-2-3 places four dots in the cell; these symbols mark the new page break.

You clear an inserted page break the same way you erase the contents of any cell—highlight the cell containing the page break and press Del.

Troubleshooting

Sometimes when I print my model, 1-2-3 cuts off some of the graphs.

Cell entries define the edges of the range that 1-2-3 prints. If a graph sticks out past the right-most column of data, it might get cut off during printing. Either move the graph a bit to the left, make it smaller, or select a restricted print range that includes one or more blank columns to the right of your data.

Several shaded areas in my spreadsheet print out as dark blocks; it's impossible to read the text in them.

Your choice of color combinations may be to blame, as well as the printer driver you're using. Some printer drivers show high contrast between shaded spreadsheet ranges and the text they contain. Others print virtually all shadings as black or near-black, thereby blotting out text in the shaded ranges. If you're going to print your spreadsheet, use highly contrasting color combinations. In fact, consider using only white-on-black or black-on-white. If your printer can work with more than one driver (many laser printers can, and so can some PostScript printers), try installing several drivers and printing with each of them until you find one that gives satisfactory results.

II

Using 1-2-3

From Here...

By now, you know enough to make 1-2-3 jump through hoops. For all your knowledge, you have to be at your computer to get such a performance. However, if you automate spreadsheet processes with macros, you might never again have to sit at your desk. OK, that's an exaggeration. Still, by automating tasks with macros, you'll cut a lot of time from a typical work session. Eventually, you might even build fully automated spreadsheets that lead less-advanced users through data-entry and analysis so they can do the work for you. Learn about macros in the following chapter:

■ Chapter 11, "Automating with 1-2-3 Macros," introduces the topic of worksheet automation with macros.

After you master 1-2-3, you can move on to the other SmartSuite applications. Get started quickly with each one by working through the first chapter in each section of this book:

■ Chapter 12, "Creating and Editing Documents," gets you started with the Ami Pro word processing application.

■ Chapter 20, "Getting Started with Freelance Graphics," shows you the power of graphics presentation software.

Chapter 11

Automating with 1-2-3 Macros

by Elaine Marmel

Will humans someday create a machine so sophisticated that it frees them from the drudgery of work to pursue more lofty ambitions? Ah, a question that philosophers and science fiction writers have explored for decades! Here's a more immediate question: Will humans someday create software so sophisticated that it frees them from the drudgery of working with a computer? Well, how about macros?

The whole point of macros is that they automate spreadsheet processes. Some macros, in fact, can replace their users at the computer. Some macros simply help users complete jobs more quickly, and other macros guide novice users through tasks they couldn't otherwise complete at all.

In this chapter, you learn to:

- ■ Record your activity in the spreadsheet to play back later as a macro

- ■ Make macros readily available in your spreadsheets

- ■ Use key concepts and commands necessary to automate complex procedures

- ■ Recognize basic philosophies and design considerations for spreadsheet macro enthusiasts

Using Macros To Automate Your Spreadsheets

◀ See "Entering Text," p. 45

A spreadsheet macro consists of a collection of labels stored in a spreadsheet. Historically, the labels corresponded to keys a user pressed to complete a task. 1-2-3's macro processor read the labels character-by-character, and pressed the keys the labels represented.

Today, 1-2-3 understands an enormous collection of programming commands that correspond to the menu and dialog options you normally choose by pointing and clicking with the mouse. Fortunately, macro commands remind you of the spreadsheet options they control, so you can surmise what a macro does simply by browsing its code. Still, with well over 300 macro commands to wrestle with, you may welcome any help 1-2-3 has to offer as you automate your spreadsheets. Before you explore those tools, you should understand the basics of creating spreadsheet macros.

Applying Simple Automation for Serious Power

The simplest macro you write might be one that types a label—your name or your company's name—in a cell. This action may be useful if you need to type the label repeatedly as you build a spreadsheet. After you write a macro, simple or complex, you name it so that pressing just two keys starts the macro running. Alternatively, you can attach the macro to a SmartIcon that prompts you for the macro's name.

Creating Macros in the Worksheet

You can write your first macro almost by accident. In fact, any label can be a macro. You merely type the label in a cell and assign the cell a range name. Then you can identify the cell to 1-2-3's macro processor and play back the entry. To get the basics of creating a macro, follow these steps:

1. Choose an out-of-the-way place to build the macro. Your best bet is to use a blank sheet in the file and build the macro there.

2. In the cell to the left of the cell in which you intend to place macro keystrokes, type a label that represents the macro's name. If you intend to place macro keystrokes in Cell B1, place the label for the macro in

cell A1. If you want the macro to type your company's name, perhaps you should call the macro n, or less cryptically, comp_name. This example uses the name \n. To enter \n, type the characters '**\n** (otherwise 1-2-3 stores n as a repeating label in the cell).

> **Note**
>
> Macro names follow the same rules as range names: you can use up to 15 characters; don't start the name with a colon or number; don't use macro keyword names; and don't use spaces, commas, semicolons, or these characters: +, *, –, /, &, <, >, @, or #.

3. In the cell to the right of the first label, type the macro. For this example, the entry is Marmel Enterprises, Inc. (see fig. 11.1).

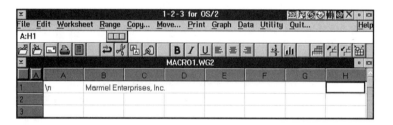

Fig. 11.1
The macro command to type a label is itself a copy of the label.

4. Assign the left-hand label as the range name for the cell holding the right-hand label. In the example, cell B1 has the name \n.

Now you can run the macro named \n and 1-2-3 types your company name so you can enter it in a cell.

◄ See "Assigning Range Names," p. 164

Running a Macro

To run a macro with a backslash (\) coupled with a single letter in the name, hold down the Ctrl key and type the letter. To run the macro in figure 11.1, select a blank cell where you want your company name to appear and press Ctrl+N. Immediately, your company name appears in the cell as if you just typed it. You can press Enter to store the name in the current cell or press Escape to clear the name from the display.

Tip
This is a perfect opportunity to take advantage of the **R**ange, **N**ame, **L**abels command to assign a name to your macro.

II

Using 1-2-3

◀ See "Saving
Your Work,"
p. 102

Caution

Always save your work before you run a newly written macro. When you run a
macro, 1-2-3 interprets it exactly as you have written it. If you have a space at the
end of a line of code, the macro processor adds a space. Misspell a macro keyword or
one of the arguments in a command, and the macro is likely to fail—or worse, act in
a way you didn't intend. You may have a chance of recovering from an errant
macro's blundering by using 1-2-3's Undo command. But you're safer not to take the
chance. Save the worksheet before running a new macro and if something goes
wrong, retrieve the saved worksheet to recover it.

If the macro's name isn't a backslash+letter combination, use the Run a
Macro dialog box to trigger the macro. To do this, follow these steps:

Tip

Before you can run
a macro, you must
open the work-
sheet file or the
macro library file
that contains the
macro.

1. Place the cell pointer where you want the macro to run.

2. Press Alt+F3. 1-2-3 displays the Run a Macro dialog box shown in
   figure 11.2.

3. Select the macro name in the Range Name listbox and click OK.

With all this work to trigger a macro, you may just as well type the simple
label the macro types rather than use the dialog box. But what if you write a
macro that prints one or more specific ranges, changing the print settings for
each range? Or what if the macro is even more complex? Working through
the Run a Macro dialog box may not seem so bothersome when the effort
saves dozens of keystrokes.

Fig. 11.2
The Run a Macro
dialog box lists
only one range
name in the
example spread-
sheet.

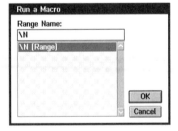

Tip
To cancel a macro,
press Ctrl+Break
and then press Esc
to clear the error
message.

Using Macro Command Keywords

If a macro could only type labels and numbers, it wouldn't be particularly
useful. Fortunately, 1-2-3 macros can use almost every key you can. Suppose,
for example, that you want 1-2-3 to press Enter for you to place the label it
types into the current cell, rather than leave the task for you. You can make

this step happen by including a tilde (˜) as the last character in the label that makes up the macro.

The tilde is one of 1-2-3's macro command keywords. The tilde means, simply, "Press Enter."

By adding another macro command, you can have 1-2-3's macro processor move the cell pointer after entering your label into the sheet. If you want the pointer to move down one cell, use the {DOWN} command (abbreviated to {D} if you prefer). Other commands to move the pointer include {RIGHT} or {R}, {LEFT} or {L}, and {UP} or {U}.

◀ See "Direction Keys," p. 87

You may recognize a theme developing: macro commands typically consist of keywords enclosed in braces. Many commands also accept arguments much like functions do. The cell pointer commands are good examples of that. While {DOWN} or {D} moves the cell pointer down one cell, you can specify a number of cells to move by including a numeric argument in the braces of the command. For example, the expression {DOWN 6} means "Press the down-arrow key six times," and the expression {D cntr} means "Press the down-arrow key as many times as specified in the cell named cntr".

In any case, figure 11.3 shows the label-typing macro modified with a {DOWN} command. Notice that the added command is in cell B2, beneath the original label. 1-2-3 still processes the command because it's in the next cell down from the first. When you trigger a macro, the macro processor reads commands from left-to-right in the macro's named cell. Then the processor looks for further commands in the next cell down, and so on until the processor encounters a blank cell or a cell that contains a numeric entry.

Certain commands can change the order in which 1-2-3 processes macro code. Understanding these commands is the key to writing macros that go beyond simple typing exercises. The "Changing the Flow of Control" section later in this chapter, explores some of these commands in greater depth.

Tip

While you can use repeat counts in pointer movement commands, such as {DOWN 3}, you may not find mention of this in 1-2-3's Help system.

Tip

Don't use macro command words as names for macros. If you use a command as a name, the range name takes precedence and 1-2-3 ignores the command in macros.

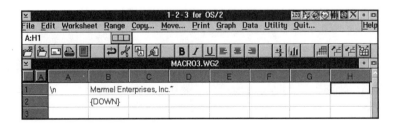

Fig. 11.3

A macro can extend several rows or several hundred rows down a column, depending on its complexity.

II

Using 1-2-3

Keeping Track of Macros

Sometimes a macro is particularly useful in conjunction with certain information in the spreadsheet. For example, when you're reviewing a particular report, you may want a macro that prints the report automatically. If you have dozens of possible reports to print in the file you're reviewing, a single macro may not be enough. Keeping track of which macro prints which report isn't a daunting task. This situation calls for using descriptive names rather than backslash names for macros. When you open the Run a Macro dialog box, you see the names you assigned to your macros in a list, so they're easily identifiable.

> **Note**
>
> You can add the Run a Macro SmartIcon to the SmartIcon bar to quickly open the Run a Macro dialog box. See "Customizing SmartIcon Palettes" in Appendix B for more information.

Getting Help When Working with Macros

By now you're aware that 1-2-3's macro language has many commands. A command coincides with virtually every setting and action you can make while working in the spreadsheet software. No sane user would try to memorize all those commands. Rather, you might learn a few key commands and then call on 1-2-3 to help with the others.

Recording Your Actions

One great source of help when creating your own macros is 1-2-3's Keystroke Recorder. This facility translates your keystrokes into macro commands on-the-fly. Every command you issue in 1-2-3 ends up as a macro command in the Keystroke Editor window.

> **Note**
>
> The Keystroke Recorder does *not* record mouse actions. You must use the keyboard to have your actions recorded.

And here's the cool part. Just go to work. When you complete the task you want to record as a macro, you're ready to copy the keystrokes into your worksheet.

Examining Macro Commands in the Keystroke Editor

To see the keystrokes 1-2-3 recorded while you were working, open the program Control menu and choose the **K**eystroke Editor command. 1-2-3 displays the window superimposed on the spreadsheet. Figure 11.4 shows a simple macro that establishes a print header and footer, specifies a print range, and then generates a printout of the range.

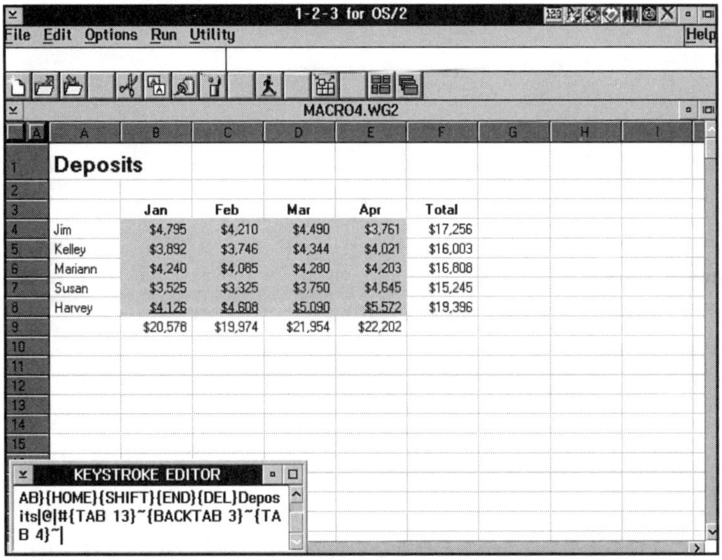

Fig. 11.4
While you work, 1-2-3 records your keystrokes in macro format in the Keystroke Editor window. By copying the commands back to the worksheet, you don't need to create macro steps—1-2-3 has already done that.

After you see the Keystroke Editor window, you can navigate its contents as you would in a word processor: use the scroll bars to move backward and forward through the text or click inside the window and use direction keys. You can also modify the information in the window by adding and deleting characters.

To make the contents more readable, resize the window by clicking the Maximize button in the top-right corner. You might want to Tile or Stack the windows by opening the program control menu and choosing the Window command. Then choose **T**ile or **S**tack. Figure 11.5 shows the macro commands in the enlarged Keystroke Editor window. Scrolling in the enlarged window makes nearly all of its contents visible.

Fig. 11.5

Because the Keystroke Editor window resides in the stack of open files in 1-2-3, you can resize and reposition it to work with it more easily.

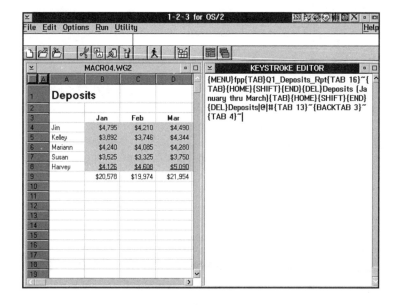

Notice that while the Keystroke Editor window is current, 1-2-3 offers a modified menu bar and its own set of SmartIcons. One particular command can be of great use: the **P**ause Recording command on the **O**ptions menu. After all, you're trying to figure out what commands apply to your macro, and in the meantime you need to move the cell pointer around. If you choose **P**ause Recording, 1-2-3 does exactly that; it doesn't record any keystrokes until you start recording again (by choosing the command again from the **O**ptions menu).

Interpreting Commands in the Keystroke Editor Window

The topic of spreadsheet macro programming could easily fill a book. So this limited introduction can't possibly turn you into a master spreadsheet developer. Still, this information should encourage you. Look over any transcript and you probably can discern the meanings of the commands it contains.

Consider some of the code in figure 11.6.

The first command is {MENU}. If you think the command means "Activate the menu bar," you're right (remember, you activate the menu bar from the keyboard by pressing Alt). The next three letters represent hot key letters for menus and commands. f means "Open the File menu," p means "choose the Print command," and p means "Choose the Print Worksheet command." {TAB} means "Press the Tab key," and the next several commands all involve selecting the print range (using a named range Q1_Deposits_Rpt) and moving the pointer through the dialog box. You'll notice a tilde (˜) after {TAB 16} indicating "Press Enter". If you followed these steps on your keyboard, you'd find that the **O**ptions button was active when 1-2-3 "pressed Enter", opening the File Print, Print Worksheet Options dialog box to set the header and footer. Other commands in the sequence are as easy to interpret.

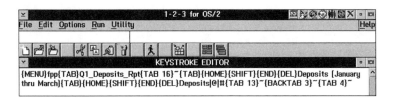

Fig. 11.6
The commands recorded in a macro transcript, shown here in an enlarged Keystroke Editor window.

The point is, despite the abundance of macro commands available, they're quite easy to interpret. What's more, because the commands reflect the menu and dialog options you would select to perform a task, you can often guess what a command might be and find it quickly in 1-2-3's online documentation if you want to know more about the command. Like @functions, you can get help about macro commands by typing one. As you type, it will appear in the contents box and you can then press F1 to get help about it. And for those of you thinking "What if I don't know the command?", type any macro command you know (such as {MENU}) and press F1. 1-2-3 gives you the option of looking through the Macro Command Index.

◀ See "A Note about Help," p. 104

Replaying the Contents of the Keystroke Editor Window

Until you develop a knack for when to activate and deactivate macro-recording, you'll rarely want to replay an entire transcript. In fact, 1-2-3 anticipates this situation and requires that you select some of the transcript to replay—you have no option to replay the entire recording. Follow these steps to replay some or all of a transcript:

1. Make sure the worksheet the macro should run in is open.

2. Move the cell pointer to the cell where the macro should start.

3. Switch to the Keystroke Editor window.

4. Highlight the section of the commands you want to replay.

 5. Choose **R**un, **G**o; or click the Run SmartIcon.

1-2-3 reactivates the spreadsheet window and processes the commands you highlighted in the Keystroke Editor window.

> **Note**
>
> The most wasteful macro is one that re-creates a spreadsheet you already created. For example, suppose you start a blank spreadsheet and record every command you issue to build a model. By replaying the recording, you can then build an exact copy of the original spreadsheet. What's the point? When you build a spreadsheet that you may want copies of, simply save the original in a file that you can retrieve later. Then you don't need to run a macro to make a copy of the spreadsheet.

When 1-2-3 records something useful in the Keystroke Editor window, move the commands to a spreadsheet to take full advantage of them. Select the text in the Keystroke Editor window, choose **E**dit, **C**opy, select a target cell in the spreadsheet, and finally choose **E**dit, **P**aste. Don't forget to name the cell containing the macro so you can run it.

> **Note**
>
> Create a spreadsheet file to hold macros only. Place related macros you might use on one project or for specific functions in one sheet of the file and then open that file so you can use the macros as you work.

Note that the macro commands in the worksheet all reside in one column and don't spill over into the next column, even when it's blank (see fig. 11.7). This causes no problem, because 1-2-3 continues processing a macro until it encounters a blank cell. Although the macro keystrokes appear jammed up, 1-2-3 has no problem running the macro.

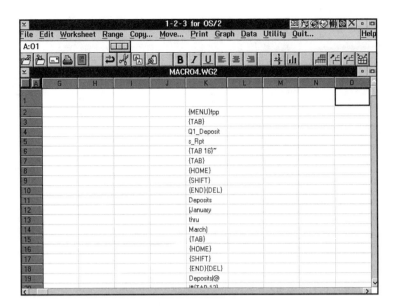

Fig. 11.7
When you copy commands from the Keystroke Editor into the worksheet, they don't appear particularly elegant. Don't worry though, 1-2-3 won't have any trouble running the macro.

Reviewing the Macro Language

Most of the macro commands in 1-2-3 serve in place of mouse clicks and keystrokes you administer manually. If you can make something happen with the mouse or the keyboard, those brace-enclosed macro commands can perform the same action.

But a realm of spreadsheet activity takes place before you press a key or use the mouse: the act of making decisions. Should this range be green or red? Should you mark this bill as paid or overdue? Should you print the entire report or just one or two summary sections? What title will you add to the graph? You get the idea.

Because of the decision-making you do, it's reasonable to assume that macros can't replace you at the keyboard. Certainly, a macro that knows only how to press keys can't replace you. But what if you can imbue the macro with some of its own decision-making powers? Or what if you can pass off decision-making to other users while forcing those decisions to take place in narrow guidelines? A subset of commands in the macro language enable you to do these things.

II

Using 1-2-3

Changing the Flow of Control

◀ See "Logical
Operators,"
p. 173

The order in which the macro processor reads and reacts to macro commands
is the macro's flow of control. At its simplest, the flow of control is from left-
to-right across a cell, then down to the next cell, and so on. 1-2-3 travels
through the commands until it encounters a blank or non-label cell. Commands that change the flow of control are fundamental to writing intelligent
macros.

Perhaps the quintessential flow-of-control diverter is the macro IF command.
Its syntax is as follows:

{IF condition}

When the macro processor encounters an IF statement, it uses Boolean logic
to interpret the condition argument(s). If the argument evaluates to a true
result (1), the processor looks for further commands to process in the cell
following the IF. If the argument evaluates to false (0), the macro processor
skips remaining commands in the cell and looks for further instructions in
the following cell.

Tip
You can use a cell
name or address in
conjunction with
the BRANCH
statement.

You typically use the IF command in conjunction with other flow of control
commands. For example, the BRANCH macro command sends control to a
specified cell. {BRANCH b12} transfers control to macro code in cell B12, and
{BRANCH printit} sends control to a cell named printit. The worksheet in
figure 11.8 suggests how IF together with BRANCH can enable a macro to
make decisions.

Fig. 11.8
IF commands
together with
BRANCH state-
ments imbue a
macro with
rudimentary
intelligence. The
number in cell B1
determines which
macro routine
1-2-3 processes.

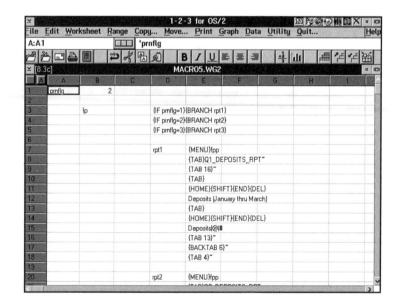

When the macro processor reads the first IF command, it sees that the value in prnflg (B1) is not 1. Because prnflg=1 is false, the processor skips the BRANCH command in cell D3 and reads the command in cell D4. That IF command's condition statement is true; prnflg does equal 2. So macro control passes to the cell named rpt2 (not shown).

Given the current value of prnflg, the macro processor never reads the command in cell D5 because the earlier IF and BRANCH combination in cell B6 diverts it. However, change the value in cell B1 to 3, and the macro's flow of control also changes.

Other commands also implement a macro's flow of control, but trying to mention all the commands goes way beyond the scope of this book. As you learn more about macros, pay special attention to the FOR and NEXT command combination and read up on subroutines. You'll use all these tools as your macro creations become more and more complex.

Establishing User Interface

If you're the only person using the macros you write, then, by all means, make them as difficult to use as you want. However, if other people will use your macros, try to make the macros friendly. If your macros are easy to use, you'll spend less time helping other people fix messes they created by using your macros.

So how can a macro be "friendly"? Well, it can walk a user through what he needs to do. 1-2-3 has an impressive complement of commands that enable you to build these kinds of controls right into your spreadsheets. Can the user choose which report to print? Then build a custom macro-driven pull-down menu, or a dialog box of selection buttons, or even a listbox of report names.

Commands to generate such OS/2-appropriate controls include these options:

- *ALERT*. Displays a warning or informational message in a dialog box.

- *DIALOG-CALL*. Creates and describes a custom dialog box that includes any type of dialog box controls. You then write supporting macro code to respond to selections a user makes in the dialog box.

- *GETLABEL*. Displays a dialog box that prompts a user for information and then stores the user's entry as a label in a cell.

- *MENU-CREATE*. Replaces the menu bar with your own custom menu.

- *MENUCALL*. Displays a dialog box of command buttons from which the user must make a selection before the macro will continue processing.

More commands are available, but this short list gives you an idea of the possibilities. Use these commands effectively, and your macros begin to look like full-fledged OS/2 applications. Casual users may be unaware that the application they're using is running inside 1-2-3.

Troubleshooting

I named a macro \t, but when I press Alt+T, the macro doesn't run.

You probably learned spreadsheets with a DOS version of 1-2-3. In 1-2-3 for OS/2, press Ctrl+T to start the \t macro.

I entered \b in a cell to name a macro, but pressing Ctrl+B has no effect.

Did you assign \b as a range name to the macro's first cell? Entering the label in the spreadsheet isn't enough, you must also use the Range Name Create dialog box (choose **R**ange, **N**ame, **C**reate) to assign the macro's name.

My macro seems to be running, but nothing is happening. Is there any way to stop it?

If you want to stop a macro before it finishes on its own, press Ctrl+Break. You may need to do this several times repeatedly before you get a response from 1-2-3. Don't be shy about it; hold down the Ctrl key and press Break several times very rapidly if you must. An error message appears when the macro stops. Press Escape to clear it, or click OK.

From Here...

Are you ready to fly solo? You probably were ready many pages ago. The beauty of 1-2-3 is that even a little knowledge of how to use the program can translate into enormous productivity. The chapters in Part II of this book have provided more than a little knowledge. If you read through all the chapters, you know far more about the high-powered electronic spreadsheet than the average user. If you find yourself excited and interested in the material, you may want to learn more to become a professional spreadsheet consultant or in-house applications developer with your company's MIS/DP group.

You have probably noticed that this isn't the end of the book. 1-2-3 addresses your spreadsheet needs, but Lotus SmartSuite for OS/2 doesn't stop there. You'll find that Ami Pro is a powerful word processing package and Freelance Graphics can produce outstanding presentations, both on paper and on-screen:

■ Chapter 12, "Creating and Editing Documents," gets you started with the Ami Pro word processing application.

■ Chapter 20, "Getting Started with Freelance Graphics," shows you the power of graphics presentation software.

II

Using 1-2-3

Part III

Using Ami Pro

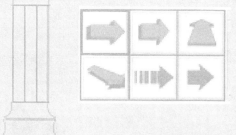

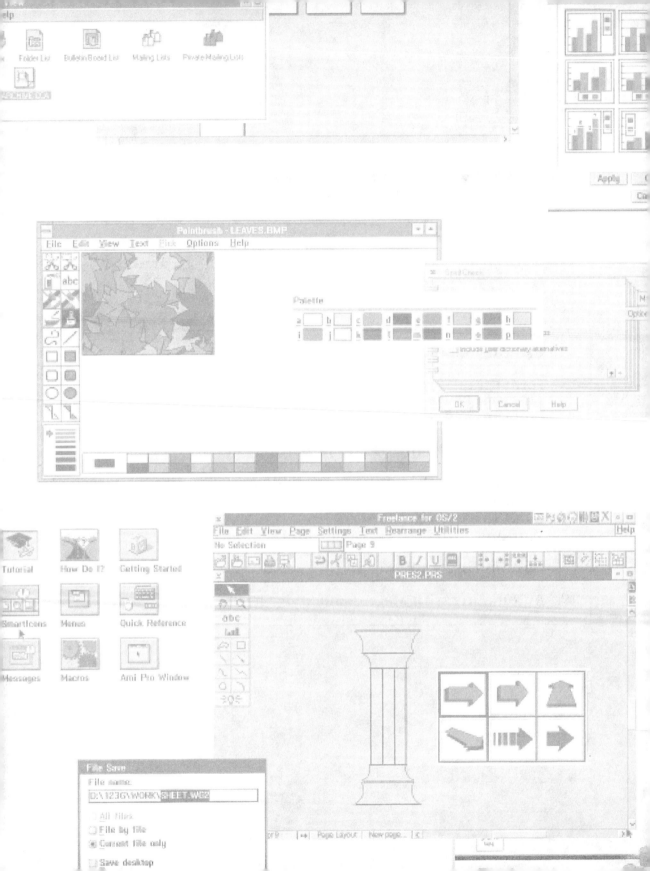

Chapter 12

Creating and Editing Documents

by Sue Plumley

Despite its advanced capabilities, Ami Pro is an easy-to-use word processing program for OS/2. You can use Ami Pro to create a variety of documents—letters, reports, memos, and faxes. You can create documents from scratch or you can use any of Ami Pro's style sheets as a base. Ami Pro also has in-depth formatting and editing features as well as graphics, tables, and drawing capabilities that let you create professional documents.

You can make your work as simple or as complex as you like. Ami Pro includes many techniques that make entering and editing text painless, from adding and moving text to deleting large blocks of text. After learning the basics, you can concentrate on the more elaborate features of the program. You'll learn how to insert and edit text, as well as create and save a document.

In this chapter, you learn to:

- Understand the Ami Pro screen
- Enter text into your document
- Select and copy text
- Undo mistakes
- Create and save new documents
- Open and close existing documents

Understanding the Ami Pro Screen

Ami Pro has several default screen elements that always appear, regardless of the document you edit. These default elements include the title bar, menu bar, SmartIcons, status bar, and scroll bars. The ruler is not a default item; however, you can easily display it using the **V**iew, Show **R**uler command. The Lotus Application Manager appears at the top of your screen if you opened it during the current session. Using the Ami Pro screen elements, you can run commands, edit text, view, and modify your document.

This section describes the separate parts of the Ami Pro screen. Figure 12.1 illustrates the default screen and shows each screen element.

Fig. 12.1
Certain default elements appear on the Ami Pro screen.

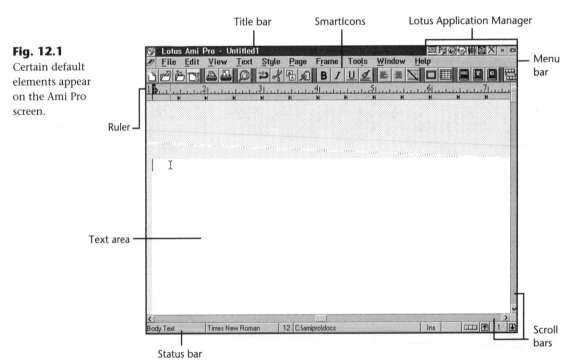

■ *Title Bar.* The title bar contains the name of the program and the current document you're editing. The title bar also contains the OS/2 Control menu and the Minimize, and Maximize or Restore buttons. These buttons shrink or enlarge your Ami Pro window. If you have saved your document, the title bar lists the document name. Otherwise, the title bar displays Untitled1. If the Application Manager is active, the icons appear in the Title bar as well.

- *Menu Bar.* The menu bar contains Ami Pro commands arranged by related groups. You can initiate any command by selecting first a menu and then the command.

- *SmartIcons.* SmartIcons are shortcuts to many common commands. There are several sets of SmartIcons that can be accessed any time—such as editing, graphics, tables, and so on—and you can customize your own. SmartIcons can be placed on the side, top, or bottom; or they can float on your Ami Pro screen.

- *Ruler.* You can visually set tabs, indents, and margins on your Ami Pro document with the ruler. You can drag margin boundaries and indent markers and place a tab location with a single mouse click.

◄ See "Viewing Parts of the Window," p. 36

- *Text area.* Enter text, create tables, or add pictures in the text area—your page or document. Ami Pro starts with a blank document each time you open the program.

- *Scroll bars.* Unless you're working with a small amount of text, you can't see it all on screen at one time. The scroll bars let you control which part of the document shows in the window. Click a scroll arrow to move up, down, left, or right, one line or character at a time. Click within the scroll bar or drag the scroll box to jump to another area of the page.

- *Status bar.* The status bar gives document information and lets you modify certain text attributes. You can click any of the buttons in the status bar to display various options and information. Click the style button to choose a text style for selected text, the font button to select a font, or the size button to change text size. If you click the fourth button from the right (the one with C:\amipro), you display the date and time; click the same button again to display the cursor position, and click the same button once more to display the current drive and directory. The fifth button from the left changes typing modes from Ins (insert), Type (typeover), to Rev (revision) each time you click it. The button with three small boxes on it displays available toolbars from which you can choose. Move from page to page using the up (previous) and down (next) arrow buttons and finally, click the page number button (between the arrows) to display the Go To dialog box.

III

Using Ami Pro

Placing Text in Your Document

You can start entering text and creating any document you want immediately after opening Ami Pro. The text you enter appears on-screen where the blinking cursor is located; the cursor moves as you enter more text.

The following sections describe basic tips for typing and selecting text, and for moving around in your document.

Typing Text

◄ See "Entering, Selecting, and Editing Text," p. 44

Entering text in Ami Pro is similar to entering text in any program. As you type, the blinking cursor moves to the right. When you reach the right margin, the text automatically *wraps* to the next line. *Word wrap* continues from line to line until you press Enter. Text also wraps to the next page when you reach the bottom of the page.

You can easily correct mistakes as you type by using the Backspace and Delete keys. Press Backspace to remove letters to the left of the cursor and press Delete to remove characters to the right of the cursor. Ami Pro includes other editing features as you'll see later in this chapter.

Using the Insertion Point

► See "Using Graphics with Ami Pro," p. 353

When you start typing, your text appears at the blinking cursor or *insertion point*. The insertion point is also where text and/or graphics are pasted from the OS/2 Clipboard and where Ami Pro frames and tables are inserted.

Before you begin entering text, make sure your cursor is positioned where you want the text to appear. Using the mouse, you can easily reposition your insertion point by clicking the I-beam anywhere in the text. You can also scroll through the document using the scroll bars, and click the location in your text where you want the new insertion point.

Tip

As you scroll through a document, the insertion point doesn't move with the document; you must click the mouse I-beam in the new area to move the insertion point.

You can also use the keyboard to move the insertion point. Table 12.1 shows how to use the keyboard to move the insertion point through the document.

Table 12.1   Maneuvering with the Keyboard

Key	Moves
←	One character to the left
Ctrl+←	One word to the left
→	One character to the right

Key	Moves
Ctrl+→	One word to the right
↑	One line up
↓	One line down
Ctrl+↑	Beginning of the paragraph
Ctrl+↓	End of the paragraph
PgUp	One screen up
PgDn	One screen down
Ctrl+PgUp	Beginning of the screen
Ctrl+PgDn	End of the screen
Home	Beginning of the line
End	End of the line
Ctrl+Home	Beginning of the document
Ctrl+End	End of the document

Selecting Text

Once you're comfortable moving the insertion point around the screen, the next step is selecting your text. Selecting text allows you to highlight only certain parts of your document on which you want to perform a specific action. For example, you may want to select a page title and change the font size, or change the style of a paragraph. You can easily identify selected text because the text becomes white highlighted in black.

Using the Keyboard

Using the keyboard, you can select text the same way you move your cursor around the screen, except that you press the Shift key as well. To select one character to your right, for example, hold down the Shift key and press the right-arrow key. You can select characters, lines, and paragraphs in this manner.

Using the Mouse

You can also use the mouse to select single characters, words, lines, or the entire document. Hold down the left mouse button and drag the cursor over the text to select it. Table 12.2 describes how to select text. Figure 12.2 shows several words highlighted within a paragraph.

III

Tip
To select all pages of your document, press Ctrl+Home to go to the beginning of the document, and press Shift+Ctrl+End.

Using Ami Pro

Fig. 12.2
You can select text
quickly and easily
with the mouse.

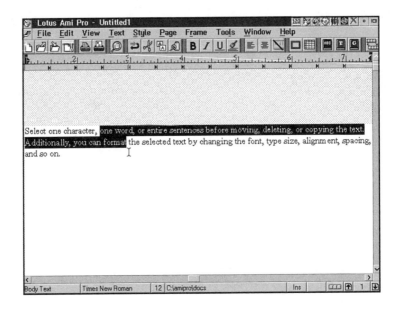

Table 12.2	Selecting Text
To Select	**Keyboard + Mouse Action**
Single word	Double-click the word
Sentence	Ctrl+click the sentence
Paragraph	Ctrl+double-click
Range of text	Click at the beginning of the text range, press Shift, click at the end of the text range or drag the mouse from the beginning of the text to the end

To deselect text, either click the mouse anywhere in the document, press an arrow key, or press Escape.

> **Caution**
>
> Selected text is automatically replaced by any character keys you type, and it's deleted if you press Delete or Backspace.

Understanding Typeover and Insert Modes

Typeover mode and *insert mode* can be used when you're creating or editing your document. Use the typeover mode to replace text to the right of your insertion point or use the insert mode to add text to your document.

While in typeover mode, you can type over existing text. Each keystroke you enter replaces an existing character on your Ami Pro screen. This feature is useful for editing documents because it replaces the text you want to change.

Insert mode ensures that any new characters you type don't overwrite existing text; the existing text simply moves to make space for the new characters. Insert mode is useful for making significant revisions because you can add new information to your document while preserving existing text.

To toggle between typeover and insert modes, press the Ins key. If you press Ins again, you return to the original typing mode. The Ami Pro status bar changes to inform you of your typing mode; it displays Ins for insert mode and Type for typeover mode. You also can click the Ins or Type button on the status bar to change the mode in which you are working.

You can also change the typing mode with your mouse. Figure 12.3 shows the button on the status bar that you click to switch between typing modes. The typing modes cycle from Ins to Type to Rev. *Rev* toggles to revision marking mode, which enables you to distinguish between original text and edited text.

▶ See "Understanding Revision Marking," p. 339

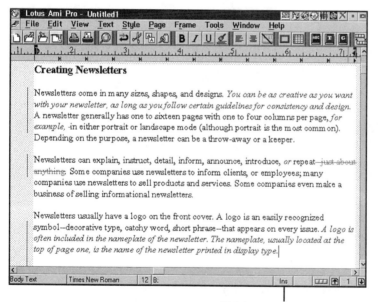

Fig. 12.3
Click the button on the status bar to change between Insert and Typeover modes.

Click here to change modes

III

Using Ami Pro

Troubleshooting

The arrow keys in the numeric keypad aren't maneuvering the insertion point around the document.

Press Num Lock to act as a toggle of your numeric keypad. If Num Lock is on, the numeric keypad displays only numbers when pressed. If Num Lock is off, the keypad keys work like standard arrow keys.

I accidentally deleted my selected text by pushing another key.

Choose **E**dit from the main menu and select the **U**ndo command to immediately reverse the last command.

Editing Text

After you've entered text into Ami Pro, you'll probably need to make changes. Whether you need to correct typographical errors or rearrange the entire document, Ami Pro simplifies the editing process.

You can easily cut, move, or modify words, sentences, and paragraphs. The Cu**t**, **C**opy, and **P**aste commands from the **E**dit menu let you move selected text around your document or to another document or application. Similarly, you can use the drag and drop feature in Ami Pro to move text on-screen without touching a key.

Of course, if you accidentally delete a paragraph or move a sentence to the wrong location, you can correct the mistake by immediately using the Undo feature (see "Undoing Mistakes," later in this chapter).

Note

This chapter discusses basic editing techniques. For more advanced editing features, such as changing fonts, setting margins, and adding page numbers, see Chapter 13, "Formatting Text and Documents."

Copying Text Using the Clipboard

The Clipboard is a built-in OS/2 feature that lets you store text or graphics directly into memory for use later in the session. The **C**opy command places a copy of the selected text onto the Clipboard; the Cu**t** command removes the text from Ami Pro to the Clipboard. Items cut or copied to the Clipboard remain there until you cut or copy another item.

You can copy the Clipboard contents to the same document or a different one with the **P**aste command. The Clipboard contents are pasted at the insertion point; you can paste the Clipboard contents over and over again until you cut or copy a different item to the Clipboard.

To copy or cut and paste text, follow these steps:

1. Select the text you want to copy to the Clipboard with your mouse or the equivalent keyboard commands.

2. Choose **E**dit, Cu**t** to move the text or **E**dit, **C**opy to duplicate the text. Or, you can click the Cut or Copy SmartIcons.

3. Click the mouse at the insertion point, either in the same document or a new one.

4. Choose **E**dit, **P**aste from the Ami Pro menu bar to paste the text, or click the Paste SmartIcon.

Moving Text by Using Drag-and-Drop

You can also move or copy text with the mouse. After selecting the text with the mouse, you can move the text by dragging it. This drag-and-drop feature allows you to see your moves and changes as you perform them.

To drag-and-drop text, follow these steps:

1. Select the text you want to move (see fig. 12.4).

2. To copy the text, press the Ctrl key and then click and hold the mouse button on the selected text. To cut the text, don't hold the Ctrl key. The mouse pointer changes from a regular arrow to an arrow with a pair of scissors.

3. Keeping the mouse button depressed, move the insertion point to the desired location. A vertical bar moves with the pointer indicating the new location of the text.

> **Note**
>
> Remember that the insertion point is actually the vertical bar, not the arrow-and-scissors cursor.

4. Release the mouse button and the highlighted text appears at the insertion point. Figure 12.5 shows the new location for the selected sentence.

Fig. 12.4
Use the drag-and-drop feature to quickly move text.

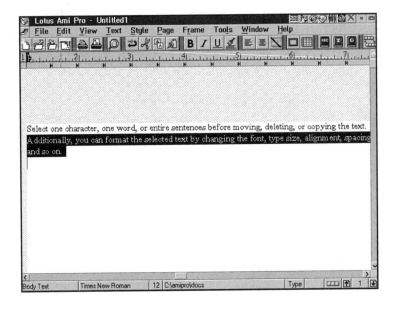

Fig. 12.5
When you release the mouse button, the text is dropped in its new position.

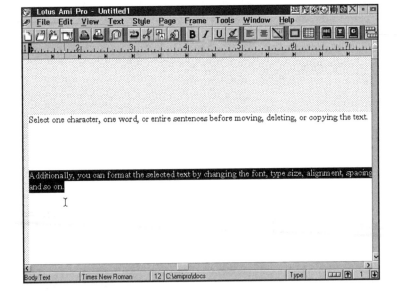

Undoing Mistakes

You may make mistakes while editing your document. For example, you might drag-and-drop the text to the wrong location or accidentally delete selected parts of the document.

Fortunately, Ami Pro has a built-in Undo feature. You can undo a text move or an accidental deletion. In fact, you can undo nearly every Ami Pro command after its completion and revert to the document's previous state. Not only can you revoke your most recent command, you can also undo multiple levels of commands. You can customize Ami Pro to set the number of recent commands you can Undo.

Caution

You can only undo the last four actions performed (set the number of actions from one to four in the Tools, User Setup dialog box); therefore, you must choose to Undo an action before performing too many subsequent actions.

▶ See "Changing Your User Setup," p. 362

To undo a command, choose **Edit** and select **Undo** from the Ami Pro menu bar. You can also press Ctrl+Z from the keyboard or click the Undo SmartIcon.

Saving Your Documents

After typing a document into Ami Pro, you usually want to save it for future reference. The document is lost if you turn the computer off or there's an interruption in power prior to saving the document. Saving enables you to retrieve the information anytime you want for further editing, proofing, or printing.

Ami Pro also includes an automatic backup feature that saves your document for you at specified times. Choose the Tools User Setup command to display the User Setup dialog box. In the File Saving area, choose the Auto **B**ackup feature and in **A**uto Timed Save, enter the number of minutes you want between saves, from one to 99. Saving your document every five to ten minutes is recommended and the auto backup takes only a couple of seconds.

Caution

Save your documents regularly, in case you have a system problem or failure. If you get into the habit of saving often, you'll never lose too much information if a computer crisis should occur.

III

Using Ami Pro

You can also save a document under a different file name or in a different drive or directory to use for a backup or for transferring files to another computer. You can also save a file as the same name in a different directory or drive.

The First Save

To save your document for the first time, follow these steps:

1. Choose **F**ile, **S**ave to open the Save As dialog box (see fig. 12.6).

Fig. 12.6
Use the Save As dialog box to specify a file name and location for your document.

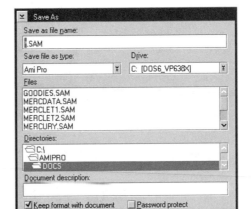

> **Note**
>
> The Save As dialog box only appears the first time you save your document or when you select **F**ile, Save **A**s.

Tip
Save a document under a new name so you can keep a copy of the old version and the revised version.

2. In the Save as File **N**ame text box, enter a name for the new file. Ami Pro automatically adds the .SAM extension.

3. Optionally, choose the D**r**ive and **D**irectory in which you want to store the file.

> **Note**
>
> If you don't choose another drive or directory, Ami Pro saves your document to the default drive and directory: C:\amipro.

4. You can also enter a summary of the document in the Document Description text box, although it's not required.

> **Note**
>
> Use the Document Description summary to track letters, memos, and other documents that you can't identify by name alone. You can enter such information as the recipient, subject, keywords, and so on that help you quickly identify a file without opening it.

5. Click the OK button or press Enter to save the document. Notice the new name replaces <UNTITLED> in the Ami Pro title bar.

> **Note**
>
> Your file name (without the extension) can be only eight characters long. Make sure you give the file a descriptive name, so you can identify it later.

You can also password-protect saved files. In the Save As dialog box, select the **P**assword Protect option. Ami Pro prompts for a password after you click OK in the dialog box. Your case-sensitive password can be a maximum of 14 characters long. Ami Pro asks you to confirm the password; enter the same password and choose OK.

You can also decide to store the document styles with the saved file using the **K**eep Format with Document option in the Save As dialog box. This option stores all paragraph styles and attributes associated with the document style sheet with the saved file. Also, Ami Pro remains compatible to version 1.2 with the Ami Pro 1.2 Format option.

▶ See "Understanding Ami Pro Styles," p. 335

> **Caution**
>
> There is no way to access an Ami Pro file if you forget the associated password.

Future Saves

Now that your document is saved, you can safely exit Ami Pro without losing any information. If you make further additions to your document, save the file again. Choose **F**ile, **S**ave to include any changes to the document. Ami Pro doesn't prompt you to name your document; it automatically uses the previous name to save the current document.

III

Using Ami Pro

As an alternative to choosing **F**ile, **S**ave, you can click the Save SmartIcon or press Ctrl+S.

Tip
Make a habit of saving your file every ten minutes or so while you work; saving takes only a few seconds whereas redoing your work can take hours.

Use the **S**ave command often to save changes to a document in case of a power interruption or computer problem. You should also save your document before attempting any large tasks such as checking grammar or spelling, finding and replacing words, phrases or characters, or assembling an index or table of contents. If, for some reason, the large task doesn't go as planned, you can choose **F**ile, **R**evert to Saved to undo all the changes since you last saved the file.

Save As

If you make major modifications to your document after saving it, and want both versions to be stored, use the Save **A**s command instead of **S**ave.

The Save **A**s command enables you to rename the new document. By choosing **F**ile, Save **A**s, you again open the Save As dialog box. You can then save the document under a new name in the same drive and directory, in a new directory or drive, or under the same name in another directory or drive. Changing the name, drive, or directory enables you to keep both the original and revised versions of a document.

Creating, Closing, and Opening Documents

Like many OS/2 programs, Ami Pro allows you to easily open previously saved files to make changes to, review, or print documents.

This section describes how to open and close previously saved files. You also learn how to create a new Ami Pro document after closing a document or while others are open, so you can switch between open documents.

Opening an Existing Document

After you have created and saved a document, you may need to access it again. Whether you need to print, make slight changes, or perform signifi-cant edits, having access to existing documents is very important.

 To open a previously saved document, choose **F**ile, **O**pen. The Open dialog box appears. Alternatively, you can press Ctrl+O to access the dialog box or you can click the Open SmartIcon. As another alternative, you could type the path and file name in the Open File **N**ame text box and choose OK.

Choose the correct **D**rive and **D**irectory, if necessary. Select the file from the list of **F**iles or type the file name in the Open File **N**ame text box. Click OK to open the file. Figure 12.7 shows the Open dialog box.

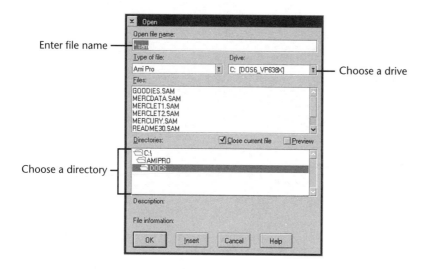

Enter file name

Choose a directory

Choose a drive

Fig. 12.7
Store the majority of your files in the default AMIPRO\DOCS directory.

By default, Ami Pro stores your saved files in the AMIPRO\DOCS directory on your hard drive. Because all your files are automatically stored in this directory, Ami Pro accesses the same directory when you choose to open a file, making it easier to keep track of your files.

Closing a Document

To close the current Ami Pro document when you're finished working on it, you can do any of the following:

- Choose **F**ile, **C**lose.

- Choose **C**lose from the document's Control menu box (see fig. 12.8).

- Press Ctrl+F4.

- Click the Close document window SmartIcon.

Closing your document before exiting the program allows Ami Pro to make sure all files are in their proper order and saved.

If changes have been made to your document since the last time you saved, Ami Pro prompts you to save your document. Choose **Y**es to save, **N**o to close the document without saving the changes, or Cancel to return to the document without closing.

Tip
You can also close your document by double-clicking the Control menu box.

III

Using Ami Pro

Document Control menu

Application Control menu

Fig. 12.8
Close the document using the document's Control menu.

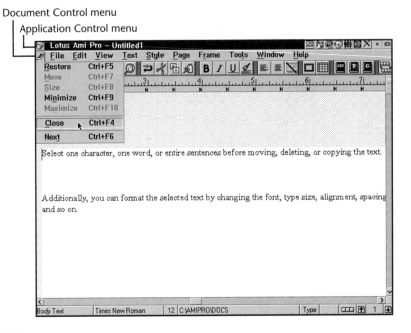

Creating a New Document

You can create a new document in Ami Pro after closing the current document or while other documents remain open, so you can switch between documents. After creating a new document, you can enter text and save it with your other documents.

To begin a new document, choose **F**ile, **N**ew to open the New dialog box. You can also click the New SmartIcon. Figure 12.9 shows the New dialog box with some of the available *style sheets*.

▶ See "Understanding Ami Pro Styles," p. 335

A style sheet is a template, or base, that Ami Pro applies to the new document. Each style sheet contains specific typefaces and sizes, page margins, columns, and other formatting choices that create a look for your document. Some of the available style sheets include fax cover sheets, memos, newsletters, reports, and so on. The DEFAULT.STY is a general style sheet on which Ami Pro bases all documents unless you choose another in the New dialog box. The default style sheet includes nine standard paragraph styles and uses the Times New Roman font.

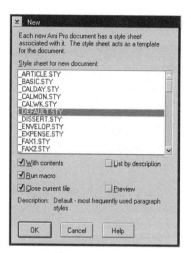

Fig. 12.9
Create a new
document
based on the
DEFAULT.STY
style sheet.

Troubleshooting

Drag-and-drop is hard to do with the mouse.

Using drag-and-drop takes practice. Load a sample document and spend some time moving text around the page. If preferred, you can disable the drag-and-drop feature. Turn to Chapter 18, "Customizing Ami Pro and Other Features," for more information.

After opening a document, I received a message saying the file was already open and I couldn't save changes. The title bar said Read-Only.

Ami Pro allows you to have multiple files open at one time, and you have the same document open twice. Choose **W**indow from the menu bar to see a list of all open documents. Close your read-only version, and switch to the original one. Or your Ami Pro file could have the read-only attribute selected. See Chapter 15 to learn how to use the Ami Pro File Manager to change this attribute.

From Here...

In this chapter, you learned how to enter and edit text in an Ami Pro document. You also became familiar with creating, saving, opening, and closing documents.

III

Using Ami Pro

For more information about working with Ami Pro, see the following chapters:

- Chapter 13, "Formatting Text and Documents," discusses changing typeface and size, setting tabs and margins, using paragraph attributes, creating headers and footers, and numbering pages.

- Chapter 14, "Proofing and Printing Documents," teaches you to use the Ami Pro spell checker, grammar checker, and thesaurus, and how to print your document and envelopes.

- Chapter 18, "Customizing Ami Pro and Other Features," covers using various views, changing defaults and other options, and comparing various versions of a document.

Chapter 13

Formatting Text and Documents

by Sue Plumley

Ami Pro's formatting features let you easily create professional documents that attract attention, are easy to read, and impress your customers and co-workers. Using these formatting features, you can change fonts and type sizes, align text, add headers and footers, and adjust margins with a click of the mouse. Ami Pro's advanced word processing features give you desktop publishing flexibility.

This chapter discusses formatting your document. You'll become familiar with changing the way your text and paragraphs look by adding various character, paragraph, and page attributes. You'll also learn how to add headers, footers, and page numbers to your Ami Pro document.

In this chapter, you learn how to:

- Change character font and size
- Change font attributes
- Use fast formatting
- Set margins and tabs
- Customize text spacing and alignment
- Create headers and footers
- Add page numbers

Changing Character Attributes

▶ See "Under-
standing Ami
Pro Styles,"
p. 335

The easiest way to modify your document design is to change character attributes. *Character attributes* are user-defined characteristics that control the
way the text appears on-screen. In Ami Pro, you can choose among several
character attributes, including font, text size, and capitalization.

To change character attributes of text already entered, you first select the text
you want to modify and then change its attributes. You can also set character
attributes before you begin entering the text.

Changing the Font

Ami Pro supplies many fonts, or typefaces, you can use in your documents.
Font refers to the way the text looks. The Times Roman font, for example,
consists of thick and thin strokes with serifs on the ends; whereas Arial has
even strokes with no serifs (see fig. 13.1).

Fig. 13.1
Serif fonts are
easier to read as
body text whereas
sans serif fonts are
great for headlines
and subheads.

> **Note**
>
> A *serif* is a small cross stroke at the end of some fonts. A font with a serif is perfect for
> body text because serifs guide your eye along the line of text, making it easier to
> read.

Tip
Although you can
use many differ-
ent fonts within
one document,
limit the number
of typefaces to
two or three so
your document
will look profes-
sional and be easy
to read.

As mentioned, serifed fonts like Times Roman work well as body text. *Sans-
serif*, or no serif fonts are good for headings and subheadings, figure captions,
and other short phrases of text. With Ami Pro you can mix and match as
many fonts as you want in your document.

> **Note**
>
> The fonts available to you depend on your printer. If your printer is able to form a
> font in your document, the font will display in Ami Pro's available font list.

To change your font, choose **T**ext, **F**ont to display the Font dialog box (see
fig. 13.2). Scroll through the **F**ace listbox to find the desired font.

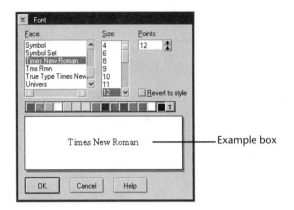

Fig. 13.2
Use the Font
dialog box to select
a typeface for the
text.

At the bottom of the Font dialog box, Ami Pro shows how the selected font
will look on-screen. When you have selected a typeface, choose OK to close
the dialog box.

You can also change the font from the Ami Pro status bar at the bottom of
the screen. After selecting the text, click the font name in the status bar to
display a pop-up list of the available fonts (see fig. 13.3). After you select the
font from the pop-up list, the list closes and the selected text changes.

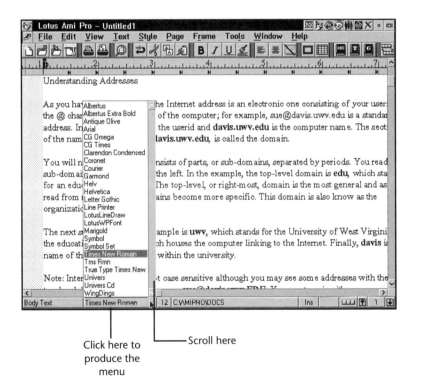

Fig. 13.3
To select a font
quickly, click the
status bar and
choose one from
the list.

III

Using Ami Pro

Adjusting Text Size

Adjusting the size of your text goes hand in hand with changing the font. You may want to reduce the font size to squeeze extra text onto the page or enlarge a few words to create a title for your document.

Font size is measured in points. In Ami Pro, you can vary your font sizes from 1 to 999 points; however, sizes less than 8-point are very difficult to read and sizes over 72-point aren't practical on standard paper sizes. For easy-to-read text, make the body text between 9- and 12-point and headings 14-, 18-, or 24-point.

To change the font size in Ami Pro, choose **T**ext, **F**ont to bring up the Font dialog box. You can select any of the preset font sizes in the **S**ize list or enter your own point size in the **P**oints box. The selected size is shown in the sample box. Choose OK to accept the change.

At the bottom of the dialog box, Ami Pro shows how the selected text will look on-screen (refer to fig. 13.2).

You can also change text size from the Ami Pro status bar. Click the current text size shown on the status bar to display a list of 19 text sizes, ranging from 4 to 72, that you can use for your text.

Changing the Font Attribute

You can customize your text in many ways besides changing the font and size. You can add bold, italic, and underline attributes to make text stand out or to set off a word or phrase.

Boldfacing text makes the lines of your letters slightly thicker and darker. *Italicizing* adds a slight slant to your selected text. Underlining draws a straight line below the selected characters and word underlining underlines only characters, not spaces. You can return your text to standard formatting by choosing the **N**ormal option in the **T**ext menu or by selecting the bold, italic, or underline option a second time, either select the icon or choose the option in the **T**ext menu.

By changing the font style, you are changing a design characteristic to set that text apart. The following table explains how to change your font style.

SmartIcon	Style	Menu	Command	Keyboard Command
B	Bold	**T**ext	**B**old	Ctrl+B
I	Italic	**T**ext	**I**talic	Ctrl+I
U	Underline	**T**ext	**U**nderline	Ctrl+U
U	Word underline	**T**ext	**W**ord Underline	Ctrl+W
N	Normal text	**T**ext	**N**ormal	Ctrl+N

Using Advanced Font Attributes

Along with boldface and italics, several other font attributes can be used to change the font style in your document. These advanced features give you the ability to completely customize the text in your document.

Commonly used in footnotes, *superscript* style changes your selected text to 7/12 of the original font size and places the text above the surrounding words. *Subscript* style is similar, except that it places the reduced text below the surrounding words. Subscripting is common in chemical equations (H_2O).

The double underline and strikethrough features are common in document editing and revision marking. By using these features, you can track editing changes. <u>Double underlining</u> places two lines below selected text; ~~strikethrough~~ places a line through the selected text. In addition to regular strikethrough, you can select a specific character to be used to overwrite your text.

To access these features, choose **T**ext, Special **E**ffects. From the Special Effects dialog box, you can select your advanced font style and click OK for your changes to take effect (see fig. 13.4).

Fig. 13.4

Choose an attribute to apply to selected text or text you are about to enter.

III

Using Ami Pro

As with other font formatting, you can apply attributes to selected text or you can make the attribute change before you type the text.

Changing Capitalization

Ami Pro lets you change the case of selected text, converting from upper- to lowercase or from uppercase to small caps, for example. This feature is especially useful if you accidentally left the Caps Lock on as you typed. Instead of deleting the text and entering it again, use the Caps feature in Ami Pro. Using uppercase or small caps to emphasize a word or phrase attracts attention to the text.

To change the case of your text, select the text you want to change, and choose **Text**, **Caps**. A cascading menu appears (see fig. 13.5). You can also select a case attribute first and then type your text in the document instead.

Fig. 13.5
Select the case attribute from the cascading menu.

Click here to display case options

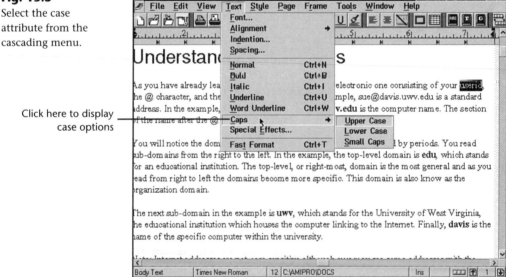

The Ami Pro **Text Caps** cascading menu offers you three options for case-formatting your documents. See Table 13.1 for examples of how your text will appear using the various capitalization options.

Table 13.1	Text Capitalization
Option	**Example**
Upper Case	THE QUICK BROWN FOX
Lower Case	the quick brown fox
Small Caps	THE QUICK BROWN FOX

Using Fast Formatting

You can use Fast Formatting to copy the format of one section of text to another text section. You can also copy formatting between documents. For example, if you have one heading in 24-point Arial with small caps and you want to apply that formatting to other headings, you can use Fast Format to quickly apply the changes.

To Fast Format paragraph styles and text formats, follow these steps:

1. Select the text that has the style you want to copy.

2. Choose **T**ext, Fas**t** Format or press Ctrl+T to display the Fast Format pointer. Or, you can click the Fast Format SmartIcon.

3. Scroll to the text you want to apply the format to and select the text.

4. When you release the mouse button, the selected text changes. The format pointer remains so you can select and change the format of more text.

5. When you're finished formatting, choose **T**ext, Fas**t** Format, press Ctrl+T, or click the Fast Format SmartIcon to stop formatting. The Fast Format pointer changes back to an I-beam.

Troubleshooting

I want to cancel all my style changes and revert to the original text style.

Select the desired text and choose **T**ext, **N**ormal. Your text loses all attribute changes and reverts to the original style.

Every time I click the mouse, I Fast Format a paragraph accidentally.

Fast Formatting is still enabled. First, choose **E**dit, **U**ndo immediately to remove the Fast Formatting from the text you accidentally highlighted; then choose **T**ext, Fas**t** Format. The Fast Format pointer should change back to the regular mouse pointer.

Changing Paragraph Attributes

You can enhance the appearance of the text on the page using many of Ami Pro's paragraph features. The paragraph features enable you to format the text in your document by changing alignment, indents, tabs, and spacing. Paragraph formatting affects the readability of the text as well as the overall design, or look, of the page.

> **Note**
>
> Ami Pro defines a paragraph as a group of sentences, one sentence, one word, or even one character with a paragraph mark at the end. A paragraph can also consist of no characters, creating a blank line. A paragraph mark is inserted each time you press the Enter key.

You use alignment to define how a paragraph fits between the left and right margins: left-aligned, centered, right-aligned, or justified. Indenting the text or using tabs in the text adjusts the way the text fits between the margins. Finally, line and paragraph spacing affects how the text looks on the page.

> **Note**
>
> When you change text alignment, tabs, indention, spacing, or margins, you change the entire paragraph, not just selected text.

Changing Tabs and Indentions

The Ami Pro ruler is a powerful text-formatting tool. Using your mouse and the ruler, you can change tabs and margins quickly for a paragraph or for the entire document. Similarly, you create various common indents, hanging indents, or full text indentation. This section shows you how to control these paragraph formats from the ruler and from Ami Pro dialog boxes.

> **Note**
>
> Each paragraph of text has its own ruler and paragraph formatting. If you click within one paragraph and change the tabs or indents, those changes don't affect the paragraph before or after the designated text. If, however, you press Enter at the end of the designated paragraph, the ruler formatting applies to the next paragraph. You can also select several paragraphs or the entire document before using the ruler to format the text.

Accessing the Ruler

Before you can change your paragraph style, you must access your ruler. In Ami Pro, the ruler appears directly below the SmartIcon palette. You can toggle the ruler on and off at will without changing your document.

> **Note**
>
> You can toggle the horizontal ruler by clicking the Show/Hide Ruler SmartIcon. Notice that the SmartIcon changes when you activate and deactivate the on-screen ruler.

To activate the ruler with the menu, choose **V**iew, Show **R**uler. The activated ruler has the tools you use to create and edit tabs and indentions. To deactivate the ruler, choose **V**iew, Hide **R**uler.

Changing Tabs with the Ruler

When you press Tab, the insertion point automatically moves right to the next established tab stop. Tabs are commonly used for documents containing columnar information and indentations.

You can customize the Ami Pro tab stops with your ruler by first clicking the ruler to activate it. See figure 13.6 for an example of an active ruler.

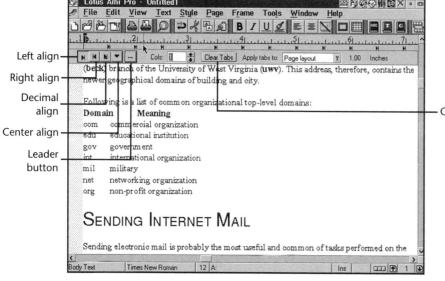

Fig. 13.6
To customize tab stops, first click the mouse anywhere on the ruler to activate it.

III

Using Ami Pro

To move a tab marker left or right, follow these steps:

1. Click anywhere on your Ami Pro ruler. A pop-up paragraph formatting bar appears (refer to fig. 13.6).

2. Drag the tab marker left or right to its new location. Notice that you can't move a tab past another existing tab stop.

Adding New Tabs

You can set four types of tabs: left-aligned, right-aligned, numeric (decimal-aligned), and centered. The following table describes the four types of tabs.

Tab Type	Description
Left	Aligns the text flush along the left edge
Right	Aligns text flush along the right edge
Numeric	Aligns text by the numeric separator (decimal point) at the tab stop
Center	Centers text to the left and right of the tab

To create a new tab, first ensure that the insertion point is in the paragraph you want to work with. Display the ruler using the **V**iew, Show **R**uler command and click anywhere in the ruler to activate the pop-up paragraph formatting bar. Next, click the type of tab you want to create. Click the ruler at the location you want the new tab marker and a new tab stop appears. You can drag the tab marker to the left or right to adjust the tab, if necessary.

Additionally, you can apply a leader to the tab by clicking the leader button before you click the ruler. A *leader* is a visual separator—such as a line of dots—added between tabs. The leader button cycles from dashed, to dot, to underline, to no leader. Each time you click the leader button, the type of leader appears above the tab alignment button.

Deleting Tabs

You may want to remove all the tabs on the ruler to start from scratch or you may only want to remove one or two tab markers from the ruler. To remove all tabs, click the Clear Tabs button in the ruler. All tab marks for that paragraph are deleted.

To remove one tab, simply click and drag the tab marker above or below the Tab & Indention area (see fig. 13.7). The tab marker disappears. Alternatively, you can click the tab marker and then press the Delete key.

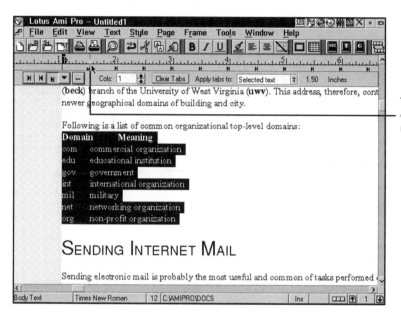

Fig. 13.7
Drag the tab down and off the ruler to delete it.

Tab stop to be dragged off the ruler

Using Indents

Indents give you the flexibility to define where your text is placed within the left and right page margins. By using the Indention dialog box or the ruler, you can create standard, hanging, or complete paragraph indention.

Using the Indention Dialog Box

You can access the Indention dialog box by choosing **T**ext, In**d**entions (see fig. 13.8).

The following table describes the four indention options.

Table 13.2 Indention Options	
Option	**Effect**
All	Indents all lines of the selected text by a specified value
First	Indents only the first line of text by a specified value

(continues)

III

Using Ami Pro

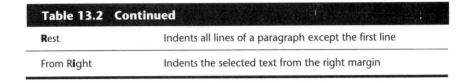

Table 13.2 Continued	
Rest	Indents all lines of a paragraph except the first line
From **R**ight	Indents the selected text from the right margin

Fig. 13.8

Select the text, then indent it using the Indention dialog box.

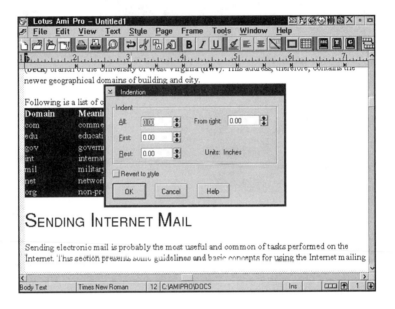

Changing Indents with the Ruler

You can also change Ami Pro indents with the ruler. Notice the two triangles on the left side of the ruler. Using these triangles, you can change the indention of your document with the mouse. The top triangle changes the first line of text; the bottom triangle indents the rest of the paragraph.

The Indention bar appears to the left of the indentation triangles. This bar controls paragraph indentations for every line in the paragraph. Figure 13.9 shows the indention markers.

You can drag all three of these elements, together or separately, on the ruler.

Left margin indicator —
Left indention bar
First line indicator
Rest indicator

Fig. 13.9
Adjust indents
quickly and easily
using the ruler.

First, click the Ami Pro ruler to activate the pop-up paragraph formatting bar; then drag the desired symbol to drag your indents left or right. Not only are the right indention bars and arrows similar to the left; they also work the same way.

Adjusting Alignment

Text alignment also enables you to adjust the way the text appears between the left and right margins. In Ami Pro, you can left-align, right-align, justify, or center your text.

Text alignment enhances the overall appearance of your document by controlling how your text flows and how readable it is. Centering headings and justifying paragraph text, for example, gives a professional appearance to your document and allows more text per page. However, justified text creates a fuller, grayer page that can sometimes be hard to read. Left-aligned headings and paragraph text, on the other hand, create a lighter and more informal page design but don't allow you to fit as much text on the page.

Click these SmartIcons to change text alignment:

To change the text alignment, follow these steps:

1. Place the insertion point in the paragraph in which you want to change the alignment. You can also select multiple paragraphs or click where you want the alignment to begin.

2. Choose **T**ext, **A**lignment and a cascading menu appears. Choose **L**eft (Ctrl+L), **C**enter (Ctrl+C), **R**ight (Ctrl+R), or **J**ustify (Ctrl+J).

   Alternatively, choose one of the text alignment icons.

3. To remove alignment, choose **T**ext, **A**lignment and then choose the alignment with the checkmark next to it.

III

Using Ami Pro

Note

You can also use the keyboard shortcuts: Ctrl+C for **C**enter, Ctrl+L for **L**eft, Ctrl+R for **R**ight, or Ctrl+J for **J**ustify.

Adjusting Spacing

Spacing controls how far apart the text lines are vertically. You may want to change the line spacing, also called *leading*, to make your document easier to read or to place more information on a page.

You have four spacing options in Ami Pro. Single spacing places lines of text directly below one another without any extra spaces between them. Single spacing fits the most text on a page and is the most commonly used line spacing. Double spacing places a space equivalent to the text size between each line. One and a half-line spacing puts a space one and one-half of the text size between your document lines.

If you don't want to use the built-in spacing options, Ami Pro permits you to custom-select the distance between your text lines.

To change the spacing of your document, first select the text you want to modify. Like alignment options, spacing options change an entire paragraph, no matter how much is selected.

After selecting text, choose **T**ext, **S**pacing. The Spacing dialog box appears (see fig. 13.10). Choose the spacing option you want to use. If you want to use custom spacing, scroll through the **C**ustom listbox or type a number in the **C**ustom text box. You can change the measuring unit from inches to centimeters, picas, or points. Click OK to apply the spacing.

Fig. 13.10
Choose the line spacing you want to apply to the selected text.

To remove any spacing specifications and change the text back to the original paragraph style, choose the **R**evert to Style option in the Spacing dialog box and click OK.

Troubleshooting

I accidentally deleted a tab marker from my ruler.

Choose the **E**dit, **U**ndo command to undo your tab deletion and place it back on your ruler.

I can't move a tab marker past an existing one.

Ami Pro won't allow you to drag a tab marker past an existing marker. Instead, you have to delete the blocking marker and drag your tab marker to the desired position.

I can't left-align and right-align two pieces of text in the same line.

Ami Pro permits only one alignment setting per line. You can, however, use multiple tabs to accomplish this goal. Set a left tab on the left side of the page and a right tab on the right side. This method enables you to emulate two alignment settings in a line.

Every time I move an indention marker, I create a tab instead.

Moving indentions with the mouse takes practice. Be patient. Often, you accidentally create tabs instead of dragging your indentation tools.

Formatting the Page

You can use page formatting to make significant design changes in your entire document in just a few seconds. Page formatting includes changing page orientation and paper size, adjusting margins, dividing the text into columns, adding headers and/or footers, and numbering your pages.

Page formatting can change the entire document or only a page or two. You can, for example, create headers for some pages and not for others; or you can display one page in portrait orientation (vertically) and another in landscape (horizontally).

When formatting the page, it's easier and often required that you change views to page layout mode. To do this, choose **V**iew, **L**ayout Mode if it isn't already selected. Layout mode is selected if a checkmark appears in front of the option on the menu.

Changing Margins and Columns

▶ See "Changing Display Modes," p. 328

Margins and columns serve to divide and organize the text on the page. You can choose Ami Pro's defaults or you can set your own measurements for these two items.

A *margin* is the blank area—or white space—around the page that borders the text. Margins balance the gray of the text area with white, making the text easier on the eye. The default Ami Pro margins are 1-inch on the top, bottom, left, and right. You can change these margins in the Page Layout dialog box.

Tip

Always use at least 1/4 inch margins in a document; even more margin is better for the eyes and makes the document easier to read.

Columns divide the page and organize the text. Ami Pro's default is one column; however, you can choose to have multiple columns of text in your Ami Pro document. You can have up to eight separate columns on a page. Multiple columns are useful for creating newsletters and reports.

To change page margins, follow these steps:

1. Choose **P**age, **M**odify Page Layout to display the Modify Page Layout dialog box (see fig. 13.11). Or, you can right-click the mouse in the page margin to get the same results.

2. Click the Margins tab if it isn't already displayed.

Fig. 13.11
Use the Modify Page Layout dialog box to change page margins.

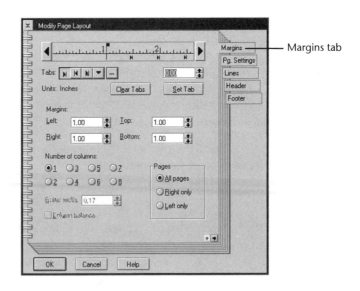

Margins tab

Tip

For maximum readability, never use more than three columns on a portrait-oriented page or four columns on a landscape-oriented page.

3. In the Margins area, click the arrows beside each margin text box or enter a value in the text boxes; the values are measured in inches, by default.

4. Click OK to accept the changes and close the dialog box.

Caution

With most laser printers, if the margin is set to less than .25 inches, the text will probably not print in that area due to the built-in no print zone.

Note

You can also choose which pages the margin changes affect if your document contains more than one page. In the Pages area, **A**ll Pages is the default. Choose **R**ight or **L**eft Only if you want to change only the margins on those pages.

To change the number of columns in your document, follow these steps:

1. Choose **P**age, **M**odify Page Layout to display the Modify Page Layout dialog box (refer to fig. 13.11); alternatively, right-click the page margin.

2. Click the Margins tab if it isn't already selected.

3. Select the number of columns you want in your Ami Pro document from the Number of Columns radio buttons.

4. Enter the gutter width (the distance between columns) in the **G**utter Width listbox.

Tip
Set the Gutter width for at least .25-inch for easier readability of columnar text.

Note

Select the **C**olumn Balance checkbox if you want Ami Pro to automatically balance your multiple columns horizontally.

5. Click the OK button. The number of columns change in your Ami Pro document.

Setting Page Options

You can change the orientation and page size of your Ami Pro document. Most printers support both landscape (horizontal) and portrait (vertical) printing orientation.

III

Using Ami Pro

You also can choose six page sizes: letter, legal, A3, A4, A5, and B5 (the default size is letter, which uses 8 1/2-by-11-inch paper). In addition, you can create your own paper size. You may want to consult your printer setup to ensure that you're using the paper size specified for your printer. Check your printer documentation if you're unsure about which paper sizes you can print.

You change your orientation and paper size in the Modify Page Layout dialog box. Choose **P**age, **M**odify Page Layout. Click the Pg Settings tab to display the page size and orientation (see fig. 13.12). Table 13.3 shows the page sizes that correspond with the option buttons in the Page Size area of the Modify Page Layout dialog box.

Table 13.3 Option Buttons and Their Page Sizes	
Button Name	**Page Size**
A**4**	8.27 x 11.69
A**5**	5.83 x 8.27
A**3**	11.69 x 16.53
B5	6.93 x 9.84

Fig. 13.12
Changing page size and orientation changes all pages in your document.

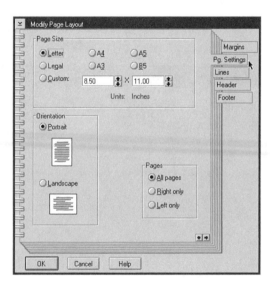

To change page size, click the appropriate option in the Page Size area. If you choose **C**ustom, you can enter your own sizes in the text boxes. To change the page orientation, click the appropriate button in the Orientation section of the dialog box. Choose OK to close the dialog box and apply the changes.

Adding Headers and Footers

Text strings that appear in the page margins are called *headers* and *footers*. Headers are located at the top of the page and footers at the bottom. Typically, headers and footers include page numbers, dates, names, and/or titles. They also can include tables, pictures, lines, and so on.

You enter the text for a header or footer one time and the header or footer appears on every page of your document. Alternatively, you can specify different header or footer text on some pages or no header or footer at all.

To create a header or footer, follow these steps:

1. Choose **P**age, **M**odify Page Layout.

2. Click either the Header or Footer tab in the Modify Page Layout dialog box; the dialog boxes for both tabs look the same. Figure 13.13 shows the Header tab.

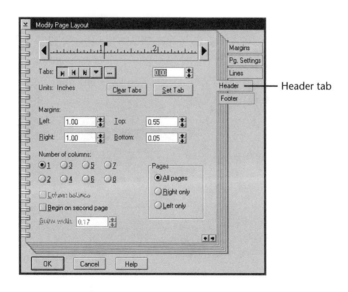

Fig. 13.13

Set margins and other options for the header in the Modify Page Layout dialog box.

III

3. As with the page options, enter the margins, tabs, and column numbers you want for the header or footer and choose OK to close the dialog box.

4. Click in the top page margin for a header or in the bottom page margin for a footer. The blinking cursor appears in the margin.

> **Note**
>
> If you don't see the page margins, choose **V**iew, **L**ayout Mode and try again.

5. Type the text you want to appear in the header or footer.

6. Click somewhere else in the Ami Pro document to stop editing your header or footer.

You can also select the text in the header or footer and format it as you would any text in Ami Pro.

Numbering Pages

Numbering the pages in your document helps you organize the document and refer to the pages as a reference. Ami Pro supports multiple page numbering by placing the page number in the header or footer.

To create page numbering for your entire document, change to layout mode and follow these steps:

1. Position the insertion point in the header or footer at the point you want to insert the page number.

2. Choose **P**age, **P**age Numbering. The Page Numbering dialog box appears (see fig. 13.14).

Fig. 13.14
Set the page number and leading text in the Page Numbering dialog box.

3. In the **S**tyle listbox, select the type of number or letter you want to use in the page number.

4. Click Start on **P**age and enter the page you want to start on if that page is other than the first in your document. Enter the page number that appears in the Page Status button on the status bar.

5. Click Start with **N**umber (if you don't want to begin numbering with number 1) and enter the first page number.

6. Type any text you want to have appear with the page number in the **L**eading Text box.

7. Click OK.

> **Note**
>
> If the insertion point isn't in a header or footer when you choose the **P**age Numbering command, Ami Pro places a number only on the current page at the current insertion point location. If this isn't what you want, choose **U**ndo and try again.

From Here...

This chapter showed you how to change your text font and style, adjust tabs and indents, change paragraph alignment and spacing, add headers and footers, and number your pages. For more information on using Ami Pro to create documents, refer to these chapters:

■ Chapter 12, "Creating and Editing Documents," covers initial text editing and saving your documents for future use.

■ Chapter 16, "Changing Views and Creating Outlines, Styles, and Revisions," covers document revision, editing and creating large documents, and using outlines.

■ Chapter 17, "Working with Frames, Tables, and Charts," discusses adding graphics to your Ami Pro documents and creating tables.

III

Using Ami Pro

Chapter 14

Proofing and Printing Documents

by Sue Plumley

You can use Ami Pro commands for proofreading and printing your document. Ami Pro's Spell Checker, Thesaurus, and Grammar Checker make it easy for you to proofread and fix mistakes in your document.

The Ami Pro dictionary contains more than 115,000 known words, allowing the spell checker to catch many spelling mistakes. The ability to add new words to your customized dictionary helps refine and tailor the Spell Checker's capabilities. The Thesaurus offers word definitions and synonyms as well as related words and antonyms. The Grammar Checker examines your document and identifies grammatical inconsistencies ranging from clichés to split infinitives.

Finally, when you finish editing and proofreading, you can print your finished product. Ami Pro supports thousands of printers for document and envelope printing. You can print your entire document immediately or choose specific print options.

In this chapter, you learn how to:

- Check your spelling
- Use the Thesaurus
- Check your grammar
- Print a document
- Print an envelope

Correcting Spelling Mistakes

Spelling mistakes are easy-to-correct errors that can be embarrassing when ignored. With Ami Pro's massive built-in dictionary, checking your spelling is quick and easy.

When you begin your spell check, Ami Pro immediately starts searching for words that aren't in its dictionary. When the program finds one, a dialog box appears, displaying other words that are similarly spelled. You can type a change, select an alternative word, ignore the word, or add the word to the custom dictionary. You also can have Ami Pro automatically fix other occurrences of the same misspelled word throughout the document.

Running a Spell Check

When Ami Pro checks the spelling in a document, it not only checks the body of the document but it can check other text streams as well. *Text streams* include tables, frames, charts, and other graphics within your document. Spell checking can be initiated in either of two ways: with the menu or with a SmartIcon.

 You can run a spell check by choosing the Tools, **S**pell Check command or by clicking the Spell Check SmartIcon to bring up the Spell Check startup dialog box (see fig. 14.1). Choose the **C**heck from Beginning of Document option if you want to start spell checking from the top of the first page; otherwise, Ami Pro checks only the text after the current insertion point location.

Fig. 14.1
Choose to check the spelling from the beginning of the document.

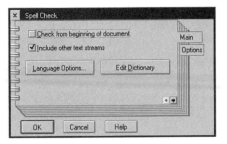

Tip
To spell check only a single word or paragraph, select the text and then run the spell checker.

The **I**nclude Other Text Streams option is selected by default. This option spell checks not only the text in graphics but the text contained in headers, footers, and footnotes.

Click the OK button and Ami Pro begins the spell check. When the program locates a word not contained in the dictionary, the Spell Check dialog box appears (see fig. 14.2). Ami Pro positions the Spell Check dialog box so you can read the sentence in your document that contains the questionable word.

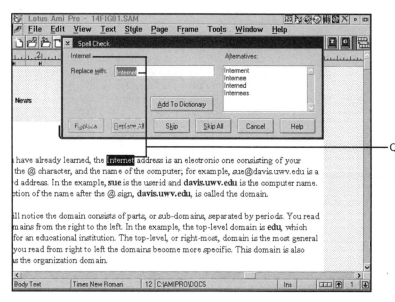

Fig. 14.2
The Spell Check dialog box alerts you to a word not found in Ami Pro's dictionary.

Questionable word

The questionable word appears at the top of the dialog box and in the Replace **W**ith text box. You can click the mouse in the Replace **W**ith text box and correct the word, or you can choose an alternative word.

The **A**lternatives list contains words that are similar to the unknown word. Click one of the alternative spellings and that word appears in the Replace **W**ith text box.

If the questionable word is correctly spelled, you can instruct Ami Pro to S**k**ip the word or add it to the dictionary so it won't be questioned again.

Table 14.1 describes the six options you can choose when Ami Pro locates an unknown word in your document.

Table 14.1	Spelling Options
Option	**Effect**
R**e**place	Substitutes the misspelled word with the word in the Replace **W**ith text box

(continues)

III

Using Ami Pro

Table 14.1 Continued	
Option	**Effect**
Replace All	Similar to **R**eplace, except that it changes all occurrences of the misspelled word in the document with the word in the Replace **W**ith text box
S**k**ip	Ignores this one occurrence of the questionable word and moves on to the next misspelled word
Skip All	Ignores all occurrences of this word for the remainder of the spell check
Add To Dictionary	Adds the current word to the dictionary so Ami Pro will recognize the word in future spell checks
Cancel	Ends the spell check

Tip
Save the document before spell checking in case you accidentally replace all occurrences of a misspelled word with the wrong spelling. That way, you can revert to the saved file and try again.

> **Caution**
>
> When you choose **R**eplace All, Ami Pro automatically makes that correction throughout the entire document without prompting you. Be careful, because in some contexts, you may not want that correction made.

Using Spell Check Options

Ami Pro has several spell check options that enable you to search for or ignore several types of words. To access these options, choose the Too**l**s, **S**pell Check command, then click the Options tab to display the spell check options (see fig. 14.3).

Fig. 14.3
Choose various options that govern spell checking.

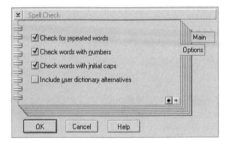

The following table describes the spell check options.

Table 14.2 Spell Check Options	
Option	**Effect**
Check for **R**epeated Words	Checks for words that appear twice in succession
Check Words with **N**umbers	Checks for any text that contains numbers (for example, FILE04)
Check Words with **I**nitial Caps	Checks for words that begin with a capital letter
Include **U**ser Dictionary Alternatives	Uses your customized dictionary to list words in the **A**lternatives list when a misspelled word is located

Using Custom Dictionary and Language Options

Two additional options are available in the Spell Check dialog box (refer to fig. 14.1). The **L**anguage and Edit **D**ictionary options give you further control of your Ami Pro dictionaries.

If you have a foreign-language dictionary installed, click the **L**anguage Options button to choose a dictionary to spell check your files. The Spell Check Language Options dialog box appears (see fig. 14.4). You can select which dictionary Ami Pro will use to spell check the current document from the list of installed dictionaries. You can also choose a default language dictionary.

The Edit **D**ictionary option opens your custom Ami Pro dictionary document file. Whenever you decide to add a word to the dictionary while running a spell check, that word is added to this file. The Edit **D**ictionary option lets you add new words to your custom dictionary before running a spell check, or to remove a word that you added accidentally.

> **Tip**
> Add technical terms and jargon particular to your job to the custom dictionary file; add your name, city, and customer's names to the file as well.

Fig. 14.4

You can choose from different language dictionaries to use for the spell check.

III

Using Ami Pro

When you finish modifying your personal dictionary, save and close the document to return to your original document.

Using Proper Grammar

Although Ami Pro's spelling dictionary is large, the spell checker doesn't catch usage errors. For example, if you meant to use the word principal instead of principle, the Ami Pro spell check won't notify you of the mistake. Fortunately, Ami Pro has a grammar checker that identifies and corrects text problems, using nearly 45 grammatical and style rules of the English language.

Using the grammar checker, you can identify many common and advanced grammatical inconsistencies within your document. For example, Ami Pro cites passive sentences and indicates when you used too many nouns or prepositions in a row.

Ami Pro can check your document for different grammatical styles; for example, although cliché phrases may not be appropriate when you're writing a report, they are acceptable when you are creating a casual letter to a friend. You can set Ami Pro to apply different grammatical rules in specific situations.

Selecting Your Preferences

To begin a grammar check, choose the Tools, Grammar Check command or click the corresponding SmartIcon. The Grammar Check dialog box appears (see fig. 14.5).

Fig. 14.5
Set the grammar checking options before checking the document.

In this dialog box, you can select the grammar check style and options, and set your preferences. Table 14.3 lists the Preferences options and their functions.

Table 14.3 Grammar Check Options	
Preference	**Effect**
Use Grammar and Style Set	Displays a list of grammar styles to choose from including Legal Writing, Technical Writing, Fiction, and so on
Show Readability **S**tatistics	Displays statistical information at the end of the grammar check, including word count, readability score, and passive verb use
Show **E**xplanations	Explains the rules and provides correct examples for each grammatical error
Check from **B**eginning of Document	Automatically begins the grammar check from the beginning of the document, no matter where the insertion point is located
Include Other Text Streams	Checks secondary streams of text in your document for grammatical errors

Ami Pro remembers the preferences that you set and saves them as default grammar check settings.

Running a Grammar Check

After choosing your preferences, click OK to begin the grammar check.

When Grammar Checker finds a sentence that contains a possible grammatical inconsistency, Ami Pro selects the sentence and displays the Grammar Checker dialog box (see fig. 14.6). The dialog box contains a detailed description of the grammar rule cited in the **S**uggestions list. You can edit your document directly or click one of the buttons in the dialog box.

Table 14.4 describes the items and buttons in the Grammar Checker dialog box.

Table 14.4 Grammar Checker Options	
Option	**Description**
Suggestions	Lists the identified problem and an explanation of the problem
Replacement **O**ptions	Highlights the problem area
S**k**ip	Ignores the grammar rule for this sentence

(continues)

III

Using Ami Pro

Table 14.4 Continued	
Option	**Description**
Skip **R**ule	Ignores this rule for the entire grammar check
Next Sentence	Skips all grammar rules for this sentence and continues the grammar check
Replace	Substitutes the highlighted sentence with one of the options in the **S**uggestions list, if Ami Pro provides a grammatical alternative (only for some grammar rules)
Cancel	Ends the grammar check

Fig. 14.6

The Grammar Checker locates a possible problem and displays the sentence in the dialog box.

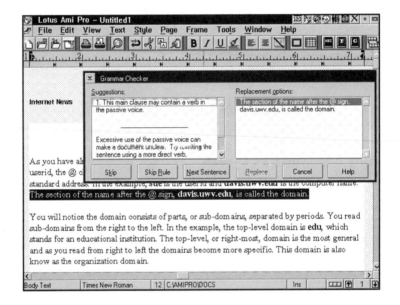

Setting Grammar Options

You can set specific options for the grammar checker including individual grammar rules, style rules, and word order rules for each style set you use. Additionally, you can save the settings to use again and again.

To change grammar options, choose the **O**ptions button in the Grammar Check dialog box. The Grammar and Style Options dialog box appears (see fig. 14.7).

Ami Pro supplies three tabs in the Grammar and Style Options dialog box: Grammar Rules, Style Rules, and Word Order Rules. In any of the three tabs you can choose which style set you want to customize in the **G**rammar and

Style Set list. Next, you select the rules you want to include in the check and those you want to ignore. Choose **S**ave to save the options for future grammar checks.

Fig. 14.7
Set specific rules for the grammar checker to use.

Note

You can create your own **G**rammar and Style Set by choosing the rules and then selecting the Save **A**s button in the Grammar and Style Options dialog box. The Save Set Name dialog box appears and you enter a new name for the set; then choose that set to check your grammar at any time.

Tip
To use every grammar rule that Ami Pro knows, choose the **A**ll Rules option in the **G**rammar and Style Set drop-down list in any tab in the Grammar and Style Options dialog box.

Finding a New Word with the Thesaurus

You no longer need to keep a thesaurus near your desk. Ami Pro can look up and define thousands of words at the click of your mouse.

Whether you need a synonym, definition, or you want to check a variation of meaning, simply select the word and start the Ami Pro Thesaurus. Ami Pro presents a list of options, from which you can choose an alternative.

To use the thesaurus, follow these steps:

1. Select the word you want to find an alternative for.

2. Choose Tools, Thesaurus or click the Thesaurus SmartIcon to access the Thesaurus dialog box.

3. Scroll through the Meaning Variations list. As you highlight a word, the definition of that word appears in the Meaning area of the dialog box (see fig. 14.8).

Fig. 14.8
Find a synonym or definition with the thesaurus.

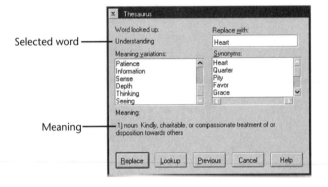

4. Choose a Meaning Variation, if applicable.

5. Scroll through the Synonyms listbox to find words that are similar to the selected word.

6. Select the word you want to use, and click the Replace button. Click Cancel to close the dialog box. If no word seems right, click Cancel to exit the Thesaurus dialog box.

Tip
If you choose the thesaurus when your insertion point is in or next to a word, the thesaurus looks up that word.

Note

You can click the Lookup button to search for synonyms of any word in the Synonym listbox. The Previous button returns you to the previous looked-up word.

Troubleshooting

I accidentally added a misspelled word to my personal dictionary.

You can modify your custom dictionary by clicking the Edit Dictionary button in the Spell Check startup dialog box. Ami Pro accesses your custom dictionary file, in which you can add and delete words.

Ami Pro is running spelling and grammar checks only in sections of my document.

Ensure that the **I**nclude Other Text Streams option is selected in the Spell Check and Grammar Check dialog boxes.

Printing Your Documents

When your document is edited and proofread, you're ready to print it. You can print your documents and envelopes with any printer that OS/2 supports. For more information, open the Information icon on the OS/2 desktop, choose Master Help Index, and look up "Printing in OS/2."

When printing, you have many options from which to choose, including number of copies, page range, and printer. Additionally, you can choose various setup options to govern the printing of each document.

Often, you print a document, such as a letter, that you need an envelope for. Ami Pro makes printing envelopes quick and easy by enabling you to save a return address and select the recipient's address in the document to use in the envelope.

◀ See "Printing Files," p. 64

Printing a Document

To print your document, follow these steps:

1. Choose **F**ile, **P**rint. The Print dialog box appears (see fig. 14.9). Alternatively, click the Print SmartIcon to display the Print dialog box.

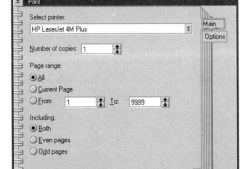

Fig. 14.9
Open the Print dialog box and choose the appropriate options to print your document.

III

Using Ami Pro

2. Verify that the printer you want to use is listed in the Select Printer listbox.

> **Note**
>
> If the correct printer isn't listed, click the down arrow and choose the right printer.

3. Specify the number of copies you want to print by using the **N**umber of Copies text box.

4. Use the option buttons in the Page Range section to set the page range for your printout. You can choose **A**ll pages, the **C**urrent page, or a specific range. To set a specific range, enter the range you want in the **F**rom and **T**o text boxes.

5. Specify whether you want to print only the odd pages, only the even pages, or all pages by using the **E**ven Pages, O**d**d Pages, or **B**oth option buttons.

6. Click OK to send the job to the printer. Ami Pro displays a message box indicating the job is printing. If you should need to stop the print job, choose Cancel.

> **Note**
>
> You can choose to print in the background so you can continue your work. Choose Too**l**s **U**ser Setup, then choose the Options tab. Choose **P**rint in Background and choose OK.

Printing Envelopes

◄ See "Printing Files," p. 64

In addition to printing entire documents, Ami Pro also enables you to print envelopes. You can directly print addresses and return addresses onto several types of envelopes. Ami Pro will even remember your return address for future use.

 The first step in printing an envelope is to choose the **F**ile, Print En**v**elope command (or click the Print Envelope SmartIcon) to access the Print Envelopes dialog box (see fig. 14.10). Ami Pro first checks the current document for an address, such as that in a letter. If it finds an address in your document, it uses that address as the recipient's address when it prints the envelope.

Note

If your document contains multiple addresses, select the address you want to use as the recipient address and then choose **F**ile, Print En**v**elope. Ami Pro uses the selected address.

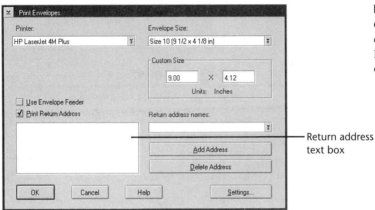

Return address text box

Fig. 14.10

Choose envelope options in the Print Envelopes dialog box.

From the Print Envelopes dialog box, select the options you want to use. If you want to enter a return address to be printed on your envelope, check the **P**rint Return Address checkbox and enter that address in the Return address text box. Table 14.5 describes the other options in the Print Envelopes dialog box.

Table 14.5 Print Envelope Options	
Option	**Description**
Printer	Specifies the selected printer to use to print envelopes; select another if you want text missing from the drop-down list
Envelope Size	Specifies which of the 11 default envelope sizes—or a custom size—is to be used
Custom Size	If you choose Custom as the envelope size, you can enter the size, in inches, in the Custom Size text boxes; otherwise, the selected envelope's size displays in the text box
Use Envelope Feeder	Feeds envelopes from a special envelope feeder to the printer; if you don't choose this option, you manually feed the envelopes

(continues)

III

Using Ami Pro

Table 14.5 Continued	
Option	**Description**
Print Return Address	Prints a return address on your envelope; if you previously saved a return address, you can select it from the Return Address Names listbox
Return address text box	Shows the return address to be printed
Return Address Names	Displays a list of saved return addresses
Add Address	Saves a new return address for future use
Delete Address	Deletes a saved return address

Choose OK. If Ami Pro didn't locate an address in your document, it prompts you with the Recipient's Address dialog box (see fig. 14.11).

> **Note**
>
> If you enter an address in the Recipient's Address dialog box, Ami Pro formats the address in a default style. However, if Ami Pro finds a formatted address in your document, it retains that formatting in the envelope address.

Fig. 14.11
Enter the recipient's address in the text box.

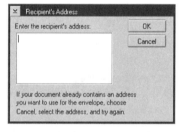

Enter the address and click OK. Ami Pro sends the job to the printer.

Changing the Default Printer

OS/2 supports multiple printer configurations. Ami Pro automatically selects the default printer when it's instructed to print a document or envelope. You can change the desired printer directly from Ami Pro.

To change your printer, follow these steps:

1. Choose **F**ile, Prin**t**er Setup to open the Select Printer dialog box shown in figure 14.12. This box lists all installed printers.

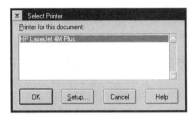

Fig. 14.12
Choose a printer
from the Select
Printer dialog box.

2. Select the printer that you want to use for this document.

3. Click OK.

> **Note**
>
> Click the **S**etup button to change printer setup options including paper source and orientation.

4. Choose **F**ile, **P**rint. The new printer's name now appears in the Print dialog box.

Troubleshooting

While Ami Pro is printing, entering and editing text seems to slow down.

Printing in the background slows all other activities until printing is complete. Disable the **P**rint in Background option by choosing Too**l**s, **User** Setup and clicking the option. Deactivating the **P**rint in Background option supplies you with faster overall printing and working.

I want to print crop marks and collate my printed copies.

You can choose those options and more in the Print dialog box. Choose the Options tab and the Print Options section appears. Choose to print in reverse order, to collate pages, print with crop marks, without pictures, or on a preprinted form.

I want to change some print setup items such as page orientation and resolution.

You'll find these options in the Print Setup dialog box; choose **F**ile, **P**rin**t**er Setup. In the Select Printer dialog box, choose **S**etup. You also can access this dialog box by choosing the Setup button in the Print dialog box.

III

Using Ami Pro

From Here...

This chapter introduced you to the Ami Pro proofreading features. You learned how to run spelling and grammar checks and how to use the thesaurus. In addition, this chapter demonstrated how to print documents and envelopes. For more information on using Ami Pro to compose documents, refer to these chapters:

■ Chapter 13, "Formatting Text and Documents," covers advanced text, paragraph, and page formatting; adding page numbers; and creating tabs and margins.

■ Chapter 18, "Customizing Ami Pro and Other Features," provides information on default style sheets, SmartIcons, and background printing.

■ Chapter 19, "Automating with Macros and Style Sheets," covers creating using Ami Pro's built-in macros, creating new macros, and using REXX in OS/2 from Ami Pro.

Chapter 15

Managing, Organizing and Importing Files

by Robert L. Weberg

Ami Pro has several features to help you easily organize tasks, files, and documents. Imagine attempting to simplify the processes in your current organization to make your daily business routines more efficient. The Merge and File Management commands are powerful tools that enable you to organize your work and files so you can spend more time concentrating on your customers.

In this chapter you learn how to:

- Use Merge to combine data and documents

- Create a merge data file

- Copy and move files

- Rename and delete files

- Open and print multiple files

Understanding Merge in Ami Pro

Customers and contacts are the lifeline of corporations and businesses. A marketing letter sent via mass mailing can be an important tool used to communicate your services and products. For example, you may want to send the same letter to 50 different contacts. You could type and print the letter 50 times, or you could even edit the name and address and then print the letter for each person. Even if you use a copy-and-paste procedure, this process would take a very long time. The most efficient process to deliver mass mailings that require personalization is to use File, Merge. You could also use the Merge command to print envelopes for the letters.

File, Merge is used to combine data, such as names and addresses, with information contained in an Ami Pro document, such as a letter or report. You could use the merge process to send and personalize each letter with an individual's name and address. You must follow three steps to perform a merge:

1. Select, create, or edit a merge data file that contains the address information. A merge data file is similar to an index card or Rolodex file. This file contains information such as contact name, company name, address, phone, fax, and any information that you deem valuable.

2. Create or edit a merge document that contains the standardized text (the letter, report, or envelope) into which the address information is merged. This text or document stays the same even when the data you are merging into it changes.

3. Merge and print the data and document.

Ami Pro prompts you for the desired information in the three-step process, allowing you to create and edit merge files in an easy fashion.

The Basics of Performing a Merge

A merge data file consists of a list of the type of information you want—such as the name, company, or address—and the data itself—the actual names and addresses. The data in a merge data file is arranged into records and fields.

A *record* contains the data for a single contact, product, or subject. A record can contain the name and address information for one contact.

Each record is divided into fields. The *field names* identify the information in the data file. For example, you can specify a record to be composed of the following fields: First Name, Last Name, Company, Address, City, State, Zip, and Phone. When creating a merge data file, you need to specify *delimiters* (discussed later in this section), which designate where records and fields begin and end.

You can create a merge data file as an Ami Pro document, use data in an Ami Pro table, or use data created in a database or spreadsheet application.

To create an Ami Pro merge data file, perform the following steps:

1. Choose **F**ile, Mer**g**e. The Welcome to Merge dialog box appears, itemizing the three steps in the merge process (see fig. 15.1).

Fig. 15.1
The three-step merge process is itemized in The Welcome to Merge dialog box.

2. Choose Select, Create or Edit a **D**ata file, and choose OK.

3. Ami Pro displays the Select Merge Data File dialog box, as shown in figure 15.2. This dialog box allows you to choose a merge data file by using the **D**irectories and D**r**ives listboxes. Since you haven't yet created a merge data file, you'll need to create a new document.

Fig. 15.2
The Select Merge Data File dialog box allows you to choose a previously created merge document or create a new one.

III

4. Click Ne**w**. Ami Pro opens an untitled document and displays the Name Merge Data File dialog box, as shown in figure 15.3. Specify a name for the merge data file in the Save As File **N**ame box, and choose OK. The Create Data File dialog box appears.

Using Ami Pro

Fig. 15.3

The Name Merge Data File dialog box allows you to specify a file name and directory location for your merge data file.

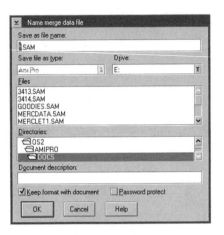

Note

Field names in a data file can contain letters and numbers, but they can neither start with numbers nor consist entirely of numbers.

5. For each field you want to create, type the text of the field name in the Field Name edit box and press Enter or click **A**dd. Ami Pro moves the field names to the Fields in Data File listbox in the exact order in which you add them. Figure 15.4 displays field names being added to build your data file.

Fig. 15.4

The Create Data File dialog box allows you to specify field names in the merge data file.

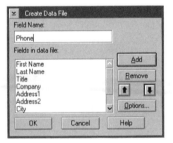

To change the order of the fields, select the desired field in the Fields in Data File listbox and choose the navigational arrow buttons to move the selected field before or after the preceding or following field.

To remove a field, select the field in the Fields in Data File listbox and click **R**emove.

Note

Plan the structure and order of your fields before inputting data into the data file. Because Ami Pro merge data files aren't relational, changing the order and sequence of your data files isn't easy.

Tip

Organize the data in the way you want to refer to it, not in the order in which the data might appear in the merge document.

6. Click **O**ptions to display the Data File Options dialog box to specify particular field and record delimiters (see fig. 15.5). This is important because the field delimiter marks the end of a field (for example, First Name), and the record delimiter marks the end of a record (for example, a complete name and address).

Fig. 15.5

The Data File Options dialog box is used to define field and record delimiters which denote the beginning and end of fields and records.

Caution

These special delimiter characters must be unique and cannot appear anywhere in the data or records because the merge process will decipher this character as one of the delimiters. Always choose a delimiter that is an uncommon character (such as ~ or l).

7. Select the desired delimiter, and choose OK to return to the Create Data File dialog box.

8. Choose OK. Ami Pro places the field and record delimiters on the first line of the merge data file and then enters the field names, separated by field delimiters and ending with the record delimiter, on the second line of the merge data file. See figure 15.6 for an example of how the merge field names and the field and record delimiters appear in the Ami Pro document.

After creating the field and record delimiter lines in the merge data file, Ami Pro displays the Data File dialog box which allows you to enter your desired data.

III

Using Ami Pro

Fig. 15.6

Field and record delimiters are on the first line. The merge field names are on the second line. Notice the fields names are separated by the field delimiter, and the record ends with the record delimiter.

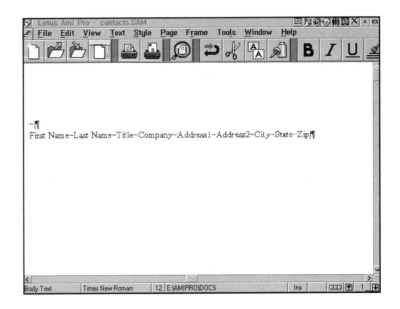

Creating Data in a Data File

After processing the data file structure you specified, Ami Pro displays the Data File dialog box, which resembles an index card (see fig. 15.7). The field names you specified appear to the left of the data text boxes with edit boxes to input data to the right.

Fig. 15.7

The Data File dialog box looks like a graphical Rolodex file and displays the field names you specified in the Create Data File dialog box.

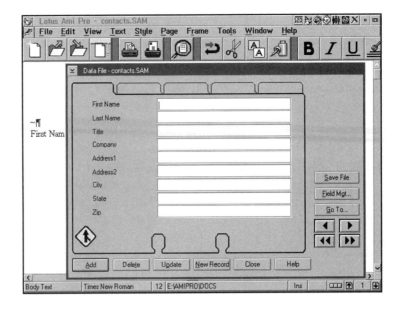

1. For each field name, type the desired data and press Enter or click **A**dd. Ami Pro places the new data record on the third and subsequent lines of the merge data file and displays a new blank record. The first 10 characters of the information you specified for the first field in the previous record appear in the tab dividers at the top of the Data File dialog box.

2. Add the information for each record you want to create. Each record is added into the merge data file in the order in which you create them. You can click **S**ave File to save the newly entered data without closing the Data File dialog box.

3. Choose Close after you finish creating all the records. If you made additions or changes to the data file and did not choose **S**ave File, Ami Pro will prompt you to save the changes. The Welcome to Merge dialog box reappears, prompting you for the next step in performing a merge.

The saved merge data file appears like the example in figure 15.8. Notice that the first line contains the field and record delimiter. The second line contains the Field Names separated by the field delimiter. The record delimiter is the last character at the end of the line.

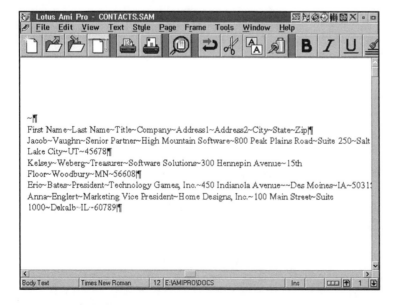

Fig. 15.8
CONTACTS.SAM is an example of a Merge data file in Ami Pro. Notice the field and record delimiters on the first line, the field names on the second line, followed by the records on the preceding lines.

III

Using Ami Pro

Selecting and Creating a Merge Document

After you create the merge data file, you need to create the merge document. The merge document contains the standardized text for the letter or report. You can either create a new Ami Pro document or use an existing Ami Pro document. The procedure you use depends on whether you just closed the merge data file.

If you just created or modified a merge data file, the Welcome to Merge dialog box appears.

1. Select Option 2 to Create or edit a merge and choose OK. A message box appears asking, `Do you want to use the current document as the merge document?`

   ◼ Choose **Y**es to use the current document as the merge document.

   ◼ Choose **N**o to utilize a previously designed merge document or create a new one based upon a different style sheet. After choosing **N**o, the Open dialog box appears allowing you to select the desired document or to click **N**ew to select a different style sheet to base your merge document upon.

2. The Insert Merge Field dialog box appears allowing you to insert fields into your merge document. The Welcome to Merge dialog box appears.

Inserting Merge fields allows you to creatively design your form to your specifications and needs. Even though your merge document is easily customized, you should carefully consider how you want your merge document to appear to save development time.

Inserting Merge Fields into a Merge Document

The Insert Merge Field dialog box now appears, listing the field names you specified when creating the merge data file, as shown in figure 15.9.

To create a merge document, you need to insert merge fields where you want the merge data to appear in the merge document. These fields contain instructions that tell Ami Pro where to insert the merge data into the designated locations when you perform the merge. To insert merge fields into a merge document, follow these steps:

▶ See "Defining the Power Fields for an Automated Style Sheet," p. 382

1. Click in the merge document and place your insertion point where you want the first data field. Select a **F**ield name in the Insert Merge Field dialog box. Choose **I**nsert to place the field name into the merge document. When you insert a field name, it becomes a merge field in the merge document. Ami Pro displays the field name within angle brackets, <>, in the document. The Insert Merge Field dialog box remains on-screen.

Fig. 15.9
The Insert Merge Field dialog box allows you to select the field names to be inserted into the merge document.

> **Caution**
>
> Ami Pro does not recognize field names and brackets that you type into the merge document. You must insert the field names using the Insert Merge Field dialog box.

2. You'll probably want to add several fields to a merge document. To add more than one field into the merge document, place the insertion point where you want to insert another field name, select the field you want in the **F**ield Names listbox and choose **I**nsert.

Tip

Using the keyboard, press Alt+F6 to move the insertion point into the document, and press Alt+F6 again to return to the Insert Merge Field dialog box.

> **Note**
>
> You can insert one or more field names on a line. If certain records do not contain information for a particular field, Ami Pro does not leave space on the line during the merge. If the field name is the only text on the line, Ami Pro sets the line spacing to 0 for that line during the merge. As long as the paragraph style has Paragraph Spacing Above and Below set to 0, no extra space appears in the printed document. To verify the paragraph spacing select **S**tyle, **M**odify Style to display the Modify Style dialog box. Select the desired paragraph style and choose S**p**acing in the Modify section and then in the Paragraph Spacing section you'll see the **A**bove and **B**elow options.

III

Using Ami Pro

3. Repeat this procedure until you insert all the desired field names into the merge document. Once you insert field names into the merge document, you can delete, copy, and move them elsewhere in the document using **C**opy, Cu**t** and **P**aste commands. Figure 15.10 has inserted several fields in the addressee section of a letter merge document.

Fig. 15.10

A completed merge document displays the inserted merge fields and the document's text.

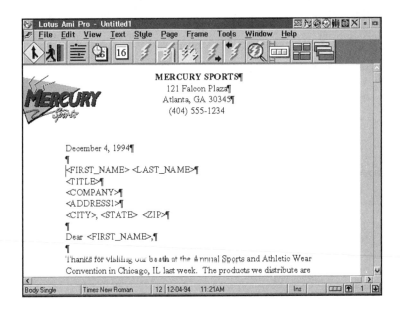

Tip

Be sure you add spaces—such as between a first and last name—and punctuation—between the city and state—between field names.

> **Note**
>
> To edit the fields inserted in the merge document, select the entire field name, including the angle brackets surrounding it, and either press the Delete key, or use Cu**t**, **C**opy, **P**aste or drag and drop to copy or move the field name to the desired location.

You can apply text formatting and text enhancements to field names using paragraph styles, SmartIcons, the status bar, or the **T**ext menu. When Ami Pro merges data into the merge document, the text displays and prints with the formatting and enhancements you applied to the field names.

4. To finish the merge, you can now choose the desired command button in the Insert Merge Field dialog box by selecting either of the following commands:

■ *Continue Merge.* Displays the Welcome to Merge dialog box with option 3 selected, allowing you to merge the data with the newly created merge document.

■ *Close.* Closes the Insert Merge Field dialog box and returns you to the merge document so you can continue to edit and format the document.

■ *Data File.* Allows you to assign a merge data file to an existing document. After clicking Data File, the Select Merge Data File dialog box appears allowing you to choose a new data file (see fig. 15.11). Click OK to return to the Insert Merge Field dialog box which displays the new merge fields contained or specified in the chosen merge data file. Select the field name(s) you want to insert into the merge document.

Tip

You can save the merge document as a new style sheet and then re-use that style sheet anytime to create a merge document. Ami Pro automatically uses the merge data file you assigned to the merge document.

Fig. 15.11

Assign a data file to the current document using the Select Merge Data File dialog box.

Merging and Printing the Data

After you have created the merge data file and merge document, assigned the desired merge data file, and inserted the desired field names into the merge document, you can perform the merge—the final step of the merge process. You can display, print, or save the merged documents. The merge will repeatedly place the information from your merge data file into the merge document until the data in each record is combined with the text in the merge document.

▶ See "Creating a New Style Sheet," p. 338

To perform the merge, follow these steps:

1. Make the merge document the active window and verify that it's in layout mode by choosing **V**iew, **L**ayout Mode.

III

Using Ami Pro

2. Choose **F**ile, Mer**g**e.

3. Select option 3 Merge and **P**rint the Data and Document and then click OK. The Merge dialog box appears, as shown in figure 15.12.

Fig. 15.12

The Merge dialog box is accessed by selecting step 3 of the three-step merge process.

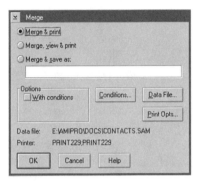

4. Select the desired type of merge:

- ■ *Merge & Print.* Sends the merge document with the information contained in the records directly to the printer.

- ■ *Merge, View & Print.* Displays the merge document with the information contained in a record so you can view and modify it before sending it to the printer. Any modifications you make will affect subsequent documents. Choosing this option tells Ami Pro to create a file containing a merge document for each record. The file could be extremely large and therefore take a long time to load, since Ami Pro creates a different letter for each record.

- ■ *Merge & Save As.* Saves the merge document with the information contained in a record to an Ami Pro file you specify for later editing or printing. Again, Ami Pro creates a merge document for each record; the saved file could be huge.

Caution

In the merge document, field names should be in the main document to successfully use Merge & **S**ave As. The field names cannot be in frames, tables, footnotes, headers, or footers. Also, the merge document should not contain pictures.

---

5. If you want to specify the number of copies, the range of pages, and additional print options, choose **P**rint Opts. Specify the desired print options and choose OK to return to the Merge dialog box.

6. Choose OK to start the merge.

◀ See "Printing Your Documents," p. 297

Ami Pro creates the documents with the information contained in the records and either displays, prints, or saves them to a file. If you selected Merge, **V**iew & Print, you can specify whether you want to print or skip the merge documents, as shown in figure 15.13.

Fig. 15.13
The Merge dialog box after selecting Merge, **V**iew & Print allows you to choose which documents you want to print or view

The following list explains the four options available when printing or previewing documents during a merge process:

- *Print and View Next.* Prints the displayed document and displays the merge document with the information contained in the next record.

- *Skip and View Next.* Skips printing the displayed merge document and displays the document with the information contained in the next record.

- *Print All.* Prints the displayed document and all remaining documents.

- *Cancel.* Cancels the merge and returns you to the merge document so you can edit or close it.

Using Merge Conditions to Select Document Recipients

You can use the **C**onditions option in the Merge dialog box to merge only certain records in the merge data file. For example, you could use conditions to send a letter only to those contacts from Illinois, or to exclude only those customers from Iowa.

To use conditions when using merge, perform the following steps:

1. Open the merge document or switch to the active window if it's already open (Alt+Tab).

2. Choose **F**ile, Mer**g**e.

III

Using Ami Pro

3. In the Welcome to Merge dialog box, select Merge and **P**rint the Data and Document option and click OK. The Merge dialog box appears.

4. Choose **C**onditions, and the Merge Conditions dialog box appears.

5. Specify the field name you want Ami Pro to use as the basis for selecting which records to merge from a list of field names in the Field **N**ame listbox.

6. Specify the Operator you want to use as the basis for selecting which records to merge. The *operator* is the relationship between the Field name and the Value you specify. Table 15.1 lists and describes these operators.

> **Note**
>
> When the insertion point is located in the Operator text box, Ami Pro displays a list of the available relational operators in an Operators listbox. Select the desired operator.

Table 15.1   Operators Available in Merge Conditions

Operator	Description
=	equal to
<	less than
>	greater than
!=	not equal to
<=	less than or equal to
>=	greater than or equal to

7. Specify the Value you want Ami Pro to use as the basis for selecting which records to merge. The *Value* is the text or number for a specified field in a particular record. Figure 15.14 displays an example of using merge conditions that will only merge records in the data file which have the state field equal to IL.

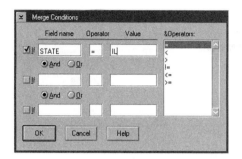

Fig. 15.14
Applying Merge Conditions and setting criteria to a data merge is easy. This technique can save you enormous time if you're working with a large data file by pinpointing specific records.

8. If you want to specify more than one set of criteria for Ami Pro to use as the basis for selecting which records to merge, select the **A**nd or **O**r options.

- *And.* This option specifies that records in the merge data file should match the Field name, Operator, and Value specified in the first set of criteria and the Field name, Operator, and Value specified in the subsequent set(s) of criteria.

- *Or.* This option specifies that records in the merge data file should match either the Field Name, Operator, and Value specified in the first set of criteria or the Field Name, Operator, and Value specified in the subsequent set(s) of criteria.

9. Choose OK to return to the Merge dialog box . Then choose OK to perform the merge based upon the conditions you specified.

Using the Ami Pro File Manager

Ami Pro provides a tool to quickly manage your files if you don't want to use the OS/2 drives folders, OS/2 or DOS commands in OS/2 and DOS windows, or the Windows File Manager. You can use the **F**ile Management command to copy, move, rename, delete, and change the attributes of your files. Plus, File Management provides options for changing directories, specifying which file names appear in the window, and displaying document information.

The Ami Pro File Manager allows you to work with files only. These files may be Ami Pro documents or style sheets or non-Ami Pro files. You cannot use File Management to create, copy or move a directory.

III

Using Ami Pro

Following is a list of the features found in File Management:

- **C**opy and **M**ove file(s)

- **R**ename file(s)

- **D**elete file(s)

- Change file **A**ttributes

- **Ch**ange Directory

Copying and Moving Ami Pro Files

You can copy or move one or more Ami Pro files at a time. In fact, you should use File Management in Ami Pro to copy, move, or rename an Ami Pro file to ensure that all necessary information and style sheets remain with the documents.

Caution

Using a Windows or DOS command to copy or move files does not guarantee that all necessary formatting information and related files remain with an Ami Pro document.

To copy or move a file, perform the following steps:

1. Choose **F**ile, **F**ile Management. The Ami Pro File Manager window appears, as displayed figure 15.15

Tip

Select a file or files by clicking the file; the selected file appears highlighted. To deselect a file, click that file again.

2. Select the files you want to copy or move. Comments previously specified in the Doc Info Description text box will be displayed next to each file name. If a file is not an Ami Pro document, the Description indicates Not an Ami Pro File.

3. Choose **F**ile, **C**opy or **F**ile, **M**ove, depending on your operation. In this example of copying a file, the Copy dialog box appears, as shown in figure 15.16.

4. Specify the full path for the destination file.

Note

If you selected multiple file names or if you want to use the same file name as the original, specify only the drive and path.

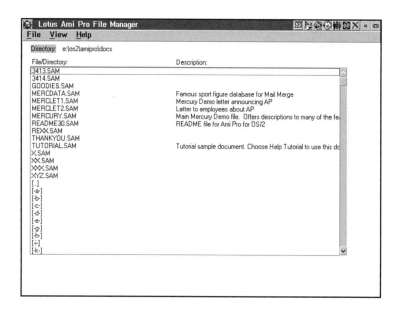

Fig. 15.15
The Ami Pro File Manager window allows you to manage and organize your Ami Pro files.

Fig. 15.16
The Copy dialog box allows you to copy a file to another location.

5. Choose OK, and the File Copy Options dialog box appears, as displayed in figure 15.17.

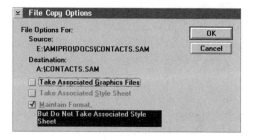

Fig. 15.17
The File Copy Options dialog box allows you to copy Ami Pro files with their associated style sheets, graphics files, and formats.

6. Select the desired format options (see fig. 15.18). The options determine whether the style sheet associated with the document and the graphics files referenced in the document are copied or moved with the document.

Tip

Use the Take Associated **G**raphics Files option when you copy or move a document containing any pictures stored as original graphics files.

■ *Take Associated **G**raphics Files.* Ami Pro copies or moves the document and any original graphics files referenced in the document to the destination you specify, even if the graphics files are stored in a different directory than the document.

Note

Do not select the Take Associated **G**raphics Files option if the pictures in the document are Ami Pro charts or drawings, were pasted from the Clipboard, or were inserted into the document using the **F**ile, **I**mport Picture, **C**opy Image option.

■ *Take Associated **S**tyle Sheet.* If you are copying or moving a document to a floppy drive, Ami Pro copies or moves the document and the style sheet to the floppy drive. If you are copying or moving a document to a hard drive, Ami Pro copies or moves the document to the directory you specify and the style sheet to the AMIPRO\STYLES directory specified in the User Setup.

Note

Select the Take Associated **S**tyle Sheet option when you copy or move an Ami Pro document that uses a style sheet you created and want to use with other documents. This ensures that the style sheet is available on the destination disk or in the destination directory and prevents `Unable to find style sheet` error messages.

Tip

Select **M**aintain Format if you're copying or moving an Ami Pro document that contains all the formatting information the document needs, and you don't plan to use another style sheet.

■ *Maintain Format.* Ami Pro doesn't copy or move the style sheet containing the page and paragraph formatting information associated with the document. Instead, the document's page layout and paragraph styles are stored in the document, and all formatting information is document specific. Also, in the Styles box, the style sheet name appears as `None`, and each paragraph style name is preceded by a bullet.

Note

When you select **M**aintain Format, even if the original style sheet is available, Ami Pro does not use it. Any changes made to the original style sheet are not reflected in the format of the document.

7. Choose OK.

Renaming Files

The Ami Pro File Management command only allows you to rename one file at a time. To rename a file, perform the following steps:

1. In the File Manager select the file you want to rename.

2. Choose **F**ile, **R**ename. The Rename dialog box appears (see fig. 15.18).

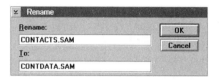

Fig. 15.18
You can use the Rename dialog box to rename a file.

3. In the **T**o box, enter the name you want to give the document. Choose OK, and the file will be renamed.

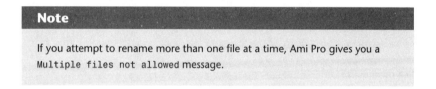

> **Note**
>
> If you attempt to rename more than one file at a time, Ami Pro gives you a
> `Multiple files not allowed` message.

Deleting Files

Using File Management, you can delete any type of file, including Ami Pro documents, style sheets, and macros. However, you cannot delete a read-only file.

To delete a file, perform the following steps:

1. In the File Manager select any files you want to delete.

2. Choose **F**ile, **D**elete, or press the Delete key. The Delete dialog box appears; choose OK to delete the files.

Using File Attributes to Protect Your Files

You can change the attributes of a document with the appropriate access rights to it. If you are on a network, your ability to change the attributes or delete files will depend on your assigned network access rights. Making files read-only can be useful if you want to protect your files from being over-written or accidentally deleted by other users.

III

Using Ami Pro

To change the file attributes of specific files, perform the following steps:

1. In the File Manager, select the file you want to change the attributes for.

2. Choose **F**ile, **A**ttributes. The File Attributes dialog box appears.

3. Select the Read **O**nly or **R**ead-Write option, and then choose OK.

> **Note**
>
> You can display and view a read-only file, but you can't save any changes to it. Ami Pro won't allow you to save over the file.

Changing the File Management Drive or Directory

Tip
Double-click a directory name in the File/Directory listbox to display the names of the subdirectories and files in that directory.

You can easily switch drives and directories in File Management. To do so, perform the following steps:

1. Choose **F**ile, **Ch**ange Directory. The Change Directory dialog box appears.

2. Specify the drive or path in the **C**hange To box.

3. Choose OK. Ami Pro displays a list of the files stored in the chosen directory.

Exiting File Management

To exit File Management when you finish managing documents, choose **F**ile, E**x**it, or double-click the Control menu box.

Tip
To keep File Management active in the background while you edit an Ami Pro document, click anywhere in the current document. To access File Management again, use the Task list by pressing Alt+Esc or Alt+Tab to switch Windows.

Troubleshooting

Why are some of my files not appearing in their path window?

You may need to change the types of files Ami Pro displays in the File Manager window. Choose **V**iew and then either choose ***.S**?M to display all file names that have extensions that begin with "S" and end with "M", including .SAM and .SMM files, choose **A**ll to display all file names in the current directory, or choose **P**artial to specify the extension for the files you want to display in the window.

When I open a file, why do I get a message saying that the file is currently protected and I cannot make changes to it?

The file currently has a Read-Only file attribute. To change to Read-Write, choose **F**ile, **F**ile Management. The Ami Pro File Manager dialog box appears. Choose **F**ile, **At**tributes, and then select the **R**ead-write option.

From Here...

This chapter showed you how to send or distribute a mass mailing to a large list of individuals using the Merge feature in Ami Pro. You now should be able to quickly create a merge data file and a merge document to deliver information to a large list of customers and clients. Plus, you learned how to use the File Management command to organize your Ami Pro documents.

For more information about creating documents, using style sheets in the merge process, and organizing your documents, refer to the following chapters:

- Chapter 1, "New Ways of Working with OS/2," explains the basics of working with applications within the OS/2 Workplace Shell.

- Chapter 4, "Introducing the 1-2-3 Worksheet," explains the basics of creating a 1-2-3 worksheet

- Chapter 12, "Creating and Editing Documents," covers the basics of creating an Ami Pro document.

- Chapter 19, "Automating with Macros and Style Sheets," shows you the basics of creating macros and automated style sheets in Ami Pro.

- Chapter 21, "Entering Slide Content," discusses how to create and build Freelance Presentations.

III

Using Ami Pro

Chapter 16

Changing Views and Creating Outlines, Styles, and Revisions

by Sue Plumley

When working with large documents, you can use several of Ami Pro's special features to edit, view, and organize your document.

Ami Pro includes various views as well as three modes, or ways, to look at the document on-screen. The views show the page at different magnifications, such as 50%, 100%, 200%, and so on. The three modes—layout, outline, and draft—present the contents in different ways so that you can organize and edit the text more easily.

In addition to enabling various views and modes, Ami Pro includes other features that help you manage and edit your documents. You can create paragraph styles to define text attributes in your document. When you create a style, you assign a typeface, type size, alignment, spacing, and so on, to selected text and save the format as a style name. Then, you can easily assign the style to other text in the document without setting each attribute again.

Revision marking is another powerful tool for editing large documents. Each editor can insert and delete text items and add notes and comments wherever necessary while revising a document. The changes appear in separate colors on-screen.

Finally, Ami Pro enables you to create outlines for your document to help you organize and rearrange the main points and text. Outlining is an effective tool for editing and organizing a long document.

In this chapter, you learn to:

- Use the Ami Pro views

- Work with layout, draft, and outline modes

- Access and use the Ami Pro Clean Screen

- Access, modify, and create paragraph styles

- Use revision marks

- Use outline mode and outline levels

Understanding Different Views

Tip

You can edit a document in any view and mode.

You can see your text in several sizes by using five built-in views. Ami Pro enables you to preview your entire page, or zoom in to display small text and graphics.

You can switch between these separate views to determine how much of the Ami Pro page you see on-screen. Use your mouse to access these five views through the **V**iew menu:

Tip

Press Ctrl+D to switch back and forth between full page and custom views.

- *Full **p**age.* This view displays the entire Ami Pro page on-screen (see fig. 16.1). Although you may not see individual lines of text, this view shows how the complete page appears. This view is available only in layout mode.

- *Standard.* This view shows your text in a standard size. You can use this view to see your true text size on-screen. If you use standard margins (one inch), you cannot see an entire line of text without using the horizontal scroll bars.

Tip

Set the percentage for the custom view by choosing the **V**iew, View **P**references command.

- *Custom.* This view displays your text in a specific percentage of the **S**tandard view. The default custom view size is 91%, which enables you to see entire lines of text without using the horizontal scroll bars. Your custom view can range from 10% to 400% of the standard view.

- *Enlarged.* This view is double the size of standard view (see fig. 16.2). At 200% text size, you can zoom into your screen to access smaller text and graphics.

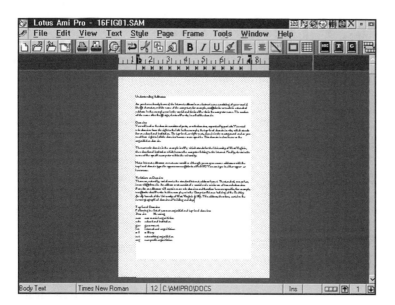

Fig. 16.1
Use the full page view to look at overall page design and margins.

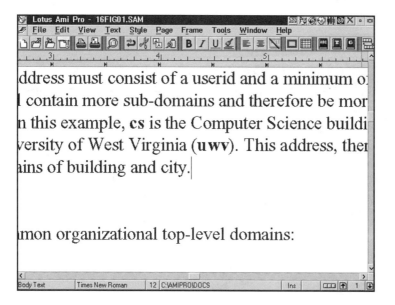

Fig. 16.2
Use the enlarged view to look at details of the screen.

■ *Facing pages.* This view, available only in layout mode, displays two pages in full-page format. Use this view to observe page and document layout and to make changes in the text and layout. Choose the **V**iew menu and a different command to change views.

III

Using Ami Pro

Changing Display Modes

In addition to the five default views, Ami Pro has three display modes. These display modes—layout, outline, and draft—show different attributes of your Ami Pro document on-screen.

Layout mode, the default mode, shows how your printed file will look, with all text formatting, pictures, headers, footers, and so on displayed in the document on-screen. Draft mode provides a continuous scrolling view and text lines that fit the window so that you can easily edit the document. Outline mode shows your document in a collapsible and expandable outline view for quick and easy organization of the headings and text. To change modes, open the **V**iew menu and choose the mode that you want to use.

Using Layout Mode

The default (and the most commonly used) display mode is layout, which shows all graphics and text formatting (see fig. 16.3). Layout mode is in *WYSIWYG* (what you see is what you get) format. WYSIWYG means that your printed document—text, graphics, and margins—will look exactly the way that it does on-screen in layout mode.

Fig. 16.3
Use layout mode to view the document in WYSIWYG format.

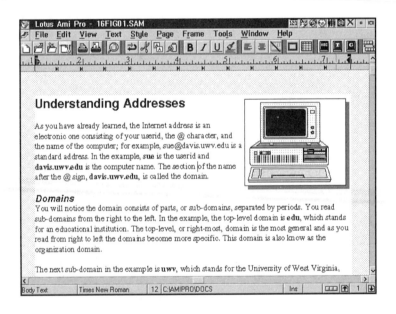

In addition to displaying your main document text, layout mode places your page headers and footers in their respective locations outside the page margins.

You can use layout mode to format your document and arrange your text and graphics on-screen. Full-page and facing-pages views are available only in layout mode; you also can use custom, standard, and enlarged views with layout mode.

Using Draft Mode

Draft mode shows your text in a less formatted manner than layout mode. Using the entire screen to display your text, you can view text and tables, as well as text or pictures in anchored frames.

Ami Pro does not display headers and footers, columns, notes, footnotes, or text and pictures in unanchored frames. Figure 16.4 shows a document in draft mode. In addition, the Ami Pro ruler does not appear in draft mode.

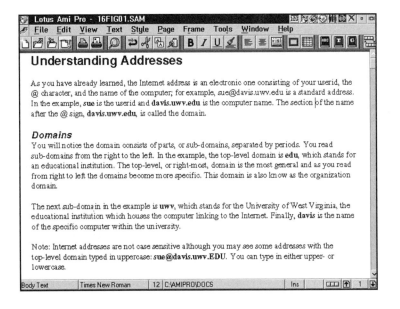

Fig. 16.4

Margins and graphics disappear from view in draft mode.

Using Outline Mode

Outline mode enables you to view, sort, and rearrange large documents easily. Using preset paragraph styles, you assign outline levels to the headings and subheadings in your document. In outline mode, each level and its text are marked and indented appropriately to show the hierarchy. You can assign up to nine levels in the outline.

Figure 16.5 shows three outline levels in outline view.

Fig. 16.5

Text indents
follow the outline
level heads.

Tip

Like draft
mode, outline
mode displays
graphics only
in anchored
frames.

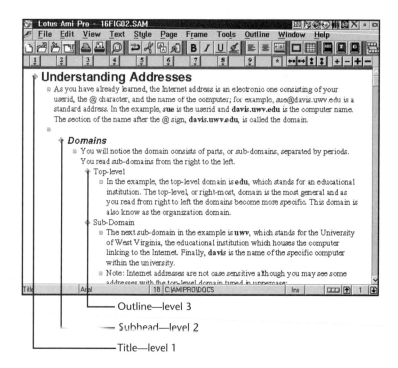

Outline—level 3

Subhead—level 2

Title—level 1

In outline mode, you can quickly and easily promote or demote level heads
and move level heads to other parts of the document. Whenever you move a
head or change its level, the text belonging to that head follows automatically.

 Use the toggle Outline/Layout View icon to quickly switch views, if you
need to.

Setting Outline Levels with Paragraph Styles

Each paragraph style can be associated with a specific outline level. To associate a paragraph style with an outline level, choose the **S**tyle, **O**utline Styles
command. Ami Pro displays the Outline Styles dialog box (see fig. 16.6).

Each associated paragraph style is listed in the Style listbox; when you select a
style, the corresponding outline level number highlights. In the figure, Title
corresponds with level 1, Subhead with level 2, and Outline3 with level 3.

To change the outline level of a paragraph style, click the paragraph style
you want to change. Click **P**romote if you want to raise the outline level,
or **D**emote if you want to lower the associated outline level. Promote and

demote enable you to change the paragraph styles assigned to the selected text with the click of the mouse. Click OK to save your new outline level associations.

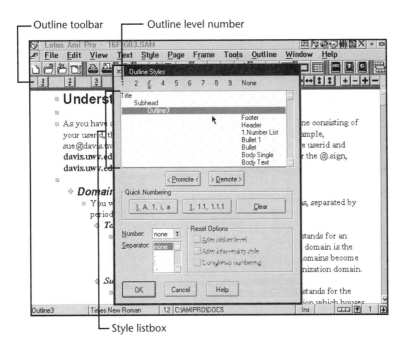

Outline toolbar ———— Outline level number

Fig. 16.6
Use the Outline Styles dialog box to associate a style with an outline level.

Style listbox

To assign a paragraph style to specific text in your document, click the text you want to change the style for. Click the style button on the status bar and select the style you want to apply (see fig. 16.7).

Maneuvering in Outline Mode

After your outline levels are applied, you can work with your document in outline mode. Although working in outline mode is slightly different from using the other display modes, you can still edit, copy, and move text around your screen.

Notice how text automatically indents to appear underneath the outline level that its paragraph style is associated with. This hierarchy allows you to list only specific outline levels of your document, if you want. If you click your mouse on the 1 in the outline toolbar, for example, only level 1 text displays. When you click 2, only text on levels 1 and 2 are shown. Displaying only certain headings is called *collapsing* the outline. Collapse an outline so you can review headings, rearrange text and headings, and track the flow of your writing.

III

Using Ami Pro

Fig. 16.7

Assign the paragraph style using the style button on the status bar.

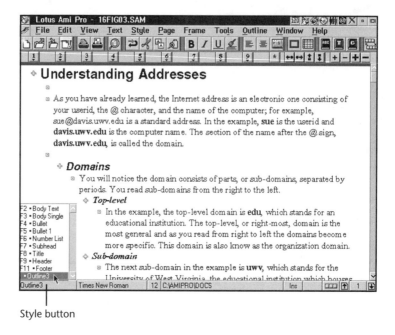

Style button

Tip

Click the asterisk on the outline toolbar to display all text and headings in the document, also called *expanding* the outline.

In addition to listing specific outline levels, you can display the text only in one level or heading. Small plus signs appear beside level headings that contain collapsed text or other headings. Double-click any plus sign to display its associated text (see fig. 16.8). Similarly, double-click the sign again to collapse the text.

You can use outline mode to view just the first level or all levels. This feature enables you to maneuver around large documents without scrolling several pages. You can expand only the levels you need to access.

Moving Text Sections in Outline Mode

You also can manipulate large blocks of text in outline mode by moving only the heading or subheading. All text moves with a heading when you drag it to another position.

> **Caution**
>
> You also can delete large amounts of text by deleting only a heading. If you accidentally delete text, choose the **E**dit, **U**ndo command.

Drag-and-drop editing works in outline mode nearly the same as in any other mode. When dragging outline text to another location, it is best to first collapse the text to its heading so that you don't inadvertently leave any text behind. After collapsing the outline level, click and drag the plus sign to a new position. As you drag, you see the drag-and-drop pointer and vertical bar drag with the text. When you release the mouse button, the outline head and its text drop into the insertion point.

Expanded level

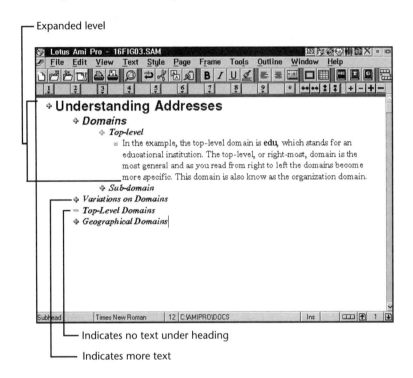

Fig. 16.8
Quickly view text or headings by expanding only one level of text.

Indicates no text under heading

Indicates more text

Using the Clean Screen

Sometimes, you want to hide certain screen elements, such as the Ami Pro menu and status bars, so that you can display only your document, thus eliminating on-screen clutter. With the Ami Pro Clean Screen feature, you can customize the on-screen elements that you want to display while editing your text.

To switch to the Ami Pro Clean Screen, choose **V**iew, Show Clean Screen (see fig. 16.9). By default, the clean screen displays a Return icon in the bottom right corner of the Ami Pro screen. To exit the clean screen, click the Return icon. Note that the ruler and the SmartSuite application manager still show on-screen.

Tip
You can use Clean Screen in all views and all modes.

III

Using Ami Pro

Fig. 16.9
You can use keyboard keys, such as Page Up and arrow keys, to move around the clean screen.

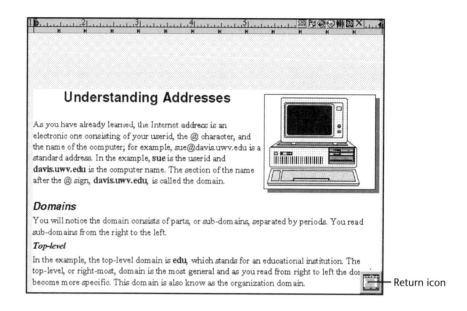

Return icon

◀ See "Viewing Parts of the Window," p. 36

You can control whether the Return icon displays, and which elements are shown while in clean screen mode, by changing your clean screen options. Choose **V**iew, View **P**references and select the Clean Screen tab. From the list, choose those items you want to display when in the clean screen; your choices are title bar, menu, SmartIcons, status bar, vertical or horizontal scroll bar, and the Return icon. Choose OK to close the dialog box.

If your menu bar is shown from your clean screen, you can also choose **V**iew, Hide Clean Scree**n** to exit clean screen mode. If the menu does not show, you can press Alt+ the corresponding letter of the menu to display the commands of that menu.

Troubleshooting

I removed all the elements from my clean screen and can't exit it.

You can access the Ami Pro menu bar even though you cannot see it. Press Alt+V to access the **V**iew menu. Then choose Hide Clean Scree**n** to escape from your clean screen.

I changed the default view from standard and now I want to change it back.

You can change the default view—the view that loads when Ami Pro starts—by choosing Too**l**s, **U**ser Setup, and then choosing the Load tab and selecting **C**ustom or **S**tandard view.

Understanding Ami Pro Styles

Style sheets are preformatted text pages that have several built-in style definitions. When you create a new document from a style sheet, you can access the style sheet's built-in styles immediately. You can choose a style sheet when you choose **F**ile, **N**ew. The New dialog box appears and enables you to select the style sheet you want to use.

> **Note**
>
> Ami Pro uses the default style sheet—one column, one-inch margins, 12-point Times Roman body text, and so on—when the program begins. You can change the default style sheet by choosing the Too**l**s, **U**ser Setup command. Choose the Load tab and select the style sheet you prefer to load by default. Choose OK.

Stored in style sheets, a *style* is a group of formatting characteristics—font, size, alignment, spacing, and so on—that you access through one command. You can use styles for headlines, body text, footnotes, and other elements of your documents. Styles are convenient to use because you can quickly format an entire document with the click of a mouse.

▶ See "Changing Your User Setup," p. 362

> **Note**
>
> You can apply a style before entering the text or after entering the text. To apply the style to text already typed, you can either select the text or position the insertion point anywhere in the paragraph; the entire paragraph changes to the selected style.

In addition to using Ami Pro's built-in styles, you can create your own styles and even alter Ami Pro's. Paragraph styles can be stored with specific documents or with Ami Pro style sheets.

Using a Built-In Style

Each Ami Pro style sheet has several default paragraph styles, or definitions. The default style sheet, for example, contains eight paragraph styles ranging from Body Text to Footer.

Each paragraph style is accessible from the Style Selection listbox (see fig. 16.10). Access the listbox by clicking the style button on the status bar, pressing Ctrl+Y, or choosing **S**tyle, **S**elect a Style.

III

Using Ami Pro

Fig. 16.10

Ami Pro provides several methods of applying styles.

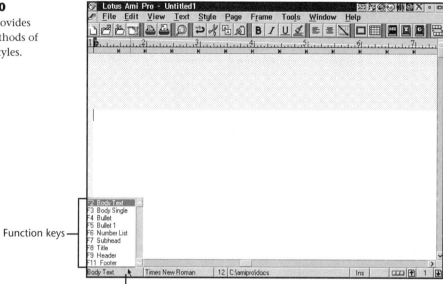

Function keys

Click here to access styles

To switch a paragraph to a new style, place the insertion point in the paragraph that you want to change, display the style list, and click the new style. Ami Pro formats your current paragraph in the new style. Alternatively, you can quickly change paragraph styles by pressing a single key. Place your insertion point in the paragraph to be changed and type the function key listed next to the style in the Style listbox.

Changing an Ami Pro Style

Ami Pro supplies various styles with its style sheet; however, you may want to make a heading larger or add more space to a footnote. You can change the Ami Pro styles stored with a document or style sheet and save them for future use.

To modify an Ami Pro style, follow these steps:

1. Choose **S**tyle, **M**odify Style to display the Modify Style dialog box (see fig. 16.11). Alternatively, press Ctrl+A or click the Modify a Paragraph Style icon.

2. In the St**y**le listbox, choose the style you want to modify from the drop-down list.

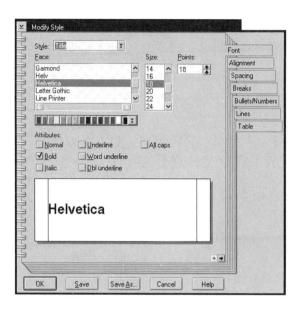

Fig. 16.11
Use the Modify Style dialog box to change the text attributes of a style.

3. Make the appropriate changes in the style. You can change the Font, Alignment, Spacing, Breaks, Bullets/Numbers, Lines, and Table options by clicking the appropriate tab.

Caution

When you change any attribute of a style in the Modify Style dialog box, all text assigned with that style in that document also changes.

---

4. Click **S**ave at the bottom of the dialog box to save your style changes if you have modified multiple styles.

5. Click OK to save your current style and return to your document.

Note

If you change a paragraph style that changes the way text looks on-screen, Ami Pro asks whether you want to save changes when you exit the document and the program. For example, if you make a style bold, Ami Pro changes the on-screen text to bold, which prompts a file save.

◄ See "Formatting the Page," p. 279

◄ See "Changing Character Attributes," p. 266

III

Using Ami Pro

Creating a New Style

Tip
Click the right
mouse button in
the text area to
directly access the
Modify Style dia-
log box. The para-
graph style you
clicked appears in
the Style listbox.

Creating a new style is similar to modifying an existing style. The difference
is that after you make changes to an existing style in the Modify Style dialog
box, you click Save **A**s rather than **S**ave at the bottom of the dialog box. Ami
Pro prompts you for a new name for the paragraph style that you defined.
Your original style remains unchanged, and the new name appears in the
Style listbox.

The other method of creating a new style is choosing the **S**tyle, **C**reate Style
command to display the Create Style dialog box (see fig. 16.12). In this dialog
box, you can create a style by typing a new name in the **N**ew Style text box.

Fig. 16.12
Create your own
style in the Create
Style dialog box.

In the Based On list, choose the style closest to the one you want to create;
for example, if the new style is a subtitle in the same font and alignment as
the style Title, choose Title as the style on which to base your new style.

Tip
If you format the
new style on-
screen using
selected text be-
fore opening the
Create Style dialog
box, you can
choose the
Selected Text
option and the
Create button to
create the new
style.

Choose the Modify button to display the Modify Style dialog box. Modify the
style as you want and choose OK to add the new style to the **S**tyle list.

Creating a New Style Sheet

You can create your own paragraph styles and save a new style sheet that can
be used with other documents, just as Ami Pro's style sheets are used over
and over again. Begin by creating new styles or modifying existing ones.
Check the page setup for margin or orientation modification. Next, add any
frames, tables, or other graphics you want to be included in the style sheet.
You can even add lines, headers and footers, and permanent text such as a
newsletter masthead.

When you are ready to save the style sheet, choose **S**tyle, Sa**v**e as Style Sheet.
The Save as a Style Sheet dialog box appears (see fig. 16.13). Enter the style
sheet name in the same manner as other Ami Pro style sheets are named—

_DEFAULT.STY, _BASIC.STY, _EXPENSE.STY, and so on. Add a **D**escription if you want, and choose **W**ith contents if you added text, tables, frames, and so on that you want to include with the style sheet. Choose OK to save as a style sheet.

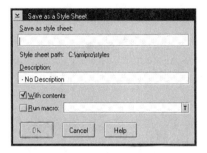

Fig. 16.13
Name your new style sheet in the Save as a Style Sheet dialog box.

▶ See "Under-standing and Using Ami Pro Macros," p. 372

> **Note**
>
> If you want, you can create a macro in your style sheet to ask the user's name, for example, or perform some other task for whoever opens the style sheet. If you add macros to the style sheet, be sure to choose **R**un Macro in the Save as a Style Sheet dialog box.

The next time you start a new document, your style sheet is listed with other Ami Pro style sheets, and you can choose it as a base on which to start a new document.

◀ See "Formatting the Page," p. 279

Understanding Revision Marking

Many large documents undergo significant revisions before they are finished. Typically, several people may read a large document before its completion, and each may have additions and edits to make on that document. Revision marking is also very common and beneficial to corporations who use group authoring.

After a book manuscript is written, for example, the information usually is read by several editors for grammatical and technical revisions. The editors make their own comments and changes in the manuscript.

When revision marks are used, Ami Pro can track what changes were made by specific people during the editing and revision process. Each person can make his or her edits in a different color or text style (such as bold or italic). Editors

III

Using Ami Pro

can even place notes in the document to ask questions about the document's content or purpose. By color-coding the revisions and notes, Ami Pro makes document revision a straightforward task.

After the document has undergone the revision process, the author can scan the suggested revisions and accept or reject each one.

Enabling Revision Marks

Revision marks enable you to edit a document easily. By using revision marks, you can insert new text, select text for deletion, or enter notes to other readers.

You can turn revision marks on by choosing Too**l**s, Re**v**ision Marking. From the Revision Marking dialog box (see fig. 16.14), select the **M**ark Revisions checkbox and click OK.

Fig. 16.14
Choose to mark revisions in the Revision Marking dialog box.

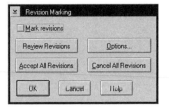

Alternatively, you can activate revision marks by choosing the mode from the status bar. Click the mode button in the status bar until it changes to display Rev. Ami Pro automatically begins to use revision marks.

To disable revision marking, choose Too**l**s, Re**v**ision Marking, deselect the **M**ark Revisions checkbox, and click OK. Alternatively, click the mode button on the status bar.

Using Revision Options

Choose from several revision options by clicking the **O**ptions button in the Revision Marking dialog box. The Revision Marking Options dialog box appears (see fig. 16.15). From this dialog box, you can specify the way your revisions appear in the document.

You can choose the style and color of your insertions and deletions. In addition, you can choose to display revision marks in the margin to identify all changes in the document.

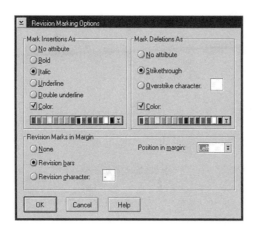

Fig. 16.15
Choose the type of revision marks you want to use in the document.

Choose to mark insertions as boldfaced, italic, underlined, or with a double underline. Additionally, you can choose to add a color to any of these attributes or to use a color alone to mark insertions.

Deletions can appear in strikethrough text or any overstrike character you choose; again, you can also choose a specific color for deletions in addition to the attribute or in lieu of the attribute.

Finally, if you choose the Revision **B**ars or Revision **C**haracter option, you can identify all document revisions quickly by looking at your page's margins. Outside your margins, thin bars indicate that a revision has been made on that specific line. You can even choose to display the character in the left, right, or both margins.

> **Note**
>
> When choosing how to mark revisions in the Revisions Marking Options dialog box, choose marks that are unique to the text so the revised text won't be confused with original text. Revision bars in the margin or a different color can help you quickly identify areas with revisions.

Placing Notes in Documents

Revision marks enable you to change and update your document directly. Sometimes, however, you need to enter a note for other people to read. You can enter several lines of text in a note, and you can place a note anywhere in the document.

To place a note in an Ami Pro document, follow these steps:

1. Place the insertion point in your document where you want to place the note.

2. Choose **E**dit, **I**nsert, **N**ote to display a new window labeled with the current date and time, as well as the author's name.

3. Type the text that you want to include in the note (see fig. 16.16).

Fig. 16.16
Insert a note in the text to clarify or ask a question.

Note marker in text

Close note box

Note box

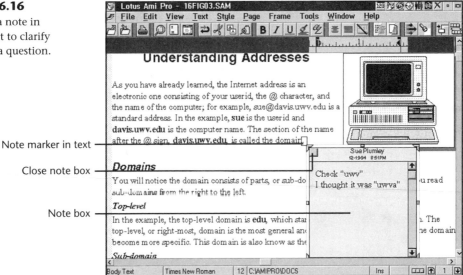

4. Double-click the Close note box in the upper-left corner of the Note box.

You can access notes by double-clicking the note marker in an Ami Pro document that represents notes.

Reviewing Revisions

After your document has undergone revision, you can review all the suggested changes. Using the built-in revision reviewing feature, you can access each revision mark individually through the Revision Marking dialog box.

Choose **T**ools, Re**v**ision Marking to access the Revision Marking dialog box. Next, click the Re**v**iew Revisions button. The Review Revision Marking dialog box appears, and the first revision is highlighted (see fig. 16.17).

Tip
If you can't see the highlighted revision, click the mouse in the title bar of the Review Revision Marking dialog box and move it off to the side.

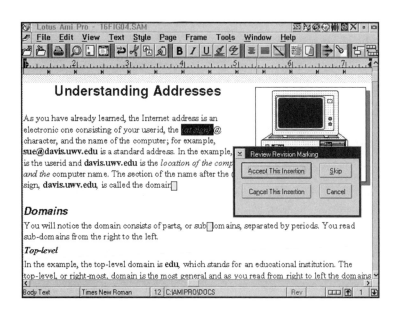

Fig. 16.17
Choose whether to
accept, cancel, or
skip the revision.

You can choose any of the following options for each revision Ami Pro finds
in your document:

- *Accept This Insertion.* Accepts the revision by changing it from a marked
  revision to fit in with the text.

- *Cancel This Insertion.* Deletes the revision from the text.

- *Skip.* Leaves the revision marked so you or someone else can consider
  the change.

Ami Pro scrolls through your document, verifying each insertion and deletion. In addition, notes are displayed for insertion or deletion.

If you prefer to accept every revision without scanning your document, you
can click **A**ccept All Revisions from the Revision Marking dialog box. Ami Pro
accepts all suggested insertions and deletions.

Similarly, you can cancel all suggested revisions by clicking **C**ancel All Revisions. The document reverts to its original form.

Troubleshooting

When I use justified alignment in layout mode, text and word spacing sometimes become misaligned.

Ami Pro constantly calculates justified text so that it fits on your screen line by line. Switch to draft mode and then back to layout mode (press Ctrl+M twice) to rejustify your text.

I want to use different styles for two sentences in the same paragraph.

Ami Pro styles affect the entire paragraph automatically. Press the Enter key between the two sentences and select a different style for each sentence. You can also change text attributes of a specific word or character.

I want to get rid of a style.

Choose **S**tyle, Style Ma**n**agement. Select the style from the Paragraph Styles list and then choose the Remove button. Choose OK to close the Style Management dialog box.

From Here...

This chapter prepared you to edit long documents. Using different views and modes helps you keep track of significant amounts of text in large documents. You learned the steps involved in formatting and revising your documents. You can learn more Ami Pro functions in the following chapters:

- Chapter 17, "Working with Frames, Tables, and Charts," describes how to add graphics and tables to your documents to make them more interesting and readable.

- Chapter 18, "Customizing Ami Pro and Other Features," shows you how to change user defaults and view preferences, as well as how to compare documents and sort lists.

Chapter 17

Working with Frames, Tables, and Charts

by Sue Plumley

Ami Pro has many features that you can use to create professional-looking documents. These desktop publishing features enable you to add pictures, produce tables, create your own images, and easily manipulate the graphics in your documents.

Additionally, you can place graphics and tables in Ami Pro frames and treat them as separate mini-documents. You can size and move frames, as well as customize and modify frame format to suit the contents and your document design.

This chapter discusses using frames, pictures, and tables in your Ami Pro documents. Specifically, you learn to:

- Create and customize frames
- Import pictures into Ami Pro frames
- Create and edit tables
- Modify column and row height and width
- Insert and delete columns and rows

Working with Ami Pro Frames

A *frame* is a container within the page that can hold either text or pictures. A *text frame* can hold a callout, quote, or specially formatted headline, for example; and a *picture frame* could hold clip art, drawings, charts, or a table.

Tip
You can use empty frames in your document to block off areas where you want to add pasted-up items after printing.

Tip
Use a frame in the margin, header, or footer of your document so you can easily move or format the text.

You can even place a frame inside of a frame, and each can hold different items.

Just as you can control the contents of the frames in your document, you can control the appearance. Each frame has its own layout options. You can adjust a frame's margins and columns; add lines, color, and shadows to a frame; and even control how the rest of the document works with the frame.

Ami Pro enables you to set a specific frame size and position, or you can adjust the size and move the frame with the mouse to suit the document's needs. As an extra bonus, you can set frame defaults so all the frames in your document follow the same layout, and you can copy and paste frames and their contents, as well.

Creating Frames

You can add an empty frame to a document to hold text, graphics, or charts. Ami Pro enables you to indicate an exact size and position for the frame before creating it, or you can draw the frame with the mouse and change size and position later. After creating the frame, you can move it around the page, add images to it, or change layout options.

 To create a frame, you can click the Insert a Frame SmartIcon and draw the frame on the page with the mouse. Alternatively, you can follow these steps:

1. Choose **F**rame, **C**reate Frame to display the Create Frame dialog box (see fig. 17.1).

Fig. 17.1
Use the Create Frame dialog box to create a frame in your document.

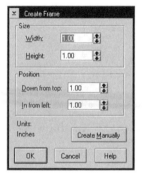

2. Customize the vertical and horizontal size of the frame by clicking the appropriate arrow buttons in the dialog box or by typing the information in the **W**idth and **H**eight selection boxes.

3. You can change the on-screen location of the frame. Use the up- or down-arrow keys or type the information you want in the **D**own from Top or **I**n from Left selection boxes in the Position section of the dialog box. The default location is one inch down from the top and one inch in from the left.

4. Click OK to have Ami Pro create the frame. The frame displays with the default formatting assigned by Ami Pro.

After Ami Pro creates the frame, you can easily move it or resize it using the mouse. Move the frame by clicking anywhere inside it and holding down the mouse button as you drag the frame to a new position. Resize a frame by positioning the mouse pointer over one of the handles until you see a double-headed arrow (see fig. 17.2). Drag the handle toward the center of the frame to reduce the frame size or away from the frame's center to enlarge its size.

Tip

Frames can span several columns. Use a frame to place a headline or graphic over multiple columns.

Tip

Resize the frame proportionally by dragging a corner handle; dragging a side handle distorts the frame size.

Frame's ruler

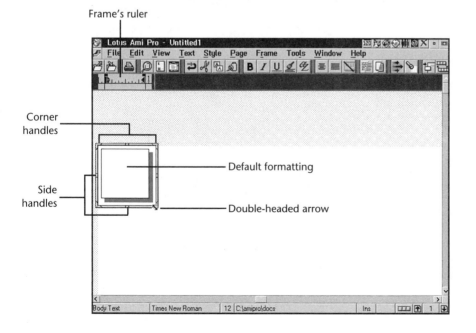

Corner handles

Side handles

Default formatting

Double-headed arrow

Fig. 17.2
Use the handles and the double-headed arrow to resize the frame.

III

Using Ami Pro

You can easily delete a frame by selecting it and then pressing the Delete key.

Frame Options

Each frame contains custom characteristics that determine on-screen appearance. By modifying frame options, you can establish text wrap around frames, set and remove frame borders, change the size and outside margins, as well as many other options.

> **Note**
>
> Choose **M**ake Default in the Modify Frame Layout dialog box to set any options you have changed as defaults. For example, set a frame as opaque with square corners with no line or border and no margins as your default; each frame you create will have this formatting until you change options again.

 You can access frame options by first selecting the frame that you want to change. A selected frame appears with a gray border and handles around it (refer to figure 17.2). To modify the layout, choose F**r**ame, **M**odify Frame Layout. Alternatively, right-click the selected frame or click the Modify Frame Layout SmartIcon. Figure 17.3 shows the Modify Frame Layout dialog box with the Type tab displaying.

Fig. 17.3
Modify specific features of the frame in the Modify Frame Layout dialog box.

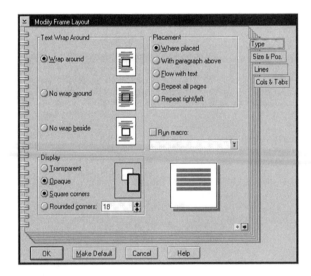

Type

Frame type includes text wrap, frame placement, and display options. To modify any of these options, choose the Type tab in the Modify Frame Layout dialog box.

Modify the text wrap options when you want to adjust how the text outside the frame flows. Use the Text Wrap Around section of the dialog box to select text wrap options. Ami Pro provides a picture next to each option demonstrating how the frame will affect wrapping text. You can wrap the text in any of the following three ways:

- ■ *Wrap Around.* Places text around all four borders of the inserted frame. This option can disrupt the flow of the text so that it is hard to read; it's best to use when you place one side of a frame against a margin or column edge.

- ■ *No Wrap Around.* Flows text behind and through the frame. This option is useful for creating images in the background of your document. Make sure you screen the image so it does not overwhelm the text in the foreground.

- ■ *No Wrap Beside.* Sets text flow above and below the frame, but not beside it. This option is useful for breaking up large streams of text with charts or graphics.

Frame placement also is important. You can place a frame in a certain spot within the text or anchor it on-screen by using the Placement options in the Type tab (refer to fig. 17.3).

Refer to the following list for a closer look at the options in the Placement section of this dialog box:

- ■ *Where Placed.* (default) The frame remains where you place it regardless of text changes and additions.

- ■ *With Paragraph Above.* Anchors the frame to a return at the end of the paragraph above it. If more text is added to the document, the frame automatically flows with the text, keeping the same relative position. The frame can be no larger than the current column.

- ■ *Flow With Text.* Anchors the frame to the last character within a paragraph. If more text is added to the document, the frame automatically flows with the text, keeping the same relative position. The frame can be no larger than the current column.

III

Using Ami Pro

- ■ *Repeat All Pages.* Repeats the frame in the same place on every page.

- ■ *Repeat Right/Left.* Repeats the frame in the same place on every alternating page. If frame is located on a left page, then it repeats on every left page.

Display options, also located on the Type tab, include the following:

- ■ *Transparent.* Sets option so you can see through the frame to whatever is printed in the background.

- ■ *Opaque.* Frame background is nontransparent, thus blocking out whatever is in the background.

- ■ *Square Corners.* Corners are squared as opposed to rounded.

- ■ *Rounded Corners.* Sets the corners as rounded; you also can enter a value between 0 (square) and 100 (circle) to define corners.

Size and Position

The Size & Pos. tab of the Modify Frame Layout dialog box enables you to set the size of the frame, its position on the page, and margins for the frame. Figure 17.4 shows the Size & Position tab of the dialog box.

Fig. 17.4
Use the Size & Pos. tab to place or size the frame exactly.

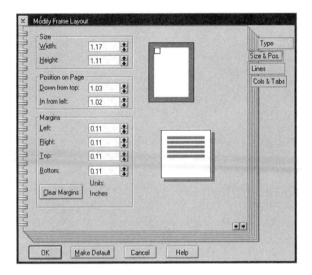

Enter the exact size of the frame in the **W**idth and **H**eight text boxes in the Size area of the Size & Pos. tab. The size of the frame is measured in inches, by default.

To change the position of the frame on the page, enter a value in **D**own from Top to move the frame vertically and **I**n from Left to move the frame horizontally. The measurements are from the edge of the page, not from the margin. Notice that the frame moves in the sample box when you enter a new value.

Finally, you can set margins for the frame in the Margins area of the Size & Pos. tab. You can set any one, two, or all margins by entering a value in the appropriate text box. The margins you set for a frame are applied to the inside and outside of the margins. Use the margins to keep both inside and outside text from running into the frame edge.

Lines

You can add a border, only one or two lines, a shadow, or color to a frame using the Modify Frame Layout dialog box. Choose the Lines tab (see fig. 17.5) and choose from the following options:

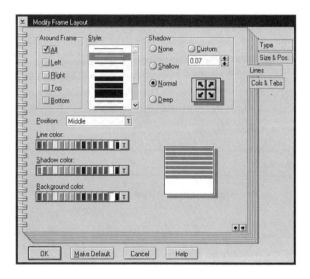

Tip
Resizing the frame also resizes the image.

▶ See "Changing Your User Setup," p. 362

Fig. 17.5
Modify lines, borders, and colors in the Lines tab of the Modify Frame Layout dialog box.

III

Using Ami Pro

- *Around Frame.* Specifies which frame borders to display. Click the checkboxes to specify **A**ll (default), **L**eft, **R**ight, **T**op, or **B**ottom. You can check one, two, or more of these checkboxes.

- *Style.* Defines the border's line style. You can choose thin, thick, or special line types to represent the frame's borders.

■ *Shadow.* Establishes the type of shadow that the frame uses. You can choose **N**one, **S**hallow, **N**ormal, **D**eep, or **C**ustom. If you choose **C**ustom, enter a value in the text box and watch the sample as it changes. In addition, you can specify which corner the shadow is placed on by clicking the arrow pointing to the corner you want to use.

In **P**osition, choose where in the frame you want the border to appear. The position of the border line is relative to the frame margin. Inside, for example, places the lines directly on the frame's margins whereas Middle creates the lines halfway between the frame margins and the frame edges. Middle is the default choice. You set the frames margins in the Size & Pos. tab of the same dialog box.

You also can choose a **L**ine Color, **S**hadow Color, and **B**ackground Color for the frame. Click the color you want to use. For more colors, click the down arrow beside the color bar and then select the color you want to use.

Columns and Tabs

◄ See "Changing Paragraph Attributes," p. 272

◄ See "Formatting the Page," p. 279

You can set columns and tabs in a frame as you would on a page of your document by using either the Cols & Tabs tab in the Modify Frame Layout dialog box or by using the frame's ruler. Ami Pro enables you to set specific tab stops and tab leaders and to move and delete tabs. Additionally, you can enter up to eight columns, set gutter width and column balance, and even add a line between columns.

Troubleshooting

No matter where I place my frame, it moves when I edit the text.

You have the wrong placement option selected. Open the Modify Frame Layout dialog box and select the Type tab. In Placement, choose **W**here Placed and choose OK. The frame now remains wherever you place it.

I just spent a long time formatting a frame, and I want all my frames to look the same. Do I have to format each frame individually?

No. Select the frame you just formatted and open the Modify Frame Layout dialog box. Choose the **M**ake Default button at the bottom of the dialog box and choose OK. All frames you now create will look the same as this formatted frame until you change the format again.

Using Graphics with Ami Pro

Graphics can refer to clip art, lines, borders, screens, tables, and so on; however, in this book, graphics refers to pictures, or clip art. You can use the clip art that comes with Ami Pro or clip art created in other applications, such as encapsulated PostScript files (EPS), Tagged Image Format files (TIFF), or OS/2 metafiles.

You can place graphics anywhere in a document and resize them to fit your spacing needs. Ami Pro automatically creates a frame for graphics added to a document. By using the frame controls described in the preceding sections, you can customize the frames that hold the clip art.

Adding an Ami Pro Graphic to a Document

Ami Pro comes with more than 100 pieces of clip art, ranging from computers to leaves. Use clip-art images to add power and interest to your documents.

To add an Ami Pro clip-art image to a document, follow these steps:

1. Place the insertion point in your document where you want to place the clip art. Alternatively, you can create a frame and select it.

2. Choose **F**ile, **I**mport Picture to display the Import Picture dialog box (see fig. 17.6). Ami Pro enables you to import images from several popular graphics packages, including Ami Pro's own AmiDraw pictures.

Fig. 17.6

Import a clip-art file using the Import Picture dialog box.

III

Using Ami Pro

3. The default file type is AmiDraw (SDW), and available files are listed in the dialog box. In the **F**iles list, select the image that you want to import.

> **Note**
>
> If you performed a Custom or Laptop installation, these images may not have been placed on your computer. You must have access to the C:\AMIPRO\DRAWSYM subdirectory.

4. Click OK to import the Ami Pro clip art. Ami Pro inserts the image into your document (see fig. 17.7).

Fig. 17.7
BIGTRUCK.SDW inserted into a frame in the document.

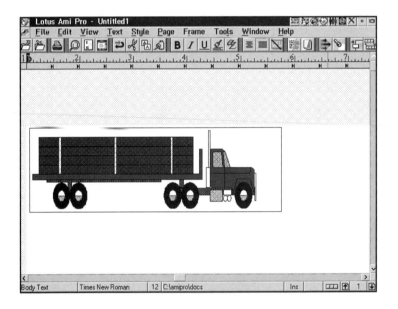

Pasting a Graphic from Another OS/2 Application

You also can paste graphic images from other OS/2 applications into your Ami Pro documents. This process, which is similar to importing files, involves using the OS/2 Clipboard to copy information from one program to another. Follow these steps:

1. In the other program, select the graphic that you want to use in Ami Pro, and then choose **E**dit, **C**opy. The Clipboard temporarily stores the image.

2. Switch to the Ami Pro application and your document.

3. In your Ami Pro document, position the insertion point where you want to place the graphic or create a frame in which to place the picture.

4. Choose **E**dit, **P**aste to paste the image from the OS/2 Clipboard into Ami Pro. Ami Pro automatically creates a frame when the new image is pasted if you did not create the frame first.

▶ See "Using the OS/2 Clipboard to Transfer Data," p. 512

Understanding Tables

Many times, you need to present information in columnar format. Whether the information is company earnings over several years or salary compari- sons, you can incorporate this data into a report, newsletter, or other Ami Pro document.

Using Ami Pro, you can create tables to store and format columnar informa- tion. You can create, edit, and delete tables that contain multiple rows and columns. Although not as sophisticated as Lotus 1-2-3 worksheets, these tables offer mathematical flexibility to Ami Pro users.

Simply create a table of any size, and then enter the required information cell by cell. When your table is complete, you can create charts and graphs from that data. You also can edit and format the table using Ami Pro's powerful editing features.

Adding a Table

You can add a table at the insertion point or within a frame in an Ami Pro document. You specify the number of rows and columns to create a table, and then you can enter and edit the data and modify the table.

To add a table to the current document, follow these steps:

1. Place the insertion point where you want the table to appear.

2. Choose **Too**ls, **Ta**bles or click the Create Table icon to display the Create Table dialog box (see fig. 17.8).

Fig. 17.8
Specify the size of the table in the Create Table dialog box.

3. Use the Number of **C**olumns and Number of **R**ows options to specify the number of rows and columns that you want to use.

4. Click OK. Ami Pro creates the table according to your specifications.

◄ See "Viewing Parts of the Window," p. 36

> **Note**
>
> The Ami Pro menu bar changes when the insertion point is in a table. A Ta**b**le menu becomes available. You also can choose the Tables SmartIcon set to make your work faster and easier.

Tip

If the table gridlines don't appear on-screen, choose **V**iew, View **P**references, and choose the Main tab in the dialog box. Check the **T**able Gridlines options and choose OK.

> **Caution**
>
> The table gridlines you show on-screen through the View Preferences dialog box don't print. If you want to print table gridlines you must apply lines using Ta**b**le, Li**n**es & Color.

Placing Information in a Table

After you create the table, you can fill it with text or graphics. You can import a picture to a cell using the same method as described previously for importing clip art. Alternatively, you can enter text into a table cell.

You can enter any amount of text in a cell. Typing text in a table is similar to typing in a regular document. The text wraps as you type, and if you press Enter, another line is added to the cell.

Additionally, moving around a table is similar to moving around in your document. You can click any cell to place the insertion point in that cell. You also can use the arrow keys to move around in a table and to move one character or line at a time, or you can press the Tab key to move one cell forward and Shift+Tab to move one cell back.

Using Drag-and-Drop to Move Cell Information

Ami Pro tables support the drag-and-drop feature, enabling you to move blocks of information within a table. To move specific cells, drag them to a new location as shown in figure 17.9.

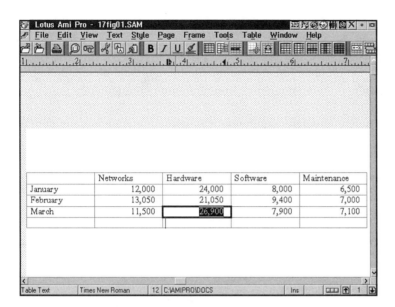

Fig. 17.9
Select the text and
drag it to a new
position within
the table.

Changing Table Attributes

You can change several table attributes, including row and column size, as
well as add table elements.

By default, all cells are the same width and height. You can, however, change
the width and row height of an entire column. In addition, you can increase
the number of columns and rows in tables to make room for additional
information.

Changing Column Width

Adjust column width to accommodate the text or data in the cells. To change
the column width, follow these steps:

1. Place the insertion point in the column that you want to change.

2. Choose Ta**b**le, Column/Row **S**ize or click the Size Columns and Rows
   SmartIcon. The Column/Row Size dialog box appears (see fig. 17.10).

Tip
You can select any
text in a table cell
and format its font,
size, alignment,
spacing, and so
on as you would
with any text in a
document.

Fig. 17.10
Change the
column width or
the row size in the
Column/Row Size
dialog box.

III

Using Ami Pro

3. Change the Column **W**idth option by clicking the arrow buttons or typing a new value in the text box. The default measurement unit is inches.

4. Click OK to save your changes and modify the table.

Alternatively, you can click the column gridline in the table and drag the double-headed arrow to adjust the width of the column.

Changing Row Height

You also can customize the height of rows in a table to make the table easier to read, so that you can add a graphic or enlarge the text in one or more cells. Follow these steps to change the row height in a table:

1. Choose the Ta**b**le, Modify Table **L**ayout command. The Modify Table Layout dialog box appears (see fig. 17.11).

Fig. 17.11
Set table defaults in the Modify Table Layout dialog box.

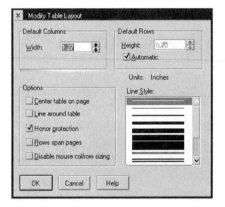

2. In the Default Rows section of the dialog box, deselect the **A**utomatic checkbox.

> **Note**
>
> If you want to change the default row height—the height of all rows in the table—enter a value in the **H**eight text box in the Default Rows area.

3. Click OK to save your changes.

4. Click in the first cell of the row you want to change.

5. Choose Ta**b**le, Column/Row **S**ize command. The Column/Row Size dialog box appears.

6. Enter the value for the row in the Row **H**eight text box and choose OK to close the dialog box.

> **Note**
>
> You can, alternatively, position the mouse on the row gridline until you see a double-arrow. Drag the gridline up or down to modify the row height.

Adding New Columns or Rows

In addition to changing table width and height, you can add new rows and columns. To create a new column or row, follow these steps:

1. Place the insertion point in the table where you want to insert new rows or columns.

> **Note**
>
> If there isn't enough room for a column, Ami Pro will not insert it; you will need to resize the other columns first to make room.

2. Choose the Ta**b**le, **I**nsert Column/Row command to display the Insert Column/Row dialog box (see fig. 17.12).

Fig. 17.12
Use the Insert Column/Row dialog box to add one or more columns or rows to the table.

III

Using Ami Pro

3. To insert a row, click the **R**ows option button. To insert a column, click **C**olumns.

4. Use the Number to Insert pop-up list to determine the number of rows to insert. In the Position section, you can select the **B**efore or **A**fter option button to determine whether you want to place the rows or columns before or after the current cursor location.

5. Click OK to insert the rows.

Note

You can, alternatively, position the mouse in the table and then click either the Insert Column or Insert Row SmartIcon.

Note

To delete a column or row, select it and then choose the Ta**b**le, **D**elete Column/Row command. From the dialog box, choose whether to delete **C**olumns or **R**ows and choose OK. Ami Pro deletes the selected column or row and its contents.

Troubleshooting

I want to place a graphic in my document without a frame around it, but Ami Pro always adds frames to my pictures.

Although you cannot remove the frame from the picture, you can remove the border lines and shadow. In the Lines section of the Modify Frame Layout dialog box, deselect the **A**ll checkbox and choose **N**one in the Shadow section. Then click OK. You now see only the information stored in the frame. Click the **M**ake Default button to have your future frames appear without borders.

From Here...

This chapter showed you how to spice up your documents with frames, tables, and pictures. You can use frames to add graphics, text, and other items to your document. In addition, you became familiar with adding and customizing columnar tables. You can learn more Ami Pro functions in the following chapters:

- Chapter 19, "Automating with Macros and Style Sheets," discusses using macros to run specific Ami Pro tasks and creating a mail merge.

- Part IV, "Using Freelance Graphics," covers using the Lotus SmartSuite presentation package.

- Chapter 20, "Getting Started with Freelance Graphics," introduces basic Freelance Graphics techniques.

Chapter 18

Customizing Ami Pro and Other Features

by Sue Plumley

Ami Pro enables you to personalize many default options to fit your working style. Customizing Ami Pro allows you to enable features you use most often or disable features that you prefer not to use. You can change your user setup and your viewing preferences.

By changing the user setup, you modify those defaults and options that directly affect your work. You can, for example, set an automatic backup, determine the number of undo levels, and disable drag and drop. You can set typographical options such as the hyphenation zone and widow and orphan control.

One of the handiest features for customization is the path you use to store documents, style sheets, backups, and so on. Ami Pro enables you to set any path you want as your user default to speed your work and make it much easier.

In addition to customizing the user setup, Ami Pro enables you to set viewing preferences such as those elements you want to view on-screen, custom view settings, and items you want to view when in clean screen mode.

In this chapter, you learn to:

- Customize user options
- Set typographic controls
- Modify your default file paths

- Change viewing options

- Customize the elements you view on-screen

Changing Your User Setup

You can change many default Ami Pro options through the User Setup dialog box. You can specify editing, notes, or file saving options that automatically take effect every time you start Ami Pro.

These options enable you to customize the look, feel, and performance of Ami Pro on your desktop. Also accessible through the User Setup dialog box are the default Ami Pro paths for saving documents, style sheets, and so on.

Choose Tools, **U**ser Setup to display the User Setup dialog box, in which you can change many default characteristics of Ami Pro (see fig. 18.1).

Fig. 18.1
The User Setup dialog box contains various tabs describing the options you can customize.

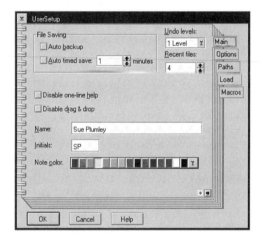

Setting Main Options

The following are descriptions of the options you can select using the Main tab in the User Default dialog box. Any options you set remain enabled until you change them.

- *Auto **B**ackup*. Automatically creates a backup of the last saved version of your Ami Pro documents. When you choose this option, the backup is saved in the path designated in the Paths tab of the dialog box.

- *A*uto *Timed Save*. Automatically saves your document at the interval that you specify in the text box.

> **Caution**
>
> If you plan to make significant changes in your document and you want to use the Save As command to save it in a separate file, disable the automatic save feature so your changes are not saved over the original document.

- *Undo Levels*. Establishes the number of recent commands you can undo, up to four. Ami Pro uses slightly more memory for each Undo level available. You also can turn Undo off.

- *Recent Files*. Changes the number (from 0 to 5) of recently activated files listed at the bottom of the *F*ile menu.

- *Disable One-Line Help*. Disables the descriptions that appear in the title bar when you choose a command.

- *Disable Drag and Drop*. Disables the drag-and-drop feature, which you use to move and copy selected text with your mouse.

- *Name*. Lists the name of the Ami Pro user.

- *Initials*. Specifies the initials used in on-screen notes.

- *Note Color*. Specifies the color of notes on your screen.

When you finish with the Main tab of the User Setup dialog box, you can choose OK to close the dialog box, or you can choose another tab.

Changing Options

The Options tab of the User Setup dialog box includes controls for setting typographic and speed options (see fig. 18.2). Typographic options are concerned with how your text looks on the page; hyphenation and widow/orphan control are two important issues in creating a professional-looking document. The speed options refer to whether Ami Pro prints in the background and whether the listbox in the Open dialog box automatically fills.

The following choices are in the Options tab of the User Setup dialog box:

- *Hyphenation Hot-Zone*. Sets the minimum number of spaces (between 2 and 9) available at the right margin before Ami Pro adds a hyphen instead of wrapping text to the next line.

- *Widow/Orphan Control*. Prevents single lines of a paragraph (first line or last) from printing at the top or bottom of a page or column.

III

Using Ami Pro

Fig. 18.2

Use the Options tab to control how your text looks and background printing.

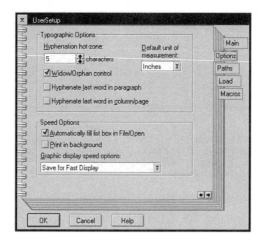

- *Hyphenate **L**ast Word in Paragraph.* Determines whether the last word of a paragraph uses a hyphen.

- *Hyphenate Last Word in **C**olumn/Page.* Determines whether the last word in a column or page uses a hyphen.

- ***D**efault Unit of Measurement.* Choose inches, centimeters, picas, or points as the default unit of measurement in dialog boxes, the ruler, and otherwise throughout Ami Pro.

- ***A**utomatically Fill List Box in File/Open.* Determines whether the Files list-box in the Open dialog box lists files in the default directory.

> **Note**
>
> The Fill List Box button is available in the File Open dialog box if the option is not selected in the User Setup dialog box. You can choose the button in the File Open dialog box to temporarily fill the Files listbox.

- ***P**rint in Background.* Makes background printing possible, which enables you to return to your document after printing, although it takes slightly longer to complete your print job. Background printing enables the Ami Pro print manager, called AmiPrint, to print your files.

- ***G**raphic Display Speed Options.* Sets graphics display for either fast display or slower. Fast display saves a copy of the graphic with the file and therefore takes up more disk space.

When you are finished choosing options, choose OK or another tab in the User Setup dialog box.

Setting Paths

You can change your default file directories by clicking the Paths tab in the User Setup dialog box. In the default paths boxes, you can access documents, style sheets, and macros in different default directories (see fig. 18.3). You also can establish a backup directory if you enable the automatic Ami Pro backup feature described earlier in the section "Setting Main Options."

Tip

All paths set in the User Setup dialog box must be set to a hard disk.

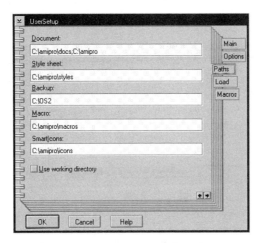

Fig. 18.3
Set paths that make accessing your work easier and faster.

To change a directory, click the desired box and type in the new drive and directory. Click OK to save your changes. Following are descriptions of each path box:

- **Document**. Sets the default drive and directory for saving (Save As dialog box) and opening (Open dialog box) documents.

- **Style Sheet**. Sets the drive and directory to store and retrieve style sheets.

- **Backup**. Sets drive and directory used to store backup files created with the Auto Backup.

> **Note**
>
> The directory specified in the Backup path must be different from that of the Document path; otherwise, the backup file overwrites the original file.

III

Using Ami Pro

■ *Macro*. Sets the drive and directory for storing and retrieving macro files. Do not set the path to a root directory; you cannot record a macro to the root.

■ *SmartIcons*. Sets the drive and directory used to store SmartIcons and icon sets.

Choosing Load Options

You can change certain document load defaults in the User Setup dialog box. Click the Load tab to change View, Mode, and Style Sheet options (see fig. 18.4).

Fig. 18.4

Set the defaults for how the screen looks when you start Ami Pro.

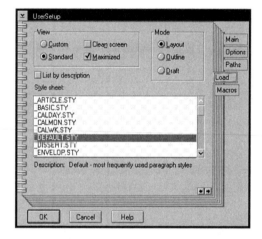

The Load tab enables you to change the default options for loading Ami Pro. The View area defines how your screen appears: in **C**ustom or **S**tandard view, in Clea**n** Screen, and/or **M**aximized. The Mode area determines whether Ami Pro displays in **L**ayout, **O**utline, or **D**raft mode.

The Default S**t**yle Sheet is the style sheet that loads when Ami Pro starts. You can change the style sheet by choosing one in the S**t**yle Sheet list. To read a description of each style sheet, check the List By Descri**p**tion option.

Setting Macro Options

Use the Macro tab of the User Setup dialog box to choose the macros you want to load every time Ami Pro starts. You can choose from Ami Pro's built-in macros or create your own. Click the down arrow in the Pro**g**ram Load listbox to display a list of Ami Pro's macros and choose the one you want to load with Ami Pro. Alternatively, click the down arrow in the Program **E**xit listbox to display the same list and choose the macro you want to run when you exit Ami Pro.

Enter the **M**acro Path if you are not using the default path in which to store your macros.

▶ See "Under-
standing and
Using Ami Pro
Macros," p. 372

Understanding View Preferences

You can customize the way a page appears as you work. Whether you want to display tab markers or change the color of your margin, Ami Pro enables you to control many page and view characteristics.

By changing these View Preferences, you can change the way pictures, margins, and tables appear on-screen while you use Ami Pro.

Change these options by choosing the **V**iew, View **P**references command to access the View Preferences dialog box shown in figure 18.5. Select the specific view preferences you want to use, and click OK to save your changes.

Fig. 18.5
Select those items you want to show on-screen as you work.

III

Changing the Main View Preferences

The Main tab of the View Preferences dialog box governs which elements display on-screen, including column guides, tabs and returns, notes, and so on. You can choose to display any element by clicking the checkbox so that a checkmark appears in the box beside the option. Following is a description of the elements you can choose to view or hide:

- *Column Guides*. Show or hide column guides with a non-printing dotted line, only in layout mode.

- *Margins in Color*. Displays a dotted or colored pattern in the page margins in layout mode.

- *Pictures*. Shows or hides pictures on-screen; if hidden, pictures appear as a box with an X in the box. Ami Pro operates faster if pictures are not displayed.

- *Tabs & Returns*. Displays symbols for tabs, returns, and line breaks.

- *Marks*. Displays symbols for column breaks, page breaks, inserted ruler or page layout, and floating headers and footers.

- *Notes*. Displays notes as colored rectangles in the text.

- *Outline Buttons*. Displays Outline buttons in outline mode.

- *Table Gridlines*. Displays non-printing lines between table columns and rows.

- *Table Row/Column Headings*. Displays the table headings (row numbers and column letters) when the insertion point is in the table.

- *Vertical Ruler*. Displays a vertical ruler in layout mode.

- *Horizontal Scroll Bar*. Displays the horizontal scroll bar in layout mode.

- *Custom View*. Specify a percentage (between 10 and 400) in which to view the screen when in custom view.

When finished setting the viewing options, choose OK to close the dialog box, or choose the Clean Screen tab to make more changes.

Using Clean Screen Options

Sometimes, you want to display your document without the clutter of the title and menu bars, SmartIcons, and status bar—maximizing your screen so that you can concentrate on your text. You can accomplish this task by using the Clean Screen feature.

◄ See "Using the Clean Screen," p. 333

A clean screen customized view displays only certain elements (menu bar, SmartIcons, and so on) on your Ami Pro screen. To customize these options, choose the Clean Screen tab in the View Preferences dialog box (see fig. 18.6).

In this dialog box, you can specify which items appear on-screen in clean screen view.

You can choose to view the title bar, menu, SmartIcons, status bar, and vertical and horizontal scroll bars. Displaying the Return icon, which appears in the lower-right corner, enables you to click it to return to your default view.

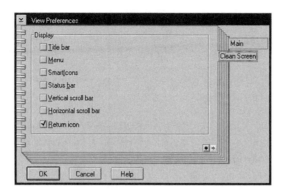

Fig. 18.6
Choose those items you want to display when using clean screen view.

Choose the options you want and click the OK button to save your changes.

Troubleshooting

I can no longer access my previous style sheets, macros, and SmartIcons.

You changed the paths in the User Setup dialog box to a new path that does not have style sheets, macros, or SmartIcons. Change your path back to its original setting.

Every time I start Ami Pro, a macro (such as the QuickStart tutorial) begins.

Deselect the Program Load checkbox in the User Setup dialog box.

In layout mode, I no longer can tell the difference between the margin and my page; the margin is no longer colored.

Choose the Margins in **C**olor option in the View Preferences dialog box, which enables you to distinguish between the Ami Pro page and the margins.

From Here...

This chapter taught you how to customize your user setup and view preferences. You learned how to have Ami Pro save your documents automatically and customize your clean screen. Use these features to make Ami Pro better fit your working style. For more information related to customizing Ami Pro, refer to these chapters:

- Chapter 14, "Proofing and Printing Documents," gives you more information on print customization and background printing.

III

Using Ami Pro

- Chapter 16, "Changing Views and Creating Outlines, Styles, and Revisions," covers the Ami Pro views and modes. This chapter also discusses using revision marks for multiple edits.

- Chapter 19, "Automating with Macros and Style Sheets," describes setting up macros for day-to-day use.

- Appendix B, "Customizing SmartIcons," discusses how to customize the location and content of SmartIcon palettes, as well as how to attach macros to customize your own SmartIcons.

Chapter 19

Automating with Macros and Style Sheets

By Robert L. Weberg

Ami Pro has many advanced features that let you work quickly and efficiently; however, they aren't found on the available menus. Using built-in tools, called macros, you can create time-saving tasks and automated style sheets.

An Ami Pro *macro* is a series of commands that perform specific tasks. You can create macros to automate routine tasks, repetitive tasks, or time-consuming tasks. Think of them as shortcuts to finishing your word processing tasks—without foregoing quality.

The quickest and easiest way to create a macro is to have Ami Pro record and save the commands used to perform a task. After saving the macro, you can play it back anytime you need to perform that task. You can even assign shortcut keys to the macros or attach the macros to SmartIcons so you can quickly implement them. You can use macros with any Ami Pro function contained in the menu commands.

You can also use the built-in macro, SMARTFLD.SMM, to create automated style sheets. This powerful tool allows you to build reusable document templates by combining macros, powerfields, and style sheets.

In this chapter, you learn to:

- Use built-in macros to automate tasks

- Create and record temporary macros

- Create and record permanent macros

- Use the SmartField macro to create reusable templates

Understanding and Using Ami Pro Macros

Macros automate a task or a set of tasks. They're mini programs that provide additional functionality in Ami Pro and an easier, faster, and more efficient way to accomplish tasks. These tasks are generally repetitive in nature or are performed the same way multiple times. Macros can range in complexity from changing a text attribute to searching files for specific pieces of text.

Lotus provides more than 40 advanced macros specifically designed to enhance Ami Pro characteristics. You can access these macros, which are installed during Ami Pro installation, from the Ami Pro menu bar and SmartIcons, and run them at any time. SmartIcons are actually icons to which specific macro functions are assigned. In Ami Pro, you can assign any permanent macro to a SmartIcon. For more information, see Appendix B, "Customizing SmartIcon Palettes."

In addition to using the installed macros, you can create your own automated processes. Your macros can perform tasks such as formatting text, changing paragraph styles, opening a specific file, or printing a range of pages when you issue or record any combination of keystroke commands.

You can create a macro by either having Ami Pro record the actions necessary to perform a task or by manually typing the desired commands in an Ami Pro document. When you write a macro, you must use the Ami Pro Macro Language to specify your instructions. This book concentrates on recording the Ami Pro commands.

> **Note**
>
> Experienced users can use the Ami Pro Macro Language commands in a document to create and manipulate powerful macros that automate groups of tasks. In fact, most of the Ami Pro Macro Language is similar to the BASIC programming language. If you aren't a computer programmer and haven't written many macros, you might have difficulty with some of the advanced macro features (not discussed in this book). If you want to learn more about the advanced macro features, start with simple macros, skipping commands and topics that you don't understand, and then build up the ones you do learn.

How can you automatically execute an Ami Pro macro?

Macros activate when you click a SmartIcon, select a new style sheet, click or select a frame, open or close a document, or load or exit Ami Pro.

> ### Note
>
> Ami Pro macros automatically copy to the AMIPRO\MACROS directory when you install Ami Pro. Save the macros you create to the AMIPRO\MACROS directory. Otherwise, you'll need to change the macro path in User Setup to find them.

Using Built-In Macros

Ami Pro has several macros available for immediate use. These built-in macros can vary in function—from searching for text in files to opening multiple documents at one time.

You can access these macros from the Ami Pro menu bar or by clicking the corresponding SmartIcon. To access the macro via the menu:

1. Choose Too**l**s, **M**acros **P**layback. The Play Macro dialog box appears (see fig. 19.1).

2. Scroll through the **M**acros listbox until you find the one you want. The Macro **D**escription explains the function of the highlighted macro. To run the macro, double-click it, or highlight the file name and choose OK. Ami Pro automatically runs the selected macro to its completion.

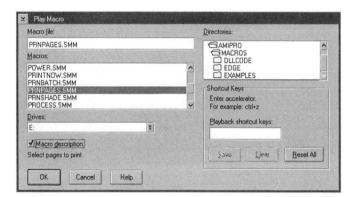

Fig. 19.1
Experiment with the various built-in macros displayed in the Play Macro dialog box by running ones that appear useful.

> ### Caution
>
> Make sure you save your open files before you experiment with various macros.

Recording and Playing Temporary Macros

Creating and playing a temporary macro for your immediate use during the current session is easy using the **Q**uick Record and **Q**uick Playback commands under the Too**l**s, **M**acros menu. These two functions allow you to automate simple repetitive tasks without saving the keystrokes to a named macro file.

> **Note**
>
> Quick Record macros are saved to the UNTITLED.SMM macro file. Only the most recently recorded Quick Record macro is available when you use Quick Playback. Keep this in mind if you use Quick Record many times in one session because you should use a quick macro only for a short-term or temporary task.

To record a temporary macro, perform the following steps:

1. Choose Too**l**s, **M**acros, **Q**uick Record. Ami Pro immediately begins recording your on-screen activities. Notice that the status bar displays Recording… in red (see fig. 19.2).

Fig. 19.2

The status bar indicates whether Ami Pro is recording a macro.

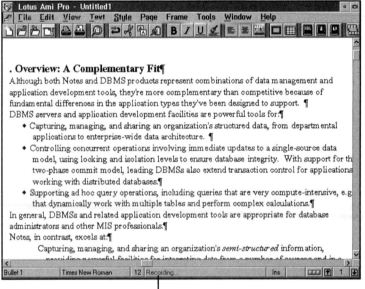

Recording macro message in red

Tip

To avoid unnecessary commands, it's best to know the keystrokes you'll want to perform beforehand.

2. You can now perform the keystrokes and tasks you want to record using the keyboard or mouse.

Ami Pro records the keystrokes, menu commands, and dialog box options you select with the mouse. It does not record mouse movements, such as moving the mouse pointer from one area of the screen to another.

> **Note**
>
> To record cursor movement in a document, you must use the keyboard and the arrow keys to move the insertion point and select text.

3. When you complete the keystrokes for the macro, choose Tools, **M**acros, End **Q**uick Record.

To play your recorded temporary macro, choose Tools, Macros **Q**uick Playback. Ami Pro plays the most recently recorded quick macro (UNTITLED.SMM).

Assigning Shortcut Keys to a Quick Macro

If you need to constantly play the temporary macro, then using the menu commands can be a time-consuming task in itself. Ami Pro possesses a great feature that allows you to assign shortcut keys to play quick macros. Just follow these steps:

1. Choose Tools, **M**acros, **R**ecord. The Record Macro dialog box appears (see fig. 19.3).

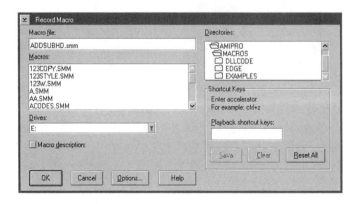

2. Choose the **O**ptions button to display the Quick Record Macro Options dialog box and then type the shortcut keys on the keyboard that you want to assign to the quick macro.

Tip
You can also click the `Recording...` message in the status bar to end the macro recording.

Fig. 19.3
The Record Macro dialog box lets you enter the name for a new permanent macro.

III

Using Ami Pro

> **Note**
>
> You can assign two shortcut key combinations. The Start/Stop record shortcut key tells Ami Pro to start or stop recording the quick macro. The Start playback shortcut key tells Ami Pro to begin playing the quick macro. You must spell out the shortcut command keys. For example, to assign Ctrl+F2, you must type the actual alphanumeric characters with no spaces. You cannot use F10, Shift+F1, or Shift+any alphanumeric key.

3. Choose OK to return to the Record Macro dialog box and then OK again to return to the current document.

You can play the quick macro by pressing the assigned shortcut keys on the keyboard.

Saving a Quick Macro

If you want to prevent a quick macro from being overwritten, you can save or rename it to a different macro file.

To save a quick macro, open UNTITLED.SMM.

1. Choose **F**ile, **O**pen and the Open dialog box appears. Choose Ami Pro Macro from the List **T**ype of File list. Make sure the current directory is \AMIPRO\MACROS in the Directories list and then choose UNTITLED.SMM in the Files list.

You can also choose Too**l**s, **M**acros, **E**dit to open UNTITLED.SMM.

2. Save the file under another name with an SMM extension. To do this, choose **F**ile, **S**ave. In the Save As dialog box, choose Ami Pro Macro as the file type and click OK.

Creating and Recording Permanent Macros

You use the same procedure for creating a permanent macro as you did to create a temporary quick macro, except you have to specify a name for the new macro before you begin recording it. Create permanent macros for actions, commands, or tasks you do frequently in Ami Pro.

By using the Too**l**s, **M**acros, **R**ecord command, you can save any action, function, or command you use frequently in Ami Pro to the macro file you designate. You can then play the macro anytime you need to perform the task.

For example, you could record a macro named ADDSUBHD.SMM to record the keystrokes required to insert or add a subheading required on company reports. You could assign Shift+F2 as the shortcut keys. Then, each time you want to add the company subheading to the current document, you only need to press Shift+F2 to play back that macro.

To record a new macro, follow these steps:

1. Choose Tools, **M**acros, **R**ecord. The Record Macro dialog box appears as shown previously in figure 19.3.

2. Enter a name for the macro you're recording, and press the shortcut keys you want to assign to the macro. Ami Pro automatically adds the SMM extension.

> **Caution**
>
> All macro files must have an SMM extension for Ami Pro to recognize them.

3. Choose OK. Ami Pro displays Recording… in red in the status bar.

4. Perform the keystrokes you want to record.

   Be certain the keystrokes you perform are the exact keystrokes you want in the macro. If you make a mistake, the mistake is saved in the macro. To edit mistakes, you can either edit the macro file or record the keystrokes again.

5. After completing the keystrokes for the macro, choose Tools, **M**acros, **E**nd Record, or click the Recording… message in the status bar to end the macro recording.

Tip

Try attaching a recorded macro to a SmartIcon that best represents the action being accomplished.

Playing a Permanent Macro

Running your newly created macro is identical to playing any built-in macro. If you assigned shortcut keys to the macro, press the appropriate keys. Otherwise, use the Playback function.

To play a macro previously saved to a file, choose Tools, **M**acros, **P**layback. When the Play Macro dialog box appears, choose the desired macro file in the **M**acros listbox. You might need to select a different drive and directory, or even type the full path and file name in the Macro **F**ile text box. Choose OK when you're finished.

III

Using Ami Pro

Tip
Double-click the
macro file name in
the **M**acros listbox
to play back the
macro.

Fig. 19.4
You can edit a
macro and the
shortcut keys
associated to it.

Assigning or Changing Shortcut Keys to a Permanent Macro

You can always modify shortcut key assignments to macros, even if you originally omitted assigning shortcut keys to your permanent macro. Just follow
these steps:

1. Choose Too**l**s, **M**acros, **E**dit. The Edit Macro dialog box appears (see
   fig. 19.4).

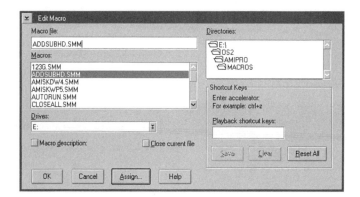

2. Select the desired macro file from the **M**acros listbox. In the **P**layback
   Shortcut Keys box, type the desired shortcut keys.

> **Note**
>
> When you assign shortcut keys, you can use either Ctrl, Shift, or any combina-
> tion of the two, with most keys. For example, you can use Shift+F2. You can-
> not use F10, Shift+F1, or Shift+any alphanumeric key.

3. Choose either **S**ave, **C**lear, or **R**eset All.

   Save. Saves the shortcut keys you specified without closing the Edit
   Macro dialog box. This allows you to assign or change shortcut keys for
   more than one macro file.

   Clear. Removes the shortcut key combination currently assigned to the
   macro.

   Reset All. Removes all the shortcut keys you assigned to all macros.

4. Choose OK to save all the macro file shortcut keys and open the currently selected macro file in a separate window to allow you to edit it; or choose Cancel to save the assigned shortcut key changes and close the Edit Macro dialog box, and then return to the document.

Playing a Macro When You Open or Close a Document

Occasionally, you might need a macro to automatically run without your assistance. Ami Pro can assign a macro to an Ami Pro document to automatically run when you open or close that file.

For example, you can assign a macro to print a document that contains a list of To Do items every time you choose **F**ile, **O**pen. Also, many style sheets in Ami Pro, such as MEMO1.STY and FAX1.STY, automatically run macros when you choose **F**ile, **N**ew.

To have a document play a macro when you open or close the document, perform the following steps:

1. Open the desired document you want to assign a File Open or File Close macro to or switch to that document to make it the active window.

2. Choose Too**l**s, **M**acros, **E**dit. The Edit Macro dialog box appears.

3. Choose **A**ssign. The Assign Macro To Run Automatically dialog box appears (see fig. 19.5).

Fig. 19.5
The PRINTNOW.SMM macro automatically runs when the TODO.SAM file opens.

4. Specify the desired Run macro options.

If you want Ami Pro to play a macro every time you open the current document, select File **O**pen and specify the desired macro (or select it from the drop-down listbox).

III

Using Ami Pro

Note

The drop-down listboxes in the Assign Macro To Run Automatically dialog box list the macros in the current default macro directory designated in the User Setup.

If you want Ami Pro to play a macro every time you close the current document, select File **C**lose and specify the desired macro (or select it from the drop-down listbox).

5. Choose OK to return to the Edit Macro dialog box. Then choose OK or Cancel to return to the current document.

Creating an Automated Style Sheet Using SmartFields

Ami Pro comes with lots of pre-designed style sheets to help create professional looking documents, such as letters, memos, faxes, and calendars, efficiently and easily. Most of these style sheets are automated, meaning that when you open a new style sheet, Ami Pro prompts you to enter information for that document. This information goes into your new document.

For example, a letter with your company's letterhead and logo could be automated to prompt for the information specific to the sender (such as name, title, and phone number) and then prompt for information specific to the recipient (such as name, company, title, address, and salutation).

Creating your own automated style sheets, tailored to your company's needs, enables you to quickly create standardized memos, letters, reports, brochures, and invoices. In fact, your managers and fellow workmates will be astonished at how you simplified many of their time-consuming administrative tasks.

An automated style sheet consists of three main elements: a document saved as a style sheet, power fields, and a macro. You can automate a style sheet by inserting pre-defined power fields, or you can utilize a powerful and easy-to-learn tool called SmartFields that enables you to quickly create automated power fields within a document. Playing back the SMARTFLD.SMM macro creates the **Sm**artFields menu.

After playing the SMARTFLD.SMM macro and displaying the SmartFields menu, there are three basic steps to creating an automated style sheet:

1. Create or modify a document you want to automate. This template contains static text or text that never changes.

2. Insert the desired power fields or SmartFields in the document using the SmartFields menu. There are two types of power fields in an automated style sheet: **P**ersonal and **O**ptional Information.

   Personal Information. These utilize default personal information data that automatically appears in a dialog box when the automated style sheet opens. This default information is initially gathered in the AMIPRO2.INI file when you first open a style sheet in Ami Pro after installation.

◀ See "Creating a New Style Sheet," p. 338

   Optional Information. These don't display in the Optional dialog box that appears when the automated style sheet opens. The user has the option of entering information into each corresponding edit box.

3. Save the document as a style sheet.

Displaying the SmartFields Menu

To make the SmartFields menu appear in Ami Pro, choose To**o**ls, **M**acros, **P**layback. Choose SMARTFLD.SMM from the list of macros, and then choose OK.

Ami Pro places SmartFields on the menu bar after **H**elp. Using the SmartFields menu, you can choose various commands to build an automated style sheet. Figure 19.6 displays the SmartFields menu.

Fig. 19.6
Using the SmartFields menu you can define Personal and Optional Information SmartFields and choose other commands to build an automated style sheet.

III

Using Ami Pro

Creating the Automated Style Sheet

To create or modify an automated style sheet, open an untitled document by choosing **F**ile, **N**ew. Choose _DEFAULT.STY, and then choose OK.

Note

If you want to use a previously created style sheet as the starting point for your auto-mated style sheet, choose **S**martFields, Edit **A**utomated Style Sheet. Choose the style sheet you want to use. This saves time over always starting a new default style sheet.

Defining the Power Fields for an Automated Style Sheet

The next step in creating an automated style sheet using the **Sm**artfields menu is to define the Personal and Optional information power fields. You can specify up to nine Personal and nine Optional power fields using the **Sm**artfields menu.

To specify your Personal and Optional Information power fields, perform the following:

1. Choose **Sm**artFields, Define **P**ersonal Information. The Personal Information dialog box appears, as shown in figure 19.7.

Fig. 19.7

Use the Personal Information dialog box to specify the field names you want to use for the default information each time you create a new document.

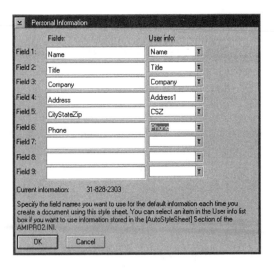

2. Type a SmartField name in the Fields text box for each field you want to include in the style sheet. You can also select a name from the User Info text box. Specify up to nine SmartField names.

The User Info listboxes contain the field names you specified the first time you chose **F**ile, **N**ew, opened a style sheet, and then selected **W**ith Contents and **R**un **m**acro. The AMIPRO2.INI file stores this informa-tion in the [AutoStyleSheet] section.

Note

To see or change what you specified in your User Info list, play back the COLLECT.SMM macro by choosing Tools, Macros, Playback. Choose COLLECT.SMM and then choose OK. The Default Information dialog box appears, shown in figure 19.8.

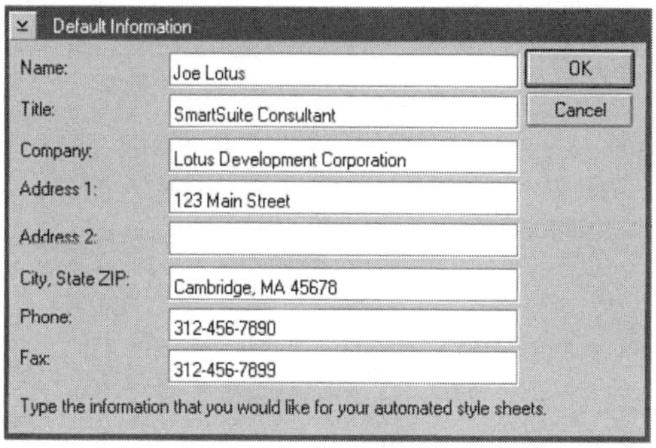

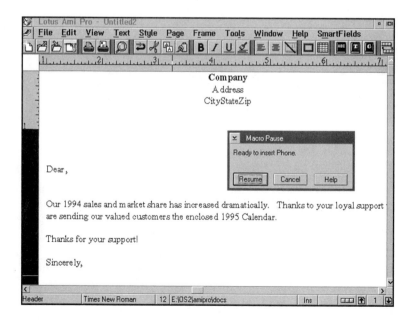

Fig. 19.8
The Default Information dialog box can be accessed by playing back the COLLECT.SMM macro. It allows you to enter or change your desired default information that appears in automated style sheets.

3. Choose OK, and Ami Pro displays the Macro Pause dialog box that prompts you to specify the locations in your document for the SmartFields you specified in the Personal Information dialog box (see fig. 19.9).

Fig. 19.9
The Macro Pause dialog box appears for every SmartField you specified in the Personal Information dialog box.

III

Using Ami Pro

4. Click in the document where you want to insert the field, and then choose Resume. The Macro Pause dialog box doesn't disappear, it becomes grayed when you click the document.

5. Repeat step 5 for each SmartField defined.

6. Choose S**m**artFields, Define **O**ptional Information. The Optional Information dialog box appears (see fig. 19.10).

> **Note**
>
> The Optional Information field names allow you to specify the field names you want to use for the optional information each time you create a document using this style sheet.

Fig. 19.10

Use the Optional Information dialog box to specify the field names for the optional information each time you create a document using this style sheet.

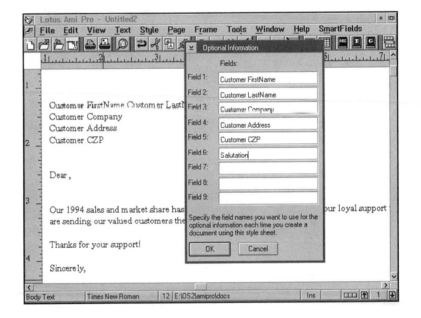

7. Specify the SmartField name for each optional information field you want to create. These SmartFields prompt you for information specific to the document you're creating. You can specify up to nine SmartFields.

8. Choose OK and Ami Pro prompts you to specify the location for the first optional SmartField name you specified. Click in the document where you want to insert the field and then choose Resume. Repeat this step for each optional information SmartField.

9. If needed, modify the page layout, paragraph styles, contents, text, objects, or pictures of the document.

10. Choose S**m**artFields, Sa**v**e Automated Style Sheet. The Save as a Style Sheet dialog box appears (see fig. 19.11). Name and describe the automated style sheet, and then click OK. Ami Pro saves the page layout, paragraph styles, contents (frames, bitmaps), and SmartFields to the style sheet.

◀ See "Changing Paragraph Attributes," p. 272

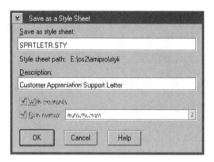

Fig. 19.11
Saving the document to be an automated style sheet.

The next time you choose **F**ile, **N**ew to create a new document using this newly saved style sheet, Ami Pro prompts you first for the Personal Information SmartFields and then the Optional Information SmartFields.

The Macro Component of the Automated Style Sheet

In order for an automated style sheet to run the Personal and Optional SmartFields that you specified by displaying dialog boxes that prompt you to enter the corresponding information, a macro needs to be selected. Fortunately, the SmartFields menu simplifies the decision of which macro to execute by automatically selecting the required macro AUTOSTY.SMM.

Figure 19.11 displays the option Run macro selected with AUTOSTY.SMM, the chosen macro.

> **Note**
>
> This option is grayed out, because AUTOSTY.SMM is required to run any automated style created from the SmartFields menu. If you designed your own power field and dialog boxes using the Ami Pro Macro Language, you could specify another macro to run.

III

Using Ami Pro

Running the Automated Style Sheet

To run the automated style sheet you created in the previous steps, do the following:

1. Choose **F**ile, **N**ew to display the New dialog box.

2. In the Style Sheet for New Document list, choose the style sheet you created and click OK. The Personal Information dialog box appears, displaying the pre-entered default information (see fig. 19.12).

Fig. 19.12

The Personal Information dialog box saves time by having information already entered for you in the designated SmartFields.

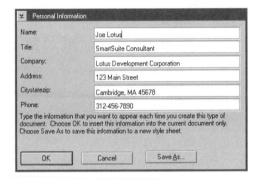

3. Enter or change any personal information as necessary, then click OK. The Optional Information dialog box appears (see fig. 19.13).

Fig. 19.13

The Optional Information dialog box prompts you to enter optional information to be placed in the automated style sheet.

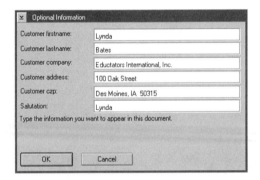

4. Enter any optional information, then click OK. The information you enter in the Personal and Optional dialog boxes replaces the SmartFields in your new document. Figure 19.14 shows the finished document.

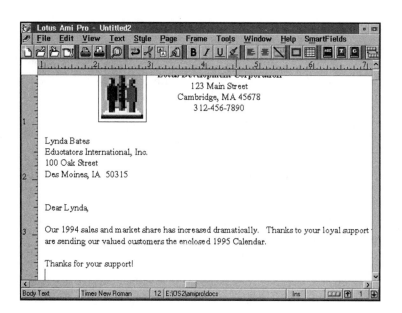

Fig. 19.14
A completed document created after selecting **F**ile, **N**ew and choosing the automated style sheet and then entering the personal and optional information.

Troubleshooting

*After inserting some Personal or Optional Information SmartFields in an automated style sheet from the S**m**artFields menu, I decided to delete a previously designated SmartField. How do I do this?*

You can choose S**m**artFields, Re**m**ove All SmartFields. But this deletes all of your Optional and Personal SmartFields. The best process to delete one SmartField is to view the SmartFields contained on your document. Choose View, Show Power Fields. The power fields and their corresponding code redisplay in brackets. Locate and highlight the SmartField and its power field code you want to delete, and then hit the delete key or choose the Cut SmartIcon.

I accidentally assigned short-cut keys that were already assigned to another macro? What can I do?

You probably received the message Keystroke already assigned as an accelerator. If you reassign this keystroke, the accelerator will no longer be accessed by this keystroke and then you clicked OK. By clicking OK, you specified and overwrote a macro playback shortcut key that's already used by Ami Pro as an accelerator key. For example, Shift+X corresponds to the Cut command; but if you specify Shift+X as the shortcut key for a new macro, it only works for the new macro. You need to reset the short-cuts keys assigned to all the macros. To do so, choose Tools, Macros, Edit. Choose Reset All to reset all the short-cut keys to their default assignments.

III

Using Ami Pro

From Here...

This chapter discussed automating tasks with Ami Pro macros and how to create automated style sheets. Automating with macros saves time, energy, and effort by performing specific tasks over and over. Use the advanced macros as additional applications and added functionality to enhance your usage of Ami Pro. To learn more about using macros to automate tasks in the SmartSuite, review the following chapters:

■ Chapter 11, "Automating with 1-2-3 Macros," describes how to create macros in 1-2-3 to automate your worksheets.

■ Chapter 12, "Creating and Editing Documents," shows the initial steps used to create and edit documents in Ami Pro, an important building block to creating automated style sheets.

■ Chapter 13, "Formatting Text and Documents," teaches you how to create professional looking documents you can use to build an automated style sheet.

■ Chapter 16, "Changing Views and Creating Outlines, Styles, and Revisions," explains the importance and foundation of styles in Ami Pro documents and style sheets.

Part IV

Using Freelance Graphics

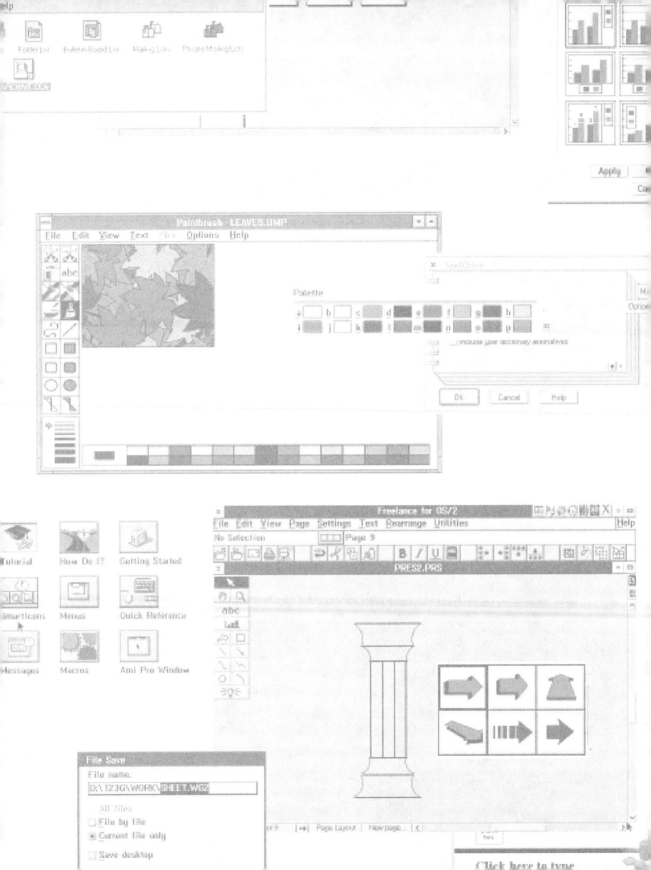

Chapter 20

Getting Started with Freelance Graphics

by Elaine Marmel

Freelance Graphics is the component of the Lotus SmartSuite that helps you create professional-quality presentations using overheads, paper, 35mm slides, photoprints, or computer screens. Before working with Freelance Graphics, you need to familiarize yourself with the Freelance Graphics window and understand the theory and process behind the way Freelance Graphics creates presentations.

In this chapter, you learn how to:

- Understand the elements of the Freelance Graphics window
- Examine components of Freelance Graphics presentations
- Understand SmartMasters, objects, and layouts
- Create a new presentation, using a variety of methods
- Change the view and order of a presentation
- Add, insert, and delete slides
- Save and close a presentation, and open an existing one

Starting Freelance Graphics

When you open Freelance Graphics, you see the dialog box shown in figure 20.1. From this dialog box, you choose either to begin working on a new presentation or to retrieve one that you have already created.

Fig. 20.1

The Welcome to Freelance Graphics dialog box starts the process of helping you begin using Freelance.

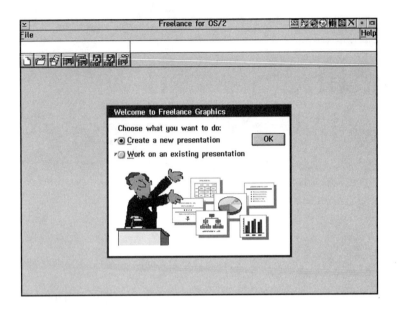

When you choose to create a new presentation, Freelance displays the next welcome dialog box, which helps you choose a look for your presentation from a list of SmartMasters (see fig. 20.2). These SmartMasters are like templates or style sheets, and provide the overall design, format, and color scheme for the presentation.

Fig. 20.2

When you start a new presentation, Freelance offers you a selection of SmartMasters upon which you can base the new presentation.

Thumbnail view of the SmartMaster

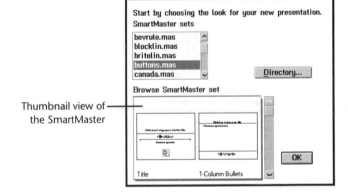

Tip

You can always modify any element of a SmartMaster, such as fonts, colors, and graphics, as you'll learn later in the chapter.

In the top-left corner of this dialog box is a list of SmartMaster sets. At the bottom of the dialog box is a thumbnail sketch of what the highlighted SmartMaster set looks like. You can get an idea of how a presentation might look based on a particular SmartMaster if you highlight the SmartMaster and then scroll through the Browse SmartMaster Set listbox.

When you select a SmartMaster and choose OK, you see the Page Choose Page Layout dialog box, shown in figure 20.3. Each SmartMaster contains several layout options for presentation pages such as title pages and bulleted lists. You use the page layouts by "filling in the blanks"—Freelance does the rest.

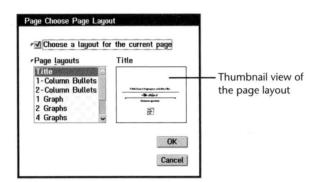

Fig. 20.3
Page layouts help you maintain a consistent look in your presentation, letting you focus on the content of the presentation rather than the design.

Finally, you come to the main Freelance Graphics screen. If you started with the default page layout suggested in the previous dialog box, you'll see the presentation's Title Page (see figure 20.4).

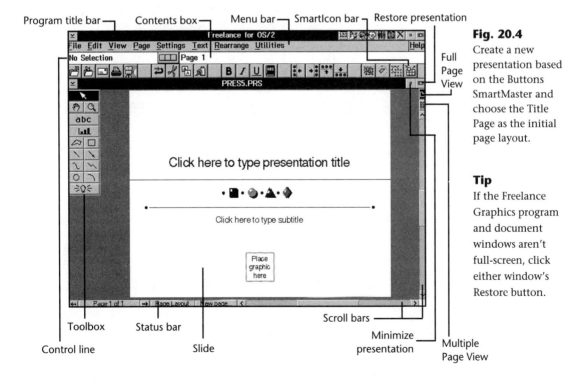

Fig. 20.4
Create a new presentation based on the Buttons SmartMaster and choose the Title Page as the initial page layout.

Tip
If the Freelance Graphics program and document windows aren't full-screen, click either window's Restore button.

Getting Familiar with the Freelance Graphics Screen

Tip

In all Lotus
SmartSuite prod-
ucts, you can find
out what a
SmartIcon does by
pointing at it and
holding down the
right mouse but-
ton. A brief expla-
nation appears in
the title bar.

Because all Lotus SmartSuite products look and feel similar, many parts of
the Freelance Graphics screen already may be familiar to you. The Freelance
Graphics menus and SmartIcons appear below the title bar at the top of the
screen. The vertical scroll bar is in its usual position at the right edge of the
window, although the horizontal scroll bar is reduced from its more traditional width (spanning the bottom edge of the window). The third bar from
the top of the screen is the control line. It displays information about the
current selection, the Show/Hide SmartIcons button, and the contents box
showing the current page.

Each presentation consists of slides. *Slides* are the individual pages in a presentation that become overheads, 35mm slides, or parts of an on-screen slide
show. The first slide in the presentation appears in the middle of the screen.

To the left of the slides, you see the Freelance Graphics toolbox, which
contains tools you use to add graphic elements such as lines or arrows
to a presentation.

At the right edge of the screen, just above the vertical scroll bar, are two icons
(refer to fig. 20.4). Each icon displays a different view of the current presentation. You learn about displaying and working with different views of your
presentation later in this chapter.

At the bottom edge of the Freelance Graphics window is the status bar (refer
to figure 20.4). The status bar shows the page number of the current slide, as
well as several buttons that enable you to move ahead or back one slide,
select or change the page layout, or create a new page.

The New Page button makes it easy for you to add a new slide to your presentation without choosing the **P**age, **N**ew command or pressing F7 (the
shortcut key for the **P**age, **N**ew command). When you click the Page Layout
button, a pop-up menu appears, from which you can choose a specially designed slide layout to apply to the page you're currently viewing. At the far
right end of the status bar is the horizontal scroll bar.

Working in a New Presentation

Virtually all presentations you create in Freelance Graphics are based on a
SmartMaster set. Each time you start a new presentation, Freelance Graphics

prompts you to select a SmartMaster set and an initial page layout. Once you understand SmartMasters and page layouts, you can easily add and delete slides.

Understanding SmartMasters

Freelance Graphics comes with a set of professionally designed templates, called *SmartMasters*, that enable you to create attractive presentations with minimal effort. You can use a SmartMaster as it comes, or you can modify it as you want. For example, you can add your company logo to a SmartMaster so that the logo automatically appears in each slide you create. You can also add pictures, text, and clip art to a SmartMaster.

When you begin to create a new presentation, you see the dialog box shown previously in figure 20.2, from which you select the SmartMaster to use as the basis for your presentation. A SmartMaster file contains all formatting and color options, graphic elements, and page layouts for a presentation. Don't worry if you decide to change the appearance of your presentation after you complete it; you can select a different SmartMaster, and Freelance Graphics changes all your slides to reflect the new design.

Working with Page Layouts

The Page Choose Page Layout dialog box lists at least nine standard page layouts that come with each SmartMaster in Freelance Graphics. In the bottom-right corner of the dialog box, you see a thumbnail sketch based on the SmartMaster that you chose. This thumbnail version shows what a slide based on a particular page layout would look like; you can see a title slide, a bulleted-list slide, and so on.

All the Page Layouts and all the SmartMaster sets are designed by professional graphic artists. Such options as background color, text color, bullet color, and text alignment are designed so you can take advantage of a professional graphic designer's expertise without actually having to be one—or having to hire one.

You can, however, change any element—text, color, graphics, and so on—within a SmartMaster set at anytime.

Understanding "Click here..." Blocks

Every page layout, except for blank pages, contains one or more "Click here..." blocks, in which you can place text, bulleted lists, symbols, graphs, or information in tables. When you add text to a "Click here..." text block, the text assumes all the attributes defined for that text block, such as font, font

Tip

You can change to a different SmartMaster set even while you're creating your presentation by choosing **S**ettings, Switch Smart**M**aster Set.

size, and background color. When you add a graphic element, such as a symbol, to a graphic "Click here..." block, the graphic is sized and positioned to reflect that block. As with all elements of a Freelance Graphics presentation, you always can go back and make any changes you want in any element.

To work with any "Click here..." block, select it and then change its content (or size, move, copy, or delete it).

Entering Text on Slides

After you choose a SmartMaster and a page layout (for example, Title), you see a screen similar to the one shown previously in figure 20.4.

Freelance Graphics makes it easy to place text in your slides. In figure 20.4, you see two "Click here..." text blocks: one for the presentation title and one for the presentation subtitle. The words you see on the SmartMaster—for example, Click here to type presentation title—won't appear on the slide. This text is here simply to help you find where to type your text. To type text, click a "Click here..." text block. When you do, a text-entry box appears (see fig. 20.5).

Fig. 20.5
Use this text-entry box to place title text on a title page.

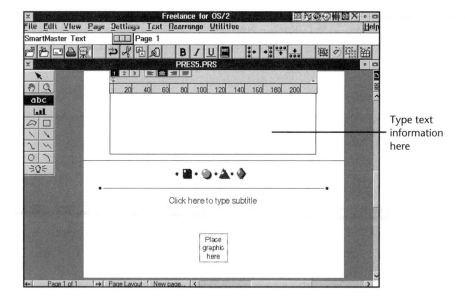

Type text information here

Tip
Press Enter to begin a new line within the text box; the font style continues to the next line.

In the box, type whatever text you want to appear on the slide, and then click anywhere outside the text box. Your text appears in the Freelance Graphics slide in the position where the "Click here..." block used to be. In figure 20.6, you see a slide that includes both a title block and a subtitle block.

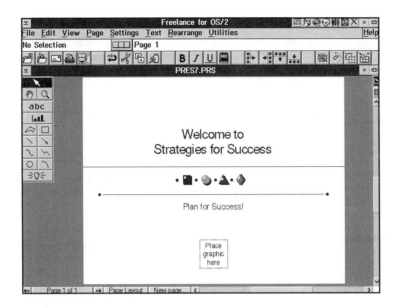

Fig. 20.6
This sample slide
includes both a
title and a subtitle.

In subsequent chapters, you learn to refine your presentation by formatting
and aligning text; inserting objects; and adding special enhancements such
as color, shadows, and patterns. You also learn to modify, create, and save
on disk new SmartMaster sets—sets that reflect, for example, your corporate
image. You then can use that new SmartMaster set from presentation to presentation to maintain a standard image in each presentation.

Note the ruler that appears when you type text. This ruler appears whenever
you type text in a text box. You'll use the ruler more when you create your
own text blocks instead of using the "Click here..." text blocks. The ruler
helps guide you while placing text on a slide.

> **Note**
>
> You can have Freelance Graphics display units of measurement in millimeters, centi-
> meters, inches, points, or picas. To change the displayed unit measurement, choose
> **S**ettings, **U**nits and Grids and then select the appropriate unit.

Adding Symbols

There's no reason for a Freelance Graphics presentation to contain dull slides
full of nothing but text. Freelance Graphics enables you to add many different types of objects to your slides to grab an audience's attention, add interest
or humor, or illustrate a particular point.

You can create some objects within Freelance Graphics and import others from other applications. To insert a standard Freelance Graphics symbol into a slide, click the Symbol tool shown in the toolbox in figure 20.7. When you click this tool, you see the Add Symbols dialog box shown in the figure.

Fig. 20.7

When you choose the Symbol tool from the Toolbox, Freelance presents you with a dialog box that helps you insert a symbol into a presentation.

Symbol tool ──

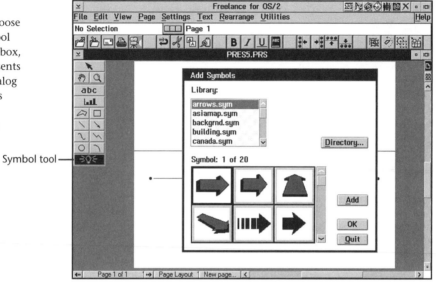

Tip

Insert your company's logo and then copy and paste the graphic to each page of your presentation for a more professional look.

From the Library list, choose the type of symbol you want. The Symbol list displays a variety of related symbols through which you can scroll. Click the symbol you want and choose OK; the symbol appears on the page. Drag the symbol to the "Place graphics here" box to let Freelance automatically resize it for you. Alternatively, you can drag the symbol to any position on the page.

If you're using a computer capable of supporting multimedia, you can add a variety of multimedia objects to your slides. For example, when you display a slide showing how far over quota annual sales are soaring, Freelance Graphics can play a WAV file of cheers and applause. Chapter 21, "Entering Slide Content," shows you how to add a variety of enhancement objects to your Freelance Graphics presentations.

Adding and Deleting Slides

After you select a SmartMaster and page layout and begin to create your presentation, you can add or delete slides whenever and wherever necessary. To add a slide after the last slide in a presentation, display the last slide, and then choose one of the following methods to open the Page Now dialog box (see fig. 20.8):

■ Click the New Page button in the status bar.

■ Click the New Page SmartIcon.

■ Choose **P**age, **N**ew.

■ Click on the Page X of Y button in the status bar. A pop-up listbox reveals the New Page command.

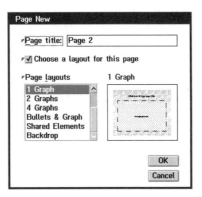

Fig. 20.8
Click the New Page button in the status bar to display the Page New dialog box.

The Page New dialog box is virtually identical to the Page Choose Page Layout dialog box (refer to fig. 20.3). In the Page New dialog box, select a page layout and click OK. Freelance Graphics displays the new page with the layout you selected.

As you refine a presentation, you may find that you don't need a slide you created. You can delete a slide at any time by displaying the slide and choosing **P**age, **R**emove.

Tip
When you want to insert a new slide between two existing slides, use the same technique, but first display the slide you want to appear before the new slide.

Troubleshooting

I tried pressing F7 to add a new page (the shortcut key). I didn't see the dialog box. What happened?

If you look at the status bar, you'll notice that you did, in fact, add a new page. When you use F7, Freelance Graphics adds a new page using the same page layout as the last slide in the presentation. Because choosing F7 duplicates the layout of the last slide, Freelance Graphics doesn't present the dialog box to choose a new page layout.

(continues)

Tip
To make your opening and closing slides the same, select the slide to copy, and choose **P**age, **D**uplicate. The slide is duplicated as the next page.

(continued)

I accidentally deleted a slide from my presentation. How can I restore it?

In any view, you can click the Undo SmartIcon in the SmartIcon palette. Alternatively, you can choose **E**dit, **U**ndo or press Alt+Backspace.

I inserted a new slide into the wrong location in my presentation. Can I move it?

Yes. It is best to use page sorter view to rearrange slides in a presentation. For specific instructions, see "Changing the Order of Presentation Slides," later in this chapter.

Viewing a Presentation

Freelance Graphics offers several ways to view your presentations, each with a particular purpose and advantage. The **V**iew menu also contains commands to switch from one view to another:

- *Current Page*. Displays individual slides in full-slide view. You can see the slide in detail and make content changes easily.

- *Page Sorter*. Displays a miniature version of every slide in the presentation, in proper order, giving you an overview of the presentation and providing you with the means to change the order of slides.

- *Screen Show*. Uses the entire screen and automatically displays each slide in your presentation for a time period you establish.

To quickly switch between current page and page sorter views, click the view buttons in the top-right corner of the Freelance Graphics document window.

Looking at Slides One at a Time

Current page view displays the individual slides in your presentation. This view is best used to get a detailed picture of each slide when you're entering or changing slide content.

At the left end of the status bar, in the bottom-left corner of the screen, you see Page 1 of 1 displayed. This display describes the slide that is currently on-screen. To the left and right of that indicator are arrows you can click to move back one slide and forward one slide. You can also press the PgUp and PgDn keys on your keyboard to move from one slide to another.

When a presentation contains a large number of slides, however, these methods may not be efficient for making large jumps—for example, from slide 3 to slide 18. You can move to a specific slide quickly by directly clicking the page number box—the one that says Page x of y. When you click this box, a pop-up list appears (see fig. 20.9). This list contains the numbers of the pages on which your slides appear. (You also see a checkmark next to the slide that currently is on-screen.) By clicking any of the other titles, you can jump directly to that slide.

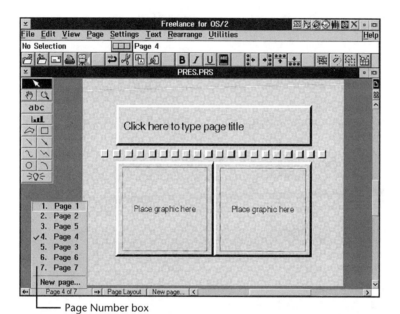

Page Number box

Fig. 20.9

You can jump quickly to a particular slide by choosing the slide's page number from the Page Number box on the status bar.

Troubleshooting

I'm having trouble seeing my slide. Can I get a close look at a portion of my slide?

When you're in current page view, each slide is displayed as a full screen at a preset percentage of its full size. The percentage varies, depending on your video driver, screen resolution, and monitor size.

If you choose **V**iew, **I**n, you zoom in on the central portion of the current slide. You can zoom in several times to get a close-up view of the center of the slide. Similarly, you can choose **V**iew, **O**ut to move the slide back and get an overview of the entire slide.

(continues)

Tip

You can use the icon with the magnifying glass on it to zoom into your presentation slide quickly.

(continued)

I zoomed in on my slide but I need to edit it. Can I edit my slide when I've zoomed in on it?

Absolutely. All the tools work the same when you zoom in. Feel free to fine-tune subtle features on your slides.

Getting an Overview of a Presentation

Page sorter view gives you an overall perspective of your presentation by displaying a miniature version of each slide in a single screen (see fig. 20.10). The number of slides you can view at any time depends on your video card, driver, and monitor.

Fig. 20.10

Page sorter view displays miniature versions of multiple slides.

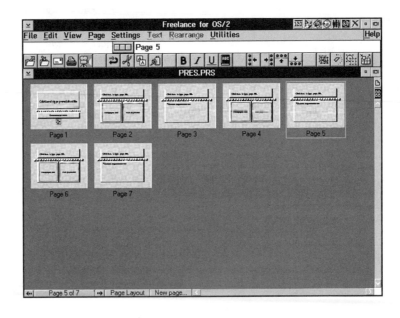

Tip

Use page sorter view to move from slide to slide quickly by double-clicking the slide you want to see. Freelance Graphics automatically switches back to current page view, displaying the slide you selected.

You can move around in page sorter view. Press Ctrl+Home to select the first slide in the presentation. Press Ctrl+End to select the last slide.

You can't edit slides in page sorter view; you must return to current page view to change the content of slides. To change the content of any particular slide you see in page sorter view, double-click that slide—you immediately return to current page view of the slide.

Troubleshooting
I'm in page sorter view and I need to add a slide. You can add or insert slides, using any of the methods described in "Adding and Deleting Slides" earlier in this chapter. In current page view, Freelance Graphics inserts a new slide after the selected slide. In page sorter view, Freelance Graphics also inserts a new slide after the selected slide unless you click the mouse button between slides before you insert the new slide.

Changing the Order of Presentation Slides

Suppose you decide, after creating several slides, that you really need them to appear in a different order. Page sorter view gives you an easy method of rearranging the slides in your presentation. To change the order of slides, follow these steps:

1. Switch to page sorter view.

2. Select a slide. To select a slide, press the direction keys to highlight the slide, or click the slide. An outline surrounds the selected slide.

3. Drag the slide to its new location. As you drag the slide, a vertical bar and the slide outline move with the slide; the vertical bar appears between other slides in the presentation.

4. When the vertical bar appears wherever you want to place the slide, release the mouse button. Freelance Graphics moves the slide to the new location.

Note

You can also use this method to move multiple slides. Suppose you want to move slides 3 and 4 to the end of the presentation. Select slides 3 and 4 (hold down the Shift key while clicking the slides you want to select), drag them to the right of the last slide in the presentation, and release the mouse button.

Troubleshooting

I thought you said page sorter view shows the slides in the proper order. When I switched to page sorter view, my slides were listed—Page 1, Page 2, Page 5, Page 9, Page 3, Page 4, Page 6, Page 7, and Page 8. What happened?

You actually are seeing your slides in the proper order—the order they would display in a slide show—while viewing them in page sorter view. Don't confuse the page number of a slide with its order in the presentation. You moved slides around in your presentation. When you first create slides, they are assigned a page number. When you move slides around in a presentation, the page numbers don't change. To avoid confusion, you can edit those page numbers. Select the appropriate slide and look immediately below the menus. In the long white box that appears immediately below the menus, you'll see the page number of the slide. Click immediately to the right of the page number and an insertion point appears. Change the page number and press Enter.

Watching a Screen Show

Using screen show view, you see each slide in your presentation at maximum size. When you use this view, the Freelance Graphics window isn't visible; each slide occupies the complete screen area (see fig. 20.11).

Fig. 20.11
In screen show view, each slide uses the entire screen area.

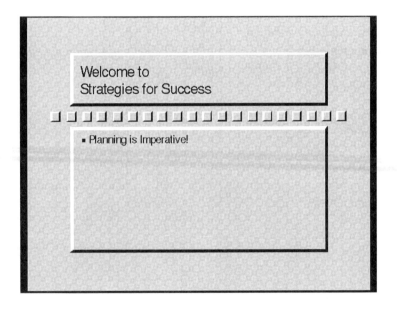

If your final presentation is to be a screen show, screen show view is useful for previewing your slides to see how they will look during the actual show. To start a screen show, choose the Screen Show SmartIcon or press Alt+F10. If you want to establish settings for the screen show, choose **V**iew, Scree**n** Show. You'll see the View Screen Show dialog box (see fig. 20.12).

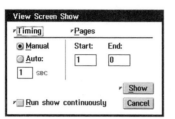

Fig. 20.12
Use this dialog box to view your slides filling the entire screen. Set **T**iming to **M**anual.

To switch from slide to slide in screen show view, press the PgUp and PgDn keys, or click the left mouse button to move forward and the right mouse button to move backward. To end the screen show, press Esc.

Saving a Presentation

When you save a presentation, Freelance Graphics saves all the components of the presentation—SmartMaster, text, graphics, and so on—in one file.

Caution

Save a file frequently so you won't lose data during a power interruption or an equipment failure.

You save a file in Freelance Graphics the same way you save a file in any other OS/2 application. Each time you save a file, Freelance Graphics displays the File Save dialog box (see fig. 20.13), whether you choose **F**ile, **S**ave or the Save SmartIcon. When you want to save an existing file under a different name, on a different disk or directory, or as a different file type, change the settings in the dialog box.

Freelance Graphics saves presentation files with the file extension PRS. When you specify the file name, you don't need to type PRS; Freelance Graphics adds the file extension to the name automatically.

Fig. 20.13
In the File Save
dialog box, select
a drive, directory,
and file type.

Opening an Existing Presentation

You open a Freelance Graphics presentation the same way you open a file in any of the Lotus SmartSuite products: by choosing **F**ile, **O**pen.

As in many applications, you can open several Freelance Graphics presentations at the same time. The active presentation appears on top of the others, and its title bar is highlighted. The names of all open presentation files are listed when you open the program control menu and choose the **W**indow command.

Closing a Presentation

To close an existing presentation, open the control menu for that presentation and choose the **C**lose command or double-click the presentation window Control menu box. If you've made changes to the file since you last saved it, Freelance Graphics asks whether you want to save these changes. Click OK to save the changes, No to ignore the changes, or Cancel to return to the presentation without saving the file.

From Here...

This chapter gave you a foundation to work in Freelance Graphics. For in-depth discussions of specific topics, see the following chapters:

- Chapter 21, "Entering Slide Content," describes the basics of entering the content of a presentation and labeling objects. This chapter also describes how to add an Ami Pro table, a 1-2-3 worksheet, and an organization chart to a Freelance Graphics presentation. You also learn how to insert objects from sources outside Freelance Graphics.

■ Chapter 22, "Working with Objects," describes what objects are; how to select and group them; and how to move, copy, resize, align, rotate, flip, and stack them.

■ Chapter 23, "Drawing Shapes, Curves, and Lines," describes how to use Freelance Graphics drawing tools to add objects to your slides.

■ Chapter 24, "Enhancing a Presentation," explains how to add color, borders, shadows, and other enhancements to objects.

■ Chapter 25, "Creating Graphs Using the Graph Tool," explains how to create and use graphs in a Freelance Graphics presentation.

Chapter 21

Entering Slide Content

by Lenny Bailes

Freelance Graphics slides can contain much more than just text. You can insert clip art, pictures, tables, worksheets, graphs, organization charts, and many other types of objects into your slides. This chapter begins by describing the standard pages provided with each Freelance Graphics SmartMaster.

In this chapter, you learn to:

- Select page layouts
- Enter and edit text
- Insert clip art, tables, and worksheets
- Insert graphs, organization charts, and other objects

Reviewing Page Layouts

In the last chapter, you were briefly introduced to page layouts, a Freelance Graphics feature that includes several professionally designed page templates for every SmartMaster set. Most of these page layouts include one or more "Click here..." blocks for such options as text, clip art, or a chart.

Using a page layout, you can choose a slide layout that contains the "Click here..." blocks you need for your current slide. A title slide, for example, contains two "Click here..." text blocks: one for a title and one for a subtitle. After you select a slide layout, you insert the actual content of your presentation—text, pictures, and graphs—into the appropriate "Click here..." blocks in the slides.

When you add a new slide to a presentation, Freelance Graphics automatically displays the New Page dialog box containing at least the nine standard page layouts for each SmartMaster (see fig. 21.1).

Fig. 21.1
In the Choose a Layout for this Page area of the Page New dialog box, you can choose a layout for a slide.

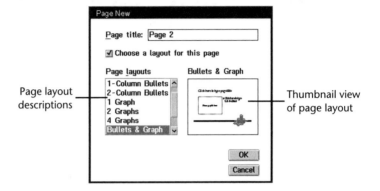

Page layout descriptions

Thumbnail view of page layout

Note

The dialog box shown in figure 21.1 is titled Choose Page Layout or Page New, depending on the method that you use to display it. The contents of the dialog box are similar, regardless of the name that appears in the title bar. To prevent confusion, this chapter calls this dialog box the Page Layout dialog box.

Take the time to scan the dialog box to see how objects are arranged in each layout. As you click each page layout, the image on the right side of the dialog box changes to display the page layout in miniature.

Besides indicating areas for text, many of the page layouts contain areas enclosed by a dashed line that indicate where charts, organization charts, tables, and symbols will be placed. You can override these locations and reposition the items manually, of course, but using the default locations gives you visual consistency from slide to slide.

Highlight the layout you want to use for your new slide and click OK, or double-click the layout you want to use. Freelance Graphics automatically applies the selected layout to the new slide. After you choose a layout, replace the sample text in each "Click here..." block with actual text or another object, such as a graph or table.

> **Note**
>
> Notice that the last slide layout in the Page Layout dialog box is titled Backdrop and is blank; it contains no "Click here…" blocks. Use this layout when you want complete control of the objects in a slide.

If you select the wrong layout or change your mind about the layout you want to use for the current slide, you can open the Page Layout dialog box at any time by clicking the Page Layout box in the status bar or by choosing **P**age, **C**hoose Page Layout.

> **Caution**
>
> After you type information in a text block, be careful about changing the slide layout. The objects containing information remain in the slide while the "Click here…" blocks for the new layout are added. Freelance Graphics tries to rearrange objects so all will fit, but this isn't always possible. The slide can become cluttered with overlapping objects and "Click here…" blocks.

Entering and Editing Text

Text is an important component of any slide presentation. Virtually every slide contains text of some kind, even if it's just a title. The following sections describe how to enter the text content of your slides and how to edit the text when necessary.

Typing the Content of Your Slides

Whenever you choose a page layout (other than the one labeled [None]), you replace the sample text in a "Click here…" text block with the content of your presentation. The slide shown in figure 21.2 includes two "Click here…" text blocks: one that contains a prompt for the title and another that contains a prompt for the subtitle. The third "Place graphic here" block is for clip art.

To select a "Click here…" text block, click anywhere within it. The prompt is replaced by an edit panel and a flashing insertion point, indicating that you can type text (see fig. 21.3). In a bulleted list "Click here…" block, the sample text disappears and the bullet remains, with the insertion point positioned where the text will begin.

Fig. 21.2
This slide layout contains two "Click here..." text blocks and one "Place graphic here..." graphic block for clip art.

Fig. 21.3
The edit panel of a selected "Click here..." text block.

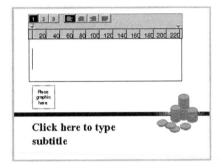

When you click a text block to enter text, Freelance Graphics automatically displays a ruler inside the edit panel, as shown in figure 21.3. At the top of the edit panel are three numbered buttons for levels of text, and four text-alignment styles. The defaults for the three "numbered" text levels and the text alignment styles are preset in the SmartMaster template. You can edit these defaults by switching to the original template page where the layout originates.

▶ See "Enhancing Text," p. 462

For now, just type the actual text for your slide in the edit panel for the selected "Click here..." text block. For titles and subtitles, press Enter only when you want to begin a new line of text. For bullets, press Enter only when you want to begin a new bulleted item. If your bullet text is too long to fit on one line, Freelance Graphics automatically wraps the text to the next line and aligns the text appropriately.

When you finish entering text, deselect the "Click here..." text block by clicking OK or by clicking a blank area of the slide outside edit panel.

Note

Unused "Click here..." blocks will neither print nor display in a screen show.

Creating New Text Blocks

Sometimes, you need to add text to a slide in a location that has no "Click here..." text block. Suppose your slide contains a title and a bulleted list like the one shown in figure 21.4, and you decide to add a note below the bulleted list. To do this, you need to make the note a separate object; otherwise, Freelance Graphics formats the note text as a bulleted-list item.

Text icon

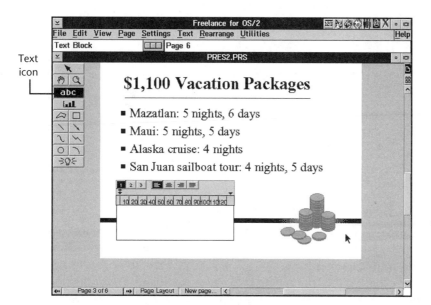

Fig. 21.4
You can add a text block wherever you need one.

Note

If you aren't certain what text you want to type in a new text box, type at least a few characters, such as Enter text here. Otherwise, Freelance Graphics deletes the text box, and you'll have to recreate it later.

To add a note at the bottom of this slide, create a new text block by clicking the Text icon in the Toolbox (refer to fig. 21.4). When you click the Text icon, move the mouse pointer into the slide area, and click the slide. Freelance Graphics creates a new text block where you clicked. As you type, the text block enlarges so the text fits in the slide.

Figure 21.5 show how the same slide looks with the new text block.

Fig. 21.5
The slide now
contains a new
text block below
the bulleted list.

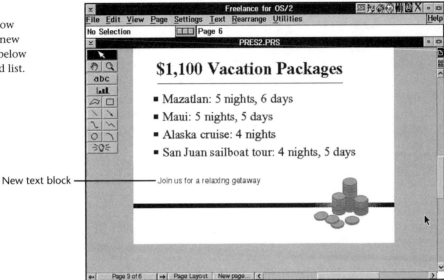

New text block ——————

Changing Text and Correcting Errors

After you type text in a text block, you may need to change the text or correct errors. Making changes in a text block is as easy as clicking and retyping. To edit text, first select the text block you want to modify, either by clicking it or by choosing the appropriate **E**dit, **S**elect command. When the text block is selected, use any of the following techniques:

- Click anywhere inside the text block. (You must let the mouse pointer linger inside the block after clicking.)

- Press F2 (Edit).

- Select the Text icon in the Toolbox and click the text block.

◀ See "Entering, Selecting, and Editing Text," p. 44

Begin typing. Whatever you type is placed at the point in the text where you clicked with the mouse.

Use standard editing conventions to change text, as summarized in table 21.1.

Table 21.1 Editing Conventions for Text Boxes

Action	Result
Press the arrow keys	Moves the insertion point right, left, up, or down within the text. (If only one line of text is present, the right arrow key moves the insertion point to the next "Click here" block.)
Press Backspace or Del	Erases characters (to the left and right, respectively) of the insertion point
Click and drag the mouse	Selects a string of characters
Double-click a word	Selects the entire word
Press Del (with block selected)	Clears selected text from the object without placing it in the Clipboard
Press Shift+Del	Cuts selected text and places it in the Clipboard
Press Ctrl+Ins	Copies selected text to the Clipboard
Press Shift+Ins	Pastes text from the Clipboard

In addition to the keyboard shortcuts listed in table 21.1, you can use the Cu**t**, **C**opy, and **P**aste commands (**E**dit menu) to edit text.

When you finish editing text in a text box, be sure to click any blank area of the slide to deselect the text box.

Checking Your Spelling

Checking the spelling in a word processing document before you print is a common practice, but you may not have developed the same good habit with Freelance Graphics. Because many presentations contain primarily text, and because slides are highly visible, remember to check your spelling before you print or produce a slide show for your presentation.

◄ See "Running a Spell Check," p. 288

When you activate the spell check feature of Freelance Graphics—by choosing **U**tilities, **C**heck Spelling, pressing Ctrl+F2, or clicking the Spell Check SmartIcon—you see the Utilities Check Spelling dialog box (see fig. 21.6). The Check Spelling feature built into Freelance Graphics performs very much like the one in Ami Pro.

Fig. 21.6
Use the Freelance
Graphics spell
checker to be sure
you haven't
misspelled any
words in your
presentation.

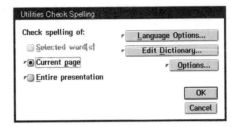

Inserting Symbols
and Other Graphics

One of the best ways to spice up a slide show is to insert a Freelance Graphics symbol or a clip-art drawing. Symbols and clip-art drawings are especially appreciated by users who don't feel confident about drawing their own pictures. The Freelance Graphics symbol set comes with hundreds of professionally drawn graphics, grouped in a wide range of categories.

You can insert a symbol into a slide by clicking the Add a Symbol icon in the Toolbox. The next step is to select a symbol category in the Add Symbols dialog box, shown in figure 21.7.

Fig. 21.7
Select a symbol in
the Add Symbols
dialog box.

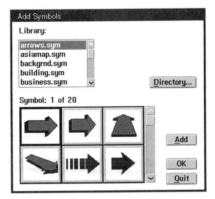

A list of categories appears at the top of the Add Symbols box. The box below the category list displays samples of the symbols in the current category. You can click or tab to each of the scroll boxes in the dialog box and then use the scroll bar, the PgUp or PgDn key, or the arrow keys to see each symbol in a category.

To add a symbol to your slide, follow these steps:

1. Display the slide you want to insert clip art into.

2. Click the Add a Symbol icon in the Toolbox.

3. Select a symbol category from the files in the Library list.

4. Select a symbol and choose OK. Freelance Graphics closes the Add Symbols dialog box and inserts the symbol into your slide.

5. If you wish to insert the symbol in a "Place Graphic Here" box, select the object with the mouse and drag it to the appropriate graphics box.

Tips for Working with Graphic Images

You can change the colors or other attributes of the object, such as the line width, fill or line color, shading, and pattern. You can change the attributes of the symbol as a whole, or you can break down the symbol into its components.

To change the attributes of a grouped object as a whole, choose **S**ettings, **A**ttributes or double-click the symbol, and make the necessary changes. For more information about changing the attributes of a collection of objects, see Chapter 24, "Enhancing a Presentation."

To change the components of the symbol, first convert the symbol to a group of Freelance Graphics objects. Select the symbol, and then choose **R**earrange, **U**ngroup. Freelance Graphics displays resize handles on every object that makes up the symbol. Select the object you want to change, and then use the appropriate command to change the object's attributes. To learn how to change object attributes, such as colors, patterns, shading, shadows, and line styles, see Chapter 24, "Enhancing a Presentation."

You can add an image from another OS/2 or Windows program by copying the image from that program to the OS/2 Clipboard and then pasting it into your Freelance Graphics presentation. Windows applications may only transfer bitmapped graphics, and the color palette of the image may become distorted. If an imported bitmap appears to be invisible, double-click it with the mouse, and select Transparent in the Bitmap Attributes dialog box.

Another method you can use is the **F**ile, **I**mport or Import **B**itmap command. When you choose **F**ile, **I**mport or Import **B**itmap, you see the Import File dialog box. Freelance Graphics can import a variety of file formats, which are summarized in table 21.2. Select the file format you want to import, and indicate the appropriate filename.

Table 21.2 Importable Graphic File Types	
File Extension	**File Type**
BMP	OS/2 Bitmap File
CGM	Computer Graphics Metafile
DRW	Freelance Graphics Draw File
MET	PM MetaFile
PFL	FreeLance Graphics Portfolio File
PRN	ASCII Text File
TIF	TIFF Bitmap File

Note

If you are importing a TIFF bitmap file, you can choose Fast, draft quality, or Slow, higher quality from the two buttons at the bottom of the File Import Bitmap dialog box.

Creating Handouts

▶ See "Understanding Output Formats and Print Options," p. 500

When you prepare slides, you may want to create handouts for your audience so they can follow discussion points you make in your presentation. Handouts containing mini-depictions of individual slides can be generated by choosing **F**ile, **P**rint, **P**rint Presentations and then choosing the **H**andout button under **F**ormat in the File Print, Print Presentation dialog box. You may select 2, 4, or 6 slides per Handout page by clicking the appropriate button option.

Creating a Table Slide

In a slide, a table can convey useful information, as long as it's simple and large enough to view easily. Creating a table in Freelance Graphics is a very straightforward task.

To begin, create a new page in your presentation by selecting the "New Page" button on the control bar at the bottom of the Presentation screen. Tables are created by copying data from an existing 1-2-3 worksheet to a presentation page, as a linked or unlinked metafile. If you import the table as a linked metafile, the data in the cells is dynamically updated when you change the worksheet in 1-2-3. To create a table for Freelance, start 1-2-3 and open an existing worksheet or create a new one. Next, format the range in the 1-2-3 worksheet you want to use. You can use the commands in the 1-2-3 **W**orksheet and **R**ange menus to add a border to the table and set foreground and background colors, and fonts. After you define the size and general appearance of your table, choose **E**dit, **C**opy. (Figure 21.8 shows a selected data range in 1-2-3 that has been formatted with commands in the **R**ange menu.)

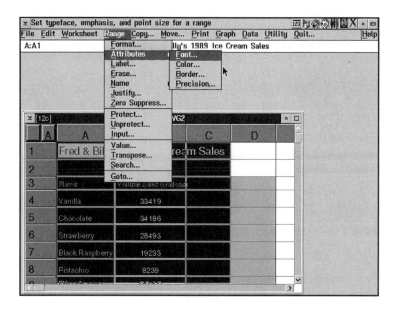

Fig. 21.8
To insert a table in a presentation, first format a selected range of cells in a 1-2-3 worksheet.

Now switch to Freelance Graphics and make sure your presentation is open to the page on which you want to insert the table. Choose **E**dit, **L**ink, **P**aste Link to add the table to the presentation page as a "Linked Metafile" (see fig. 21.9). Whenever you change the worksheet data in 1-2-3, the table in the presentation is updated automatically, provided both the worksheet and the presentation files are open at the same time.

If you wish to create an unlinked metafile, you can paste the 1-2-3 data range into your presentation with the **E**dit, **P**aste command, instead of choosing **L**ink.

Fig. 21.9

Copy the selected 1-2-3 worksheet range to the OS/2 Clipboard, and insert on a Freelance presentation page using the **E**dit, **L**ink, **P**aste Link command.

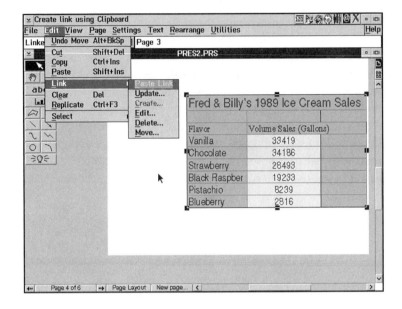

To edit information in table cells of a linked metafile, open the worksheet in 1-2-3 and make changes using the standard worksheet editing commands. To edit information in an unlinked table, you have to perform the additional step of copying it to the OS/2 Clipboard again and repasting.

You can easily reposition and resize the table in your presentation slide by selecting it and dragging any of the eight handles that surround the table box (as shown in fig. 21.10).

Fig. 21.10

The table can be resized by clicking and dragging any of its eight object handles.

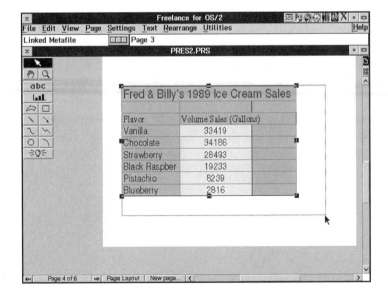

Inserting a Graph

Charts are graphic representations of data in worksheets. In a presentation, a bar, pie, or area chart often depicts data much more clearly than words. In Freelance Graphics, you can insert a chart into a slide by using the program's charting capabilities.

Because charting is such a powerful capability, Chapter 25, "Creating Graphs Using the Graph Tool," is devoted to this subject. Turn to this chapter for instructions on creating data for your chart, charting the data, and enhancing the chart in your Freelance Graphics slide.

Creating an Organization Chart Slide

Organization charts are commonly included in slide presentations. These charts convey information about new management, a group or department reorganization, or people to contact for specific types of information. If you've tried to create an organization chart in a word processing program or a drawing application, you probably have discovered how challenging that task can be.

To build an organization chart into a Freelance Graphics slide:

1. Create a new page using the New Page button on the control bar at the bottom of the presentation screen.

2. Set up a grid so you can draw properly aligned boxes of uniform size. Choose **S**ettings, **U**nits and Grids. Check the **D**isplay Grid and **S**nap to Grid checkboxes in the Setting Units and Grids dialog box. Enter **H**orizontal and **V**ertical space measurements to set up the grid at a convenient size (see fig. 21.11).

3. Next set the Text Block defaults by double-clicking the Text icon in the Toolbar (refer to fig. 21.4). Change **J**ustification and **V**ertical Justification to Centered. Click the **E**dge & area button and change **E**dge **S**tyle to a solid line.

   `abc`

4. The next step is to add the text blocks for your organization chart. Select the Text icon in the Toolbox and drag a large text box to the top of the page for a title.

5. Now create additional text boxes and position them appropriately on the page for your chart entries. (If you need to make several text blocks

of the same size, press Replicate (Ctrl+F3) to duplicate the selected text block.)

Fig. 21.11

Start your organization chart by turning on the Display Grid and Snap to Grid options.

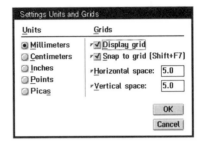

6. To enter text, select each text block and begin typing. Press Enter to move to the next line in an entry. Pressing Tab or clicking the 1, 2, and 3 buttons at the top of the text box moves the entry to subordinate positions within the box. You can adjust the Font style and size for each entry.

7. To complete the organization chart, draw lines that connect the text blocks by selecting the line tool in the text box. When you are finished, turn off the **D**isplay Grid from the **U**nits and Grids option in the **S**ettings menu.

Figure 21.12 shows an organization chart that results from following the steps outlined previously and with some enhancements added. (You learn to modify text and lines in Chapter 24, "Enhancing a Presentation.")

Fig. 21.12

The organization chart resulting from building a set of text boxes and connecting them with graphic lines.

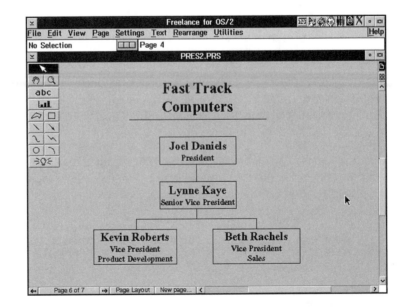

From Here...

Refer to the following chapters for information related to entering slide content:

- Chapter 22, "Working with Objects," describes how to manipulate objects, including moving, copying, deleting, resizing, grouping, and ungrouping.

- Chapter 23, "Drawing Shapes, Curves, and Lines," describes how to use Freelance Graphics' drawing tools to add drawn objects to your slides.

- Chapter 24, "Enhancing a Presentation," explains how to add color, borders, shadows, and other enhancements to objects.

- Chapter 25, "Creating Graphs Using the Graph Tool," teaches you how to create a wide variety of chart types from worksheet data.

Chapter 22

Working with Objects

by Sue Plumley

You were introduced to objects in Chapter 20, "Getting Started with Freelance Graphics," and you learned more about entering content in objects in Chapter 21, "Entering Slide Content." Objects are the building blocks of slides. *Objects* contain primarily text, graphics, or pictures; but they also can contain other elements, such as tables, worksheets, and organization charts. You need to understand how to work with objects, because they are key components of a Freelance Graphics slide.

In this chapter, you learn to:

- Select and group objects

- Move, copy, resize, and delete objects

- Align objects

- Use the grid

- Rotate and flip objects

- Stack objects

Selecting and Grouping Objects

Before you can make any kind of change in an object—add color, change its size, move it, or delete it, for example—you must select the object. To select a single object, simply click it. When you click an object, such as a chart, clip art, or organization chart, handles appear around the object (see fig. 22.1). *Handles* are small boxes that appear at the corners and along the sides of the object. When you see these handles, you know that the object is selected. In

◀ See "Managing
Objects," p. 52
the "Resizing and Scaling Objects" section later in this chapter, you learn
how to use these handles to change the size of an object.

Fig. 22.1
Handles appear on
the corners and
sides of an object
when you click it.

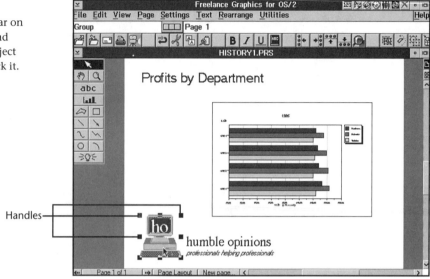

Fig. 22.2
Choose the way
you want to select
objects using the
Edit menu.

You also can select an object in a Freelance Graphics slide by choosing Edit,
Select. When you do, the menu shown in figure 22.2 appears. These options
enable you to select objects in a variety of ways, as described in table 22.1.

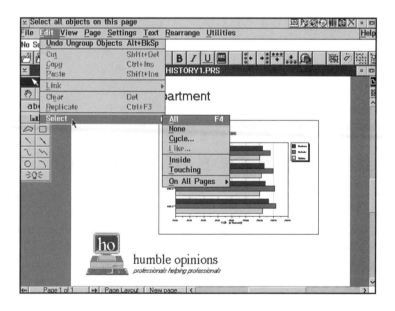

Table 22.1 Edit Select Options	
Option	**Description**
All (or F4)	Selects all objects on the page.
None	Deselects all objects on the page.
Cycle	Cycles through selecting objects in sequence. This option can be particularly helpful when you have several overlapping objects on the page.
Like	Selects only those objects on the page that have the attributes that you specify.
Inside	Selects all objects inside a box that you create by dragging your mouse.
Touching	Selects all objects inside or touching a box that you drag, using your mouse.

Note

"Click here..." text blocks behave a little differently, depending on whether they contain text. If a "Click here..." text block contains text, a single click selects that text block as an object. If you haven't yet typed any text in the block, a single click places you in edit mode, enabling you to enter text.

Selecting Multiple Objects

In Freelance Graphics, you generally select an object to move, copy, or resize it, or to change one or more of its attributes. An *attribute* is any characteristic applied to an object, such as color, border, fill, and shadow.

Sometimes you may want to select more than one object at a time. Selecting multiple objects can save you time, compared with applying the same attribute to several objects individually. When you select multiple objects, any attribute that you change is applied to all selected objects. To change the color of several objects to blue, for example, select all the objects, and then apply the blue fill color.

Note

To cancel any multiple selection, click a blank area of the slide. To remove an object from a multiple selection, hold down the Shift key, and then click the object that you want to remove.

To select multiple objects with the mouse, hold down the Shift key and then click each object you want to include in the selection. Handles appear around each object you select (see fig. 22.3). If you select an object by mistake and want to remove it from your selection, continue holding down the Shift key and click the object again. Freelance Graphics removes that object from the selection. Release the Shift key when you've selected all objects.

Another way to select multiple objects is to click the Selector icon (the top button, shaped like a mouse pointer) in the Freelance Graphics toolbox. Click the Selector icon, and then drag the mouse across all objects that you want to include in the selection. As you drag the mouse, Freelance Graphics draws a dashed rectangle that encloses all selected objects. When you release the mouse button, the rectangle disappears, and handles appear around each object in the selection.

Fig. 22.3
Hold down the Shift key while clicking multiple objects to be selected.

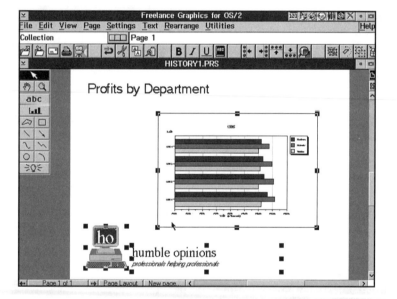

Note

You must enclose all parts of the object in the selection box. If a portion of the object is not enclosed in the rectangle, that object is excluded from the selection. You can add an object to any selection by holding down the Shift key and clicking the object.

To select every object in a slide quickly, choose **E**dit, **S**elect, **A**ll or press F4 (Select All). Freelance Graphics immediately displays selection handles around all objects in the slide.

Troubleshooting

When I draw a selection box around several objects, some objects are not selected. Why?

You must enclose in the selection box all objects that you want to select. If a portion of an object falls outside the selection box, it won't be selected.

Can I select objects in multiple slides at the same time?

No. The only way to view multiple slides at the same time is to use page sorter view, and you cannot select objects in this view.

I try to select the company logo in my slide, and nothing happens. Why?

The logo probably was inserted into the SmartMaster page layout rather than into the individual slide. To select the logo, modify the SmartMaster page layout by choosing **V**iew, SmartMaster Pages or pressing Shift+F9, and then select the object. Any changes you make affect the object in all slides that use that page layout.

Grouping Objects

Grouping enables you to treat several objects as a single object. Suppose that you created a logo for your company using a symbol and two text objects. Without grouping the three objects that compose the logo (see fig. 22.4), moving, copying, or resizing the logo as a whole is more difficult. You might inadvertently move or delete a component, or change one of its attributes by mistake. But when you select and group all the objects that make up the logo, the logo is treated as a single object. Any attributes that you choose are applied to the entire object as a whole; and you can move, copy, resize, scale, rotate, or flip the object as a whole.

Tip
You can select all objects on a page by pressing the Select All shortcut key, F4.

To group several objects, select the objects using one of the methods that you learned in the preceding section. Handles appear around the selected objects. Then choose **R**earrange, **G**roup. The collective object, made up of all the objects that you selected, is now surrounded by an invisible rectangle, indicated by handles at the corners and along the sides of the rectangle. When you select the object in the future, it appears as a single object with one set of handles (see fig. 22.5). You now can modify all the objects as though they are one.

Fig. 22.4
Select the components of the logo and group them.

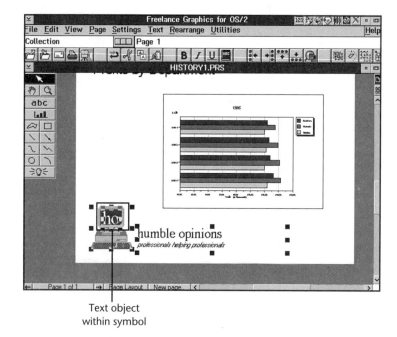

Text object
within symbol

Fig. 22.5
The grouped objects now have only one set of handles.

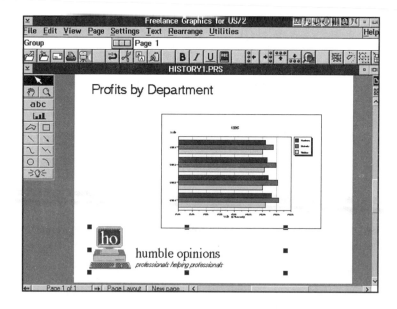

> **Note**
>
> You can't use the **R**earrange, **G**roup command if one or more of the selected objects is a "Click here…" block. If the selected objects contain one or more "Click here…" blocks, hold down the Shift key and click the "Click here…" blocks to deselect them. Then use the **R**earrange, **G**roup command to group the remaining objects.

◀ See "Understanding 'Click here…' Blocks," p. 395

> **Note**
>
> If you adjusted your SmartIcon set so that the Select All and Group SmartIcons are displayed, you can click the Select All and Group SmartIcons instead of using menu commands. You can ungroup objects by clicking the Ungroup SmartIcon. For more information, see Appendix B, "Customizing SmartIcons."

You may want to group multiple objects only temporarily. Suppose that you moved or resized your logo, and now you want to apply different attributes to the various components of the text. To separate grouped objects, select the grouped object and then choose **R**earrange, **U**ngroup. Freelance Graphics separates the objects, and each object's selection handles are visible in the slide. You can now apply attributes to each object separately.

Moving and Copying Objects

Occasionally, you need to move or copy objects in a presentation. To move an object in a slide, simply click and drag the object to a new location. As you drag, the original object stays in its current location in the slide, and a "ghost" image (a dotted-line frame) of the object follows your mouse movements around the screen. Release the mouse button when the frame is positioned correctly. Freelance Graphics then moves the object to its new location.

To move an object from one slide to another, or from one presentation to another, follow these steps:

1. If you are moving an object from one presentation to another, open both presentations, making the active presentation the one that contains the object to be moved.

2. Select the object to be moved.

Tip
When you move an object, press the arrow keys on the keyboard to make minor adjustments in the object's position. Click outside the object when it is positioned correctly.

3. Choose **E**dit, Cu**t** or press Shift+Del. Freelance Graphics removes the selected object from the current slide and places it in the Clipboard.

4. If you are moving the object to another slide in the same presentation, display that slide.

   If you are moving the object to another presentation, make it the active presentation and display the correct slide.

5. Choose **E**dit, **P**aste or press Shift+Ins. Freelance Graphics pastes the object in the current slide.

6. Position the object appropriately by clicking and dragging the object to the correct position.

7. Click any blank area of the slide to deselect the object.

The steps for copying an object are similar to those for moving an object, except that you use the **E**dit, **C**opy command rather than the **E**dit, Cu**t** command. As you can when moving an object, you can copy an object within a slide, within a presentation, or to another presentation.

To copy an object, follow these steps:

1. If you are copying an object from one presentation to another, open both presentations, making the active presentation the one that contains the object to be copied.

2. Select the object to be copied.

3. Choose **E**dit, **C**opy or press Ctrl+Ins. The selected object remains unchanged in the current slide, and a copy is placed on the Clipboard.

4. If you are copying the object to another slide in the same presentation, display that slide.

   If you are copying the object to another presentation, make it the active presentation, and display the correct slide.

5. Choose **E**dit, **P**aste or press Shift+Ins. Freelance Graphics pastes the object in the current slide.

6. Position the object appropriately by clicking and dragging the object to the correct position.

7. Click any blank area of the slide to deselect the object.

Resizing and Scaling Objects

Throughout this chapter, you have seen several examples of the handles that become visible when you select an object. To resize an object, you first click the object to select it and then drag any handle to a new position.

The handles that appear on the sides of the selection box resize the object in one dimension only. If you click the resize handle at the top of the selection box, for example, you can stretch or shrink only the top of the object; the bottom remains anchored. If you click the right handle, you can stretch or shrink only the right side of the object; the left side remains anchored. Release the mouse button when the object is the size you want.

The handles that appear at the corners of an object enable you to resize an object in two directions at the same time. If you click the handle at the upper-right corner of an object, for example, you can change the height and width of the object by dragging the handle in any direction. Whenever you drag a corner handle, the handle in the opposite corner remains anchored while you expand or contract the object's height and width.

Tip

If you change your mind about an object's new size, choose **E**dit, **U**ndo or press Alt+Backspace.

Tip

To maintain the object's height-to-width ratio, hold down the Shift key as you drag a corner resize handle.

Aligning Objects

Sometimes you want to align objects in a slide to give the slide a neater, more polished appearance. Freelance Graphics takes the guesswork out of aligning objects by offering a variety of automatic alignment options. You can use the traditional left, center, and right alignment styles; or you can align the tops, bottoms, and middles of objects.

Figure 22.6 illustrates these alignment options in page sorter view. In the figure, slide 1 shows how the objects—three text blocks—originally were arranged. Slides 2 through 5 show the objects aligned at the left, right, top, and bottom of the arrangement, respectively. Slides 6 and 7 show the objects centered in a column and in a row. The final choice, Center on a Point, is not shown; however, it would overlap the three objects in the center of the page.

◀ See "Viewing a Presentation," p. 400

You can perform four alignments using SmartIcons, as noted in table 22.2.

Table 22.2	SmartIcons To Use for Aligning Objects
Icon	**Description**
	Align right
	Align left
	Align top
	Align bottom

Fig. 22.6

Align selected objects using the Rearrange, Align command.

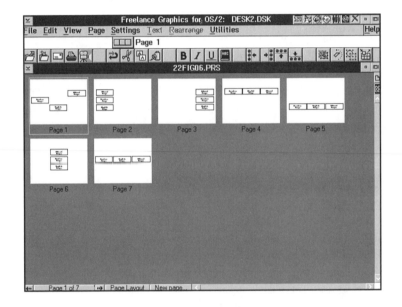

Caution

It's a good idea to save any file before aligning the graphics so you can revert back to the saved file if you make a mistake in alignment.

To use any Freelance Graphics alignment options, follow these steps:

1. Select the objects that you want to align.

2. Choose **R**earrange, **A**lign. (You must select two or more objects in the current slide to make the **R**earrange, **A**lign command available.) The Rearrange Align dialog box appears (see fig. 22.7).

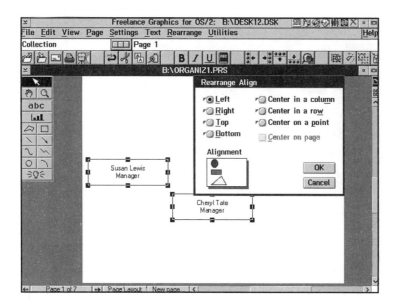

Fig. 22.7
Choose an
alignment in the
Rearrange Align
dialog box.

3. Choose an alignment option and press OK. Freelance Graphics realigns
the selected objects.

Using Grids

To help you align and position objects in a slide, Freelance Graphics includes
grids, which you can toggle on and off by choosing menu commands. The
grid is a set of lines that run horizontally and vertically on a slide. You can
turn on the grid and use it to align objects in your slides manually, or you
can make Freelance Graphics objects snap to the grid. When the **S**nap to Grid
option is turned on, objects that you draw or move snap into alignment with
the nearest intersection of the grid. Use of the grid helps make aligning objects easier. Use the grid when you want to align objects at precise locations.

You can specify the grid units and the density of intersections by choosing
Settings, **U**nits and Grids. When you do, you see the dialog box shown in
figure 22.8.

In this dialog box, you can select the units that will be used for the grid and
specify the horizontal and vertical spacing density for grid points. Finally,
you can specify whether you want the grid to appear on-screen and whether
you want drawn objects to snap to the grid.

Fig. 22.8
Set the grid units and display the grid in the Settings Units and Grids dialog box.

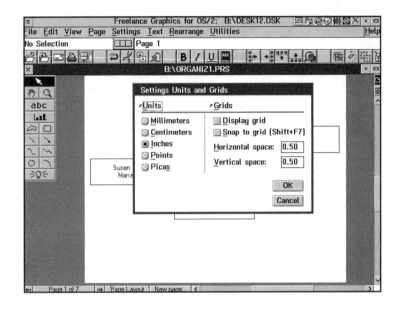

Tip
You can quickly turn the snap feature on and off by pressing Shift+F7.

Figure 22.9 shows a zoomed-in view of a Freelance Graphics slide with a 0.5-inch grid displayed. Notice that the text box on the right side of the window was created with the **S**nap to Grid selected; its edges and corners align with grid intersection points. The text box on the left side of the window was created without the **S**nap to Grid option selected; it can be placed anywhere in the slide, without reference to the grid intersection points.

Fig. 22.9
Use the grid to ensure that the objects are properly aligned.

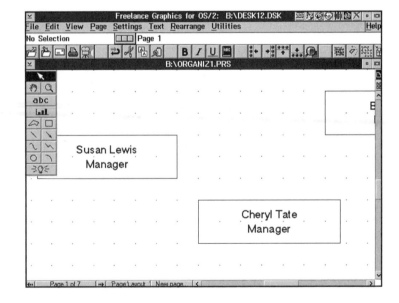

Rotating and Flipping Objects

One way to add visual interest to your slides is to rotate or flip an object. *Rotating* means turning an object by up to 180 degrees, either clockwise or counterclockwise. *Flipping* means turning an object over—either left to right or top to bottom—to create a mirror image of that object. You can rotate or flip any Freelance Graphics object except a "Click here…" text block, a chart, a table, or an organization chart.

> **Note**
>
> Freelance Graphics objects that can be rotated are those created within Freelance Graphics or imported from another program and then converted to a Freelance Graphics object.
>
> To convert an object to a Freelance Graphics object, you must be able to ungroup its components. You can then regroup the components, if necessary, by using the **R**earrange, **G**roup command.

Freelance Graphics enables you to rotate an object either clockwise or counterclockwise. As you rotate an object, the degrees of positive rotation (counterclockwise) or negative rotation (clockwise) appear in the edit line, just below the menu bar at the top of your screen.

When you flip an object, you flip it either left to right or top to bottom by 180 degrees. Use the **R**earrange, **R**otate or **F**lip commands to manipulate a selected object.

To flip an object 180 degrees, follow these steps:

1. Select the object that you want to flip.

2. Choose either the **R**earrange, **F**lip, **L**eft-to-Right or **T**op-to-Bottom command, or click the Flip Left to Right or the Flip Top to Bottom SmartIcon.

3. Click any blank area of the slide or press Esc to deselect the object.

To rotate an object manually by any amount, choose **R**earrange, **R**otate or click the Rotate SmartIcon. When you do, the mouse pointer changes to a curved arrow with a plus sign and you can drag the graphic with the mouse.

Tip

You can constrain, or force, the rotation of objects to 45-degree increments by holding down the Shift key as you perform the rotation.

To rotate an object to any angle, follow these steps:

1. Select the object that you want to rotate.

2. Choose **R**earrange, **R**otate or click the Rotate SmartIcon. The mouse pointer changes to the rotation pointer.

3. Hold down the left mouse button as you rotate the object clockwise or counterclockwise. You see the rectangular outline of the object rotate.

4. When the outline is in the correct position, release the mouse button.

5. Click any blank area of the slide to deselect the object.

You can rotate or flip several objects at the same time. You also can rotate or flip grouped objects as though they were one object, as shown in figure 22.10.

Fig. 22.10
Rotate several objects by first grouping them.

Changing the Priority Order

As you add objects to a slide and overlap them, you quickly discover that the object you drew first appears below all the others, and that the object you drew most recently appears on top of the others. Think of the objects being stacked on the slide as you draw them. The most recently drawn object appears at the top of the stack unless you change the priority order.

In figure 22.11, the truck was created first, followed by the white oval on the side of the truck, the "HUMBLE OPINIONS" text, and then the "ho." No matter where you move the objects in the slide, the order remains the same.

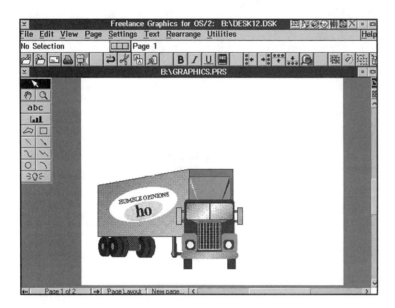

Fig. 22.11

Objects stack in the order you draw, type, or place them.

Freelance Graphics enables you to change the stacking order of objects in several ways. Suppose that you add another oval to place behind the "ho." You can select the oval and choose the **R**earrange, **P**riority menu. From the cascading menu, choose **F**all Back One. The oval moves back one level so that it appears behind the "ho" rather than covering it.

Also on the **P**riority menu are the **T**op and **B**ottom commands, which enable you to move the selected object to the top or bottom of the stack—that is, in front of or behind all other objects, respectively. The **S**end Forward One (Shift+F8) command enables you to move an object forward through a stack of objects one step at a time. If, for example, you have six objects stacked on top of one another and the sixth object is selected, that object becomes the fifth object in the stack if you choose the **S**end Forward One command.

You can, alternatively, click the Forward One or Back One SmartIcons to move objects in a stack one level at a time. To quickly send an object to either the front or the back of all objects, click the Bring to Front or Send to Back SmartIcons.

In figure 22.12, the "ho" now appears on top of all the objects.

Fig. 22.12
Arrange the stacking order of the objects using the Rearrange menu.

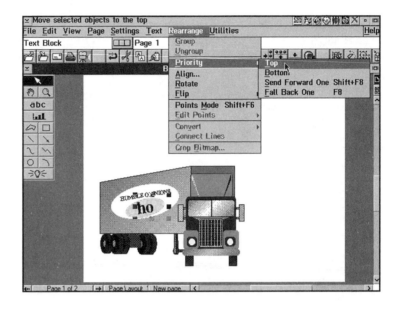

Small objects can be obscured by larger ones. If you can't find an object to select it, choose **E**dit, **S**elect, **C**ycle. When you do, you see the dialog box shown in figure 22.13. By clicking the **N**ext, **P**revious, and **S**elect buttons, you can cycle through the various objects in your slide, selecting one or more as appropriate.

Fig. 22.13
Use the Edit Select Cycle dialog box to find hidden objects.

Tip
If the Edit Select Cycle dialog box obscures a part of the slide that you need to view, click the title bar of the dialog box and drag it to a new location.

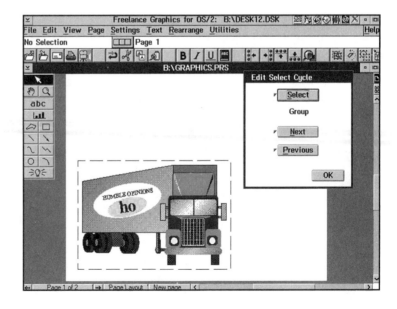

From Here...

In this chapter, you learned all the skills that you need to work with objects, including selecting and grouping, moving and copying, aligning, rotating, flipping, and stacking. For related information about working with objects, refer to the following chapters:

- Chapter 23, "Drawing Shapes, Curves, and Lines," describes how to use Freelance Graphics' drawing tools to add drawn objects to your slides.

- Chapter 24, "Enhancing a Presentation," describes how to add color, borders, shadows, and other enhancements to objects.

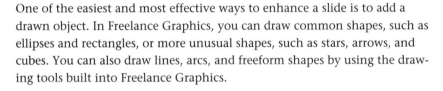

Chapter 23

Drawing Shapes, Curves, and Lines

by Lenny Bailes

One of the easiest and most effective ways to enhance a slide is to add a drawn object. In Freelance Graphics, you can draw common shapes, such as ellipses and rectangles, or more unusual shapes, such as stars, arrows, and cubes. You can also draw lines, arcs, and freeform shapes by using the drawing tools built into Freelance Graphics.

In this chapter, you learn how to:

- Use the drawing tools in Freelance Graphics
- Draw shapes, including perfect squares and circles
- Draw lines, arcs, and freeform shapes
- Modify shapes

Using Freelance Graphics Drawing Tools

The drawing toolbox in Freelance Graphics is displayed in the Freelance Graphics window automatically whenever you open a presentation. The tools in the toolbox are used to add or change the appearance of objects in a slide.

In this chapter, you learn how to use the drawing tools in the toolbox. These tools are described in table 23.1.

Table 23.1	Drawing Tools in Freelance Graphics' Toolbox	
Tool	**Tool Name**	**Function**
Selector	Selector	Displays an arrow-shaped mouse pointer that lets you select objects in a slide.
Polygon	Polygon	Draws a figure with three or more connected straight-line edges.
Rectangle	Rectangle	Draws a rectangle or a square.
Line	Line	Draws a line.
Arrow	Arrow	Draws an arrow with an arrowhead at the endpoint.
Curve	Curve	Draws a Bézier curve.
Polyline	Polyline	Draws multisegmented, connected straight lines.
Circle	Circle	Draws an oval or a circle.
Arc	Arc	Draws an arc.
Symbol	Symbol	Adds a predesigned, saved symbol to a page.

To activate a drawing tool, simply click it. When you click the Text tool, a text box opens wherever you position the cursor and click. When you click the Chart or Symbol tool, Freelance Graphics opens an appropriate dialog box so you can create a graph or add a symbol. When you click any of the remaining tools, the mouse pointer changes to a crosshair pointer, enabling you to begin drawing the relevant shape.

▶ See "Using Shading and Patterns," p. 467

Drawing Shapes

In the context of this chapter, a *shape* is a closed object that you draw with a Freelance Graphics drawing tool. Shapes include circles, ellipses, squares, and rectangles.

To draw one of these regular shapes, follow these steps:

1. In the toolbox, click the Rectangle or Circle icon to select that shape.

2. Move the mouse pointer to the approximate location in the slide where you want to draw the object. The mouse pointer changes to a crosshair pointer.

3. Click and drag the mouse in any direction. As you drag the mouse, a dotted outline of the shape appears in the slide.

4. When the object is the shape and size you want, release the mouse button. The object is selected automatically.

5. Click any blank area of the slide to deselect the object.

Figure 23.1 illustrates what you see on-screen while you draw an object. As you draw, don't feel that you must position your object perfectly the first time; you can move, copy, resize, rotate, flip, color, or align any object you draw.

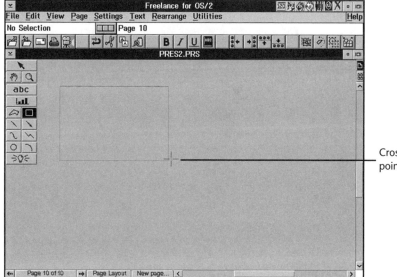

Fig. 23.1
As you draw, a dotted outline indicates the size and shape of the object.

Crosshair mouse pointer

Note

Depending on the SmartMaster you're using when you draw an object, Freelance Graphics automatically fills the object with a color called the fill color. (In some SmartMasters, the fill color may be white.) The *fill color* is determined by the color scheme of the template you're using. In Chapter 24, "Enhancing a Presentation," you learn how to change the colors of individual objects and the default color for any type of object. For now, don't worry about changing the colors of the objects that you draw.

Drawing Perfect Shapes

To draw a perfect square or circle, follow the basic steps for drawing a shape, except you use the Shift key as the constraint key. Holding down the Shift key while you click the Circle or Rectangle icon in the toolbox maintains the same horizontal and vertical distance from the original point to the mouse pointer as you draw. Figure 23.2 shows several sample shapes.

To draw a perfect square or circle, follow these steps:

1. In the toolbox, click the Rectangle or Circle tool to select that shape.

2. Place the mouse pointer in the slide where you want to draw the object. The mouse pointer changes to a crosshair pointer.

3. Hold down the Shift key, and then click and drag the mouse in any direction.

4. When the object is the uniform shape and size that you want, release the mouse button. The object is selected automatically.

5. Click any blank area of the slide to deselect the object.

Fig. 23.2

Examples of shapes drawn with the Rectangle and Circle tools.

An oval drawn with the Circle tool

A circle drawn with the Circle tool, using the Shift key

A rectangle drawn with the Rectangle tool

A square drawn with the Rect-angle tool, using the Shift key

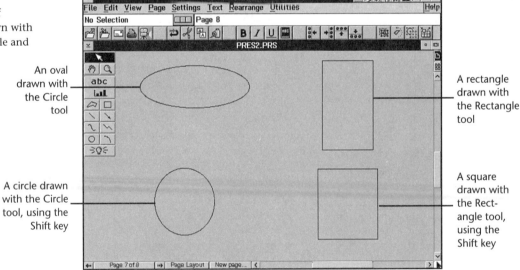

> **Note**
>
> After you draw a shape, you may want to modify its size, shape, position, or rotation. All these changes are covered in detail in Chapter 22, "Working with Objects." You can also modify the colors used to outline and fill objects. These techniques are covered in Chapter 24, "Enhancing a Presentation."

Drawing Lines, Arrows, and Arcs

The technique for drawing lines, arrows, and arcs is similar to the technique for drawing shapes. The only difference is that lines, arrows, and arcs aren't enclosed objects; they have a beginning point and an end point, with resize handles at each of those points. Figure 23.3 shows a drawing made with lines and arcs.

To draw an arc, follow these steps:

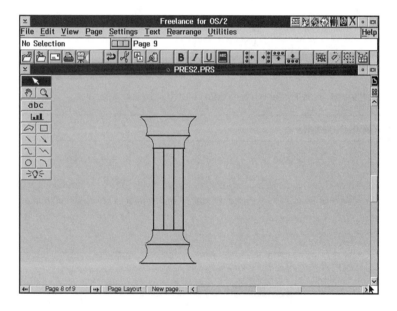

Fig. 23.3
Examples of lines and arcs in a drawing.

Tip
An arc is defined by eight handles: one at each corner and one on each side of the rectangle that contains it. Drag any of the eight handles to change the size or shape of an arc.

1. Click the Arc tool in the toolbox.

2. Place the mouse pointer in the slide area. The mouse pointer changes to a crosshair pointer.

3. Click where you want the arc to begin, and then drag the mouse until you reach the end point of the arc.

Tip

A line is defined by the rectangle that contains it. As you can with all such objects, drag any handle to change the length of a line or its direction.

Tip

When drawing a line or an arrow, you can limit the line to horizontal, vertical, or 15 degree angles by holding down the Shift key as you draw the line.

Alternatively, you can just click where you want the arc to begin and click again where you want it to end.

4. After you define the end points of the arc, click and drag the center of the arc until the shape is what you want.

5. Release the mouse button. The arc is selected automatically.

6. Click any area of the slide to deselect the arc.

To draw a line or an arrow, follow these steps:

1. In the toolbox, click the Line or Arrow icon to select that shape.

2. Place the mouse pointer in the slide area. The mouse pointer changes to a crosshair pointer.

3. Click where you want the line or arrow to begin, and then drag the mouse until the shape is complete.

Alternatively, you can just click where you want the line or arrow to begin and click again where you want it to end.

4. Release the mouse button. The line or arrow is selected automatically.

5. Click any area of the slide to deselect the line or arrow.

Troubleshooting

I created a line, but I meant to make it an arrow. Can I add an arrowhead?

You can turn either a line or a Bézier curve into an arrow. To do so, double-click the line or curve. When you do, you see the dialog box shown in figure 23.4. You can use the right side of the dialog box to define the placement of the arrowhead, as well as the size of the arrowhead.

Fig. 23.4

Use the Line & Curve Attributes dialog box to add arrowheads and change the attributes of selected items.

Define various line attributes in this area

Define arrowheads here

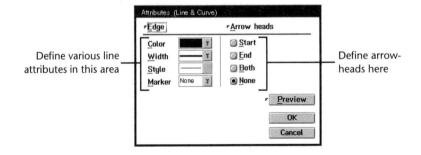

Drawing Polylines and Curves

A polyline is a line consisting of multiple, connected line segments. To draw a polyline, follow these steps:

1. Click the Polyline tool in the toolbox.

2. Place the mouse pointer in the slide area. The mouse pointer changes to a crosshair pointer.

3. Click where you want the polyline to begin, and then drag the mouse until you reach the end point of the first line segment. Continue with this process for each segment.

   Alternatively, you can just click where you want the polyline to begin and click again where you want each segment to end.

4. After you define the entire polyline, double-click or press Esc to indicate the final point. The polyline is selected automatically.

5. Click any area of the slide to deselect the polyline.

Drawing a curve gives you more flexibility than using the Arc tool. To draw a curve, follow these steps:

1. Click the Curve tool in the toolbox.

2. Place the mouse pointer in the slide area. The mouse pointer changes to a crosshair pointer.

3. Click where you want the curve to begin, and then drag the mouse until you reach the end point of the first portion of the curve.

   Alternatively, you can just click where you want the curve to begin and click again where you want each segment of the curve to end.

4. After you define the entire curve, double-click or press Esc to indicate the final point. The curve is selected automatically.

5. Click any area of the slide to deselect the curve.

For details on reshaping or otherwise adjusting the curve after you draw it, see "Editing Shapes" later in this chapter.

Tip

You can place arrowheads at the ends of polylines, just as you can with lines and curves.

▶ See "Working with Colors and Line Styles," p. 465

Drawing Polygons

Use the Polygon tool to draw closed objects made up of multiple line segments or line segments and curves. To draw a polygon, follow these steps:

1. Click the Polygon tool in the toolbox.

2. Place the mouse pointer in the slide area. The mouse pointer changes to a crosshair pointer.

3. Click where you want the polygon to begin, and then drag the mouse until you reach the end point of the first line segment of the polygon. Continue with this process for each segment to end.

   Alternatively, you can just click where you want each line segment to begin and click again where you want each segment to end.

4. After you define the line segments, double-click or press Esc to close the polygon. (If your line segments don't close the polygon, double-clicking or pressing Esc will close it for you.) The polygon is selected automatically.

5. Click any area of the slide to deselect the polygon.

> **Note**
>
> You can create polygons that include curved sides by selecting the Polygon tool first and then selecting and using the Polyline, Curve, and Polygon tools as necessary. When you start with the Polygon tool, Freelance Graphics closes the polygon for you when you double-click or press Esc at the end of your drawing.

Drawing Text Blocks

You can create a text block anywhere you want, even on slides that the page layout doesn't include a "Click here…" text block. To create a text block, follow these steps:

1. Click the Text tool in the toolbox.

2. Place the mouse pointer where you want to begin the text, and click.

3. Type the text. (Text can be formatted just as it is when entered into a preconfigured "Click-here…" box.)

4. Click any area of the slide to deselect the text block.

Editing Shapes

Any shape you create in Freelance Graphics is accompanied by a variety of attributes. A shape has a size, shape, position on the page, line surrounding it (if it's a closed figure), and perhaps color and shading effects. You can modify all these attributes to fit your needs.

You've already experimented with repositioning an object on the page by dragging it to a new location. Chapter 24, "Enhancing a Presentation," explains how to modify many of the other attributes.

Editing an Object by Using Its Surrounding Rectangle

When you create any shape in Freelance Graphics, you can modify it by clicking it to display the standard eight handles on the rectangle surrounding the figure. By dragging a handle, you can resize and reshape the entire object inside the rectangle.

In figure 23.5, for example, the shape on the left was drawn with the Polygon tool in the Freelance Graphics toolbox; it then was copied to the Clipboard, pasted back into the image, and moved to the location on the right. The new figure was selected to display the handles on the rectangle surrounding it, and the bottom-right handle was moved to change the size and shape of the object. If you click a handle on one side of an object and drag it far enough towards the other side, the object rotates, allowing you to stretch or contract its mirror image (see fig. 23.6).

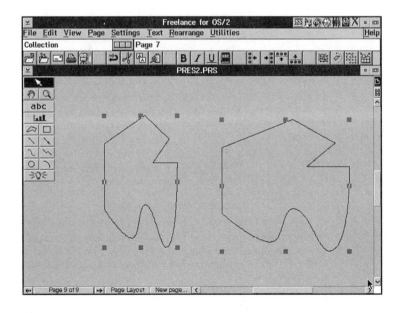

Fig. 23.5

The shape on the right, which is based on the left one, was copied, repositioned, and resized by dragging the bottom-right handle on the surrounding rectangle.

Fig. 23.6

The shape can be manually "flipped" either vertically or horizontally by dragging a center handle over the border of a corresponding center handle on the opposite side of the shape.

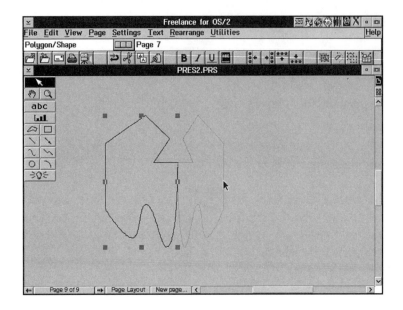

Editing an Object by Using Its Points

In addition to modifying an object by resizing the surrounding rectangle, you can fine-tune objects by modifying the individual points that make up an object. You can modify the points on lines, curves, arcs, polygons, polylines, and freehand objects. You can also modify the points on circles or ellipses and squares or rectangles by converting them to polygons.

Edit points on an object by selecting the object and then choosing **R**earrange, Points **M**ode or pressing Shift+F6. When you do, small hollow squares appear at vertices and along the curves that make up your object. Also, an Edit Pts prompt appears on the title bar, and the mouse pointer changes to the shape shown in figure 23.7.

Figure 23.8 shows the object from figure 23.7 in points mode. When you're in points mode, you can move individual points on a figure to new positions, thus changing the shape of the object. In figure 23.8, the same figure was copied to the right side of the page. In the shape on the right, the handle at the top of the object has been moved to reshape the figure.

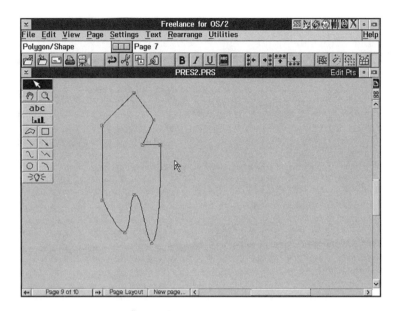

Fig. 23.7
Points enable you
to fine-tune the
size and shape of
objects.

IV

Using Freelance Graphics

The mouse pointer in edit points mode

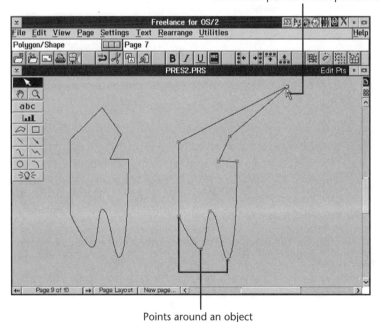

Fig. 23.8
Moving the top
point on the
object changes its
shape.

Points around an object

When you click a point that's located on a curve, you can both move the point, and change the shape of the curve by moving the two additional control points that appear, as shown in the close-up view in figure 23.9.

Fig. 23.9

You have even more control of a curve by adjusting the two additional control points.

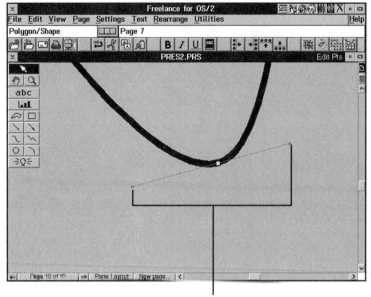

Additional control points for adjusting curves

Adjusting these additional points results in the image shown on the right side of figure 23.10.

If no point appears at a particular location on an object, you can add one or more points wherever you need them. To do so, switch to points mode and select the object you want to add points to. (Use Shift+F6, or select Points mode from the **R**earrange menu.) Then choose **R**earrange, **E**dit Points, **A**dd Point or simply press the Ins key. A small plus sign appears in the middle of the mouse pointer, as shown in figure 23.11.

Click the outline of the object where you want the new point to appear. You can adjust the new point as you would any other. Figure 23.11 shows the same figure on the left. It's reproduced on the right, and a point has been added on the top-right segment and adjusted.

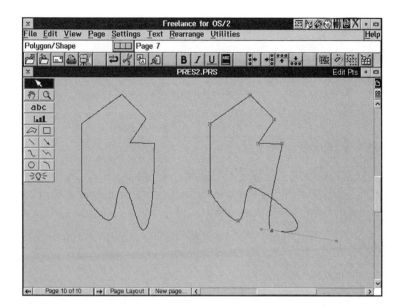

Fig. 23.10
Adjust the figure by modifying the curve control points.

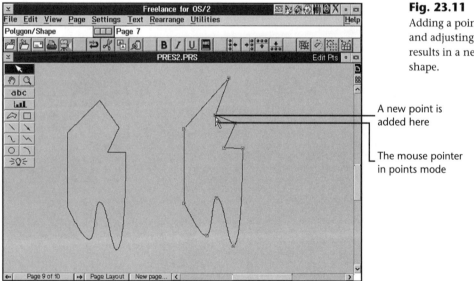

Fig. 23.11
Adding a point and adjusting it results in a new shape.

A new point is added here

The mouse pointer in points mode

Note

To work with small or detailed objects easily, click the Zoom Page icon or choose the **V**iew, **I**n command to zoom in on an object.

From Here...

In this chapter, you learned how to create all types of shapes and objects with Freelance Graphics' drawing tools. Refer to the following chapters for more information about working with objects:

- Chapter 22, "Working with Objects," describes how to manipulate objects by moving, copying, deleting, resizing, grouping, and ungrouping them.

- Chapter 24, "Enhancing a Presentation," describes how to work with templates; enhance text; and add color, borders, and shadows to objects.

Chapter 24

Enhancing a Presentation

by Sue Plumley

Audiences appreciate interesting slides! Nothing is worse than sitting through a presentation of dull slides that contain no color, patterns, shadows, or special fonts. You can do many things to enhance the appearance of slides in a presentation, whether the slides contain text objects, drawn objects, or inserted objects. When you take the time to add special touches to objects, your slides are easier to read and help hold your audience's attention.

At the other extreme, nothing can detract from a presentation more than slides with too much color, too many patterns, or too many fonts or special effects. Freelance Graphics' SmartMasters give you professionally created bases to work from, as well as the option of customizing a SmartMaster set so that it reflects you and your organization.

This chapter covers the many techniques you can use to give your slides a powerful presence. You don't have to be a graphic arts expert; the SmartMasters provide you a professional base from which to work. Even the simplest touches can personalize and make a world of difference in the appearance of a presentation.

In this chapter, you learn how to:

- Work with SmartMasters

- Enhance text by changing the font, style, and color

- Work with line spacing, bullets, and alignment of text

- Work with colors, fills, and line styles of objects

- Add patterns, shading, borders, and shadows to objects
- Work with color palettes

Working with SmartMasters

In Chapter 20, "Getting Started with Freelance Graphics," you learned that SmartMasters are saved formats, including page layouts, special graphic elements, colors, font sizes, font styles, backgrounds, and other special effects. Freelance Graphics includes SmartMasters specially designed for black-and-white overheads, color overheads, and on-screen slide shows. Because all SmartMaster sets contain the same page layouts, you can easily change the appearance of your entire presentation by selecting another SmartMaster set.

◀ See "Under-standing SmartMasters," p. 395

Using a SmartMaster is by far the quickest and easiest way to create professional-looking presentations, because a SmartMaster takes the guess-work and experimentation out of designing a presentation. Freelance Graphics' SmartMasters are designed by professional graphic artists who understand the elements required to achieve a certain effect and to convey a particular attitude. In figures 24.1, 24.2, and 24.3, you see that the title pages convey very different impressions, depending on the SmartMasters used to create them.

Fig. 24.1
GRADLINE.MAS conveys a somewhat lackluster, tedious background.

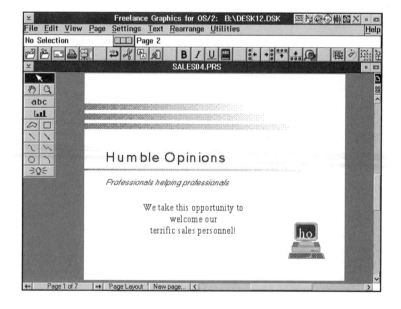

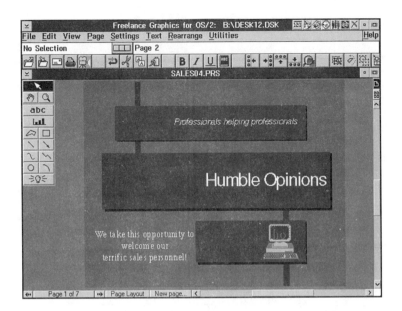

Fig. 24.2
COLLAGE.MAS presents a modern, zestful title page.

IV

Using Freelance Graphics

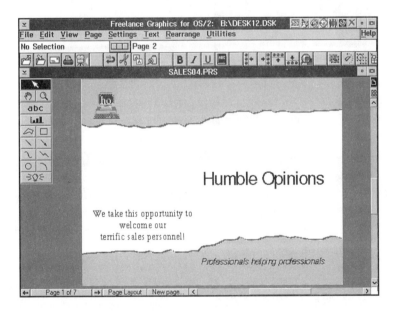

Fig. 24.3
TORNPAPR.MAS offers an informal, unrestricted appearance.

Choosing a SmartMaster

You can specify a SmartMaster when you create a new presentation; choose the **C**reate a New Presentation option in the Welcome to Freelance Graphics dialog box, which appears automatically when you start the program. Alternatively, choose **F**ile, **N**ew when you're already in Freelance Graphics, and then select a SmartMaster in the File New dialog box that appears.

◀ See "Working in a New Presentation," p. 394

To change the SmartMaster being used for the current presentation, follow these steps:

1. Choose **S**ettings, Switch Smart**M**aster Set or choose the Choose SmartMaster Set SmartIcon. The Settings Switch SmartMaster Set dialog box appears.

2. Select a SmartMaster in the SmartMaster Sets list (see fig. 24.4).

Fig. 24.4
When you choose a SmartMaster set, samples appear in the Browse SmartMaster Set area of the dialog box.

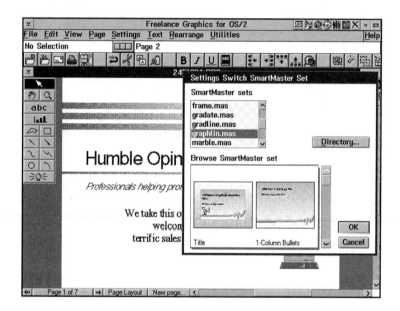

3. If the SmartMaster that you want is not in the list of SmartMasters, click the **D**irectory button and locate the directory in which it is located. After you return to the Settings Switch SmartMaster Set dialog box, select the SmartMaster that you want.

> **Note**
>
> Freelance Graphics automatically previews each SmartMaster as you highlight it in the list. You can preview all the layouts in any SmartMaster by scrolling the samples in the Browse SmartMaster Set area.

Altering a SmartMaster

After you select a SmartMaster for your presentation, you may want to change several of its characteristics. You may decide to use a different font and larger point size for your slide titles, for example; or you may want to add a graphic element (such as your company logo) to the SmartMaster. To make these changes, which affect all slides in the presentation, you change the Basic Layout page of the SmartMaster set after you choose **V**iew, Smart**M**aster Pages. The gray area (work area) is striped when viewing SmartMaster view and not striped when viewing Presentation Pages to visually help people edit in the right view. When you are finished editing the SmartMaster page, choose **V**iew, **P**resentation Pages.

You do not have to edit the SmartMaster set to change the colors defined for a SmartMaster. Instead, choose the **S**ettings, Switch **P**alette command or select the Choose Palette SmartIcon to display the Settings Switch Palette dialog box shown in figure 24.5. In this dialog box, you can specify a different color scheme for the current SmartMaster set. For more about color palettes, see "Working with Color Palettes" later in this chapter. Alternatively, you can change individual colors in the current color scheme.

Tip
Press Shift+F9 to toggle the view between the SmartMaster pages and the Presentation pages.

IV

Using Freelance Graphics

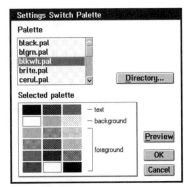

Fig. 24.5
Choose a different color scheme for the SmartMaster.

Troubleshooting

I want one slide in my presentation to stand out from the others but all the slide backgrounds are the same. What can I do?

SmartMasters apply to all slides in a presentation; you cannot use more than one SmartMaster in a single presentation. You can, however, change colors, fonts, shadows, patterns, and other enhancements in individual slides, as described throughout this chapter.

(continues)

(continued)

Every time I create a presentation, I like to use my own custom SmartMaster. Is there any way I can save it so I don't have to re-create it every time?

Yes. First, choose **F**ile, **O**pen and change the file type to SmartMaster Set (MAS). Then select the directory in which the SmartMasters are located (usually, \FLW\TEMPLATE) and choose the SmartMaster set on which you want to base your customization.

Open the SmartMaster set and modify it as needed. Finally, save the customized SmartMaster set with a new file name and store it in the correct SmartMaster subdirectory. Now you can apply the custom SmartMaster to any new or existing presentation.

If I make changes to the SmartMaster used in my presentation, how is the Freelance Graphics SmartMaster set affected?

Any changes that you make to a SmartMaster affect only the current presentation; the Freelance Graphics SmartMaster set file that you are using is not altered.

Enhancing Text

When you type text in a slide, the font, attributes (normal, bold, italic, or underline), color, and size of the text conform to the settings specified in the current SmartMaster. In the TORNPAPR.MAS SmartMaster, for example, the title is black, Helvetica, 48-point, normal text; and the subtitle is black, Helvetica, 24-point, italic.

If you want to use a different font, attribute, size, or color, you can change these settings for all slides in a presentation, or for individually selected text objects, by altering the SmartMaster.

Choosing a Font, Attribute, Size, or Color for Text

To change font settings, as well as attribute, size, color, and so on, you change the settings in one dialog box from the SmartMaster base. When you change settings on the SmartMaster base, the settings change for the entire presentation.

To change font settings in a SmartMaster, follow these steps:

1. Choose **V**iew, Smart**M**aster Pages and then double-click the text you want to change.

2. The Attributes (Text) dialog box appears (see fig. 24.6).

3. Choose the **F**ace, **A**ppearance, **S**ize, **C**olor, and other settings that you want to use.

4. Click OK to apply the changes.

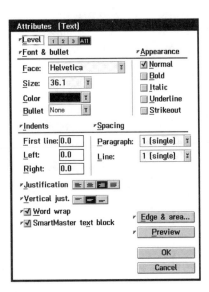

Fig. 24.6
Change fonts, bullets, indents, and so on for the entire Smart-Master set in the Attributes dialog box.

You also can change specific format settings by clicking the following buttons in the SmartIcon palette:

Button	Name	Description
N	Normal	Returns the selected text to normal (turns off bold, italic, strikeout, and/or underline)
B	Bold	Turns bold on or off for the selected text
I	Italic	Turns italic on or off for the selected text
U	Underline	Turns underline on or off for the selected text

Changing Line and Paragraph Spacing

Just as the SmartMaster defines colors, fonts, and other characteristics of a presentation, it also defines the line spacing for text in text objects. Freelance Graphics enables you to set the spacing between lines, as well as the amount of space between paragraphs. In most SmartMasters, the default line and paragraph spacing is 1, although the default paragraph spacing for bullets is 1.15.

You may want to change line or paragraph spacing, depending on the content of your slides. If a slide contains only four bullets, for example, you may want to increase the line spacing so that the bullets fill the slide. If your slide contains several paragraphs of text, you may want to set the space between paragraphs to 1.5 so that each paragraph is distinctly separate from the ones before and after it.

To change line and paragraph spacing, double-click the text in SmartMaster view. The Attributes dialog box appears. Choose the line and paragraph spacing in the **S**pacing area of the dialog box (see fig. 24.7).

Fig. 24.7

The bullet text Attribute dialog box with 1.15 default paragraph spacing.

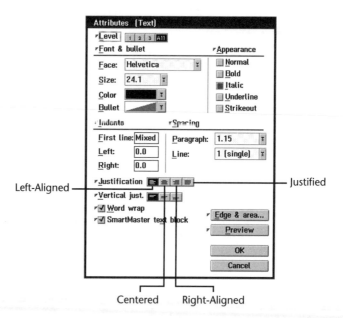

Note

To change indents for SmartMaster text, double-click the text in SmartMaster view and enter the amount of indent you want for **F**irst line, **L**eft, or **R**ight in the **I**ndents area of the dialog box.

Aligning Text

Justification, in the Attributes dialog box, refers to the horizontal positioning of text in a text block. In presentation slides, text often is left-aligned (for paragraphs or bullets) or centered (for titles). In some SmartMasters, text is right-aligned or justified.

The Justification buttons are, from left to right, Left-Aligned, Centered, Right-Aligned, and Justified (refer to fig. 24.7). Left alignment aligns text along the left edge of a text object leaving a ragged right edge. The center alignment option aligns text at the center point of the text object so that an equal number of characters appear to the right and left of the center point. Right alignment aligns text along the right edge with a ragged left. The justify option aligns text along both the right and left edges so that the characters in a line cover the entire width of a text object.

Because alignment involves horizontal positioning of text at margins or at the center point, alignment affects entire paragraphs. In other words, you cannot align a single word or line in a paragraph. You don't have to select any text to align a single paragraph; Freelance Graphics aligns the entire text object in which the insertion point is located.

To change the alignment of text, follow these steps:

1. Double-click the text in the SmartMaster view. The Attributes dialog box appears.

2. In **J**ustification, click the icon that aligns the text the way you want it.

3. Choose OK to close the dialog box. Freelance Graphics realigns the current paragraph or selected paragraphs.

Working with Colors and Line Styles

All objects that you draw in Freelance Graphics have an area color (except lines), an edge color, width, and style. The *area color* is the color inside an object; the *edge* is the frame that defines the boundaries of an object; and the *edge color*, *width*, and *style* define the color, width, and style (type of line, such as dashed or solid) of the object's frame.

For any object, you can turn off the area pattern and the edge style. Turning off both options makes an object invisible (unless it contains text), so this practice is not as common as turning off one option or the other. In most SmartMasters, for example, the edge style and area pattern for a text object are turned off, because text generally looks better in a slide without an edge or area pattern. For other objects, such as shapes that you create with the drawing tools, the object's edge usually is visible, and the object has an area color.

In most SmartMasters, an object's edge width and style produce a narrow solid line. The edge color generally is the same as the area color, however, so the edge is not apparent initially.

You can choose any of eight line widths. In addition, you can change a solid line to a dashed, dotted, or mixed line by choosing one of the six dashed-line options. If an object is any type of line rather than a solid shape, you can add arrowheads to either or both ends of the line or arc. You also can add shadows to objects and round the edges of rectangles.

Changing the Edge and Area

The *edge* refers to a line you can add to the text block. You can choose a color for the line, a line width, and a line style, such as solid, dashed, or dotted.

The *area* refers to the background of the text block. You can choose any color in the palette for the block background, and you can even change the area to a pattern, such as dots, stripes, or graded shading.

To choose the edge and area for a SmartMaster set, follow these steps:

1. Double-click the text in SmartMaster view. The Attributes (Text) dialog box appears.

2. Click the **E**dge & Area button; the Attributes (Text Edge & Area) dialog box appears (see fig. 24.8).

Fig. 24.8

Add lines and color to a text box in the Attributes (Text Edge & Area) dialog box.

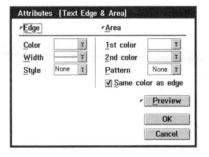

3. Choose the **W**idth arrow button to view the available line widths; and choose the **S**tyle arrow button to view the list of line styles (see fig. 24.9).

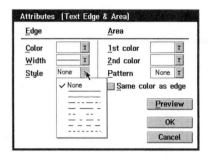

Fig. 24.9
Choose a style
from the list of
available styles.

IV

Using Freelance Graphics

4. Choose a color for the text block in the **A**rea part of the dialog box under **1**st color.

◄ See "Creating
an Organiza-
tion Chart
Slide," p. 421

5. Choose OK to close the dialog box and OK again to close the Attributes (Text) dialog box.

Using Shading and Patterns

In a slide presentation, filled objects often are more interesting than plain ones. Two effective variations for filled objects are shading and patterns.

A *shaded color* is a dark-to-light or light-to-dark variation of a filled object's color. This variation can run vertically, horizontally, diagonally, from the center outward, or from any corner. You also can adjust the intensity of the color.

Add shading and patterns to text blocks in the Attributes (Text Edge & Area) dialog box.

To shade an object, follow these steps:

1. Double-click the object that you want to shade. The Attributes (Text) dialog box appears.

2. Choose the **E**dge & Area button. The Attributes (Text Edge & Area) dialog box appears.

3. Click to open the **P**attern drop-down list, which displays the options shown in figure 24.10.

4. To add shading to the current object, choose one of the last 16 Pattern options.

5. Pick a color from the **1**st Color palette to change one of the colors for your shading.

Fig. 24.10
Choose a shade or
a pattern from the
drop-down list.

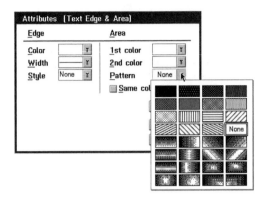

6. Pick a color from the **2**nd Color palette to change the other color for your shading.

7. If you want, click the **P**review button to preview the shading for the selected object.

8. Choose OK to close the dialog box. Freelance Graphics applies the shading to the selected object.

An alternative to adding shading to an object is adding a non-shaded pattern. A *pattern* is a design (such as lines, dots, bricks, or checkerboard squares) that contains two colors: a first color and a second color.

To add a pattern to a filled object, follow all the preceding steps for adding shading except step 4. For that step, choose one of the first 14 patterns.

Working with Color Palettes

A *color palette* is a set of colors that complement one another. As you learned earlier in this chapter, every SmartMaster has a predefined color palette that consists of specific colors for the slide background, title text, text and edges, and areas. You can use the colors defined in a SmartMaster, choose a different color palette, or change individual colors in a color palette.

Choosing a Different Color Palette

Each SmartMaster set uses specific colors for text, background, and foreground. You can choose to change the color palette with preset color combinations that apply automatically to the SmartMaster in your presentation.

To change the color palette in your presentation, follow these steps:

1. Choose the **S**ettings, Switch **P**alette command. The Settings Switch Palette dialog box appears (see fig. 24.11).

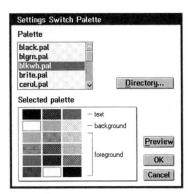

IV

Using Freelance Graphics

Fig. 24.11

Switch palettes for the entire presentation in the Settings Switch Palette dialog box.

2. In the Palette area, choose the palette that you want to change. The Selected Palette area displays colors for the text, background, and foreground.

3. Choose OK to apply the new palette to the presentation.

Editing a Color Palette

After selecting the palette you want to use in your presentation, you can edit individual colors on the palette to better suit your presentation and your tastes. You can change the color of the text, background, and foreground.

To change a color in the palette, follow these steps:

1. Select the **S**ettings, **E**dit Palette command. Freelance Graphics displays the Settings Edit Palette dialog box.

2. Select a color in the text, background, or foreground area of the **C**hoose Color area. The color appears in the **M**odify color box.

3. Click the down arrow in the **M**odify Color box and another color palette appears (see fig. 24.12).

4. Click OK to apply the new colors.

Tip

Choose the **P**review button in the Settings Switch Palette dialog box to see what the selected palette looks like in your presentation.

Fig. 24.12
Choose colors that
better suit your
tastes in the
Settings Edit
Palette dialog box.

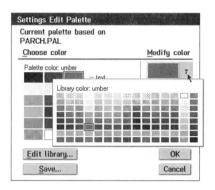

Troubleshooting

*The line style I chose in the Attributes (Text Edge & Area) dialog box doesn't show up
against my selected SmartMaster background.*

Go back into the Attributes (Text Edge & Area) dialog box. Under **E**dge, choose
Width and select a thicker line width. You can also select **C**olor under **E**dge and
choose a color that better contrasts with the SmartMaster background.

*I want a shaded color for a background to my slides but there are no solid SmartMasters
Can I create a SmartMaster set with a shaded background?*

Yes. Open the Settings Switch SmartMaster Set dialog box, select the PLAIN.MAS set,
and choose OK. Next, edit the Basic Layout page as discussed in "Altering a
SmartMaster" earlier in this chapter. Create an object, such as a rectangle, and apply
shading to it. Size the rectangle so that it fits the background for your slides.

From Here...

This chapter discussed the variety of techniques that you can use to enhance
objects in a Freelance Graphics presentation. Refer to the following chapters
for more information about working with objects:

■ Chapter 23, "Drawing Shapes, Curves, and Lines," describes how to use
Freelance Graphics' drawing tools to add drawn objects to your slides.

■ Chapter 25, "Creating Graphs Using the Graph Tool," teaches you how
to create, format, and enhance graphs in your Freelance Graphics slides.

Chapter 25

Creating Graphs Using the Graph Tool

by Elaine J. Marmel

If you've worked with spreadsheet programs such as Lotus 1-2-3, you know you can create graphical representations of the data you enter in a spreadsheet. A chart (or graph, as Lotus calls it) is an effective tool for presenting data in a clear way and for providing instant visual impact. In other words, graphs often are easier to understand at a glance than are rows and columns of data. Because of the high impact that graphs provide, especially in a presentation, Freelance Graphics has a powerful built-in tool, called the Graph Tool. The Graph Tool is shared with 1-2-3, making it easy to add graphs to your slides.

In this chapter, you learn to:

- Use the Type Gallery to select a graph type

- Enter and edit graph data

- Choose colors, patterns, borders, and fonts

- Edit an existing graph

Using the Graph Tool

When you use Freelance Graphics' built-in charting facility, you use the Graph Tool to create or edit bar graphs, pie graphs, area graphs, and line graphs for a presentation slide. The Graph Tool enables you to identify the axes of a graph, provide a title, subtitle, and legend for the graph, and enhance the appearance of a graph by adding lines, text, or arrows to point out important information. The Graph Tool can display the data in two separate modes: graph view and data view. Graph view displays the data as a bar, line, pie, or other chart. Data view displays the data in a worksheet, similar to a 1-2-3 worksheet.

When you create a new graph in Freelance, the Graph Tool supplies a Data View window you can use to set up data on which a graph is based. Or you can use data stored in a 1-2-3 worksheet. If you already created a graph in a 1-2-3 file, you can simply add that graph to a Freelance presentation file.

▶ See "Linking 1-2-3 Data to a Freelance Presentation," p. 534

If you use 1-2-3 for OS/2, you may already be familiar with the Graph Tool, and you won't need to learn much to use the facility in Freelance. You can use graphs you create in 1-2-3 in presentations you create in Freelance. The graph is stored in whatever file it was created in; that is, you don't need to save the graph in a separate graph file. If you create a graph in a 1-2-3 worksheet and then save the worksheet, the graph is part of the worksheet. If you then use the graph in Freelance, but change the type from a bar to a line graph, the line graph version is stored in the Freelance presentation, and you don't affect the graph created and stored in the 1-2-3 file. However, because the two files (1-2-3 and Freelance) are linked by graph information, if you change the data in the source file (1-2-3, in this case), you also update the graph in the destination file—your Freelance presentation file

Tip

See Chapter 6, "Working with Charts and Graphics To Present Your Data," for more information on using the Graph Tool with 1-2-3.

Start the Graph Tool from inside Freelance Graphics (or 1-2-3, but we'll focus on Freelance in this chapter). When you create or view a graph, Freelance automatically displays the Graph Tool (see fig. 25.1).

Fig. 25.1
When you open the Graph Tool by displaying or creating a graph, the menus and SmartIcons change.

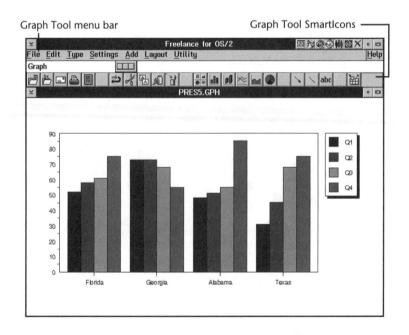

Creating a New Graph

Typically, when you want to add a graph to a presentation, you start by using a SmartMaster page layout that contains at least one "Click here..." graph block. Each SmartMaster set contains four page layouts that hold one, two, or four graphs, and one page layout holds a graph with a bulleted list to its left.

Once you display an appropriate SmartMaster page layout, start the Graph Tool by clicking the Graph icon in the Freelance Graphics toolbox. Freelance Graphics displays the Add Graph dialog box shown in figure 25.2 and starts Graph Tool.

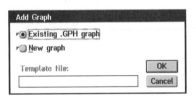

Fig. 25.2
From the Add Graph dialog box, you can create an entirely new graph or you can add an existing graph to a presentation.

If you choose to add a **N**ew graph, Graph Tool displays the Data View window. There you enter the data to base your graph on (see fig. 25.3).

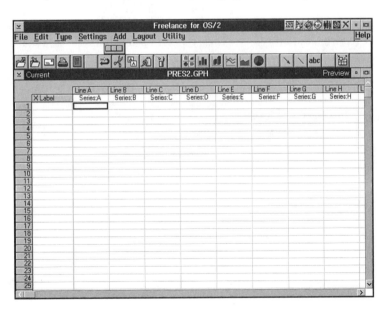

Fig. 25.3
The Data View window, maximized, resembles a spreadsheet and lets you supply data to base your graph on.

Tip

You can place a graph on a page without a "Click here..." box. Click the Graph Tool in the toolbox and choose **N**ew. The graph appears on the page and you can move and resize it.

> **Note**
>
> You don't need to manually enter data to create a new graph. You can take advantage of data or a graph that already exists in a 1-2-3 worksheet. Or, you can use a graph you previously created in a different Freelance Graphics presentation. See "Adding Existing Graphs to a New Presentation" later in this chapter.

A Graph Tool Data View window is made up of rows and columns, similar to a Lotus 1-2-3 worksheet or an Ami Pro table. Rows are numbered 1 through 4,000, and columns are labeled Line A, Line B, Line C, and so on, through Line W. The intersection of each row and column is a cell, into which you enter text or a number. Unlike a 1-2-3 worksheet or an Ami Pro table, however, a Graph Tool window can't use formulas.

> **Troubleshooting**
>
> *The "Click here..." text gets in the way of my graph and I want to size the graph larger than the allotted space in the graph SmartMaster.*
>
> Choose either the Backdrop or Shared Elements as the page layout in the Page New dialog box. Then click the Graph button in the Toolbox and enter your data and other information to create the graph. Freelance draws the graph for you on the new page. When the graph is selected (handles appear around it) you can resize and shape the graph, and reposition it on the page, as you wish.

Understanding How Data Is Plotted

In figure 25.4, a sample Graph Tool shows data for four states, entered in rows.

◄ See "Entering Data," p. 81

A data series contains individual data points that are plotted along the y-axis (vertical axis) of a graph on line, bar, or area slides. The first column of the Data View window is X Label; the entries in this column identify the data series, which are translated into labels below the x-axis (horizontal axis) in the graph shown in figure 25.5. The column headings near the first row of the dialog box (the row above row 1) represent categories of data and are translated, as indicated in the figure, into legends.

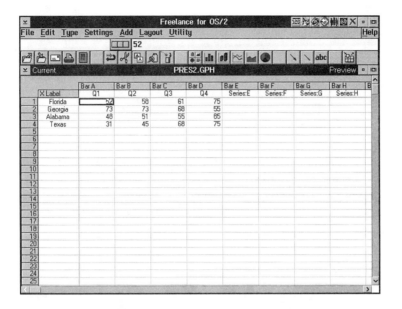

Fig. 25.4
Enter data in the
Data View window
as you would in a
worksheet.

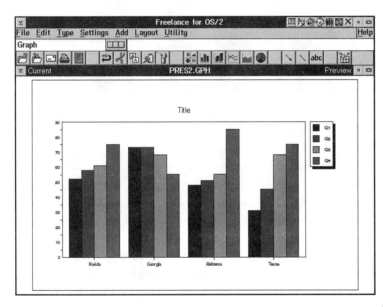

Fig. 25.5
The data shown
in figure 25.4
produces a bar
graph like this
one.

Note

By default, Graph Tool produces a line graph; but this is shown as a bar graph to
make the picture easier to see and read.

The type and style of the graph you create affects the visual impact of the final graph. For example, the bar graph shown in figure 25.5 shows relative sales of a particular product line in each state, quarter by quarter. The graph shows that sales in Georgia declined over the course of the year. Plotting the same data as a stacked bar graph, however, shows that sales in Georgia in fact exceeded sales in the other states for the cumulative four quarters (see fig. 25.6).

Fig. 25.6
Showing the same data differently allows a different analysis.

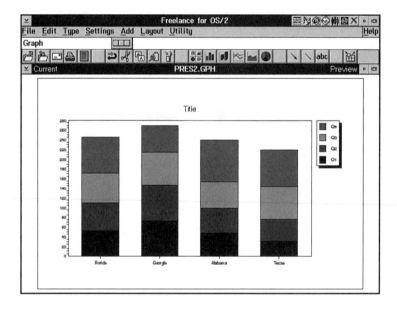

Entering Data

When you're ready to enter data in the Graph Tool, display the Data View window (click the Graph icon in the Toolbox), and then type the information into the appropriate cells in the window. Move from cell to cell by pressing the arrow keys or by clicking the next cell. The active cell is outlined with a bold border. Overtype mode always is active in the Data View window, so any entry you type in a cell automatically replaces the current contents of a cell. To complete an entry, press Enter, or press any of the arrow keys to move to another cell.

When you finish entering data in the Data View window, choose **L**ayout, **G**raph. Graph Tool automatically creates a line graph of the data in a window that appears as an object behind the Data View window.

Editing Data

Editing refers to changes that you make in data after it's entered in the Data View window. Of course, if you chose to view the graph, you must switch back to the Data View window. Choose **L**ayout, **D**ata View if you're in Graph view in the Graph Tool. If you're viewing a slide in Freelance Graphics, double-clicking the graph object Graph Tool redisplays the graph object in its own window (see fig. 25.7). Then choose **L**ayout, **D**ata View to switch the display from the graph to the data it's based on.

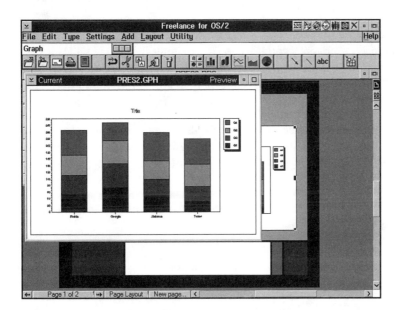

Fig. 25.7

When you switch back to the Graph Tool after creating a graph and placing it in a Freelance presentation slide, you see the graph in its own window in the Graph Tool.

You change data in the window the same way you do in Lotus 1-2-3. Editing includes changing individual entries; cutting, moving, and copying entries; and inserting and deleting rows and columns. Before you can edit cells, you must know how to select them.

Selecting Cells, Rows, and Columns

You already know that to select a single cell, you press the arrow keys or click a cell. But as you enter and edit data in the Data View window, you may want to work with a group of cells rather than just one. You may want to move a group of cells to a new location, for example. In the Data View window, you can select a range of cells, entire rows, or entire columns.

◀ See "Selecting Ranges," p. 92

A *range* is any rectangular group of cells. To select a range, click the cell in the top-left corner of the range and drag the mouse to the cell in the bottom-right corner of the range. The entire range appears highlighted.

In the Data View window, select an entire row or column by clicking the row number or column letter. You can also select multiple rows or columns by dragging the mouse across row numbers and column letters. To select rows 1, 2, and 3, for example, click and drag the mouse across the row numbers 1, 2, and 3. All cells in each row are highlighted. You can also press and hold down the Shift key as you highlight cells with the arrow keys.

To cancel any selection—a range of cells, or a group of columns or rows—press Esc or click any cell.

Correcting a Cell Entry

Earlier in this chapter, you learned that to enter new data in a Data View window, you simply type the data in a cell. This method, however, isn't the only way to change data in a cell. When an entry contains a minor error, you may want to edit the entry rather than type over it.

Tip

Alternatively, double-click the cell; the cursor appears in the edit line.

Editing allows you to change only selected characters in an entry. If a cell contains a part number such as BXN-231-781S and you discover that the B should be a C, you can correct the error rather than retype the entire part number.

To edit an entry, click the cell and then click the entry in the edit line at the top of the screen (see fig. 25.8).

Fig. 25.8

When you click in the edit line, an insertion point appears.

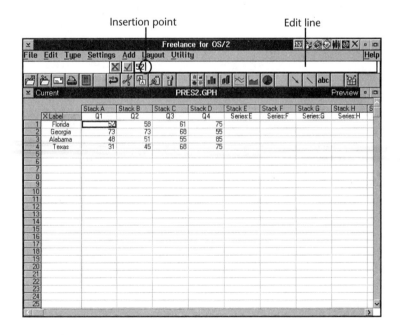

Insertion point   Edit line

Press the arrow keys or click to position the insertion point; then press Backspace or Del to delete the error. Pressing Backspace deletes characters to the left of the insertion point; pressing Del deletes characters to the right of the insertion point. New characters that you type appear to the left of the insertion point.

When you finish editing, press Enter or press the up- or down-arrow keys to move to another cell.

Clearing Cells

Clearing refers to removing the contents of a cell (a number or text character that appears in the cell) if you entered incorrect data or if the data has changed. To clear one or more cells, select the cells to be cleared, and choose the **E**dit, Cl**e**ar command or press Del.

Moving and Copying Data

Two common editing tasks are moving and copying information. Moving information means removing information from its original location and placing the removed information in a new location. Copying information means leaving the information at its original location and also placing a copy at a new location.

Moving information is a two-part process. First, you cut the information from the original location and then paste it in the new location. Cutting information removes the contents of selected cells and places the data on the Clipboard.

Tip

You can enter changes by clicking the Confirm (checkmark) button in the edit line. You can cancel changes by clicking the Cancel (X mark) in the edit line.

Tip

If you clear a cell or cells by accident, choose **E**dit, **U**ndo, the Undo SmartIcon, or press Alt+Backspace.

> **Caution**
>
> At first glance, **E**dit, Cl**e**ar and **E**dit, Cu**t** may seem to perform the same function: removing data from selected cells. The commands perform the task in entirely different ways, however. **E**dit, Cu**t** removes the data but places it on the Clipboard, while **E**dit, Cl**e**ar permanently removes the data without storing it anywhere. Be sure to cut data if you want to move the data elsewhere in the Data View window.

Copying information is also a two-part process. First, you place the original information on the Clipboard, and then paste the information from the Clipboard to the new location. Copying is like cutting because it places information on the Clipboard; unlike cutting, however, copying also leaves the information at the original location.

> **Note**
>
> When you move or copy data, you can restore the data to its original location—click the Undo SmartIcon, choose **E**dit, **U**ndo, or press Alt+Backspace. In Freelance Graphics, **E**dit, **U**ndo remembers the last 10 actions you performed. Choosing **U**ndo repeatedly, progresses through all 10 of the most recent actions.

To move information in the Data View window, follow these steps:

1. Select the cells you want to remove data from.

2. Choose **E**dit, **Cut**, click the Cut SmartIcon, or press Shift+Del. The data is removed from the worksheet and placed in the Clipboard.

3. Select the first cell in the range to move the data to. The new location you choose shouldn't contain data; if it does, the data you move overwrites the existing data.

4. Choose **E**dit, **P**aste, click the Paste SmartIcon, or press Shift+Ins. The data appears in the new location in the Data View window.

Unlike moving, copying leaves the original data intact in the Data View window, and a copy of the data is placed in the Clipboard. After the data is in the Clipboard, you can paste it anywhere in the Data View window. Again, the new location should not contain data; if it does, the original data is overwritten.

To copy data, follow these steps:

1. In the Data View window, select the cells to copy from.

2. Choose **E**dit, **C**opy, click the Copy SmartIcon, or press Ctrl+Ins. The data is copied to the Clipboard.

3. Select the first cell in the range to copy to. The new location you choose shouldn't contain data; if it does, the data you copy overwrites the existing data.

4. Choose **E**dit, **P**aste, click the Past SmartIcon or press Shift+Ins. The data is copied to the new location in the Data View window, and it remains intact in the original location.

Choosing a Graph Type

Freelance Graphics comes with 13 graph types, as indicated on the left side of the Type Gallery dialog box. Most graph types have six different styles, as shown on the right side of the dialog box. The graph styles listed on the right side of the dialog box depend on which graph type is selected on the left side of the dialog box. To display this dialog box, you must be working in the graph view of the Graph Tool. From a graph window, choose **L**ayout, **G**raph. Then choose **T**ype, **G**allery to open the Type Gallery dialog box. After you choose a graph type, the right side of the dialog box changes to illustrate the styles available for that type of graph.

Adding Visual Elements to a Graph

Aside from the graph itself—that is, the actual bars, lines, slices, columns, and areas—most graphs contain elements that make the graph easier to read. For example, you can add a title and a subtitle to describe the graph's purpose. You can also add titles (such as Thousands of Dollars, Percentage of Budget, or 1995 Sales) to identify the units used in the horizontal x-axis and the vertical y-axis.

A *data series* is one set of numbers you're plotting. On a line graph, each line is a data series; on a bar graph, one data series is distinguished from another by color or by pattern. Legends are used to identify each data series represented in a graph. You can also add grid lines, which help readers find the values of data points more accurately (see fig. 25.9).

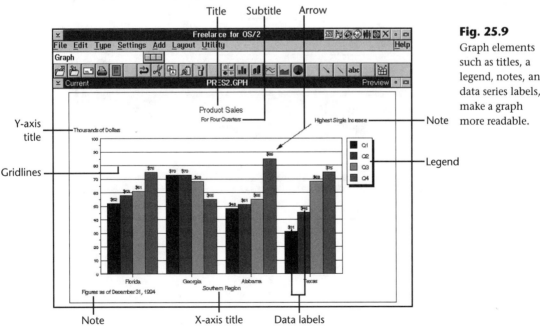

Fig. 25.9
Graph elements such as titles, a legend, notes, and data series labels, make a graph more readable.

Titling a Graph

By default, when Graph Tool creates a graph, it leaves placeholders on the
graph for a title, an x-axis title, and a y-axis title. You also see a legend on the
graph. But the words Graph Tool supplies aren't meaningful—you see "Title"
where you're expected to place a title, and "X-Axis" where the title of the
x-axis belongs.

To modify any of these titles, follow the same basic steps:

1. Double-click the item you want to modify. The contents of the text
   object you double-clicked appear in the edit line (see fig. 25.10).

2. Edit the information so it describes your graph.

3. Press Enter. Graph Tool updates the text object in the graph.

To change the font or type size of a graph title or axis title, select the title
and then choose **S**ettings, **F**ont to display the Settings Font dialog box (see
fig. 25.11).

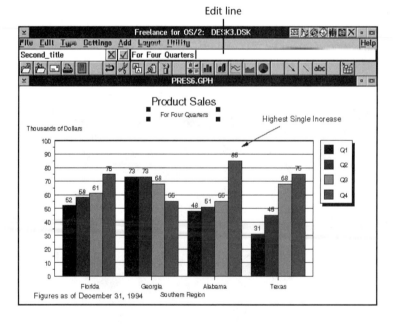

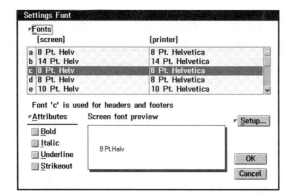

Fig. 25.11
Using this dialog box, you can change the font and point size of a text object, as well as add special effects such as bold or italics.

To change the color or alignment of a text object, select the title and then choose **S**ettings, **T**ext Style to open the Settings Text Style dialog box (see fig. 25.12).

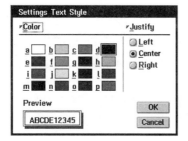

Fig. 25.12
Use this dialog box to change the color and alignment of the text within a text object.

Suppose you feel that a graph title is insufficient—you need a subtitle as well. Not a problem. Choose **A**dd, **T**itle, **S**econd. Graph Tool adds a subtitle to the graph, immediately below the title.

If you need to add notes to the graph, choose **A**dd, **N**otation, **T**ext. Graph Tool adds a note to the upper-left corner of the graph (see fig. 25.13).

If you need additional notes, repeat the process described above. Be aware that Graph Tool always adds notes to the upper-left corner of the graph—even if a note already appears there. If you intend to add more notes, move the graph note to a different location by dragging it.

Tip
You can modify the content, font, and text style of a subtitle or note the same way you modify other text objects, such as the graph title.

Fig. 25.13
Adding notes can help clarify your graph.

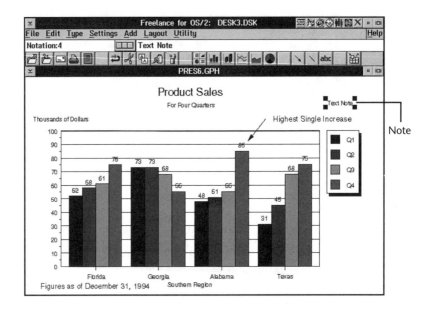

> **Caution**
>
> While the idea of notes sounds like a good one, remember, you're trying to tell a story with pictures. Be careful not to add excessive numbers of notes to a graph; too many notes on a graph clutter it and make it more difficult to read.

Positioning a Legend

Tip
When you select the graph type in the Type Gallery, the example styles display a legend if it's included with the style.

A legend uses color-coded boxes to identify the data series in a graph. If the East data series is represented in a bar graph by red bars, for example, the legend shows a small red box next to the word East. Most of the graph styles offered by Graph Tool include a legend in the graph, so you don't need to choose a special command to add one.

> **Note**
>
> You can suppress the legend by deleting it. Select it and press Del. You can add it by choosing **A**dd, **L**egend. Choose **F**rame or **L**abel. This command is available only if no legend appears on the graph.

Tip
You also can drag the legend to a new position in the graph.

You can change the location of the legend in various types of graphs. In figure 25.13, shown earlier in this chapter, the legend appears to the right of and outside the frame surrounding the graph. To change the location of the legend, select the legend by clicking it, and then choose **S**ettings, **P**osition, **L**egend. You see the dialog box shown in figure 25.14.

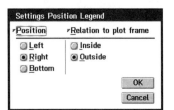

Fig. 25.14
Use the Settings Position Legend dialog box to change the location of the legend.

Adding Data Labels

Data labels show the exact value or percentage represented by a data point. Data labels often are used in bar graphs to pinpoint values when data points are close together.

Once you display data labels, you can control the position of the data labels in relation to the data point. You can also control the number formatting Graph Tool uses to display the data label.

To add data labels to a graph one data series at a time, follow these steps:

1. Select the first data series to show data labels for.

2. Choose **S**ettings, Series **O**ptions to display the Settings Series Options dialog box.

3. Place a check in the **S**how Data Label checkbox.

4. Choose OK. Data labels appear for the series you selected. You can see data labels above each bar in figure 25.13, shown previously.

Once you display data labels, you may want to change their position in relation to the data series:

1. Choose **S**ettings, **D**ata Labels. The Settings Data Labels dialog box appears.

2. Choose a position: **A**bove, **C**enter, **B**elow, **L**eft, or **R**ight. Note that **L**eft and **R**ight may not work, depending on the type of graph you have defined. They don't work, for example, in bar graphs.

3. Choose OK. Graph Tool repositions the data labels.

Tip
You can change the position of all data labels simultaneously by clicking anywhere on the plot frame—the box that outlines the graph.

Changing the position of data labels may not be adequate; perhaps you'd like to change the appearance—the number format—of data labels:

Tip
You can change the appearance of all data labels simultaneously by clicking anywhere on the plot frame—the box that outlines the graph.

1. Choose **S**ettings, **N**umber Format, **D**ata Labels. The Settings Number Format dialog box appears (see fig. 25.15).

2. Choose a number format. Watch the Preview box for a sample of the format you chose.

3. Choose OK. Graph Tool redisplays your graph using the new number format for data labels.

The graph shown in figure 25.9, earlier in this chapter, displays value labels above the bars formatted to appear as currency.

Fig. 25.15
From this dialog box, change the way Graph Tool displays data label numbers.

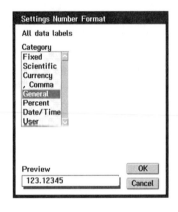

Controlling the Y-Axis

Tip
Use 0 decimals places when formatting a number format to keep from crowding the chart data and to avoid confusion.

◀ See "Formatting Numbers for Clarity," p. 108

In figure 25.22 later in this chapter, it would be helpful to have the second y-axis reflect dollars ($100,000) instead of just the figure 100,000. You change axis label number formats the same way you changed data label number formats. Select the axis and then choose **S**ettings, **N**umber Format, **Y** Labels. In the Settings Number Format dialog box choose a format and click OK.

As you've noticed, Graph Tool creates a scale for the y-axis automatically. That scale always appears measured in a power of 10 (that is, 100,000 is represented as 100, and (in thousands) appears on the axis). Suppose, however, that you'd like to set the lower and upper limits of the scale and specify the increment of numbers appearing on the scale. Choose **S**ettings, **S**cale. From the submenu, choose **Y.** The Settings Scale Y dialog box, shown in figure 25.16, appears.

Upper Limit and **L**ower Limit do exactly what you'd expect—they let you set the upper and lower values on the scale.

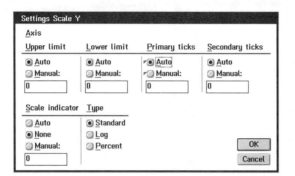

Fig. 25.16
Use this dialog box to control the appearance of the y-axis.

Primary Ticks control the distance between major tick marks on the y-axis and also determine the increment of values on the scale. For example, in figure 25.17, primary tick marks are set to auto, while in figure 25.18, primary tick marks are set to manual, and the distance between them is 10.

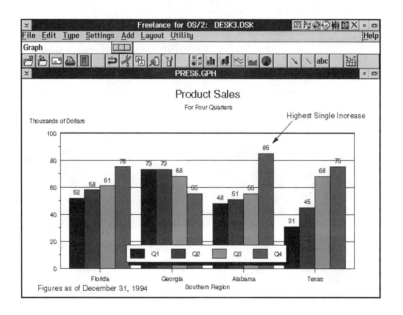

Fig. 25.17
In this graph, all limits and tick marks are set to automatic.

Secondary Ticks work just like primary ticks but for minor tick marks on the scale. Compare figures 25.18 and 25.19. In figure 25.18, the secondary tick marks are set to auto, while in figure 25.19, primary tick marks are set to auto, but the secondary tick marks are set to manual and the distance between them is 5.

Fig. 25.18

In this figure, primary tick marks are set to manual, and the distance between them is 10.

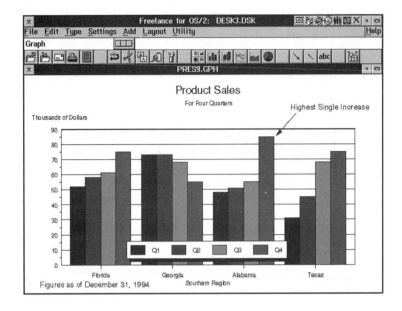

Fig. 25.19

In this figure, the secondary tick marks are set to manual and the distance between them is 5.

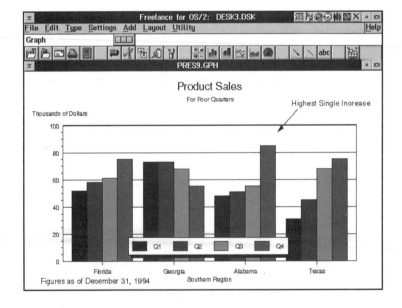

> **Note**
>
> If you change any of these limits to manual, use the following guidelines:
>
> - The lower limit must be less than the upper limit.
>
> - The Graph Tool doesn't display any data that falls outside the upper and lower limits.
>
> - The value for the primary ticks must be less than the difference between the upper and lower limits.
>
> - The value for the secondary ticks must be less than the value for the primary ticks.

Creating a Second Y-Axis

With certain sets of data—for example, the set shown in figure 25.20—you're measuring two different things (in this case, units sold and total sales revenue).

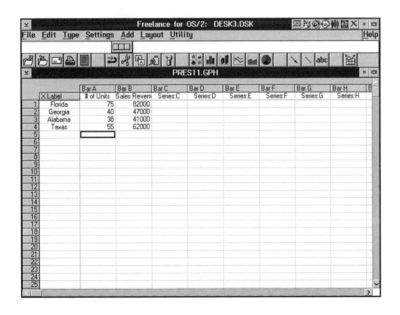

Fig. 25.20

Data sets with different units of measurement: units sold and total sales revenue.

Creating a standard bar graph for this data produces a graph like the one shown in figure 25.21. Because the units for the two data sets are different, the graph is confusing at best and misleading at worst. The y-axis goes from 0 to 100,000 so that it can display the largest dollar figures, even though units range only from 0 to 7,500. The bars for the units barely appear on the graph because the y-axis scale is so large, but Graph Tool left spaces where the bars for the units would appear. It would be better to have the two data sets plotted with their scales on different axes.

Fig. 25.21

Plotting data measured in different units in the same graph can lead to difficult interpretation.

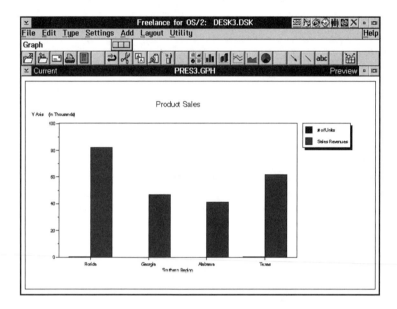

Before we create a second y-axis, let's reposition the existing y-axis so the axis measuring dollar revenue appears on the right side of the graph. Follow these steps:

1. Click any of the sales revenue bars to select them all.

2. Choose **S**ettings, **P**osition, **Y**-axis. The Settings Position Y-axis dialog box appears.

3. Choose **R**ight.

4. Click OK. Graph Tool moves the current y-axis to the right side of the graph.

Now we've got a place to put the other y-axis that represents sales in units—on the left side of the graph. To add a second y-axis, follow these steps:

1. Choose **S**ettings, Series **O**ptions.

2. Choose the 2Y-axis option button.

3. Click OK. Your graph now has two y-axes (see fig. 25.22).

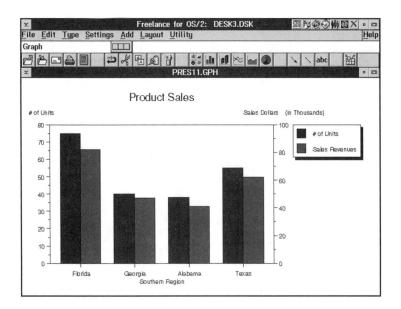

Fig. 25.22
The first data set—
units sold—is
plotted on the y-
axis on the left;
and the dollar
volume is plotted
on the y-axis on
the right.

Change the number formatting and titles for the second y-axis the same way
you changed the first y-axis.

Specifying Colors or Patterns in a Graph

Throughout this chapter, you've seen how Freelance Graphics can create a
variety of graphs from your data. Just as you can change the graph type, you
can change the colors and patterns used in your graphs. Changing these attributes can greatly improve the appearance of a graph.

You can apply colors or patterns to almost any element of a graph. In the
sample Bar graph shown in figure 25.23, columns that represent the data
series use hatching patterns and are black, but they could have appeared in
color. The legend box and the walls of the graph (made visible by the horizontal grid lines) appear in white, and the gridlines themselves appear in
black. You can change the colors of the legend, but not the gridlines. You can
change the color of the frame that appears around the graph as well. You also
can change the background color of the area inside the frame, the area outside the frame, and the inside of the legend box.

Suppose you want to create a black and white graph because you're going to
reproduce it on paper to appear in multiple copies of a report and you don't
have access to a color photocopy machine. The process for changing the
color or pattern of any element is basically the same.

Fig. 25.23

You can specify colors and patterns for most elements of a graph.

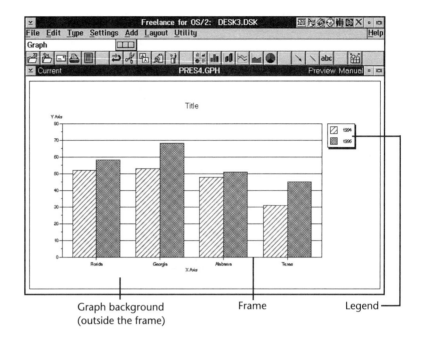

Graph background
(outside the frame)   Frame   Legend

Select the element you want to change. If you want to change the background outside the plot frame, just click in that area. For all elements except the background outside the frame, you'll see selection handles. Choose **S**ettings, Area Style. The Settings Area Style dialog box appears. You can use this dialog box to change the color and fill patterns of the background. Regardless of the element you select, this dialog box looks basically the same. Make appropriate choices from the dialog box (watch the preview box) and choose OK.

Tip

3D bar graphs, pie graphs, and radar graphs have no frame.

You can also change the line style for the edges of bars, the legend box, and the frame. Choose **S**ettings, Line/Edge Style to display the Settings Line/Edge Style dialog box. From this dialog box, you can change line styles for the outside edges of various elements of a graph.

Placing the Graph in a Presentation Slide

Now that you've done all this work and created a graph, it's time to switch back to Freelance Graphics and place the graph on a slide. To switch back to Freelance Graphics, click the title bar of the Presentation window or anywhere in the presentation window. If you can't see the Presentation window because you maximized the Graph Tool window, restore the Graph Tool window to its original size. When you switch back to the Presentation window, the Graph Tool window disappears and the graph object appears selected—note the black handles surrounding it (see fig. 25.24).

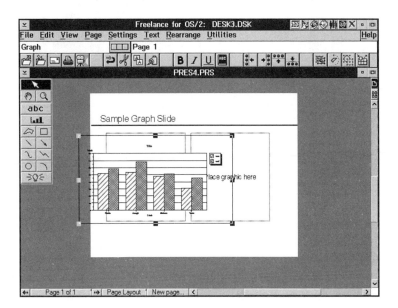

Fig. 25.24
When you switch back to Freelance Graphics, the graph object is already selected.

While it may seem like a long time ago, you started this process by selecting a Freelance Graphics page layout that contained at least one graph block. Drag the graph on top of a "Click Here..." graph block, and Freelance Graphics automatically adjusts the graph object so it fits into the "Click Here..." graph block (see fig. 25.25).

Saving Graphs

If you want, you can save your graphs in separate graph files; this isn't entirely necessary, however, because any graph you use in a presentation is also stored automatically by Freelance Graphics in the presentation file.

> **Note**
>
> By the way, the same applies to graphs in 1-2-3. They are also stored as part of the 1-2-3 file in which they appear.

Tip
If you need to reopen the Graph Tool window to modify the graph, double-click the graph in the Presentation window.

Fig. 25.25
Drag the object on top of a "Click here..." graph block, and Freelance Graphics automatically sizes the object to fit in the graph block.

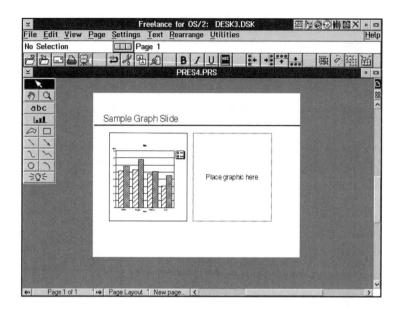

Tip
To delete a graph, select it while viewing it in a Freelance slide and press Delete.

To save a graph as part of the Presentation file, simply save the Presentation file. To save the graph separately from the Presentation file, display the graph in Graph Tool (double-click the graph in Freelance Graphics) and then save the file. In the File Save dialog box, choose the **C**urrent File Only option and change the name of the graph file.

> **Caution**
>
> Be sure to use a unique name for the graph. *Don't* use the suggested name—the same name as the presentation file with a .GPH extension. The presentation filename with a .GPH extension is reserved for the graph associated with the presentation file. If you use this name, you might lose data.

Adding Existing Graphs to a New Presentation

Suppose you had already created a graph in 1-2-3 and saved it separately as a graph file. Now you decide that you want to use that graph in a presentation. Do you need to recreate the graph in Freelance Graphics using the Graph Tool? Nope. You simply bring in the existing graph.

Select an appropriate page layout on which you want the graph to appear. Click the Graph icon in the Toolbox. When you see the Add Graph dialog box, choose **E**xisting .GPH file and click OK. You'll see the Add Existing Graph dialog box, from which you can navigate to the drive and directory that contains the graph file you want to use. Select it and choose OK. The graph appears selected in your presentation file. Drag-and-drop it on one of the "Click Here..." graph objects in the page layout. If you want to make changes to the graph, double-click it to open the Graph Tool and go from there.

From Here...

In this chapter, you learned how to create graphs for your presentation slides. Refer to the following chapters for information about other types of objects you can add to slides:

- Chapter 21, "Entering Slide Content," describes the basics of entering the content of a presentation and labeling objects. This chapter also describes all aspects of enhancing text.

- Chapter 23, "Drawing Shapes, Curves, and Lines," describes how to use Freelance Graphics' drawing tools to add drawn objects to your slides.

- Chapter 24, "Enhancing a Presentation," describes how to add color, borders, shadows, and other enhancements to objects.

Chapter 26

Printing and Displaying Your Presentation

by Lenny Bailes

As you learned in Chapter 20, "Getting Started with Freelance Graphics," you can print both slides (on paper or overhead transparencies) and audience handouts. You also can prepare an on-screen slide show as a special kind of output.

In this chapter, you learn to:

- Choose a setup for presentation components
- Print presentation components (slides and handouts)
- Create and run an on-screen slide show

Choosing a Page Setup for Your Presentation

A page setup determines the dimensions and orientation to be used for printing each component of a presentation. Freelance Graphics' default setting is to print slides on 8 1/2-by-11-inch paper. The unprintable margin area for each page is a function of the printer that you're using. If your printer supports them, you can produce slides in landscape or portrait orientation; you also can place headers or footers on each page. You set these options by choosing **F**ile, **P**rint, **O**ptions; the File Print Options dialog box appears, as shown in figure 26.1.

◀ See "Printing and Print Options," p. 64

Fig. 26.1

Use the File Print Options dialog box to set headers, footers, orientation, and margins.

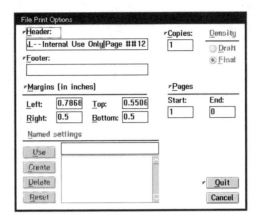

Setting Headers and Footers

As in other Lotus SmartSuite products, you can print a header at the top and/ or a footer at the bottom of every page in Freelance Graphics.

> **Note**
>
> Headers and footers don't appear in screen shows, only in printouts.

Headers and footers can contain any text you choose. By default, text you type in the **H**eader or **F**ooter text box in the File Print Options dialog box is left-aligned in the printout. If you precede header or footer text with a vertical bar (|), that text is centered. If you precede the text with two vertical bars (||), the text is right-aligned.

You can also have Freelance Graphics place specific information into headers and footers by incorporating special symbols into your header and footer text entries. Table 26.1 describes these symbols.

Table 26.1 Symbols to Use in Headers and Footers

Symbol	Effect
#	Inserts the sequential page number at this location
##N	Inserts the page number at this location, beginning with the number specified by N (for example, ##12 prints page number 12 on the first page and numbers pages sequentially from there)
@	Inserts the current date at this location

Symbol	Effect
|	Centers the following text
||	Right-aligns the following text

You can combine these symbols to obtain a variety of header and footer printouts. For example, type this text as a header

@|CONFIDENTIAL-Internal Use Only|Page ##12

and it results in the printout shown in figure 26.2.

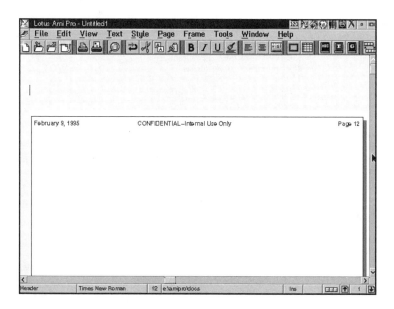

Fig. 26.2
You can customize header and footer text in your printout.

Setting Margins

Margins are set according to the units you specify in the Settings Units & Grids dialog box. The numerical settings are specified by selecting **F**ile, **P**rint, **O**ptions.

Understanding Output Formats and Print Options

When you choose **F**ile, **P**rint, **P**rint Presentation, you see the dialog box shown in figure 26.3. The **F**ormat section of this dialog box contains a variety of options, which are described in table 26.2.

Fig. 26.3

The File Print, Print Presentation dialog box enables you to control the way your slide show looks on paper.

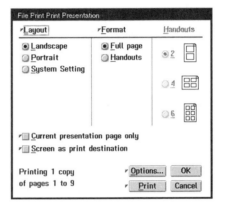

Table 26.2	Print Format Options
Format	**Output**
Full Page	Prints each page of your presentation on a separate output page
Landscape	Prints each presentation page in landscape mode (11" x 8.5")
Portrait	Prints each presentation page in portrait mode (8.5" x 11")
System Setting	Positions each presentation page according to the orientation setting in the OS/2 Driver Setup dialog box
Handouts	Produces printout in any of three styles: Portrait mode with two presentation pages per printout page Landscape mode with four presentation pages per printout page Portrait mode with six presentation pages per printout page
Current Presentation Page Only	Prints only the current page of your presentation
Screen as Print Destination	Opens the View Screen Show dialog box when you select the **P**rint button. This allows you to create a screen show instead of sending output to the printer (see fig. 26.4)

Format	Output
Options	Opens the Print Options dialog box, used to set margins, headers, and footers (Print Options can also be accessed directly from the **F**ile, **P**rint menu)
Print	Sends the presentation to the printer

Note

Be sure to set the page orientation to reflect the orientation of the slides in your presentation. Most of Freelance Graphics' SmartMasters are designed to be presented in landscape mode.

You can also specify exactly what you want to print. For example, you can specify the number of copies to be printed and the range of pages to be printed (for example, only pages 7 through 12). You can also print only the page that currently appears on-screen.

Creating a Screen Show

One of the most effective ways to present your slides is to use your computer screen as an output medium. When you use your computer for an on-screen slide show (called a *screen show*), the entire screen area is used; Freelance Graphics' title bar, menu, and toolbars are cleared from the screen, and each slide is presented in full-screen display. You can hook your computer up to a projection device that projects your slides onto a large screen so audience members can view them.

The advantage a screen show offers over transparencies or 35mm slides is that a screen show saves you the expense of producing slides; it requires no projection equipment, and you can use your computer's color capabilities to their fullest extent.

You can run a Freelance Graphics slide show manually, using the mouse or keyboard to advance to the next slide when you're ready; you can set up a slide show to run in a continuous loop for demonstration purposes; or you can set up a slide show to advance slides automatically. To learn how to run a slide show manually or in a continuous loop, see "Setting Slide Timing" later in this chapter.

You can also create a screen show for display on another PC, even if it doesn't have Freelance Graphics loaded. For information, see "Creating a Stand-Alone Screen Show" later in this chapter.

Setting Slide Timing

When you set up a slide show to advance to the next slide automatically, you can set the amount of time that each slide remains on-screen. To set timing, choose **V**iew, Scree**n** Show and then choose the appropriate options in the View Screen Show dialog box (see fig. 26.4).

Fig. 26.4

You can set the timing for each slide and choose the starting pages in the View Screen Show dialog box.

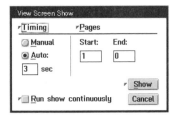

Choose **M**anual to set slides to advance manually when you click the left mouse button and to return to the preceding slide when you click the right mouse button. Choose **A**uto to set slides to advance automatically, and specify the number of seconds of transition time (from 1 to 60) between slides.

If you want the screen show to run continuously, choose **R**un Show Continuously. This causes the show to loop back to the first slide and repeat itself each time the last slide is shown. You can use either **M**anual or **A**uto timing with this option.

To run the screen show, choose **V**iew, **S**creen Show, Show, press Alt+F10, or click the Run Screen Show SmartIcon.

To quit viewing a screen show, press the Esc key.

Creating a Stand-Alone Screen Show

Sometimes, you may want to prepare a slide show for use on another computer that doesn't have access to Freelance Graphics. You can prepare your slides so they can be shown on virtually any DOS computer that's capable of displaying graphics.

Choose **F**ile, **Ex**port and select the Freelance (**S**HW) option in the File Export dialog box, as shown in figure 26.5.

Fig. 26.5

Use the File Export dialog box to prepare a stand-alone screen show.

By default, Freelance creates a file with the SHW extension in the same directory and with the same name as your presentation. If you want to designate another file name or directory, click the **L**ist Files button. In the example shown in figure 26.6, the slide show will be saved under the filename DEMOSHOW.SHW onto drive A. After Freelance Graphics finishes creating the screen show on the disk in drive A, the following files will be located on that disk:

SHOW.EXE

DEMOSHOW.SHW

DEMOSH1.GX2

DEMOSH2.GX2

DEMOSH3.GX2

To run your screen show from a computer that doesn't have Freelance Graphics, place the disk in the A (or B) drive, and type the following DOS command at the A (or B) prompt:

A>SHOW DEMOSHOW

Your stand-alone screen show runs, even without access to Freelance Graphics.

Fig. 26.6

The **L**ist Files button in the File Export dialog box opens another dialog box that allows you to specify a source drive, directory and filename for a slideshow to be saved.

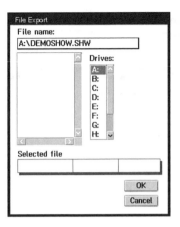

Troubleshooting

All my screen show files fill more than one floppy disk. How do I transport my screen show to another computer that doesn't have Freelance Graphics?

Before you create your stand-alone screen show, create a subdirectory on your hard drive named, for example, C:\SHOWTEMP. Create all your stand-alone files in that subdirectory. Then if you have access to a disk compression program, you can compress the files and copy the compressed version to a floppy disk. (Remember to take the decompression program with you to the other computer!) Decompress the screen show into an equivalent subdirectory on the second computer.

If you don't have compression software, you can use the OS/2 Drives Object or an equivalent program to copy files individually to a number of floppy disks from C:\SHOWTEMP. Copy them onto an equivalent directory on the second computer and run the slide show from there.

From Here...

This chapter described how to print a slide show and run a slide show in Freelance Graphics and concludes the Freelance Graphics part of Using OS/2 Lotus SmartSuite. To review information about Freelance Graphics, refer to any of the following chapters:

- Chapter 20, "Getting Started with Freelance Graphics," describes how to start and exit Freelance Graphics. In this chapter, you also learn about SmartMasters, page layouts, and objects you can add to a Freelance Graphics presentation.

■ Chapter 21, "Entering Slide Content," describes the basics of entering the content of a presentation and labeling objects. The chapter also describes how to create an organization chart in a Freelance Graphics presentation.

■ Chapter 22, "Working with Objects," describes what objects are; how to select and group them; and how to move, copy, resize, align, rotate, flip, and stack them.

■ Chapter 24, "Enhancing a Presentation," describes how to work with SmartMasters, as well as how to add color, borders, shadows, and other enhancements to objects.

For additional information on using Freelance Graphics with other SmartSuite applications, refer to the following chapters:

■ Chapter 28, "Sharing Data between Applications with DDE," teaches you how to share data between a Freelance presentation and another SmartSuite program.

■ Chapter 29, "Using the OS/2 Workplace Shell to Create an Integrated Desktop," discusses how to bring a variety of SmartSuite documents, or portions of documents, into a Freelance Graphics presentation.

IV

Using Freelance Graphics

Part V

Working Together with Lotus SmartSuite Applications

Chapter 27

Copying and Pasting Information between SmartSuite Applications

by Robert L. Weberg

Projects, assignments, and various work situations arise that require you to create detailed reports, memos, faxes, proposals, and so on using information or data stored previously in one of the SmartSuite packages. Imagine the time you can save by not having to re-create the same income statement, budget analysis, marketing proposal, or loan review. A simple copy and paste allows you to share or move important pieces of information between SmartSuite files. The techniques discussed in this chapter show you how to copy and share information between Ami Pro documents, 1-2-3 worksheets, and Freelance Graphics presentations.

In this chapter, you learn to:

- Copy text, data, and pictures between SmartSuite applications
- Use Paste Special to get a different format

Understanding How To Integrate the SmartSuites

Of course your goal in creating professional-appearing proposals, reports, and presentations is to convince your managers, customers or colleagues of a specific idea or solution. You can influence decisions by designing sharp, convincing documents that utilize information from the various SmartSuite applications.

Building and creating documents by using integration of the SmartSuites and other applications is simple and easy. The key to successful document integration is understanding how to switch between applications and open documents for effective data manipulation, and knowing what objects, data, or pieces of information you can share between the SmartSuite applications. In fact, there is no easier way in the SmartSuite for OS/2 to accomplish this than using the simple copy and paste procedure.

Arranging Documents

Tip
The **C**ascade command in Ami Pro is the same as the **S**tack command in 1-2-3 and Freelance.

Before transferring data between files or applications you may need to arrange windows to see more than one file at a time. To arrange the open files and windows, follow these steps:

1. Open the files you want to view. Each open file is in a separate window.

2. Choose **W**indow, **T**ile or **C**ascade. The documents are tiled or cascaded. Figure 27.1 illustrates three opened documents tiled on-screen in Ami Pro. You can now click back and forth between active and inactive document windows using the mouse.

Fig. 27.1
Try tiling open documents when you need to visually compare or copy data. Tiling automatically sizes your documents to fit on the screen for easy viewing.

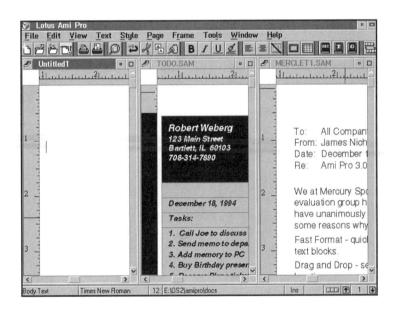

- If you choose **T**ile, each open window reduces in size so all open windows can fit on the screen (the more open windows, the smaller each window).

- If you choose **C**ascade, all windows display at one time, but they overlap so that only the title bar of each window (excluding the top one) displays.

- In 1-2-3 and Freelance, you need to open the Document Control menu and select the **W**indow command. Then choose the **S**tack command to cascade the open document windows or **T**ile to tile the open document windows.

3. You can change and size the windows by positioning the mouse pointer on the window border and then holding down the left mouse button and dragging.

When you click the title bar of any tiled or cascaded/stacked window, that window becomes active. An active window has a dark title bar. Menu commands, SmartIcon buttons, and shortcut-key combinations apply to the active window. You can open several files and then minimize the files until you need them. To minimize a file window, click the Minimize button; the document changes to a small icon that appears at the bottom of the application's window. Figure 27.2 illustrates two documents in 1-2-3 minimized and a new file window adjusted for size so you can see the two icons.

Tip

Close the files you don't want to view by double-clicking the control menu button for each window.

◄ See "Switching between Documents," p. 67

Tip

To move a window, drag the title bar.

V

Working Together

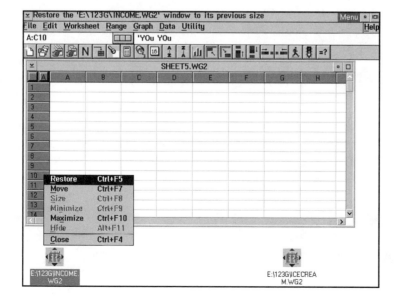

Fig. 27.2

You can click a file icon to reveal the Control menu, then choose the **R**estore or Ma**x**imize command to open the file window.

Transferring Data between Applications

You can transfer data between the SmartSuite applications in various ways such as using File, **O**pen and selecting the appropriate file type, using the **F**ile, **E**xport and **F**ile, **I**mport commands (Freelance), using DDE commands, using the OS/2 Clipboard, or using the drag-and-drop technique.

Using the OS/2 Clipboard To Transfer Data

Generally, the OS/2 Clipboard is a faster, more convenient, and more selective method of transferring data because you can copy, cut, and paste data as you require it, without having to save or retrieve separate files. The OS/2 Clipboard is not limited to OS/2 applications. All applications running under the OS/2 environment, including Windows and DOS applications, share a common Clipboard that can transfer information from one application to another.

> **Note**
>
>
> In all the SmartSuite applications except cc:Mail, you can use the Paste SmartIcon.

◄ See "Cutting, Copying, and Pasting," p. 49

To copy data, use the **C**opy command; to move data, use the Cu**t** command. The data remains on the Clipboard until you copy or cut another selection of data to the Clipboard. For example, if you copy text on the current page and then copy a picture, the Clipboard contains only the most recently copied item—the picture. You can then switch to the application or document you want to paste the data into and use the **P**aste command.

◄ See "Shortcut-Key Combinations," p. 42

> **Caution**
>
> When switching between Windows applications to OS/2 applications, you need to remember the Cut, Copy, and Paste keystroke differences between OS/2 and Windows. The shortcut keystrokes in Windows applications are: Cut (Ctrl+X), Copy (Ctrl+C) and Paste (Ctrl+V).

Using the Drag-and-Drop Technique To Transfer Data

A quick and efficient way to move data and text within Ami Pro to another location in the same document is to use the mouse to drag-and-drop information. Drag-and-drop is similar to using the Cut and Paste procedure because it removes selected text from its current location and then places it in a new location. The difference is that you are performing the procedure with the mouse and the selected information is not copied into the Clipboard.

To use drag-and-drop to move and copy text, perform the following steps:

1. Select the text you want to move or copy; then click the mouse anywhere in the selected data and begin to drag the mouse to the desired location or position.

As you drag, the mouse pointer changes to an arrow with scissors attached and a vertical insertion point.

2. Release the right mouse button when you reach your destination and Ami Pro places the text in the desired location.

To copy text, select the data and hold down the Ctrl key as you drag.

Copying between Ami Pro Documents

If you enjoy saving time and being productive when typing—and especially hate typing the same text, sentences, and paragraphs repeatedly—learning how to copy text between documents is worthwhile. This is useful when the information you are gathering is dispersed throughout existing documents.

◀ See "Using Built-in Macros," p. 373

The initial step in working with multiple documents in Ami Pro is opening all the documents you need by using the **F**ile, **O**pen command.

> ### Note
>
> An alternate and more efficient process to open multiple documents is to run a macro called OPENDOCS.SMM. To do so, choose **T**ools, **M**acros, **P**layback. Select OPENDOCS.SMM. The Multiple File Open dialog box appears, as shown in figure 27.3. This macro allows you to open up to nine Ami Pro files at a time. In the File and Drives listbox, choose the drive and directory of the files you want to open. Click or select each of the files you want to open and then select OK.

Now you're ready to copy or move text between the open Ami Pro documents using the **E**dit, **C**opy or the **E**dit, **C**ut command; switch to the desired document you want to receive the information and then choose the **E**dit, **P**aste command to insert the copied data.

V

Working Together

Fig. 27.3
The OPENDOCS.SMM macro is a great time-saver when you need to open a lot of related documents.

◀ See "Using Fast Formatting," p. 271

After the text has been copied into your document, you may have to reformat the text so it matches the surrounding text.

> **Note**
>
> Use the Fast Format icon to copy formats between text; or choose **T**ext, Fas**t** Format. Highlight the text with the insertion point that has the format you want, and click the Fast Format button. A paintbrush indicator appears. Drag the mouse-pointer paintbrush across the text you want to change. When you release the button, the selected text changes format.

Tip
Choose **E**dit, **G**o To; or double-click the page number on the right portion of the status bar to move around large documents. Select the page number item type you wish to move to.

◀ See "Creating Frames," p. 346

◀ See "Using Graphics with Ami Pro," p. 353

Copy Ami Pro Frames and Pictures

You can also use the OS/2 Clipboard to cut, copy, and paste pictures and frames. The picture can be one you created in another application or a picture in an Ami Pro document. You can create a frame of the desired size before pasting the picture or let Ami Pro create the frame for you using predefined settings.

To copy and paste a picture in Ami Pro, select the picture you want to cut or copy and then perform the usual Cut, Copy, or Paste commands.

Ami Pro copies the picture into the document. If you let Ami Pro create the frame, the Placement option in the Modify Frame Layout dialog box is set to **F**low with Text. If you placed the picture into a frame you created, the picture is sized to fit in the frame, and the aspect ratio is maintained.

> **Note**
>
> You can use Paste **S**pecial to select the format for the picture. See "Using Paste Special" later in this chapter.

Copying Ami Pro Table Information

Ami Pro tables are a great way to enhance your documents. They allow you to align data and lists, plus you can highlight important areas by utilizing shading, lines, and borders. When you paste Ami Pro table text into a document or frame, Ami Pro creates a table and inserts the information into the table cells.

Tip

To modify the options for a frame, choose **F**rame, **M**odify Frame Layout.

> **Note**
>
> In order for the table to be created when pasting from another table, you need to highlight all of the original table. If you only highlight a section or a few cells, only the text will be copied.

However, you may only need to copy or cut a smaller amount of text or graphics from an Ami Pro table. In these situations, you can cut or copy the contents of one or more cells and paste the information in other cells in the same table or in another table. The cells can contain text, numbers, pictures, or table formulas.

◀ See "Understanding Tables," p. 355

To cut, copy, and paste table information:

1. Select or highlight the data in one or more cells if you wish to copy the data into another table. If you want a table to be automatically created for you, select the entire table.

2. You can now perform the usual Cut, Copy, and Paste commands to copy or move the data.

Tip

To select the entire table, choose Ta**b**le, Select Entire Ta**b**le.

When pasting table information into a table you need to be aware of the following results:

■ When you paste text from one cell into another cell, Ami Pro appends the text to the existing cell contents, starting at the location of the insertion point within the cell.

■ When you paste the contents of multiple cells, text separated by tabs, or formulas into other cells, Ami Pro overwrites any existing cell contents, starting in the cell in which the insertion point is located.

■ Ami Pro doesn't insert any columns to accommodate the information. Information in additional columns isn't pasted. To have all the data pasted, you can increase the number of columns and paste the data again.

V

Working Together

◄ See
"Changing
Table
Attributes,"
p. 357

- Ami Pro automatically increases the size of the cells to accommodate the pasted data if you selected Automatic Row Height in the Modify Table Layout dialog box. If you didn't select Automatic and text in the cells is greater than the size of the receiving cells, some of the pasted text may not appear. If so, you need to manually size the cells to display the text.

- Ami Pro automatically inserts additional rows into the table if the destination table doesn't have enough rows to accept the pasted data.

Copying from Ami Pro to 1-2-3 and Freelance

When designing business proposals, worksheets, presentations, or reports, you need to exchange and combine spreadsheet, presentation, and document data. The steps for copying information from Ami Pro to a 1-2-3 worksheet or a Freelance Presentation are essentially the same as copying between two Ami Pro documents, as discussed in the previous section.

To copy Ami Pro data into 1-2-3, copy or cut the desired data in Ami Pro, switch to 1-2-3 and then paste the data. Figure 27.4 displays Ami Pro text copied into a 1-2-3 worksheet.

Fig. 27.4

Ami Pro text has been pasted into cell A1 in a 1-2-3 worksheet and it won't retain its formatting attributes.

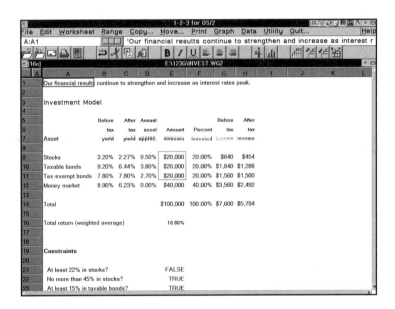

Caution

The pasted text copied from Ami Pro to 1-2-3 is placed into one cell as a label and isn't word wrapped. Meaning that you lose the visual effect of wrapping paragraphs and the text continues from left to right in 1-2-3.

Note

Ami Pro tables also paste into 1-2-3. Each table cell in the Ami Pro table is pasted into separate cells in 1-2-3. However, you lose the formatting attributes (such as lines, colors, and alignment) contained in the Ami Pro table.

◄ See "Using Edit Copy and Edit Paste," p. 147

When copying Ami Pro data into Freelance you can copy the Clipboard data into pre-existing text boxes or directly into the presentation.

To transfer Ami Pro data into a Freelance presentation, select the desired data you want to copy; choose **E**dit, **C**opy; switch to Freelance; and choose **E**dit, **P**aste. Pasting data in Freelance depends on whether you are copying the data into a preexisting text box or creating a new text box.

■ To place the data in a preexisting text box, click the desired text box where you want the data to appear. With your cursor in the text block, press Shift+Insert, or choose **E**dit, **P**aste.

◄ See "Entering Text on Slides," p. 396

■ To copy the data directly into the presentation, choose **E**dit, **P**aste. Freelance automatically creates a new text box with the copied data in it (see fig. 27.5) The new text box appears at the top of your presentation page and can then be moved and sized to another location.

Copying from 1-2-3 to Ami Pro and Freelance

You may need to display worksheet information like income statements, sales analysis, and budget estimates in an Ami Pro document or Freelance presentation. You can then add attributes like frames, shading, and borders to enhance your document.

To copy information or data from a 1-2-3 worksheet to an Ami Pro document, select the range of data you want to copy; choose **E**dit, **C**opy; switch to Ami Pro or Freelance; and choose **E**dit, **P**aste.

Fig. 27.5
Ami Pro text
pasted into a text
box in Freelance
can be moved and
sized to a new
location.

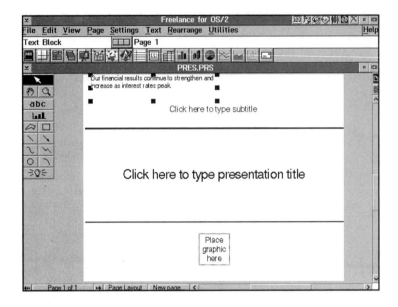

◄ See "General
Effects of Copy-
ing Informa-
tion," p. 142

If you copy a 1-2-3 range and then paste it into Ami Pro, you get a table, as
shown in figure 27.6. If you don't want your worksheet data to appear as a
table, or if you want the 1-2-3 styles and formatting to be transferred, use the
Edit, Paste **S**pecial command and choose Metafile from the list of available
formats. See "Understanding Paste Special" later in this chapter.

Fig. 27.6
The 1-2-3
information
pasted into an Ami
Pro table. Notice
that each cell in
1-2-3 becomes a
cell in an Ami Pro
table.

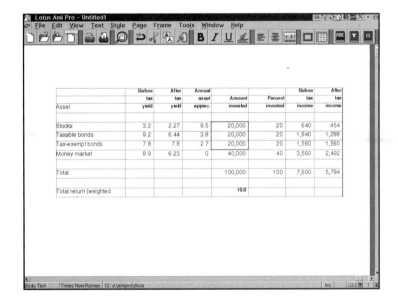

> **Note**
>
> When using a normal paste operation, the pasted information is placed into a table in Ami Pro, as shown in figure 27.6. The light grid lines won't print, unless you change the formatting and borders of the table by choosing Ta**b**le, Li**n**es & Colors.

Figure 27.7 shows how the above copied 1-2-3 range would appear if it was pasted into a Freelance presentation. Note that the data appears in metafile format and that Freelance doesn't create a table.

◄ See "Under-standing Tables," p. 355

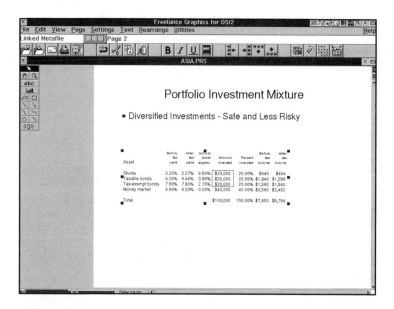

Fig. 27.7
The 1-2-3 information pasted into a Freelance presen-tation. You could also Paste Link the 1-2-3 range so the data would automatically update whenever the 1-2-3 data changed.

► See "Sharing Data between Applications with DDE," p. 525

V

Working Together

Copying from Freelance to Ami Pro and 1-2-3

Copying text or data from within the SmartSuites can help you express your thoughts or ideas in a document, but you may want to copy more visual data like text, charts, or pictures from a Freelance presentation to enhance a drab business report or document. The procedure is essentially the same as copy-ing data between two Ami Pro documents or a 1-2-3 worksheet to an Ami Pro document.

Select the object, picture, or chart; choose **E**dit, **C**opy; switch to Ami Pro or 1-2-3; and choose **E**dit, **P**aste.

> **Note**
>
> Ami Pro uses a frame border to highlight a selected picture object, not black handles.

◀ See "Creating Frames in Ami Pro," p. 346

To select the copied Freelance object, picture, or chart, click it. Now, you can move the picture to a new location or drag the frame borders to change the size of the picture.

Freelance allows you to copy an entire presentation page to Ami Pro and 1-2-3, which enables you to display entire presentations or important pages in a report or worksheet.

To copy an entire presentation page in Freelance, follow these steps:

1. In Freelance, copy the desired page to the Clipboard.

Tip
You can switch to the page sorter view to view all your current presentation pages by clicking the page sorter icon on the right window border, or choose **View**, **P**age Sorter.

2. Switch to Ami Pro using the Lotus Application Manager, the Window List dialog box, or Alt+Tab and then position your insertion point in the Ami Pro document where you want to place the copied Freelance presentation page.

3. Choose **E**dit, **P**aste, or press Shift+Ins. The Freelance presentation page appears in your Ami Pro document (see fig. 27.8). Figure 27.9 shows how the page would appear in 1-2-3 after sizing.

Fig. 27.8
A Freelance Presentation Page pasted into an Ami Pro document allows you to integrate your Freelance presentations into reports and proposals.

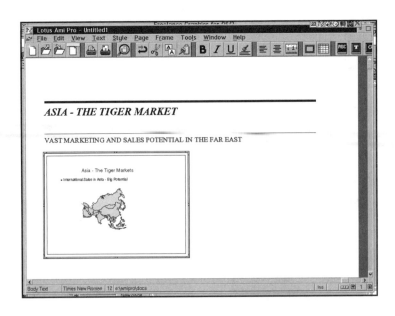

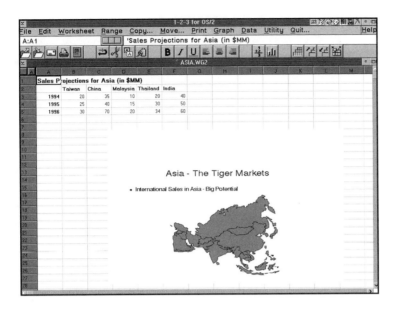

Fig. 27.9
You can include the same presentation page in a 1-2-3 worksheet for easy reference or to spruce up a worksheet.

Understanding Paste Special

When you choose the **E**dit, **P**aste command to paste information, the corresponding SmartSuite application checks the location of the insertion point and automatically uses the format that seems most suitable for that location.

Sometimes you may want to select a different format than the application normally uses. As a case in point, Ami Pro defaults to Ami Text Format or Metafile when you paste text or a picture from the Clipboard, but you may want the pasted data to be linked or appear with its original attributes. In this situation, you must use the Paste **S**pecial command.

> **Note**
>
> The Paste Special command is not available in either Freelance Graphics or cc:Mail.

When pasting 1-2-3 data into an Ami Pro document you may want the text to appear as body text and not in a table. To use the Paste Special option with 1-2-3 spreadsheet data in the Clipboard, choose **E**dit, Paste **S**pecial. The Paste Special dialog box appears (see fig. 27.10).

Fig. 27.10

The Paste Special dialog box allows you to paste the Clipboard data into a different format. The formats displayed depend on the application you are copying from.

The Paste Special dialog box has options that enable you to DDE link data and specify a different format for the Clipboard data (spreadsheet in this example):

- *Text.* Inserts the spreadsheet with tabs separating the data that was in the columns. If you select this option, you probably will have to select the data and change the tabs if you want the information to align (see fig. 27.11).

▶ See "Sharing Data between Applications with DDE," p. 525

- *Rich Text Format.* Inserts the spreadsheet as a table in your document, getting the same result as choosing **E**dit, **P**aste.

- *DDE Link.* Links information to the source spreadsheet. Both files must be open for DDE Link to work.

◀ See "Changing Tabs and In- dentions," p. 272

- *OS/2 Metafile.* Scales well but it doesn't always retain text formatting.

- *OS/2 Bitmap.* Provides exact representations of a graphic but it doesn't scale well.

Fig. 27.11

After copying information from a 1-2-3 spread- sheet, set tabs to separate the items that were in columns in the worksheet. In this example, the ruler displays that the data has been formatted using right-aligned tabs.

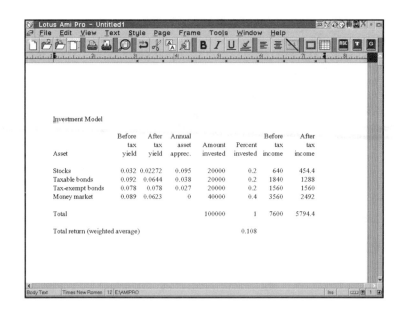

From Here...

In this chapter you learned how to copy information between the SmartSuite applications. However, in some situations you may want to link copied information instead. *Linking* means that when the source document or object changes, the link automatically updates the target document. For more information on integrating within the SmartSuites products, refer to the following chapters:

- Chapter 7, "Editing Worksheets," covers the basic requirements for manipulating worksheets, plus how to use cut, copy, paste, and paste special.

- Chapter 12, "Creating and Editing Documents," reviews how to insert text, copy text using the Clipboard, and move text using drag-and-drop.

- Chapter 21, "Entering Slide Content," dives into creating and building a Freelance presentation.

- Chapter 28, "Sharing Data between Applications with DDE," reviews the concepts of linking information between SmartSuite applications so that documents remain updated.

- Chapter 34, "Using Notes with SmartSuite Applications," discusses how Notes interacts with the SmartSuites.

V

Working Together

Chapter 28

Sharing Data between Applications with DDE

by Robert L. Weberg

Dynamic Data Exchange (DDE) is a standard used by Presentation Manager (OS/2) and Windows programs to share data among applications. Of the SmartSuite applications for OS/2, only cc:Mail doesn't support DDE. DDE is a method that allows you to create a data link between a file created in one OS/2 application and a file created in another OS/2 application; you can even link to a Windows application. Using DDE links, you can modify information in one file and automatically update other files using the same information.

> **Note**
>
> You cannot create links between two files in the same application, such as two Ami Pro documents.

DDE is very similar to the functionality of the OS/2 Clipboard (copy and paste), in that both DDE and the Clipboard display data created with other Presentation Manager and Windows applications within your files. But DDE extends the capabilities of the Clipboard by making links or connections to other files that can be reactivated and updated. Creating a DDE link is like building a pipeline between two files from different applications. You can open the pipeline so that data flows between the source application and the target file. If the data in the source file is changed, it will be updated in the target file. Both applications must be running before you can create or activate a link.

In this chapter, you learn how to:

■ Use DDE and DDE Linking

■ Use Paste Special and Paste Link to DDE Link two files

■ Edit, display, and link DDE linked files

> **Caution**
>
> Running two or more applications simultaneously uses a lot of memory.

Understanding Links

When you create a DDE link in a SmartSuite document, you are inserting a location pointer to information in an external source file. Since the link connects to the original data, any changes made to the original file are reflected in the target linked document. Imagine the DDE link as a telephone converstation between the SmartSuite document and the source file it's linked to. If the "phone connection" is active, the target file "hears" the source.

All links have a *server* and a *client*. The server contains the original information, while the client uses and links to the original information.

For example, suppose you want to include the latest sales figures from a Lotus 1-2-3 spreadsheet in an Executive Summary document in Ami Pro. As the data changes in the spreadsheet, you want the changes reflected in the report. However, you want to use Ami Pro paragraph styles to format the data. Instead of frequently pasting, importing, or retyping the sales figures to keep them updated, you can create a link from the 1-2-3 file in your Executive Summary document in Ami Pro. In this scenario, the 1-2-3 spreadsheet is the server because it contains the original source information and the Ami Pro document is the client because it uses (and is the target for) the original information.

> **Note**
>
> Server and client files can be any files created in OS/2 or Windows applications that support DDE.

When Should You Use DDE Linking?

DDE linking provides a convenient way to manage and organize data files that keep changing within numerous SmartSuite documents. Plus, it's a terrific way to combine the different sources into one compact and integrated document. When should you use DDE Linking between files?

■ When you want a central place to store certain information that you and others can link to.

■ When the source file (server) won't be moved or deleted (or the link will have to be re-created).

■ When all users who need to edit the information have access to the server application and the source file on the same file server. In other words, all users must use the same directory mapping in order to activate or update the linked data.

However, linking data or using DDE is not always the best solution for integrating data. When should you *not* use DDE linking?

■ When the original data doesn't need to change—use the Clipboard (copy and paste).

■ When users need to edit the data and don't have the source application available—use Import or the Clipboard. This situation generally occurs when the documents are accessed by remote users who don't have the source application on their laptops.

■ When the source application doesn't support DDE—use file attachments, Import, or the Clipboard.

■ When the original file has the possibility of being moved to a new directory or server. Moving the source file invalidates all the links. Although the links might still show the information from the last link update, you'll receive error reports when you attempt to refresh the link to a nonexistent file.

▶ See "Linking SmartSuite Data with Notes," p. 656

General Requirements for Using DDE

Implementing and initializing DDE between files is easy; however, certain rules need to be followed before you can successfully link data between two different applications. To avoid confusion or situations where DDE doesn't seem to be working, always remember the following DDE Linking guidelines or rules:

V

Working Together

- Save the source file before you create a DDE link because the Clipboard requires a named file to paste a link. It can't be an untitled or unnamed document.

- Launch the server application and file before you activate a DDE link because the server must already be running and the linked file must already be open before you can activate a DDE link.

- You can't create links between two files in the same application, such as two Ami Pro documents.

- Ami Pro doesn't support DDE links to Freelance OS/2 or Freelance for Windows 2.1.

- You must edit the linked information in the server application. You can't edit it in the client application.

Setting Up and Creating a Standard Paste Link

Most users envision linking only two SmartSuite files, but in fact, a single SmartSuite file can be linked from several different applications. For example, you could link a 1-2-3 worksheet to a Freelance Presentation and to an Ami Pro document. This enables you to share a lot of information across the SmartSuite products.

Establishing a link is a simple three step process: copy the data to the Clipboard, switch to the target application, and then choose the Edit, Paste Special or Paste Link command. Essentially, you're copying the source information from the server application to the Clipboard, switching to the client application and placing the cursor in the target location, and then choosing the Edit, Paste Link command to link the data. You could also choose the Edit, Paste Special command and then select the DDE Link option.

Note

Unfortunately, the linking commands and hot keys vary between the SmartSuites. The commands for paste linking data are Paste Link and Paste Special in Ami Pro, Paste Link and Paste Special in 1-2-3, and Link, Paste Link in Freelance Graphics.

Once you become acquainted with the techniques used to create linked data, you'll realize the potential for integrating important pieces of your data. For instance, you might maintain a 1-2-3 worksheet or Ami Pro document that contains variables for formulas in financial calculations like cost of capital, interest rate, prime rate, or some other economic indicator. These numbers in the document could be linked to other files or templates, thus requiring you to change the number only in one location.

Using Paste Special and Paste Link

Generally, copying and pasting data via the Clipboard is the simplest method available to transfer data between documents and applications. By using the **E**dit, **P**aste command, the current application automatically uses the format that seems most suitable for that location and information. But sometimes you may want to select a different format than the one the current Smart-Suite application uses. The Edit, Paste Special and Paste Link commands allow you to be selective in how you want your data to appear.

◄ See "Cutting, Copying, and Pasting," p. 49

What's the difference between the Paste Special and Paste Link commands? If you choose the Paste Link command, the information you copied to the Clipboard appears in the SmartSuite document unformatted. By choosing Paste Special, the data you selected has formatting but it won't be linked, depending upon the format option you select in the Paste Special dialog box.

◄ See "Under-standing Paste Special," p. 521

When you copy information to the OS/2 Clipboard, the current application will render the formats in which the information is available or can be used. The available formats will be displayed upon selecting the Paste Special command. The most common formats that appear in the Paste Special dialog box are OS/2 Metafile (Picture), OS/2 Bitmap, RTF (Rich Text Format), Text and DDE Link.

The application you're working with doesn't always support a specific format (see fig. 28.1).

When should you Paste Link data? Generally, when you don't care about the final appearance of the data or when all you require is a number or a small line of text.

Fig. 28.1
This error message appears when trying to link Freelance data into an Ami Pro document.

V

Working Together

Paste Special on the other hand should be used when you want the format of the original data to be maintained. For example, if you want the data contained in a 1-2-3 for OS/2 spreadsheet to maintain its formatting when you paste it into an Ami Pro document, you should use Paste Special. You could Paste Link the data—but Ami Pro defaults to Text when Paste Linking spreadsheet data—and this defeats your need to retain the attributes, fonts, and colors of the original worksheet data. The workaround is using Paste Special and selecting Metafile or Bitmap so the formatting and attributes you applied in 1-2-3 appear; however, the data isn't linked.

> **Note**
>
> When linking Ami Pro data into a 1-2-3 worksheet, the Paste Special command isn't available. Also, Freelance doesn't have a Paste Special command.

Linking 1-2-3 Data to an Ami Pro Document

Linking 1-2-3 worksheet data to Ami Pro is the most common link you'll perform because there is no better way to improve a dull textual report in Ami Pro than with numbers or tables. For example, you may have copied some important forecasting numbers from a 1-2-3 worksheet to a Report document in Ami Pro and want any changes made in that forecasting worksheet to be reflected in the report. Instead of continually copying the data every time it changes, the best solution is to link the forecasting data to the Ami Pro report document.

> **Note**
>
> Ami Pro doesn't support DDE links to or from Freelance Graphics for OS/2 or Freelance Graphics for Windows.

To create a link to an Ami Pro document from a 1-2-3 worksheet (or any application that supports DDE), follow these steps:

1. Switch to or launch 1-2-3 and open the desired 1-2-3 file.

> **Caution**
>
> The file must be a named file. It can't be an untitled worksheet or document.

2. Select the object or highlight the range of cells you want to include in the link to the Ami Pro document (see fig. 28.2).

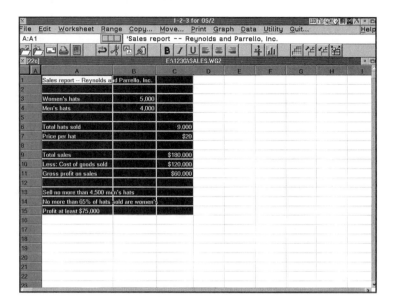

Fig. 28.2
The selected range of worksheet data in SALES.WG2 will be paste-linked into an Ami Pro document.

3. Choose **E**dit, **C**opy to copy the information to the OS/2 Clipboard. You can also press Ctrl+Ins.

4. Switch to Ami Pro and open the Ami Pro document you want to contain the information and then place the insertion point where you want the information to appear.

   If you want the information to appear in a table, place the insertion point in the desired table cell.

   ◄ See "Placing Information in a Table," p. 356

   If you want the information to appear in a frame, create, size, and select an empty frame.

5. Choose **E**dit, Paste **L**ink. The data appears unformatted in an Ami Pro table, as shown in figure 28.3.

You could choose the Paste **S**pecial command in Ami Pro and select another format option so that the original formatting attributes used in the 1-2-3 worksheet are retained, but the two files wouldn't be linked.

◄ See "Creating Frames," p. 346

V

Working Together

Fig. 28.3

The pasted 1-2-3 worksheet data is linked to the original source file. Any changes or modifications in the worksheet are reflected here.

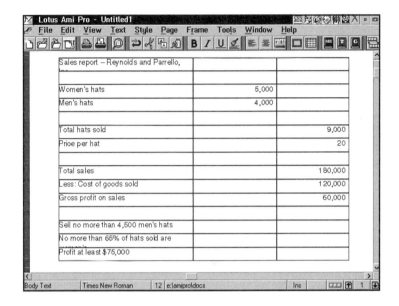

Note

Ami Pro encloses DDE links for main document text with the information in blue left and right square brackets. You can see the blue brackets by choosing **V**iew, View **P**references, **M**arks.

Troubleshooting

I am trying to move some text in an Ami Pro document into another area and I received the following message: `DDE link(s) in the selected cells will be termi-nated. Continue?` *What does this mean?*

You tried to use Drag and Drop to move or copy data into a column, row, or cell that contains a DDE link. If you continue, the DDE link will be deleted. Choose Yes to delete the DDE link and move or copy the data. Choose No to cancel moving or copying the data.

Linking an Ami Pro Document to 1-2-3

Occasionally, you may need to reverse the flow of data or information (as described in the previous section) and link pieces of an Ami Pro document to a 1-2-3 worksheet. For example, you may need to include a paragraph from a company report in a 1-2-3 spreadsheet, or have your company's prime interest rate or discount interest rate (used in calculating loans or other deals) be updated from an Ami Pro weekly report into your 1-2-3 spreadsheets.

To create a link from an Ami Pro document to a 1-2-3 worksheet (or any other application that supports DDE), follow these steps:

1. Open the Ami Pro document that contains the data you want to link to 1-2-3.

> **Caution**
>
> The file must be a named file. It can't be an Untitled worksheet or document.

2. Select the text or table information you want to use in the 1-2-3 worksheet (see fig. 28.4).

3. Choose **E**dit, **C**opy to copy the information to the OS/2 Clipboard. You can also press Ctrl+Ins.

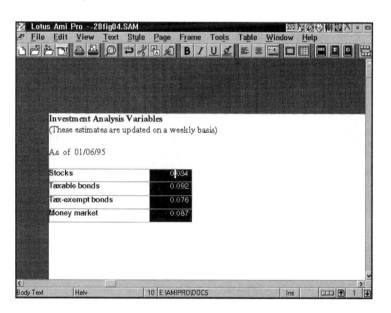

Fig. 28.4
Copying the four investment analysis variables which will be linked to a 1-2-3 worksheet. These changing variables will automatically be updated in the 1-2-3 worksheet or template.

4. Switch to 1-2-3 and open the 1-2-3 worksheet you want to contain the information and then place the insertion point in the cell where you want the information to appear.

5. Choose **E**dit, Paste **L**ink. The data appears as unformatted (see fig. 28.5).

V

Working Together

Fig. 28.5

The linked Ami Pro data appears in the 1-2-3 worksheet. These investment variables will be updated whenever the numbers change in the source file in Ami Pro.

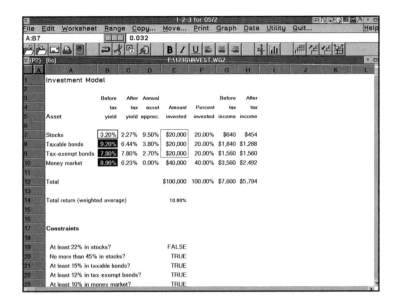

Linking 1-2-3 Data to a Freelance Presentation

Just as numbers and tables can spruce up and enhance an Ami Pro document, the same can be argued for improving a Freelance presentation. In fact, you can create a table in Freelance Graphics using data from a 1-2-3 for OS/2 worksheet by means of a linked Metafile. A linked Metafile is the graphics format that supports the DDE standard of Presentation Manager.

Linking a range of 1-2-3 worksheet data to Freelance Graphics is very similar to the steps and commands taken to link other types of data within the SmartSuite, except that the linked 1-2-3 data appears in Freelance as a Linked Metafile.

  Figure 28.6 displays selecting a range of 1-2-3 data to be copied to the Clipboard using Edit, Copy. You can then switch to Freelance for OS/2, placing your cursor on the page that you want to add the table to, and choose **E**dit, **L**ink, **P**aste Link to display the 1-2-3 information as a Linked Metafile (see fig. 28.7).

Note

The control line identifies the object type as a "Linked Metafile."

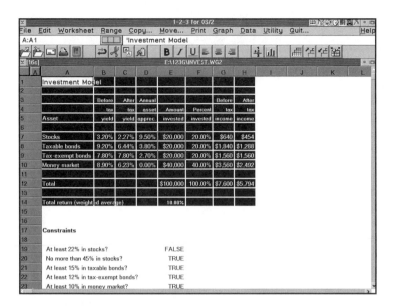

Fig. 28.6
Selecting and copying a range of 1-2-3 data to be linked to a Freelance Presentation.

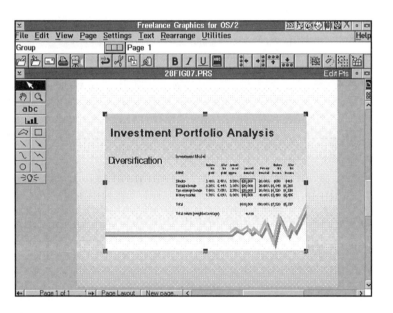

Fig. 28.7
The linked metafile can be sized and moved to any location desired on the presentation page. The data will need to be modified in the 1-2-3 worksheeet.

The new metafile will be linked to the 1-2-3 worksheet. Plus, whenever you modify the worksheet, the table in the presentation is updated automatically, provided both the worksheet and the presentation files are open.

V

Working Together

Using the Graph Tool To Create an Automatic Link

Freelance Graphics and 1-2-3 for OS/2 were designed to work seamlessly with each other. When used together, Freelance Graphics and 1-2-3 for OS/2 run on a common desktop, share a common user interface, have similar commands, and share graphs and data.

This integration allows Freelance Graphics and 1-2-3 for OS/2 to share the Graph Tool, which you use to create and edit graphs. You can bring graphs created in 1-2-3 directly into a Freelance Graphics presentation page and edit the graph without losing the links to the worksheet data. When the worksheet data changes, Freelance Graphics recomposes the graph automatically with the changed data.

This seamless integration is made possible by the shared Graph Tool. With the Graph Tool you can create a new graph, place an existing graph on a presentation page or worksheet, or edit any graph in your presentation or worksheet. In fact, the Graph Tool incorporates automatic linking of spreadsheet and Freelance presentation information—no DDE is required.

To create a new graph, you can either enter data manually or link to data in a 1-2-3 for OS/2 worksheet. You can even set up links to one or more 1-2-3 for OS/2 worksheets to create a Series graph.

◀ See "The Shared Graph Tool (between 1-2-3 and Freelance Graphics)," p. 129

There are several methods and ways to place a graph in your presentation. The first method is to simply retrieve the name of the existing graph and let Freelance Graphics copy it to your presentation. A copied graph remains linked to its source data when you move, size, or edit the graph. The second method is to copy and paste data between the two applications:

For example, to create a graph in Freelance that is linked to 1-2-3 worksheet data, follow these steps:

1. In 1-2-3, open the worksheet file that contains the range of data you want to link and copy that range to the Clipboard.

2. Switch to Freelance and select the presentation page that contains a graph or a "Click here..." graph block.

3. Double-click the graph to open the Graph Tool window or, if needed, click the graph icon in the toolbox and choose **N**ew graph to create a graph. Figure 28.8 shows the windows for the worksheet and graph that will be linked. Figure 28.9 displays an empty data view that you will copy data into to create the graph.

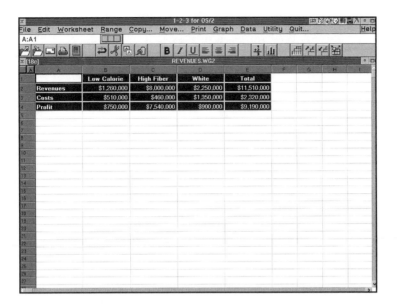

Fig. 28.8
The range in the 1-2-3 worksheet REVENUES.WG2 will be linked to the presentation displayed. In this example, a new graph will be created to display the highlighted and pasted data.

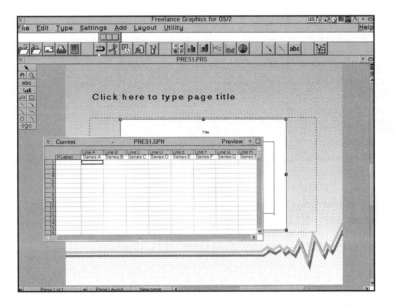

Fig. 28.9
The Graph Tool window or data view appears empty after creating a new graph. A previously created graph will have data entered that you can modify if desired.

4. In the Graph Tool window, choose **E**dit, **L**ink, **C**reate to open the Edit Link Create dialog box as shown in figure 28.10.

Fig. 28.10

The Edit Link Create dialog box allows you to specify the source and destination. In this situation you just need to choose [from clipboard] because the range of 1-2-3 data was copied to the Clipboard.

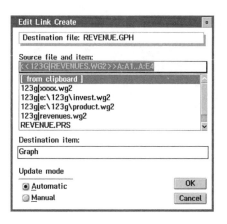

5. Specify the source file item in the Source File and Item listbox. In this example, choose [from clipboard] as the source file.

Tip

Press F3 to list Destination items that can be linked.

6. Now, choose Graph as the Destination item (if it isn't already selected as the default) in the Destination Item listbox.

7. Choose the Update Mode (**A**utomatic or **M**anual) and click OK. This inserts the linked 1-2-3 data into the data view in the Graph Tool window, as shown in figure 28.11.

8. You can now modify the graph type (the default is a line graph), attributes, labels, and so on using the menu commands. Then close and save the graph. This creates the linked graph in the Freelance presentation (see fig. 28.12). Notice that the graph isn't contained in the graph block. Drag and drop the graph onto the area and it will resize to that area.

> **Note**
>
> You can also create a series graph that is linked to separate data ranges in different worksheet files. Choose Series as the Destination Item in the Edit Link Create dialog box for each data range or source file you want to represent in the graph.

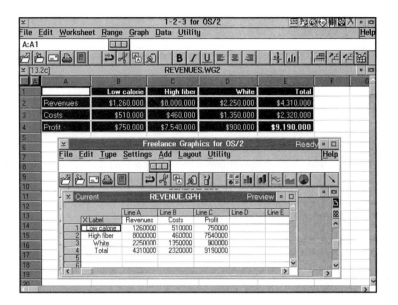

Fig. 28.11
The linked data is inserted into a data view that will be used for the graph. At this point you can change the graph type and other attributes.

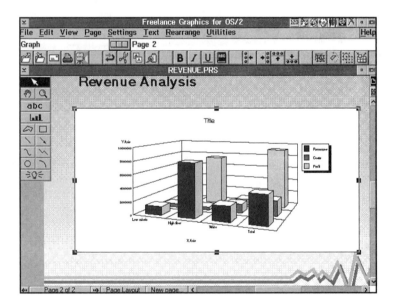

Fig. 28.12
The resulting graph has been modified to be a 3D Bar graph and then dropped into the graph block on the presentation.

Editing and Displaying Links

After adding or pasting a link to a document, you may need to edit the link. For example, you may want to change how the link is updated from automatic to manual or unlink the link from updating. The procedures to edit and modify links in the SmartSuite applications are easy, but the steps and menus required to edit links in Ami Pro are subtly different than those for 1-2-3 and Freelance (which utilize identical steps). The following two sections cover the differences between editing links in Ami Pro, 1-2-3, and Freelance Graphics.

Modifying Links in Ami Pro

To edit or create links via menu commands in an Ami Pro document, you can choose **E**dit, Link **O**ptions. This allows you to display information about existing DDE links and to update, unlink, deactivate, edit, or create a link anywhere in an Ami Pro document.

> **Note**
>
> The Link **O**ptions command is greyed if the current document or application doesn't contain links from another OS/2 or Windows application

Tip
Ami Pro allows you to choose File, Doc Info to verify or check for existing links in the current document.

To create or modify a link in Ami Pro, follow these steps:

1. Choose **E**dit, Link **O**ptions to display the Link Options dialog box (see fig. 28.13) which lists the existing links in the current document. These links are listed in the order in which they were pasted into the document. The links can be text, frame, or table links.

Fig. 28.13
The Link Options dialog box in Ami Pro allows you to select the links in the current document and then choose between the command buttons.

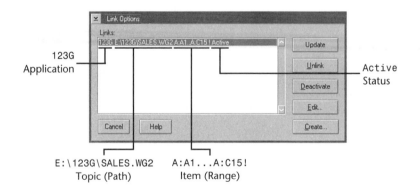

123G
Application

Active
Status

E:\123G\SALES.WG2
Topic (Path)

A:A1...A:C15!
Item (Range)

2. At this point you need to decide whether to create, modify, or edit a link. Most likely you'll need to modify an existing link.

> **Note**
>
> When possible, try pasting the data to the Clipboard when creating a link because the information in the Link dialog box will already be entered. This is usually easier than remembering the program's topic and the item (range).

To modify a link, select the desired link in the Links listbox and select one of the following buttons:

- *Update.* Updates the linked information with the latest version of the original source data. The source file must be open to update a link.

- *Unlink.* Terminates the link. The data is still pasted but changes to the source are no longer reflected in the document.

- *Deactivate.* Stops updating the linked information without terminating the link. Changes won't appear until you reactivate or update the linked data.

- *Edit.* Displays the Link dialog box as shown in figure 28.14. Here you can specify a different application, path, or range for the original source information, without having to open or switch to the other application.

Fig. 28.14
The Link dialog box allows you to edit an existing link or create a new link. Here the file is linked to a 1-2-3 for OS/2 worksheet using the range indicated.

In the Link dialog box, you need to specify the following options:

- *Application.* The name and path of the application that contains the original information

- *Topic.* The drive, directory, and name for the file that contains the original information.

- *Item.* The location or name for the original information, such as a name or range of cells, a bookmark, or a graphic reference.

V

Working Together

To create a link, deselect an existing link if you have already selected one in the Links listbox, then choose the **C**reate button to display the Link dialog box. You can now create a new link even if you did not copy information to the Clipboard.

Since 1-2-3 and Freelance share a lot of the same tools and windows, the menus and commands to modify and edit links are almost identical. To create or modify a link in a 1-2-3 worksheet or Freelance Graphics presentation, open the file that contains the link you want to modify. Then choose **E**dit, **L**ink, which cascades to more available menu selections. Here you can now choose between several linking commands: **U**pdate, **C**reate, **E**dit, **D**elete, and **M**ove. Depending on your selection the corresponding dialog box appears for that command:

- *Create.* Lets you create a new link.

- *Update.* Updates a link contained in the current file.

- *Edit.* Lets you edit an existing link by displaying the Edit Link Edit dialog box.

- *Delete.* Removes or erases a link in the current document.

- *Move.* Lets you move a link to a different source by displaying the Edit Link Move dialog box.

Troubleshooting

Why do I get the error message `Cannot establish DDE link. Acceptable DDE format is not available.` *when trying to Paste Link data from the OS/2 Clipboard?*

You tried to create or update a DDE link, and the program either can't paste the data or reestablish the link. Choose OK. Check the following before you retry:

- Close any unnecessary running applications to increase the amount of available memory.

- Make certain there is sufficient disk space available on the drive where the SWAPPER.DAT file is located. If necessary move or delete some files on that drive.

- Make certain the other application is available.

- Make certain the other application can supply data in a format Ami Pro can use. To check this, recopy the data from the other application, then open the OS/2 Clipboard object located in your OS/2 System folder to display the data you copied. Choose Display and make certain Bitmap, Picture, and Text are available options.

Why am I getting the following message after opening a file containing a DDE link:
`Cannot update DDE (link name) (topic name) (item name) because the`
`server does not respond.?`

Make sure the source file in the server application is open and then try to update the DDE Link. If necessary, also check the list described in the first troubleshooting question.

From Here...

In this chapter you learned how to transfer information between the SmartSuite applications using the copy and paste routine. Copy and Paste is a quick and efficient process, however, in some situations you may want to link copied information instead. Linking means that when the source document or object changes, the link automatically updates the target document, which, in turn, can save you tremendous amounts of time in updating related documents. For more information on automating and integrating within the SmartSuites products, refer to the following chapters:

- Chapter 21, "Entering Slide Content," discusses how to create and build a Freelance presentation from the ground up.

- Chapter 29, "Using the OS/2 Workplace Shell To Create an Integrated Desktop," shows you how the SmartSuite can be used to build integrated project files and how they can be organized on the OS/2 Workplace Shell.

- Chapter 34, "Using Notes with SmartSuite Applications," discusses how Notes interacts and shares data with the various SmartSuite applications.

Chapter 29

Using the OS/2 Workplace Shell to Create an Integrated Desktop

Robert L. Weberg

The previous chapters in this book have focused on the functions and features specific to each SmartSuite application, integrating the SmartSuite packages, and even some OS/2 Workplace Shell fundamentals. *Integration* means not only cohesiveness between the SmartSuite applications, but also how the SmartSuite can be intertwined with the OS/2 Desktop to build integrated data files for all projects or assignments. A project could include an Ami Pro report or proposal, a Freelance Graphics presentation, a shared graph between 1-2-3 and Freelance or a detailed analysis prepared in a 1-2-3 worksheet, and a cc:Mail message template.

The OS/2 Workplace Shell expands your opportunities to integrate your data files with the "outside world" or operating environment.

The goal of this chapter is to incorporate a lot of the lessons and skills previously learned to build integrated project files that are OS/2 Aware. *OS/2 Aware* means that your data files are accessible—a point and click away; noticeable—represented by sharp looking icons; and organized—contained in folders. This awareness theme forces you to scrap some old philosophies or habits you have grown accustomed to when working with PC files; like choosing File, Open to open a document, or File, Print to print it—when all you have to do is drag and drop that data file icon to a printer device object. By thinking objects and icons you can break the bounds of conventional personal computing.

In this chapter you learn to:

- Create a folder to store data files relating to a specific project

- Create data files from templates

- Print, delete, and open data files using drag-and-drop

- Use Desktop files related to a project for quick easy access to data files

Taking Advantage of the OS/2 Workplace Shell

Many OS/2 users aren't aware of what OS/2 really has to offer. Many users continue to utilize their applications as before—using menu driven commands like **F**ile, **O**pen, **F**ile, **P**rint, and **F**ile, **S**ave. These actions aren't incorrect, but they don't take advantage of the OS/2 Workplace Shell.

The OS/2 Desktop environment is comprised of a thrilling world of icons that represent objects. The OS/2 Workplace Shell contains four types of objects:

- *Datafile.* Object that has information in it, such as a WG2, SAM, PRE, or a GPH file

- *Program.* Executable object, such as Ami Pro

- *Device.* Object that represents a physical device, such as a printer

- *Folder.* Object that contains other objects or folders

As you probably know, double-clicking a program icon starts that program. But you can use the other kinds of objects in the OS/2 Workplace Shell in similar ways to speed up your work and make you more efficient. You can create any of these objects using a template. A *template* is an object you can use as a model to create additional objects. When you drag and drop a template from the Template folder onto the OS/2 Desktop, you create another of the original objects, as though you were peeling one of the objects off a stack. The new object has the same settings and contents as the template. To modify any settings, you need to use the templates notebook settings to update the settings specific to that new object.

> **Note**
>
> You can customize the different types of objects on your desktop using their Settings Notebook and the pop-up menu. After you select an object, click the right mouse button to view the pop-up menu. The menu varies depending on the type of object you select. Choose **O**pen, **S**ettings to view the different properties you can set for the object. In OS/2 Warp, the **S**ettings command appears on the pop-up menu.

Figure 29.1 lists the available data file templates in the Templates folder. This depends on which SmartSuite applications you have installed.

> **Note**
>
> During installation of a new application (for example, the SmartSuite applications) OS/2 recognizes and associates any new templates. These templates appear in the Templates folder.

You can create new objects by using the objects in the Templates folder. To open the Templates folder, double-click the Templates object on your OS/2 Desktop.

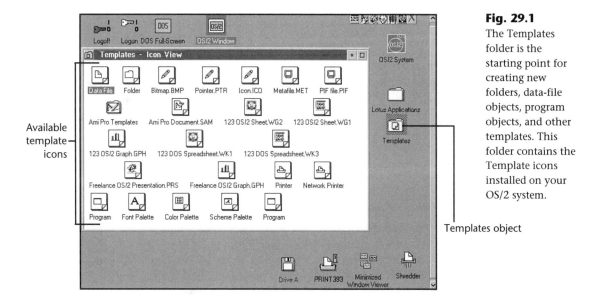

Available template icons

Templates object

Fig. 29.1
The Templates folder is the starting point for creating new folders, data-file objects, program objects, and other templates. This folder contains the Template icons installed on your OS/2 system.

V

Working Together

Creating Folder Objects To Organize Your Project Files

Have you ever experienced a moment when your manager taps you on your shoulder looking for that late report, proposal, or document? Hopefully, with preparation, you can grab your mouse, open your project folder on the OS/2 desktop, locate and select the required data icon, then drag it to your printer object to print the document. Using the SmartSuite applications and the OS/2 Workplace Shell, you can eliminate the pressure related to unfinished business by properly preparing all of your project-related files.

Objects eliminate the need for menu-driven commands. No longer do you need to open each application and search drives and directories for every file associated with your report or project. To build an integrated compound document in SmartSuite for OS/2, you probably need to include an Ami Pro document file, a 1-2-3 spreadsheet, and a Freelance presentation. With a little thought and effort you can design work-related project folders to organize your data files on the OS/2 Workplace Shell.

When creating folders, you should try to visualize your subdirectories on your hard drive and network drives as manila folders. Contained within those folders are the data-file objects. To use the Folder template to create a new folder, follow these steps:

1. Click the Templates object to open the Templates folder (refer to fig. 29.1).

2. Point to the Folder template and hold down the right mouse button to drag a copy of that template to the OS/2 Desktop or to another folder, and release the mouse button (see fig. 29.2). An empty folder is created.

Tip
To quickly rename a folder icon, select the icon and then click the left mouse button while holding down the Alt key. Type the new name and click the icon to save it.

3. Rename the folder. In figure 29.3 the folder has been renamed to "Airline Industry Analysis."

> **Note**
>
> To rename a folder, click the right mouse button on the newly created folder icon. Click **O**pen, **S**ettings to display the Settings Notebook window (in OS/2 Warp, right click and select **S**ettings). To change the name of the folder displayed, click the **G**eneral tab and edit the text in the Title edit box. Save your changes by double-clicking the top-left corner of the Settings notebook.

The selected Folder template

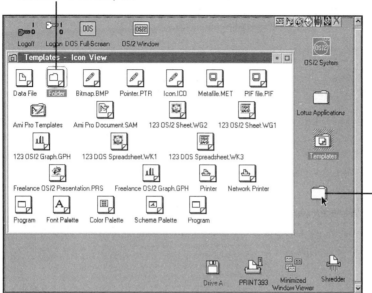

Fig. 29.2
Select the Folder template and drag and drop it to the OS/2 Desktop to create a new folder. This folder will be the storage location for your desired project files.

Dragging and dropping to the OS/2 Desktop

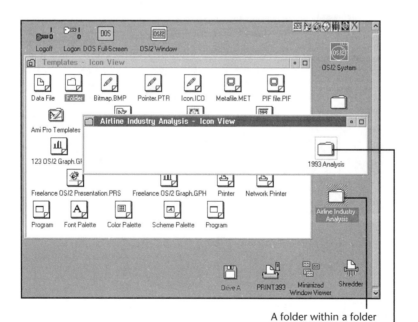

Fig. 29.3
The newly created "Airline Industry Analysis" folder. To illustrate how you can more easily organize your data files, a second file folder, "1993 Analysis," has been created to store historical files.

Tip
You can have folders within folders.

A folder within a folder
The new folder has been opened

Creating Data-File Objects

Data-file objects act as pointers to your data files. A simple double-click on the object opens the application and the data file. To use data-file templates to create a data-file object, follow these steps:

1. Open the Templates folder and move the mouse to the desired data-file template.

2. Drag and drop the template into your newly created "Airline Industry Analysis" folder. This creates a new data-file object based upon the template selected. Figure 29.4 shows how to create an Ami Pro document data file.

Fig. 29.4

Creating an Ami Pro data file using the Ami Pro Document.SAM template.

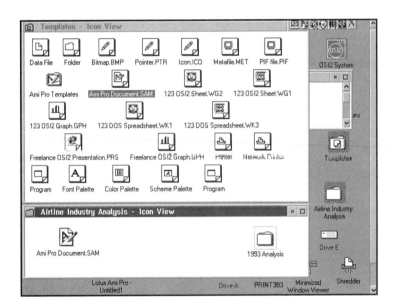

3. You can now rename the file. Double-click the new icon to open the file and then begin entering the desired text. Figure 29.5 displays the renamed data file AIRLINES.SAM and its open document window.

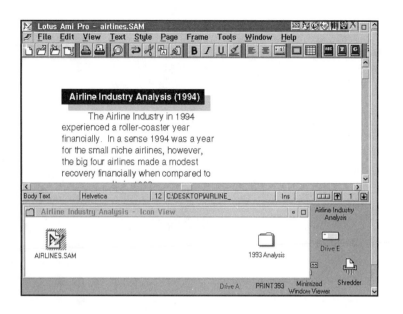

Fig. 29.5
The newly created
Ami Pro data file
AIRLINES.SAM has
been opened and
modified with new
text. Notice that
the icon of the
open data file has
diagonal lines,
which signify that
it is open.

Creating Program Objects

A program object is slightly different from a data-file object because it starts an application or program session with an untitled document while data-file objects start the application and then open the selected data file. However, program icons provide another convenient route to opening files using drag-and-drop, especially if you want to open a new file in a separate program session.

> **Note**
>
> The recommended method of creating a program object is to run the Add Programs program in the System Setup folder contained in the OS/2 System folder, but you can also do it manually when needed.

To create a new program icon for a desired application, follow these steps:

1. Open the Templates folder and select the Program Template.

2. Drag the Program template to a folder on the Desktop.

The Settings notebook appears blank, allowing you to customize the program object by selecting or entering the path, file name and session type, naming the program object, and establishing any file associations. See figure 29.6 for an example of creating an Ami Pro program object.

V

Working Together

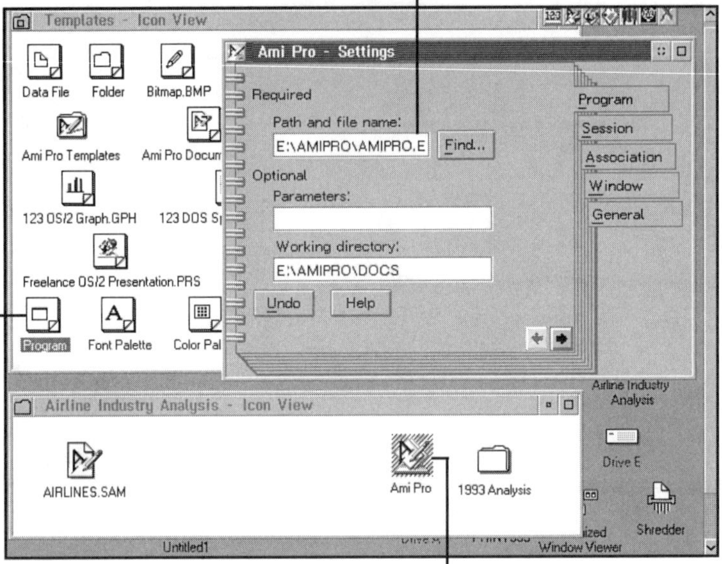

The settings are established for the Program icon

Fig. 29.6
Creating an Ami
Pro for OS/2
program object.
The Path and File
Name edit box
represents where
the program
(Ami Pro, in this
example) is
installed.

Dragging and dropping the Program template creates the Program icon

Dragging and Dropping Objects

The concept and functionality of dragging and dropping objects is an appeal-
ing and fun process. Not only is it visually enticing, but it's efficient and
effective in accomplishing personal computing tasks. Plus, it's much faster
than using the basic menu commands (like **F**ile, **P**rint and **F**ile, **O**pen) contained in each application.

You can use the OS/2 Workplace Shell drag-and-drop feature to perform some
common tasks like printing, opening, deleting, and copying files on any of
the SmartSuite files. When using drag-and-drop you can:

- Open a presentation, graph, or desktop data-file object by dragging and
  dropping it onto the corresponding SmartSuite work area.

- Start a SmartSuite session by dragging and dropping a data file on the
  corresponding program object.

- Print a document, presentation, worksheet, or a graph data-file object
  by dragging and dropping it on a Printer object.

- Delete a document, presentation, worksheet, or a graph data-file object
  by dragging and dropping it on the Shredder object.

You can quickly and easily open a data file in your project folder by dragging and dropping the data file into an open work area for the corresponding work area. Figure 29.7 shows opening the file AIRLINES.SAM by dragging and dropping the file into the Ami Pro for OS/2 work area. This data file becomes the active window in the SmartSuite application.

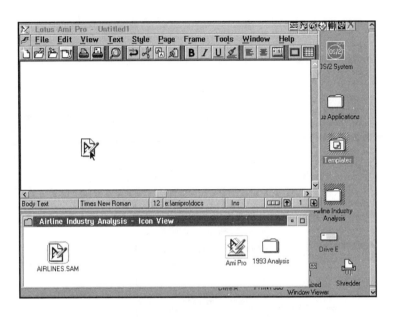

Fig. 29.7

Using drag-and-drop to open AIRLINES.SAM by dropping it on the open work area for its corresponding application. Another method would be to open the **F**ile menu in that application and choose the **O**pen command.

Note

You can't drag and drop an object like a Freelance Graphics presentation (PRS) file onto an Ami Pro program object. Nor can you open a file by dragging and dropping it on an open application not associated with that data file.

There is one exception to dragging and dropping data files in a work area not associated with the corresponding data file: opening a WK4, WK3, or WK1 spreadsheet into an Ami Pro file or session. This can quickly be performed by following these steps:

1. Drag a WK1, WK3, or WK4 data-file object onto the Ami Pro work area (see fig. 29.8).

2. Select Open or Insert. The Import dialog box appears as shown in figure 29.9.

Fig. 29.8

Using drag-and-drop to open a 1-2-3 WK3 file by dropping it on the open Ami Pro work area.

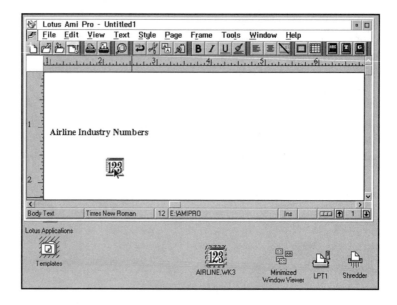

Fig. 29.9

The Import dialog box allows you to select an entire file, an active worksheet, or specify a named range.

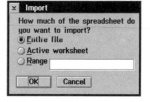

3. Select the desired option and Ami Pro creates a table containing the 1-2-3 spreadsheet information (see fig. 29.10).

You can also open a data file and start another Ami Pro for OS/2 session by dragging and dropping the data-file object on the corresponding program icon. Follow these steps:

1. Open the folder containing your document files. Select a data-file object; drag the data-file object to the Ami Pro object and release it on top, as shown in figure 29.11. (The Ami Pro icon can be in any state: closed, minimized, or open.)

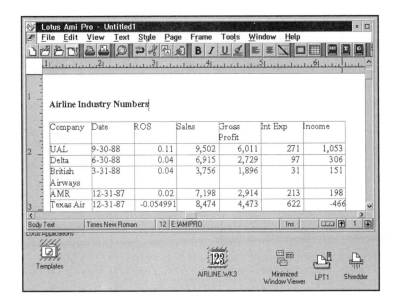

Fig. 29.10
A table of 1-2-3 data is created using the simple functionality of dragging and dropping a data file.

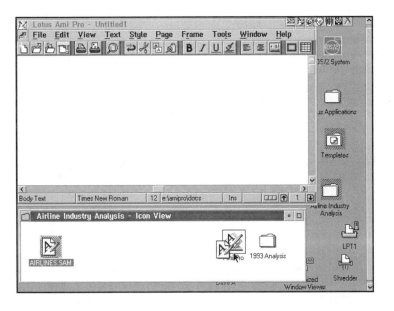

Fig. 29.11
Using drag-and-drop to open a file by dropping the selected data file (AIRLINES.SAM) on the corresponding program object that you created (Ami Pro).

You can also very easily print and delete data-file objects utilizing the same techniques described above, except that you need to locate your printer and shredder device objects so you can drag and drop the data-file objects onto these device objects. To print or delete a data-file object, follow these steps:

1. Open the folder that contains your document files and select a data-file object with the mouse.

2. Holding down the right mouse button, drag the data-file object to the Printer device (to print the object) or the Shredder object (to delete the object) and release it on top of the object, as shown in figure 29.12.

Fig. 29.12
Use drag-and-drop to print the file (AIRLINES.SAM) on a network printer object designated on your OS/2 Workplace Shell. To delete the data file, drop it over the Shredder device object.

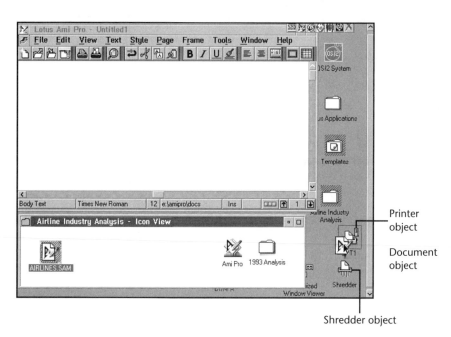

Printer object

Document object

Shredder object

Using Desktop Files To Get Organized

Another great feature of 1-2-3 and Freelance integration is the ability to save your desktop setup as a (.DSK) file. A desktop file integrates the graph, worksheet, and presentation files on your desktop and remembers their names, links, status, placement, and window size. A desktop file doesn't contain data, but contains information about the state of all windows that were open when you saved the desktop file. This information includes locations and size of all windows, links between files, paths to all data files on the desktop, and the status of the desktop itself.

Using a desktop file as a container for files saves the time it would take to find individual application files, link them together, and position them. You can use the File Desktop commands to create new desktop files, open and retrieve existing desktop files, and erase existing files.

Tip

In OS/2, files must be open for links to be updated. Using desktop files is a good way to ensure that all necessary files are open.

Note

Desktop files only work with 1-2-3 for OS/2 and Freelance Graphics for OS/2 work areas, not Ami Pro, cc:Mail for OS/2, or other OS/2 folders and windows.

Saving a Desktop File

Saving a desktop file is an excellent way to organize related data files and graphs together with the utilities you use with them. Plus, you'll most likely use a desktop file to start your next work session with the desktop in the same state it was in when you ended your last work session.

You can save information about the state of all open windows on the desktop file with the **S**ave Desktop checkbox in the File Save dialog box. This information includes the location and size of all windows, links, and paths to all the data files. You can include as many data files as you want in a desktop file. The files need not be in the same directory. You can even save the same data file with more than one desktop file. To save a desktop file, perform the following steps:

1. Organize, size, and open the data files and graphs you want to include in the desktop file.

2. Choose **F**ile, **S**ave to display the File Save dialog box.

3. Choose **A**ll Files and select the **S**ave desktop option.

4. Edit or enter a new name in the File Name box. Freelance or 1-2-3 automatically adds the .DSK extension. Click OK.

Note

You can set up your system to automatically save the desktop when you end a Freelance Graphic or 1-2-3 session and restore that desktop when you start up again. Choose **U**ser, **S**ettings, **S**tartup in the Window Control-menu box. Select **R**estore and click the **U**pdate button to save your new settings.

Opening and Retrieving Desktop Files

Opening a desktop file restores the work session exactly as you left it when you saved the desktop file. The desktop and windows appear with the same size, position, and status they had when you saved it. To open a desktop file, perform the following steps:

◀ See "Launching from the Desktop," p. 30

V

Working Together

1. Choose **F**ile, **O**pen to display the File Open dialog box (see fig. 29.13).

Fig. 29.13
Using the File
Open dialog box
to open a
previously saved
desktop file
(.DSK).

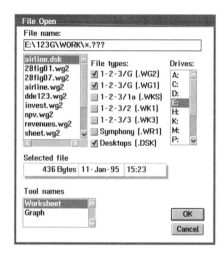

2. Select the Desktops (.DSK) option to display the names of desktop files in the current directory. Change the directory and drive if necessary.

3. Double-click the name of the desktop file you want to open. The data files with their previous sizes and locations appear as shown in figure 29.14.

Fig. 29.14
Opening
the selected
AIRLINE.DSK file
opens the data
files to their
previous locations
and size.

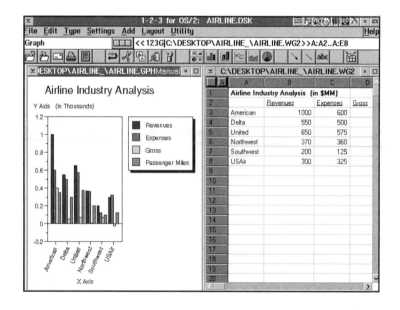

If you use **F**ile, **O**pen to open a desktop when no other data files are open, the appropriate work session is restored and the Desktop title bar displays the current desktop file name after the current program name. If you open a desktop file when other desktop files or data files are open, Freelance or 1-2-3 adds the new windows to the open windows. However, the Desktop title bar retains the name of the previous desktop file while all files are open. When you close the data files and desktop files, Freelance or 1-2-3 restores them to their original status, unless you save them all as a single desktop file.

> **Note**
>
> If you open a desktop file and can't get the reservation for one or more of the data files, Freelance or 1-2-3 asks if you want to open the data file in read-only mode. Select Yes if you need to copy some data from the file to the Clipboard, or if you want to save the file to another file name.

When you use **F**ile, **R**etrieve to retrieve a desktop file, the current desktop is cleared and you're asked if you want to save your changes to the current desktop. To retrieve a desktop file, follow these steps:

1. Choose **F**ile, **R**etrieve to display the File Retrieve dialog box (see fig. 29.15).

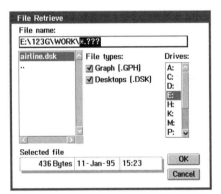

Fig. 29.15
Opening a desktop file using the File, Retrieve command clears the current desktop files and then open the files contained in the selected desktop file.

2. Check the Desktops checkbox and then select the desired Desktop.

> **Note**
>
> If you use **F**ile, **E**rase to delete a desktop file, you don't delete the associated data files contained in the desktop file.

Troubleshooting

*When I use **F**ile, **R**etrieve to open a desktop file, why do my files that are currently open disappear?*

Retrieving a desktop file closes any open files. If you want files to appear with the ones that are currently open, you should use the **F**ile, **O**pen command.

When I open a desktop file that I've saved and used previously, one of my files doesn't appear.

Verify that you haven't deleted or moved the file to a new location. The desktop file can't locate and open the file if it has been moved or deleted.

From Here...

Now that you understand the basics of creating integrated project files using not only the SmartSuite applications but also the OS/2 Workplace Shell, you're ready to start integrating your own applications and projects to simplify your work flow and processes. Other chapters that relate to integrating the SmartSuite applications and the OS/2 Workplace Shell include the following:

- Chapter 3, "Managing Files and Work Areas," reviews using the OS/2 Workplace Shell to create files, subdirectories, desktop files, and other functionalities unique to OS/2.

- Chapter 28, "Sharing Data between Applications with DDE," discusses how to use DDE linking between the various SmartSuite applications to share and maintain information.

- Chapter 30, "Using cc:Mail with SmartSuite Applications," provides an introduction to sending messages and attachments to other users via cc:Mail.

- Chapter 34, "Using Notes with SmartSuite Applications," covers the details of using DDE linking between Notes and the SmartSuite applications.

Part VI

Communicating with Others Using the Lotus Suite of Products

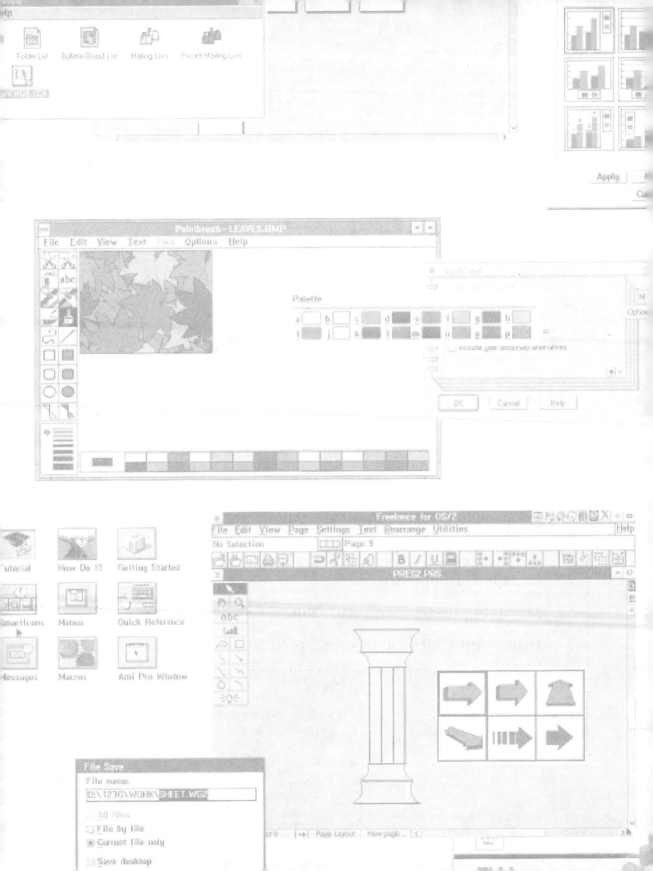

Chapter 30

Using cc:Mail with SmartSuite Applications

by Robert L. Weberg

Using cc:Mail for OS/2 Workplace Shell is an easy, powerful and flexible way to send data for use in the other SmartSuite applications. You can use cc:Mail to send or receive an entire file, a specified range, chart, or drawing, or virtually anything created on your workstation as an electronic message to people connected to your network. Plus, you can customize cc:Mail for OS/2 to make the application work the way you want it to.

> **Note**
>
> cc:Mail allows you to exchange messages and attachments with cc:Mail users running OS/2 2.1 or above (including OS/2 Warp) and with those using the MS-DOS, Windows, Macintosh, and UNIX versions of cc:Mail. In addition, cc:Mail for OS/2 allows you to communicate with users running other mail messaging systems.

In this chapter you learn to:

- Prepare and read cc:Mail messages
- Customize the cc:Mail work area
- Send a cc:Mail message
- Insert a selection in a cc:Mail message
- Attach files to a cc:Mail message
- Receive notification of a cc:Mail message

Is cc:Mail Paper Mail in Disguise?

The basic concepts and building blocks of cc:Mail for OS/2 are based upon a very simple and logical business metaphor—paper mail. To use this electronic mailing application, just apply your knowledge of how letters and packages are delivered and received within your office every business day.

Imagine that cc:Mail is the post office and carrier of your electronic messages. You can connect with cc:Mail users on a LAN or dedicated PC through a cc:Mail post office. *Messages* are envelopes that signify the basic unit of exchange in the cc:Mail system. The messages can contain text (letters), and *attachments* (files), and can be addressed to more than one individual. Messages delivered to you are contained in the *Inbox*. The messages you read can be saved to *folders*.

When sending paper mail to individuals, you can find their names in your corporate directory. In cc:Mail, the cc:Mail Directory lists all the people and post offices you exchange mail with. cc:Mail has public and private Mailing Lists that allow you to send messages to groups of people, such as "Finance Department" or "District Sales Managers."

Of all the features mentioned above, the most important concept to remember is that cc:Mail for OS/2 saves time in delivering important information by allowing you to quickly communicate with other users in your corporation.

Accessing cc:Mail for OS/2

Before starting cc:Mail for OS/2 you need to get the following information from the cc:Mail Administrator:

- Your log-in name

- Your cc:Mail password

- The network drive and directory where cc:Mail is installed (Path)

To start cc:Mail for OS/2:

1. Double-click the cc:Mail folder icon, or right-click the cc:Mail folder icon and choose the Open command in the pop-up menu. The cc:Mail window appears as shown in figure 30.1.

Title bar icon

Fig. 30.1
The cc:Mail folder allows you to access the features of cc:Mail.

The cc:Mail folder is the starting point for mailing operations like preparing new messages, reading messages in your inbox and on bulletin boards, and previewing folders and mailing lists. Within the cc:Mail folder you can double-click the icons or highlight the desired icon and then open the **W**indow menu and choose one of the desired commands.

Note

If you aren't currently logged onto cc:Mail, the cc:Mail login window appears after selecting any of the icons in the cc:Mail folder (see fig. 30.2).

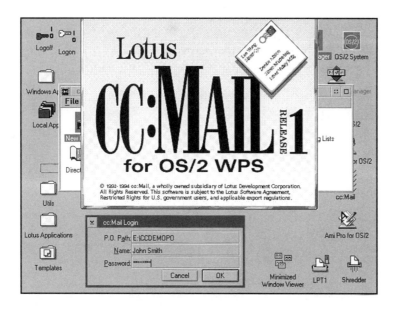

Fig. 30.2
The cc:Mail login window allows you to access your messages and prevents other users from accessing your mail.

VI

Communicating

Preparing a Simple cc:Mail Text Message

Preparing and sending electronic-mail messages to recipients in cc:Mail for OS/2 is simple and quick. You'll soon learn that there are more options to fit your mailing needs. To prepare and send a simple text message:

1. Double-click the cc:Mail folder object to open the main cc:Mail window.

2. Choose **W**indow, **P**repare a Message. You can also press Alt+P, or double-click the Prepare a Message object. The New Message window appears (see fig. 30.3).

> **Note**
>
> You can also set up cc:Mail so the Address Message window is displayed first by changing your cc:Mail settings. To do so, choose **F**ile, **O**ptions in the main cc:Mail window. The cc:Mail Settings notebook appears. Click the message tab to display the Message Options page. Then click the Start in Address Window option to have the Address Message window appear when you begin preparing a message.

3. In the To box begin typing the name of the recipient. cc:Mail automatically fills in the rest of the name as you type. Once the name you want is completed, press Enter to add the name to the address list.

4. Move the cursor to the Subject line by pressing Enter or by clicking in the Subject line area.

5. Enter a subject for your message, and then press Enter or Tab. You can enter up to 60 characters for the subject. Your cursor appears in the message box to allow you to type your message. Figure 30.3 shows a prepared message before sending.

6. After composing your message, choose **M**essage, **S**end, or press Ctrl+N.

> **Note**
>
> Before sending a message, you can save it in the Drafts folder instead. To do so, choose **M**essage, Save **D**raft. This works well in situations if you're not ready to send a message and want to return to the memo and send it at a later time. To work with the draft message you need to open the Folder List icon in the cc:Mail folder and then select the Draft folder. Your drafts are listed in the Draft folder.

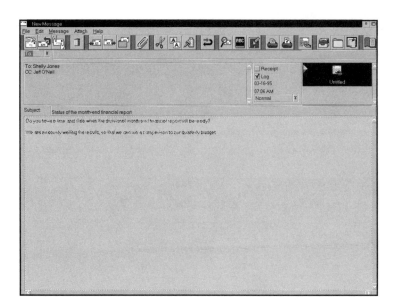

Fig. 30.3
Preparing and
addressing a new
cc:Mail message.

To exit cc:Mail for OS/2, do either of the following:

1. In the main cc:Mail window or on any message window, choose **F**ile,
   Log out.

2. Double-click the title bar icon in the top-left corner of the cc:Mail folder
   window (refer to fig. 30.1).

Reading and Managing cc:Mail Messages

Most of the cc:Mail messages you receive will consist of a single item of text.
These are easy to read and handle. All incoming messages are stored in your
inbox. The cc:Mail Status window, shown in figure 30.4 tells you how many
new and total messages there are in your inbox. You can click the **I**nbox
button to quickly display the Inbox window (see fig. 30.5).

Fig. 30.4
The cc:Mail status
window displays
message and folder
activity.

VI

Communicating

To read and handle simple text messages, you can also perform the following steps:

1. Open the cc:Mail folder by double-clicking the cc:Mail folder object. The main cc:Mail window appears.

2. Double-click the Inbox folder and the Inbox window appears listing your messages as shown in figure 30.5. You can also highlight the Inbox folder and then press Enter, or choose **W**indow, **I**nbox.

Fig. 30.5

The Inbox window displays a list of messages sent to you.

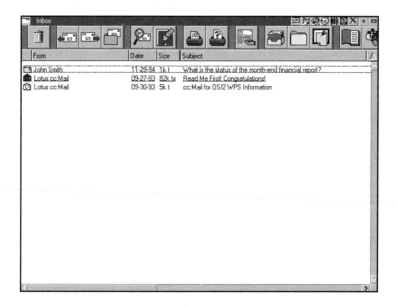

3. To read a message in the Inbox, highlight the message, and double-click it, or click the right mouse button and select the Open command in the pop-up menu. The message appears as shown in figure 30.6.

Replying to a Message

After opening a message, you can handle and perform various actions on the message. For instance you can reply, forward, store, or delete the message. You may also want to read the next read or unread messages in the Inbox list.

To send a reply message, follow these steps:

1. Choose **M**essage, **R**eply, or press Ctrl+R. The reply is displayed with Re: and the original subject in the window title. The first text item in the message is displayed, and the cursor appears at the beginning (see fig. 30.7).

Subject appears in title bar

Fig. 30.6
The message
window appears
allowing you to
read the message.
The subject line
appears in the
window title bar.

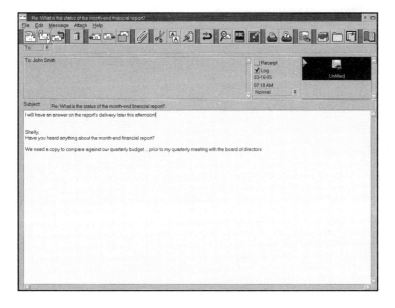

Fig. 30.7
A Reply message is
designated by the
Re: in the window
title.

2. Type your message and change any message settings, then click the
Send icon or choose **M**essage, **S**end.

VI

Tip
When replying, type above the previous message and press Enter twice for white space.

> **Note**
>
> You can also reply to all the recipients by choosing **M**essage, Repl**y** to All, or by pressing Ctrl+Y.

Forwarding a Message

To forward the message to other people, choose **M**essage, **F**orward, or press Ctrl+F. You can also forward a message as if it were a new message by choosing **M**essage, **F**orward As New or by pressing Ctrl+W. The forwarding message is displayed with an empty To box (see fig. 30.8). Type your comments above the previous message and then send the message like any other mail message.

Fig. 30.8
Forwarding a message to another user to include them in the flow of information.

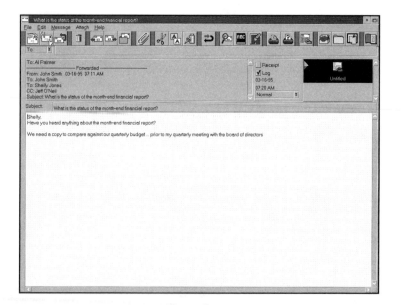

Storing Messages

To store the message in a folder, choose **M**essage, S**t**ore, or press Ctrl+T. The Store Message window appears as shown in figure 30.9.

Tip
Drag the selected message to a folder in the Folder List to move it.

Select a folder for storing the message by typing the name or pulling down the drop-down folder menu. If the folder doesn't currently exist, create it by typing a name for the folder. This example demonstrates creating a new folder called "Month-End Reports." Select the **C**opy or **M**ove option to copy or move the message to the folder and then choose OK.

Fig. 30.9
Storing a message
to a cc:Mail folder.

Note

To copy the text of the message to the Clipboard, select and highlight the text you wish to copy, and click the Copy icon, or choose **E**dit, **C**opy, or press Ctrl+Insert.

Searching for Text in a Message

To search for text in a message, choose **E**dit, **S**earch, or press F5. The Search window appears (see fig. 30.10). Enter the text to search for in the Find box and click the Fin**d** button. You can also search for and replace existing text using the Change **T**o: box and clicking **C**hange or Change **A**ll.

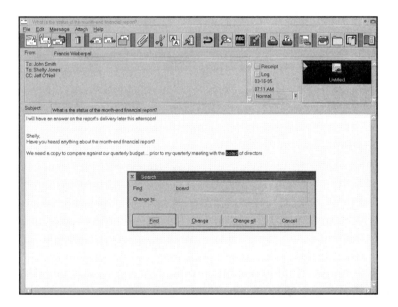

Fig. 30.10
The Search window
is used to find text
and even replace
located text items.

VI

Communicating

Saving Messages

To save the message to disk, choose **F**ile, Save **A**s. The Save dialog box appears allowing you to enter a file name and change the file type, drive, and directory. Select the Save button to save the message to a new file name.

Deleting a Message

To delete a message, choose **M**essage, **D**elete message.

Once you have deleted a message, you may recover it from the Trash folder. To do so, open the Folder list object in the main cc:Mail window and then open the Trash folder.

The Trash folder may be cleared out periodically, depending on your settings. Also, the Trash folder may not be enabled for your post office. Contact your cc:Mail administrator for more information.

Reading and Viewing Messages

To read the message immediately after the current message in the Inbox window choose **M**essage, **N**ext Message, or press Alt+Right Arrow, or press the plus key (+) on the keypad. You can also choose **M**essage, N**e**xt Unread, or press F4 to display the next unread message.

Delete and Read Next Message

You can click the Delete, Get Next Message icon or press Shift+Alt+Right Arrow to delete the current message and go on to the next message in the Inbox.

Go Back to Previous Message

To go back to the previous message in the Inbox, you can click the Previous Message icon, choose **M**essage, **P**revious, press Alt+Left Arrow, or press the minus key (-) on the keypad. You can also choose **M**essage, Pre**v**ious Unread, or press Shift+F4 to display the next unread message.

Delete and Return to Previous Message

You can also click the Delete, Get Previous Message icon, or press Shift+Alt+Left Arrow to delete the current message and go back to the previous message in the Inbox.

Close Current Message

To close the current message, double-click the title-bar icon in the top-left corner of the message window (refer to fig. 30.1), or click the right mouse button and select the Close command from the pop-up menu.

Note

You can minimize a message and not have it appear on your desktop. To do so, click the minimize box, or press Alt+F9. You can also click the right mouse button to display the pop-up menu and select the Minimize command. An icon for the minimized message is placed in the Minimized Window Viewer, and its name appears in the Window List.

Customizing the cc:Mail Work Area

Since the OS/2 Workplace Shell is customizable you can easily change and modify your cc:Mail windows and folders to your preferences. For example, you can open, size, and position cc:Mail windows and then save this arrangement. This allows you to customize the work area that opens up when you start cc:Mail. To customize the cc:Mail for OS/2 Workplace Shell work area you can open, size, and position cc:Mail windows, such as the main window and the Inbox, as you wish. Figure 30.11 shows an example of a cc:Mail work area with various window sizings and icon placements.

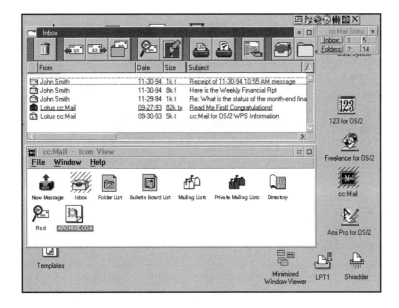

Fig. 30.11
Positioning and customizing cc:Mail to coincide with your work habits.

You can also create a work-area folder in which you can place objects related to a specific task. For example, you might create a work-area folder to include current reports, previous reports, and a printer with customized settings; or, you might create a work-area folder to include charts, documents, and a plotter. To create a work-area folder, follow these steps:

1. Point at the cc:Mail folder and click the right mouse button to display the pop-up menu.

2. Select the **O**pen command by clicking the left mouse button on the arrow to the right of the Open command.

3. Select the **S**ettings command.

4. Select the **F**ile tab to display the Settings menu.

5. Click on the option **W**ork Area.

6. Close the cc:Mail Settings notebook to have your changes take effect. You can also click Undo to return to the current settings.

◀ See "Using the OS/2 Workplace Shell," p. 10

Work-area folders have two special features. When you close the folder, all windows belonging to the objects within the folder are closed automatically and the view of each object is saved. When you open the folder the next time, the windows for the objects in the folder are displayed with their previous view.

The other feature is that when you hide the window of a work-area folder, all windows belonging to the objects in the folder are hidden automatically. When you show the work-area folder (from the Window List), the windows for the objects in the folder are displayed with their previous view. If you minimize a work-area folder, only the icon for the work-area folder is displayed in the Minimized Window Viewer or on the desktop. The windows belonging to the objects in the work-area folder are not displayed.

> **Caution**
>
> Work-area folders function with the icon or details view, but not with the tree view.

Sending a cc:Mail Message from within the SmartSuites

Using cc:Mail is an easy way to send data and files to others for use with the other SmartSuite applications. You can use the File, Send Mail command from within the other SmartSuites to send an attached file, a specified range, chart, or drawing as an electronic-mail message.

Occasionally, it's easier to send a message or file from within Ami Pro, Freelance, or 1-2-3 rather than directly accessing cc:Mail and preparing a message with an attachment. From the other SmartSuite applications you can send a message without attaching a document or you can attach either a titled document or selected text in a document.

When using any of the SmartSuite applications to send a worksheet, document, or presentation file, the application reacts differently to the status of the current file. If a file has been previously saved, the cc:Mail dialog box appears after selecting the Send **M**ail command. Otherwise, untitled worksheets, documents, or presentation files force the File Save As dialog box to appear prompting you to save the file.

> **Note**
>
> Ami Pro doesn't attach the style sheet associated with a document to the message. If you want to maintain the formatting in a titled Ami Pro document when you attach it to a message, save the document under a different name and select the Keep Format with Document option when using **F**ile, **S**ave or **F**ile, Save **A**s before you open the **F**ile menu and choose the Send **M**ail command.

Tip

To send table information from within Ami Pro you can open the Ta**b**le menu and choose Select Entire Ta**b**le.

To send a text message or a message with the current file attached from within the other SmartSuite applications, perform the following steps:

1. Make the document, worksheet, or presentation you want to attach to a cc:Mail message the active window. If you want to send just part of the document, select the desired text to incorporate the selected text or table data into the message.

2. In Ami Pro, choose **F**ile, Send **M**ail or select the Mail SmartIcon. In 1-2-3 or Freelance, choose **F**ile, Send Mail. The Send Mail dialog box appears with the **A**ttach option as shown in figure 30.12.

VI

Communicating

> **Caution**
>
> The hot key in the Send Mail command within Ami Pro, 1-2-3, and Freelance is different. In Ami Pro the hot key is the letter **M**, while the hot key utilized in 1-2-3 and Freelance is the letter **L**.

Fig. 30.12

The Send Mail dialog box allows you to quickly send a message or a message with an attachment to a colleague

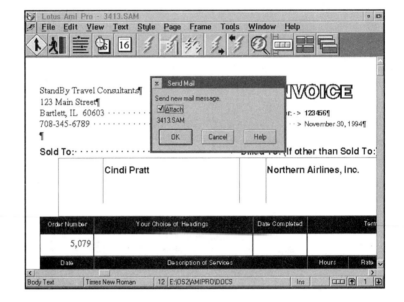

3. Select **A**ttach to send and attach the current document. If you only want to send a message and not include the current file as an attachment you can deselect the **A**ttach option.

> **Note**
>
> If you selected text, the **A**ttach option is dimmed. If you edited the current document since the last save, or if the current document is Untitled, the option is **S**ave and Attach, as shown in figure 30.13. The Save As dialog box appears if the document is Untitled or read-only. Specify the desired file name, select Keep Format with Document, and choose OK.

Fig. 30.13
Using the Save
and Attach option
for an Untitled
or modified
document.

4. If the current document is untitled or has been recently modified
    choose File, Save and Attach File. The File Save dialog box appears.
    Name the file and click OK.

5. A cc:Mail window appears. After preparing and sending a cc:Mail
    message, you return to the application.

Automating the Process to Send cc:Mail Messages

You can easily create new-message templates with specific customized settings to automate sending cc:Mail messages. For example, you may want to
have a template message for sending a weekly financial report to certain individuals. By creating a new-message template you never have to retype the
message, reenter the addresses, or change the settings.

To create a new-message template, perform the following steps:

1. Open the Templates folder on your OS/2 desktop.

2. Drag a copy of the Message Template object onto the desktop or to
    another folder by holding down the right mouse button, as shown in
    figure 30.14. The Address page for the message template appears.

VI

Communicating

Fig. 30.14
Creating a cc:Mail
message template
by dragging and
dropping the
cc:Mail Message
template icon on
the OS/2 Work-
place Shell.

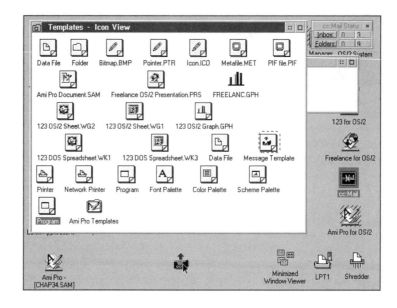

3. Click the **A**ddress tab and then address the message by adding the individuals you want to receive it. Figure 30.15 shows a cc:Mail message
   template being addressed to specific individuals.

Fig. 30.15
The Address page
for setting Message
Template options
for a new-message
template.

4. Type a short subject and change the priority or receipt setting.

5. Select the **S**end Automatically option if you want to drag a file onto
   this new-message template for automatic sending. Or you could select
   Prompt before sending if you want to be asked to confirm before sending when you drag a file onto this new-message template.

6. Click the **G**eneral tab to change the name of the template in the Title: edit box.

7. Save the template by closing the Message Template Settings window.

You can now use the new-message template by either clicking the message template icon or by dragging any file icon onto the message template. Figure 30.16 shows a 1-2-3 worksheet file being dragged and dropped onto a message template named "Weekly Financial Report." The worksheet file is delivered as an attachment to the addressees listed in the message template and uses the entered subject line.

Fig. 30.16
Dragging and dropping the weekly financial report created in 1-2-3 for OS/2 onto the new-message template which automatically creates and sends the cc:Mail message.

Receiving Notification of a cc:Mail Message

If you're logged onto cc:Mail you can be notified about incoming mail in several ways:

- The cc:Mail Status window informs you of the number of new and total messages in your inbox and folders.

- cc:Mail Notify alerts you when new messages arrive in your inbox.

- When working within a SmartSuite application, the application notifies you when you get new mail by beeping and displaying an envelope in the status bar. Click the envelope icon that appears to switch to your mail application.

To configure how cc:Mail uses notification, perform the following steps:

1. Choose **F**ile, **O**ptions in the main cc:Mail window or in any message window. The cc:Mail Settings notebook appears.

2. Click the Notify tab to display the Notify Options page as shown in figure 30.17.

VI

Communicating

Fig. 30.17
The cc:Mail
Settings Notebook
allows you to
establish how you
want to be notified
of new mail.

3. Select the Mail-Check Interval ranging from 1 minute to 24 hours, and if you want to be notified by a Beep or a Show Window. When cc:Mail Notify finds new mail in your inbox, it will beep or show a Notify window in the middle of your screen, depending on the settings you choose.

> **Caution**
>
> Don't set the Mail-Check Interval too low, because that will create excessive network traffic. Your Network Administrator will appreciate this concern. A setting of 5-10 minutes is recommended.

cc:Mail It! Mailing Files Directly from the Workplace Shell

If you like working with icons and objects on the OS/2 Workplace shell, cc:Mail for OS/2 features a quick and efficient method to mail files directly from the Workplace Shell. The method is called cc:Mail It!

1. Select a file icon on the desktop.

2. Click the right mouse button to display the pop-up menu.

3. Select cc:Mail It! from the menu as shown in figure 30.18.

4. The New Message window appears with the file-item icon attached in the item-icon list. Finish preparing and sending the message.

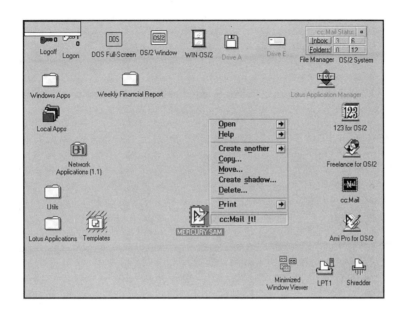

Fig. 30.18
cc:Mail It! allows
you to select a file
to send directly
from the OS/2
Workplace Shell.

Printing from cc:Mail for OS/2

There are several different ways to print a copy of a cc:Mail message. If you like reading your messages before printing them, you can perform the following steps:

1. Open the message to print by double-clicking the message.

2. Choose **F**ile, **P**rint.

Instead of opening the message and using the top menu commands as previously described, you can save a step by performing the following steps:

1. Select and highlight the message.

2. Click the right mouse button and select **P**rint from the pop-up menu.

A third way to print a cc:Mail message is to drag-and-drop the selected message onto a specific printer object installed on your OS/2 Workplace Shell:

1. Select and highlight the message.

2. Hold down the left mouse button and then click and hold down the right mouse button. Drag a message to the Printer object on your Workplace Shell, as shown in figure 30.19.

Fig. 30.19

Dragging and dropping a cc:Mail message to a Printer object on the Workplace shell.

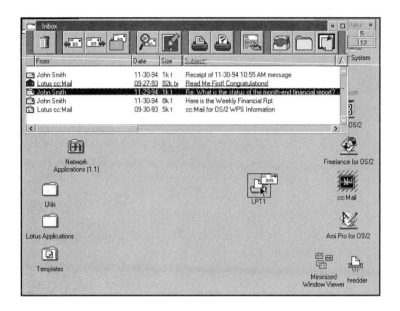

Troubleshooting

After receiving an Ami Pro file via cc:Mail I got an error message that the associated style sheet can't be found when attempting to open the file.

The person who sent you the file needs to send you the associated style sheet or when saving the file, select the Keep Format option. Ami Pro doesn't attach the style sheet associated with a document to the message. To maintain the formatting in a titled document when you attach it to a message, save the document with a different name and select Keep Format with Document before you choose **F**ile, Send **M**ail.

When I try to drag a message listed in the Inbox window to a Printer icon on the OS/2 Workplace Shell nothing happens.

Make sure you hold down the right mouse button before moving. The mouse pointer should change to an icon that can be dragged onto the Printer icon. A lot of users make the mistake of pressing the wrong mouse button or simultaneously clicking both mouse buttons.

From Here...

This chapter explained how to work with cc:Mail and the other SmartSuite applications to send electronic messages to people in your corporation and on your network. Mailing electronic messages to people over a network is an efficient and effective mode of communication, and will change your "paper mail" thinking of how you and others in your organization share files and disseminate information.

- Chapter 2, "Using Common Features," shows you the intricacies of using the OS/2 Workplace Shell, how to launch the applications, open and close files, move between programs and documents, and more.

- Chapter 3, "Managing Files and Work Areas," shows you how to name, save, and print files; and describes the work areas of the SmartSuite applications and the OS/2 Workplace Shell.

- Chapter 29, "Using the OS/2 Workplace Shell to Create an Integrated Desktop," describes how to create project folders, integrated data files, and desktop files.

Chapter 31

Understanding Notes

by Derek S. Anderson

A big part of Lotus Development's game plan for the coming decade is its "working together" strategy. SmartSuite is the result of at least some of that intent.

Lotus went to great lengths to provide a consistent interface and high degree of integration among the products that comprise SmartSuite for OS/2. You benefit from a comprehensive set of software tools that really do work well together.

But the working together concept is more than mere synergy between software programs. Lotus envisions a future where products that help people work together more effectively are the big winners. So it's no surprise that a software product that lets you communicate with people near and far, and lets you share all manner of business knowledge easily and on existing hardware platforms, represents the very heart of Lotus' strategy. That all-important product is Lotus Notes.

> **Note**
>
> Lotus Notes isn't part of Lotus SmartSuite. We include chapters on Notes because it's central to Lotus Development's product strategy and because one of the great benefits of SmartSuite is that all its products integrate so easily with Lotus Notes.

In this chapter, you learn about:

- The features and functions of Lotus Notes

- Communicating with Notes

- Using Notes in your business

VI

Communicating

Notes: A Document-Oriented Database

Lotus Notes is a program that enables you to store, retrieve, organize, and share data. In that sense, Notes is similar to a database. But Notes differs from conventional relational databases in the way it handles data. Conceptually, relational databases organize data in tables of records that each consist of a specific number of rigidly defined fields.

Unlike Approach and other relational databases, Notes organizes data into documents. Although you can think of documents as similar to records in a traditional database, a closer analogy is to think about documents as something like the documents produced by a word processor.

A Notes document usually contains fields similar to those you find in a record of a relational database. But a Notes document also typically contains a special kind of field called Rich Text. Figure 31.1 shows an example of Rich Text. Note that the text varies in format, with some words appearing in italic or bold, or with an underline.

Fig. 31.1

The body of this Notes memo is a Rich Text field that contains text, graphics, and an embedded file attachment.

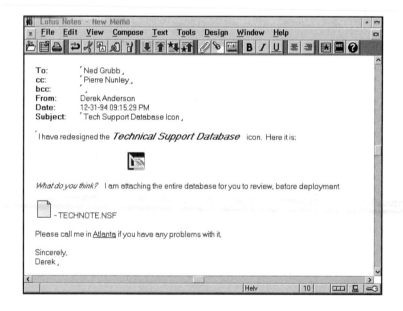

A Rich Text field can contain text, tables, graphics, file attachments, and even embedded data from other program files. Unlike a normal text field, you can style areas of text in a Rich Text field with different fonts, colors, sizes, and styles (bold, italic, and so on). This capability to store varying text formatting and data types in a single field isn't something you typically find in a database.

Notes' document orientation makes the program ideal for storing loosely defined, or unstructured, data. A relational database may be better for storing structured data, such as a large list of inventory parts, descriptions, and prices. Notes, on the other hand, excels at storing unstructured documents such as legal contracts, corporate policy statements, memos, letters, and so on.

Sharing Data on a Network

Of course, if all Notes did was organize and store documents, it wouldn't be the best-selling program that it is. What really makes Notes powerful is the way it enables disparate users to share Notes documents through a computer network.

Notes represents the first and foremost example of a new category of software with a work-together capability. Computer industry pundits have dubbed this new generation of products *groupware*. You also may hear people call Notes a group information manager.

Whatever you call it, Notes is like a well-organized, corporate filing cabinet. Anyone with the proper authority can read, modify, or add documents to any file as needed. The big difference between Notes files and those in a metal filing cabinet is that you don't have to get up from your desk to find the document you need. Furthermore, the filing cabinet doesn't even need to be nearby; it may be in the next office, the next building, the next city, the next country, or nearly anywhere in the world!

Communicating with Notes

Considering Notes' strong points—document management and communications—it's hardly surprising that Notes is an outstanding platform for electronic mail (e-mail). Your first practical use for Notes may well be as an e-mail system. As with any e-mail program, you can type memos to specific people or to entire groups of people.

Notes transfers your messages and offers some measure of assurance to those who receive them that the messages really are from you. You can be reasonably confident about a memo's author because Notes enables you to sign your messages with a unique electronic signature. This capability is only one of many security features that makes Notes suitable for the electronic exchange of sensitive information. Another feature is encryption. Notes can optionally encode a message so that only the intended recipients can read it. When you send e-mail, Notes asks whether you want to use either of these primary security features. In general, you should always choose both these security features.

Of course, Notes enables you to do more than just send simple text. You can dress up your e-mail with graphics. For example, you can create a custom form to match your corporate letterhead. You can add pictures or charts to the body of your letter or use a scanned image of your signature at the closing. Notes also enables you to format the body of your e-mail using a variety of fonts, colors, and styles, much the way you do in a word processor like Ami Pro.

After you get a memo looking the way you like, you may want to include some electronic attachments. Notes offers several ways to share disk files or data in those files with other people. For example, you can attach a copy of any disk file to a mail memo. The memo's recipient need only detach the file to copy it to his or her hard disk. And if you're concerned about transmission time for sending such files, Notes can compress file attachments for you. This feature is especially useful when you're sending e-mail by modem. A compressed file attachment takes much less time to transmit.

Another useful way to share data in a file is to embed it as an OLE (Object Linking and Embedding) object in the body of your e-mail. You simply copy or cut data from an OLE-capable application, such as 1-2-3 for Windows, and then paste it into the body of your Notes memo. The recipient can see the data right in the Notes memo and can even open it in the source application (like 1-2-3) by double-clicking the embedded object.

Using Notes To Organize, Access, Track, and Participate

Besides e-mail, corporations can use Notes for a wide variety of distributed, unstructured-database applications. You may be able to find real-world examples of Notes databases on your server. You also can explore the sample databases that ship with Lotus Notes. These examples can show you some of the applications that are possible in Notes and maybe even give you ideas on how best to make use of Notes in your organization.

Notes is most useful for the following types of applications:

- *Broadcast.* These databases contain information of interest to a large number of people. Such an application may broadcast company news, industry reports, or work schedules. The Notes News database (NOTENEWS.NSF) that ships with Notes is a broadcast application.

- *Discussion.* Notes is great for creating discussion databases, which may center on any number of topics such as quality control, process improvement, or research and development. The Support Conference database (SUPPCONF.NSF) that ships with Notes is a discussion application.

- *Reference.* You can store any and all corporate data for easy reference in a database. For example, policies and procedures manuals, inventory photographs and descriptions, and legal contracts are all candidates for a Notes reference application. The Electronic Library file (HRDOCS.NSF) that ships with Notes is a reference application.

- *Tracking.* Your company may want to use Notes to keep track of documents containing a variety of information. Such databases can follow the trail of sales leads, keep an eye on advertising performance, or track project status. The Call Tracking Database (CALLTRAK.NSF) that ships with Notes is a tracking application.

- *Workflow.* One of the most advanced uses of Notes, workflow applications can automate a whole range of company procedures. You might create a database to handle the routing and tracking of purchases, advertising copy reviews, or new investment approvals. The Product Catalog & Requisitions database (PRODCAT.NSF) is part of an example workflow application that ships with Notes.

Notes is more than a simple e-mail system. Companies can use Notes to develop all kinds of sophisticated workgroup applications. The focus on Notes in this book is to help you make the best use of such applications in your own daily work.

VI

Communicating

From Here...

This chapter described the Lotus Notes program and how you can use it in your business. For related information about using Lotus Notes, refer to the following chapters:

- Chapter 32, "Getting Started with Notes," takes you through some actual hands-on tutorials for using Notes.

- Chapter 33, "Managing Information with Notes," shows you how to organize documents in a Notes database.

- Chapter 34, "Using Notes with SmartSuite Applications," teaches you how to get the most out of Notes and other SmartSuite programs.

Chapter 32

Getting Started with Notes

by Derek S. Anderson

Your first practical use of Notes will likely involve sending and receiving Notes mail. Not every company that uses Notes uses it for e-mail, but most do. Notes mail is really just another Notes database application, so the information covered here is applicable to most Notes databases.

In this chapter, you learn to:

- Send and receive Notes mail
- Open a Notes database
- Create a Notes document
- Spot Notes fields
- Use buttons
- Create DocLinks

Using the Mail Database

When you open Notes, you see the Notes workspace. Your Notes-mail icon should be visible on the first tabbed page of the workspace. If you don't see it, click the far left tab to make sure you're looking at the first tabbed page. The default Notes-mail database shows your user name and a small picture of an envelope.

Opening the Mail

Tip

To get Notes to display the number of unread documents from the workspace, go to View and choose Show Unread.

To open the mail database, double-click its icon or press Enter when highlighting the icon. Notes opens the database and shows what Lotus calls a *view* of all the documents in that database. If you don't have any mail documents in your mail database, the view will be empty.

By default, Notes puts stars in the left margin beside unread mail documents. The stars are a different color from those put next to mail items that you've already read. When you open the database for the first time, Notes scans the fields in every document and uses the information to present a sorted and categorized list.

Many Notes databases have views that organize documents by categories and some even have subcategories. A categorized view is very much like an expandable outline. As shown in figure 32.1, you can *collapse* or *expand* a categorized view to see exactly the level of detail you need.

- To collapse all categories in a view, choose **V**iew, Collapse All. Or you can press Shift+ – (minus key).

- To expand all categories choose **V**iew, Expand All. Or press Shift++ (hold down the Shift key and press the plus key).

- To collapse a specific category, highlight the category heading and choose **V**iew, Collapse (or press –).

- To expand a specific category, highlight the heading and choose **V**iew, Expand (or press +).

Fig. 32.1

You can collapse a categorized view to see only the category headings. Here, the user collapsed all categories and then expanded only the Not-Categorized category to reveal two unread documents.

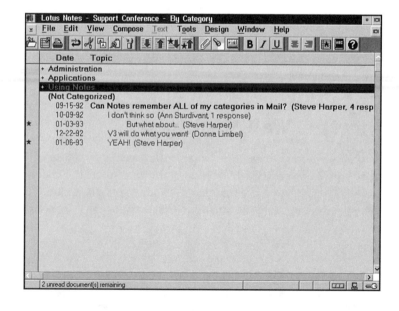

Some database designers set up views to function like a table of contents. For example, the Notes help system, which is just another Notes database file, has a Table of Contents view. To open this database, choose **H**elp, **T**able of Contents. You can quickly locate a topic by scanning through the list. To view the list presented in figure 32.2, choose **H**elp, **T**able of Contents, **V**iew, Show Only **C**ategories.

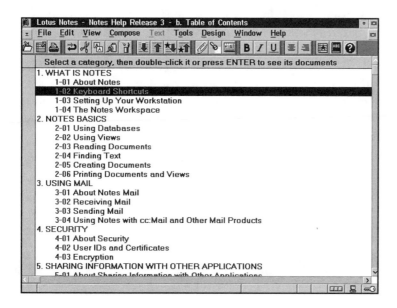

Fig. 32.2
The Notes help database provides you with easy-to-find information.

Changing the View

Most Notes databases offer more than one view of documents, and each database must have a default view—the view displayed when you first open the file. By default, the Notes-mail database offers eight views. To switch to another view, choose **V**iew and scan the list in the bottom third of the **V**iew menu. (The views vary from database to database.) The last view you use in a database will be the view you see the next time you open it.

With the exception of category and subcategory headings, each horizontal row in a view is a document. The vertical columns of the view show information based on the contents of the documents. To open a document you either double-click it or highlight it and press the Enter key.

Reading and Organizing Mail

Most often, Notes mail is simple correspondence. Use the scroll bar or the PgDn key to scroll down a document as needed.

VI

Communicating

When you finish reading the Notes mail, you may want to send a reply. To do that, just click the Reply button at the top of the document or choose **C**ompose, **R**eply. Notes automatically fills in the address and subject; enter only the contents of your memo and then send it (see "Sending a Message," later in this chapter).

 You also have the option of forwarding your mail to someone else. In fact, you can use Notes mail to forward any document you're reading in any Notes database. To forward a message, just choose **M**ail, **F**orward and type the recipient's address. You can also click the Forward SmartIcon. Notes automatically enters the contents of the forwarded document, including representations of all visible fields, in the body of the mail memo. You can edit the contents of the forwarded message as you see fit. Typically, you add introductory text at the top of the message to give the recipients some context for the forwarded message.

 To help keep your mail organized, Notes lets you assign each mail document to a category. To assign a mail document to a category, click the Categorize button at the top of the document or choose **T**ools, **C**ategorize. Notes presents you with a list of all available categories. The categories you see in your own mail database will, of course, be different.

> **Note**
>
> The first time you use Notes mail, there probably won't be any categories. To add one, just enter a category name in the New categories edit box at the bottom of the Categorize dialog box.

You can't use the backslash character (\) when creating a category name because Notes recognizes the backslash character as a separator between a category and subcategories. For example, figure 32.3 shows three subcategories under the main category Software.

Fig. 32.3
Using the backslash character (\), you can add subcategories that further organize documents in a Notes database.

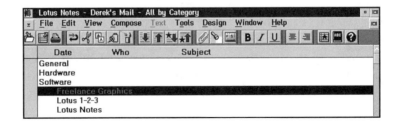

To categorize three documents within these three subcategories (Lotus 1-2-3, Lotus Notes, and Freelance Graphics), enter the new subcategories in the **N**ew categories edit box for each, as follows:

- Software\Lotus 1-2-3

- Software\Lotus Notes

- Software\Freelance Graphics

If you really want to get organized, Notes lets you go even further. You could, for example, subdivide each subcategory by region. You might use ACME Inc.\Notes Consulting\East and ACME Inc.\Notes Consulting\West. Usually, a single level of descriptive categories is enough to keep your mail organized.

Sending a Message

You can compose a mail memo from anywhere in Notes. You don't have to be in your Notes mail database, nor does the database have to be open. That means you can dash off a memo to anyone at any time, even when you're in the middle of reading a document from a reference database.

To create a mail memo, open Mail and then choose **C**ompose, **M**emo. Notes displays a blank memo like the one shown in figure 32.4. This blank memo is a new Notes mail document. When you choose **M**emo from the **C**ompose menu, you're telling Notes to use the Memo form when creating the new document. A *form* is a specific template for creating or looking at a document. A form isn't the same as the document itself, but the terms are sometimes used interchangeably.

Notes identifies *editable fields*—the places in a form that you can edit—with small angle brackets. The four editable fields—To:, cc:, bcc:, and Subject:—are located at the top of the Notes mail form.

- *To:*. Enter the address or addresses of the primary recipient(s).

- *cc:*. Enter the address or addresses of any secondary recipients you want to send a copy of the memo to.

- *bcc:*. Enter the address or addresses of secondary recipients you can send hidden or blind copies to. The recipients identified in the To: field and the cc: field don't see the contents of the bcc: field. Therefore the To: recipients don't know you've sent copies of the memo to bcc: recipients. Even bcc'ed people don't know about each other, only themselves.

VI

Communicating

■ *Subject:*. Enter a brief description of the memo. Most of the mail database's views use this description in the subject column.

Fig. 32.4

To send Notes mail, fill in the appropriate fields of the mail memo form.

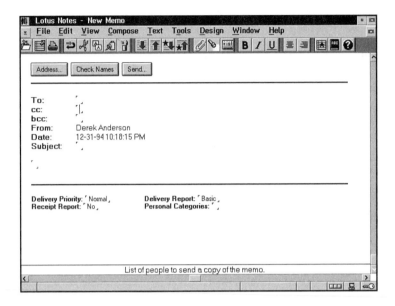

The only field you must fill in is the To: field. You should, however, always enter something in the Subject: field as well. Otherwise, the recipient's view of the memo doesn't provide an indication of the memo's topic.

Addressing a Notes Mail Memo

The rules for entering information in the address fields (To:, cc:, and bcc:) apply to all three fields. For example, you can enter the following:

■ A single name or multiple names separated by commas

■ Either the names of individuals or groups identified in your personal Name & Address Book (NAMES.NSF) or the public N&A book

■ Only a first name or last name, if the name is unique in your Name & Address Book

Note

If you enter only a first or last name that isn't unique, Notes presents a list of all matches in the Name & Address books.

If the full name of a recipient doesn't appear in your personal Name & Address Book or in any public Name & Address Book on your mail server, you must specify the name of the recipient's domain. A domain is simply the name of a group of Notes servers that share the same public Name & Address Book database. For example, if you need to send a memo to Joe Yu and his domain is named Support, use the address **Joe Yu @ Support**. For this to work, the Name & Address Book on your server must identify the Support domain. If it doesn't, check with your Notes administrator.

Most often, you'll be sending mail to people and groups already identified in your public Name & Address Book. You can either type an address yourself or you can choose it from the Mail Address dialog box by clicking the Address button in the upper-left corner of the mail form. Or you can open the Mail Address dialog box by choosing **M**ail, **A**ddress.

You can use the Mail Address dialog box to enter correctly spelled addresses in any field in the memo (see fig. 32.5). Most often, you'll use it to get an address or addresses for the To field. But you can get the correct spelling of names for use in the body of the memo as well. To specify where you want the dialog to enter addresses, select from the To drop-down listbox. The options are: To, cc, bcc, and Current field.

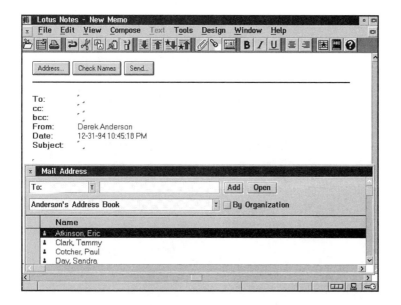

Fig. 32.5
Use the Mail Address dialog box to select any addresses you want to add to a Notes mail memo.

If you have a personal and public address list available, you can choose either one from the address book drop-down listbox (such as "Anderson's Address Book" in fig. 32.5). To add addresses to the selected memo field, double-click the names from the scrolling list in the dialog box. If you choose more than one name, Notes automatically separates the addresses with a comma in the memo's field.

Formatting Your Message

▶ See "Sharing Information with Other Applications," p. 639

After you address the memo and enter a subject, you're ready to write your mail message. The body of the mail memo is just below the Subject field. This is a rich text field, and you can enter text in it just as you would in Ami Pro or any other word processor. Although Notes doesn't offer as many features as Ami Pro, it has plenty of options for formatting the text you enter in any rich text field. You can also include information or objects from other Windows applications. The most common method for including information from other applications involves pasting data or graphics from the Clipboard with the **E**dit, **P**aste command.

▶ See "Using Notes with 1-2-3," p. 647

▶ See "Using Notes with Ami Pro," p. 652

To change the look of text in the body of your memo, highlight it and choose **T**ext. The **T**ext menu provides several ways to format selected text. You'll often want to choose **U**nderline (Ctrl+U), **I**talic (Ctrl+I), **N**ormal (Ctrl+T), or **B**old (Ctrl+B) text, so Notes includes these quick, simple operations in the **T**ext menu.

More formatting options are available through the Font dialog box (see fig. 32.6). To open the Font dialog box, choose Text, **F**ont. You can select a font for your screen display or for printing. Selecting a font for printing is a handy feature because not all screen fonts are available on all printers. You can also specify the size and color of the selected text in the Font dialog box and you can select from three additional formatting styles: St**r**ikethrough, Supe**r**script, and Sub**s**cript.

Fig. 32.6
Use the Font dialog box to choose a specific screen or printer font and to set its color and formatting attributes.

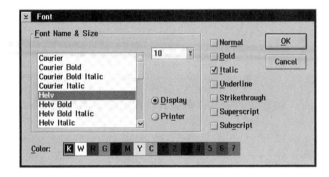

Using the mouse is the easiest way to select text for formatting. As with Ami Pro, you can select a single word by double-clicking it. To select larger sections of text, move the insertion point while holding down the left mouse button. Or place the insertion point where you want to start your selection, hold down the Shift key, and click where you want to end the selection.

From the keyboard, you can select text by holding down the Shift key and moving the insertion point with the arrow keys. Keyboard selection commands include the following:

- Ctrl+Shift and the left/right arrow keys move one word at a time.

- Shift+End selects text to the end of the line.

- Shift+Home selects text from the insertion point to the beginning of the line.

- Shift+Ctrl+End selects text to the end of the rich text field.

- Shift+Ctrl+Home selects text to the beginning of the body field.

You can also use keyboard combinations to apply formatting to selected text. Table 32.1 summarizes these keyboard formatting options.

Table 32.1 Function Keys and Combinations That Format Text	
Key(s)	**Action**
F2	Enlarges selected text
Shift+F2	Reduces selected text
F7	Indents first line of paragraph
Shift+F7	Eliminates indentation of first line of paragraph
F8	Indents entire paragraph
Shift+F8	Eliminates indentation of entire paragraph
Ctrl+L	Creates a forced page break
Ctrl+K	Opens the Font dialog box
Ctrl+J	Opens the Text Paragraph dialog box

Tip

To create a hanging indent, press Shift+F7 and then press F8.

VI

Communicating

Setting Memo Options

There are four fields at the bottom of the Notes-mail form: Delivery Priority, Delivery Report, Receipt Report, and Personal Categories. The first three are special *keyword fields*, which means you can select from a list of appropriate entries. There are two ways to select from the list when the edit cursor is on a keyword field:

- Press the space bar, which cycles through the list.

- Press Enter, which displays the Select Keywords dialog box shown in figure 32.7.

Fig. 32.7
When you press Enter on a keyword field, a dialog box appears, listing all the entries available for that field.

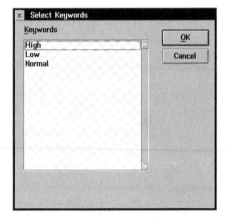

If you know the options for a keyword field, you can select your choice immediately by typing just the first letter of the desired option. For example, typing the letter H when the insertion point is in the Delivery Priority field selects the High option.

The choices for Delivery Priority are High, Normal (the default), and Low. If you're connected to a Local Area Network (LAN), the Delivery Priority field doesn't determine when Notes delivers your memo to the recipient. The Delivery Priority only specifies when to send memos through a modem or across a Wide Area Network (WAN). The priority levels are described in the following list:

- *High.* Sends the memo almost immediately.

- *Normal.* Sends the memo at the next scheduled connection.

- *Low.* Sends the memo sometime between midnight and 6 a.m.

Unlike Delivery Priority, Delivery Report affects all Notes memos whether you're connected to LAN or not. Delivery Report provides feedback on the message delivery. The options are Basic (the default), Confirmed, No Report, and are described in the following list:

- *Basic.* Notifies you only when it can't deliver the memo.

- *Confirmed.* Tells you the outcome of the memo's delivery even if it's successful. You'll probably never use this option because you really only need to know the memo's delivery status when delivery fails. (Even if the network successfully delivers a memo, there's no guarantee the recipient opened the file and read it.)

- *No Report.* Eliminates notification; it won't tell you if your memo fails to reach your designated recipients.

If you want to know whether the recipient read your memo, set the Receipt Report field to Yes. This setting provides you with a memo telling you that the recipient opened your memo or deleted it. Because you usually don't need that information, the Notes default setting for Receipt Report is No.

Specifying Categories

Personal Categories serve the same function as the Categorize button that appears in memos you already saved in your database. You can categorize mail documents by setting up the categories in Personal Categories. Categorizing mail documents makes it easier to find memos containing specific information.

You can enter the name of an existing category or create a new one. Keep in mind that category names are case-sensitive, so maintain a consistent naming pattern. Notes thinks MyBigCategory and Mybigcategory are different categories.

To save a memo in more than one category, separate the category names with commas. These categories are for your database only. The recipients don't receive this category information.

Sending the Mail

When you finish creating your memo and setting its options, you can send it by either clicking the Send button in the top-right corner of the document or by enabling Mail and then choosing **S**end. The Mail Send dialog box enables you to **S**ign and **E**ncrypt the memo (see fig. 32.8). The **S**ign and **E**ncrypt features are security measures that help prevent unscrupulous individuals from sending mail in someone else's name and help prevent someone from reading another person's private mail.

Fig. 32.8

The Sign and Encrypt features are security measures that discourage misuse of Notes mail.

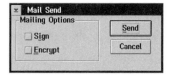

You probably should always check the **Si**gn box, which adds an electronic signature to your memo. This security feature assures the recipient that the document indeed comes from you. Of course, no security feature is foolproof, and you should be aware that a clever person could send a memo using someone else's electronic signature. To reduce that risk, assign a password to your ID using the T**o**ols, User **I**D, **P**assword, **S**et command.

If you check the **E**ncrypt box, Notes encodes the mail document so that only the intended recipients can read it. This prevents other users and even the Notes administrator from reading your private mail on the Notes server.

Troubleshooting

I tried to use the Mail Address dialog box to insert names in the body of a mail memo, but it kept adding the names to the end of the memo's To field.

Don't use the Address button in the mail memo to open the Mail Address dialog box. The button puts the insertion point at the top of the memo, which is the To field, before opening the dialog box. Instead, move the insertion point to where you want to insert the addresses and then open the dialog box by enabling Mail, and then choosing the **A**ddress menu. Be sure to select Current Field from the first drop-down list before you start selecting names.

Exploring Other Notes Databases

Most techniques you use in managing your Notes mail file apply to all manner of Notes databases. Like your mail file, all Notes databases are comprised of documents and you use views to find specific documents.

If your company's Information Services department installed Notes on your computer, there may already be interesting Notes database icons on the tabbed pages in your Notes workspace. You can arrange the icons in your workspace any way you prefer. To move an icon to a new position, simply drag it with the mouse to wherever you want. You can even move database icons to other tabbed pages by dragging the icon to the tab of the page where you want to place the icon.

The tabbed pages help you easily organize your databases to your preference. To display a tabbed page, simply click the tab. To name a tabbed page or change the color of its tab, double-click the tab to access the Workspace Page Name dialog box (see fig. 32.9).

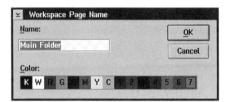

Fig. 32.9
By double-clicking a tab, you can change the tab's color or label.

Getting Notes Help

One database that should be on your system is HELP.NSF. Notes uses this file as an online help system. It's a reference database you'll probably use several times. You may have unknowingly referenced it already. If, for example, you open a document in a Notes database and press F1, Notes displays the About Reading Documents document in section 2-03 of the HELP.NSF file.

To open the Help system, double-click the Notes Help icon in your workspace and choose **V**iew, **b**. Table of Contents. If you don't see the icon, choose **H**elp, **T**able of Contents to open the file as shown in figure 32.10. If you've never used the HELP.NSF file, Notes first displays a special help document called About Database. Close this document with the **F**ile, **C**lose Window command (or Ctrl+W) to see the view.

In the Help file, open a document the same way as in Notes mail: either double-click it or highlight it and press Enter. Change views of the database the same way: by choosing **V**iew and choosing a particular view from the bottom of the pull-down menu. The same is true for all Notes databases after you learn how to use one, it's easy to learn how to use others.

The Help file offers the following views:

- Index
- Table of Contents

VI

Communicating

- Messages

- Release Notes

- @Functions

Fig. 32.10

The Lotus Notes help system is simply a Notes database.

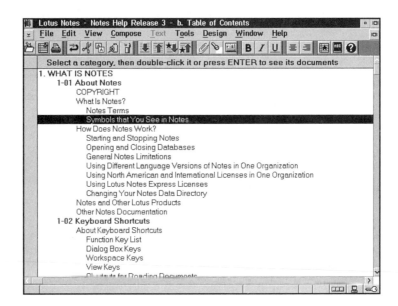

Table of Contents is the default, and Index is the other view you'll probably use most often. Table of Contents is expanded by default and Index is collapsed by default (see fig. 32.11). This feature enables you to scan the index until you find a specific topic. When you locate your information, double-click the topic (or category header) to reveal the documents categorized under that topic.

With its well-organized views, the Notes help file provides generic help and instructions. The instructions you find there apply to every database you're ever likely to use in Notes. Beyond this generic help, each individual database application typically offers at least some specific help. Whenever you use a database application, you should have access to two special help documents: About and Using.

For example, the Business Card Request database offers these two help documents about itself. To view either of these help documents for that database, select the database, then choose **H**elp, **A**bout Business Card Request, or **H**elp, **U**sing Business Card Request.

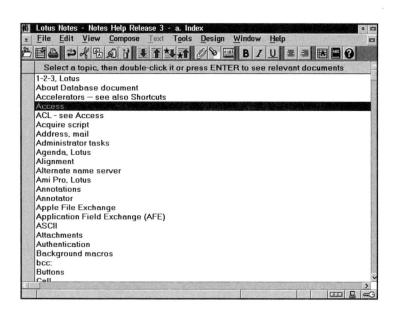

Fig. 32.11
The Index view of
the Notes help file
appears collapsed
by default. The
topics shown here
are the same as
categories, and
you can double-
click any topic to
reveal related
information.

Although the content of these documents is determined by the database's designer, documents typically contain specific information. The About Database document answers the following type of questions:

■ What is this database?

■ What does it do?

■ What's its benefit?

The Using Database document generally answers the following type of questions:

■ How do I get started?

■ How do I use it?

■ How do I accomplish a specific task?

Because the About Database document introduces the spreadsheet to users, Notes automatically displays it when you first open any database file. The About Database document usually contains information about a database's intended audience, the name and phone number of the database's manager, and guidelines on using the application. The About Database document typically contains any copyrights or legal information. Figure 32.12 shows the About document for the Notes Help Release 3 file. The Using Database document contains information about using the database.

VI

Communicating

Fig. 32.12
Every Notes database should have an About document. Even the Notes help file provides one, as shown here.

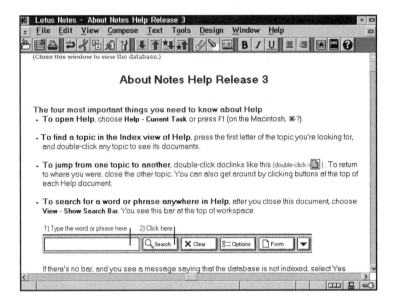

Browsing Database Titles

You can also use the About document to determine whether you're interested in a particular file. You can review the About document of a database before you bother adding it to your workspace by browsing through the available databases on your Notes server.

Browsing the server for Notes database files is similar to browsing your own hard disk for files. Start by choosing File, **O**pen Database, which displays the Open Database dialog box shown in figure 32.13.

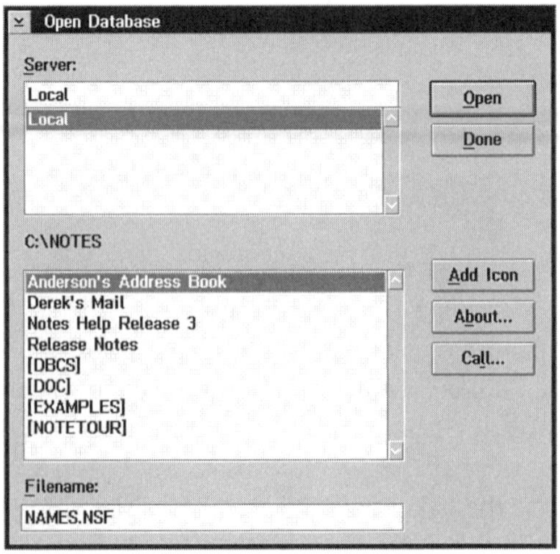

Fig. 32.13
The Open Database dialog box lists the Notes database files available on your local computer, and on all the Notes servers to which your computer connects.

First select the server you want to browse from the list of available servers and click **O**pen (or double-click the name of the server). Notes lists the databases available in the Notes directory of the server. If you scroll to the bottom of the listbox, you may find subdirectories enclosed in square brackets. To browse a subdirectory, double-click it or highlight it and press Enter. To switch back to the main Notes directory, double-click the parent directory, which appears as two periods enclosed between square brackets ([..]).

The scrolling listbox displays Notes database files by description. The actual file name for each database appears in the **F**ilename box. If you see a description that interests you, click **Ab**out to display more information. **Ab**out displays a simplified version of the database's About document. Specifically, it strips out all graphics and formatting and displays only the text information available in the database's About document (see fig. 32.14). If the About information piques your interest, you can either click **A**dd Icon to add the database's icon to your Notes workspace or click **O**pen to both add the icon to the workspace and open it.

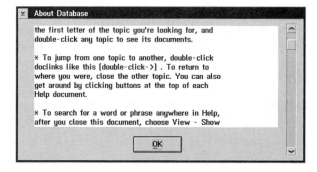

Fig. 32.14
Clicking About in the Open Database dialog box displays a text-only version of the highlighted database's About document.

Call is the same as the **T**ools, Ca**l**l menu command. You only need to use it if you're connecting to a server with a modem. In that case, you can use it to call a server and add it to the list of available servers, which will probably only list Local initially.

Understanding Database Access

Sometimes when browsing Notes databases on a server, Notes won't allow access to a database. If you're not supposed to see any data in a particular file, Notes flashes a message. If you believe you should have access to the database, check with the database's manager, if you know who that is, or the Notes administrator. The database manager can update the file to provide you with access.

VI

Communicating

Notes lets database managers restrict access to sensitive information by completely locking some users out of a particular database. For example, you may be allowed to open a database, but you may not be able to add or change any documents. The database manager can restrict you to merely reading documents created by others. The manager might also restrict you to reading only specific documents or even specific sections of documents. In other databases, you may be able to create your own documents but you may not be able to edit documents created by others.

Database designers or managers determine your access to a particular database. They control access with an Access Control List (ACL), which determines the users, groups, and servers that can access a database and determines the extent of that access. Each ACL has a default access level, which is your access level unless the ACL specifically lists you or your group.

The following list includes the basic access levels to a database, the icon that represents them (in the lower-right corner of the screen) and their descriptions:

- ■ *Manager*. Small key icon means you have unlimited access to a database file. You can read, write, and edit all documents, forms, views, and even the database's icon. You also can change all database settings, including the ACL, or you can delete the database altogether. Each Notes database has at least one manager.

> **Note**
>
> To locate the name of the open database's manager(s), enable Mail and then choose **C**ompose, M**e**mo to Manager. Notes automatically fills in the To field with the addresses of the users, groups, and servers assigned manager access. This Notes feature is handy if you want to request an access-level change. Just send the manager(s) the request via Notes mail.

- ■ *Designer*. Ruler and compass icon means you have access similar to the Manager, except you can't change the ACL, User Activity, Replication, and Other settings available in the Database Information dialog box. You also can't delete the database.

- ■ *Editor*. Pencil and paper icon means you can read, write, and edit all documents, but you can't change forms, views, or any database settings.

- ■ *Author*. Quill pen and ink bottle icon means you can read existing documents and create new documents, but you can only edit documents you've authored.

- *Reader.* Pair of glasses icon means you can only read documents; you can't edit or add to them.

- *Depositor.* Ballot box icon means you can add new documents but you can't read existing ones.

- *No Access.* Not able to open a database.

Troubleshooting

I can't edit documents in a particular database even though I'm a member of a group that has Editor access to it.

Make sure you're listed as a member of the group, and make sure the group has Editor access to the database. Another likely problem is that the database's manager listed your name specifically in the ACL and assigned a lower access level to it. Check with the database manager to ensure that you have the proper access.

Another member of my group has more privileges than I do.

There are two ways that a user might gain access privileges that are higher than those of the group in which they're a member. If the ACL also lists the user as an individual, the individual access level takes precedence over the group access level. Or if the user is a member of another listed group with a higher privilege level, that higher privilege level takes precedence.

Creating Documents

Most Notes files let users add documents as well as reference databases. The process is similar to the one used in the mail database. Although you can create a Notes mail memo any time, you must first open most databases before you can compose a document. After the database is open and current, you create a new document or a response to the currently selected document by choosing **C**ompose and selecting the appropriate form from the pull-down menu.

The options in the **C**ompose menu vary from database to database. Some databases, such as the Notes help file, don't offer any options because they don't let you add documents. Many databases offer only one compose option and others, such as the NOTESNEWS.NSF example file, offer several options. Each option enables you to compose a new document using the specified form.

VI

Communicating

For example, the Newswire **A**rticle option in the **C**ompose menu creates a document in the form shown in figure 32.15. In contrast, the News**l**etter option creates a document in the form shown in figure 32.16. Despite the obvious differences between these forms, each creates documents in the same database.

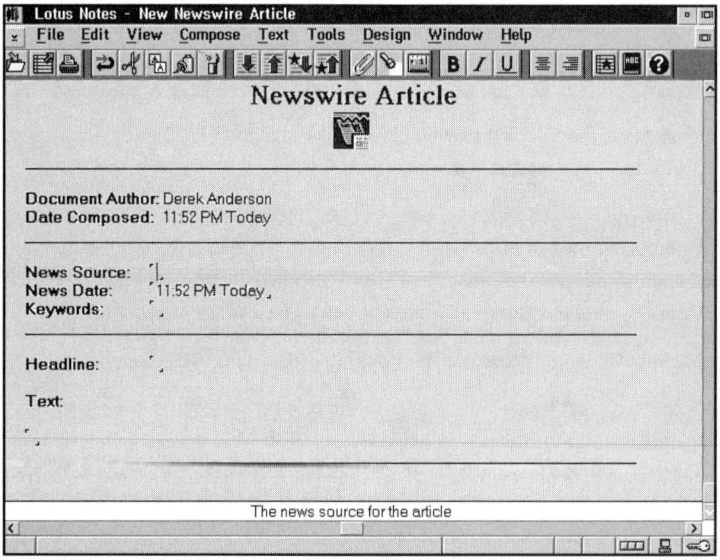

Fig. 32.15

When you choose Compose, Newswire Article in the Notes News database, Notes displays this form.

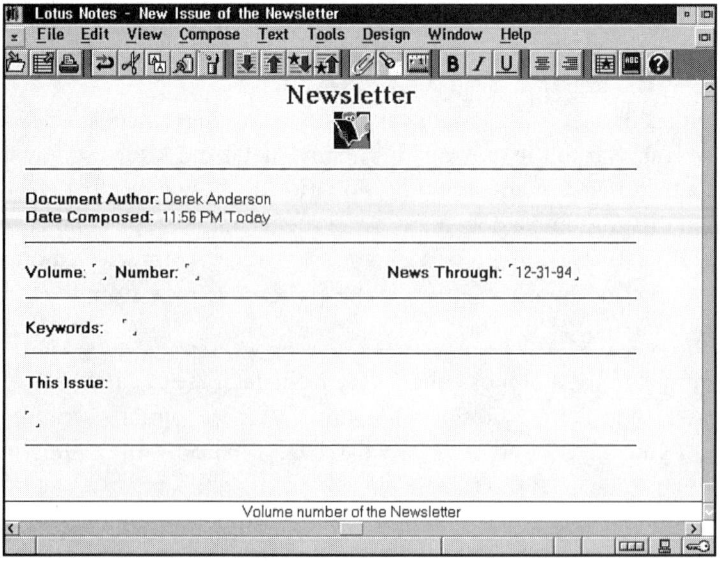

Fig. 32.16

The Compose Newsletter option displays a different form to add documents to the same database.

Understanding Fields

Every form in Notes started as a blank sheet for the database's designer. The designer then adds text, graphics, and fields to make the form useful. *Editable* fields enable you to enter or select information in a form. A Notes database designer also can add computed fields to a form that display information or a calculation for you. These are special fields that you can't edit.

You can use several data types in editable fields. The database designer determines the type of data to be used. For example, you can't enter your name in a *numeric* field because that field only accepts numbers. If you enter a non-numeric character, Notes won't let you save the document until you change the characters to numbers.

Although Notes doesn't tell you the data type for every field, it should be obvious because of the context of the form. A good database designer sets up the database so that it provides adequate information in the form to guide you through data entry. Typically, there is a textual prompt preceding the editable field. Also, when the insertion point is in an editable field, Notes typically provides field help at the bottom of the screen (see fig. 32.17). If you don't see field help, choose **V**iew, Show **F**ield Help.

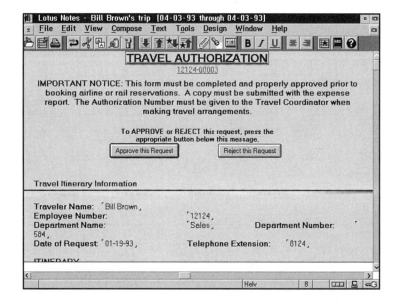

Fig. 32.17

A well-designed form makes it easy for you to enter data. This includes form prompts and field help.

VI

Communicating

Here is a list of the field types you're likely to encounter in Notes databases:

- *Text.* Enables you to enter alphanumeric characters and punctuation. Unlike rich text fields, you can't format the text (with features such as bold and italic), and you can't insert OLE/DDE objects or links.

- *Number.* Enables you to enter numbers, plus or minus signs, a decimal point, a dollar sign for currency, and an E if you're using scientific notation (such as 1.23E36).

- *Rich Text.* Enables you to enter text, tables, OLE/DDE objects and links, and graphics. You can format the text the same as you would in a word processor.

- *Keywords.* Special text fields that enable you to select from a predefined list. The database designer has three display options (Standard, Check Box, and Radio Button) for Keywords fields (see fig. 32.18).

Fig. 32.18
This document shows three Keyword fields that contain the same list of options.

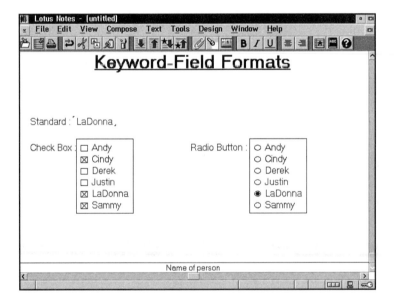

- *Checkbox.* Enables you to select one or more of the options. Radio button enables you to select only one option. To see the list of options in the Standard format, move the insertion point to that field and press Enter. Sometimes the standard format lets you choose more than one option and sometimes it doesn't. That's determined by the database designer. If it allows more than one option, enter commas between your choices.

■ *Time/Date.* Enables you to enter time and date information. Enter dates in the form MM/DD/YY or MM/DD/YYYY. You also can enter Today or Yesterday. Enter times in the form HH:MM or HH:MM:SS. You can either append AM or PM to a time, or enter it in military (24-hour clock) format. For example, you could either enter 21:30 or 9:30 PM for the same result.

Note

Depending on specifications set forth by the database designer, the Time/Date field may or may not display the date and time as you entered it. For example, some fields only display dates, not time.

Spotting Available Pop-Up Instructions

Some document forms offer additional information in pop-up annotations. Pop-up annotations are hidden instructions normally associated with a block of text. When you hold down the left mouse button with the pointer anywhere on the text, Notes displays a pop-up window (see fig. 32.19). The Travel Authorization database is an example file that ships with Lotus Notes.

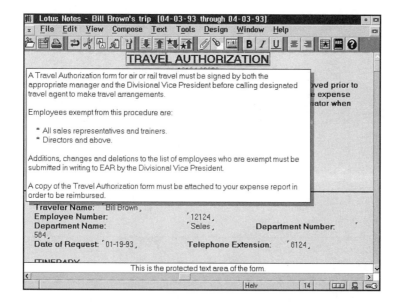

Fig. 32.19

If you open any document in the example Travel Authorization file, clicking and holding on Travel Authorization displays pop-up help for the form.

VI

Communicating

Most documents won't contain any pop-up help. When a document contains a pop-up annotation, you can usually spot it because the database designer typically identifies a pop-up annotation with a green border around the associated area.

Using Buttons

Notes documents often contain buttons that perform various tasks. You probably already used the Address and Send buttons in Notes mail documents, and you'll encounter others as you use Notes.

When you click a button, you're telling Notes to run a macro that's associated with that button. A macro is a short set of instructions that's condensed into one step (such as the aforementioned button). For example, when you click the Send button in a mail document, Notes processes a macro that checks to make sure that you addressed the memo properly and then issues the equivalent of a **M**ail, **S**end command.

The Insert Button dialog box reveals the actual macro code, which Notes lists in cryptic form, for the Send button (see fig. 32.20). For your sake, the database designer is responsible for determining the complex details of how the button works.

Fig. 32.20

To view the macro code associated with any button in a Notes document, hold down the Ctrl key and click the button.

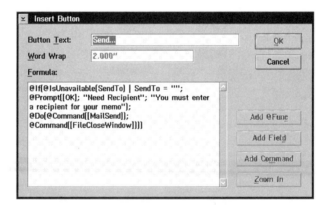

> **Caution**
>
> Be aware that the Notes macro language is reasonably powerful. While this is good for creating flexible and feature-rich database applications, it also means an unscrupulous individual could wreak havoc on the computer systems of the unwary.

Figure 32.21 shows a Notes mail memo with a macro button ClickMe! in the body of the document. Such a message should arouse suspicion if it comes from someone you don't know. There aren't many reasons for mailing a button-based macro to another person, and you should realize that there's no telling what the button might do if you click it. It could erase your hard disk, launch a virus, or even send a nasty memo to your boss from you!

If you receive a suspicious macro button, examine it by holding down the Ctrl key and clicking it. If you're not familiar with Notes macros, have a Notes expert examine the suspicious button before you use it. If you do click a button and it seems to take a long time to run, immediately press Ctrl+Break, which aborts most Notes macros. Then have the resident Notes expert take a look at the suspicious button to make sure it's harmless.

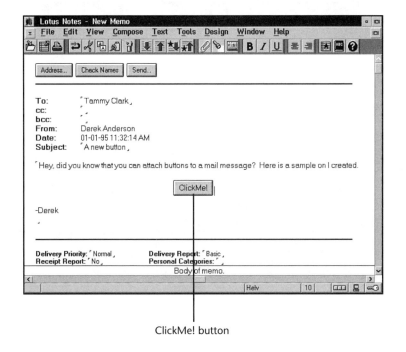

Fig. 32.21
You can send and receive macro buttons such as the ClickMe! button pictured. But be wary of macro buttons you receive from users you don't know; there's no telling what the button might do if you click it.

ClickMe! button

VI

Communicating

Note

Save suspicious mail documents until there's an opportunity to examine their button macros. If a button turns out to be malevolent, the mail document contains the name of the sender and that's a good start toward further investigation.

Creating DocLinks

Fortunately, most Notes macro buttons are beneficial and don't contain any mischievous code. You often see a DocLink, which is another handy graph icon used in documents. DocLinks are references to other Notes documents. When you double-click a DocLink, Notes opens the linked-to document even if the document is in a different view or a different database. Of course, you must have the proper access privileges to the database containing the linked-to document, and that database must be on a Notes server in your network.

To see information on the linked-to document before opening it, point the mouse at the DocLink and press and hold down the left mouse button. Notes displays a pop-up annotation on the DocLink as shown in figure 32.22.

Fig. 32.22

Hold down the left mouse button over any DocLink to see a pop-up annotation that identifies the linked-to document.

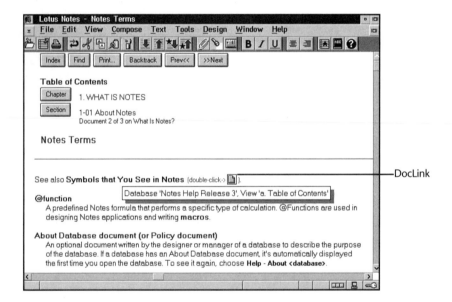

DocLink

You can add your own DocLinks to any rich text field you edit. DocLinks are a convenient way to reference text in other documents and other databases. To add a DocLink, follow these steps:

1. Open the document you want to link, or select it in a view.

2. Choose Edit, **M**ake DocLink; or click the Edit Make DocLink icon, to place a DocLink on the Windows Clipboard.

3. With the DocLink on the Clipboard, place the insertion point where you want the DocLink to appear in the rich text field of the target document, and then choose **E**dit, **P**aste.

Occasionally, Notes won't be able to open a linked-to document. Usually it's because a user has deleted the document, deleted the view containing the document when first linked, or deleted the entire database that contained the document.

Notes tells you whether you don't have the proper access level to view the linked-to document.

Troubleshooting

Notes says it can't find a critical database, but I can't believe that anyone would have deleted such an important file.

Check with your Notes administrator. Someone may have moved the database to another server.

A form in a particular database won't let me enter information in any fields below a horizontal line in the document.

The horizontal line shows the start of a restricted section. The database manager can set separate access levels for special sections of documents. This lets designers and managers create applications in which one set of users creates one part of each document and another set of users (typically managers) edits another part of each document. If you feel you should have access to the fields in the restricted section, check with the database manager.

From Here...

This chapter introduced you to the basics of Lotus Notes. There's still a lot to learn about the product. Review the following chapters to learn more about Notes and how you can use Notes with SmartSuite applications:

- Chapter 33, "Managing Information with Notes," covers how to find information in Notes databases.

- Chapter 34, "Using Notes with SmartSuite Applications," covers using Lotus's field-exchange technology with Notes and SmartSuite programs.

VI

Communicating

Chapter 33

Managing Information with Notes

by Derek S. Anderson

Notes is great for sharing and routing documents through a computer network. It also provides tools for organizing and finding documents or information you need in one or more Notes databases. For some end users, Notes' Full Text search capability is its most useful feature. Understanding how to use Notes to organize and find the information you want is vital, especially if you want to integrate Notes with any of the SmartSuite applications.

In this chapter, you learn how to:

- Index Notes databases

- Search for information

- Minimize the size of indexes

- Perform advanced queries

- Add custom views

Searching for Information

There are two ways to search for words or phrases in a Notes database: Find and Full Text search. You can use the Find dialog box to search for words or phrases in any Notes database. To perform a Full Text search, the database must first be indexed. While a Full Text search is faster and offers many more options, the Find dialog box suffices for most simple searches.

To use Find, open the non-indexed database in question and start in a view that you're sure contains the document. To open the dialog box, choose **E**dit, **F**ind (see fig. 33.1).

Fig. 33.1

Choose Edit, Find to search for a word or phrase in any Notes database.

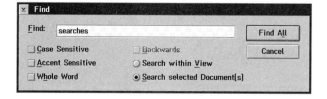

The Find dialog box lets you find all documents containing a word or phrase in the current view. To search more than one view, you must search each view separately. Most often, you should select the view that shows all database documents, if there is one.

When you click Find A**ll**, Notes searches all documents according to the options you set in the Find dialog box, and selects those documents that contain the word or phrase. If you preselect a number of documents before searching with Find, Notes searches only those documents.

By default, Notes ignores case. So, for example, given the dialog box shown earlier in figure 33.1, Notes would find all documents containing *Searches*, *SEARCHES*, *searches*, or any other upper- and lowercase combination of that word. If you want Notes to find only the word as typed, choose the **C**ase Sensitive checkbox.

The **A**ccent Sensitive checkbox tells Notes to search only for occurrences of the word or phrase that has the appropriate accented (ANSI) characters. For example, if you want to search for the word résumé, leaving this box unchecked finds documents containing both résumé and resume. With the box checked, Notes finds only those documents containing résumé.

Choose the W**h**ole Word checkbox if you want Notes to search only for occurrences of a word with white space around it. For example, use this option if you want to find documents that contain "Jack" while ignoring documents that contain only "Jackie." With W**h**ole Word unchecked, Notes would select documents containing either or both.

Notes normally searches forward from the currently highlighted document. If you want to search backward, toward the top of the view, choose the **B**ackwards checkbox.

If you want Notes to search through all the document titles in a view without searching the actual contents of the documents, click the Search within **V**iew button. The **S**earch Selected Document(s) button results in a search of both titles and contents of all selected (checkmarked) documents. If no documents are selected, Notes searches through all documents in the view under this option.

Database Indexes

If you want better performance or want to conduct more advanced queries, you must index the Notes database. Creating an index lets you use Full Text search and create queries that search one or more databases for words, phrases, or complex combinations of text, wild cards, logical operators, and more.

If you have at least Designer-level access, you can index any local Notes database or Server database. If you want a database indexed that you don't have Designer-level access to, check with your Notes administrator or that database's manager.

If you have the appropriate access, you can create an index by choosing File, **F**ull Text Search, **C**reate Index. When you do this, Notes displays the Full Text Create Index dialog box shown in figure 33.2.

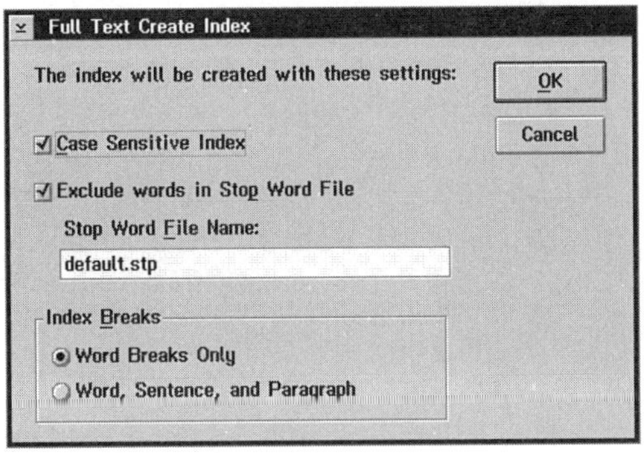

Fig. 33.2
When creating most indexes, use the options shown here. Other option combinations result in larger indexes, and may offer more options than you need.

Figure 33.2 shows the best choice of options for most situations. The Exclude Words in Sto**p** Word File option excludes all words contained in the specified Stop Word file (default.stp) from the resulting index. The Stop Word file is simply an ASCII-text file that contains a list of very common words (for example, a, all, after, also, an, and, and so on) that you'd probably never want to use in a query. By specifically excluding common words from an index, you can reduce the size of the index files by as much as 20 percent. Of course, by choosing this option, you can't search for any words contained in the Stop Word file. Using a Stop Word file is usually a good idea and, if needed, you can edit DEFAULT.STP or create and select your own similar file.

If you want to do Full Text searches and differentiate words on the basis of case, you must choose **C**ase Sensitive Index. This option typically increases the size of the resulting index anywhere from 5 to 10 percent. While case-sensitivity lets you increase the precision of your searches, it adds some complexity to the querying process. For example, you must use the EXACTCASE operator when doing a case-sensitive search. For general purposes, don't use this option.

The Index **B**reaks options affect your ability to do proximity searches. If you want to search for words based on how close together they are, you must choose Word, Sentence, and Paragraph. Of course, this increases the size of the index (by about 50 percent) since it adds information into the index about how close words are to one another. With this option you can use the proximity operators NEAR, SENTENCE, and PARAGRAPH on the resulting index.

Once your options are set, choose OK or press Enter to create the Full Text index. Be forewarned that indexing a large Notes database can take a long time. A 20 M database might take an hour or more to index, even on a fast machine. The resulting index is typically anywhere from 20 to 50 percent of the size of the original database file.

When you create a Full Text index, Notes adds a subdirectory to the directory containing the original database. Notes creates the index files in this subdirectory, which has an FT extension. For example, if you Full Text index the help file, C:\NOTES\HELP.NSF, Notes creates a subdirectory named C:\NOTES\HELP.FT\. The files in this subdirectory comprise the index for the Notes help file.

Index files typically contain all text contained in Text, Number, Time, Keywords, and Rich Text fields. Notes also indexes the text visible in linked and embedded objects if the display format for these objects is either Text or Rich Text. Even hidden and privileged text ends up in the index along with Author Names, Names, Reader, and all computed fields.

Notes won't, however, index words in the Stop Word file, nor does it index any computed-for-display fields.

Search Bar Basics

Notes makes a search bar available for every indexed database in your workspace. If the search bar isn't visible for an indexed database, choose **V**iew, Show Search Ba**r**. Initially, the search bar appears as shown at the top of figure 33.3.

Search bar

Fig. 33.3

To search for a word or phrase, enter the query in the text box of the search bar and either click the Search button or press Enter.

Usually, you need only enter a query in the text box and click the Search button. Clicking the Search button (or pressing Enter) processes the query you enter in the text box. Notes searches the index for matches to your query and then displays all matching documents in the current view.

The Clear button clears the text box, displays all documents appropriate for the current view, and clears the search options. Basically, the Clear button resets all search options and query results so you can start over.

Search Options

When you click the Options button, Notes displays the Search Options dialog box as shown in figure 33.4. Your first option is to turn Include Word Variants (**St**emming) off. When on (the default), Notes searches for variations on the words in your query. For example, if you search for the word jump, Notes also finds jumping, jumper, and jumped. Had you turned the option off, Notes would have only found occurrences of the exact word, jump.

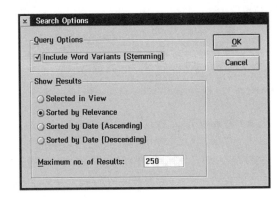

Fig. 33.4

The Search Options dialog box lets you specify how Notes should conduct a query and how it should display the query results.

VI

Communicating

The rest of this dialog box lets you specify how you want Notes to display the results of the query. By default, Notes displays all matching documents, Sorted by Relevance, in the current view. Notes indicates how well each document matches the criteria with varying shades of gray in the left margin as shown in figure 33.5 once the search is performed. The darker the shade, the higher the density of matches in the document. Notes determines this density by dividing the number of matches in the document by the number of indexed words.

Fig. 33.5
When Notes displays query results listed by relevance, it uses shades of gray in the left margin to rate documents by the "density" of the match.

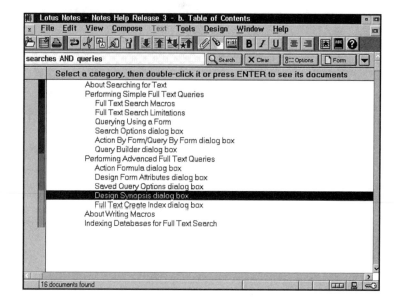

If you prefer, you can click one of the other listing options:

- *Selected in View.* Selects all matching documents the same way **E**dit, **F**ind does on non-indexed databases.

- *Sorted by Date (either ascending or descending).* Displays documents in date-sorted order, with the newest (last modified) document appearing at the top when you choose descending order.

The **M**aximum No. of Results box lets you set an upper limit on the number of documents Notes can list as matching a query. This number can prevent Notes from searching too long when a query isn't specific enough to return a small subset of documents.

The Form Button

Notes also lets you conduct a query by form from the search bar. With query by form, you can use a Notes form to create a query. You start by clicking the

Form button on the search bar and selecting from the list of available forms as shown in figure 33.6.

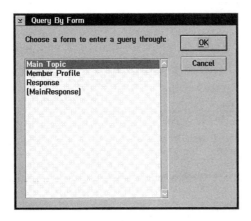

Fig. 33.6
Select a form for the query-by-form search after clicking the Form button on the Search bar. The dialog box displays the forms available in the standard Notes-mail file.

Notes displays the selected form for you to build a query. Figure 33.7 shows how you might build a query in the Memo form of the Notes-mail database. When you enter words or phrases in more than one field, Notes searches for documents where both fields meet the criteria. In other words, Notes builds a query in the form of a logical AND. So, for the example shown in figure 33.7, Notes finds all documents where the SendTo field contains "Philip Melund" AND the Body field contains the phrase "database."

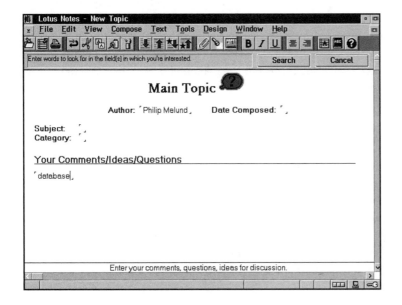

Fig. 33.7
When you press the Search button for this query-by-form, Notes creates and processes the query ([SendTo] CONTAINS (Philip Melund)) AND ([Body] CONTAINS (database)).

VI

Communicating

You can type any valid query into a field. For example, you could type Daniel OR Jennifer in the SendTo field to find all documents sent to anyone named either Daniel or Jennifer. You can enter multiple items separated by commas and use wild cards, logical operators, proximity operators, field operators, the EXACTCASE operator, and the TERMWEIGHT operator as appropriate. Using query by form makes it relatively easy to construct complex queries that can really narrow your search in large databases.

The Expanded Search Bar

When you click the down-arrow icon at the right side of the search bar, Notes displays an expanded search bar as shown in figure 33.8. Of all the additional options the expanded search bar offers, the most useful is the Refine button (located directly below the Search button).

Fig. 33.8

The expanded search bar gives you more querying options. Click the up-arrow icon in the upper-right corner of the search bar to return the search bar to its normal display.

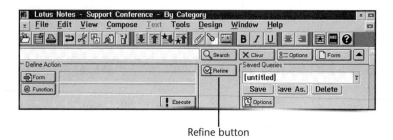

Refine button

You can use the Refine button to narrow your search for documents. For example, you could start the query by typing "Lotus" in the text box and clicking the Search button. Suppose this query lists two hundred matching documents. To narrow the search, you could type "Notes" in the text box and then click the Refine button in the expanded search bar. The new search criterion ("Notes") is applied only to the documents already returned by the previous query ("Lotus"). Had you instead clicked the Refine button, Notes would have searched for the word "Notes" in all the database's documents rather than just in the documents already found by the previous query.

The buttons in the Saved Queries section offer ways to save queries for later use. Once you've created a query, you need only click the Save button in the expanded search bar to display the Saved Query As dialog box. Enter a description for the current query to save it for future use. Once saved, you can select any of your saved queries from a second dialog box that appears when you choose Save As in the Saved Queries section. Notes displays all the saved queries in alphabetical order as shown in figure 33.9.

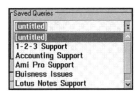

Fig. 33.9
You can locate specific queries easily because Notes displays your list of saved queries in alphabetical order.

Most often, you run a saved query by selecting it from the menu that appears when you choose Save As from the Saved Queries section. When you select a query, Notes enters the saved query's text in the search text box of the search bar. Click the Search (or Refine) button to run the query.

If you want to run a specific query automatically, click the Options button to display the Saved Query Options dialog box as shown in figure 33.10. Click the **E**nable Background Execution of Query checkbox to set the selected query to run automatically, in the background, at some specific time interval. Click the pop-up **F**requency list to specify how often Notes should run the query. The options are Hourly, Daily, Weekly, or Never. Select where you want Notes to run the query from the **S**erver/Workstation on Which To Run Query list. Finally, click the **S**tore Query Highlights with Document check box if you want Notes to store query highlights (word or phrase matches to the query) with matched documents. If you decide to store the query highlights, Notes displays the query highlights whenever you open the document. Choose **O**K (or press Enter) to set the options or Cancel to leave them as they were.

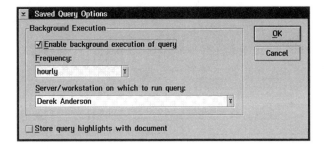

Fig. 33.10
Use the options in the Saved Query Options dialog box to run a saved query periodically in the background.

VI

To save a query in a database, you must have at least Designer-level access. Since you automatically have Manager status for all local databases, you can save a query for any database on your own hard disk.

Communicating

Multi-Database Searches

Notes lets you search for documents in more than one indexed database at a time. To search in more than one database, select multiple database icons from the Notes workspace by holding down the Shift key while clicking each icon. Then choose **E**dit, **F**ind. You can also open all the databases by double-clicking the last database icon while still holding down the Shift key. Then you can choose **V**iew, Show Search Ba**r** to display the search bar.

Either technique opens multiple databases into a special collapsed view. From this view, you can create and execute queries just as you would for a single database.

When you move the selection bar to a different database name, Notes uses the current view of that database to format the column titles at the top of the screen. You can expand the view of any of the databases by clicking the arrow in the left margin, by double-clicking the database's name, or by pressing Enter when the selection bar is on the name of the database. Figure 33.11 shows the Notes Help database expanded in the view to show the matching documents.

You can search multiple databases just as you would a single database. The primary difference is that you can't use the expanded search bar for querying multiple databases.

Fig. 33.11

You can expand the view of any database listed in the multi-database view to see the matching documents returned by the multi-database search.

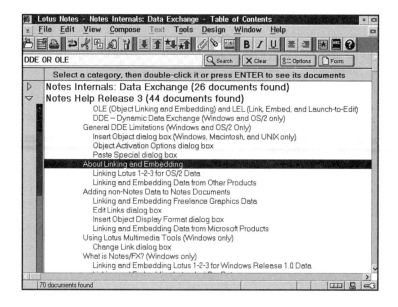

Using Sophisticated Queries To Search for Information

Most of the time, you can keep search queries fairly simple. For example, you can search for a name, like Anderson. But sometimes such simple searches just don't cut it. When you need to narrow or broaden a query, you can use selection operators and wild cards to create complex searches.

The AND operator sets Notes to select documents that contain the criteria on both sides of the operator. For example, the query Derek AND Sammy selects all documents containing both Derek and Sammy, and ignores documents that contain only one or the other of these criteria. You can abbreviate the AND operator with the ampersand (&). So Derek & Sammy is equivalent to Derek AND Sammy.

The OR operator sets Notes to find documents that contain either of two criteria. For example, the query Derek OR Sammy selects all documents containing either Derek or Sammy (or both). You can abbreviate the OR operator with a vertical bar (|). So Derek | Sammy is equivalent to Derek OR Sammy.

The ACCRUE operator is similar to OR. The difference is that the relevance ranking increases when a document contains more than one of the criteria words. This is not the case with OR. The abbreviation for ACCRUE is the comma (,) and that's the way you'll use it most often. For example, the query Derek ACCRUE Sammy ACCRUE Tammy is equivalent to Derek, Sammy, Tammy. Using either results in a list where a document with one incidence of Derek and one of Sammy would rank higher than one containing three occurrences of Derek.

The NOT operator sets Notes to find documents that don't contain the criteria. For example, NOT Anderson selects all documents that do not contain the word Anderson. The abbreviation for NOT is the exclamation point (!). So !Anderson and NOT Anderson are equivalent.

The EXACTCASE operator sets Notes to find documents containing words or phrases that match the criteria exactly. For example, EXACTCASE Anderson would find Anderson but not ANDERSON. This function only works if you've indexed a database to be case-sensitive.

Using Wild Cards

Notes lets you use standard, DOS-style wild cards in queries. You can use a question mark to stand in for any single character. For example, "T?m" finds "Tim," "Tom," and "Tum" but not "Team."

VI

Communicating

For a multi-character wild card, use the asterisk (*). For example, "ont*" finds "Ontario" and "ontology," while "*ont" finds both "Vermont" and "font."

Using Proximity Operators

If you indexed the current database with the Word, Sentence, and Paragraph option, you can use proximity operators in your query. The proximity operators are NEAR, SENTENCE, and PARAGRAPH.

The NEAR operator finds documents containing both criteria, ranking the documents according to how close they are to one another. For example, Nicholas NEAR Cynthia finds all documents that contain both Nicholas and Cynthia and displays the matching documents sorted by how close together these words appear to each other.

The SENTENCE operator finds all documents where two words can be found in the same sentence. For example, Delonas SENTENCE Casner finds all documents where the words Delonas and Casner appear in the same sentence.

The PARAGRAPH operator works the same way SENTENCE does. The difference is that Notes expands the proximity from occurrences in the same sentence to occurrences in the same paragraph. So PARAGRAPH is less restrictive and tends to find more matching documents.

Using the TERMWEIGHT Operator

The TERMWEIGHT operator lets you adjust the way Notes relevance ranks matching documents in a query. For example, TERMWEIGHT 80 Derek OR TERMWEIGHT 20 Fred finds all documents containing either Derek or Fred and ranks those that contain Derek much higher than those containing Fred.

Use the TERMWEIGHT operator to apply something like a weighted average to your queries. You can use any integer, from 0 to 100 inclusive, to weight the ranking for each expression in a complex query.

> **Note**
>
> The TERMWEIGHT operator allows you to control the content of your answer set more closely than if you simply asked for a normal contains query. For instance, if you wanted to see all documents relating to swimming in the ocean to write a report about swimming, you are going to be more interested in the swimming references than the ocean ones. In this way you can eliminate most of the articles that discuss mainly the ocean and happen to mention a shark "swimming."

Using Parentheses To Clarify What You Want To Find

The best way to ensure that operators in a complex query execute the way you expect is to enclose them in parentheses. For example, "FIELD Subject CONTAINS (Notes OR ViP)" finds all documents where the Subject field contains either "Notes" or "ViP." By contrast, "(FIELD Subject CONTAINS Notes) OR ViP" finds all documents that contain "ViP" anywhere in the document or that have "Notes" in the Subject field. Using parentheses clarifies what you want Notes to find.

For those of you with a programming background, you might be interested in the order of precedence for the query operators. Notes evaluates operators in the following order:

- NOT

- AND

- ACCRUE

- OR

Searching for a Phrase

To search for a phrase instead of a word, enclose the phrase in quotation marks. This is especially important when the phrase contains a word that Notes would interpret as an operator. For example, suppose you want to find documents that contain the string "DDE and OLE." You can't simply use DDE and OLE as your query without any quotation marks.

Notes interprets the "and" in that query as the logical operator AND. So to find the literal string "DDE and OLE" you must use the query shown in the search text box in figure 33.12.

Searching for Symbols

Notes doesn't index most non-alphanumeric symbols. So you can't typically search for words containing symbols like the dollar sign ($). Notes simply ignores such characters when searching.

One exception is the hyphen. If you include a hyphen in a query, Notes treats it almost like a special wild character. For example, the query "anti-aircraft" finds "anti-aircraft," "anti aircraft," and "antiaircraft."

Notes also handles periods (.), ampersands (&), colons (:), and backslashes (\), but only when they don't occur at the beginning or end of a word. For example, Notes would not index the backslash in "NOTES\" but it would index the backslash in "C:\NOTES."

VI

Communicating

Fig. 33.12
This query finds all documents containing the exact literal string, "DDE and OLE."

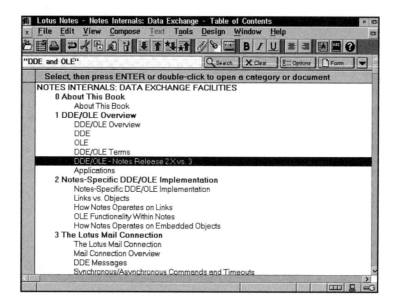

Notes treats the @ symbol similarly, but only indexes it when it appears at the beginning of a word (not the end). So Notes indexes "@BINOMIAL" separately from "BINOMIAL."

Searching for Numbers and Dates

Notes doesn't normally let you search for numbers in the Text or Rich Text fields of a database. The default Stop Word file (DEFAULT.STP) explicitly excludes numbers from an index. If you want to be able to search for numeric text in a database, don't index it using the DEFAULT.STP file or change the DEFAULT.STP file so that it doesn't contain the line [0-9]+.

Normally, though, you'll only want to search for numbers in numeric fields. You can leave the DEFAULT.STP file as is because Notes includes these in its index. You search for values in number fields using the FIELD operator with a comparative operator. For example, the query "FIELD Balance >1000" finds all documents where the Balance field contains a value greater than 1,000.

You can use the same comparative operators on Time fields or you can use the BEFORE or AFTER operators.

Troubleshooting

I'm used to doing plain-text searches on non-indexed databases and I often use the Search within View and Search Selected Documents options. Unfortunately, these options aren't available in the Full Text search bar.

Hold down the Shift key and choose **E**dit, **F**ind to display the simple Edit Find dialog box rather than the Full Text search dialog box, even on indexed databases.

I was searching a database for a document containing the value $1500 in a Number field. The query found no documents even though documents containing this value exist.

You must search for the value using the query "1500" instead of "$1500." Notes doesn't recognize the "$" character for numeric queries.

I entered a valid query to search a large database and Notes responded with the message `Query is not understandable.`

If the query results in too many matching documents, Notes may be unable to keep track of all the matches. Refine the query so that Notes matches fewer documents. One way to do that is to query by form. Another is to use fewer generic wild card combinations in your query text.

Adding Custom Views

Views in Notes are like tables of contents. They list some or all of the documents in a Notes database based on the contents of one or more fields in those documents. Most database designers provide several useful shared views that everyone with access to the database can use. While these shared views may meet all your needs, there may be some large databases that you'd like to organize differently. If you have at least Reader-level access to the database, you can create your own private views to organize the database any way you like.

Creating a private view is essentially a way to filter information. Properly applied, such information filtering is one of the most powerful and important features of Lotus Notes for the average user.

Before you can create a private view you have to decide what you want the view to do and how you want it to appear. Once you know what you want a view to do, deciding how you want the view to display documents should be fairly straightforward. Most often, you simply want something similar to an existing view but perhaps more restrictive. For example, you might want a particular view to display only those documents that mention the name of your department or perhaps only those that mention you specifically.

Copying an Existing View

To make a copy of an existing view, open the Design Views dialog box by choosing **D**esign, **V**iews.

To create a copy of an existing view, highlight the existing view and choose the New **C**opy button in the Design Views dialog box. That creates an un-named copy of the selected view and then opens it in design mode as shown in figure 33.13.

Fig. 33.13
Opening the selected view in design mode.

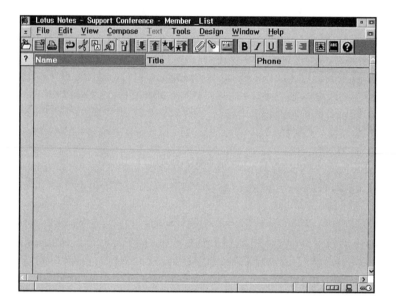

When you're in design mode, the **D**esign menu changes to include five new commands. You can use these commands to change view attributes, define document selection criteria, specify which forms to use in the view, or add and define new columns.

One way to name the new view is to choose **D**esign, View **A**ttributes and enter a name as shown in figure 33.14. If you have Designer or higher access to the database, you must also specify the type of view as **P**rivate.

> **Caution**
>
> Private views can greatly increase the size of your DESKTOP.DSK file and typically take longer to load.

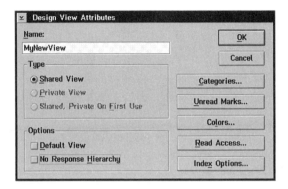

Fig. 33.14
The Design View Attributes dialog box lets you name the view and set several view attributes.

The Design View Attributes dialog box also lets you set numerous other characteristics of the view. You can click the **C**ategories button to specify whether the view should initially display categories in the view as expanded or collapsed. The **U**nread Marks button lets you specify whether the view displays unread marks next to new documents. You can use the Co**l**ors button to change the view's color scheme. Finally, the Inde**x** Options button lets you specify how frequently Notes should update the index for the view. (Each Notes view is itself an index and Notes needs to update that index periodically to keep the view up to date.)

Understanding View Formulas

Sometimes you may only wish to create a private view to change the basic attributes of another view. For example, you might not like the colors or may want the categories to be initially expanded or collapsed.

More often, you'll want to change the way the view selects documents or the kind of information it displays about those documents. To do that, you need to know something about Notes formulas.

Notes uses formulas to do all kinds of things. Notes database designers use formulas in forms, views, and macros. In views, designers often use formulas in columns and to select the documents that the view displays.

VI

Communicating

Tip
To learn more about the @functions available in Notes, choose Help, @Functions.

Formulas consist of any of the following components:

- @functions

- Keywords

- Commands

- Numbers

- Dates and times

- Operators

- Fields

- Text strings

You combine these components to create a formulaic statement. If you need more than one statement in a large formula, you must separate the statements with semicolons (;).

Figure 33.15 shows an example of a column formula in the Design Column Definition dialog box for the first column of the view shown previously in figure 33.13. To display this dialog box for any column, double-click the column's header, or with the column selected, choose **D**esign, Column **D**efinition.

Fig. 33.15
Double-click any column header to modify the column's definition.

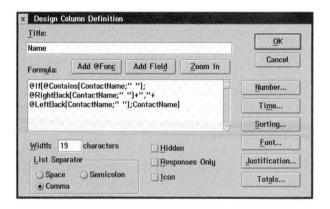

The formula for the column is fairly complex, though some column formulas can get far more sophisticated. This one takes the name of a contact, reverses it, and adds a comma between the last and the first name. So "Tom Smith" becomes "Smith, Tom."

Sometimes column formulas are much simpler. A column formula might be the name of a document field, as is the case with the rest of the columns in this example view. For example, the column formula for the Company column is simply CompanyName, which is the name of the field in the database documents that hold the name of each contact's company. When you want to add a field to a column formula, click the Add Field button to display a list of all available fields defined in the current database.

Adding Selection Formulas

To specify what documents a view should include, choose **D**esign, **S**election Formula. Notes opens the Design Selection Formula dialog box as shown in figure 33.16. From here, you can change the selection formula as necessary.

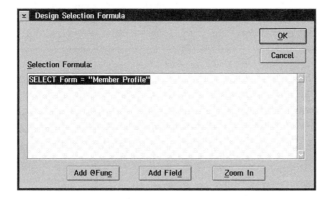

Fig. 33.16
You can change the selection formula in a private view to suit your needs.

Selection formulas must always start with the keyword SELECT. After that, you can use a combination of field names, Notes @functions, and operators to define a selection criterion. Typically, you'll create a formula that selects based on the contents of some field. For example, you might want to select documents in a project document that are past due. The formula might be:

    SELECT ResponseDue <= @NOW

Another common technique is to search for your name in a specific field. Suppose, for example, you wanted to see all documents where you were mentioned in a field named Responsible. You could create the following selection formula:

    SELECT @Contains(Responsible; @UserName)

Tip
To learn more about the @functions available in Notes, choose Help, @Functions.

VI

Communicating

Troubleshooting

How do I get rid of a private view?

To delete a private view, choose **D**esign, **V**iews, select the private view you want to delete, and then choose the Clear button.

Our Notes administrator has moved a database on the server and that database now has a different name. When I tried to open the database from my worksheet, I got the message Server not responding. I don't want to delete the current icon and start over because I'll lose all my private views.

To retain your private views, don't delete the database icon from your worksheet. Instead, highlight the icon and choose **F**ile, **D**atabase, Use Different **S**erver. Enter the name of the new server in the resulting dialog box. If Notes tells you the old server is not responding, click Cancel. Notes will then say that your unread marks won't be exchanged. Choose Yes.

From Here...

Chapters 31, 32, and 33 introduced you to the basics of using Lotus Notes. There is a lot more to learn about Notes and also about how to get Notes to work together with other SmartSuite applications. For more about using Notes, read the documentation that came with your copy of the program. Also, browse the Notes help facility by choosing **H**elp, Table of Contents.

For more on using Notes with SmartSuite applications, refer to the following chapter:

- Chapter 34, "Using Notes with SmartSuite Applications," shows you how to integrate the power of your SmartSuite programs with the communication capabilities of Notes.

Chapter 34

Using Notes with SmartSuite Applications

by Robert L. Weberg

Groups within corporations can attain a lot of work productivity using Lotus Notes alone, by using discussion databases, exchanging information, and managing documents.

But Notes for OS/2 (and Notes for Windows) enables you to integrate data from other programs by importing, exporting and linking the information. Although Notes for Windows can run under OS/2, we will focus on the features of Notes for OS/2. Both versions essentially possess the same functionality when integrating with the SmartSuites (like importing, exporting, and DDE), except Notes for OS/2 isn't capable of using Object Linking and Embedding (OLE) and Notes F/X.

In this chapter, you learn to:

- Exchange data with other applications

- Link data files to Notes documents

- Use Notes with 1-2-3, Ami Pro, and Freelance Graphics

Sharing Information with Other Applications

Lotus Notes provides several ways to import information from other programs into Notes documents or views. Conversely, Notes data can be exported to other software programs and file formats.

In Notes, the **F**ile, **I**mport and **F**ile, **E**xport commands enable you to transfer information through a variety of standard file formats. Whether you want to exchange data with an OS/2, Windows, or DOS application or with your company's mainframe, you'll discover an easy way to do it.

Transferring data to or from Notes is performed from a view or from within a specific document. You use views to exchange tabular information between the Notes database and another application and you use documents when you only want to transfer data from a specific document. In most cases, you'll probably be importing or exporting large amounts or records and will need to work from a view.

Notes supports the following file formats when exporting or importing tabular data at the *view level*:

- 1-2-3 Worksheet (.WKS, .WK1, and .WK3 files)
- Structured Text (.LTR, .CGN, .STR, and others)
- Tabular Text (.TAB, .TXT, .PRN, and .RPT)
- Lotus Agenda (.STF)

When exporting or importing rich-text data at the *document level*, Notes supports the following file formats:

- MultiMate
- DisplayWrite DCA
- Lotus 1-2-3 (import only)
- Ami Professional
- Lotus Manuscript
- WordStar
- Microsoft Word (RTF)
- Structured Text (import only)
- Tabular Text (import only)
- ASCII text
- WordPerfect

Importing Structured-Text Files

Importing data from ASCII file reports is relatively painless, and with a little preparation and setup, Notes can offer quite a bit of flexibility. For example, if your Management Information Systems reporting department provides your group with a weekly report listing outstanding loans or new deals in ASCII file format (generally, mainframe downloads are in ASCII or tabular-text format), you can set up Notes to make importing the weekly report a simple matter.

By choosing **F**ile, **I**mport, you can select from four basic types of data files in the Import dialog box:

- Structured Text

- Tabular Text

- 1-2-3 Worksheet

- Agenda STF

If working with ASCII text files, you must select either the Structured Text or Tabular Text type. An example of a structured-text file is shown in figure 34.1. Structured-text is an ASCII text file that contains labels that identify each field. This file delimits records with a form-feed character (ASCII 12). Each line starts with a field name followed by a colon and then the contents of the field. Generally, records in structured-text files are separated by a form feed ASCII character or delimiter.

> **Note**
>
> The ASCII symbol for the form feed character (code 12) is the ankh (universal symbol for female).

When importing data into a view, the field labels in the structured-text file must correspond and match the names of the fields in the target form of the Notes database. Figure 34.1 shows an example structured-text file that imports data into PRODCAT.NSF, which is an example database installed with Notes. To import the file into the PRODCAT.NSF example database, follow these steps:

1. Choose **F**ile, **I**mport. The Import dialog box appears. Select the path and name of the structured-text file.

2. In the **T**ype of File listbox, choose Structured Text as the file type.

VI

Communicating

3. Choose I**m**port. Notes then displays the Structured Text Import dialog box.

4. Select the Approved Product form in the **U**se Form listbox and then choose Character-Code 12 as the record delimiter. Click OK and Notes imports the data into the fields in your Notes database.

Fig. 34.1

A structured-text file can be imported into a Notes view. The field labels in the structure-text file correspond to the fields in your Notes database.

Field names and data

Record delimiter

◀ See "Understanding Fields," p. 611

With the structured-text format, you can even bring multiple paragraphs of text into a rich-text field. Figure 34.2 shows how to transfer data from a mainframe mail program, a press release from a bulletin board or online service, a deal announcement from a company news release, or a research paper from the Internet, for import into a Notes database. Figure 34.3 shows the document created in Notes.

> **Note**
>
> The order of the labeled fields doesn't have to match the order of fields in your Notes form. Each record could have messages of various sizes. However, you must separate records with a specific delimiter, such as ASCII-code 12 (form-feed).

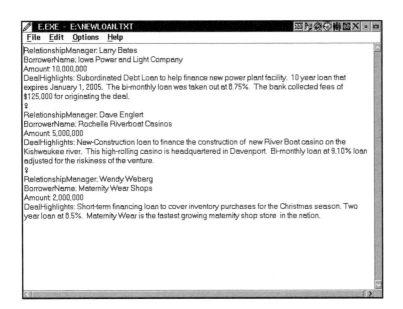

Fig. 34.2
In the
NEWLOAN.TXT
file, the
Relationship-
Manager,
Borrower-
Name,
Amount, and the
DealHighlights
field labels go into
a Notes form with
identical field
names.

Fig. 34.3
One of the
documents created
in Notes using the
data from
NEWLOAN.TXT.

Importing Tabular-Text Files

Reports from mainframe programs are also downloaded in the form of tabular-text files. Tabular-Text files contain data in distinct rows and columns
because records and fields are separated with equal amounts of tabs or spaces.
If you have a Notes database with a view that exactly matches the contents of
the tabular view, both in terms of field names and widths, you might be able
to import it directly into the view with little trouble. Generally, the safest
approach is to create a column-descriptor file to clarify the contents of the
tabular-text file for Notes, because the spaces and tabs in the Tabular-Text file
may not always be consistently equal.

Suppose you want a listing of new contacts from the corporate customer contact system. This file will be downloaded in tabular-text format (see fig. 34.4).

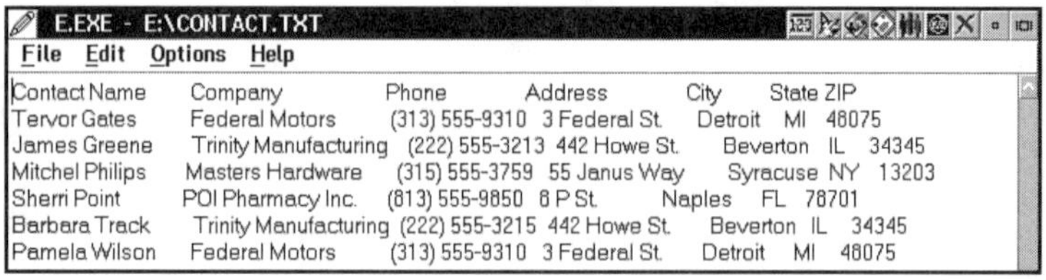

Fig. 34.4

The tabular-text file CONTACT.TXT shows records as rows and fields as columns.

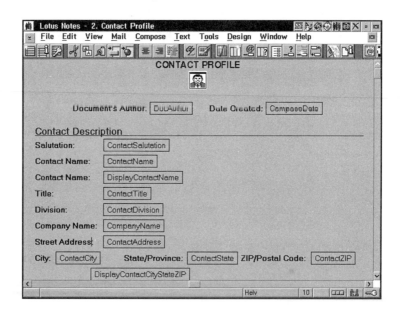

Now suppose you want to import this file into a Notes database you designed. The employee form you'll be importing into that database might contain the fields shown in figure 34.5.

Fig. 34.5

The target form can contain more fields than the tabular-text file, and the fields can be in a different order.

The tabular-text file doesn't provide data for all the target fields and also doesn't properly identify the contents of each field for Notes. The best way to handle such an import is to create a .COL file, as shown in figure 34.6. A .COL is used by Notes to specify how a tabular-text file is imported into a Notes database.

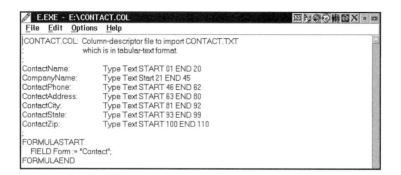

Fig. 34.6
The
CONTACT.COL
file tells Notes how
to interpret and
import the
contents of the
tabular-text file
shown in fig. 34.4
into documents
using the form
shown in fig. 34.5.

Examining the Contents of a .COL File

.COL files like the CONTACT.COL file shown in figure 34.6, can be created
with any ASCII-text editor, such as the OS/2 Editor. To start an editor session,
open an OS/2 window, type the letter E and hit enter. You can also double-
click the OS/2 Editor icon.

This .COL file starts with three comment lines. Comment lines in .COL files
start with a semicolon. Next, enter how each field (or column) will be imported into Notes.

Start each field line by naming the field (column) with the appropriate field
name in the Notes form. These names must match exactly! Enter a colon at
the end of the field name. Follow the colon with one or more space characters and then the keyword **TYPE**. After TYPE, enter one or more spaces and
identify the field type in the Notes form. The following are your keyword
choices:

Tip
Notes is very sensi-
tive to the syntax
of this section and
in .COL files, so
you might want to
stick to the format
presented here.

- Text

- Number

- DateTime

- Automatic

The **TYPE** expression is optional. If you omit it, Notes works as if you had
specified Type automatically and attempts to guess the field type based on
the contents of the field.

Next, you need to specify the character length of each field by describing the
starting and ending point. The fields are identifiable by their specific positions in each record. For example, the CompanyName field in the earlier

VI

Communicating

figure 34.4 starts at character offset 21 in every row. To identify the starting point of each field, you can type the keyword **START** followed by the character offset from the beginning of the line.

> **Note**
>
> The first character on any line is at offset 1, not 0.

To specify the width of the field, you must type the **END** keyword, enter one or more spaces, and then specify the position of the last character in the field.

If you use START, you have to determine the starting point of each field, so finding the ending point of the previous field is easy (one character less). Notes strips off any trailing space characters, so you don't have to bother counting back to find the exact end of a particular field for text fields.

Importing Comma-Delimited Files

Because comma-delimited files are so common in exchanging data within and between all corporations, you should know how to import these file types into a Notes database.

Suppose you want to import data from a comma-delimited file containing the following fields in each record:

- CustNum

- Name

- City

- Age

- Company

- Date

A typical comma-delimited file might be structured as shown in figure 34.7.

Each record is a single line in the file. So the major difference between the comma-delimited structure and that of the tabular-text file shown earlier in figure 34.4 is that the fields don't have a fixed width. You need to use the **UNTIL** keyword rather than START and END in the .COL file to identify the fields in each record.

The set of commands listed in a .COL file displayed in figure 34.8 would import such a comma-delimited file.

Fig. 34.7
CUST.TXT is an example of a comma-delimited ASCII file.

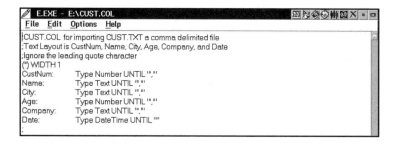

Fig. 34.8
This CUST.COL file is being used to import the comma-delimited data in CUST.TXT into a Notes database.

It's advisable when working or sharing your information with others to specify field types as a matter of clarity or documentation in describing any .COL file. Notes accepts a date-string in the form of MM/DD/YY as a date into a Time field, so you don't usually have to specify the field type. However, you may need to specify the field type in certain situations, for example, if you want Notes to read a string of code numbers, such as Customer Numbers or Zip Codes which often can begin with zero, as text.

Using Notes with 1-2-3

The simplest way you can get Notes to work together with other programs is by importing or exporting data using 1-2-3 as the intermediary file format. Since Notes can export and import data to and from a 1-2-3 worksheet, any program that can read or write a .WK* file can effectively export and import data with Notes.

Exporting Data from Notes to 1-2-3

To export data from Notes to a 1-2-3 worksheet file, you must first start from a view because you can't export to a worksheet file from within an open document. The view doesn't need to display all the fields available in the Notes database, but it must contain all the fields you want to export.

◀ See "Changing the View," p. 593

VI

Communicating

◄ See "Deleting Rows, Columns, and Sheets," p. 157

When you export a view, Notes creates a worksheet file where each field in the original view becomes a column, and every document becomes a row of data.

Suppose you want to export the airline financial information from the view shown in figure 34.9. This view can be found in the sample database AIRLINE.NSF installed with Notes.

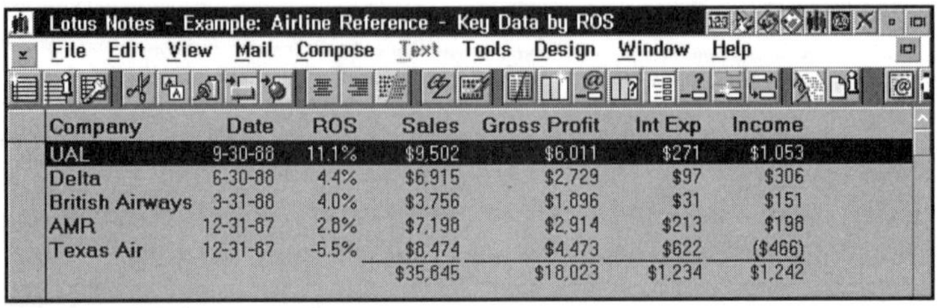

Fig. 34.9

The Key Data by ROS view in AIRLINE.NSF contains all the fields necessary to create the airline financial information for analysis in a 1-2-3 worksheet.

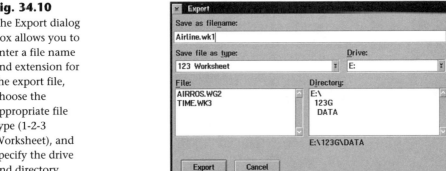

With the view selected, perform the following steps:

1. Choose **F**ile, **E**xport to open the Export dialog box (see fig. 34.10).

Fig. 34.10

The Export dialog box allows you to enter a file name and extension for the export file, choose the appropriate file type (1-2-3 Worksheet), and specify the drive and directory where you want to save the file.

2. Enter a filename in the Save as File**n**ame box, as shown in figure 34.10. Then choose 123 Worksheet in the Save File as **T**ype listbox.

> **Note**
>
> It's advisable to designate a .WK1 extension. You could designate a .WG2 extension used by 1-2-3 for OS/2 but you'll get a warning message when opening this saved file in 1-2-3 for OS/2 that states you won't be able to change the file extension when opening this exported file. After clicking OK to the message, the data appears in 1-2-3 for OS/2 but you have to rename the file even though the one appearing has a .WG2 extension.

4. Specify the **D**rive and **Di**rectory where you want to save the file, and click the E**x**port button. The Worksheet Export Settings dialog box appears as shown in figure 34.11.

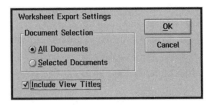

Fig. 34.11
The Worksheet Export Settings dialog box allows you to specify how you want to export the data.

5. Choose **A**ll Documents if you want to export all the documents appearing in the view, or choose **S**elected Documents if you preselected a subset of the ones available.

6. Check the **I**nclude View Titles box if you want to export the column titles along with the data.

7. Click OK and the view information is imported into 1-2-3 worksheet format. Open the exported file in 1-2-3 (see fig. 34.12).

	A	B	C	D	E	F	G	H	I
1	Company	Date	ROS	Sales	Gross Profit	Int Exp	Income		
2	UAL	9-30-88	11.1%	$9,502	$6,011	$271	$1,053		
3	Delta	6-30-88	4.4%	$6,915	$2,729	$97	$306		
4	British Airways	3-31-88	4.0%	$3,756	$1,896	$31	$151		
5	AMR	12-31-87	2.8%	$7,198	$2,914	$213	$198		
6	Texas Air	12-31-87	-5.5%	$8,474	$4,473	$622	($466)		
7				$35,845	$18,023	$1,234	$1,242		
8									

Fig. 34.12
The exported data from the Notes view appears in 1-2-3. The fields in the original view become columns and every document becomes a row in 1-2-3.

VI

Importing Data into Notes

Usually, the 1-2-3/Notes connection is often the best way to import data from other programs into Notes, because they can usually export to a 1-2-3 worksheet file format.

However, importing data from a worksheet file into Notes requires more preparation than does exporting from Notes. If you won't be importing all of a worksheet file, the first step is to assign a range name to the data range that you want to import.

Tip
Don't include any column headings in this range name; otherwise, Notes imports those column headings as a document.

Communicating

◄ See "Naming
Ranges," p. 163

◄ See "Adding
Custom
Views," p. 633

Open or switch to the Notes view into which you want to import the
worksheet. The columns in the receiving view shouldn't be categorized and
must exactly match the columns in the 1-2-3 worksheet. For example, if the
first column in the 1-2-3 worksheet's range contains a name, you should set
the first column of the view to contain those names.

In this example, you'll be importing some time sheet information into the
sample Client Tracking database installed with Notes. Figure 34.13 shows
time sheet information to be imported into a Notes view. If necessary, recreate the data shown and then perform the following steps:

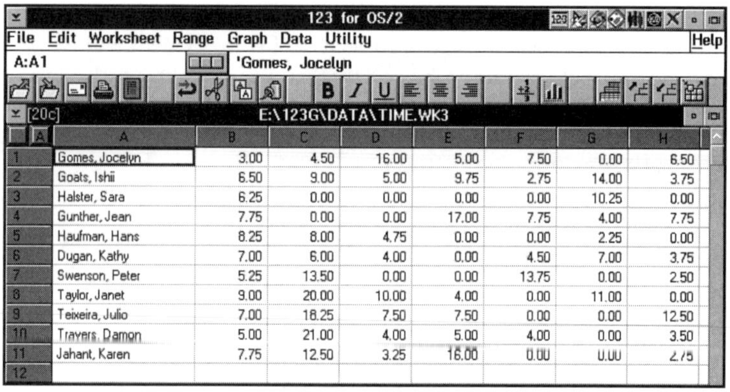

Fig. 34.13

The time sheet
information
contains individ-
uals and their
corresponding
hours worked.
This worksheet
data will be
imported into a
Notes view.

1. Switch to the "8. Weekly Summary" view in TRACKING.NSF because
   this is the view you'll be importing the data into. Choose **F**ile, **I**mport
   to display the Import dialog box (see fig. 34.14).

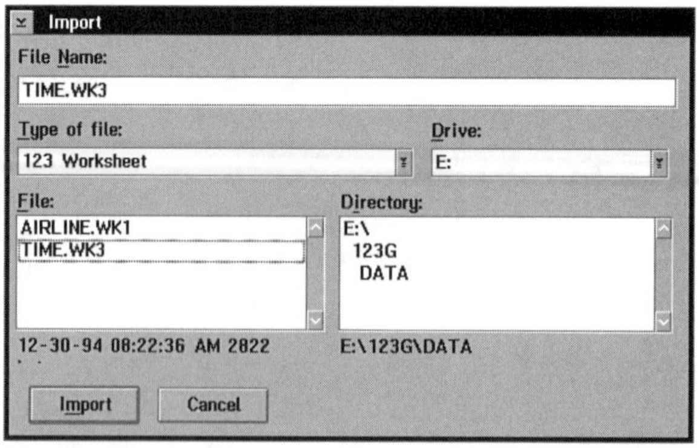

Fig. 34.14

The Import dialog
box is similar to
the Export dialog
box. Use it to
select the file type
and file to import.

2. Choose the file to import (TIME.WK3) and specify 123 Worksheet in
   the **T**ype of File listbox.

3. Click I**m**port to open the Worksheet Import Settings dialog box shown
in figure 34.15.

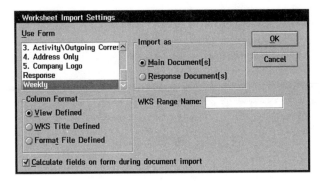

Fig. 34.15
In the Worksheet
Import Settings
dialog box, choose
the appropriate
Notes form to use
for importing the
data.

4. In the **U**se Form list, choose the form (Weekly) that will receive the
data. This form should be the one that contains the fields that most
closely match the data to import.

5. Next, select the desired column format. This example uses **V**iew Defined because you're mapping the columns in 1-2-3 to the Notes view.
The following describes when to use the different column format
options:

  ■ *View Defined.* Notes maps the data in the worksheet file to the
    columns in the current view.

  ■ *WKS Title Defined.* Notes creates database-form field names based
    on labels in the first row of the worksheet range.

  ■ *Format File Defined.* Choose Forma**t** File Defined (the most reliable
    import method) if you have created a separate column format
    descriptor (.COL) file.

6. In the Import As section select the desired option. Generally, you want
to import each worksheet row as a main document, so leave the **M**ain
Document(s) option chosen. However, if needed you can import the
1-2-3 data into **R**esponse Document(s).

VI

Communicating

7. If you're importing the whole worksheet, leave the WKS Range Name box blank. Otherwise, enter the name of the named range you want to import.

8. In this example, choose **C**alculate Fields on Form During Document Import because the Weekly form has a computed field called Total that totals the weekly billable hours for each person. Choosing this option enables Notes to calculate any computed fields on the form during the import procedure.

9. Choose OK or press Enter to import the data into the Notes database. The resulting documents are listed in the current view (see fig. 34.16) as unread documents (asterisks on left).

Fig. 34.16

The imported timesheet data appears in the 8. Weekly Summary view. You can open the documents to see that the Total field has been calculated.

Asterisks signify unread documents

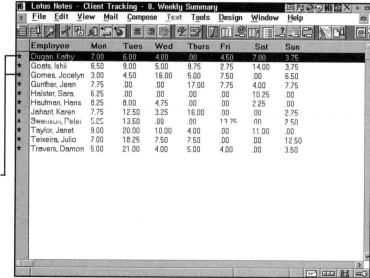

Employee	Mon	Tues	Wed	Thurs	Fri	Sat	Sun
Dugan, Kathy	7.00	6.00	4.00	.00	4.50	7.00	3.75
Goats, Ishii	6.50	9.00	5.00	9.75	2.75	14.00	3.75
Gomes, Jocelyn	3.00	4.50	16.00	5.00	7.50	.00	6.50
Gunther, Jean	7.75	.00	.00	17.00	7.75	4.00	7.75
Halster, Sara	6.25	.00	.00	.00	.00	10.25	.00
Haufman, Hans	8.25	8.00	4.75	.00	.00	2.25	.00
Jahant, Karen	7.75	12.50	3.25	16.00	.00	.00	2.75
Swensun, Peter	5.05	13.50	.00	.00	13.75	.00	2.50
Taylor, Janet	9.00	20.00	10.00	4.00	.00	11.00	.00
Teixeira, Julio	7.00	18.25	7.50	7.50	.00	.00	12.50
Travers, Damon	5.00	21.00	4.00	5.00	4.00	.00	3.50

Using Notes with Ami Pro

As with 1-2-3, you can get Ami Pro and Notes to work together in many ways. From importing or exporting data and sending attached files to DDE Linking, you can increase the effectiveness of a work group using Ami Pro with the groupware capabilities of Lotus Notes.

Exchanging data between Notes and Ami Pro is structurally and fundamentally different from the import and export process between Notes and 1-2-3. Notes exchanges data with 1-2-3 at the *view level* but exchanges data with Ami Pro at the *document level*.

For example, you can easily export any Notes document, such as the one shown in figure 34.17, to an Ami Pro .SAM file. To do so, follow these steps:

1. Open the desired Notes document or select it from the view.

2. Choose **F**ile, **E**xport to display the Export dialog box and then choose Ami Professional as the file type, enter a file name, then select a drive and directory to save the file to (see fig. 34.17).

3. Click E**x**port to export the Notes document to Ami Pro.

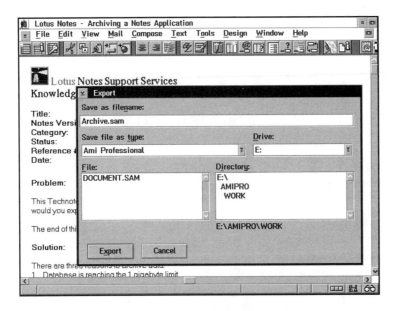

Fig. 34.17
You can choose any Notes document and export it to an Ami Pro .SAM file.

Figure 34.18 shows the results of an export to Ami Pro from Notes. In general, text and text formatting translates quite well. Bitmaps and pictures tend not to export well, if at all. Any file attachments are displayed as disconnected bitmaps because Notes doesn't export the actual attachments.

Note

Importing an Ami Pro file into Notes is very similar to Exporting data from Notes to Ami Pro, except that you choose **F**ile, **I**mport and select the desired Ami Pro file. However, you can import an Ami Pro document only into a rich-text field.

VI

Communicating

Fig. 34.18
Exporting does an excellent job with text and formatting, but results with pictures and bitmaps are mixed. Notice that the lighthouse bitmap shown in figure 34.18 is lost in the conversion.

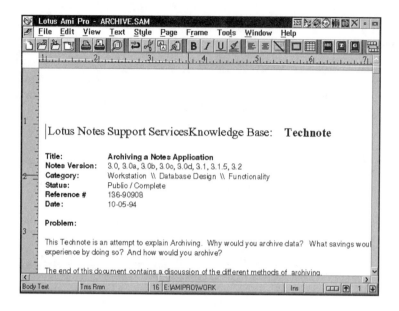

Using DDE To Bring in Data from Other Applications

◀ See "Understanding Fields," p. 611

Notes enables you to copy and paste data from other OS/2 applications and even Windows applications. You can paste text into any editable field. Just be sure to paste data that's appropriate to the field. You can't, for example, try to paste your name into a Date field. Notes rejects inappropriately pasted data the same way it sometimes rejects inappropriate entries you've typed when composing a document. Besides text, rich-text fields also enable you to paste Rich Text, Picture, and Bitmap data formats.

With Notes, you can link data from a server, such as 1-2-3 for OS/2, to the client, Notes. Both client and server must have built-in support for DDE.

Notes functions only as a DDE client, not as a DDE server. This means Notes documents can receive linked data, but can't provide linked data via DDE to other applications. To provide Notes data to other applications, either copy and paste the data using the OS/2 Clipboard, or export Notes documents and views to the required file format.

After pasting the selected data to the Clipboard, the DDE server application renders the data in one or more formats and you select the one you want to use. Then you paste the data as a linked object. If you select DDE Link, a DDE link is established between the Notes document and the source file.

Creating a DDE Link

How do you create DDE Links from the SmartSuite packages to Notes?

1. Select the data you want to link and choose **E**dit, **C**opy to copy the data to the Clipboard. The data selected can be paragraphs from an Ami Pro document, a range from a 1-2-3 spreadsheet, or a page from a Freelance presentation.

> **Caution**
>
> The file in the server application must be saved. Without a file name, Notes won't know where to create the link from.

2. Open the Notes document in edit mode by choosing **E**dit, **E**dit Document. You can also compose a new document to hold the DDE object.

3. Place the insertion point in the desired Rich Text field where you want to link to appear.

4. Choose **E**dit, Paste **S**pecial to display the Paste Special dialog box.

5. Select the DDE Link option as the data format and click OK to paste your data as a DDE Link. If the Link button isn't available, the source application might not be a valid DDE server.

Preparing To Link Data from Other Applications

You can easily link data from the SmartSuite applications to Notes. But before you can use DDE with 1-2-3 for OS/2 you must make some changes to your NOTES.INI file and make a configuration change within 1-2-3 for OS/2. If you're not familiar with editing the NOTES.INI file, ask your Notes administrator for assistance.

First, to create embedded links with 1-2-3 for OS/2, Notes needs to know where to find your 1-2-3 executable and data directories. To designate the location of 1-2-3 for OS/2 you need to modify the DDE line in your NOTES.INI file.

Edit this DDE line in your NOTES.INI file assuming 1-2-3 for OS/2 is your executable directory and 123G\DATA is your data directory.

    OS2DDE_LOTUS=OC,C:\123G to:

    OS2DDE_LOTUS=OC,C:\123G,C:\123G\DATA

> **Note**
>
> If you don't make this designation, you'll need to type the full path name for every link you create with 1-2-3 for OS/2. If you do make this change, Notes supplies the correct path for you.

Second, you need to tell 1-2-3 for OS/2 not to confirm when saving. This configuration change must be made within 1-2-3 for OS/2 to override its default Confirm option when saving. Otherwise, 1-2-3 for OS/2 won't be able to save any files that are linked to Notes. To do so perform the following steps:

1. Within 1-2-3 for OS/2, choose **U**tility, **U**ser Settings, **P**references. The User Settings Preference dialog box appears.

2. Change the **S**ave Options to either **R**eplace or **B**ackup instead of **C**onfirm and then click **U**pdate to save your changes.

> **Caution**
>
> Lotus 1-2-3 for OS/2 doesn't support Picture format for DDE links or embedded files.

Linking SmartSuite Data with Notes

You can only link data to a rich-text field, not to any other type of field in Notes. When you do, Notes maintains a link to the original data in the source application's data file. Thus whenever the original data changes, the link in Notes changes accordingly. This feature is handy whenever you want a Notes document to reflect the latest information in some other application.

Tip

To insert graphs from 1-2-3 for OS/2 into Notes, use the Clipboard (regular copy and paste) rather than DDE.

Suppose your financial research department keeps a number of industry analysis worksheets from past quarters, years, etc. A few of these worksheets such as the one shown in figure 34.20 analyze the key numbers for the airline industry. The goal is to keep these numbers and worksheets in a central location (like a Notes database) so users have quick and easy access. Simply paste linking the data allows you to keep the Notes documents current with any changes made to the source 1-2-3 worksheets used by the financial research department. Whenever those numbers change in the original 1-2-3 worksheets, the new information is available to all the Notes documents that contain the linked numbers. That way, no one has to open and edit all the documents with the new information. Notes handles the updates automatically any time someone goes to read the document.

To DDE link 1-2-3 worksheet data into a Notes document, follow these steps:

1. Highlight the desired range in 1-2-3 and choose **E**dit, **C**opy.

2. Switch to Notes and place your cursor in the Rich-Text field that will hold the data. The current document needs to be in Edit mode (**E**dit, **E**dit Document).

3. Choose **E**dit, Paste **S**pecial to open the Paste Special dialog box.

4. Choose the desired format and select **L**ink. The data is pasted into the document as a DDE Link (see fig. 34.19).

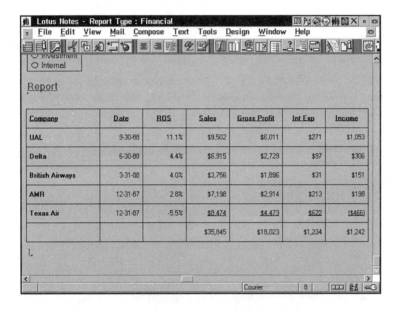

Fig. 34.19
Here, the airline industry information is linked to a 1-2-3 worksheet.

Whenever you open a document containing data links, Notes asks you whether you want to refresh the links. Select OK to close the message box. To update the linked data perform the following steps:

1. Choose **E**dit, Lin**k**s to display the Edit Link dialog box as shown in figure 34.20.

2. Select the desired link listed in the **L**inks box and click **U**pdate to update the link. You can also choose the options **A**ctivate, U**n**link, **D**eactivate, and **C**hange Link depending on the current link and the desired task you want to perform.

Fig. 34.20
The Edit Links dialog box allows you to update or modify the linked data. Updating the link retrieves the most current data from the source file.

You can also easily DDE link Ami Pro documents and Freelance presentations to a Notes document. Figures 34.21 and 34.22 show examples of linking to these SmartSuite applications.

Fig. 34.21
A Freelance Presentation is inserted and linked to a Notes document.

Tip
Double-click the linked DDE object to switch to the source file.

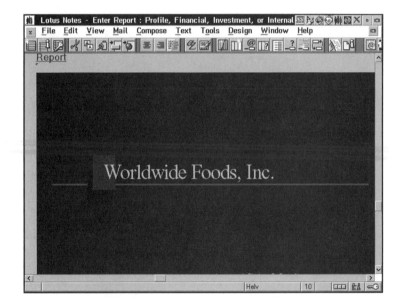

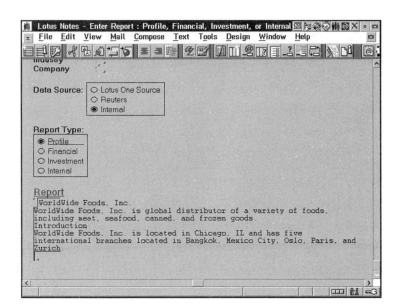

Fig. 34.22
You can also DDE Link Ami Pro documents within a Notes document. Even though you lose the formatting and attributes from the source file, you can still update the linked data.

As you can see, linking provides a convenient way to keep changing data current in numerous Notes documents. Plus, it's a great way to organize and manage worksheets, documents and presentations.

◄ See "Under-standing Links," p. 526

Troubleshooting

I get a Lotus Notes DDE Error Report when I try to refresh or activate a DDE link in Notes.

Someone has moved or deleted the original, linked to data file. Notes can't update the link, since it can't find the original source file.

After importing data from a text file into Notes several of my views in Notes display documents as "Not Categorized".

These "Not Categorized" documents are missing data in the fields that are being categorized in the view. An important thing to realize is that Notes imports only data actually in the text file. For example, the Approved Product form file (shown earlier in figure 34.1) contains several more fields than each record of the structured-text. Thus the resulting, imported documents don't contain those fields. Depending on the database, this situation might cause problems like categorization in views. In the case of PRODCAT.NSF, you have to create a new view to display the new documents, edit the selection criteria in an existing view, or open each document and enter the data in the empty fields because all the views in the file depend on the contents of a field that the import process doesn't create.

VI

Communicating

From Here...

Now that you understand the basics of working together with Lotus Notes and the Lotus SmartSuite products, you are ready to start integrating your own applications.

Other chapters that relate to using Notes include the following:

- Chapter 28, "Sharing Data Between Applications with DDE," shows you how to implement Dynamic Data Interchange (DDE) with the other SmartSuites.

- Chapter 29, "Using the OS/2 Workplace Shell To Create an Integrated Desktop," teaches you how to organize and integrate project related files in the OS/2 and SmartSuite environment.

- Chapter 32, "Getting Started with Notes," provides an introduction to creating documents, fields and other specific items in Notes.

- Chapter 33, "Managing Information with Notes," takes a close-up look at searching databases, creating views, and creating selection formulas.

Part VII

Appendixes

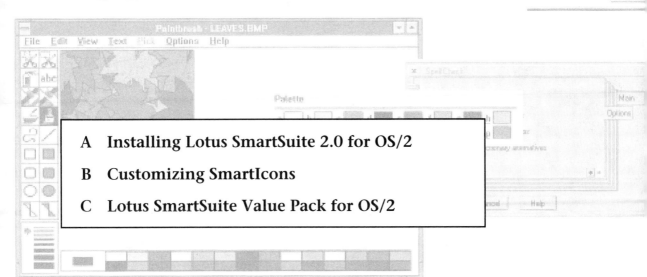

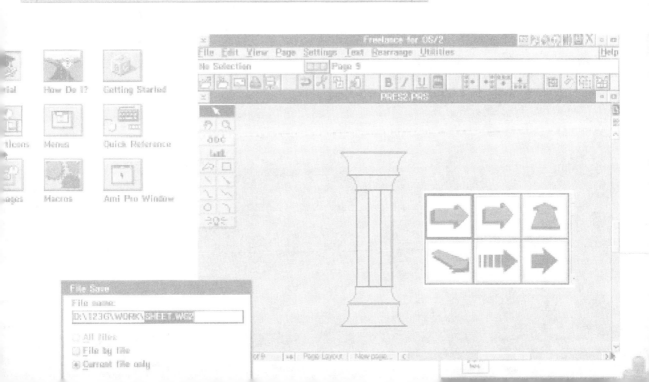

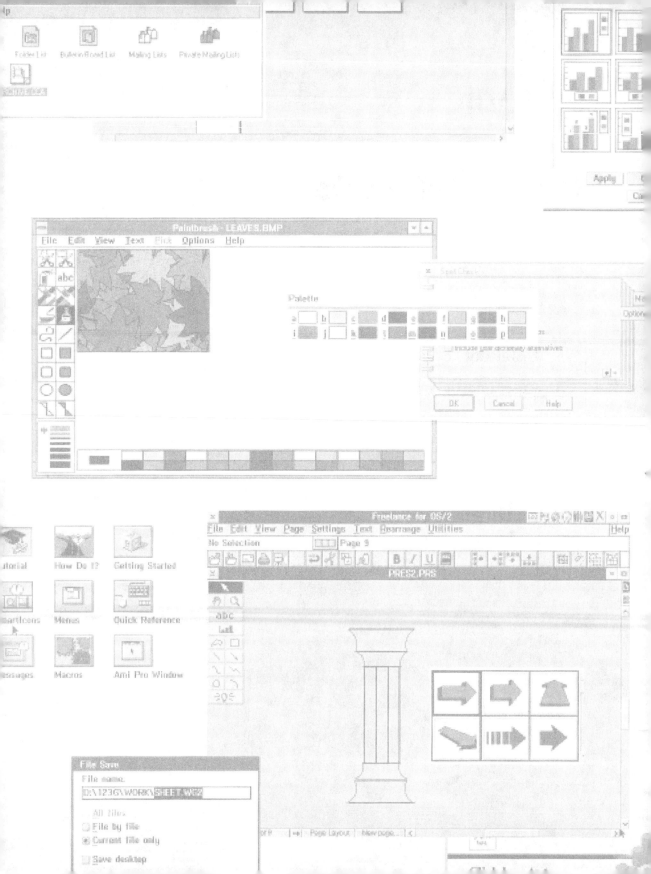

Appendix A

Installing Lotus SmartSuite 2.0 for OS/2

by Lenny Bailes

Lotus SmartSuite for OS/2 2.0 includes installation disks for the following applications: 1-2-3 for OS/2, Ami Pro for OS/2, Freelance Graphics for OS/2, cc:Mail for OS/2 (WorkStation), Lotus Application Manager, Adobe Type Manager, and the Value Pack (which includes Lotus SmartCenter, and a set of bonus icons and templates for 1-2-3, Ami Pro, and Freelance). These applications can be installed in any order from the appropriate set of disks.

> **Note**
>
> The Lotus Value Pack began shipping with SmartSuite v.2.0. If you have an earlier version, you may need to order the Value Pack separately. See Appendix C for details.

In this appendix, you learn how to:

- Check system requirements for installing SmartSuite

- Install SmartSuite the first time

- Install SmartSuite to a network

- Update SmartSuite and any of its applications

Preparing To Install SmartSuite

Before installing Lotus SmartSuite, check the system requirements to make sure you can run the applications. In addition, you should make backups of important system files. This section describes hardware and software requirements and backup procedures.

Checking the System Requirements

To install Lotus SmartSuite, you need at least an 80386-based computer; and 80486 CPU is recommended. In addition, you must use an EGA, VGA, or higher video adapter.

To operate one SmartSuite application at a time, you need a minimum of 12M of RAM. If, however, you want to use two or more SmartSuite applications at one time, you need at least 16M of RAM. In addition to your computer's active RAM, the SmartSuite applications also require an OS/2 Swap file. With the minimum amount of system memory (12M), you should allow 24M or more on your hard drive to accommodate OS/2's SWAPPER.DAT file. To configure the size of the OS/2 Swap file, check your CONFIG.SYS for the statement that specifies its location and size, or type **help swappath** at an OS/2 command prompt for online help on how to do this.

Depending on the applications and optional features you choose to install, you can use anywhere from 25.4M to 41.4M of disk space. You need 25.4M disk space to install minimum features of all SmartSuite applications; you need 41.4M disk space to install all features, tutorials, templates, sample, and demonstration files.

> **Note**
>
> To use the Node Edition of 1-2-3 for OS/2, you need 20KB (kilobytes) of available disk space on the drive that will contain your 1-2-3 personal directory. To use the Node Edition of Freelance Graphics for OS/2, it must be installed in the same personal directory as 1-2-3 for OS/2. You'll need another 200KB of available disk space on the drive that will hold your 1-2-3 and Freelance files.

Checking Software Requirements

Lotus SmartSuite requires that you have OS/2 version 2.1 or higher installed on your computer. It's also recommended that you use a mouse with the SmartSuite applications. As with all OS/2 programs, you can, however, use only the keyboard if you want. A mouse offers shortcuts and easy access to applications, features, and tools.

Backing Up the Desktop

Before installing any new applications, it's a good idea to make backups of your OS/2 desktop and INI files. If you encounter any problems with installing or running Windows after installation, you can always restore the backup files to your system.

If you're using OS/2 Warp v.3, all you need to do is click the desktop with the right mouse button held down, select settings, click the Archives Tab, and select Create archive at each system restart. If you shut down OS/2 and reboot, a backup of your current configuration will be saved in the OS/2\ ARCHIVES directory. After you use this feature to save your system configuration once, you may want to reopen the Desktop, Settings, Archives tab, and turn it off, since successive backups consume hard disk storage space.

If you are using OS/2 v. 2.xx, there is no automated procedure for creating a backup, but you can make one manually. Insert a formatted floppy disk into drive A, make your OS/2 boot drive current, and type the following command:

backup \desktop*.* /s a:

Additionally, users of both Warp and OS/2 2.xx may want to back up the CONFIG.SYS file stored in the root directory of the OS/2 boot drive:

copy \config.sys config.bak

> **Note**
>
> In addition to backing up your system files, you may want to back up your SmartSuite program disks. To do so, use high-density disks that are the same size as the originals. You can use DOS or Windows to back up the files.

Backing Up Data Files from Old SmartSuite Applications

In preparation for installing the SmartSuite applications, you should determine whether previous versions of any OS/2 SmartSuite application exist on your hard drive. For each application that will be upgraded, you should create a backup data directory. Copy any spreadsheets, graphs, templates, word processing documents, or other datafiles you wish to save to this backup directory. (If you like, you can store the data files from more than one SmartSuite application in the same data directory.) The backup directory must be separate from and located above the directories for the old SmartSuite applications that you're going to replace. (See the section on installing the individual SmartSuite applications later in this appendix for more details.)

Installing SmartSuite Applications

After checking that your system can run SmartSuite and backing up any data files created by a previous version, you can begin the installation. The following directions assume you are installing from the floppy drive A; if you're installing from a different drive, substitute the letter of that drive.

The following table represents the minimum and default disk space required to install each of the SmartSuite applications:

Application	Minimum	Default
1-2-3	8.2M	8M
Ami Pro	8M	17M
Freelance Graphics	8M	8M
Adobe Type Manager	1.4M	1.4M
cc:Mail	3M	3M
Lotus Application Manager	125K	125K
SmartSuite Value Pack	590K	5M

Installing for the First Time on a Stand-Alone Computer

Use the following instructions to install SmartSuite applications for the first time.

Insert the first Install disk for the first application in drive A. Open the drive A object from the Warp Launch Pad or from the OS/2 Drives Object and click INSTALL.EXE. (Alternatively, you may open an OS/2 command prompt and type **a:\install**.) Install displays the introductory screen; choose the Standard installation option (Local workstation), and click OK to begin Install.

As the SmartSuite application installs, a series of dialog boxes appears, prompting you for information. You are asked, for example, to enter your name and your company's name, to choose a directory to install, and to select the type of installation you want: Default features, Customized features. The Default feature places all files—program, help, tutorial, example, and so on—on your hard drive. The Customize feature enables you to choose which files you want to install, and the minimum features places only those files essential for running the program.

Follow the instructions on-screen, and insert the disks as specified.

Installing 1-2-3 for OS/2

1-2-3 for OS/2 resides in a hard disk directory called 123G. If this directory already exists, you may want to back up any data files that you wish to save to another directory on your hard disk. (By default, the new installation procedure won't overwrite them, but it pays to be safe.)

1. Open an OS/2 command prompt and make the drive that contains the previous version of 1-2-3 the current drive.

2. Type **cd** and press Enter.

3. Make a new data directory on the drive with the MD command. Example: **md \123gdata**.

4. Copy all the worksheets and templates you wish to save from the 123G, 123G\TEMPLATES, and 123G\WORK directories to the 123GDATA directory. (You may wish to copy files with the .WG1, .WG2, .WKS, .WK4, *.GPH, .DSK, .DBF, and .PRS file extensions.)

Installing Freelance Graphics for OS/2

Freelance Graphics for OS/2 resides in a hard disk directory called FLG, if it has been installed as a stand-alone application. If it has been installed as part of SmartSuite, the recommended procedure is to install it in a shared directory with 1-2-3 for OS/2. If FLG or 123G directories exist from a previous version of Freelance, you may want to transfer any data files you wish to save to another directory on your hard disk.

1. Open an OS/2 command prompt and make the drive that contains the previous version of Freelance Graphics the current drive.

2. Type **cd** and press Enter.

3. Make a new data directory on the drive with the MD command. Example: **md \flgdata**.

4. Copy all the worksheets and templates you wish to save from the old FLG or 123G and FLG\TEMPLATE or 123G\TEMPLATE directories to the FLGDATA directory. (You may wish to copy files with the .MAS, .SYM, .GPH, and .PRS file extensions.)

Freelance 2.0 may be installed directly over an older version without deleting the program files in the Freelance 1.0 directory. If you have created a custom dictionary in Freelance 1.0, and are using the same directories for version 2.0, the dictionary is automatically renamed and updated for use with the new version. If you install Freelance 2.0 into a different directory, then copy the CUSTOM.SPL file you backed up to the new Freelance directory, and rename it LTUSER1.DIC.

Installing Ami Pro for OS/2

Ami Pro for OS/2 resides in a hard disk directory called \AMIPRO. If this directory already exists, you may want to back up any data files that you wish to save to another directory on your hard disk.

1. Open an OS/2 command prompt and make the drive that contains the previous version of Ami Pro the current drive.

2. Type **cd** and press Enter.

3. Make a new data directory on the drive with the MD command. Example: **md \amidata**.

4. Copy all the documents, macros, and style sheets you wish to save from the AMIPRO\DOCS, AMIPRO\MACROS, and AMIPRO\STYLES directory to the /AMIDATA directory. (You may want to copy files with the .SAM, .SDW, .SMM, and .STY file extensions.)

5. After the data files have been copied, you may generally install Ami Pro 3.0b directly over a previous version of Ami Pro in the same directory. The install program prompts you to specify where you want to install style sheets, documents, and macros for the new version. If you haven't backed up your existing files, you should specify new directories for style sheets, documents, and macros, to avoid overwriting the old files.

VII

> **Note**
>
> Some users may encounter difficulties when installing the current version of Ami Pro over an older version. If your Ami Pro installation doesn't proceed normally, or if you experience problems with the program after installation, you need to perform a clean reinstallation. This entails deleting all program files in the \AMIPRO directory and purging references to previous versions in OS/2's INI files. Refer to the file called README.INS on Ami Pro Installation disk 1 for detailed instructions.

Installing cc:Mail for OS/2

If you're installing cc:Mail from a disk, insert WorkStation Install Disk 1 in the appropriate floppy drive and locate the INSTALL.EXE object. Run the INSTALL.EXE program and press Enter or click OK to accept the default path for the cc:Mail files. To relocate the files, type in another drive and directory in the Install Path dialog box. When prompted, remove the first WorkStation Install disk and insert WorkStation Install disk 2.

If you're installing cc:Mail from a directory on a network drive, locate the cc:Mail program directory and run the INSTALL.EXE program. (You may type **install.exe** from an OS/2 command prompt, or locate and double-click the file object in the OS/2 Drives Window.)

Installing Adobe Type Manager

To add the Adobe fonts provided in SmartSuite to your Workplace Shell applications, you must install them with the Font Palette object located in the OS/2 System Setup folder:

1. Click an empty area of the desktop with the right mouse button held down and select System Setup.

2. When the System Setup folder opens, double-click the Font Palette object to open it.

3. Click the Edit Font button to open the Edit Font dialog box.

4. Insert the Adobe Type Font disk in an appropriate floppy drive, click Add in the Edit Font dialog box you opened, and enter the drive that contains the Adobe Font disk.

5. Click the .AFM font files for the fonts you want to add to the Workplace Shell. A set of corresponding font names appears in the Font names window on the right.

6. When you've finished selecting fonts, make sure the OS/2 font directory specified in the lower portion of the screen is correct (usually C:\PSFONTS), and click the Add button underneath it. This will install the fonts you've selected and return you to the Edit Font dialog box.

7. Press Alt+F4 four times to return to the desktop.

Installing Lotus Application Manager

To install Application Manager, insert the Lotus Application Manager disk in an appropriate floppy drive, and locate the INSTALL.EXE object as you did when installing the other SmartSuite applications. Double-click INSTALL.EXE or run it from an OS/2 command prompt.

Installing the SmartSuite Value Pack

To install the Lotus Value Pack for OS/2, insert Install Disk 1 in an appropriate floppy drive, locate the INSTALL.EXE object and double-click it, or run it from an OS/2 command prompt. You may selectively install all or none of the Value Pack components. An introductory screen appears, allowing you to specify drive and directory paths for Lotus SmartCenter, bonus Freelance templates, 1-2-3 file translators, and Ami Pro bonus icons.

> **Note**
>
> The Lotus Application Manager and SmartCenter toolbars should be installed on local workstations only. See the section that follows for instructions on installing the Value Pack templates, file translators, and bonus icons on a network.

Installing SmartSuite Applications on a Network

You can install SmartSuite applications to a network server if you have the license agreement to allow use by multiple users. After installing to the server, users can then install the application to their workstations.

Installing on a Network

To install SmartSuite on a network, the system administrator must log on as a supervisor. Insert Install Disk 1 for the first application in the server's floppy drive, run the Install program, and select Network Install at the opening screen. When choosing the path for installation, make sure you choose a network drive path. Follow any other directions, such as entering a path for shared files and choosing a location for shared files. Installation then proceeds just as it does for a stand-alone computer.

After the application has been copied and installed to the network drive, the system administrator should create appropriate user aliases to allow individual client nodes to access the application directory.

> **Note**
>
> To allow client nodes to access cc:Mail, this application should be installed on the server using the Standard Installation procedure. If you wish to establish individual demo post offices for cc:Mail users, these demo post offices should be installed individually on each local workstation.

You may optionally install the Adobe Type Manager fonts on a network drive to allow end users to conveniently access them in individual OS/2 nodes.

For individual node users to take advantage of SmartSuite Value Pack file translators, templates, SmartIcons, and macros, they must be installed in the appropriate application directories on the network drive. The system administrator should log onto the network as a supervisor to obtain write-access to the network drive, insert Value Pack Disk 1 in a floppy drive on the server, and run the INSTALL.EXE program just like you do when installing the Value Pack on single-user workstations. All components of the Value Pack should be installed in appropriate application directories, except for Lotus SmartCenter. The Lotus SmartCenter component of Value Pack should be installed only on individual user-node workstations.

Installing to Workstation Nodes

After the application is installed to the server, the end user can install it to a workstation, license permitting.

> **Note**
>
> Ami Pro provides an automated process for setting up user workstations. After the network administrator installs the program to the server, the administrator runs the NODE.EXE program (located in the NODE directory specified during installation) from each workstation. Complete information on the Ami Pro install procedure is provided in a file called READNET.TXT on Install Disk 1.

To install the program on a network node, you must know the drive and directory for the application on the server (for example, the network drive might be F, and the 1-2-3 application located in the F:\SMARTSUITE\123G directory). Ask your network administrator if you're unsure of the application's location.

To start the Node install process for 1-2-3 or Freelance Graphics:

1. Open an OS/2 command prompt from the local workstation and log onto the network drive or alias where the SmartSuite application resides. (If necessary, type **cd** followed by the name of your 1-2-3 or Freelance Graphics program directory and press Enter.)

2. Once you're logged into the application directory on the server, type **install** and press Enter. The first screen you see is an introductory screen that explains how the INSTALL program works. Press Enter to start the program. The Standard and Network Install option buttons are grayed out, allowing you to select the Node option and complete the installation procedure.

Answer questions from the dialog boxes as in a normal installation.

Returning to Install

Tip

If you notice that your system is sluggish when switching from application to application, consider installing more RAM.

Tip

Customize an Install by choosing only certain applications to install now; later, you can add other Lotus applications features, more Help files, and so on.

You can return to the Install program for any SmartSuite application at any time to add application files you didn't originally install. To install items you didn't originally install, you must use Customized Install with the Install disks from the appropriate application.

Insert the first application installation disk in the floppy drive. Open an OS/2 command prompt, or use the Drives object to locate the INSTALL.EXE file. Type **install.exe** and press Enter, or double-click the object in the Drives Window and follow the instructions on-screen. Choose a Customize Features installation and select the features you want to install. You will be prompted to insert the correct disks.

Note

If after installing cc:Mail you discover that the OS/2 desktop won't shut down correctly, you can solve this problem in three ways:

1. Make a shadow of the cc:Mail INBOX object and place it on the desktop.

2. Always keep the cc:Mail folder open when you perform a system shutdown.

3. Enter the following statement in the OS/2 CONFIG.SYS:
   set ccnoanimatedicon=yes

Appendix B

Customizing SmartIcons

by Robert L. Weberg

All the SmartSuite applications come with multiple default SmartIcon palettes and each palette is designed for different circumstances. For example, in Ami Pro, you can use the Graphics SmartIcon palette when adding and modifying graphics or pictures; use the Tables SmartIcon palette when creating and modifying Ami Pro tables. These customized palettes save you time and steps from searching the menus for the proper commands.

In this appendix, you learn to:

- Change the location of your SmartIcon palette

- Add, delete, and move SmartIcons within a palette

- Save and delete entire SmartIcon palettes

- Modify custom SmartIcons

- Assign macros to customized SmartIcons

Note

A new toolbar called the Lotus OS/2 SmartCenter is now available in SmartSuite for OS/2 2.0 (SmartCenter for OS/2 1.1 users must order separately). Appendix C discusses the OS/2 SmartCenter, which is a customizable object-oriented toolbar that makes it incredibly easy to navigate the OS/2 Workplace Shell by clicking an icon.

Using SmartIcons

SmartIcons are icons that represent shortcuts for functions, commands, and macros within a corresponding SmartSuite application. These powerful tools enable you to run many SmartSuite tasks by simply choosing a button. Most SmartIcons are standard icons like Cut, Copy, and Paste. However, some SmartIcons are flexible and customizable. You can do the following to manipulate the available SmartIcons:

- Select the set of SmartIcons you want to display.

- Show or hide the SmartIcons on-screen.

- Specify the screen position for a set of SmartIcons.

- Specify the display size for the SmartIcons.

- Specify the order of the SmartIcons in the displayed set.

- Add, move, group, and remove icons, and then save the changes to either the selected icon set or a new set.

- Delete a set of SmartIcons.

- Create and modify custom icons and assign macros to them.

> **Note**
>
> Depending on the SmartSuite application you're in, the menus to access or customize SmartIcons vary. The menus and dialog boxes used to manipulate SmartIcons in 1-2-3 and Freelance are identical, but the same procedures in Ami Pro require different commands. The situations where the menu commands and dialog boxes differ between applications are noted in this Appendix.

 To use the SmartIcons dialog box in Ami Pro, choose Tools, SmartIcons (see fig. B.1).

 To use the Utility SmartIcons Customize dialog box in 1-2-3 and Freelance, choose Utility, SmartIcons, Customize (see fig. B.2).

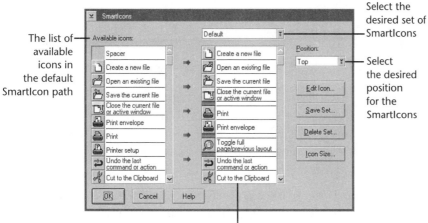

The list of available icons in the default SmartIcon path

Select the desired set of SmartIcons

Select the desired position for the SmartIcons

The icons listed and ordered in the selected SmartIcon set

Fig. B.1
The SmartIcons dialog box in Ami Pro allows you to customize the icons and palettes for your work area.

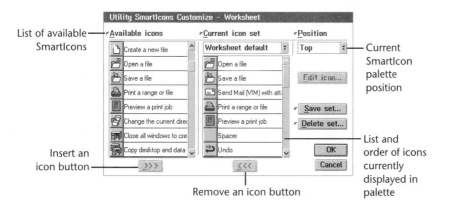

List of available SmartIcons

Insert an icon button

Remove an icon button

Current SmartIcon palette position

List and order of icons currently displayed in palette

Fig. B.2
The Utility SmartIcons Customize dialog box in 1-2-3 and Freelance is very similar to Ami Pro's SmartIcons dialog box.

To find out what an icon does, position the mouse pointer on the desired icon and hold down the right mouse button. Ami Pro displays information about that SmartIcon in the title bar.

By default, SmartIcons appear below the menu bar. If desired, you can relocate SmartIcon palettes to the left, right, and bottom borders of your screen. The palettes can even float anywhere on the screen.

There are two types of SmartIcons: standard and custom. Each SmartSuite application has its own set of standard icons. You can't modify standard icons. However, the ability to customize SmartIcons varies between the SmartSuites. Ami Pro and 1-2-3 allow you to create custom icons and assign macros to them. Freelance only allows you to modify or rearrange the standard icons and create new palettes using the standard icons since it doesn't have a macro programming language.

You can modify the existing SmartIcon palettes to fit your specifications by moving, adding, and deleting SmartIcons within a selected palette. The capability to modify existing palettes comes in handy when you want to change only a few SmartIcons in a specific palette.

Displaying the SmartIcon Palettes

Occasionally you may want to hide the SmartIcon palette; especially if you require more working area in your current application window. To toggle between displaying or hiding the SmartIcon palette, perform the following commands:

■ In Ami Pro, if the SmartIcons don't display on-screen, choose **V**iew, Show SmartIcons. If they are currently displayed, choose **V**iew, Hide SmartIcons. Pressing Ctrl+Q toggles the two commands.

■ In 1-2-3 and Freelance, if the SmartIcons don't display on-screen, choose **U**tility, Smart**I**cons, **S**how SmartIcons. You can also click the Show/Hide SmartIcons toggle button in the control line.

Changing the Location and Size of SmartIcon Palettes

Tip

Click the close box in the title bar to hide the SmartIcons in a floating palette.

SmartIcon palettes typically appear at the top of the screen (below the menu bar). However, you can display the set of SmartIcons in either a fixed location at the left, right, top, or bottom of the window, or in a floating position inside or outside the Ami Pro application window.

To position a set of SmartIcons, follow these steps:

1. In Ami Pro, choose Too**l**s, Smart**I**cons. The SmartIcons dialog box appears.

   In 1-2-3 or Freelance, choose **U**tility, Smart**I**cons, **C**ustomize to display the Utility SmartIcons Customize dialog box.

2. In the **P**osition box, select the desired position for the SmartIcons— Float, Left, Top, Right, or Bottom. Choose OK to save your changes. The application displays the relocated SmartIcons in the selected position and remembers the change in subsequent sessions. Figure B.3 shows a floating SmartIcon palette in Ami Pro.

Tip

Floating allows you to position the set of SmartIcons anywhere on the screen and adjust the size of the set.

In Ami Pro (but not 1-2-3 and Freelance), you can also select the display size for the SmartIcons. The size of the icons determines the number of icons Ami Pro displays in a set in the selected location. The default display size is automatically chosen based upon the type of video you're using.

Close box

Fig. B.3
This floating
SmartIcon palette
has been resized
for ease of use.
Click the Close
box to hide the
palette.

To size SmartIcons, follow these steps:

1. Choose Tools, SmartIcons to open the SmartIcons dialog box.

2. Click the Icon Size button, and in the Icon Size dialog box, select Small
   (VGA) or Large (Super VGA) as the desired size.

3. Choose OK to return to the SmartIcons dialog box and then choose OK
   again to return to the document. Ami Pro displays the SmartIcons in
   the selected size.

Switching between SmartIcon Palettes

You can access and switch between your various SmartIcons in several ways,
but you can use only one set of SmartIcons at a time. All the SmartSuite
applications provide several different sets of SmartIcons for performing
various tasks.

In Ami Pro, click the SmartIcons button in the status bar and then click the
set you want to show (see fig. B.4).

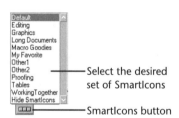

Select the desired
set of SmartIcons

SmartIcons button

Fig. B.4
In Ami Pro, switch
your SmartIcons
palette directly
through the status
bar. This method is
quick and always
accessible.

You can change the current SmartIcon palette in the SmartSuites via menu
commands, by performing the following commands:

■ In Ami Pro, choose Tools, SmartIcons. In the SmartIcons dialog box,
  select the desired set of SmartIcons and choose OK. Ami Pro displays
  the selected icon set in the selected position.

■ In 1-2-3 and Freelance, choose Utility, SmartIcons, Customize. In the
  Utility SmartIcons Customize dialog box you can click the Current icon
  set listbox to view and select the icon set you want to use. Choose OK
  and the selected icon set appears in the position you specified.

> **Note**
>
> The next time you start Ami Pro, the icon set selected when you last exited the application is displayed.

Modifying SmartIcon Palettes

You can customize the SmartIcon palettes in the SmartSuite applications to fit your working habits, needs, and preferences.

You can modify a SmartIcon set by:

- Reordering the icons in a set

- Inserting an available icon into a set

- Creating a new custom icon

- Editing and assigning a macro for a custom icon

Customizing SmartIcon Palettes in Ami Pro

You can modify any set of SmartIcons in Ami Pro by adding, moving, grouping, or removing icons. You can then save the changes to either the selected icon set or a new set. The icon sets are stored in the AMIPRO\ICONS directory. Each set of SmartIcons is stored in a separate file with an .SMI extension. To add, move, group, or remove an icon in Ami Pro, follow these steps:

Tip
Add as many SmartIcons to a palette as you like. You can use floating palettes to display more SmartIcons.

1. Choose Tools, SmartIcons. The SmartIcons dialog box appears, as shown in figure B.5.

2. From the SmartIcons dialog box, add new icons to your current palette by dragging them from the Available Icons list and dropping them on a new location on the current selected palette list.

The Available icons include all the icons provided with Ami Pro, any custom icons you create, and any bitmap files located in either the AMIPRO\ICONS directory or the default SmartIcons directory.

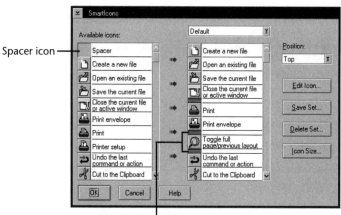

Spacer icon

Spacer icon used to visually group
and organize sets of SmartIcons

Fig. B.5
The SmartIcons
dialog box in Ami
Pro enables you to
customize and save
various palettes of
SmartIcons. Spacer
icons allow you to
organize and
group related
SmartIcons.

VII

Appendixes

The following table explains how to use the SmartIcons dialog box to customize a SmartIcon palette in Ami Pro.

Task	Procedure
Delete a SmartIcon	Drag the SmartIcon out of the palette.
Add a SmartIcon	Drag the SmartIcon you want from the Available Icons list to the new location in the palette.
Move a SmartIcon	Drag the SmartIcon to the new location in the palette.
Add a spacer to your palette	Drag the Spacer icon to the correct location on your SmartIcon palette.

Tip
Use Spacer icons to
separate or group
related icons from
other SmartIcons
in the set.

Note

You can move an icon to the end of the set by using the right mouse button to drag the icon outside the set. Ami Pro moves any icons following that icon forward one position.

Creating and Modifying Custom SmartIcons in Ami Pro

Some of the SmartIcons provided with Ami Pro are custom icons. *Custom icons* represent shortcuts for macros developed to take advantage of tasks not available via Ami Pro menu selections or commands. You can create a macro incorporating Ami Pro functions or commands, assign it to a custom icon, and then use the icon as a shortcut to execute the macro.

The custom icons are bitmap files located in either the AMIPRO\ICONS directory or a designated default SmartIcons directory. These icons appear in the Available icons list in the SmartIcons dialog box.

A new custom icon can be created from an existing icon or from an existing bitmap designed in another graphic application. You can also modify a custom icon by editing an existing icon and saving it to another file name, editing the colors in the original icon, or assigning a macro to a custom icon.

To create a custom icon in Ami Pro, follow these steps:

1. Choose Tools, SmartIcons. The SmartIcons dialog box appears.

2. Choose the Edit Icon button to display the Edit SmartIcon dialog box (see fig. B.6).

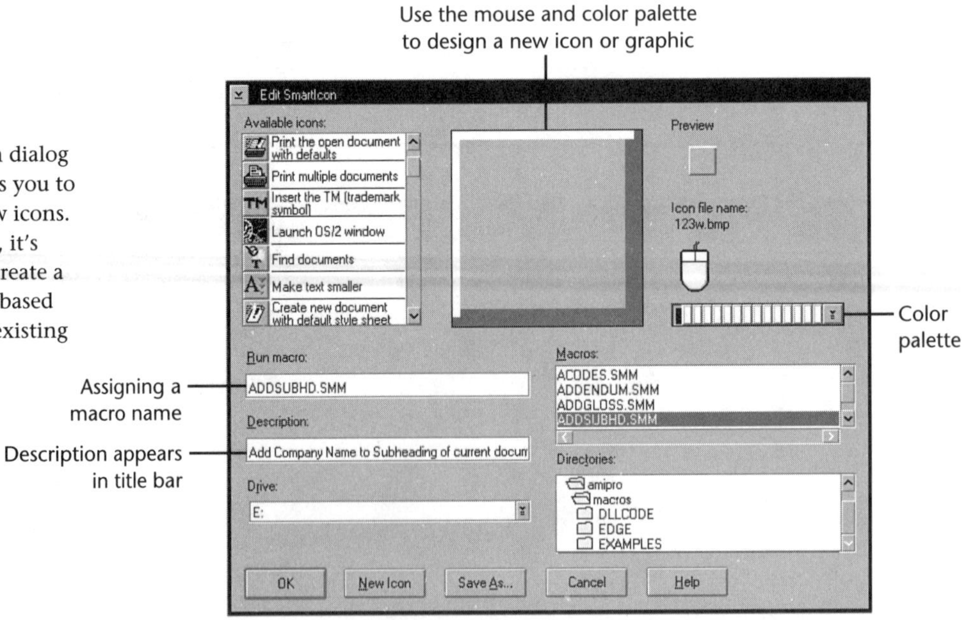

Use the mouse and color palette
to design a new icon or graphic

Fig. B.6
The Edit SmartIcon dialog box allows you to create new icons. Generally, it's easier to create a new icon based upon an existing icon.

Assigning a macro name

Description appears in title bar

Color palette

3. Choose **N**ew Icon to create a new icon that isn't based on an existing icon. Ami Pro displays the Save As New SmartIcon dialog box. Specify a file name and choose OK. Make any necessary design changes to the icon and click OK to update the icon.

> **Note**
>
> You can use an existing bitmap to create a new icon. Before you choose Tools, SmartIcons, copy the desired bitmap to the Clipboard. Choose Tools, SmartIcons, **E**dit Icon, and then press Shift+Ins to paste the bitmap into the blank button.

4. You could also choose **E**dit Icon to create a new icon that is based upon an existing icon. Ami Pro displays the Save As New SmartIcon dialog box. Specify a file name and choose OK to create the custom icon.

5. You must now assign a macro to the custom icon in order for that icon to run some action or task. Select the desired macro file name in the **M**acros listbox.

   If necessary, use the Directories listbox to change the path to locate the desired macro file. Ami Pro displays the macro description in the **D**escription text box. You can use the existing text as the description for the icon or modify it because Ami Pro doesn't change the original macro description.

6. Choose OK to return to the SmartIcons dialog box. Ami Pro displays the icon as a new icon at the bottom of the Available icons listbox. If necessary, add the custom icon to an icon set. Choose OK to return to the current open document.

Customizing SmartIcon Palettes in 1-2-3 and Freelance

The procedure or process for modifying SmartIcon palettes in 1-2-3 and Freelance is very similar to those steps used in Ami Pro. You can create SmartIcon sets and custom icons, add or delete icons or SmartIcon sets, or change the position of the SmartIcon palette.

> **Note**
>
> You can't edit custom icons in Freelance Graphics. Freelance only allows you to modify the standard icons and the SmartIcon sets they are contained in.

The icon sets are stored in your specified program directory. Each set of SmartIcons is stored in a separate file with an .SMI extension.

To add, move, group, or remove an icon, follow these steps:

1. Choose **U**tility, SmartIcons, **C**ustomize. The Utility SmartIcons Customize dialog box appears (see fig. B.7).

Fig. B.7
The Utility SmartIcons Customize dialog box in 1-2-3 and Freelance enables you to customize and save various palettes of SmartIcons.

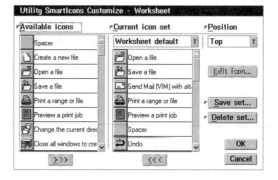

2. To reposition the icons in the Current Icon Set, you can drag the selected icon to a new location in the palette.

3. Adding an icon from the **A**vailable Icons list to the **C**urrent Icon Set list can be performed by dragging and dropping a selected icon from the Available Icons list to the **C**urrent Icon Set. You can also use the right-arrow button to add the selected icon to your **C**urrent Icon Set.

4. Removing an icon from the **C**urrent Icon Set can be managed by selecting the desired icon and then dragging and dropping the icon over the **A**vailable Icons list. You can also choose the left-arrow button to remove the selected icon from the **C**urrent Icon Set.

Modifying Custom Icons in 1-2-3

SmartIcons that perform 1-2-3 commands and functions are called *standard icons*. Each tool (for example, Graph) has its own set of standard SmartIcons. You can't modify standard icons.

> **Note**
>
> A tool in 1-2-3 for OS/2 can refer to a worksheet, a graph, desktop, and so on. Each of these tools has its own set of predesigned SmartIcons.

Working with custom SmartIcons in 1-2-3 is different than the steps used to create custom SmartIcons in Ami Pro. In Ami Pro you could create new icons by clicking the New Icon button and then making any modification. In 1-2-3 you must first copy an icon (.BMP file) to your personal working directory or to a user-defined directory (for example, C:\123G\ICONS). Then select that directory to display the icon in your Available list.

Custom icons in 1-2-3 are displayed in the **A**vailable Icons list (along with the standard icons) in the Utility SmartIcons Customize dialog box. After copying the .BMP file to a directory, reopen the Utility SmartIcons Customize dialog box to view the new custom icon in the **A**vailable Icons list. If you can't find your custom icon, use the scroll bar or be sure to copy the bitmap (.BMP) file to the specified custom icon directory. The icons description will display Custom Icon.

In order for a custom icon to run a task you need to create or provide a macro (.MAC) file. After creating and editing a macro, 1-2-3 automatically creates the macro file name (using .MAC) to match the .BMP file name.

You can specify a directory to store the custom icons for each tool. After specifying the directory and adding the custom icons to your Current Icon Set, you can display the custom and standard icons in the icon palette on your screen.

> **Caution**
>
> The bitmap must be in OS/2 bitmap file format, otherwise you get an error message when you open the Utility SmartIcons Customize dialog box.

The first step in modifying custom icons in 1-2-3 is to change or specify the custom icons directory. The current directory specified for SmartIcons informs 1-2-3 where to locate the current set of icons and palettes. To change the custom icons directory, follow these steps:

1. Choose **U**tility, Smart**I**cons, **D**irectory. The Utility SmartIcons Directory-Worksheet dialog box appears, as shown in figure B.8.

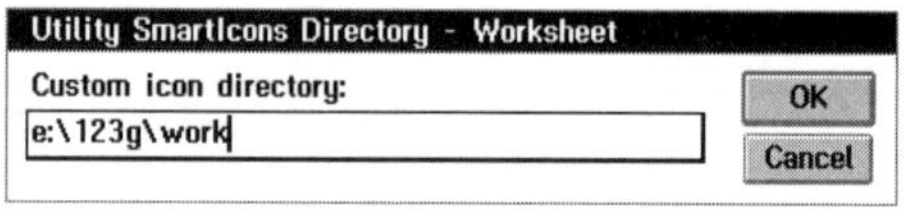

Fig. B.8

Specify the directory for your SmartIcons.

Utility SmartIcons Directory - Worksheet

Custom icon directory:

e:\123g\work

OK

Cancel

2. Enter the path your custom icons are located in (for example, C:\123G\ICONS) and click OK to save and exit.

3. Choose **U**tility, Smart**I**cons, **C**ustomize to display the Utility SmartIcons Customize dialog box. Your custom icons appear along with the standard icons.

You can modify custom icons in 1-2-3 in the following ways:

■ *Modify the default description.* To change the default text "Custom icon" that appears next to a selected custom icon in the **A**vailable Icons list, choose **U**tility, Smart**I**cons, **C**ustomize. Then choose **E**dit Icon to display the Utility SmartIcons Customize Edit Icon dialog box. Enter the description text into the description field. This text appears in the Title bar and next to the icon in the USC dialog box when you press and hold the right mouse button.

■ *Create a macro for the custom icon.* After creating a .BMP file for a custom icon, you can create an optional macro (.MAC) file. The macro file contains a one-line description of the custom macro in the first line of the file and macro commands. The macro commands are on subsequent lines in the file.

Tip

If you want to use the custom icon with several tools, place the .BMP file for the custom icon in each tool's custom icon directory.

To create a macro for a custom icon, follow these steps:

1. Choose **U**tility, Smart**I**cons, **C**ustomize. Find your custom icon in the **A**vailable Icons list.

2. Select the custom icon in the **A**vailable Icons list.

3. Click the **E**dit Icon button. This allows you to create or modify a custom macro .MAC file for the custom icon.

4. Enter a short description of the macro in the **D**escription box. The maximum size for the macro description is 80 characters and this information appears in the title bar when you press the right mouse button.

5. You can now enter the necessary macro commands directly into the **M**acro text box to create the macro for the custom icon (see fig. B.9). This is different from how you assign a macro to a custom icon in Ami Pro, because you're directly inputting the macro code and not just selecting a previously created macro.

◀ See "Using
Macros To
Automate Your
Spreadsheets,"
p. 230

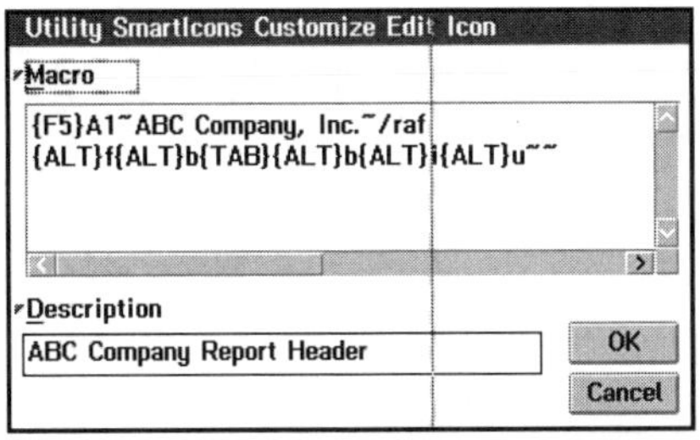

Utility SmartIcons Customize Edit Icon

Macro

```
{F5}A1~ABC Company, Inc.~/raf
{ALT}f{ALT}b{TAB}{ALT}b{ALT}i{ALT}u~~
```

Description

`ABC Company Report Header`

OK

Cancel

Fig. B.9
Creating a macro
for a custom
macro in 1-2-3,
that enters the
company name
(ABC Company,
Inc.) in bold,
italic, and
underline to a
worksheet.

6. Choose OK to save the macro and exit the dialog box. The macro is saved to a .MAC file in the custom icon directory under the same name as your custom icon but with the .MAC file extension.

Tip
Press Ctrl+Enter to
insert new lines in
your macro.

7. Add the custom icon in your **C**urrent Icon Set list and then choose OK to exit the Utility SmartIcons Customize dialog box.

You can now click the custom icon in the icon palette to start the custom macro. If you can't find the new custom icon in the icon palette, rearrange the icons in your Current Icon Set or if you're using a floating palette, adjust the size and shape of the icon palette.

Tip
You can also copy
text from a macro
that exists in your
current worksheet
to the Clipboard
and then use
Shift+Ins to paste
the text in the
Macro text box.

Note

Any changes you make to the custom icon in the **C**urrent Icon Set list don't affect the definition of the custom icon in the **A**vailable Icons list. Any changes to your custom macro in the **C**urrent Icon Set list are saved in the SMI file. The maximum size of the macro file is 32766 KB.

Saving SmartIcon Palettes

You can save a palette under a new name for future reference. After you save a palette, you can access it from the status bar or from the SmartIcons dialog box in Ami Pro, or from the Utility SmartIcons Customize dialog box in 1-2-3 and Freelance.

To save a SmartIcon palette, follow these steps:

1. Make the desired modification by adding, moving, grouping, or removing icons.

2. In Ami Pro, choose the **S**ave Set button in the SmartIcon dialog box to bring up the Save SmartIcons Set dialog box. In the **F**ilename text box, type a new name for your palette of SmartIcons (see fig. B.10). The file extension for SmartIcon palettes is .SMI. In the **N**ame of SmartIcons Set text box, type a unique description for your SmartIcon palette. Choose OK or press Enter to save the set. Ami Pro places the .SMI file in the default SmartIcons directory.

Fig. B.10

Saving a SmartIcon palette based upon your preferences and uses in Ami Pro.

3. In 1-2-3 and Freelance, choose the **S**ave Set button in the Utility SmartIcons Customize dialog box to display the Utility SmartIcons Customize Save Set dialog box (see fig. B.11). In the **F**ilename text box, type a new name for your palette of SmartIcons. Choose OK twice to exit the Save Set and Utility SmartIcons Customize dialog boxes.

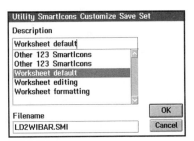

Fig. B.11
The Utility SmartIcons Customize Save Set dialog box allows you to create and save new SmartIcon palettes for 1-2-3 and Freelance.

Tip
Use a descriptive name for your SmartIcon palette (for example, *My Favorites*). This name helps you remember which SmartIcons the palette contains.

Note

In Ami Pro, you can type up to 15 characters, including spaces and punctuation, for the name of the icon set. In 1-2-3 and Freelance, you can type up to 80 characters for the description. You can type up to 8 characters for the file name of the icon set. The file name must have an .SMI extension.

Caution

If you type the name of an existing palette in the **F**ilename text box, you overwrite the original palette of SmartIcons with your changes.

Deleting SmartIcon Palettes

You can delete palettes of SmartIcons in the SmartIcons dialog box. To delete a SmartIcon palette, follow these steps:

1. In Ami Pro, choose the **D**elete Set button in the SmartIcons dialog box to access the Delete Set dialog box. Choose the palette of SmartIcons you want to delete (see fig. B.12). Then choose OK or press Enter to delete that palette.

Fig. B.12
Ami Pro allows you to delete older palettes of SmartIcons for better organization.

2. In 1-2-3 and Freelance, choose the **D**elete Set button in the Utility SmartIcons Customize dialog box to display the Utility SmartIcons Customize Delete Set dialog box (see fig. B.13). Select the SmartIcon set you want to delete from the list and then choose OK twice to exit the Delete Set and the Utility SmartIcons Customize dialog boxes.

Fig. B.13
Removing a
SmartIcon palette
from within 1-2-3
or Freelance.

> **Note**
>
> In 1-2-3 and Freelance you can't delete an icon set when it's your Current Icon set. To delete the Current Icon set, you must select and confirm another icon set or None. After doing so, you can delete the icon set.

Customizing SmartIcons in cc:Mail for OS/2

The ability to customize which SmartIcons appear on the cc:Mail windows allows you to modify the cc:Mail interface according to the functions you use most. cc:Mail doesn't have the capability to create custom icons; you can only customize the entire set of SmartIcons or individual icons in the set. You can add, move, remove, and group SmartIcons to customize your set.

To add, move, or remove SmartIcons from the displayed set, follow these steps:

1. Choose **E**dit, Smart**I**cons to display the SmartIcons dialog box.

2. You can drag selected icons from the **A**vailable Icons list and drop them to the desired position in the set, move icons currently in the selected set to a new position using drag and drop, and remove icons from the selected set by dragging and dropping an icon out of the set. After making the desired changes, click OK.

To visually enhance the organization of SmartIcons within your SmartIcon sets, you should strategically place spacer icons at either end of related icons to separate these icons from other icons in the set. This is done by dragging and dropping the Spacer icon from the **A**vailable Icons list in the SmartIcons dialog box to the desired positions in the set.

VII

Appendixes

Appendix C

Lotus SmartSuite Value Pack for OS/2

by Robert L. Weberg

During the writing of this book Lotus released an OS/2 SmartCenter Application Manager and several other welcome enhancements. These new features are contained in the Lotus SmartSuite Value Pack for OS/2.

The SmartSuite Value Pack for OS/2 not only enhances the performance and integration of Lotus SmartSuite for OS/2, it actually supercharges the OS/2 Workplace Shell. The Lotus Value Pack is an essential addition to your Lotus SmartSuite applications and contains the following features:

- Lotus SmartCenter

- Bubble Help in the Lotus SmartCenter

- Bonus pack with a set of Ami Pro SmartIcons

- Additional SmartMaster templates and business symbols for Freelance Graphics

- New file translators for Lotus 1-2-3 and Freelance Graphics

Lotus SmartCenter

Like its counterpart in SmartSuite for Windows, the SmartCenter is a customizable object-oriented toolbar that appears at the top or bottom of the Workplace Shell and lets you launch or switch to other packages with a single click on an icon. Also, the SmartCenter lets you shut down your PC, find a file or other object, open an OS/2 window, click directly on an icon to launch a commonly used application or document, retrieve all documents for a project with a single click, access SmartCenter, and monitor system resources (such as available disk space).

The innovative Lotus SmartCenter icon bar makes it incredibly easy to navigate the Workplace Shell. You gain one-click access to your files, folders, SmartSuite applications, other applications, or anything else on the Workplace Shell. Figure C.1 displays the SmartCenter icon bar at the bottom of the Workplace Shell. Notice that new Bubble Help describes each icon, so everything is easy to find.

Fig. C.1

The SmartCenter for OS/2 makes it quicker to launch or switch applications, locate files, keep tabs on system resources like disk space, and handle other common tasks.

SmartCenter icon bar

Tip

To create a new SmartCenter button on the toolbar for an object, just drag it to the SmartCenter icon bar.

Note

The SmartCenter doesn't overwrite or replace the Lotus Application Manager (LAM) but is a greatly expanded version of the LAM introduced in SmartSuite Release 1.1 for OS/2. If desired, you can continue to display the Lotus Application Manager in the top right corner of your applications and Workplace Shell.

Other Features and Value Pack Information

The SmartSuite Value Pack for OS/2 also features a Bonus Pack with a set of Ami Pro SmartIcons. Like its counterpart in SmartSuite for Windows, this Bonus Pack includes Ami Pro macros that perform all kinds of tasks. You can collect data from 1-2-3 or Freelance and paste them in Ami Pro, prepare meeting handouts in Ami Pro using a Freelance Graphics presentation, and collect multiple pages in a Freelance Graphics presentation and paste them, all in one step, into an Ami Pro document.

Also, a series of Quick Calculator SmartIcons gives you 1-2-3 number crunching power in Ami Pro allowing you to quickly carry out specialized calculations such as figuring mortgage payments and calculating savings investments by filling in the blanks (see fig. C.2).

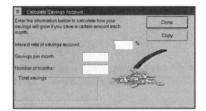

Fig. C.2
The Calculate Savings Account macro allows you to quickly calculate investments and savings numbers in Ami Pro and then copy the results into a document.

Note

In Ami Pro, you can open the BONUSPAK.SAM file in the AMIPRO\DOCS directory for information about selecting the Bonus Pack icon set and using the macros.

The Value Pack includes new file translators for Lotus 1-2-3 and Freelance Graphics to allow you to quickly exchange files between OS/2 and Windows versions (.WK4 and .PRE) of the SmartSuite applications.

The presentation capabilites of Freelance Graphics are enhanced via the addition of over 40 OS/2 Freelance SmartMaster sets equivalent to the Freelance Graphics for Windows SmartMaster sets, and 30 business related symbols. Producing great-looking meeting visuals, business proposals, and marketing plans is now more automatic—whatever your industry or objective. These SmartMaster sets include fill-in-the-blank sections specific to the type of presentation you're preparing.

You can also easily access SmartCenter for OS/2 help, Working Together help, and Customer Support help (phone numbers and policies) with a click of the Help icon in the SmartCenter toolbar.

The new Value Pack is a very welcome addition to the SmartSuite for OS/2 family and shows that Lotus is becoming a little more aggressive in keeping the OS/2 applications line up to date. The Value Pack works with OS/2 versions up to 2.1. If you have OS/2 SmartSuite Version 2.0, you already have the Value Pack. If you have OS/2 SmartSuite Version 1.1, you can order the Value Pack for a $10 shipping charge; call 1-800-872-3387.

Note

You need 5MB of available hard disk space to install all the Value Pack tools.

Index

J-K

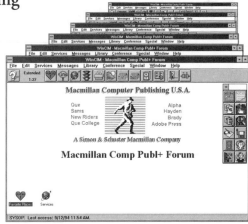

PLUG YOURSELF INTO...

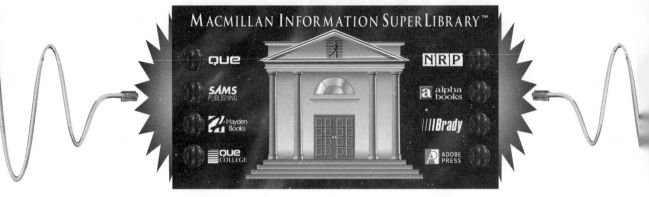

THE MACMILLAN INFORMATION SUPERLIBRARY™

Free information and vast computer resources from the world's leading computer book publisher—online!

FIND THE BOOKS THAT ARE RIGHT FOR YOU!

A complete online catalog, plus sample chapters and tables of contents give you an in-depth look at *all* of our books, including hard-to-find titles. It's the best way to find the books you need!

- STAY INFORMED with the latest computer industry news through our online newsletter, press releases, and customized Information SuperLibrary Reports.

- GET FAST ANSWERS to your questions about MCP books and software.

- VISIT our online bookstore for the latest information and editions!

- COMMUNICATE with our expert authors through e-mail and conferences.

- DOWNLOAD SOFTWARE from the immense MCP library:
    - Source code and files from MCP books
    - The best shareware, freeware, and demos

- DISCOVER HOT SPOTS on other parts of the Internet.

- WIN BOOKS in ongoing contests and giveaways!

TO PLUG INTO MCP: →

GOPHER: gopher.mcp.com

FTP: ftp.mcp.com

WORLD WIDE WEB: **http://www.mcp.com**